THE BIRTH OF BRITAIN

"A memorable history, illumined by flashes of genius, character and style, and one that is bound to prove an ever-enduring record of our common race."

"Full of growl and glory, and the English pride of Churchillian prose . . . A book of heroes and heroines, and of the myths that make heroes."

"For all English-speaking peoples, indeed for the whole world, this magnificent account of the pageant of our own past should be for us what THE ILIAD and THE ODYSSEY were to the Greeks and what the Old Testament was to the Hebrews."

"CHURCHILL AT HIS

"Magnificent history—magnificent because of the personality that colors it, and because herein is done full justice to a remarkable race."

LADIES HOME JOURNAL

"This is history seen through a temperament. But to paraphrase its author's comments on another occasion: 'Some history! Some temperament!' "

PROVIDENCE JOURNAL

"This is a magnificent accomplishment, a history of man in war, peace, love and work, by a writer probably better qualified to tell this story than anyone else in the world. It is a major contribution to the literature of our times."

NEW BEDFORD STANDARD-TIMES

SCINTILLATING BEST"

"His writing brings alive hundreds of years of history, whether he is describing the landing of Caesar's legions or the business-like invasion of William the Conqueror in 1066. . . . This is far more than any ordinary history book. It is superb writing that captures the whole pageantry of a land and its people over many centuries."

WORCESTER TIMES

"Churchill has given us one of his greatest works to enshrine his greatest theme."

SAN FRANCISCO CHRONICLE

A HISTORY OF THE ENGLISH–SPEAKING PEOPLES

THE BIRTH OF BRITAIN is the first volume of Churchill's monumental work, A HISTORY OF THE ENGLISH-SPEAKING PEOPLES. The remaining volumes are:

THE NEW WORLD
THE AGE OF REVOLUTION
THE GREAT DEMOCRACIES

Volume One

A HISTORY OF THE
ENGLISH-SPEAKING PEOPLES

WINSTON S. CHURCHILL

THE BIRTH
OF BRITAIN

CASSELL · LONDON

CASSELL & COMPANY LTD

an imprint of
Cassell & Collier Macmillan Publishers Ltd
35 Red Lion Square, London WC1R 4SG
and at Sydney, Auckland, Toronto, Johannesburg

and an affiliate of The Macmillan Company Inc., New York

First edition April 1956
Eleventh edition, fourth impression August 1972
(I.S.B.N. 0 304 91647 1)

First cheap edition April 1962
Fourth cheap edition, third impression March 1971
(I.S.B.N. 0 304 91646 3)

First "Churchill's People" paperback edition September 1974
(I.S.B.N. 0 304 29500 0)

W. F. Hall Printing Company
Chicago, Illinois
674

sources may be—folkright brought from beyond the seas by Danes, and by Saxons before them, maxims of civil jurisprudence culled from Roman codes—is being welded into one Common Law. This is England in the thirteenth century, the century of Magna Carta, and of the first Parliament.

As we gaze back into the mists of time we can very faintly discern the men of the Old Stone Age, and the New Stone Age; the builders of the great megalithic monuments; the newcomers from the Rhineland, with their beakers and tools of bronze. Standing on a grassy down where Dover now is, and pointing to the valley at his feet, one of them might have said to his grandson, "The sea comes farther up that creek than it did when I was a boy," and the grandson might have lived to watch a flood-tide, a roaring swirl of white water, sweeping the valley from end to end, carving its grassy sides into steep chalk edges, and linking the North Sea with the Channel. No wanderings, henceforth, of little clans, in search of game or food-yielding plants, from the plains of France or Belgium, to the wooded valleys and downs of Southern England; no small ventures in dugout canoes across narrow inlets at slack water. Those who come now must come in ships, and bold and wary they must be to face and master the Channel fogs and the Channel tides, and all that may lie beyond them.

Suddenly the mist clears. For a moment the Island stands in the full light of historic day. In itself the invasion of Britain by Julius Cæsar was an episode that had no sequel; but it showed that the power of Rome and the civilisation of the Mediterranean world were not necessarily bounded by the Atlantic coast. Cæsar's landing at Deal bridged the chasm which nature had cloven. For a century, while the Roman world was tearing itself to pieces in civil war, or slowly recovering under a new Imperial form, Britain remained uneasily poised between isolation and union with the Continent, but absorbing, by way of trade and peaceful intercourse, something of the common culture of the West. In the end Rome gave the word and the legions sailed. For nearly four hundred years Britain became a Roman province. This considerable period was characterised for a great part of the time by that profound tranquillity which leaves little for history to record. It stands forth sedate, luminous, and calm. And what remained? Noble roads, sometimes overgrown with woodland; the stupendous work of the Roman Wall, breached and crumbling; fortresses, market towns, country houses, whose very ruins the next comers contemplated with awe. But of Roman speech, Roman law, Roman institutions, hardly a vestige. Yet we should be mistaken if we therefore supposed that the Roman occupation could be dismissed as an incident without consequence. It had given time for the Christian faith to plant itself. Far in the West, though severed from the world by the broad flood of barbarism, there remained, sorely beset, but defended by its mountains, a tiny Christian realm. British Christianity converted Ireland. From Ireland the faith recrossed the seas to Scotland. Thus the newcomers were enveloped in the old civilisation; while at Rome men remembered that Britain had been Christian once, and might be Christian again.

This island world was not wholly cut off from the mainland. The south-east at all events kept up a certain intercourse with its Frankish cousins across the straits, and hence came the Roman missionaries. They brought with them a new set of beliefs, which, with some brief, if obstinate, resistance here and there, were accepted with surprising readiness. They brought a new political order, a Church which was to have its own rulers, its own officers, its own assemblies, and make its own laws, all of which had somehow or other to be fitted into the ancient customs of the English people. They planted the seed of a great problem, the problem of Church and State, which will grow until a thousand years later it almost rives the foundations of both asunder. But all this lies in the future. What mattered at the moment was that with her conversion England became once more part of the Western World. Very soon English missionaries would be at work on the Continent; English pilgrims would be making their way across the Alps to see the wonders of Rome, among them English princes, who, their work in this world being done, desired that their bones should rest near the tomb of the Apostles.

Nor was this all, because the English people now have an institution which overrode all local distinctions of speech, or custom, or even sovereignty. Whatever dynastic quarrels might go on between the kingdoms, the Church was one and indivisible: its rites are everywhere the same, its ministers are sacred. The Kingdom of Kent may lose its ancient primacy, Northumbria make way for Mercia; but Canterbury and York remain. The contrast is startling between the secular annals of these generations, with their meagre and tedious records of forays and slaughter, and the brilliant achievements of the English Church. The greatest scholar in Christendom was a Northumbrian monk. The most popular stylist was a West Saxon abbot. The Apostle of Germany was Boniface from Devon. The revival of learning in the Empire of Charlemagne was directed by Alcuin of York.

But this youthful, flourishing, immature civilisation lacked any solid military defence. The North was stirring again: from Denmark up the Baltic, up the Norwegian fiords, the pirate galleys were once more pushing forth in search of plunder, and of new homes for a crowded people. An island without a fleet, without a sovereign to command its scattered strength, rich in gold pieces, in cunning metal-work, and rare embroideries, stored in defenceless churches and monasteries, was a prize which the heathen men might think reserved for them whenever they chose to lay hands on it. Those broad, slow rivers of the English plain invited their galleys into the very heart of the country, and once on land how were rustics hurriedly summoned from the plough to resist the swift and disciplined march of armed bands, mounted or on foot? When the storm broke the North, the Midlands, the East, went down under its fury. If Wessex had succumbed all would have been lost. Gradually however it became manifest that the invaders had come not only to ravage but to settle.

At last the hurricane abated and men could take count of their losses. A broad strip of land along the middle of the eastern coast and stretching inland as far as Derby was in Danish hands; seafarers turned farmers were still holding together as an army. But London, already one of the great ports of Northern Europe, had been saved, and all the South, and here was the seat and strength of the royal house. The tie with the mainland had not been severed. Year by year, sometimes by treaty, sometimes by hard fighting, King Alfred's dynasty laboured to establish its ascendancy and reunite the land; so successfully that the temporary substitution of a Danish for an English king made little mark on history. He too was a Christian; he too made the pilgrimage to Rome. After this brief interlude the old line returned to the throne, and might have remained there from one generation to another. Yet in three short winter months, between October and Christmas Day in 1066, the astounding event had happened. The ruler of one French province—and that not the largest or most powerful—had crossed the Channel and made himself King of England.

* * *

The structure into which the Norman enters with the strong hand was a kingdom, acknowledged by all who spoke the King's English, and claiming some vague sovereignty over the

Welsh and the Scots as well. It was governed, we may say, by
the King in Council, and the Council consisted of his wise
men, laymen and clerics; in other words, bishops and abbots,
great landowners, officers of the Household. In all this it departed in no way from the common pattern of all kingdoms
which had been built out of fragments of the Roman Empire.
It had also been showing, since the last of the strong kings
died, a dangerous tendency to split up into provinces, or earl-
doms, at the expense of the Crown and the unity of the nation;
a tendency only, because the notion still persisted that the
kingdom was one and indivisible, and that the King's Peace
was over all men alike. Within this peace man was bound to
man by a most intricate network of rights and duties, which
might vary almost indefinitely from shire to shire, and even
from village to village. But on the whole the English doctrine
was that a free man might choose his lord, following him in
war, working for him in peace, and in return the lord must
protect him against encroaching neighbours and back him in
the courts of law. What is more, the man might go from one
lord to another, and hold his land from his new lord. And
these lords, taken together, were the ruling class. The greatest
of them, as we have seen, sat in the King's Council. The lesser
of them are the local magnates, who took the lead in shire or
hundred, and when the free men met in the shire or hundred
court to decide the rights and wrongs of a matter it was their
voice which carried weight. We cannot yet speak of a nobility
and gentry, because the Saxons distinguished sharply between
nobles and peasants and there was no room for any middle
rank. But there were the makings of a gentry, to be realised
hereafter.

Such was the state of England when the new Norman order
was imposed on it. The Conqueror succeeded to all the rights
of the old kings, but his Council now is mainly French-born,
and French-speaking. The tendency to provincialisation is arrested; the King's Peace is everywhere. But the shifting pattern
of relationships is drastically simplified to suit the more advanced, or more logical, Norman doctrine, that the tie of man
to lord is not only moral and legal, but material, so that the
status of every man can be fixed by the land he owns, and the
services he does for it, if he is a tenant, or can demand, if he is
a lord. In Norman days far more definitely than in Saxon the
governing class is a landowning class.

In spite of its violent reannexation to the Continent, and its
merger in the common feudalism of the West, England re-

tained a positive individuality, expressed in institutions gradually shaped in the five or six hundred years that had passed since its severance, and predestined to a most remarkable development. The old English nobility of office made way for the Norman nobility of faith and landed wealth. The lesser folk throve in a peaceful but busy obscurity, in which English and Norman soon blended, and from them will issue in due course the Grand Jurors, the Justices of the Peace, the knights of the shire; ultimately overshadowing, in power if not in dignity, the nobility, and even the Crown itself. These days are far off. In the meantime we may picture the Government of England in the reign of Henry II, let us say, somehow thus. A strong monarchy, reaching by means of its judges and sheriffs into every corner of the land; a powerful Church that has come to a settlement with the Crown, in which the rights of both sides are acknowledged; a rich and self-willed nobility, which the Crown is bound by custom to consult in all matters of State; a larger body of gentry by whom the local administration is carried on; and the king's Household, his personal staff, of men experienced in the law and in finance. To these we must add the boroughs, which are growing in wealth and consequence now that the peace is well kept, the roads and seaways safe, and trade is flourishing.

* * *

Standing at this point, and peering forward into the future, we see how much depends on the personality of the sovereign. In the period after the Conquest we have had three powerful rulers: in William a ruthless and determined soldier-prince who stamped the Norman pattern on the land; in his son Henry I a far-sighted, patient administrator; in Henry's grandson, the second Henry, a great statesman who had seen that national unity and the power of the Crown hung together, and that both could only be served by offering, for a price, even justice to all men, and enforcing it by the royal authority. Certain strains are developing in that compact fabric of Plantagenet England. The Crown is pressing rather hard on the nobility; the king's Household is beginning to oust the ancient counsellors of the kingdom. We need a strong king who will maintain the law, but a just king who will maintain it for the good of all, and not only for his private emolument or aggrandisement. With King John we enter on a century of political experiment.

Anyone who has heard from childhood of Magna Carta,

who has read with what interest and reverence one copy of it
was lately received in New York, and takes it up for the first
time, will be strangely disappointed, and may find himself
agreeing with the historian who proposed to translate its title
not as the Great Charter of Liberties, but the Long List of
Privileges—privileges of the nobility at the expense of the
State. The reason is that our notion of law is wholly different
from that of our ancestors. We think of it as something constantly changing to meet new circumstances; we reproach a
Government if it is slow to pass new legislation. In the Middle
Ages circumstances changed very gradually; the pattern of society was settled by custom or Divine decree, and men thought
of the law rather as a fixed standard by which rights and duties
could in case of wrongdoing or dispute be enforced or determined.

The Great Charter therefore is not in our sense of the word
a legislative or constitutional instrument. It is an agreed statement of what the law is, as between the king and his barons;
and many of the provisions which seem to us to be trifling and
technical indicate the points at which the king had encroached
on their ancient rights. Perhaps, in their turn, the victorious
barons encroached unduly on the rights of the Crown. No one
at the time regarded the Charter as a final settlement of all outstanding issues, and its importance lay not in details but in the
broad affirmation of the principle that there is a law to which
the Crown itself is subject. *Rex non debet esse sub homine, sed
sub Deo et lege*—the king should not be below man, but below
God and the law. This at least is clear. He has his sphere of
action, within which he is free from human control. If he steps
outside it he must be brought back. And he will step outside it
if, ignoring the ancient Council of the kingdom, and refusing
to take the advice of his wise men, he tries to govern through
his Household, his favourites, or his clerks.

In other words, personal government, with all its latent possibilities of oppression and caprice, is not to be endured. But it
is not easy to prevent. The King is strong, far stronger than
any great lord, and stronger than most combinations of great
lords. If the Crown is to be kept within its due limits some
broader basis of resistance must be found than the ancient
privileges of the nobility. About this time, in the middle of the
thirteenth century, we begin to have a new word, Parliament.
It bears a very vague meaning, and some of those who first
used it would have been startled if they could have foreseen
what it would some day come to signify. But gradually the idea

spreads that if it is not enough for the King to "talk things over" with his own Council; so, on the other hand, it is not enough for the barons to insist solely on their right to be considered the Council of the kingdom. Though they often claim to speak for the community of the realm, in fact they only represent themselves, and the King after all represents the whole people. Then why not call in the lesser gentry and the burgesses? They are always used in local matters. Why not use them in national concerns? Bring them up to Westminster, two gentlemen from every shire, two tradesmen from every borough. What exactly they are to do when they get there no one quite knows. Perhaps to listen while their betters speak; to let them know what the grievances of the country are; to talk things over with one another behind the scenes; to learn what the king's intentions are in Scotland and France, and to pay the more cheerfully for knowing. It is a very delicate plant, this Parliament. There is nothing inevitable about its growth, and it might have been dropped as an experiment not worth going on with. But it took root. In two or three generations a prudent statesman would no more think of governing England without a Parliament than without a king. What its actual powers are it would be very hard to say. Broadly, its consent is necessary to give legal sanction to any substantial act of authority: an important change of ancient custom can only be effected by Act of Parliament; a new tax can only be levied with the approval of the Commons. What more it can do the unfolding of time will show. But its authority is stabilised by a series of accidents. Edward III needed money for his French wars. Henry IV needed support for his seizure of the crown. And in the Wars of the Roses both the contending parties wanted some sort of public sanction for their actions, which only Parliament could provide.

Thus when in the fifteenth century the baronial structure perished in faction and civil war there remained not only the Crown, but the Crown in Parliament, now clearly shaped into its two divisions, the Lords sitting in their own right, and the Commoners as representatives of the shires and boroughs. So far nothing has changed. But the destruction of the old nobility in battle or on the morrow of battle was to tip the balance of the two Houses, and the Commons, knights and burgesses, stood for those elements in society which suffered most from anarchy and profited most by strong government. There was a natural alliance between the Crown and the Commons. The Commons had little objection to the Crown extending its prerogative at the expense of the nobility, planting Councils of the North and Councils of Wales, or in the Star Chamber exercising a remedial jurisdiction by which the small man could be defended against the great. On the other hand, the Crown was willing enough to leave local administration to the Justices of the Peace, whose interest it was to be loyal, to put down sturdy beggars, and to grow quietly and peacefully rich. As late as 1937 the Coronation service proclaimed the ideal of Tudor government in praying that the sovereign may be blessed with "a loyal nobility, a dutiful gentry, and an honest, peaceable, and obedient commonalty." Some day perhaps that commonalty might ask whether they had no more to do with Government than to obey it.

*　*　*

Thus by the end of the fifteenth century the main characteristics and institutions of the race had taken shape. The rough German dialects of the Anglo-Saxon invaders had been modified before the Norman conquest by the passage of time and the influence of Church Latin. Vocabularies had been extended by many words of British and Danish root. This broadening and smoothing process was greatly hastened by the introduction into the islands of Norman French, and the assimilation of the two languages went on apace. Writings survive from the early thirteenth century which the ordinary man of to-day would recognise as a form of English, even if he could not wholly understand them. By the end of the fourteenth century, the century of Geoffrey Chaucer, it is thought that even the great magnates had ceased to use French as their principal language and commonly spoke English. Language moreover was not the only institution which had achieved a distinctively English character. Unlike the remainder of Western Europe, which still retains the imprint and tradition of Roman law and the Roman system of government, the English-speaking peoples had at the close of the period covered by this volume achieved a body of legal and what might almost be called democratic principles which survived the upheavals and onslaughts of the French and Spanish Empires. Parliament, trial by jury, local government run by local citizens, and even the beginnings of a free Press, may be discerned, at any rate in primitive form, by the time Christopher Columbus set sail for the American continent.

Every nation or group of nations has its own tale to tell. Knowledge of the trials and struggles is necessary to all who would comprehend the problems, perils, challenges, and opportunities which confront us to-day. It is not intended to stir a new spirit of mastery, or create a mood in the study of history which would favour national ambition at the expense of world peace. It may be indeed that an inner selective power may lead to the continuous broadening of our thought. It is in the hope that contemplation of the trials and tribulations of our forefathers may not only fortify the English-speaking peoples of to-day, but also play some small part in uniting the whole world, that I present this account.

W.S.C.

Chartwell
　Westerham
　　Kent
January 15, 1956

Contents

BOOK I

THE ISLAND RACE

BOOK II

THE MAKING OF THE NATION

BOOK III

THE END OF THE FEUDAL AGE

MAPS AND GENEALOGICAL TABLES

BOOK ONE

THE
ISLAND RACE

Britannia

IN the summer of the Roman year 699, now described as the year 55 before the birth of Christ, the Proconsul of Gaul Gaius Julius Cæsar, turned his gaze upon Britain. In the midst of his wars in Germany and in Gaul he became conscious of this heavy Island which stirred his ambitions and already obstructed his designs. He knew that it was inhabited by the same type of tribesmen who confronted the Roman arms in Germany, Gaul, and Spain. The Islanders had helped the local tribes in the late campaigns along the northern coast of Gaul. They were the same Celtic stock, somewhat intensified by insular life. British volunteers had shared the defeat of the Veneti on the coasts of Brittany in the previous year. Refugees from momentarily conquered Gaul were welcomed and sheltered in Britannia. To Cæsar the Island now presented itself as an integral part of his task of subjugating the Northern barbarians to the rule and system of Rome. The land not covered by forest or marsh was verdant and fertile. The climate, though far from genial, was equable and healthy. The natives, though uncouth, had a certain value as slaves for rougher work on the land, in mines, and even about the house. There was talk of a pearl fishery, and also of gold. "Even if there was not time for a campaign that season, Cæsar thought it would be of great advantage to him merely to visit the island, to see what its inhabitants were like, and to make himself acquainted with the lie of the land, the harbours, and the landing-places. Of all this the Gauls knew next to nothing." [1] Other reasons added their weight. Cæsar's colleague in the Triumvirate, Crassus, had excited the imagination of the Roman Senate and people by his spirited march towards Mesopotamia. Here, at the other end of the known world, was an enterprise equally audacious. The Romans hated and feared the sea. By a supreme effort of survival they had two hundred years before surpassed Carthage upon its own element in the Mediterranean, but the idea of Roman legions landing in the remote, unknown, fabulous Island of the vast ocean of the North would create a novel thrill and topic in all ranks of Roman society.

[1] Cæsar, *The Conquest of Gaul*, translated by S. A. Handford, Penguin Classics, 1951.

Moreover, Britannia was the prime centre of the Druidical religion, which, in various forms and degrees, influenced profoundly the life of Gaul and Germany. "Those who want to make a study of the subject," wrote Cæsar, "generally go to Britain for the purpose." The unnatural principle of human sacrifice was carried by the British Druids to a ruthless pitch. The mysterious priesthoods of the forests bound themselves and their votaries together by the most deadly sacrament that men can take. Here, perhaps, upon these wooden altars of a sullen island, there lay one of the secrets, awful, inflaming, unifying, of the tribes of Gaul. And whence did this sombre custom come? Was it perhaps part of the message which Carthage had given to the Western world before the Roman legions had strangled it at its source? Here then was the largest issue. Cæsar's vision pierced the centuries, and where he conquered civilisation dwelt.

Thus, in this summer fifty-five years before the birth of Christ, he withdrew his army from Germany, broke down his massive and ingenious timber bridge across the Rhine above Coblenz, and throughout July marched westward by long strides towards the Gallic shore somewhere about the modern Calais and Boulogne.

Cæsar saw the Britons as a tougher and coarser branch of the Celtic tribes whom he was subduing in Gaul. With an army of ten legions, less than fifty thousand soldiers, he was striving against a brave, warlike race which certainly comprised half a million fighting men. On his other flank were the Germans, driven westward by pressure from the East. His policy towards them was to hurl their invading yet fleeing hordes into the Rhine whenever they intruded beyond it. Although all war was then on both sides waged only with tempered iron and mastery depended upon discipline and generalship alone, Cæsar felt himself and his soldiers not unequal to these prodigies. A raid upon Britannia seemed but a minor addition to his toils and risks. But at the seashore new problems arose. There were tides unknown in the Mediterranean; storms beat more often and more fiercely on the coasts. The Roman galleys and their captains were in contact with the violence of the Northern sea. Nevertheless, only a year before they had, at remarkable odds, destroyed the fleet of the hardy, maritime Veneti. With sickles at the end of long poles they had cut the ropes and halyards of their fine sailing ships and slaughtered their crews with boarding-parties. They had gained command of the Narrow Seas which separated Britannia from the main-

land. The salt water was now a path and not a barrier. Apart
from the accidents of weather and the tides and currents, about
which he admits he could not obtain trustworthy information,
Julius Cæsar saw no difficulty in invading the Island. There
was not then that far-off line of storm-beaten ships which
about two thousand years later stood between the great Corsi-
can conqueror and the dominion of the world. All that mattered was to choose a good day in the fine August weather,
throw a few legions on to the nearest shore, and see what there
was in this strange Island after all.

While Cæsar marched from the Rhine across Northern
Gaul, perhaps through Rheims and Amiens, to the coast, he
sent an officer in a warship to spy out the Island shore, and
when he arrived near what is now Boulogne, or perhaps the
mouth of the Somme, this captain was at hand, with other
knowledgeable persons, traders, Celtic princes, and British
traitors, to greet him. He had concentrated the forces which
had beaten the Veneti in two ports or inlets nearest to Britannia, and now he awaited a suitable day for the descent.

* * *

What was, in fact, this Island which now for the first time
in coherent history was to be linked with the great world?
We have dug up in the present age from the gravel of Swans-
combe a human skull which is certainly a quarter of a million
years old. Biologists perceive important differences from the
heads that hold our brains to-day, but there is no reason to
suppose that this remote Palæolithic ancestor was not capable
of all the crimes, follies, and infirmities definitely associated
with mankind. Evidently, for prolonged, almost motionless,
periods men and women, naked or wrapped in the skins of
animals, prowled about the primeval forests and plashed
through wide marshes, hunting each other and other wild
beasts, cheered, as the historian Trevelyan finely says,[1] by the
songs of innumerable birds. It is said that the whole of Southern Britain could in this period support upon its game no
more than seven hundred families. Here indeed were the lords
of creation. Seven hundred families, all this fine estate, and
no work but sport and fighting. Already man had found out
that a flint was better than a fist. His descendants would bur-
row deep in the chalk and gravel for battle-axe flints of the
best size and quality, and gained survival thereby. But so far
he had only learned to chip his flints into rough tools.

[1] *History of England.*

At the close of the Ice Age changes in climate brought about the collapse of the hunting civilisations of Old Stone Age Man, and after a very long period of time the tides of invasion brought Neolithic culture into the Western forests. The newcomers had a primitive agriculture. They scratched the soil and sowed the seeds of edible grasses. They made pits or burrows, which they gradually filled with the refuse of generations, and they clustered together for greater safety. Presently they constructed earthwork enclosures on the hilltops, into which they drove their cattle at night-time. Windmill Hill, near Avebury, illustrates the efforts of these primitive engineers to provide for the protection of herds and men. Moreover, Neolithic man had developed a means of polishing his flints into perfect shape for killing. This betokened a great advance; but others were in prospect.

It seems that at this time "the whole of Western Europe was inhabited by a race of long-headed men, varying somewhat in appearance and especially in colouring, since they were probably always fairer in the north and darker in the south, but in most respects substantially alike. Into this area of long-headed populations there was driven a wedge of round-headed immigrants from the east, known to anthropologists as 'the Alpine race.' Most of the people that have invaded Britain have belonged to the Western European long-headed stock, and have therefore borne a general resemblance to the people already living there; and consequently, in spite of the diversities among these various newcomers, the tendency in Britain has been towards the establishment and maintenance of a tolerably uniform long-headed type." [1]

A great majority of the skulls found in Britain, of whatever age, are of the long- or medium-headed varieties. Nevertheless it is known that the Beaker people and other round-headed types penetrated here and there, and established themselves as a definite element. Cremation, almost universal in the Later Bronze Age, has destroyed all record of the blending of the long-headed and round-headed types of man, but undoubtedly both persisted, and from later traces, when in Roman times burials were resumed instead of cremation, anthropologists of the older school professed themselves able to discern a characteristic Roman-British type, althought in point of fact this may have established itself long before the Roman conquest. Increasing knowledge has rendered these early categories less certain.

[1] Collingwood and Myres, *Roman Britain*.

In early days Britain was part of the Continent. A wide plain joined England and Holland, in which the Thames and the Rhine met together and poured their waters northward. In some slight movement of the earth's surface this plain sank a few hundred feet, and admitted the ocean to the North Sea and the Baltic. Another tremor, important for our story, sundered the cliffs of Dover from those of Cape Gris Nez, and the scour of the ocean and its tides made the Straits of Dover and the English Channel. When did this tremendous severance occur? Until lately geologists would have assigned it to periods far beyond Neolithic man. But the study of striped clays, the deposits of Norwegian glaciers, shows layer by layer and year by year what the weather was like, and modern science has found other methods of counting the centuries. From these and other indications time and climate scales have been framed which cover with tolerable accuracy many thousand years of prehistoric time. These scales enable times to be fixed when through milder conditions the oak succeeded the pine in British forests, and the fossilised vegetation elaborates the tale. Trawlers bring up in their nets fragments of trees from the bottom of the North Sea, and these when fitted into the climatic scale show that oaks were growing on what is now sixty fathoms deep of stormy water less than nine thousand years ago. Britain was still little more than a promontory of Europe, or divided from it by a narrow tide race which was gradually enlarged into the Straits of Dover, when the Pyramids were a-building, and when learned Egyptians were laboriously exploring the ancient ruins of Sakkara.

While what is now our Island was still joined to the Continent another great improvement was made in human methods of destruction. Copper and tin were discovered and worried out of the earth; the one too soft and the other too brittle for the main purpose, but, blended by human genius, they opened the Age of Bronze. Other things being equal, the men with bronze could beat the men with flints. The discovery was hailed, and the Bronze Age began.

The invasion, or rather infiltration, of bronze weapons and tools from the Continent was spread over many centuries, and it is only when twenty or thirty generations have passed that any notable change can be discerned. Professor Collingwood has drawn us a picture of what is called the Late Bronze Age. "Britain," he says, "as a whole was a backward country by comparison with the Continent; primitive in its civilisation, stagnant and passive in its life, and receiving most of what progress it enjoyed through invasion and importation from overseas. Its people lived either in isolated farms or in hut-villages, situated for the most part on the gravel of river-banks, or the light upland soils such as the chalk downs or oolite plateaux, which by that time had been to a great extent cleared of their native scrub; each settlement was surrounded by small fields, tilled either with a foot-plough of the type still used not long ago by Hebridean crofters, or else at best with a light ox-drawn plough which scratched the soil without turn-ing the sod; the dead were burnt and their ashes, preserved in urns, buried in regular cemeteries. Thus the land was inhabited by a stable and industrious peasant population, living by agri-culture and the keeping of livestock, augmented no doubt by hunting and fishing. They made rude pottery without a wheel, and still used flint for such things as arrow-heads; but they were visited by itinerant bronze-founders able to make swords, spears, socketed axes, and many other types of implement and utensil, such as sickles, carpenter's tools, metal parts of wheeled vehicles, buckets, and cauldrons. Judging by the ab-sence of towns and the scarcity of anything like true fortifica-tion, these people were little organised for warfare, and their political life was simple and undeveloped, though there was certainly a distinction between rich and poor, since many kinds of metal objects belonging to the period imply a considerable degree of wealth and luxury."

The Late Bronze Age in the southern parts of Britain, ac-cording to most authorities, began about 1000 B.C. and lasted until about 400 B.C.

At this point the march of invention brought a new factor upon the scene. Iron was dug and forged. Men armed with iron entered Britain from the Continent and killed the men of bronze. At this point we can plainly recognise across the van-ished millenniums a fellow-being. A biped capable of slaying another with iron is evidently to modern eyes a man and a brother. It cannot be doubted that for smashing skulls, whether long-headed or round, iron is best.

The Iron Age overlapped the Bronze. It brought with it a keener and higher form of society, but it impinged only very gradually upon the existing population, and their customs, formed by immemorial routine, were changed only slowly and piecemeal. Certainly bronze implements remained in use, par-ticularly in Northern Britain, until the last century before Christ.

The impact of iron upon bronze was at work in our Island

before Julius Cæsar cast his eyes upon it. After about 500 B.C. successive invasions from the mainland gradually modified the whole of the southern parts of the Island. "In general," says Professor Collingwood, "settlements yielding the pottery characteristic of this culture occur all over the south-east, from Kent to the Cotswolds and the Wash. Many of these settlements indicate a mode of life not perceptibly differing from that of their late Bronze Age background; they are farms or villages, often undefended, lying among their little fields on river-gravels or light upland soils, mostly cremating their dead, storing their grain in underground pits and grinding it with primitive querns, not yet made with the upper stone revolving upon the lower; keeping oxen, sheep, goats, and pigs; still using bronze and even flint implements and possessing very little iron, but indicating their date by a change in the style of their pottery, which, however, is still made without the wheel." [1]

The Iron Age immigrations brought with them a revival of the hill-top camps, which had ceased to be constructed since the Neolithic Age. During the third and fourth centuries before Christ a large number of these were built in the inhabited parts of our Island. They consisted of a single rampart, sometimes of stone, but usually an earthwork revetted with timber and protected by a single ditch.

The size of the ramparts was generally not very great. The entrances were simply designed, though archæological excavation has in some instances revealed the remains of wooden guardrooms. These camps were not mere places of refuge. Often they were settlements containing private dwellings, and permanently inhabited. They do not seem to have served the purpose of strongholds for invaders in enemy land. On the contrary, they appear to have come into existence gradually as the iron age newcomers multiplied and developed a tribal system from which tribal wars eventually arose.

The last of the successive waves of Celtic inroad and supersession which marked the Iron Age came in the early part of the first century B.C. "The Belgic tribes arrived in Kent and spread over Essex, Hertfordshire, and part of Oxfordshire, while other groups of the same stock . . . later . . . spread over Hampshire, Wiltshire, and Dorset and part of Sussex." [2] There is no doubt that the Belgæ were by far the most enlightened invaders who had hitherto penetrated the recesses of the

[1] *Op. cit.*
[2] Darby, *Historical Geography of England*, p. 42.

Island. They were a people of chariots and horsemen. They were less addicted to the hill-forts in which the existing inhabitants put their trust. They built new towns in the valleys, sometimes even below the hilltop on which the old fort had stood. They introduced for the first time a coinage of silver and copper. They established themselves as a tribal aristocracy in Britain, subjugating the older stock. In the east they built Wheathampstead, Verulam (St Albans), and Camulodunum (Colchester); in the south Calleva (Silchester) and Venta Belgarum (Winchester). They were closely akin to the inhabitants of Gaul from whom they had sprung. This active, alert, conquering, and ruling race established themselves wherever they went with ease and celerity, and might have looked forward to a long dominion. But the tramp of the legions had followed hard behind them, and they must soon defend the prize they had won against still better men and higher systems of government and war.

Meanwhile in Rome, at the centre and summit, only vague ideas prevailed about the western islands. "The earliest geographers believed that the Ocean Stream encircled the whole earth, and knew of no islands in it." [1] Herodotus about 445 B.C. had heard of the tin of mysterious islands in the far West, which he called the Cassiterides, but he cautiously treated them as being in the realms of fable. However, in the middle of the fourth century B.C. Pytheas of Marseilles—surely one of the greatest explorers in history—made two voyages in which he actually circumnavigated the British Isles. He proclaimed the existence of the "Pretanic Islands Albion and Ierne," as Aristotle had called them. Pytheas was treated as a story-teller, and his discoveries were admired only after the world he lived in had long passed away. But even in the third century B.C. the Romans had a definite conception of three large islands, Albion, Ierne, and Thule (Iceland). Here all was strange and monstrous. These were the ultimate fringes of the world. Still, there was the tin trade, in which important interests were concerned, and Polybius, writing in 140 B.C., shows that this aspect at least had been fully discussed by commercial writers.

* * *

We are much better informed upon these matters than was Cæsar when he set out from Boulogne. Here are some of the impressions he had collected:

"The interior of Britain is inhabited by people who claim,

[1] *Antiquity*, vol. i, p. 189.

on the strength of an oral tradition, to be aboriginal; the coast, by Belgic immigrants who came to plunder and make war—nearly all of them retaining the names of the tribes from which they originated—and later settled down to till the soil. The population is exceedingly large, the ground thickly studded with homesteads, closely resembling those of the Gauls, and the cattle very numerous. For money they use either bronze, or gold coins, or iron ingots of fixed weights. Tin is found inland, and small quantities of iron near the coast; the copper that they use is imported. There is timber of every kind, as in Gaul, except beech and fir. Hares, fowl, and geese they think it unlawful to eat, but rear them for pleasure and amusement. The climate is more temperate than in Gaul, the cold being less severe.

"By far the most civilised inhabitants are those living in Kent (a purely maritime district), whose way of life differs little from that of the Gauls. Most of the tribes in the interior do not grow corn but live on milk and meat, and wear skins. All the Britons dye their bodies with woad, which produces a blue colour, and this gives them a more terrifying appearance in battle. They wear their hair long, and shave the whole of their bodies except the head and the upper lip. Wives are shared between groups of ten or twelve men, especially between brothers and between fathers and sons; but the offspring of these unions are counted as the children of the man with whom a particular woman cohabited first."

* * *

Late in August 55 B.C. Cæsar sailed with eighty transports and two legions at midnight, and with the morning light saw the white cliffs of Dover crowned with armed men. He judged the place "quite unsuitable for landing," since it was possible to throw missiles from the cliffs on to the shore. He therefore anchored till the turn of the tide, sailed seven miles farther, and descended upon Albion on the low, shelving beach between Deal and Walmer. But the Britons, observing these movements, kept pace along the coast and were found ready to meet him. There followed a scene upon which the eye of history has rested. The Islanders, with their chariots and horsemen, advanced into the surf to meet the invader. Cæsar's transports and warships grounded in deeper water. The legionaries, uncertain of the depth, hesitated in face of the shower of javelins and stones, but the eagle-bearer of the Tenth Legion plunged into the waves with the sacred emblem, and Cæsar brought his warships with their catapults and arrow-fire upon the British flank. The Romans, thus encouraged and sustained, leaped from their ships, and, forming as best they could, waded towards the enemy. There was a short, ferocious fight amid the waves, but the Romans reached the shore, and, once arrayed, forced the Britons to flight.

Cæsar's landing however was only the first of his troubles. His cavalry, in eighteen transports, which had started three days later, arrived in sight of the camp, but, caught by a sudden gale, drifted far down the Channel, and were thankful to regain the Continent. The high tide of the full moon which Cæsar had not understood wrought grievous damage to his fleet at anchor. "A number of ships," he says, "were shattered, and the rest, having lost their cables, anchors, and the remainder of their tackle, were unusable, which naturally threw the whole army into great consternation. For they had no other vessels in which they could return, nor any materials for repairing the fleet; and, since it had been generally understood that they were to return to Gaul for the winter, they had not provided themselves with a stock of grain for wintering in Britain."

The Britons had sued for peace after the battle on the beach, but now that they saw the plight of their assailants their hopes revived and they broke off the negotiations. In great numbers they attacked the Roman foragers. But the legion concerned had not neglected precautions, and discipline and armour once again told their tale. It shows how much food there was in the Island that two legions could live for a fortnight off the cornfields close to their camp. The British submitted. Their conqueror imposed only nominal terms. Breaking up many of his ships to repair the rest, he was glad to return with some hostages and captives to the mainland. He never even pretended that his expedition had been a success. To supersede the record of it he came again the next year, this time with five legions and some cavalry conveyed in eight hundred ships. The Islanders were overawed by the size of the armada. The landing was unimpeded, but again the sea assailed him. Cæsar had marched twelve miles into the interior when he was recalled by the news that a great storm had shattered or damaged a large portion of his fleet. He was forced to spend ten days in hauling all his ships on to the shore, and in fortifying the camp of which they then formed part. This done he renewed his invasion, and, after easily destroying the forest stockades in which the British sheltered, crossed the Thames

near Brentford. But the British had found a leader in the chief
Cassivellaunus, who was a master of war under the prevailing
conditions. Dismissing to their homes the mass of untrained
foot-soldiers and peasantry, he kept pace with the invaders
march by march with his chariots and horsemen. Cæsar gives
a detailed description of the chariot-fighting:

In chariot fighting the Britons begin by driving all over the field
hurling javelins, and generally the terror inspired by the horses and
the noise of the wheels are sufficient to throw their opponents'
ranks into disorder. Then, after making their way between the
squadrons of their own cavalry, they jump down from the chariots
and engage on foot. In the meantime their charioteers retire a
short distance from the battle and place the chariots in such a
position that their masters, if hard pressed by numbers, have an
easy means of retreat to their own lines. Thus they combine the
mobility of cavalry with the staying-power of infantry; and by
daily training and practice they attain such proficiency that even
on a steep incline they are able to control the horses at full gallop,
and to check and turn them in a moment. They can run along the
chariot pole, stand on the yoke, and get back into the chariot as
quick as lightning.

Cassivellaunus, using those mobile forces and avoiding a
pitched battle with the Roman legions, escorted them on their
inroad and cut off their foraging parties. None the less Cæsar
captured his first stronghold; the tribes began to make terms
for themselves; a well-conceived plan for destroying Cæsar's
base on the Kentish shore was defeated. At this juncture Cassivellaunus, by a prudence of policy equal to that of his tactics,
negotiated a further surrender of hostages and a promise of
tribute and submission, in return for which Cæsar was again
content to quit the Island. In a dead calm, "he set sail late in
the evening and brought all the fleet safely to land at dawn."
This time he proclaimed a conquest. Cæsar had his triumph,
and British captives trod their dreary path at his tail through
the streets of Rome; but for nearly a hundred years no invading army landed upon the Island coasts.

Little is known of Cassivellaunus, and we can only hope
that later defenders of the Island will be equally successful and
that their measures will be as well suited to the needs of the
time. The impression remains of a prudent and skilful chief,
whose qualities and achievements, but for the fact that they
were displayed in an outlandish theatre, might well have
ranked with those of Fabius Maximus Cunctator.

Subjugation

DURING the hundred years which followed Julius Cæsar's invasion the British Islanders remained unmolested. The Belgic cities developed a life of their own, and the warrior tribes enjoyed amid their internecine feuds the comforting illusion that no one was likely to attack them again. However, their contacts with the mainland and with the civilisation of the Roman Empire grew, and trade flourished in a wide range of commodities. Roman traders established themselves in many parts, and carried back to Rome tales of the wealth and possibilities of Britannia, if only a stable Government were set up.

In the year A.D. 41 the murder of the Emperor Caligula, and a chapter of accidents, brought his uncle, the clownish scholar Claudius, to the throne of the world. No one can suppose that any coherent will to conquest resided in the new ruler, but the policy of Rome was shaped by the officials of highly competent departments. It proceeded upon broad lines, and in its various aspects attracted a growing and strong measure of support from many sections of public opinion. Eminent senators aired their views, important commercial and financial interests were conciliated, and elegant society had a new topic for gossip. Thus, in this triumphant period there were always available for a new emperor a number of desirable projects, well thought out beforehand and in harmony with the generally understood Roman system, any one of which might catch the fancy of the latest wielder of supreme power. Hence we find emperors elevated by chance whose unbridled and capricious passions were their only distinction, whose courts were debauched with lust and cruelty, who were themselves vicious or feeble-minded, who were pawns in the hands of their counsellors or favourites, decreeing great campaigns and setting their seal upon long-lasting acts of salutary legislation.

The advantages of conquering the recalcitrant island Britannia were paraded before the new monarch, and his interest was excited. He was attracted by the idea of gaining a military reputation. He gave orders that this dramatic and possibly lucrative enterprise should proceed. In the year 43, almost one hundred years after Julius Cæsar's evacuation, a powerful, well-organised Roman army of some twenty thousand men was prepared for the subjugation of Britain. "The soldiers were indignant at the thought of carrying on a campaign outside the limits of the known world." But when the Emperor's favourite freedman, Narcissus, attempted to address them they felt the insult. The spectacle of a former slave called in to stand sponsor for their commander rallied them to their duty. They taunted Narcissus with his slave origin, with the mocking shout of *"Io Saturnalia!"* (for at the festival of Saturn the slaves donned their masters' dress and held festival), but none the less they resolved to obey their chief's order.

"Their delay, however, had made their departure late in the season. They were sent over in three divisions, in order that they should not be hindered in landing—as might happen to a single force—and in their voyage across they first became discouraged because they were driven back in their course, and then plucked up courage because a flash of light rising in the east shot across to the west, the direction in which they were sailing. So they put in to the Island, and found none to oppose them. For the Britons, as the result of their inquiries, had not expected that they would come, and had therefore not assembled beforehand." [1]

The internal situation favoured the invaders. Cunobelinus (Shakespeare's Cymbeline) had established an overlordship over the south-east of the Island, with his capital at Colchester. But in his old age dissensions had begun to impair his authority, and on his death the kingdom was ruled jointly by his sons Caractacus and Togodumnus. They were not everywhere recognised, and they had no time to form a union of the tribal kingdom before Plautius and the legions arrived. The people of Kent fell back on the tactics of Cassivellaunus, and Plautius accordingly had much trouble in searching them out; but when at last he did find them he first defeated Caractacus, and then his brother somewhere in East Kent. Then, advancing along Cæsar's old line of march, he came on a river he had not heard of, the Medway. "The barbarians thought that the Romans would not be able to cross without a bridge, and consequently bivouacked in rather careless fashion on the opposite bank"; but the Roman general sent across "a detachment of Germans, who were accustomed to swim easily in full armour across the most turbulent streams. These fell unexpectedly upon the enemy, but instead of shooting at the men

[1] Dio Cassius, chapter lx, pp. 19–20.

they disabled the horses that drew the chariots, and in the ensuing confusion not even the enemy's mounted men could save
themselves." [1] Nevertheless the Britons faced them on the second day, and were only broken by a flank attack, Vespasian—
some day to be Emperor himself—having discovered a ford
higher up. This victory marred the stage-management of the
campaign. Plautius had won his battle too soon, and in the
wrong place. Something had to be done to show that the Emperor's presence was necessary to victory. So Claudius,
who had been waiting on events in France, crossed the seas,
bringing substantial reinforcements, including a number of
elephants. A battle was procured, and the Romans won.
Claudius returned to Rome to receive from the Senate the
title of "Britannicus" and permission to celebrate a triumph.

But the British war continued. The Britons would not come
to close quarters with the Romans, but took refuge in the
swamps and the forests, hoping to wear out the invaders, so
that, as in the days of Julius Cæsar, they should sail back with
nothing accomplished. Caractacus escaped to the Welsh border, and, rousing its tribes, maintained an indomitable resistance for more than six years. It was not till A.D. 50 that he
was finally defeated by a new general, Ostorius, an officer of
energy and ability, who reduced to submission the whole of
the more settled regions from the Wash to the Severn. Caractacus, escaping from the ruin of his forces in the West, sought
to raise the Brigantes in the North. Their queen however
handed him over to the Romans. "The fame of the British
prince," writes Suetonius, "had by this time spread over the
provinces of Gaul and Italy; and upon his arrival in the
Roman capital the people flocked from all quarters to behold
him. The ceremonial of his entrance was conducted with great
solemnity. On a plain adjoining the Roman camp the Pre-
torian troops were drawn up in martial array. The Emperor
and his court took their station in front of the lines, and behind
them was ranged the whole body of the people. The procession commenced with the different trophies which had been
taken from the Britons during the progress of the war. Next
followed the brothers of the vanquished prince, with his wife
and daughter, in chains, expressing by their supplicating looks
and gestures the fears with which they were actuated. But not
so Caractacus himself. With a manly gait and an undaunted
countenance he marched up to the tribunal, where the Emperor was seated, and addressed him in the following terms:

[1] *Ibid.*

"If to my high birth and distinguished rank I had added the virtues of moderation Rome had beheld me rather as a friend than a captive, and you would not have rejected an alliance with a prince descended from illustrious ancestors and governing many nations. The reverse of my fortune is glorious to you, and to me humiliating. I had arms, and men, and horses; I possessed extraordinary riches; and can it be any wonder that I was unwilling to lose them? Because Rome aspires to universal dominion must men therefore implicitly resign themselves to subjection? I opposed for a long time the progress of your arms, and had I acted otherwise would either you have had the glory of conquest or I of a brave resistance? I am now in your power. If you are determined to take revenge my fate will soon be forgotten, and you will derive no honour from the transaction. Preserve my life, and I shall remain to the latest ages a monument of your clemency.

"Immediately upon this speech Claudius granted him his liberty, as he did likewise to the other royal captives. They all returned their thanks in a manner the most grateful to the Emperor; and as soon as their chains were taken off, walking towards Agrippina, who sat upon a bench at a little distance, they repeated to her the same fervent declarations of gratitude and esteem." [1]

* * *

The conquest was not achieved without one frightful convulsion of revolt. "In this year A.D. 61," according to Tacitus, "a severe disaster was sustained in Britain." Suetonius, the new governor, had engaged himself deeply in the West. He transferred the operational base of the Roman army from Wroxeter to Chester. He prepared to attack "the populous island of Mona [Anglesey], which had become a refuge for fugitives, and he built a fleet of flat-bottomed vessels suitable for those shallow and shifting seas. The infantry crossed in the boats, the cavalry went over by fords: where the water was too deep the men swam alongside of their horses. The enemy lined the shore, a dense host of armed men, interspersed with women clad in black like the Furies, with their hair hanging down and holding torches in their hands. Round this were Druids uttering dire curses and stretching their hands towards heaven. These strange sights terrified the soldiers. They stayed motionless, as if paralysed, offering their bodies to the blows. At last, encouraged by the general, and exhorting each other not to quail before the rabble of female fanatics, they advanced their

[1] C. Suetonius Tranquillus, *The Lives of the Twelve Cæsars*, trans. by Alexander Thomson, revised by T. Forester.

standards, bore down all resistance, and enveloped the enemy in their own flames.

"Suetonius imposed a garrison upon the conquered and cut down the groves devoted to their cruel superstitions; for it was part of their religion to spill the blood of captives on their altars, and to inquire of the gods by means of human entrails."

This dramatic scene on the frontiers of modern Wales was the prelude to a tragedy. The king of the East Anglian Iceni had died. Hoping to save his kingdom and family from molestation he had appointed Nero, who had succeeded Claudius as Emperor, as heir jointly with his two daughters. "But," says Tacitus, "things turned out differently. His kingdom was plundered by centurions, and his private property by slaves, as if they had been captured in war; his widow Boadicea [relished by the learned as Boudicca] was flogged, and his daughters outraged; the chiefs of the Iceni were robbed of their ancestral properties as if the Romans had received the whole country as a gift, and the king's own relatives were reduced to slavery." Thus the Roman historian.[1]

Boadicea's tribe, at once the most powerful and hitherto the most submissive, was moved to frenzy against the Roman invaders. They flew to arms. Boadicea found herself at the head of a numerous army, and nearly all the Britons within reach rallied to her standard. There followed an up-rush of hatred from the abyss, which is a measure of the cruelty of the conquest. It was a scream of rage against invincible oppression and the superior culture which seemed to lend it power. "Boadicea," said Ranke, "is rugged, earnest and terrible." [2] Her monument on the Thames Embankment opposite Big Ben reminds us of the harsh cry of liberty or death which has echoed down the ages.

In all Britain there were only four legions, at most twenty thousand men. The Fourteenth and Twentieth were with Suetonius on his Welsh campaign. The Ninth was at Lincoln, and the Second at Gloucester.

The first target of the revolt was Camulodunum (Colchester), an unwalled colony of Roman and Romanised Britons, where the recently settled veterans, supported by the soldiery, who hoped for similar licence for themselves, had been ejecting the inhabitants from their houses and driving them away from their lands. The Britons were encouraged by

---

[1] Extracts from Tacitus' *Annals* are from G. G. Ramsay's translation; passages from the *Agricola* come from the translation of Church and Brodribb.
[2] *History of England*, vol. i, p. 8.

omens. The statue of Victory fell face foremost, as if flying from the enemy. The sea turned red. Strange cries were heard in the council chamber and the theatre. The Roman officials, business men, bankers, usurers, and the Britons who had participated in their authority and profits, found themselves with a handful of old soldiers in the midst of "a multitude of barbarians." Suetonius was a month distant. The Ninth Legion was a hundred and twenty miles away. There was neither mercy nor hope. The town was burned to ashes. The temple, whose strong walls resisted the conflagration, held out for two days. Everyone, Roman or Romanised, was massacred and everything destroyed. Meanwhile the Ninth Legion was marching to the rescue. The victorious Britons advanced from the sack of Colchester to meet it. By sheer force of numbers they overcame the Roman infantry and slaughtered them to a man, and the commander, Petilius Cerialis, was content to escape with his cavalry. Such were the tidings which reached Suetonius in Anglesey. He realised at once that his army could not make the distance in time to prevent even greater disaster, but, says Tacitus, he, "undaunted, made his way through a hostile country to Londinium, a town which, though not dignified by the title of colony, was a busy emporium for traders." This is the first mention of London in literature. Though fragments of Gallic or Italian pottery which may or may not antedate the Roman conquest have been found there, it is certain that the place attained no prominence until the Claudian invaders brought a mass of army contractors and officials to the most convenient bridgehead on the Thames.

Suetonius reached London with only a small mounted escort. He had sent orders to the Second Legion to meet him there from Gloucester, but the commander, appalled by the defeat of the Ninth, had not complied. London was a large, undefended town, full of Roman traders and their British associates, dependants, and slaves. It contained a fortified military depot, with valuable stores and a handful of legionaries. The citizens of London implored Suetonius to protect them, but when he heard that Boadicea, having chased Cerialis towards Lincoln, had turned and was marching south he took the hard but right decision to leave them to their fate. The commander of the Second Legion had disobeyed him, and he had no force to withstand the enormous masses hastening towards him. His only course was to rejoin the Fourteenth and Twentieth Legions, who were marching with might and main from Wales to London along the line of the Roman road now known as Watling Street, and, unmoved by the entreaties of the inhabitants, he gave the signal to march, receiving within his lines all who wished to go with him.

The slaughter which fell upon London was universal. No one was spared, neither man, woman, nor child. The wrath of the revolt concentrated itself upon all of those of British blood who had lent themselves to the wiles and seductions of the invader. In recent times, with London buildings growing taller and needing deeper foundations, the power-driven excavating machines have encountered at many points the layer of ashes which marks the effacement of London at the hands of the natives of Britain.

Boadicea then turned upon Verulamium (St Albans). Here was another trading centre, to which high civic rank had been accorded. A like total slaughter and obliteration was inflicted. "No less," according to Tacitus, "than seventy thousand citizens and allies were slain" in these three cities. "For the barbarians would have no capturing, no selling, nor any kind of traffic usual in war; they would have nothing but killing, by sword, cross, gibbet, or fire." These grim words show us an inexpiable war like that waged between Carthage and her revolted mercenaries two centuries before. Some high modern authorities think these numbers are exaggerated; but there is no reason why London should not have contained thirty or forty thousand inhabitants, and Colchester and St Albans between them about an equal number. If the butcheries in the countryside are added the estimate of Tacitus may well stand. This is probably the most horrible episode which our Island has known. We see the crude and corrupt beginnings of a higher civilisation blotted out by the ferocious uprising of the native tribes. Still, it is the primary right of men to die and kill for the land they live in, and to punish with exceptional severity all members of their own race who have warmed their hands at the invaders' hearth.

"And now Suetonius, having with him the Fourteenth Legion, with the veterans of the Twentieth, and the auxiliaries nearest at hand, making up a force of about ten thousand fully armed men, resolved . . . for battle. Selecting a position in a defile closed in behind a wood, and having made sure that there was no enemy but in front, where there was an open flat unsuited for ambuscades, he drew up his legions in close order, with the light-armed troops on the flanks, while the cavalry was massed at the extremities of the wings." The day was bloody and decisive. The barbarian army, eighty thousand strong, attended, like the Germans and the Gauls, by their women and children in an unwieldy wagon-train, drew out their array, resolved to conquer or perish. Here was no thought of subsequent accommodation. On both sides it was all for all. At heavy adverse odds Roman discipline and tactical skill triumphed. No quarter was given, even to the women.

"It was a glorious victory, fit to rank with those of olden days. Some say that little less than eighty thousand Britons fell, our own killed being about four hundred, with a somewhat larger number wounded." These are the tales of the victors. Boadicea poisoned herself. Pœnius Postumus, camp commander of the Second Legion, who had both disobeyed his general and deprived his men of their share in the victory, on hearing of the success of the Fourteenth and Twentieth ran himself through with his sword.

Suetonius now thought only of vengeance, and indeed there was much to repay. Reinforcements of four or five thousand men were sent by Nero from Germany, and all hostile or suspect tribes were harried with fire and sword. Worst of all was the want of food; for in their confident expectation of capturing the supplies of the Romans the Britons had brought every available man into the field and left their land unsown. Yet even so their spirit was unbroken, and the extermination of the entire ancient British race might have followed but for the remonstrances of a new Procurator, supported by the Treasury officials at Rome, who saw themselves about to be possessed of a desert instead of a province. As a man of action Suetonius ranks high, and his military decisions were sound. But there was a critical faculty alive in the Roman state which cannot be discounted as arising merely through the jealousies of important people. It was held that Suetonius had been rashly ambitious of military glory and had been caught unaware by the widespread uprising of the province, that "his reverses were due to his own folly, his successes to good fortune," and that a Governor must be sent, "free from feelings of hostility or triumph, who would deal gently with our conquered enemies." The Procurator, Julius Classicianus, whose tombstone is now in the British Museum, kept writing in this sense to Rome, and pleaded vehemently for the pacification of the warrior bands, who still fought on without seeking truce or mercy, starving and perishing in the forests and the fens. In the end it was resolved to make the best of the Britons. German unrest and dangers from across the Rhine made even military circles in Rome disinclined to squander forces in re-

moter regions. The loss in a storm of some of Suetonius's warships was made the pretext and occasion of his supersession.
The Emperor Nero sent a new Governor, who made a peace
with the desperate tribesmen which enabled their blood to be
perpetuated in the Island race.

* * *

Tacitus gives an interesting account of the new province.

The red hair and large limbs of the inhabitants of Caledonia [he
says] pointed quite clearly to a German origin, while the dark
complexion of the Silures, their usually curly hair, and the fact
that Spain lies opposite to them are evidence that Iberians of a
former date crossed over and occupied these parts. Those who are
nearest to the Gauls are also like them, either from the permanent
influence of original descent, or because climate had produced
similar qualities. . . . The religious beliefs of Gaul may be traced
in the strongly marked British superstition [Druidism]. The language differs but little. There is the same boldness in challenging
danger, and when it is near the same timidity in shrinking from it.
The Britons however exhibit more spirit, being a people whom a
long peace has not yet enervated. . . . Their sky is obscured by
continual rain and cloud. Severity of cold is unknown. The days
exceed in length those of our world; the nights are bright, and in
the extreme north so short that between sunset and dawn there is
but little distinction. . . . With the exception of the olive and
vine, and plants which usually grow in warmer climates, the soil
will yield all ordinary produce in plenty. It ripens slowly, but
grows rapidly, the cause in each case being excessive moisture of
soil and atmosphere.

In A.D. 78 Agricola, a Governor of talent and energy, was
sent to Britannia. Instead of spending his first year of office in
the customary tour of ceremony, he took field against all who
still disputed the Roman authority. One large tribe which had
massacred a squadron of auxiliary cavalry was exterminated.
The island of Mona, from which Suetonius had been recalled
by the rising of Boadicea, was subjugated. With military
ability Agricola united a statesmanlike humanity. According
to Tacitus (who had married his daughter), he proclaimed
that "little is gained by conquest if followed by oppression."
He mitigated the severity of the corn tribute. He encouraged
and aided the building of temples, courts of justice, and dwelling-houses. He provided a liberal education for the sons of the
chiefs, and showed "such a preference for the natural powers
of the Britons over the more laboured style of the Gauls" that
the well-to-do classes were conciliated and became willing to

adopt the toga and other Roman fashions. "Step by step they were led to practices which disposed to vice—the lounge, the bath, the elegant banquet. All this in their ignorance they called civilisation, when it was but part of their servitude."

Although in the Senate and governing circles in Rome it was constantly explained that the Imperial policy adhered to the principle of the great Augustus, that the frontiers should be maintained but not extended, Agricola was permitted to conduct six campaigns of expansion in Britannia. In the third he reached the Tyne, the advances of his legions being supported at every stage by a fleet of sea-borne supplies. In the fifth campaign he reached the line of the Forth and Clyde, and here on this wasp-waist of Britain he might well have dug himself in. But there was no safety or permanent peace for the British province unless he could subdue the powerful tribes and large bands of desperate warriors who had been driven northwards by his advance. Indeed, it is evident that he would never of his own will have stopped in any direction short of the ocean shore. Therefore in his sixth campaign he marched northwards again with all his forces. The position had now become formidable. Past misfortunes had taught the Britons the penalties of disunion.

Agricola's son-in-law tells us:

Our army, elated by the glory they had won, exclaimed that they must penetrate the recesses of Caledonia and at length in an unbroken succession of battles discover the farthest limits of Britain. But the Britons, thinking themselves baffled not so much by our valour as by our general's skilful use of an opportunity, abated nothing of their arrogance, arming their youth, removing their wives and children to a place of safety, and assembling together to ratify, with sacred rites, a confederacy of all their states.

The decisive battle was fought at Mons Graupius, a place which remains unidentified, though some suggest the Pass of Killiecrankie. Tacitus describes in unconvincing detail the course of this famous struggle. The whole of Caledonia, all that was left of Britannia, a vast host of broken, hunted men, resolved on death or freedom, confronted in their superiority of four or five to one the skilfully handled Roman legions and auxiliaries, among whom no doubt many British renegades were serving. It is certain that Tacitus greatly exaggerated the dimensions of the native army in these wilds, where they could have no prepared magazines. The number, though still considerable, must have been severely limited. Apparently, as in so

ROMAN BRITAIN

ANTONINE WALL

MAEATAE

HADRIAN'S WALL

BRIGANTES

Eburacum

Mona

Devo

Abus

Lindum

ORDOVICES

Ratae

ICENI

Venta
Icenorum

SILURES

CATUVELLAUNI

Camulodunum

Isca
Silurum

Glevum

Verulamium

Sabrina

Aquae Sulis

Londinium

P. Lemanis

Venta Belgarum

Regnum

Isca
Dumnoniorum

Vectis

Vectis

STATUTE MILES

0 5 10 20   30   40   50

many ancient battles, the beaten side were the victims of mis-understanding and the fate of the day was decided against them before the bulk of the forces realised that a serious en-gagement had begun. Reserves descended from the hills too late to achieve victory, but in good time to be massacred in the rout. The last organised resistance of Britain to the Roman power ended at Mons Graupius. Here, according to the Roman account, "ten thousand of the enemy were slain, and on our side there were about three hundred and sixty men." Clive's victory at Plassey, which secured for the British Empire a long spell of authority in India, was gained against greater odds, with smaller forces and with smaller losses.

The way to the entire subjugation of the Island was now open, and had Agricola been encouraged or at least supported by the Imperial Government the course of history might have been altered. But Caledonia was to Rome only a sensation: the real strain was between the Rhine and the Danube. Coun-sels of prudence prevailed, and the remnants of the British fighting men were left to moulder in the Northern mists.

Dio Cassius, writing over a century later, describes how they were a perpetual source of expense and worry to the settled regions of the South.

There are two very extensive tribes in Britain, the Caledonians and the Mæatæ. The Mæatæ dwell close up to the cross-wall which cuts the island in two, the Caledonians beyond them. Both live on wild, waterless hills or forlorn and swampy plains, without walls or towns or husbandry, subsisting on pastoral products and the nuts which they gather. They have fish in plenty, but do not eat it. They live in huts, go naked and unshod; make no separate marriages, and rear all their offspring. They mostly have a democratic gov-ernment, and are much addicted to robbery. . . . They can bear hunger and cold and all manner of hardship; they will retire into their marshes and hold out for days with only their heads above water, and in the forest they will subsist on bark and roots.

* * *

In the wild North and West freedom found refuge among the mountains, but elsewhere the conquest and pacification were at length complete and Britannia became one of the forty-five provinces of the Roman Empire. The great Augustus had proclaimed as the Imperial ideal the creation of a com-monwealth of self-governing cantons. Each province was or-ganised as a separate unit, and within it municipalities received their charters and rights. The provinces were divided between those exposed to barbarian invasion or uprising, for which an Imperial garrison must be provided, and those which required no such protection. The military provinces were under the direct supervision of the Emperor. The more sheltered were controlled, at least in form, through the medium of the Senate, but in all provinces the principle was followed of adapting the form of government to local conditions. No prejudice of race, language, or religion obstructed the universal character of the Roman system. The only divisions were those of class, and these ran unchallenged throughout the ordered world. There were Roman citizens, there was an enormous mass of non-Roman citizens, and there were slaves, but movement to full citizenship was possible to fortunate members of the servile class. On this basis therefore the life of Britain now developed.

BOOK ONE · CHAPTER THREE

The Roman Province

FOR nearly three hundred years Britain, reconciled to the Roman system, enjoyed in many respects the happiest, most comfortable, and most enlightened times its inhabitants have ever had. Confronted with the dangers of the frontiers, the military force was moderate. The Wall was held by the auxiliaries, with a legion in support at York. Wales was pinned down by a legion at Chester and another at Caerleon-on-Usk. In all the army of occupation numbered less than forty thousand men, and after a few generations was locally recruited and almost of purely British birth. In this period, almost equal to that which separates us from the reign of Queen Elizabeth I, well-to-do persons in Britain lived better than they ever did until late Victorian times. From the year 400 till the year 1900 no one had central heating and very few had hot baths. A wealthy British-Roman citizen building a country house regarded the hypocaust which warmed it as indispensable. For fifteen hundred years his descendants lived in the cold of unheated dwellings, mitigated by occasional roastings at gigantic wasteful fires. Even now a smaller proportion of the whole population dwells in centrally heated houses than in those ancient days. As for baths, they were completely lost till the middle of the nineteenth century. In all this long, bleak intervening gap cold and dirt clung to the most fortunate and highest in the land.

In culture and learning Britain was a pale reflection of the Roman scene, not so lively as the Gallic. But there was law; there was order; there was peace; there was warmth; there was food, and a long-established custom of life. The population was free from barbarism without being sunk in sloth or luxury. Some culture spread even to the villages. Roman habits percolated; the use of Roman utensils and even of Roman speech steadily grew. The British thought themselves as good Romans as any. Indeed, it may be said that of all the provinces few assimilated the Roman system with more aptitude than the Islanders. The British legionaries and auxiliaries were rated equal or second only to the Illyrians as the finest troops in the Empire. There was a sense of pride in sharing in so noble and widespread a system. To be a citizen of Rome was to be a citizen of the world, raised upon a pedestal of unquestioned superiority above barbarians or slaves. Movement across the great Empire was as rapid as when Queen Victoria came to the throne, and no obstruction of frontiers, laws, currency, or nationalism hindered it. There is a monument at Norwich erected to his wife by a Syrian resident in Britain. Constantius Chlorus died at York. British sentinels watched along the Rhine, the Danube, and the Euphrates. Troops from Asia Minor, peering through the mists at the Scottish raiders, preserved the worship of Mithras along the Roman Wall. The cult of this Persian Sun-god spread widely throughout the Roman world, appealing especially to soldiers, merchants, and administrators. During the third century Mithraism was a powerful rival to Christianity, and, as was revealed by the impressive temple discovered at Walbrook in 1954, it could count many believers in Roman London.

The violent changes at the summit of the Empire did not affect so much as might be supposed the ordinary life of its population. Here and there were wars and risings. Rival emperors suppressed each other. Legions mutinied. Usurpers established themselves in the provinces affected on these occasions. The British took a keen interest in the politics of the Roman world and formed strong views upon the changes in the Imperial power or upon the morale of the capital. Many thrusting spirits shot forward in Britain to play a part in the deadly game of Imperial politics, with its unparalleled prizes and fatal forfeits. But all were entirely reconciled to the Roman idea. They had their law; they had their life, which flowed on broad, and, if momentarily disturbed, in the main unaltered. A poll in the fourth century would have declared for an indefinite continuance of the Roman régime.

In our own fevered, changing, and precarious age, where all is in flux and nothing is accepted, we must survey with respect a period when, with only three hundred thousand soldiers, widespread the peace in the entire known world was maintained from generation to generation, and when the first pristine impulse of Christianity lifted men's souls to the contemplation of new and larger harmonies beyond the ordered world around them.

The gift which Roman civilisation had to bestow was civic and political. Towns were planned in chessboard squares for communities dwelling under orderly government. The buildings rose in accordance with the pattern standardised throughout the Roman world. Each was complete with its forum, temples, courts of justice, gaols, baths, markets, and main drains. During the first century the builders evidently took a sanguine view of the resources and future of Britannia, and all their towns were projected to meet an increasing population. It was a period of hope.

The experts dispute the population of Roman Britain, and rival estimates vary between half a million and a million and a half. It seems certain that the army, the civil services, the townsfolk, the well-to-do, and their dependants amounted to three or four hundred thousand. To grow food for these, under the agricultural methods of the age, would have required on the land perhaps double their number. We may therefore assume a population of at least a million in the Romanised area. There may well have been more. But there are no signs that any large increase of population accompanied the Roman system. In more than two centuries of peace and order the inhabitants remained at about the same numbers as in the days of Cassivellaunus. This failure to foster and support a more numerous life spread disappointment and contraction throughout Roman Britain. The conquerors who so easily subdued and rallied the Britons to their method of social life brought with them no means, apart from stopping tribal war, of increasing the annual income derived from the productivity of the soil. The new society, with all its grace of structure, with its spice of elegance and luxury—baths, banquets, togas, schools, literature, and oratory—stood on no more sumptuous foundation than the agriculture of prehistoric times. The rude plenty in which the ancient Britons had dwelt was capable of

supporting only to a moderate extent the imposing façade of
Roman life. The cultivated ground was still for the most part
confined to the lighter and more easily cultivated upland soils,
which had for thousands of years been worked in a primitive
fashion. The powerful Gallic plough on wheels was known in
Britain, but it did not supplant the native implement, which
could only nose along in shallow furrows. With a few exceptions, there was no large-scale attempt to clear the forests,
drain the marshes, and cultivate the heavy clay soil of the
valleys, in which so much fertility had been deposited. Such
mining of lead and tin, such smelting, as had existed from
times immemorial may have gained something from orderly
administration; but there was no new science, no new thrust
of power and knowledge in the material sphere. Thus the economic basis remained constant, and Britain became more
genteel rather than more wealthy. The life of Britain continued
upon a small scale, and in the main was stationary. The new
edifice, so stately and admirable, was light and frail.

These conditions soon cast their shadows upon the boldly
planned towns. The surrounding agricultural prosperity was
not sufficient to support the hopes of their designers. There
are several excavations which show that the original boundaries were never occupied, or that, having been at first occupied, portions of the town fell gradually into decay. There was
not enough material well-being to make things go. Nevertheless men dwelt safely, and what property they had was secured
by iron laws. Urban life in Britannia was a failure, not of
existence, but of expansion. It ran on like the life of some
cathedral city, some fading provincial town, sedate, restricted,
even contracting, but not without grace and dignity.

We owe London to Rome. The military engineers of Claudius, the bureaucracy which directed the supply of the armies,
the merchants who followed in their wake, brought it into a
life not yet stilled. Trade followed the development of their
road system. An extensive and well-planned city with mighty
walls took the place of the wooden trading settlement of
A.D. 61, and soon achieved a leading place in the life of the
Roman province of Britain, superseding the old Belgic capital,
Colchester, as the commercial centre. At the end of the third
century money was coined in the London mint, and the city
was the headquarters of the financial administration. In the
later days of the province London seems to have been the
centre of civil government, as York was of the military,
although it never received the status of a *municipium*.

The efflorescence of Rome in Britain was found in its villa population all over the settled area. The villas of country gentlemen of modest station were built in the most delightful spots of a virgin countryside, amid primeval forests and the gushing of untamed streams. A very large number of comfortable dwellings, each with its lands around it, rose and thrived. At least five hundred have been explored in the southern counties. None is found farther north than Yorkshire or farther west than the Glamorgan sea-plain. The comparative unsuccess of urban life led the better-class Roman Britons to establish themselves in the country, and thus the villa system was the dominant feature of Roman Britain in its heyday. The villas retained their prosperity after the towns had already decayed. The towns were shrunken after the third century. The villas still flourished in the fourth, and in some cases lingered on into the darkening days of the fifth.

The need for strong defences at the time when the expansion of the Empire had practically reached its limits was met by the frontier policy of the Flavian emperors. Domitian was the first to build a continuous line of fortifications. About A.D. 89 the great earth rampart was constructed on the Black Sea, and another connecting the Rhine with the Danube. By the end of the first century a standard type of frontier barrier had been evolved. The work of Agricola in Northern Britain had been left unfinished at his hasty recall. No satisfactory line of defence had been erected, and the position which he had won in Scotland had to be gradually abandoned. The legions fell back on the line of the Stanegate, a road running eastwards from Carlisle. The years which followed revealed the weakness of the British frontier. The accession of Hadrian was marked by a serious disaster. The Ninth Legion disappears from history in combating an obscure rising of the tribes in Northern Britain. The defences were disorganised and the province was in danger. Hadrian came himself to Britain in 122, and the reorganisation of the frontier began.

During the next five years a military barrier was built between the Tyne and the Solway seventy-three miles long. It consisted of a stone rampart eight to ten feet thick, sustained by seventeen forts, garrisoned each by an auxiliary cohort, about eighty castles, and double that number of signal towers. In front of the wall was a 30-foot ditch, and behind it another ditch which seems to have been designed as a customs frontier and was probably controlled and staffed by the financial administration. The works needed a supporting garrison of about

fourteen thousand men, not including some five thousand
who, independent of the fighting units in the forts, were engaged in patrol work along the wall. The troops were pro-
visioned by the local population, whose taxes were paid in
wheat, and each fort contained granaries capable of holding
a year's supply of food.

Twenty years later, in the reign of the Emperor Antoninus
Pius, the Roman troops pushed northwards again over the
ground of Agricola's conquests, and a new wall was built
across the Forth-Clyde isthmus thirty-seven miles in length.
The object was to control the tribes of the eastern and central
Lowlands; but the Roman forces in Britain were not able to
man the new defences without weakening their position on
Hadrian's Wall and in the West. The middle years of the second century were troubled in the military area. Somewhere
about the year 186 the Antonine Wall was abandoned, and the
troops were concentrated on the original line of defence.
Tribal revolts and Scottish raids continually assailed the northern frontier system, and in places the Wall and its supporting
camps were utterly wrecked.

It was not until the Emperor Severus came to Britain in 208
and flung his energies into the task of reorganisation that
stability was achieved. So great had been the destruction, so
massive were his repairs, that in later times he was thought to
have built the Wall, which in fact he only reconstructed. He
died at York in 211; but for a hundred years there was peace
along the Roman Wall.

We can measure the Roman activity in road-building by the
milestones which are discovered from time to time, recording
the name of the emperor under whose decree the work was
done. These long, unswerving causeways stretched in bold
lines across the Island. Ordinarily the road was made with a
bottoming of large stones, often embedded in sand, covered
with a surface of rammed gravel, the whole on an average
eighteen inches thick. In special cases, or after much repairing,
the formation extended to a 3-foot thickness. Over Blackstone
Edge, where the road was laid upon peat, a 16-foot road-span
was made of square blocks of millstone grit, with a kerb on
either side and a line of large squared stones down the middle.
Upon these the wheels of ancient carts going down the steep
hill, braked by skid-pans, have made their grooves.[1]

The first half-century after the Claudian invasion was very
active in road-building. In the second century we find most of

[1] *An Economic Survey of Ancient Rome*, iii, 24.

the work concentrated upon the frontiers of the military districts. By the third century the road system was complete, and needed only to be kept in repair. It is true that for the period of Constantine no fewer than four milestones have been unearthed, which point to some fresh extension, but by 340 all new work was ended, and though repairs were carried out as long as possible no later milestones proclaim a forward movement. The same symptoms reproduced themselves in Gaul after the year 350. These pedestrian facts are one measure of the rise and decline of the Roman power.

If a native of Chester in Roman Britain could wake up to-day [1] he would find laws which were the direct fulfilment of many of those he had known. He would find in every village temples and priests of the new creed which in his day was winning victories everywhere. Indeed the facilities for Christian worship would appear to him to be far in excess of the number of devotees. Not without pride would he notice that his children were compelled to learn Latin if they wished to enter the most famous universities. He might encounter some serious difficulties in the pronunciation. He would find in the public libraries many of the masterpieces of ancient literature, printed on uncommonly cheap paper and in great numbers. He would find a settled government, and a sense of belonging to a worldwide empire. He could drink and bathe in the waters of Bath, or if this were too far he would find vapour baths and toilet conveniences in every city. He would find all his own problems of currency, land tenure, public morals and decorum presented in a somewhat different aspect, but still in lively dispute. He would have the same sense of belonging to a society which was threatened, and to an imperial rule which had passed its prime. He would have the same gathering fears of some sudden onslaught by barbarian forces armed with equal weapons to those of the local legions or auxiliaries. He would still fear the people across the North Sea, and still be taught that his frontiers were upon the Rhine. The most marked changes that would confront him would be the speed of communications and the volume of printed and broadcast matter. He might find both distressing. But against these he could set chloroform, antiseptics, and a more scientific knowledge of hygiene. He would have longer history books to read, containing worse tales than those of Tacitus and Dio. Facilities would be afforded to him for seeing "regions Cæsar never knew," from which he would probably return in sorrow and

[1] Written in 1939.

wonder. He would find himself hampered in every aspect of foreign travel, except that of speed. If he wished to journey to Rome, Constantinople, or Jerusalem, otherwise than by sea, a dozen frontiers would scrutinise his entry. He would be called upon to develop a large number of tribal and racial enmities to which he had formerly been a stranger. But the more he studied the accounts of what had happened since the third century the more satisfied he would be not to have been awakened at an earlier time.

* * *

Carefully conserved, the resources of the Empire in men and material were probably sufficient to maintain the frontiers intact. But they were often wasted in war between rival emperors, and by the middle of the third century the Empire was politically in a state of chaos and financially ruined. Yet there was much vitality still, and from the Illyrian armies came a succession of great soldiers and administrators to restore the unity of the Empire and consolidate its defences. By the end of the century Rome seemed as powerful and stable as ever. But below the surface the foundations were cracking, and through the fissures new ideas and new institutions were thrusting themselves. The cities are everywhere in decline; trade, industry, and agriculture bend under the weight of taxation. Communications are less safe, and some provinces are infested with marauders, peasants who can no longer earn a living on the land. The Empire is gradually dissolving into units of a kind unknown to classical antiquity, which will some day be brought together in a new pattern, feudal and Christian. But before that can happen generations must pass, while the new absolutism struggles by main force to keep the roads open, the fields in cultivation, and the barbarian at bay.

Nevertheless the Roman Empire was an old system. Its sinews and arteries had borne the strain of all that the ancient world had endured. The Roman world, like an aged man, wished to dwell in peace and tranquillity and to enjoy in philosophic detachment the good gifts which life has to bestow upon the more fortunate classes. But new ideas disturbed the internal conservatism, and outside the carefully guarded frontiers vast masses of hungry, savage men surged and schemed. The essence of the Roman peace was toleration of all religions and the acceptance of a universal system of government. Every generation after the middle of the second century saw an increasing weakening of the system and a gathering movement towards a uniform religion. Christianity asked again all the questions which the Roman world deemed answered for ever, and some that it had never thought of. Although the varieties of status, with all their grievous consequences, were accepted during these centuries, even by those who suffered from them most, as part of the law of nature, the institution of slavery, by which a third of Roman society was bound, could not withstand indefinitely the new dynamic thoughts which Christianity brought with it. The alternations between fanatic profligacy and avenging puritanism which marked the succession of the emperors, the contrast between the morals at the centre of power and those practised by wide communities in many subject lands, presented problems of ever-growing unrest. At the moment when mankind seemed to have solved a very large proportion of its secular difficulties and when a supreme Government offered unlimited freedom to spiritual experiment inexorable forces both within and without drove on the forward march. No rest; no stay. "For here have we no continuing city, but we seek one to come." Strange standards of destiny were unfurled, destructive of peace and order, but thrilling the hearts of men. Before the Roman system lay troubles immeasurable—squalor, slaughter, chaos itself, and the long night which was to fall upon the world.

From outside the uncouth barbarians smote upon the barriers. Here on the mainland were savage, fighting animals, joined together in a comradeship of arms, with the best fighting men and their progeny as leaders. In the rough-and-tumble of these communities, with all their crimes and bestialities, there was a more active principle of life than in the majestic achievements of the Roman Empire. We see these forces swelling like a flood against all the threatened dykes of the Roman world, not only brimming at the lip of the dam, but percolating insidiously, now by a breach, now in a mere ooze, while all the time men become conscious of the frailty of the structure itself. Floods of new untamed life burst ceaselessly from Asia, driving westward in a succession of waves. Against these there was no easy superiority of weapons. Cold steel and discipline and the slight capital surplus necessary to move and organise armies constituted the sole defences. If the superior virtue of the legion failed all fell. Certainly from the middle of the second century all these disruptive forces were plainly manifest. However, in Roman Britain men thought for many generations that they had answered the riddle of the Sphinx. They misconceived the meaning of her smile.

The Lost Island

NO one can understand history without continually relating the long periods which are constantly mentioned to the experiences of our own short lives. Five years is a lot. Twenty years is the horizon to most people. Fifty years is antiquity. To understand how the impact of destiny fell upon any generation of men one must first imagine their position and then apply the time-scale of our own lives. Thus nearly all changes were far less perceptible to those who lived through them from day to day than appears when the salient features of an epoch are extracted by the chronicler. We peer at these scenes through dim telescopes of research across a gulf of nearly two thousand years. We cannot doubt that the second and to some extent the third century of the Christian era, in contrast with all that had gone before and most that was to follow, were a Golden Age for Britain. But by the early part of the fourth century shadows had fallen upon this imperfect yet none the less tolerable society. By steady, persistent steps the sense of security departed from Roman Britain. Its citizens felt by daily experience a sense that the world-wide system of which they formed a partner province was in decline. They entered a period of alarm.

The spade of the archæologist, correcting and enlarging the study of historians, the discovery and scrutiny of excavations, ruins, stones, inscriptions, coins, and skeletons, the new yields of aerial photography, are telling a tale which none can doubt. Although the main impressions of the nineteenth century are not overthrown modern knowledge has become more true, more precise, and more profound. The emphasis placed by Victorian writers upon causes and events and their chronology has been altered, especially since the First World War. Their dramas have been modified or upset. A host of solid gradations and sharp-cut refinements is being marshalled in stubborn array. We walk with shorter paces, but on firmer footholds. Famous books which their writers after a lifetime's toil believed were final are now recognised as already obsolete, and new conclusions are drawn not so much from new standpoints as from new discoveries. Nevertheless the broad story holds, for it is founded in a dominating simplicity.

From the end of the third century, when Roman civilisation in Britain and the challenge to the supreme structure were equally at their height, inroads of barbarian peoples began, both from Europe and from the forlorn Island to the westward. The Scots, whom nowadays we should call the Irish, and the Picts from Scotland began to press on Hadrian's Wall, to turn both flanks of it by sea raids on a growing scale. At the same time the Saxons rowed in long-boats across the North Sea and lay heavy all along the east coast from Newcastle to Dover. From this time forth the British countryside dwelt under the same kind of menace of cruel, bloody, and sudden inroad from the sea as do modern nations from the air. Many proofs have been drawn from the soil in recent years. All point to the same conclusion. The villa life of Britain, upon which the edifice of Roman occupation was now built, was in jeopardy. We see the signs of fear spreading through the whole country. Besides the forts along the east and south coasts, and the system of galleys based upon them, a host of new precautions becomes evident. The walls of London were furnished with bastion towers, the stones for which were taken from dwelling-houses, now no longer required by a dwindling town-population. Here and there the broad Roman gateways of townships were narrowed to half their size with masonry, a lasting proof of the increasing insecurity of the times. All over the country hoards of coins have been found, hardly any of which are later than the year A.D. 400. Over this fertile, peaceful, ordered world lay the apprehension of constant peril.

Like other systems in decay, the Roman Empire continued to function for several generations after its vitality was sapped. For nearly a hundred years our Island was one of the scenes of conflict between a dying civilisation and lusty, famishing barbarism. Up to the year 300 Hadrian's Wall, with its garrisons, barred out the Northern savages, but thereafter a new front must be added. At the side of the "Duke of the Northern Marches" there must stand the "Count of the Saxon Shore." All round the eastern and southern coasts, from the Wash to Southampton Water, a line of large fortresses was laboriously built. Eight have been examined. Of these the chief was Richborough, known to the generation of the First World War as an invaluable ferry-port for the supply of the armies in France.

There is some dispute about the strategic conceptions upon which these strongholds were called into being. Many disparaging judgments have been passed upon a policy which is accused of seeking to protect four hundred miles of coastline from these eight points. Obviously these strictures are unjust. The new line of coastal fortresses could only have had any value or reason as bases for a British-Roman fleet.

Such a fleet, the Classis Britannica, had been maintained from the first century. Tiles with an Admiralty mark show that it had permanent stations at Dover and Lympne. But the whole coast was organised for defence, and for long periods these measures proved effective. Vegetius, writing in the fourth century on the art of war, mentions a special kind of light galley attached to the British fleet. These vessels, the hulls, sails, the men's clothes, and even faces, were painted sea-green, to make them invisible, and Vegetius tells us that in naval parlance they were called "the Painted Ones." As the Imperial and British sea-power gradually became unequal to the raiders the ramparts of the fortresses grew higher and their usefulness less. Flotilla defence by oared galleys working from bases fifty to a hundred miles apart could not contend indefinitely with raiding thrusts. Even a High Sea Fleet capable of keeping the sea for months at a time off the coasts of what are now called Holland, Germany, and Denmark, though a powerful deterrent, would have been too slow to deal with oared boats in calm weather.

The Roman Britons were lively and audacious members of the Empire. They took a particularist view, yet wished to have a hand in the game themselves. As time passed the Roman garrison in Britain steadily became more British, and towards the end of the third century it assumed a strong national character. While glorying in the name of citizens and Romans, and having no desire for independence, both province and army adopted a highly critical attitude towards the Imperial Government. Emperors who disregarded British opinion, or sacrificed British interests, above all those who could be accused of neglecting the defences of the province, were the objects of active resentment. A series of mutinies and revolts aggravated the growing dangers of the times. No one can suppose that the Roman military centres at Chester, York, or Caerleon-on-Usk threw up claimants for the Imperial diadem unsupported by a strong backing in local opinion. These were not merely mutinies of discontented soldiers. They were bold bids for control of the Roman Empire by legions only a few thousand strong, but expressing the mood, sentiments, and ambitions of the society in which they lived. They left the local scene for the supreme theatre, like players who wish to quit the provinces for the capital. Unhappily they took away with them at each stage important elements of the exiguous military forces needed to man the dykes.

* * *

The Emperor Diocletian has gone down to history principally as the persecutor of the early Christians, and the enormous work which he achieved in restoring the frontiers of the ancient world has remained under that shadow. His policy was to construct a composite Cæsarship. There were to be two Emperors and two Cæsars, he himself being the senior of the four. In due course the Emperors would retire in favour of the Cæsars, new ones would be appointed, and thus the succession would be preserved. The co-Emperor Maximian, sent to Gaul in 285, and responsible for Britannia, was deeply concerned by the raiding of the Saxon pirates. He strengthened the Channel fleet, and put at its head a sea officer from the Low Countries named Carausius. This man was tough, resolute, ambitious, and without scruple; from his base at Boulogne he encouraged the raiders to come and pillage, and then when they were laden with plunder he fell upon them with Roman-British flotillas, captured them by scores, and destroyed them without mercy. His success did not satisfy the British community; they accused him of having been in league with those he had destroyed. He explained that this was all part of his ambush; but the fact that he had retained all the spoil in his own hands told heavily against him. Maximian sought to bring him to execution, but Carausius, landing in Britain, declared himself Emperor, gained the Island garrison to his cause, and defeated Maximian in a sea battle. On this it was thought expedient to come to terms with the stubborn rebel, and in the year 287 Carausius was recognised as one of the Augusti in command of Britain and of Northern Gaul.

For six years this adventurer, possessing sea-power, reigned in our Island. He seems to have served its interests passably well. However, the Emperor Diocletian and his colleagues were only biding their time, and in the year 293 they cast away all pretence of friendship. One of the new Cæsars, Constantius Chlorus, besieged and took Boulogne, the principal Continental base of Carausius, who was soon assassinated by one of his officers. The new competitor sought to become Emperor in his stead. He did not gain the support of the British nation and the whole country fell into confusion. The Picts were not slow to seize their advantage. The Wall was pierced, and fire and sword wasted the Northern districts. Chlorus crossed the Channel as a deliverer. His colleague, with part of the force, landed near Portsmouth; he himself sailed up the Thames, and was received by London with gratitude and submission. He restored order. A gold medallion discovered at Arras in 1922 reveals him at the head of a fleet which had sailed up the Thames. He drove back the Northern invaders, and set to work to restore and improve the whole system of defence.

* * *

Continuous efforts were made by the Roman-British community to repel the inroads, and for two or three generations there were counter-strokes by flotillas of galleys, and hurried marchings of cohorts and of British auxiliaries towards the various thrusts of raid or invasion. But although the process of wearing down was spread over many years, and misery deepened by inches, we must recognise in the year 367 circumstances of supreme and murderous horror. In that fatal year the Picts, the Scots, and the Saxons seemed to work in combination. All fell together upon Britannia. The Imperial troops resisted manfully. The Duke of the Northern Marches and the Count of the Saxon Shore were killed in the battles. A wide-open breach was made in the defences, and murderous hordes poured in upon the fine world of country houses and homesteads. Everywhere they were blotted out. The ruins tell the tale. The splendid Mildenhall silver dinner service, now in the British Museum, is thought to have been buried at this time by its owners, when their villa was surprised by raiders. Evidently they did not live to dig it up again. The villa life of Britain only feebly recovered from the disaster. The towns were already declining. Now people took refuge in them. At least they had walls.

The pages of history reveal the repeated efforts made by the Imperial Government to protect Britannia. Again and again, in spite of revolts and ingratitude, officers and troops were sent to restore order or drive back the barbarians. After the disasters of 367 the Emperor Valentinian sent a general, Theodosius, with a considerable force to relieve the province. Theodosius achieved his task, and once again we find on the coastal fortifications the traces of a further strong reconstruction. Untaught however by continuing danger, the garrison and inhabitants of Britain in 383 yielded themselves willingly to a Spaniard, Magnus Maximus, who held the command in Britain and now declared himself Emperor. Scraping together all the troops he could find, and stripping the Wall and the fortresses of their already scanty defenders, Maximus hastened to Gaul, and defeated the Emperor Gratian near Paris. Gratian was murdered at Lyons by his troops, and Maximus became master of Gaul and Spain as well as Britain. For five years he struggled to defend his claim to these great dominions, but Theodosius, who had succeeded Gratian, at length defeated and slew him.

Meanwhile the Wall was pierced again, and Britain lay open to the raiders both from the North and from the sea. Seven years more were to pass before Theodosius could send his general, Stilicho, to the Island. This great soldier drove out the intruders and repaired the defences. The writings of Claudian, the court poet, describe in triumphant terms the liberation of Britain from its Saxon, Pictish, and Scottish assailants in the year 400. In celebrating the first consulship of Stilicho he tells how Britain has expressed her gratitude for her deliverance from the fear of these foes. This sentiment soon fades.

Stilicho had returned to Rome, and was in chief command when in the same year Alaric and the Visigoths invaded Italy. He was forced to recall a further part of the British garrison to defend the heart of the Empire. In 402 he defeated Alaric in the great battle of Pollentia, and drove him out of Italy. No sooner was this accomplished than a new barbarian invasion swept down upon him under Radagaisus. By 405 Stilicho had completely destroyed this second vast host. Italy was scarcely clear when a confederacy of Suevi, Vandals, Avars, and Burgundians broke through the Rhine frontiers and overran Northern Gaul. The indomitable Stilicho was preparing to meet this onslaught when the British army, complaining that the province was being neglected, mutinied. They set up a rival Emperor named Marcus, and on his speedy murder elected a Briton, Gratianus, in his stead. After his assassination four months later the soldiers chose another Briton, who bore the famous name of Constantine. Constantine, instead of protecting the Island, found himself compelled to defend upon the Continent the titles he had usurped. He drained Britain of troops, and, as Magnus Maximus had done, set forth for Boulogne to try his fortune. In the supreme theatre for three years, with varying success, he contended with Stilicho, and was finally captured and executed, as Maximus had been before him. None of the troops who had accompanied him ever returned to Britain. Thus in these fatal years the civilised parts of the Island were stripped of their defenders, both in order to aid the Empire and to strike against it.

By the beginning of the fifth century all the legions had gone on one errand or another, and to frantic appeals for aid the helpless Emperor Honorius could only send his valedictory message in 410, that "the cantons should take steps to defend themselves."

* * *

The first glimpse we have of the British after the Roman Government had withdrawn its protection is afforded by the visit of St Germanus in 429. The Bishop came from Auxerre in order to uproot the Pelagian heresy, which in spite of other preoccupations our Christian Island had been able to evolve. This doctrine consisted in assigning an undue importance to free will, and cast a consequential slur upon the doctrine of original sin. It thus threatened to deprive mankind, from its very birth, of an essential part of our inheritance. The Bishop of Auxerre and another episcopal colleague arrived at St Albans, and we are assured that they soon convinced the doubters and eradicated the evil opinions to which they had incautiously hearkened. What kind of Britain did he find? He speaks of it as a land of wealth. There is treasure; there are flocks and herds; food is abundant; institutions, civil and religious, function; the country is prosperous, but at war. An invading army from the North or the East is approaching. It was an army said to be composed of Saxons, Picts, and Scots in ill-assorted and unholy alliance.

The Bishop had been a distinguished general in his prime. He organised the local forces. He reconnoitred the surrounding districts. He noticed in the line of the enemy's advance a valley surrounded by high hills. He took command, and lay in ambush for the ferocious heathen hordes. When the enemy were entangled in the defile, suddenly "The priests shouted a triple Alleluia at their foes. . . . The cry was taken up with one mighty shout and echoed from side to side of the enclosed valley; the enemy were smitten with terror, thinking that the rocks and the very sky were falling upon them; such was their fear that they could hardly run quickly enough. They threw away their arms in their disorderly flight, glad to escape naked; a river devoured many in their headlong fear, though in their advance they had crossed it in good order. The innocent army saw itself avenged, a spectator of a victory gained without exertion. The abandoned spoils were collected, . . . and the

Britons triumphed over an enemy routed without loss of blood; the victory was won by faith and not by might. . . . So the Bishop returned to Auxerre, having settled the affairs of that most wealthy Island, and overcome their foes both spiritual and carnal, that is to say, both the Pelagians and Saxons." [1]

Another twelve years passed, and a Gaulish chronicler records this sombre note in A.D. 441 or 442: "The Britons in these days by all kinds of calamities and disasters are falling into the power of the Saxons." What had happened? Something more than the forays of the fourth century: the mass migration from North Germany had begun. Thereafter the darkness closes in.

Upon this darkness we have four windows, each obstructed by dim or coloured glass. We have the tract of Gildas the Wise, written, approximately, in A.D. 545, and therefore a hundred years after the curtain fell between Britannia and the Continent. Nearly two hundred years later the Venerable Bede, whose main theme was the history of the English Church, lets fall some precious scraps of information, outside his subject, about the settlement itself. A compilation known as the *Historia Britonum* contains some documents earlier than Bede. Finally, in the ninth century, and very likely at the direction of King Alfred, various annals preserved in different monasteries were put together as the *Anglo-Saxon Chronicle*. Checking these by each other, and by such certainties as archæology allows us to entertain, we have the following picture.

Imitating a common Roman practice, the dominant British chief about A.D. 450 sought to strengthen himself by bringing in a band of mercenaries from over the seas. They proved a trap. Once the road was open fresh fleet-loads made their way across and up the rivers, from the Humber perhaps as far round as Portsmouth. But the British resistance stiffened as the invaders got away from the coast, and their advance was brought to a standstill for nearly fifty years by a great battle won at Mount Badon. If now we draw a V-shaped line, one leg from Chester to Southampton, and the other back from Southampton to the Humber, we shall observe that the great bulk of pagan Saxon remains, and that place-names in *ing* or *ings*, usually evidence of early settlement, are to the east of this second line. Here then we have the England of about A.D. 500. The middle sector is the debatable land, and the West is still Britain.

So far this tale is confirmed, historically and geographically.

[1] Constantine of Lyons, a near contemporary biographer of St Germanus.

Gildas could have heard the story of the mercenaries from old men whom he had known in his youth, and there is no real ground for doubting the statements of Nennius, a compiler probably of the ninth century, and Bede, who agree that the name of the deceived chief who invited these deadly foes was Vortigern. Hengist, a name frequently mentioned in Northern story, like a medieval mercenary was ready to sell his sword and his ships to anyone who would give him land on which to support his men; and what he took was the future kingdom of Kent.

Gildas has a tale to tell of this tragedy.

No sooner have they (the Britons) gone back to their land than the foul hosts of the Picts and Scots land promptly from their coracles. . . . These two races differ in part in their manners, but they agree in their lust for blood, and in their habit of covering their hang-dog faces with hair, instead of covering with clothing those parts of their bodies which demand it. They seize all the northern and outlying part of the country as far as to the Wall. Upon this Wall stands a timorous and unwarlike garrison. The wretched citizens are pulled down from the Wall and dashed to the ground by the hooked weapons of their naked foes. What shall I add? The citizens desert the high Wall and their towns, and take to a flight more desperate than any before. Again the enemy pursue them, and there is slaughter more cruel than ever. As lambs by butchers, so are our piteous citizens rent by their foes, till their manner of sojourning might be compared to that of wild beasts. For they maintained themselves by robbery for the sake of a little food. Thus calamities from outside were increased by native feuds; so frequent were these disasters that the country was stripped of food, save what could be procured in the chase.

Therefore again did the wretched remnants send a letter to Ætius, a powerful Roman—"To Ætius, three times Consul, the groans of the Britons": "The barbarians drive us to the sea, the sea drives us to the barbarians: between these two methods of death we are either massacred or drowned." But they got no help. Meantime dire famine compelled many to surrender to their spoilers. . . . But others would in no wise surrender, but kept on sallying from the mountains, caves, passes, and thick coppices. And then, for the first time, trusting not in man but in God, they slaughtered the foes who for so many years had been plundering their country. . . . For a time the boldness of our enemies was checked, but not the wickedness of our own countrymen: the enemy left our citizens, but our citizens did not leave their sins.

Nennius also tells us, what Gildas omits, the name of the British soldier who won the crowning mercy of Mount Badon, and that name takes us out of the mist of dimly remembered history into the daylight of romance. There looms, large, uncertain, dim but glittering, the legend of King Arthur and the Knights of the Round Table. Somewhere in the Island a great captain gathered the forces of Roman Britain and fought the barbarian invaders to the death. Around him, around his name and his deeds, shine all that romance and poetry can bestow. Twelve battles, all located in scenes untraceable, with foes unknown, except that they were heathen, are punctiliously set forth in the Latin of Nennius. Other authorities say, "No Arthur; at least, no proof of any Arthur." It was only when Geoffrey of Monmouth six hundred years later was praising the splendours of feudalism and martial aristocracy that chivalry, honour, the Christian faith, knights in steel and ladies bewitching, are enshrined in a glorious circle lit by victory. Later this would have been retold and embellished by the genius of Malory, Spenser, and Tennyson. True or false, they have gained an immortal hold upon the thoughts of men. It is difficult to believe it was all an invention of a Welsh writer. If it was he must have been a marvellous inventor.

Modern research has not accepted the annihilation of Arthur. Timidly but resolutely the latest and best-informed writers unite to proclaim his reality. They cannot tell when in this dark period he lived, or where he held sway and fought his battles. They are ready to believe however that there was a great British warrior, who kept the light of civilisation burning against all the storms that beat, and that behind his sword there sheltered a faithful following of which the memory did not fail. All four groups of the Celtic tribes which dwelt in the tilted uplands of Britain cheered themselves with the Arthurian legend, and each claimed their own region as the scene of his exploits. From Cornwall to Cumberland a search for Arthur's realm or sphere has been pursued.

The reserve of modern assertions is sometimes pushed to extremes, in which the fear of being contradicted leads the writer to strip himself of almost all sense and meaning. One specimen of this method will suffice.

It is reasonably certain that a petty chieftain named Arthur did exist, probably in South Wales. It is possible that he may have held some military command uniting the tribal forces of the Celtic or highland zone or part of it against raiders and invaders (not all of them necessarily Teutonic). It is also possible that he may have engaged in all or some of the battles attributed to him; on the other hand, this attribution may belong to a later date.

This is not much to show after so much toil and learning. None the less, to have established a basis of fact for the story of Arthur is a service which should be respected. In this account we prefer to believe that the story with which Geoffrey delighted the fiction-loving Europe of the twelfth century is not all fancy.[1] If we could see exactly what happened we should find ourselves in the presence of a theme as well founded, as inspired, and as inalienable from the inheritance of mankind as the *Odyssey* or the Old Testament. It is all true, or it ought to be; and more and better besides. And wherever men are fighting against barbarism, tyranny, and massacre, for freedom, law, and honour, let them remember that the fame of their deeds, even though they themselves be exterminated, may perhaps be celebrated as long as the world rolls round. Let us then declare that King Arthur and his noble knights, guarding the Sacred Flame of Christianity and the theme of a world order, sustained by valour, physical strength, and good horses and armour, slaughtered innumerable hosts of foul barbarians and set decent folk an example for all time.

We are told he was Dux Bellorum. What could be more natural or more necessary than that a commander-in-chief should be accepted—a new Count of Britain, such as the Britons had appealed to Ætius to give them fifty years before? Once Arthur is recognised as the commander of a mobile field army, moving from one part of the country to another and uniting with local forces in each district, the disputes about the scenes of his actions explain themselves. Moreover the fourth century witnessed the rise of cavalry to the dominant position in the battlefield. The day of infantry had passed for a time, and the day of the legion had passed for ever. The Saxon invaders were infantry, fighting with sword and spear, and having little armour. Against such an enemy a small force of ordinary Roman cavalry might well prove invincible. If a chief like Arthur had gathered a band of mail-clad cavalry he could have moved freely about Britain, everywhere heading the local resistance to the invader and gaining repeated victories. The memory of Arthur carried with it the hope that a deliverer would return one day. The legend lived upon the increasing tribulations of the age. Arthur has been described as the last of the Romans. He understood Roman ideas, and used them

[1] See Sir Frank Stenton, *Anglo-Saxon England* (1943), p. 3: "The silence of Gildas may suggest that the Arthur of history was a less imposing figure than the Arthur of legend. But it should not be allowed to remove him from the sphere of history, for Gildas was curiously reluctant to introduce personal names into his writing."

for the good of the British people. "The heritage of Rome," Professor Collingwood says, "lives on in many shapes, but of the men who created that heritage Arthur was the last, and the story of Roman Britain ends with him."

Arthur's "twelfth battle," says Nennius, "was on Mount Badon, in which there fell in one day nine hundred and sixty men from the onslaught of Arthur only, and no one laid them low save he alone. And in all his battles he was victor. But they, when in all these battles they had been overthrown, sought help from Germany and increased without intermission."

All efforts to fix the battlefield of Mount Badon have failed. A hundred learned investigations have brought no results, but if, as seems most probable, it was fought in the Debatable Land to check the advance from the East, then the best claimant to the title is Liddington Camp, which looks down on Badbury, near Swindon. On the other hand, we are able to fix the date with unusual accuracy. Gildas speaks of it as having occurred forty-three years and a month from the date when he was writing, and he says that he remembers the date because it was that of his own birth. Now we know from his book that the King of North Wales, Maelgwyn, was still alive when he wrote, and the annals of Cambria tell us that he died of the plague in 547. Gildas thus wrote at the latest in this year, and the Battle of Mount Badon, forty-three years earlier, would have been fought in 503. We have also a cross-check in the Irish annals, which state that Gildas died in 569 or 570. His birth is therefore improbable before 490, and thus the date of the battle seems to be fixed between 490 and 503.

* * *

A broader question is keenly disputed. Did the invaders exterminate the native population, or did they superimpose themselves upon them and become to some extent blended with them? Here it is necessary to distinguish between the age of fierce forays in search of plunder and the age of settlement. Gildas is speaking of the former, and the scenes he describes were repeated in the Danish invasions three centuries later. But to the settler such raids are only occasional incidents in a life mainly occupied in subduing the soil, and in that engrossing task labour is as important as land. The evidence of place-names suggests that in Sussex extermination was the rule. Farther west there are grounds for thinking that a substantial British population survived, and the oldest West Saxon code of A.D. 694 makes careful provision for the rights of "Welshmen" of various degrees—substantial landowners, and "the King's Welshmen who ride his errands," his native gallopers in fact, who know the ancient track-ways. Even where self-interest did not preserve the native villagers as labourers on Saxon farms we may cherish the hope that somewhere a maiden's cry for pity, the appeal of beauty in distress, the lustful needs of an invading force, would create some bond between victor and vanquished. Thus the blood would be preserved, thus the rigours of subjugation would fade as generations passed away. The complete obliteration of an entire race over large areas is repulsive to the human mind. There should at least have been, in default of pity, a hearing for practical advantage or the natural temptations of sex. Thus serious writers contend that the Anglo-Saxon conquest was for the bulk of the British community mainly a change of masters. The rich were slaughtered; the brave and proud fell back in large numbers upon the Western mountains. Other numerous bands escaped betimes to Brittany, whence their remote posterity were one day to return.

The Saxon was moreover a valley-settler. His notion of an economic holding was a meadow for hay near the stream, the lower slopes under the plough, the upper slopes kept for pasture. But in many places a long time must have passed before these lower grounds could be cleared and drained, and while this work was in progress what did he live on but the produce of the upland British farms? It is more natural to suppose that he would keep his natives working as serfs on the land with which they were familiar until the valley was ready for sowing. Then the old British farms would go down to grass, and the whole population would cluster in the village by the stream or the spring. But the language of the valley-settlers, living in compact groups, would be dominant over that of the hill-cultivators, scattered in small and isolated holdings. The study of modern English place-names has shown that hill, wood, and stream names are often Celtic in origin, even in regions where the village names are Anglo-Saxon. In this way, without assuming any wholesale extermination, the disappearance of the British language can be explained even in areas where we know a British population to have survived. They had to learn the language of their masters: there was no need for their masters to learn theirs. Thus it came about that both Latin and British yielded to the speech of the newcomers so completely that hardly a trace of either is to be found in our earliest records.

There was no uniformity of practice in the Island. There is good reason to think that the newcomers in Kent settled down beside the old inhabitants, whose name, Cantiaci, they adopted. In Northumbria there are strong traces of Celtic law. In Hants and Wilts a broad belt of British names, from Liss to Deverill, seems to show the natives still cultivating their old fields on the downs, while the Saxon was clearing the valleys. There was no colour bar. In physical type the two races resembled each other; and the probabilities are that in many districts a substantial British element was incorporated in the Saxon stock.

The invaders themselves were not without their yearnings for settled security. Their hard laws, the rigours they endured, were but the results of the immense pressures behind them as the hordes of avid humanity spread westward from Central Asia. The warriors returning from a six months' foray liked to sprawl in lazy repose. Evidently they were not insensible to progressive promptings, but where, ask the chiefs and elders, could safety be found? In the fifth century, as the pressure from the East grew harder and as the annual raiding parties returned from Britain with plunder and tales of wealth there was created in the ruling minds a sense of the difficulty of getting to the Island, and consequently of the security which would attend its occupation by a hardy and valiant race. Here, perhaps, in this wave-lapped Island men might settle down and enjoy the good things of life without the haunting fear of subjugation by a stronger hand, and without the immense daily sacrifices inseparable from military and tribal discipline on the mainland. To these savage swords Britain seemed a refuge. In the wake of the raiders there grew steadily the plan and system of settlement. Thus, with despair behind and hope before, the migration to Britain and its occupation grew from year to year.

* * *

Of all the tribes of the Germanic race none was more cruel than the Saxons. Their very name, which spread to the whole confederacy of Northern tribes, was supposed to be derived from the use of a weapon, the seax, a short one-handed sword. Although tradition and the Venerable Bede assign the conquest of Britain to the Angles, Jutes, and Saxons together, and although the various settlements have tribal peculiarities, it is

probable that before their general exodus from Schleswig-
Holstein the Saxons had virtually incorporated the other two
strains.

The history books of our childhood attempted courageously
to prescribe exact dates for all the main events. In 449 Hengist
and Horsa, invited by Vortigern, founded the Jutish kingdom
of Kent upon the corpses of its former inhabitants. In 477
Ella and his three sons arrived to continue the inroad. In 495
Cerdic and Cynric appeared. In 501 Port, the pirate, founded
Portsmouth. In 514 the West Saxons Stuf and Wihtgar descended in their turn and put the Britons to flight. In 544
Wihtgar was killed. In 547 came Ida, founder of the kingdom
of Northumberland. All that can be said about these dates is
that they correspond broadly to the facts, and that these successive waves of invaders, bringing behind them settlers, descended on our unhappy shores.

Other authorities draw an alternative picture. "The bulk of
the homesteads within the village," J. R. Green tells us,

were those of its freemen or ceorls; but amongst these were the
larger homes of eorls, or men distinguished among their fellows by
noble blood, who were held in an hereditary reverence, and from
whom the leaders of the village were chosen in war-time or rulers
in times of peace. But the choice was a purely voluntary one, and
the man of noble blood enjoyed no legal privilege amongst his
fellows.[1]

If this were so we might thus early have realised the democratic ideal of "the association of us all through the leadership
of the best." In the tribal conceptions of the Germanic nation
lie, no doubt, many of those principles which are now admired,
and which have formed a recognisable part of the message
which the English-speaking peoples have given to the world.
But the conquerors of Roman Britain, far from practising these
ideals, introduced a whole scheme of society which was funda-
mentally sordid and vicious. The invaders brought into Britain
a principle common to all Germanic tribes, namely, the use
of the money power to regulate all the legal relations of men.
If there was any equality it was equality within each social
grade. If there was liberty it was mainly liberty for the rich. If
there were rights they were primarily the rights of property.
There was no crime committed which could not be compounded by a money payment. Except failure to answer a call

[1] *Short History of the English People*, p. 4.

to join an expedition, there was no offence more heinous than that of theft.

An elaborate tariff prescribed in shillings the "wergild" or exact value or worth of every man. An ætheling, or prince, was worth 1500 shillings, a shilling being the value of a cow in Kent, or of a sheep elsewhere; an eorl, or nobleman, 300 shillings; a ceorl, now degraded to the word "churl," who was a yeoman farmer, was worth 100 shillings; a læt, or agricultural serf, 40–80 shillings, and a slave nothing. All these laws were logically and mathematically pushed to their extremes. If a ceorl killed an eorl he had to pay three times as much in compensation as if the eorl were the murderer. And these laws were applied to the families of all. The life of a slaughtered man could be compounded for cash. With money all was possible; without it only retribution or loss of liberty. However, the ætheling, valued at 1500 shillings, suffered in certain respects. The penalty for slander was the tearing out of the tongue. If an ætheling were guilty of this offence his tongue was worth five times that of an eorl and fifteen times as much as that of a common læt, and he could ransom it only on these terms. Thus the abuse of a humble tongue was cheap. Wergild at least, as Alfred said long afterwards, was better than the blood feud.

The foundation of the Germanic system was blood and kin. The family was the unit, the tribe was the whole. The great transition which we witness among the emigrants is the abandonment of blood and kin as the theme of their society and its replacement by local societies and lordship based on the ownership of land. This change arose, like so many of the lessons learned by men, from the grim needs of war. Fighting for life and foothold against men as hard pressed as themselves, each pioneering band fell inevitably into the hands of the bravest, most commanding, most fortunate war-leader. This was no longer a foray of a few months, or at the outside a year. Here were settlements to be founded, new lands to be reclaimed and cultivated, land which moreover offered to the deeper plough a virgin fertility. These must be guarded, and who could guard them except the bold chieftains who had gained them over the corpses of their former owners?

Thus the settlement in England was to modify the imported structure of Germanic life. The armed farmer-colonists found themselves forced to accept a stronger state authority owing to the stresses of continued military action. In Germany they had no kings. They developed them in Britain from leaders who claimed descent from the ancient gods. The position of the king continually increased in importance, and his supporters or companions gradually formed a new class in society, which carried with it the germ of feudalism, and was in the end to dominate all other conventions. But the lord was master; he must also be protector. He must stand by his people, must back them in the courts, feed them in time of famine, and they in return must work his land and follow him in war.

The king was at first only the war-leader made permanent; but, once set up, he had his own interests, his own needs, and his own mortal dangers. To make himself secure became his paramount desire. "To be thus is nothing, but to be safely thus . . ." But how was this to be achieved? Only by the king gathering round him a band of the most successful warriors and interesting them directly in the conquest and in the settlement. He had nothing to give them except land. There must be a hierarchy. The king must be surrounded by those who had shared his deeds and his bounty. The spoils of war were soon consumed, but the land remained for ever. Land there was in plenty, of varying quality and condition, but to give individual warriors a title to any particular tract was contrary to the whole tradition of the Germanic tribes. Now under the hard pressures of war and pioneering land increasingly became private property. Insensibly, at first, but with growing speed from the seventh century onwards, a landed aristocracy was created owing all they had to the king. While the resistance of the Britons was vigorously maintained, and the fortunes of the struggle swung this way and that way for nearly two hundred years, this new institution of personal leadership established in the divinely descended war-chief sank deeply into the fibre of the Anglo-Saxon invaders.

But with this movement towards a more coherent policy or structure of society there came also a welter of conflicting minor powers. Distances were usually prohibitive, and writing virtually unknown. Districts were separated from each other like islands in rough seas, and thus a host of kings and kinglets sprang into existence behind the fighting frontier of the intruding tribes. In marking the many root faults and vices which they possessed a high place must be assigned to their inability to combine. For a long time the Island presented only the spectacle of a chaos arising from the strife of small fiercely organised entities. Although from the time of the immigration the people south of the Humber were generally subject to a common overlord, they were never able to carry the evolution of kingship forward to a national throne. They remained marauders; but they had taken more pains to be sure of their booty.

Much has been written about the enervating character of Roman rule in Britain, and how the people were rendered lax and ineffectual by the modest comforts which it supplied. There is no doubt that Gildas, by his writings, imparted an impression, perhaps in this case well founded, of gross incompetence and fatuity in the society and administration which followed the decay of Roman power. But justice to this vanished epoch demands recognition of the fact that the Britons fought those who are now called the English for nearly two hundred and fifty years. For a hundred years they fought them under the ægis of Rome, with its world organisation; but for a hundred and fifty years they fought them alone. The conflict ebbed and flowed. British victories were gained, which once for a whole generation brought the conquest to a halt; and in the end the mountains which even the Romans had been unable to subdue proved an invincible citadel of the British race.

BOOK ONE · CHAPTER FIVE

England

A RED sunset; a long night; a pale, misty dawn! But as the light grows it becomes apparent to remote posterity that everything was changed. Night had fallen on Britannia. Dawn rose on England, humble, poor, barbarous, degraded and divided, but alive. Britannia had been an active part of a world state; England was once again a barbarian island. It had been Christian, it was now heathen. Its inhabitants had rejoiced in well-planned cities, with temples, markets, academies. They had nourished craftsmen and merchants, professors of literature and rhetoric. For four hundred years there had been order and law, respect for property, and a widening culture. All had vanished. The buildings, such as they were, were of wood, not stone. The people had lost entirely the art of writing. Some miserable runic scribblings were the only means by which they could convey their thoughts or wishes to one another at a distance. Barbarism reigned in its rags, without even the stern military principles which had animated and preserved the Germanic tribes. The confusion and conflict of petty ruffians sometimes called kings racked the land. There was nothing worthy of the name of nationhood, or even of tribalism; yet this is a transition which the learned men of the nineteenth century banded themselves together to proclaim as an onward step in the march of mankind. We wake from an awful and, it might well have seemed, endless nightmare to a scene of utter prostration. Nor did the seeds of recovery spring from the savage hordes who had wrecked the Roman culture. They would certainly have continued to welter indefinitely in squalor, but for the fact that a new force was stirring beyond the seas which, moving slowly, fitfully, painfully, among the ruins of civilisation, reached at length by various paths the unhappy Island, to which, according to Procopius, the souls of the dead upon the mainland were ferried over by some uncouth Charon.

Christianity had not been established as the religion of the Empire during the first two centuries of the Roman occupation of Britain. It grew with many other cults in the large and easy tolerance of the Imperial system. There arose however a British Christian Church which sent its bishops to the early councils, and had, as we have seen, sufficient vitality to develop the Pelagian heresy from its own unaided heart-searchings. When the evil days overtook the land and the long struggle with the Saxons was fought out the British Church fell back with other survivors upon the western parts of the Island. Such was the gulf between the warring races that no attempt was made at any time by the British bishops to Christianise the invaders. Perhaps they were not given any chance of converting them. After an interval one of their leading luminaries, afterwards known as St David, accomplished the general conversion of what is now Wales. Apart from this British Christianity languished in its refuges, and might well have become moribund but for the appearance of a remarkable and charming personality.

St Patrick was a Roman Briton of good family dwelling probably in the Severn valley. His father was a Christian deacon, a Roman citizen, and a member of the municipal council. One day in the early fifth century there descended on the district a band of Irish raiders, burning and slaying. The young Patrick was carried off and sold into slavery in Ireland. Whether he dwelt in Connaught or in Ulster is disputed, and the evidence is contradictory. It may well be that both versions are true and that both provinces may claim the honour. For six years, wherever it was, he tended swine, and loneliness led him to seek comfort in religion. He was led by miraculous promptings to attempt escape. Although many miles separated him from the sea he made his way to a port, found a ship, and persuaded the captain to take him on board. After many wanderings we find him in one of the small islands off Marseilles, then a centre of the new monastic movement spreading westward from the Eastern Mediterranean. Later he consorted with Bishop Germanus of Auxerre. He conceived an earnest desire to return good for evil and spread the tidings he had learned among his former captors in Ireland. After fourteen years of careful training by the Bishop and self-preparation for what must have seemed a forlorn adventure Patrick sailed back in 432 to the wild regions which he had quitted. His success was speedy and undying. "He organised the Christianity already in existence; he converted kingdoms which were still pagan, especially in the West; he brought Ireland into connection with the Church of Western Europe, and made it formally part of universal Christendom." On a somewhat lower plane, although also held in perpetual memory, was the banishing of snakes and reptiles of all kinds from the Irish soil, for which from age to age his fame has been celebrated.

It was therefore in Ireland and not in Wales or England that the light of Christianity now burned and gleamed through the darkness. And it was from Ireland that the Gospel was carried to the North of Britain and for the first time cast its redeeming spell upon the Pictish invaders. Columba, born half a century after St Patrick's death, but an offspring of his Church, and imbued with his grace and fire, proved a new champion of the faith. From the monastery which he established in the island of Iona his disciples went forth to the British kingdom of Strathclyde, to the Pictish tribes of the North, and to the Anglian kingdom of Northumbria. He is the founder of the Scottish Christian Church. Thus the message which St Patrick had carried to Ireland came back across the stormy waters and spread through wide regions. There was however a distinction in the form of Christianity which reached England through the mission of St Columba and that which was more generally accepted throughout the Christianised countries of Europe. It was monastic in its form, and it travelled from the East through Northern Ireland to its new home without touching at any moment the Roman centre.

The Celtic churches therefore received a form of ecclesiastical government which was supported by the loosely knit communities of monks and preachers, and was not in these early decisive periods associated with the universal organisation of the Papacy.

* * *

In spite of the slow means of travel and scanty news, the Papacy had from an early stage followed with deep attention the results of St Columba's labours. Its interest was excited not only by the spread of the Gospel, but also by any straying from the true path into which new Christians might be betrayed. It saw with thankfulness an ardent Christian movement afoot in these remote Northern islands, and with concern that it was from the outset independent of the Papal throne. These were the days when it was the first care of the Bishop of Rome that all Christ's sheep should be gathered into one fold. Here in the North, where so much zeal and fervour were evident, the faith seemed to be awkwardly and above all separately planted.

For various reasons, including the spreading of the Gospel, it was decided in the closing decade of the sixth century that a guide and teacher should be sent to England to diffuse and stimulate the faith, to convert the heathen, and also to bring about an effective working union between British Christians and the main body of the Church. For this high task Pope Gregory, afterwards called "the Great," and the ecclesiastical statesmen gathered in Rome selected a trusty and cultured monk named Augustine. St Augustine, as he is known to history, began his mission in 596 under hopeful auspices. Kent had always been the part of the British Island most closely in contact with Europe, and in all its various phases the most advanced in culture. The King of Kent had married Bertha, a daughter of the Frankish king, the descendant of Clovis, now enthroned in Paris. Although her husband still worshipped Thor and Woden Queen Bertha had already begun to spread the truth through courtly circles. Her chaplain, an earnest and energetic Frank, was given full rein, and thus a powerful impulse came to the people of Kent, who were already in a receptive mood towards the dominant creed of Western Europe. St Augustine, when he landed in Kent, was therefore aware that much had been prepared beforehand. His arrival infused a mood of action. With the aid of the Frankish princess he converted King Ethelbert, who had for reasons of policy long meditated this step. Upon the ruins of the ancient British church of St Martin he refounded the Christian life of Canterbury, which was destined to become the centre and summit of religious England.

Ethelbert, as overlord of England, exercised an effective authority over the kingdoms of the South and West. His policy was at once skilful and ambitious; his conversion to Christianity, however sincere, was also in consonance with his secular aims. He was himself, as the only English Christian ruler, in a position where he might hold out the hand to the British princes, and, using the Christian faith as a bond of union, establish his supremacy over the whole country. This, no doubt, was also in accordance with the ideas which Augustine had carried from Rome. Thus at the opening of the seventh century Ethelbert and Augustine summoned a conference of the British Christian bishops. The place chosen in the Severn valley was on the frontier between the English and British domains, and far outside the bounds of the Kentish kingdom. Here, then, would be a chance of a general and lasting peace for both races, reconciled in the name of Christ; and of this settlement Ethelbert and his descendants could securely expect to be the heirs. We must regret that this hope, sustained by sagacious and benevolent politics, was not realised. It failed for two separate reasons: first, the sullen and jealous temper of the British bishops, and, secondly, the tactless arrogance of St Augustine.

There were two conferences, with an interval. The discussions were ostensibly confined to interesting but uncontroversial questions. There was the date of Easter, which is still debated, and also the form of the tonsure. Augustine urged the Roman custom of shaving only the top of the head. The British bishops had perhaps imitated the Druidical method of shaving from the centre to the ears, leaving a fringe on the forehead. It was a choice of the grotesque. These were matters which might well be capable of adjustment, but which conveniently offered ample pasture upon which the conferences could browse in public, while the vital issues were settling themselves in an atmosphere of goodwill, or being definitely compacted behind the scenes.

But the British bishops were found in no mood to throw themselves into the strong embraces of Rome. Why should they, who had so long defended the Faith against horrible cruelties and oppression, now receive their guidance from a Saxon Kentish king whose conversion was brand-new, and whose political designs, however inspiring, were none the less obvious? The second conference ended in a complete rupture. When Augustine found himself in the presence of what he deemed to be unreasonable prejudice and deep-seated hostility, when he saw the few bishops who had been won over reproached by their brethren as backsliders and traitors, he fell back quite quickly upon threats. If British Christianity would not accept the fair offers now made the whole influence and prestige of Rome would be thrown against them upon the English side. The Saxon armies would be blessed and upheld by Rome and the unbroken traditions of the main Christian Church, and no sympathy would be felt for these long-faithful British Christians when they had their throats cut by the new English convert states. "If," the Saint exclaimed, "you will not have peace from your friends you shall have war from your foes." But this was no more than the British had faced for two hundred years. It was language they understood. The conference separated in enmity; the breach was irreparable. All further efforts by Rome through Ethelbert and the Kentish kingdom to establish even the slightest contact with Christian Britain were inexorably repulsed.

Augustine's mission therefore drew to a dignified but curtailed end. Except for the consecration of Mellitas as Bishop of the East Saxons in a church on the site of St Paul's, he had made little attempt to proselytise outside Kent. From the title loosely accorded him of "Apostle of the English" he enjoyed for many centuries the credit of having re-converted the once-famous Roman province of Britannia to the Christian faith; and this halo has shone about him until comparatively recent times.

* * *

Almost a generation passed before envoys from Rome began to penetrate into Northern England and rally its peoples to Christianity, and then it came about in the wake of political and dynastic developments. By a series of victories Redwald, King of the East Angles, had established a wide dominion over the lands of Central England from the Dee to the Humber. With Redwald's aid the crown of Northumbria was gained by an exiled prince, Edwin, who by his abilities won his way, step by step, to the foremost position in England. Even before the death of his ally Redwald, Edwin was recognised as overlord of all the English kingdoms except Kent, and the isles of Anglesey and Man were also reduced by his ships. He not only established his personal primacy, but the confederation

founded by him foreshadowed the kingdom of all England
that was later to take shape under the kings of Mercia and
Wessex. Edwin married a Christian princess of Kent, whose
religion he had promised to respect. Consequently, in her train
from Canterbury to Edwin's capital at York there rode in 625
the first Roman missionary to Northern England, Paulinus, an
envoy who had first come to Britain in the days of St Augustine, twenty-four years before.

We have a picture agreeable and instructive of Edwin:
"There was then a perfect peace in Britain wheresoever the
dominion of King Edwin extended, and, as it is still prover-
bially said, a woman with her new-born babe might walk
throughout the Island from sea to sea without receiving any
harm. That King took such care for the good of his nation that
in several places where he had seen clear springs near the
highways he caused stakes to be fixed with proper drinking-
vessels hanging on them for the refreshment of travellers, nor
durst any man touch them for any other purpose than that for
which they were designed, either for the great fear they had
of the King or for the affection which they bore him." He
revived the Roman style: "Not only were his banners borne
before him in battle, but even in peace when he rode about
his cities, townships, or provinces with his thanes. A standard-
bearer was always wont to go before him when he walked anywhere in the streets in the Roman fashion."

Such in his heyday was the prince to whom Paulinus resorted. Paulinus converted Edwin, and the ample kingdom of
Northumbria, shaped like England itself in miniature, became
Christian. But this blessed event brought with it swift and dire
consequences. The overlordship of Northumbria was fiercely
resented by King Penda of Mercia, or, as we should now say,
of the Midlands. The drama unfolded with staggering changes
of fortune. In 633 Penda, the heathen, made an unnatural
alliance with Cadwallon, the Christian British King of North
Wales, with the object of overthrowing the suzerainty of
Edwin and breaking the Northumbrian power. Here for the
first time noticed in history British and English fought side by
side. Politics for once proved stronger than religion or race. In
a savage battle near Doncaster Edwin was defeated and slain,
and his head—not the last—was exhibited on the ramparts of
captured York. It may be that York, long the home of a legion,
still preserved Roman-British traditions which led them to welcome the British victors. This sudden destruction of the greatest king who had hitherto ruled in the Island brought in recoil

an equally speedy vengeance. British Cadwallon had triumphed over Northumbria. Here at last was the chance, so long expected, of British vengeance upon their Saxon foes. Here was the faithful paying off of very old but very heavy debts. We might almost be seeing again the spirit of Boadicea.

But the inherent power of Northumbria was great. The name and fame of the slaughtered Edwin rang through the land. His successor, Oswald, of the house of Bernicia, which was one of the two provinces of the kingdom, had but to appear to find himself at the head of the newly Christianised and also infuriated Saxon warriors. Within a year of the death of Edwin Oswald destroyed Cadwallon and his British forces in a hard battle which fell out along the line of the Roman Wall. This was the last pitched battle between the Britons and the Saxons; and it must be admitted that the Britons fared as badly in conduct as in fortune. They had joined with the heathen Saxon Midlands to avenge their wrongs, and had exploited an English movement towards the disunity of the land. They had shattered this bright hope of the Christianity they professed, and now they were themselves overthrown and cast aside. The long story of their struggle with the invaders ended thus in no fine way; but what is important to our tale is that it had ended at last.

The destruction of Cadwallon and the clearance from Northumbria of the wild Western Britons, whose atrocities had united all the Saxon forces in the North, was the prelude to the struggle with King Penda. He was regarded by the Saxon tribes as one who had brought boundless suffering and slaughter upon them through a shameful pact with the hereditary foe. Nevertheless he prospered for a while. He upheld the claims of Thor and Woden with all the strength of Mercia for seven years. He defeated, decapitated, and dismembered King Oswald, as he had destroyed his predecessor before him. But a younger brother of Oswald, Oswy by name, after a few years, settled the family account, and Penda fell by the sword he had drawn too often. Thus the power of Northumbria rose the stronger from the ordeal and eclipse through which its people had passed.

The failure of Ethelbert's attempt to make a Christian re-union of England and Britain left the direction of the immediate future with the Northumbrian Court. It was to York and not to Canterbury that Rome looked, and upon English, not British, armies that the hopes of organised Christendom were placed. When the disasters had overtaken Northumbria

Paulinus had hastened back by sea to Canterbury. Neither he nor Augustine was the kind of man to face the brutal warfare of those times. Carefully trained as they were in the doctrines, interests, and policy of the Papacy, they were not the stuff of which martyrs or evangelists are made. This British incursion was too rough. But the lieutenant of Paulinus, one James the Deacon, stuck to his post through the whole struggle, and preached and baptised continually in the midst of rapine and carnage. Still more important than his work was that of the Celtic mission to Northumbria under St Aidan. Much of Mercia and East Anglia, as well as Northumbria, was recovered to Christianity by the Celtic missionaries. Thus two streams of the Christian faith once more met in England, and the immediate future was to witness a struggle for supremacy between them.

With the defeat and death of Penda, and upon the surge of all the passions which had been loosed, Anglo-Saxon England was definitely rallied to the Christian faith. There was now no kingdom in which heathen practices prevailed. Indeed, apart from individuals, whose private adherence to Woden was overlooked, the whole Island was Christian. But this marvellous event, which might have brought in its train so many blessings, was marred by the new causes of division which now opened between the English and British peoples. To the ferocious British-English racial feud there was added a different view of Church government, which sundered the races almost as much as the difference between Christianity and heathenism. Henceforward the issue is no longer whether the Island shall be Christian or pagan, but whether the Roman or the Celtic view of Christianity shall prevail. These differences persisted across the centuries, much debated by the parties concerned.

The celebrated and largely successful attempt to solve them took place at the Synod of Whitby in 664. There the hinging issue was whether British Christianity should conform to the general life-plan of Christendom or whether it should be expressed by the monastic orders which had founded the Celtic Churches of the North. The issues hung in the balance, but in the end after much pious dissertation the decision was taken that the Church of Northumbria should be a definite part of the Church of Rome and of the Catholic system. Mercia soon afterwards conformed. Though the Celtic leader and his following retired in disgust to Iona, and the Irish .clergy refused to submit, the importance of this event cannot be overrated. Instead of a religion controlled by the narrow views of abbots pursuing their strict rule of life in their various towns or remote resorts there was opened to every member of the English Church the broad vista of a world-state and universal communion. These events brought Northumbria to her zenith. In Britain for the first time there was achieved a unity of faith, morals, and Church government covering five-sixths of the Island. The decisive step had been taken in the spiritual sphere. The Island was now entirely Christian, and by far the greater and more powerful part was directly associated with the Papacy.

Rome had little reason to be satisfied with the mission of either Augustine or Paulinus. The Papacy realised that its efforts to guide and govern British Christianity through the kingdom of Kent had been misplaced. It now made a new plan, which illustrates the universal character of the Catholic Church. Two fresh emissaries were chosen in 668 to carry the light into the Northern mists, the first a native of Asia Minor, Theodore of Tarsus, the second an African named Hadrian from Carthage. These missionaries were of a stronger type than their precursors, and their character and integrity shone before all. When they arrived at Canterbury there were but three bishops from all England to greet them. When their work was finished the Anglican Church raised its mitred front in a majesty which has not yet been dimmed. Before he died in 690 Theodore had increased the number of bishoprics from seven to fourteen, and by his administrative skill he gave the Church a new cohesion. The Church has not canonised him as a saint. This remarkable Asiatic was the earliest of the statesmen of England, and guided her steps with fruitful wisdom.

* * *

There followed a long and intricate rivalry for leadership between the various Anglo-Saxon kings which occupied the seventh and eighth centuries. It was highly important to those whose span of life was cast in that period, but it left small marks on the subsequent course of history. Let a few words suffice. The primacy of Northumbria was menaced and finally ended by the inherent geographical and physical weakness of its position. It was liable to be beset from every quarter, from the north by the Picts, on the west by the British kingdom of Strathclyde, in the south by Mercia, those jealous Midlands still smarting from the suppression of Penda and the punishments inflicted upon his adherents. These antagonisms were too much for Northumbria to bear, and although great efforts were made and amid the exhausting feuds of rival kings some wise chieftains occasionally prevailed, its collapse as the leading community in the Island was inevitable.

Northumbria was fortunate however in having in this twilight scene a chronicler, to whom we have already referred, whose words have descended to us out of the long silence of the past. Bede, a monk of high ability, working unknown in the recesses of the Church, now comes forward as the most effective and almost the only audible voice from the British islands in these dim times. Unlike Gildas, Bede wrote history. The gratitude of the Middle Ages bestowed on Gildas the title of "the Wise," and the name of "the Venerable Bede" still carries with it a proud renown. He alone attempts to paint for us, and, so far as he can, explain the spectacle of Anglo-Saxon England in its first phase: a Christian England, divided by tribal, territorial, dynastic, and personal feuds into what an Elizabethan antiquary called the Heptarchy, seven kingdoms of varying strength, all professing the Gospel of Christ, and striving over each other for mastery by force and fraud. For almost exactly a hundred years, from 731 to 829, there was a period of ceaseless warfare, conducted with cruelty and rapine under a single creed.

The leadership of Saxon England passed to Mercia. For nearly eighty years two Mercian kings asserted or maintained their ascendancy over all England south of the Humber. Ethelbald and Offa reigned each for forty years. Ethelbald had been an exile before he became an autocrat. As a fugitive he consorted with monks, hermits, and holy men. On attaining power he did not discard his Christian piety, but he found himself much oppressed by the temptations of the flesh. St Guthlac had comforted him in misfortune and poverty, but St Boniface was constrained to rebuke him for his immorality.

The moral sense had grown so strong in matters of sex that Churchmen could now brand a king as licentious. Boniface from Germany censured Ethelbald for the "twofold sin" which he committed in nunneries by using the advantages of his royal position to gain himself favours otherwise beyond his reach. The chronicles of this sovereign are scanty. He showed charity to the poor; he preserved law and order; in the South in 733 he raided Wessex; and in 740 he laid parts of Northumbria waste while its harassed chief was struggling with the Picts. After this last victory he took to styling himself "King of the Southern English" and "King of Britain." South of the Humber these claims were made good.

* * *

Ethelbald, having been at length murdered by his guards, was succeeded by a greater man. Little is known of Offa, who reigned for the second forty years, but the imprint of his power is visible not only throughout England but upon the Continent. Offa was the contemporary of Charlemagne. His policy interlaced with that of Europe; he was reputed to be the first "King of the English," and he had the first quarrel since Roman times with the mainland.

Charlemagne wished one of his sons to marry one of Offa's daughters. Here we have an important proof of the esteem in which the Englishman was held. Offa stipulated that his son must simultaneously marry a daughter of Charlemagne. The founder of the Holy Roman Empire appeared at first incensed at this assumption of equality, but after a while he found it expedient to renew his friendship with Offa. It seems that "the King of the English" had placed an embargo upon Continental merchandise, and the inconvenience of this retaliation speedily overcame all points of pride and sentiment. Very soon Offa was again the Emperor's "dearest brother," and Charlemagne is seen agreeing to arrange that there should be reciprocity of royal protection in both countries for merchants, "according to the ancient custom of trading." Apparently the commodities in question were "black stones," presumably coal, from France, in return for English cloaks. There were also questions of refugees and extradition. Charlemagne was interested in repatriating a Scot who ate meat in Lent. He sent presents of an ancient sword and silken mantles. Thus we see Offa admitted to equal rank with the greatest figure in Europe. It is evident that the Island Power must have counted for a great deal in these days. Monarchs of mighty empires do not make marriage contracts for their children and beat out the details of commercial treaties with persons of no consequence.

The advantage given by these two long reigns when everything was in flux had reinstated the Island again as a recognisable factor in the world. We know that Offa styled himself not only *rex Anglorum,* but also "King of the whole land of the English" (*rex totius Anglorum patriæ*). This expression *rex Anglorum* is rightly signalised by historians as a milestone in our history. Here was an English king who ruled over the greatest part of the Island, whose trade was important, and whose daughters were fit consorts for the sons of Charles the Great. We learn about Offa almost entirely through his impact on his neighbours. It is clear from their records that he suppressed the under-kings of the Severn valley, that he defeated the West Saxons in Oxfordshire and subjugated Berkshire, that he decapitated the King of East Anglia, that he was master of London, that he extirpated the monarchy which Hengist had founded in Kent, and put down a Kentish rising with extreme severity. Henceforth he gave his own orders in Kent. He captured their mint and inscribed his name upon the coins issued by the Archbishop of Canterbury. One of these coins tells its own quaint tale. It is a gold dinar, nicely copied from an Arabic die, and is stamped with the superscription *rex Offa*. The Canterbury mint evidently regarded the Arabic as mere ornamentation, and all men would have been shocked had they known that it declared "There is no God but one and Mahomet is his Prophet." Offa established a good understanding with the Pope. The Supreme Pontiff addressed him as *rex Anglorum*. The Papal envoys in 787 were joyfully received in the hall of Offa, and were comforted by his assurances of reverence for St Peter. These professions were implemented by a small annual tribute to the Papacy, part of it unwittingly paid in these same infidel coins which proclaimed an opposite creed.

In studying Offa we are like geologists who instead of finding a fossil find only the hollow shape in which a creature of unusual strength and size undoubtedly resided. Alcuin, one of the few recorders of this period at the Court of Charlemagne, addresses Offa in these terms: "You are a glory to Britain and a sword against its enemies." We have a tangible monument of Offa in the immense dyke which he caused to be built between converted Saxon England and the still unconquered British. The tables were now turned, and those who had never faltered in the old faith and had always maintained their independence had sunk in the estimation of men from the mere fact that they lived in barren mountainous lands, while their successful ravishers strode on in pomp and even dignity. This dyke, which runs over the hills and dales, leaving gaps for the impenetrable forests, from the mouth of the Severn to the neighbourhood of the Mersey, attests to our day the immense authority of the state over which Offa presided. When we reflect how grim was the struggle for life, and how the getting of enough food to keep body and soul together was the prime concern not only of families but of whole peoples, the fact that this extensive rampart could have been mainly the work of the lifetime and the will of a single man is startling. It conveys to us an idea of the magnitude and force of Offa's kingdom. Such works are not constructed except upon a foundation of effective political power. But "Offa's dyke" shows policy as well as man-power. In many sections it follows lines favourable to the British, and historians have concluded that it was a boundary rather than a fortification, and resulted from an agreement reached for common advantage. It was not a Roman wall, like those of Antonine and Hadrian, between savagery and civilisation, but rather the expression of a solemn treaty which for a long spell removed from Offa's problem the menace of a British incursion, and thus set him free with his back secure to parley and dispute with Europe.

* * *

Art and culture grew in the track of order. The English had brought with them from their Continental home a vigorous barbaric art and a primitive poetry. Once established in the Island, this art was profoundly affected by the Celtic genius for curve and colour, a genius suppressed by Roman provincialism, but breaking out again as soon as the Roman hand was removed. Christianity gave them a new range of subjects to adorn. The results are seen in such masterpieces as the Lindisfarne Gospels and the sculptured crosses of Northern England. A whole world of refinement and civilisation of which the monasteries were the home, and of which only fragments have come down to us, had come into being. Bede was universally honoured as the greatest scholar of his day. It is to his influence that the world owes the practice, adopted later, of reckoning the years from the birth of Christ. Aldhelm of Malmesbury was the most popular writer in Europe; of no author were more copies made in the monasteries of the Continent. Vernacular poetry flourished; in Wessex the first steps had been taken in the art of prose-writing. Another West Saxon, Boniface, from Crediton, near Exeter, was the Apostle of Germany. In the eighth century indeed England had claims to stand in the van of Western culture.

After the shapeless confusion of darker centuries, obscure to history and meaningless to almost all who lived through them, we now see a purpose steadily forming. England, with an independent character and personality, might scarcely yet be a part of a world civilisation as in Roman times, but there was a new England, closer than ever before to national unity, and with a native genius of her own. Henceforward an immortal spirit stood for all to see.

The Vikings

AFTER the fall of Imperial Rome the victorious barbarians were in their turn captivated and enthralled by the Gospel of Christ. Though no more successful in laying aside their sinful promptings than religious men and women are today, they had a common theme and inspiration. There was a bond which linked all the races of Europe. There was an international organisation which, standing erect in every country, was by far the most powerful, and indeed the only coherent surviving structure, and at the head of which the Bishop of Rome revived in a spiritual, or at least in an ecclesiastical form, the vanished authority of the Cæsars. The Christian Church became the sole sanctuary of learning and knowledge. It sheltered in its aisles and cloisters all the salvage of ancient days. It offered to men in their strife and error "the last solace of human woe, the last restraint of earthly power." Thus, while the light of pagan civilisation was by no means wholly extinguished, a new effulgence held, dazzled, and dominated the barbaric hordes, not only in our Island but throughout Europe. They were tamed and uplifted by the Christian revelation. Everywhere, from the Euphrates to the Boyne, old gods were forsworn, and a priest of Christ could travel far and wide, finding in every town an understanding brotherhood and a universal if sometimes austere hospitality.

Amid the turbulence and ignorance of the age of Roman decay all the intellectual elements at first found refuge in the Church, and afterwards exercised mastery from it. Here was the school of politicians. The virtual monopoly of learning and the art of writing made the Churchmen indispensable to the proud and violent chieftains of the day. The clerics became the civil servants, and often the statesmen, of every Court. They fell naturally, inevitably, into the place of the Roman magistrates whose garb they wore, and wear to-day. Triumphant barbarism yielded itself insensibly to a structure, reliance upon which was proved on numberless occasions to give success in the unending struggle for power. After the convulsions and disorders of the Dark Ages, when at last daylight fell again on the British Island, she awoke to a world also profoundly changed, but devoid neither of form nor majesty. There was even a gentler breeze in the air.

The fervour of the converted heathen brought in its train mischiefs which opened new calamities. The Church was bound by its spirit to inculcate mildness and mercy. It was led by zeal and by its interests to fortify in every way the structure of its own power. The humility and faith of the descendants of the invaders soon exposed them, in their human frailty, to an organised exploitation which during the sixth and seventh centuries led in many countries to an engrossment by the Church of treasure and lands out of all proportion to its capacity to control events. We see, then, Christendom pious but froward; spiritually united, but a prey to worldly feuds; in a state of grace, but by nо means free from ambition.

Upon this revived, convalescent, loosely-knit society there now fell two blasting external assaults. The first came from the East. In Arabia Mahomet unfurled the martial and sacred standards of Islam. His celebrated escape from Mecca to Medina, called the Hejira, or emigration, from which the Moslem era dates, took place in 622. During the decades that followed, Mahomet and his successors, the Caliphs, made themselves masters of all Arabia, Persia, much of the Byzantine Empire, and the whole North African shore. At the beginning of the next century, Islam crossed the Straits of Gibraltar and prevailed in Spain, whence it was not finally to be dislodged for nearly eight hundred years. At one moment France, too, seemed about to succumb, but the Arabs were beaten back by Charles Martel, grandfather of Charlemagne, in 732 at Poitiers. Thus, all the way from Mecca, the power of Islam came almost to within striking distance of these islands.

For Britain, however, was reserved the second invading wave. It came from the North. In Scandinavia the Vikings fitted out their long-boats for sea. This double assault by Arab infidels and Nordic pirates distracted the weakened life of Europe for ten generations. It was not until the eleventh century that the steel-clad feudalism of medieval Christendom, itself consisting largely of the converted descendants of the Vikings, assigned limits to the Arab conquests, and established at the side of the Christian Church ample and effective military power.

* * *

Measure for measure, what the Saxon pirates had given to the Britons was meted out to the English after the lapse of four hundred years. In the eighth century a vehement manifestation of conquering energy appeared in Scandinavia. Norway, Sweden, and Denmark threw up bands of formidable fighting men who, in addition to all their other martial qualities, were the hardy rovers of the sea. The causes which led to this racial ebullition were the spontaneous growth of their strength and population, the thirst for adventure, and the complications of dynastic quarrels. There was here no question of the Danes or Norsemen being driven westward by new pressures from the steppes of Asia. They moved of their own accord. Their prowess was amazing. One current of marauding vigour struck southwards from Sweden, and not only reached Constantinople, but left behind it potent germs which across the centuries influenced European Russia. Another contingent sailed in their long-boats from Norway to the Mediterranean, harried all the shores of the inland sea, and were with difficulty repulsed by the Arab kingdoms of Spain and the north coast of Africa. The third far-ranging impulse carried the Scandinavian buccaneers to the British Isles, to Normandy, to Iceland, and presently across the Atlantic Ocean to the American continent.

The relations between the Danes and the Norwegians were tangled and varying. Sometimes they raided in collusion; sometimes they fought each other in desperate battles; but to Saxon England they presented themselves in the common guise of a merciless scourge. They were incredibly cruel. Though not cannibals, they were accustomed to cook their feasts of victory in cauldrons placed upon, or on spits stuck in, the bodies of their vanquished enemies. When, after a battle in Ireland between Northmen and Danes, the local Irish inhabitants—themselves none too particular—expressed horror at this disgusting habit, and, being neutral, asked them why they did it, they received the answer, "Why not? They would do it to us if they won." It was said of these Scandinavian hunters that they never wept for their sins, nor for the death of their friends. It is certain however that in many places where the raiding war-bands settled down they soon developed luxurious habits. They took baths. They wore silken robes. Their ships carried tents and beds for use on shore. Their war-chiefs in every land into which they penetrated practised polygamy, and in the East adopted quite readily the harem system. One conquering leader was credited with possessing no fewer than eight hundred concubines; but this was probably a Biblical illustration. When Limerick was captured from them in the year 936 the Irish were staggered by the beauty of the womenfolk already in the hands of the marauders, and by the mass of silks and embroideries with which they were decked. No doubt they recovered their poise before long.

* * *

The soul of the Vikings lay in the long-ship. They had evolved, and now, in the eighth and ninth centuries, carried to perfection, a vessel which by its shallow draught could sail far up rivers, or anchor in innumerable creeks and bays, and which by its beautiful lines and suppleness of construction could ride out the fiercest storms of the Atlantic Ocean.

We are singularly well informed about these ships. Half a dozen have been dug up almost intact. The most famous was unearthed at Gokstad, in Norway, in 1880, from a tumulus. It is almost complete, even to the cooking-pots and draught-boards of the sailors. It was remeasured with precision in 1944 in spite of other distractions. This ship was of the medium size, 76 feet 6 inches from stem to stern, 17 feet 6 inches beam, and drawing only 2 feet 9 inches amidships. She was clinker-built of sixteen strakes a side of solid oak planks, fastened with tree-nails and iron bolts, and caulked with cord of plaited animal-hair. Her planks fastened to the ribs with bast ties gave the framework great elasticity. She had a deck of loose unnailed boards, but no doubt her stores were contained in lockers which have perished. Her mast was stepped in a huge solid block, which, says Professor Collingwood (whose description I have revised to date), was so cunningly supported "that while the mast stands steady and firm there is no strain on the light elastic frame of the ship." She had sixteen oars a side, varying in length between 17 and 19 feet; the longer oars were used at the prow and stern, where the gunwale was higher above the water-line; they were all beautifully shaped, and passed through circular rowlocks cut in the main strake, which were neatly fitted with shutters that closed when the oars were shipped. Her rudder, stepped to the starboard quarter, was a large, short oar of cricket-bat shape, fitted with a movable tiller, and fastened to the ship by an ingenious contrivance which gave the blade full play. The mast, 40 feet high, had a long, heavy yard with a square sail. She could carry a smaller boat or dinghy, three of which were discovered with her. The Gokstad ship would carry a crew of fifty, and if necessary another thirty warriors or captives, in all weathers, for a month.

Such was the vessel which, in many different sizes, bore the Vikings to the plunder of the civilised world—to the assault of

Constantinople, to the siege of Paris, to the foundation of Dublin, and the discovery of America. Its picture rises before us vivid and bright: the finely carved, dragon-shaped prow; the high, curving stern; the long row of shields, black and yellow alternately, ranged along the sides; the gleam of steel; the scent of murder. The long-ships in which the great ocean voyages were made were of somewhat stouter build, with a higher freeboard; but the Gokstad model was reproduced in 1892 and navigated by a Norwegian crew across the Atlantic in four weeks.

Yet this superb instrument of sea-power would have been useless without the men who handled it. All were volunteers. Parties were formed under leaders of marked ability. In the sagas we read of crews of "champions, or merry men": a ship's company picked no doubt from many applicants, "as good at the helm or oar as they were with the sword." There were strict regulations, or early "Articles of War," governing these crews once they had joined. Men were taken between the ages of sixteen and sixty, but none without a trial of his strength and activity. No feud or old quarrel must be taken up while afloat or on service. No woman was allowed on board. News was to be reported to the captain alone. All taken in war was to be brought to the pile or stake, and there sold and divided according to rule. This war booty was personal; that is to say, it was not part of the property which passed by Scandinavian law to a man's kindred. He was entitled to have it buried with him.

"With anything like equal numbers," says Oman, "the Vikings were always able to hold their own, but when the whole countryside had been raised, and the men of many shires came swarming up against the raiders, they had to beware lest they might be crushed by numbers." It was only when a fleet of very exceptional strength had come together that the Norsemen could dare to offer their opponents battle in the open field. Fighting was after all not so much their object as plunder, and when the land was rallied in overwhelming force the invaders took to their ships again and sailed off to renew their ravages in some yet intact province. They soon learned moreover to secure for themselves the power of rapid locomotion on land. When they came to shore they would sweep together all the horses of the neighbourhood and move themselves and their plunder on horseback across the land. It was with no intention of fighting as cavalry that they collected the horses, but only for swift marching. The first mention of this practice in England comes in the year 866, when "a great heathen army came to the land of the East Angles, and there was the army a-horse." [1]

When we reflect upon the brutal vices of these salt-water bandits, pirates as shameful as any whom the sea has borne, or recoil from their villainous destruction and cruel deeds, we must also remember the discipline, the fortitude, the comradeship and martial virtues which made them at this period beyond all challenge the most formidable and daring race in the world.

* * *

One summer's day, probably in 789, while "the innocent English people, spread through their plains, were enjoying themselves in tranquillity and yoking their oxen to the plough," news was carried to the King's officer, the Reeve of Dorchester, that three ships had arrived on the coast. The Reeve "leapt on his horse and rode with a few men to the harbour [probably Portland], thinking that they were merchants and not enemies. Giving his commands as one who had authority, he ordered them to be sent to the King's town; but they slew him on the spot and all who were with him." This was a foretaste of the murderous struggle which, with many changes of fortune, was to harry and devastate England for two hundred and fifty years. It was the beginning of the Viking Age.

In 793, on a January morning, the wealthy monastic settlement of Lindisfarne (or Holy Island), off the Northumbrian coast, was suddenly attacked by a powerful fleet from Denmark. They sacked the place, devoured the cattle, killed many of the monks, and sailed away with a rich booty in gold, jewels, and sacred emblems, and all the monks who were likely to fetch a good price in the European slave-market. This raid had been planned with care and knowledge. It was executed by complete surprise in the dead of winter before any aid from the shore could reach the island. The news of the atrocity travelled far and wide, not only in England but throughout Europe, and the loud cry of the Church sounded a general alarm. Alcuin, the Northumbrian, wrote home from the Court of Charlemagne to condole with his countrymen:

Lo, it is almost three hundred and fifty years that we and our forefathers have dwelt in this fair land, and never has such a horror before appeared in Britain, such as we have just suffered from the heathen. It was not thought possible that they could have made

[1] *Anglo-Saxon Chronicle*, A.D. 866.

such a voyage. Behold the church of St. Cuthbert sprinkled with the blood of the priests of Christ, robbed of all its ornaments. . . . In that place where, after the departure of Paulinus from York, the Christian faith had its beginning among us, there is the beginning of woe and calamity. . . . Portents of this woe came before it. . . . What signifies that rain of blood during Lent in the town of York?

When the next year the raiders returned and landed near Jarrow they were stoutly attacked while harassed by bad weather. Many were killed. Their "king" was captured and put to a cruel death, and the fugitives carried so grim a tale back to Denmark that for forty years the English coasts were unravaged. In this period the Vikings were little inclined for massed invasion or conquest, but, using their sea-power, made minor descents upon the east coast of Scotland and the Scottish islands. The monastic colonies which had hitherto found a safe retreat in these islands now found themselves as a particularly vulnerable prey. Their riches and their isolation left them the most attractive quarry of the sea-rovers. Iona was pillaged and destroyed in 802. The Irish religious establishments also presented attractive prizes to marauding greed, and from now onward their sufferings were unceasing. The vitality of the Church repaired the ruin with devoted zeal. The Vikings, having a large choice of action, allowed an interval of recovery before paying another visit. Iona was sacked thrice, and the monastery of Kildare no fewer than fourteen times.

Buccaneering had become a steady profession, and the Church was their perpetually replenished treasure-house. Charlemagne's historian, Eginhard, records that the ravages were continuous, and a new shadow of fear spread over Christendom. No effective measures were however taken, and the raiding business was so profitable that the taste for it spread throughout Scandinavia. "These merry, clean-limbed, stouthearted gentlemen of the Northlands," as one of their Scottish eulogists describes them, sailed every year in greatly increasing numbers upon their forays, and returned triumphant and enriched. And their example inspired all audacious spirits and younger sons. Other fleets ranged more widely. They broke into the Mediterranean. Charlemagne, gazing through a window in a town near Narbonne, saw these sinister ships haunting the coast and uttered an impressive warning of the wrath to come.

* * *

It was not till 835 that the storm broke in fury, and fleets, sometimes of three or four hundred vessels, rowed up the rivers of England, France, and Russia in predatory enterprises on the greatest scale. For thirty years Southern England was constantly attacked. Paris was more than once besieged. Constantinople was assaulted. The harbour towns in Ireland were captured and held. Dublin was founded by the Vikings under Olaf. In many cases now the raiders settled upon the conquered territory. The Swedish element penetrated into the heart of Russia, ruling the river towns and holding the trade to ransom. The Norwegian Vikings, coming from a still more severe climate, found the Scottish islands good for settlement. They colonised the Shetlands, the Faroes, and Ireland. They reached Greenland and Stoneland (Labrador). They sailed up the St Lawrence. They discovered America; but they set little store by the achievement.

For a long time no permanent foothold was gained in Britain or France. It was not until 865, when resistance on the Continent had temporarily stiffened, that the great Danish invasion of Northumbria and Eastern England began.

Saxon England was at this time ripe for the sickle. The invaders broke in upon the whole eastern seaboard, once guarded by the "Count of the Saxon Shore," with its Imperial fortresses in ruins, buried already under the soil of centuries. No Roman galleys plied their oars upon the patrol courses. There was no Imperial Government to send a great commander or a legion to the rescue. But on all sides were abbeys and monasteries, churches, and even cathedrals, possessed in that starveling age of treasures of gold and silver, of jewels, and also large stores of food, wine, and such luxuries as were known. The pious English had accepted far too literally the idea of the absolution of sins as the consequence of monetary payment to the Church. Their sins were many, their repentances frequent, and the Church had thrived. Here were easy prizes for sharp swords to win.

To an undue subservience to the Church the English at this time added military mismanagement. Their system of defence was adapted to keeping the survivors of the ancient Britons in their barren mountain-lands or guarding the frontier against an incursion by a Saxon neighbour. The local noble, when called upon by his chief or king, could call upon the able-bodied cultivators of the soil to serve in their own district for about forty days. This service was grudgingly given, and when it was over the army dispersed without paying any serious regard to the enemies who might be afoot or the purposes for which the campaign had been undertaken. Now they found themselves in contact with a different type of enemy. The Danes and Norsemen had not only the advantages of surprise which sea-power so long imparted, but they showed both mobility and skill on land. They adopted the habit of fortifying their camps with almost Roman thoroughness. Their stratagems also have been highly praised. Among these "feigned flight" was foremost. Again and again we read that the English put the heathen army to rout, but at the end of the day the Danes held the field. On one occasion their leader, who was besieging a town, declared himself to be dying and begged the bishop of the place to give him Christian burial. The worthy Churchman rejoiced in the conversion and acceded to the request, but when the body of the deceased Viking was brought into the town for Christian burial it suddenly appeared that the attendants were armed warriors of proved quality, disguised in mourning, who without more ado set to work on sack and slaughter. There are many informing sidelights of this kind upon the manners and customs of the Vikings. They were, in fact, the most audacious and treacherous type of pirate and shark that had ever yet appeared, and, owing to the very defective organisation of the Saxons and the conditions of the period, they achieved a fuller realisation of their desires than any of those who have emulated their proficiency—and there have been many.

* * *

In Viking legend at this period none was more famous than Ragnar Lodbrok, or "Hairy-breeches." He was born in Norway, but was connected with the ruling family of Denmark. He was a raider from his youth. "West over seas" was his motto. His prow had ranged from the Orkneys to the White Sea. In 845 he led a Viking fleet up the Seine and attacked Paris. The onslaught was repulsed, and plague took an unforeseeable revenge upon the buccaneers. He turned his mobile arms against Northumbria. Here again fate was adverse. According to Scandinavian story, he was captured by King Ælle of Northumbria, and cast into a snake-pit to die. Amid the coiling mass of loathsome adders he sang to the end his death-song. Ragnar had four sons, and as he lay among the venomous reptiles he uttered a potent threat: "The little pigs would grunt now if they knew how it fares with the old boar." The skalds tell us how his sons received the news. Bjorn "Ironside" gripped his spear shaft so hard that the print of his fingers remained stamped upon it. Hvitserk was playing chess, but he clenched his fingers upon a pawn so tightly that the blood started from under his nails. Sigurd "Snake-eye" was trimming his nails with a knife, and kept on paring until he cut into the bone. But the fourth son was the one who counted. Ivar, "the Boneless," demanded the precise details of his father's execution, and his face "became red, blue, and pale by turns, and his skin appeared puffed up by anger." [1]

A form of vengeance was prescribed by which sons should requite the killer of their fathers. It was known as the "Blood-red Eagle." The flesh and ribs of the killer must be cut and sawn out in an aquiline pattern, and then the dutiful son with his own hands would tear out the palpitating lungs. This was the doom which in legend overtook King Ælle. But the actual consequences to England were serious. Ivar "the Boneless" was a warrior of command and guile. He was the master-mind behind the Scandinavian invasion of England in the last quarter of the ninth century. He it was who planned the great campaigns by which East Anglia, Deira in Northumbria, and Mercia were conquered. Hitherto he had been fighting in Ireland, but he now appeared in 866 in East Anglia. In the spring of 867 his powerful army, organised on the basis of ships' companies, but now all mounted not for fighting but for locomotion, rode north along the old Roman road and was ferried across the Humber.

He laid siege to York. And now—too late—the Northumbrians, who had been divided in their loyalties between two rival kings, forgot their feuds and united in one final effort. They attacked the Danish army before York. At first they were successful; the heathens were driven back upon the city walls. The defenders sallied out, and in the confusion the Vikings defeated them all with grievous slaughter, killing both their kings and destroying completely their power of resistance. This was the end of Northumbria. The North of England never recovered its ascendancy.

As Hodgkin has put it:

The schools and monasteries dwindled into obscurity or nothingness; and the kingdom which had produced Bede and Alcuin, which had left the great stone crosses as masterpieces of Anglican art, and as evidences of Anglican poetry the poems of Cædmon and the Vision of the Rood, sank back in the generation following the de-

---

[1] From *The Vikings and their Voyages*, by A. MacCallum Scott, "The Universal History of the World," ed. J. A. Hammerton, vol. iv.

feat of the year 867 sank back into the old life of obscure barbarism. . . . A dynasty was broken, a religion was half smothered,
and a culture was barbarised.[1]

Simeon of Durham, writing a hundred and fifty years after
this disastrous battle at York, confirms these lamentations:

The army raided here and there and filled every place with
bloodshed and sorrow. Far and wide it destroyed the churches and
monasteries with fire and sword. When it departed from a place it
left nothing standing but roofless walls. So great was the destruction that at the present day one can scarcely see anything left of
these places, nor any sign of their former greatness.[2]

But Ivar's object was nothing less than the conquest of
Mercia, which, as all men knew, had for nearly a hundred
years represented the strength of England. Ivar lay before Nottingham. The King of Mercia called for help from Wessex. The
old King of Wessex was dead, but his two sons, Ethelred and
Alfred, answered the appeal. They marched to his aid, and
offered to join him in his attack upon the besiegers' lines; but
the Mercians flinched, and preferred a parley. Ivar warred with
policy as well as arms. He had not harmed churches at York
and Ripon. He was content to set up a vassal king, one Egbert,
in Northumbria, and after ending the campaign of 868 by a
treaty which left him master of Nottingham he spent the winter
fortifying himself in York.

While the Danes in their formidable attempt at conquest
spread out from East Anglia, subdued Mercia, and ravaged
Northumbria, the King of Wessex and his brother Alfred
quietly built up their strength. Their fortunes turned on balances so delicate and precarious that even the slightest addition
to their burdens must have been fatal. It was therefore a deliverance when Ivar, after breaking the Treaty of Nottingham
and subjecting King Edmund of East Anglia to martyrdom,
suddenly quitted England for ever. The annals of Ulster explain that Olaf and Ivar, the two kings of the Northmen, came
again to Dublin in 870 from Scotland, and "a very great spoil
of captives, English, British, and Pictish, was carried away to
Ireland." But then there is this final entry: "872. Ivar, King
of the Northmen of all Ireland and Britain, ended his life." He
had conquered Mercia and East Anglia. He had captured the
major stronghold of the kingdom of Strathclyde, Dumbarton.
Laden with loot and seemingly invincible, he settled in Dublin,

and died there peacefully two years later. The pious chroniclers report that he "slept in Christ." Thus it may be that he had the best of both worlds.

* * *

The Danish raiders now stayed longer every year. In the summer the fleets came over to plunder and destroy, but each year the tendency was to dally in a more genial and more verdant land. At last the warrior's absence on the raids became long enough and the conditions of his conquest sure enough for him to bring over his wife and family. Thus again behind piracy and rapine there grew the process of settlement. But these settlements of the Danes differed from those of the Saxons; they were the encampment of armies, and their boundaries were the fighting fronts sustained by a series of fortified towns. Stamford, Nottingham, Lincoln, Derby, Leicester were the bases of the new invading force. Behind their frontier lines the soldiers of one decade were to become the colonists and landowners of the next. The Danish settlement in England was essentially military. They cut their way with their swords, and then planted themselves deeply in the soil. The warrior type of farmer asserted from the first a status different from the ordinary agriculturist. Without any coherent national organisation to repel from the land on which they had settled the ever-unknowable descents from the seas, the Saxons, now for four centuries entitled to be deemed the owners of the soil, very nearly succumbed completely to the Danish inroads. That they did not was due—as almost every critical turn of historic fortune has been due—to the sudden apparition in an era of confusion and decay of one of the great figures of history.

BOOK ONE · CHAPTER SEVEN

Alfred the Great

THE story of Alfred is made known to us in some detail in the pages of Asser, a monk of St David's, who became Bishop of Sherborne. The Bishop dwells naturally upon the religious and moral qualities of his hero; but we must also remember that, in spite of ill-health, he was renowned as a hunter, and that his father had taken him to Rome as a boy, so that he had a lively comprehension of the great world. Alfred began as second-in-command to his elder brother, the King. There were no jealousies between them, but a marked difference of temperament. Ethelred inclined to the religious view that faith and prayer were the prime agencies by which the heathen would be overcome. Alfred, though also devout, laid the emphasis upon policy and arms.

In earlier years the overlordship of Mercia had never been popular, and her kings had made the serious mistake of quarrelling with the See of Canterbury. When, in 825, the Mercian army, invading Wessex, was overthrown by Alfred's grandfather, King Egbert, at Ellandun, near Swindon, all the South and East made haste to come to terms with the victor, and the union of Kent, the seat of the Primate, with Wessex, now the leading English kingdom, created a solid Southern block. This, which had been the aim of West Saxon policy for many generations, was achieved just in time to encounter the invasion from the North. And Wessex was strategically strong, with sharp ridges facing north, and none of those long, slow rivers up which the Danes used to steer their long-ships into the heart of Mercia. Wessex had moreover developed a local organisation which gave her exceptional resiliency under attack: the alderman at the head of the shire could act on his own account. The advantages of this system were later to be proved. Definite districts, each under an accepted commander, or governor, for civil and military purposes, constituted a great advance on the ancient tribal kingdoms, or the merely personal union of tribes under a single king. When the dynasties of Kent, Northumbria, and Mercia had disappeared all eyes turned to Wessex, where there was a royal house going back without a break to the first years of the Saxon settlement.

The Danes had occupied London, not then the English capital, but a town in the kingdom of Mercia, and their army had fortified itself at Reading. Moving forward, they met the forces of the West Saxons on the Berkshire downs, and here, in January 871, was fought the Battle of Ashdown. Both sides divided their forces into two commands. Ethelred tarried long at his devotions. The Vikings, with their brightly painted shields and banners, their finery and golden bracelets, made the West Saxons seem modest by contrast. As they slowly approached they clashed their shields and weapons and raised long, repeated, and defiant war-cries. Although archery was not much in use, missiles began to fly. The King was still at his prayers. God came first, he declared to those who warned him that the battle must soon be joined. "But Alfred," according to Bishop Asser, who had the account from "truthful eye-witnesses,"

seeing the heathen had come quickly on to the field and were ready for battle . . . could bear the attacks of the enemy no longer, and he had to choose between withdrawing altogether or beginning the battle without waiting for his brother. At last, like a wild boar, he led the Christian forces boldly against the army of the enemy . . . in spite of the fact that the King had not yet arrived. And so, relying on God's counsel and trusting to His help, he closed the shield-wall in due order and thereupon moved his standards against the enemy.[1]

The fight was long and hard. King Ethelred, his spiritual duty done, soon joined his brother. "The heathens," said the Bishop, "had seized the higher ground, and the Christians had to advance uphill. There was in that place a single stunted thorn-tree which we have seen with our own eyes. Round about this tree, then, the opposing ranks met in conflict, with a great shouting from all men—one side bent on evil, the other side fighting for life and their loved ones and their native land." At last the Danes gave way, and, hotly pursued, fled back to Reading. They fled till nightfall; they fled through the night and the next day, and the whole breadth of Ashdown— meaning the Berkshire hills—was strewn with their corpses, among which were found the body of one of the Viking kings and five of his jarls.

The results of this victory did not break the power of the Danish army; in a fortnight they were again in the field. But the Battle of Ashdown justly takes its place among historic en- counters because of the greatness of the issue. If the West Saxons had been beaten all England would have sunk into heathen anarchy. Since they were victorious the hope still burned for a civilised Christian existence in this Island. This was the first time the invaders had been beaten in the field. The last of the Saxon kingdoms had withstood the assault upon it. Alfred had made the Saxons feel confidence in themselves again. They could hold their own in open fight. The story of this conflict at Ashdown was for generations a treasured memory of the Saxon writers. It was Alfred's first battle.

All through the year 871 the two armies waged deadly war.

[1] Hodgkin, vol. ii, pp. 544–545.

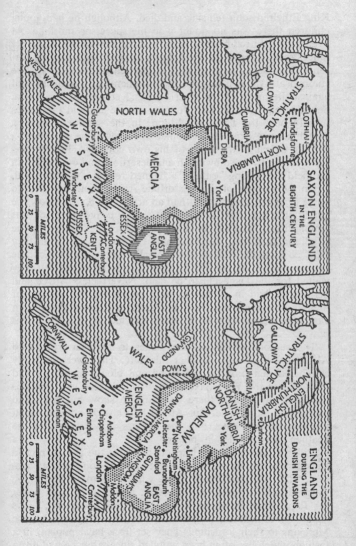

SAXON ENGLAND IN THE EIGHTH CENTURY

WEST WALES
NORTH WALES
MERCIA
WESSEX
Glastonbury
Winchester
SUSSEX
KENT
London
Canterbury
ESSEX
EAST ANGLIA
CUMBRIA
STRATHCLYDE
GALLOWAY
LOTHIAN
NORTHUMBRIA
Lindisfarne
DEIRA
York

0 25 50 75 100
MILES

ENGLAND DURING THE DANISH INVASIONS

CORNWALL
WESSEX
Glastonbury
Wareham
Ethandun
Chippenham
Ashdown
London
Maldon
Canterbury
WALES
POWYS
GWYNEDD
ENGLISH MERCIA
DANISH MERCIA
Derby
Nottingham
Leicester
Stamford
Lincoln
Brunanburh
GUTHRUM'S KINGDOM
EAST ANGLIA
DANELAW
DANISH NORTHUMBRIA
York
Durham
ENGLISH NORTHUMBRIA
CUMBRIA
GALLOWAY
STRATHCLYDE

0 25 50 75 100
MILES

King Ethelred soon fell sick and died. Although he had young children there was no doubt who his successor must be. At twenty-four Alfred became King, and entered upon a desperate inheritance. To and fro the fighting swayed, with varying fortunes. The Danes were strongly reinforced from overseas; "the summer army," as it was called, "innumerable," "eager to fight against the army of the West Saxons," arrived to join them. Seven or eight battles were fought, and we are told the Danes usually held the field. At Wilton, in the summer, about a month after Alfred had assumed the crown, he sustained a definite defeat in the heart of his own country. His numbers had been worn down by death and desertion, and once again in the field the Vikings' ruse of a feigned retreat was successful.

On the morrow of this misfortune Alfred thought it best to come to terms while he still had an army. We do not know the conditions, but there is no doubt that a heavy payment was among them. "The Saxons made peace with the heathen on the condition that they should depart from them, and this they did," declares the *Chronicle* laconically. But as they took three or four months before retiring upon London it seems that they waited for the Danegeld to be paid. Nevertheless Alfred and his Saxons had in all this fighting convinced the Vikings of their redoubtable force. By this inglorious treaty and stubborn campaign Alfred secured five years in which to consolidate his power.

The reasons which led the Danes to make a truce with Alfred are hard to analyse at this date. They were certainly convinced that only by prolonged and bloody fighting could they master the West Saxons. Both sides liked war, and this had been ding-dong: there was little to show but scars and corpses on either side. But Alfred had always counted upon the invaders dividing, and the stresses at work within the heathen army justified his policy.

Still maintaining their grip on London, the Danes moved back to the Midlands, which were now in complete submission. "The Mercians made peace with the army." Their king Burgred in 874 was driven overseas, and died in piety under the Papal compassion in Rome. "After his expulsion," says Asser, "the heathen subjected the whole kingdom of the Mercians to their lordship." They set up a local puppet, in a fashion which has often been imitated since, after he had given hostages and taken an oath "that he would not obstruct their wishes, and would be obedient in everything."

* * *

But now in the last quarter of the century a subtle, profound change came over the "Great Heathen Army." Alfred and the men of Wessex had proved too stubborn a foe for easy sub-jugation. Some of the Danes wished to settle on the lands they already held; the rest were for continuing the war at a suitable moment till the whole country was conquered. Perhaps these two bodies acted in concert, the former providing a sure and solid base, the latter becoming an expeditionary force. Thus, after mauling the kingdom of Strathclyde and carrying off the stock and implements of agriculture nearly half of the sea-pirates settled themselves in' Northumbria and East Anglia. Henceforward they began "to till the ground for a livelihood." Here was a great change. We must remember their discipline and organisation. The ships' companies, acting together, had hitherto fought ashore as soldiers. All their organisation of settlements was military. The sailors had turned soldiers, and the soldiers had turned yeomen. They preserved that spirit of independence, regulated only by comradeship and discipline for vital purposes, which was the life of the long-ship.

The whole of the East of England thus received a class of cultivator who, except for purposes of common defence, owed allegiance to none; who had won his land with the sword, and was loyal only to the army organisation which enabled him to keep it. From Yorkshire to Norfolk this sturdy, upstanding stock took root. As time passed they forgot the sea; they forgot the army; they thought only of the land—their own land. They liked the life. Although they were sufficiently skilful agricul-turists, there was nothing they could teach the older inhabit-ants; they brought no new implements or methods, but they were resolved to learn.

They were not dependent wholly upon their own labour. They must have exploited the former possessors and their serfs. The distribution of the land was made around a unit which could support a family. What eight oxen could plough in a certain time under prescribed conditions, much disputed by students, became the measure of the holding. They worked hard themselves, but obviously they used the local people too.

Thus the Danish differs in many ways from the Saxon settle-ment four hundred years earlier. There was no idea of ex-terminating the older population. The two languages were not very different; the way of life, the methods of cultivation, very much the same. The colonists—for such they had now become —brought their families from Scandinavia, but also it is cer-tain that they established human and natural relations with

the expropriated English. The blood-stream of these vigorous
individualists, proud and successful men of the sword, mingled
henceforward in the Island race. A vivifying, potent, lasting,
and resurgent quality was added to the breed. As modern steel
is hardened by the alloy of special metals in comparatively
small quantities, this strong strain of individualism, based upon
land-ownership, was afterwards to play a persistent part, not
only in the blood but in the politics of England. When in the
reign of Henry II, after much disorder, great laws were made
and· royal courts of justice were opened descendants of these
hardy farmers—not only "sokemen" or independent peasants,
but much smaller folk—were found in a state of high assertive-
ness. The tribulations of another three hundred years had not
destroyed their original firmness of character nor their deep attachment to the conquered soil. All through English history
this strain continues to play a gleaming part.

The reformed and placated pirate-mariners brought with
them many Danish customs. They had a different notation,
which they would have been alarmed to hear described as the
"duodecimal system." They thought in twelves instead of tens,
and in our own day in certain parts of East Anglia the expression "the long hundred" (i.e., 120) is heard on market-days.

They had a different view of social justice from that entertained by the manorialised Saxons. Their customary laws as
they gradually took shape were an undoubted improvement
upon the Saxon theme.

With East Anglia we enter the region within which Danish influence endured. Long before the Norman Conquest it had developed a distinctive form of rural society, which preserved many
Scandinavian features, and in which the free man of peasant condition was holding his own successfully against the contemporary
drift towards manorialism.[1]

Scandinavian England reared a freed peasant population
which the burdens of taxation and defence had made difficult
in Wessex and English Mercia. And this population related itself so closely to the original invaders that students seek in the
Domesday Book of the eleventh century for the means of esti-
mating the size of the Viking armies in the ninth. We shall
see presently the equitable, deferential terms which even after
their final victory the Anglo-Saxon monarchs proffered to the
districts settled by the Danes, known as the Danelaw. It remained only for conversion to Christianity to mingle these

[1] F. Stenton, The Danes in England, 1927, p. 13.

races inextricably in the soul and body of a nation. These considerations may aptly fill the five years' breathing-space which Alfred had gained by courageous fighting and politic Danegeld. In this interval Halfdene, the Viking king, departed like Ivar from the scene. The tortured, plundered Church requited his atrocities by declaring that God punished him in the long run by madness and a smell which made his presence unendurable to his fellows.

At Lindisfarne, in Dane-ravaged Northumbria, a pathetic tale is told. The ruined monks quitted their devastated, polluted sanctuary and carried on their shoulders the body of St Cuthbert and the bones of St Aidan. After seven years of pilgrimage by land and sea they establised themselves in a new patrimony of St Cuthbert as Chester-le-Street. The veneration felt throughout the North for St Cuthbert brought such wealth to his see that in 995 its bishops began to build a new cathedral on the rock at Durham. Thither St Cuthbert's bones were taken, and so great was his prestige that until the nineteenth century the Bishops of Durham were Prince-Bishops, exercising immense power in North-Eastern England.

* * *

Alfred's dear-bought truce was over. Guthrum, the new war-leader of the mobile and martial part of the heathen army, had formed a large design for the subjugation of Wessex. He operated by sea and land. The land army marched to Wareham, close to Portland Bill, where the sea army joined him in Poole harbour. In this region they fortified themselves, and proceeded to attack Alfred's kingdom by raid and storm from every quarter. The prudent King sought peace and offered an indemnity. At the same time it seems probable that he had hemmed in the land army very closely at Wareham. The Danes took the gold, and "swore upon the Holy Ring" they would depart and keep a faithful peace. With a treachery to which all adjectives are unequal they suddenly darted away and seized Exeter. Alfred, mounting his infantry, followed after, but arrived too late. "They were in the fortress, where they could not be come at." But let all heathen beware of breaking oaths! A frightful tempest smote the sea army. They sought to join their comrades by sea. They were smitten in the neighbourhood of Swanage by the elements, which in those days were believed to be personally directed by the Almighty. A hundred and twenty ships were sunk, and upwards of five thousand of these perjured marauders perished as they deserved. Thus the whole careful plan fell to pieces, and Alfred, watching and besetting Exeter, found his enemies in the summer of 877 in the mood for a new peace. They swore it with oaths of still more compliant solemnity, and they kept it for about five months.

Then in January 878 occurred the most surprising reversal of Alfred's fortunes. His headquarters and Court lay at Chippenham, in Wiltshire. It was Twelfth Night, and the Saxons, who in these days of torment refreshed and fortified themselves by celebrating the feasts of the Church, were off their guard, engaged in pious exercises, or perhaps even drunk. Down swept the ravaging foe. The whole army of Wessex, sole guarantee of England south of the Thames, was dashed into confusion. Many were killed. The most part stole away to their houses. A strong contingent fled overseas. Refugees arrived with futile appeals at the Court of France. Only a handful of officers and personal attendants hid themselves with Alfred in the marshes and forests of Somerset and the Isle of Athelney. which rose from the quags. This was the darkest hour of Alfred's fortunes. It was some months before he could even start a guerrilla. He led "with thanes and vassals an unquiet life in great tribulation. . . . For he had nothing wherewith to supply his wants except what in frequent sallies he could seize either stealthily or openly, both from the heathen and from the Christians who had submitted to their rule." He lived as Robin Hood did in Sherwood Forest long afterwards.

This is the moment when those gleaming toys of history were fashioned for the children of every age. We see the warrior-king disguised as a minstrel harping in the Danish camps. We see him acting as a kitchen-boy to a Saxon housewife. The celebrated story of Alfred and the Cakes first appears in a late edition of Bishop Asser's Life. It runs: "It happened one day that the countrywoman, who was the wife of the cowherd with whom King Alfred was staying, was going to bake bread, and the King was sitting by the fireside making ready his bow and arrows and other weapons. A moment came when the woman saw that her bread was burning; she rushed up and removed it from the fire, upbraiding the undaunted King with these words (recorded, strangely, in the original in Latin hexameters): 'Alack, man, why have you not turned over the bread when you see that it is burning, especially as you so much like eating it hot.' The misguided woman little thought that she was talking to King Alfred, who had fought so vigorously against the heathens and won so many victories over them." Low were the fortunes of the once ruthless English. Pent in their mountains, the lineal descendants of the Ancient Britons, slatternly, forlorn, but unconquered, may well have grinned.

The leaders of the Danish army felt sure at this time that mastery was in their hands. To the people of Wessex it seemed that all was over. Their forces were dispersed, the country overrun; their King, if alive, was a fugitive in hiding. It is the supreme proof of Alfred's quality that he was able in such a plight to exercise his full authority and keep contact with his subjects.

Towards the end of Lent the Danes suffered an unexpected misfortune. The crews of twenty-three ships, after committing many atrocities in Wales, sailed to Devon and marched to the attack of one of Alfred's strongholds on Exmoor. The place was difficult to assail, but

in besetting it they thought that the King's thanes would soon give way to hunger and thirst . . . since the fortress had no supply of water.

The Christians, before they endured any such distress, by the inspiration of heaven judged it to be better either to suffer death or to gain the victory. Accordingly at daybreak they suddenly rushed forth against the heathen, and at the first attack they laid low most of the enemy, including their king. A few only by flight escaped to their ships.[1]

Eight hundred Danes were killed, and the spoils of the victory included an enchanted banner called the Raven, of which it was said that the three daughters of Ragnar Lodbrok had woven it in a single day, and that "in every battle in which that banner went before them the raven in the middle of the design seemed to flutter as though it were alive if they were going to have the victory." On this occasion it did not flutter, but hung listlessly in its silken folds. The event proved that it was impossible for the Danes to win under these conditions.

Alfred, cheered by this news and striving to take the field again, continued a brigand warfare against the enemy while sending his messengers to summon the "fyrd," or local militia, for the end of May. There was a general response; the King was loved and admired. The news that he was alive and active caused widespread joy. All the fighting men came back. After all, the country was in peril of subjugation, the King was a hero, and they could always go home again. The troops of Somerset, Wiltshire, and Hampshire concentrated near Sel-

[1] Quoted in Hodgkin, *loc. cit.*, vol. ii, pp. 565–566.

wood. A point was chosen near where the three shires met, and we can see from this the burdens which lay upon Alfred's tactics. Nevertheless here again was an army: "and when they saw the King they received him like one risen from the dead, after so great tribulations, and they were filled with great joy."

Battle must be sought before they lost interest. The Danes still lay upon their plunder at Chippenham. Alfred advanced to Ethandun, now Edington, and on the bare downs was fought the largest and culminating battle of Alfred's wars. All was staked. All hung in the scales of fate. On both sides the warriors dismounted; the horses were sent to the rear. The shield-walls were formed, the masses clashed against each other, and for hours they fought with sword and axe. But the heathen had lost the favour of God through their violated oath, and eventually from this or other causes they fled from the cruel and clanging field. This time Alfred's pursuit was fruitful. Guthrum, king of the Viking army, so lately master of the one unconquered English kingdom, found himself penned in his camp. Bishop Asser says, "the heathen, terrified by hunger, cold, and fear, and at the last full of despair, begged for peace." They offered to give without return as many hostages as Alfred should care to pick and to depart forthwith.

But Alfred had had longer ends in view. It is strange that he should have wished to convert these savage foes. Baptism as a penalty of defeat might lose its spiritual quality. The workings of the spirit are mysterious, but we must still wonder how the hearts of these hard-bitten swordsmen and pirates could be changed in a single day. Indeed these mass conversions had become almost a matter of form for defeated Viking armies. It is reported that one old veteran declared he had been through this washing twenty times, and complained that the alb with which he was supplied was by no means up to the average standard. But Alfred meant to make a lasting peace with Guthrum. He had him and his army in his power. He could have starved them into surrender and slaughtered them to a man. He wished instead to divide the land with them, and that the two races, in spite of fearful injuries given and received, should dwell together in amity. He received Guthrum with thirty prominent buccaneers in his camp. He stood godfather to Guthrum; he raised him from the font; he entertained him for twelve days; he presented him and his warriors with costly gifts; he called him his son.

This sublime power to rise above the whole force of circumstances, to remain unbiased by the extremes of victory or defeat, to persevere in the teeth of disaster. to greet returning fortune with a cool eye, to have faith in men after repeated betrayals, raises Alfred far above the turmoil of barbaric wars to his pinnacle of deathless glory.

* * *

Fourteen years intervened between the victory of Ethandun and any serious Danish attack. In spite of much uneasiness and disturbance, by the standards of those days there was peace. Alfred worked ceaselessly to strengthen his realm. He had been content that the Danes should settle in East Anglia, but he cultivated the best relations with the harassed kingdom of Mercia, which had become tributary to the Danes, though still largely unoccupied by them. In 886 he married his eldest daughter to the regent, Ethelred, who was striving to bear the burden abandoned to him by the fugitive king, Burhred. There had already been several inter-marriages in the Mercian and Wessex royal families, and this set the final seal upon the co-operation of the South and the Midlands.

The first result of this new unity was the recovery of London in 886. London had long been the emporium of Christian England. Ancient Rome had seen in this bridgehead of the Thames, at the convergence of all the roads and sea routes, the greatest commercial and military centre in the Island. Now the City was set on the road to becoming the national capital. We read in the *Chronicle:* "King Alfred restored London, and all the English—those of them who were free from Danish bondage —turned to him, and he then entrusted the borough to the keeping of the ealdorman Ethelred." It would seem that heavy fighting and much slaughter attended the regaining of London, but of this nothing has been recorded. We know little more than the bare fact, and that Alfred after the victory made the citizens organise an effective defence force and put their walls in the highest order.

King Alfred's main effort was to restore the defences and raise the efficiency of the West Saxon force. He reorganised the "fyrd," dividing it into two classes which practised a rotation of service. Though his armies might be smaller, Alfred's peasant soldiers were encouraged not to desert on a long campaign, because they knew that their land was being looked after by the half of the militia that had stayed at home. The modesty of his reforms shows us the enormous difficulties which he had to overcome, and proves that even in that time of mortal peril it was almost impossible to keep the English under arms. The

King fortified the whole country by boroughs, running down
the Channel and then across to the Severn estuary and so back
by the Thames valley, assigning to each a contributory district
to man the walls and keep the fortifications in repair. He saw
too the vision of English sea-power. To be safe in an island it
was necessary to command the sea. He made great departures
in ship design, and hoped to beat the Viking numbers by fewer
ships of much larger size. These conclusions have only recently
become antiquated.

Then King Alfred commanded to be built against the Danish
warships longships which were well-nigh twice as long as the others.
Some had sixty oars, some more. They were both swifter and
steadier, and also higher than the others. They were shaped neither
as the Frisian nor as the Danish, but as it seemed to himself that
they might be most useful.[1] .

But the big ships were beyond the skill of their inexperienced seamen to handle. In an action when nine of them
fought six pirate vessels several were run ashore "most awkwardly," says the *Chronicle*, and only two of the enemy fell
into Alfred's hands, to afford him the limited satisfaction of
hanging their crews at Winchester. Still, the beginning of the
English Navy must always be linked with King Alfred.

In spite of the disorders a definite treaty was achieved after
the reconquest of London in 886. Significance attaches to the
terms in which the contracting parties are described. On Alfred's side there are "the counsellors of the English nation,"
on Guthrum's "the people who dwell in East Anglia." The
organisation of the Danelaw, based entirely upon the army and
the subjugated inhabitants, had not yet assumed the form of a
State. The English, on the other hand, had already reached
the position of "King and Witan"; and none did more to enforce the idea than Alfred himself. The treaty defined a political boundary running up the Thames, up the Lea, along the
Lea to its source, then straight to Bedford, and after by the
Ouse to Watling Street, beyond which no agreement was made.
This line followed no natural frontiers. It recognised a war
front. It was drawn in No Man's Land.

The second part of the treaty is curious and instructive.
Both sides were familiar with the idea of "wergeld." In order
to deal with the ceaseless murders and physical injuries which
the anarchic conditions had produced, a scale for compensation or revenge must at all cost be agreed. Nothing would stop

[1] Quoted in Hodgkin, vol. ii, p. 584.

the Danes from killing and robbing the English, and *vice versa;* but if there was to be any cessation of war a tariff must be agreed. Both Danish and English independent peasants were accordingly valued at 200 silver shillings each, and men of higher rank were assigned a wergeld of 8½ marks of pure gold. In accepting this clause of the treaty Guthrum was in fact undertaking not to discriminate in wergelds between his English and his Danish subjects. Alfred had gained an important point, which is evidence of the reality of his power.

* * *

King Alfred's Book of Laws, or Dooms, as set out in the existing laws of Kent, Wessex, and Mercia, attempted to blend the Mosaic code with Christian principles and old Germanic customs. He inverted the Golden Rule. Instead of "Do unto others as you would that they should do unto you," he adopted the less ambitious principle, "What ye will that other men should *not* do to you, that do ye not to other men," with the comment, "By bearing this precept in mind a judge can do justice to all men; he needs no other law-books. Let him think of himself as the plaintiff, and consider what judgment would satisfy him." The King, in his preamble, explained modestly that "I have not dared to presume to set down in writing many laws of my own, for I cannot tell what will meet with the approval of our successors." The Laws of Alfred, continually amplified by his successors, grew into that body of customary law administered by the shire and hundred courts which, under the name of the Laws of St Edward (the Confessor), the Norman kings undertook to respect, and out of which, with much manipulation by feudal lawyers, the Common Law was founded.

The King encouraged by all his means religion and learning. Above all he sought the spread of education. His rescript to the Bishop of Worcester has been preserved:

I would have you informed that it has come into my remembrance what wise men there formerly were among the English race, both of the sacred orders and the secular; and what happy times those were throughout the English race, and how the kings who had the government of the folk in those days obeyed God and His Ministers; and they on the one hand maintained their peace and morality and their authority within their borders, while at the same time they enlarged their territory abroad; and how they prospered both in war and in wisdom, . . . how foreigners came to this land for wisdom and instruction. . . . So clean was it fallen

away in the English race that there were very few on this side
Humber who could understand their Mass-books in English, or
translate a letter from Latin into English; and I ween that there
were not many beyond the Humber.[1]

He sought to reform the monastic life, which in the general
confusion had grossly degenerated.

If anyone takes a nun from a convent without the King's or the
bishop's leave he shall pay 120 shillings, half to the King, half to
the bishop. . . . If she lives longer than he who abducted her, she
shall inherit nothing of his property. If she bears a child it shall
inherit no more of the property than its mother.[2]

Lastly in this survey comes Alfred's study of history. He it
was who set on foot the compiling of the *Saxon Chronicle*. The
fact that the early entries are fragmentary gives confidence that
the compilers did not draw on their imagination. From King
Alfred's time they are exact, often abundant, and sometimes
written with historic grasp and eloquence.

We discern across the centuries a commanding and versatile
intelligence, wielding with equal force the sword of war and of
justice; using in defence arms and policy; cherishing religion,
learning, and art in the midst of adversity and danger; welding
together a nation, and seeking always across the feuds and
hatreds of the age a peace which would smile upon the land.

This King, it was said, was a wonder for wise men. "From
his cradle he was filled with the love of wisdom above all
things," wrote Asser. The Christian culture of his Court sharply
contrasted with the feckless barbarism of Viking life. The older
race was to tame the warriors and teach them the arts of peace,
and show them the value of a settled common existence. We
are watching the birth of a nation. The result of Alfred's work
was the future mingling of Saxon and Dane in a common
Christian England.

In the grim time of Norman overlordship the figure of the
great Alfred was a beacon-light, the bright symbol of Saxon
achievement, the hero of the race. The ruler who had taught
them courage and self-reliance in the eternal Danish wars, who
had sustained them with his national and religious faith, who
had given them laws and good governance and chronicled their
heroic deeds, was celebrated in legend and song as Alfred the
Great.

* * *

[1] Quoted in Hodgkin, *History of the Anglo-Saxons*, p. 609.
[2] *Ibid.*, p. 612.

One final war awaited Alfred. It was a crisis in the Viking story. In 885 they had rowed up the Seine with hundreds of ships and an army of forty thousand men. With every device known to war they laid siege to Paris, and for more than a year battered at its walls. They were hampered by a fortified bridge which the Franks had thrown across the river. They dragged their long-ships overland to the higher reaches and laid waste the land; but they could not take Paris. Count Odo, a warrior prince, defended it against these shameless pirates, and far and wide the demand was made that the King of the Franks should come to the rescue of his capital. Charles the Great had not transmitted his qualities to his children. The nicknames which they received as their monuments sufficiently attest their degeneracy. Charles the Bald was dead, and Charles the Fat reigned in his stead. This wretched invalid was at length forced to gather a considerable army and proceed with it to the aid of Paris. His operations were ineffectual, but the city held firm under its resolute governor. The Viking attack flagged and finally collapsed. All the records are confused. We hear at this time of other battles which they fought with Germanic armies, in one of which the dyke was filled with their corpses. Evidently their thrust in all directions in Western Europe encountered resistance, which, though inefficient, was more than they could overcome. For six years they ravaged the interior of Northern France. Famine followed in their footsteps. The fairest regions had been devoured; where could they turn? Thus they began again to look to England: something might have had time to grow there in the interval. On the Continent their standards were declining, but perhaps again the Island might be their prey. "It was," says Hodgkin in his admirable account, "a hungry monster which turned to England for food as well as plunder." A group of pagan ruffians and pirates had gained possession of an effective military and naval machine, but they faced a mass of formidable veterans whom they had to feed and manage, and for whom they must provide killings. Such men make plans, and certainly their descent upon England was one of the most carefully considered and elaborately prepared villainies of that dark time.

Guthrum died in 891, and the pact which he had sworn with Alfred, and loosely kept, ended. Suddenly in the autumn of 892 a hostile armada of two hundred and fifty ships appeared off Lympne, carrying "the Great Heathen Army" that had ravaged France to the invasion of England. They disembarked and fortified themselves at Appledore, on the edge of the forest.

They were followed by eighty ships conveying a second force
of baffled raiders from the Continent, who sailed up the
Thames and established themselves on its southern bank at
Milton, near Sittingbourne. Thus Kent was to be attacked from
both sides. This immense concerted assault confronted Alfred
with his third struggle for life. The English, as we may call
them—for the Mercians and West Saxons stood together—had
secured fourteen years of unquiet peace in which to develop
their defences. Many of the Southern towns were fortified;
they were "burhs." The "fyrd" had been improved in organisation, though its essential weaknesses had not been removed.
There had been a re-gathering of wealth and food; there was a
settled administration, and the allegiance of all was given to
King Alfred. Unlike Charlemagne, he had a valiant son. At
twenty-two Edward could lead his father's armies to the field.
The Mercians also had produced an Ethelred, who was a fit
companion to the West Saxon prince.. The King, in ill-health,
is not often seen in this phase at the head of armies; we have
glimpses of him, but the great episodes of the war were centred,
as they should be, upon the young leaders.

The English beat the Vikings in this third war. Owning the
command of the sea, the invaders gripped the Kentish penin-
sula from the north and south. Alfred had tried to buy them
off, and certainly delayed their full attack. He persuaded
Hæsten, the Viking leader, at least to have his two young sons
baptised. He gave Hæsten much money, and oaths of peace
were interchanged, only to be broken. Meanwhile the Danes
raided mercilessly, and Alfred tried to rouse England to action.
In 893 a third expedition composed of the Danish veterans
who had settled in Northumbria and East Anglia sailed round
the south coast, and, landing, laid siege to Exeter. But now the
young leaders struck hard. Apparently they had a strong
mounted force, not indeed what we should call cavalry, but
possessing swiftness of movement. They fell upon a column
of the raiders near the modern Aldershot, routed them, and
pursued them for twenty miles till they were glad to swim the
Thames and shelter behind the Colne. Unhappily, the army
of the young princes was not strong enough to resume the attack, and also it had run out of provisions. The pursuit therefore had to be abandoned and the enemy escaped.

The Danes had fortified themselves at Benfleet, on the
Thames below London, and it is said that their earthworks can
be traced to this day. Thence, after recovering from their defeat, they sallied forth to plunder, leaving a moderate garrison

in their stronghold. This the princes now assaulted. It had very rarely been possible in these wars to storm a well-fortified place; but Alfred's son and his son-in-law with a strong army from London fell upon Benfleet and "put the army to flight, stormed the fort, and took all that there was within, goods as well as women and children, and brought all to London. And all the ships they either broke in pieces or burnt or brought to London or Rochester." Such are the words of the *Saxon Chronicle*. When in the nineteenth century a railway was being made across this ground the charred fragments of the ships and numbers of skeletons were unearthed upon the site of Benfleet. In the captured stronghold the victors found Hæsten's wife and his two sons. These were precious hostages, and King Alfred was much criticised at the time, and also later, because he restored them to Hæsten. He sent back his wife on broad grounds of humanity. As for the two sons, they had been baptised; he was godfather to one of them, and Ethelred of Mercia to the other. They were therefore Christian brethren, and the King protected them from the consequences of their father's wrongful war. The ninth century found it very hard to understand this behaviour when the kingdom was fighting desperately against brutal marauders, but that is one of the reasons why in the after-time the King is called "Alfred the Great." The war went on, but so far as the records show Hæsten never fought again. It may be that mercy and chivalry were not in vain.

In this cruel war the Vikings used their three armies: the grand army that Hæsten had brought from the Continent, the army which had landed near Lympne, and the third from the Danelaw. But in the end they were fairly beaten in full and long fight by the Christians from Mercia, Wessex, and Wales.

One other incident deserves to be noticed. The *Saxon Chronicle* says:

Before the winter [the winter of A.D. 894–5] the Danes . . . towed their ships up the Thames and then up the Lea . . . and made a fort twenty miles above Lunden burh. . . . In the autumn [895] the King camped close to the burh while they reaped their corn, so that the Danes might not deprive them of the crop. Then one day the King rode up by the river, and looked at a place where it might be obstructed, so that they could not bring their ships out. . . . He made two forts on the two sides of the river; . . . then the army perceived that they could not bring their ships out. Therefore they left them and went across country, . . . and the men of Lunden burh fetched the ships, and all that they could not take away they broke up, and all that were worth taking they brought into Lunden burh.

In 896 the war petered out, and the Vikings, whose strength seemed at this time to be in decline, dispersed, some settling in the Danelaw, some going back to France. "By God's mercy," exclaims the *Chronicle,* in summing up the war, "the [Danish] army had not too much afflicted the English people." Alfred had well defended the Island home. He had by policy and arms preserved the Christian civilisation in England. He had built up the strength of that mighty South which has ever since sustained much of the weight of Britain, and later of her Empire. He had liberated London, and happily he left behind him descendants who, for several generations, as we shall see, carried his work forward with valour and success.

* * *

Alfred died in 899, but the struggle with the Vikings had yet to pass through strangely contrasted phases. Alfred's blood gave the English a series of great rulers, and while his inspiration held victory did not quit the Christian ranks. In his son Edward, who was immediately acclaimed King, the armies had already found a redoubtable leader. A quarrel arose between Edward and his cousin, Ethelwald, who fled to the Danelaw and aroused the Vikings of Northumbria and East Anglia to a renewed inroad upon his native land. In 904 Ethelwald and the Danish king crossed the upper reaches of the Thames at Cricklade and ravaged part of Wiltshire. Edward in retaliation ordered the invasion of East Anglia, with an army formed of the men of Kent and London. They devastated Middle Anglia; but the Kentish contingent, being slow to withdraw, was overtaken and brought to battle by the infuriated Danes. The Danes were victorious, and made a great slaughter; but, as fate would have it, both Eric, the Danish king, and the renegade Ethelwald perished on the field, and the new king, Guthrum II, made peace with Edward on the basis of Alfred's treaty of 886, but with additions which show that the situation had changed. It is now assumed that the Danes are Christians and will pay their tithes, while the parish priest is to be fined if he misleads his flock as to the time of a feast-day or a festival.

In 910 this treaty was broken by the Danes, and the war was renewed in Mercia. The main forces of Wessex and Kent had already been sent by Edward, who was with the fleet, to the aid of the Mercians, and in heavy fighting at Tettenhall, in Staffordshire, the Danes were decisively defeated.

This English victory was a milestone in the long conflict. The Danish armies in Northumbria never recovered from the battle, and the Danish Midlands and East Anglia thus lay open to English conquest. Up to this point Mercia and Wessex had been the defenders, often reduced to the most grievous straits. But now the tide had turned. Fear camped with the Danes.

Edward's sister had been, as we have seen, married to Earl Ethelred of Mercia. Ethelred died in 911, and his widow, Ethelfleda, succeeded and surpassed him. In those savage times the emergence of a woman ruler was enough to betoken her possession of extraordinary qualities. Edward the Elder, as he was afterwards called, and his sister, "the Lady of the Mercians," conducted the national war in common, and carried its success to heights which Alfred never knew. The policy of the two kingdoms, thus knit by blood and need, marched in perfect harmony, and the next onslaught of the Danes was met with confident alacrity and soon broken. The victors then set themselves deliberately to the complete conquest of the Danelaw and its Five Boroughs. This task occupied the next ten years, brother and sister advancing in concert upon their respective lines, and fortifying towns they took at every stage. In 918, when Edward stormed Tempsford, near Bedford, and King Guthrum was killed, the whole resistance of East Anglia collapsed, and all the Danish leaders submitted to Edward as their protector and lord. They were granted in return their estates and the right to live according to their Danish customs. At the same time "the Lady of the Mercians" conquered Leicester, and received even from York offers of submission. In this hour of success Ethelfleda died, and Edward, hastening to Tamworth, was invited by the nobles of Mercia to occupy the vacant throne.

Alfred's son was now undisputed King of all England south of the Humber, and the British princes of North and South Wales hastened to offer their perpetual allegiance. Driving northwards in the next two years, Edward built forts at Manchester, at Thelwall in Cheshire, and at Bakewell in the Peak Country. The Danes of Northumbria saw their end approaching. It seemed as if a broad and lasting unity was about to be reached. Edward the Elder reigned five years more in triumphant peace, and when he died in 925 his authority and his gifts passed to a third remarkable sovereign, capable in every way of carrying on the work of his father and grandfather.

The Saxon Dusk

A THELSTAN, the third of the great West Saxon kings, sought at first, in accordance with the traditions of his house, peaceful relations with the unconquered parts of the Danelaw; but upon disputes arising he marched into Yorkshire in 926, and there established himself. Northumbria submitted; the Kings of the Scots and of Strathclyde acknowledged him as their "father and lord," and the Welsh princes agreed to pay tribute. There was another uneasy interlude; then in 933 came a campaign against the Scots, and in 937 a general rebellion and renewed war, organised by all the hitherto defeated characters in the drama. The whole of North Britain—Celtic, Danish, and Norwegian, pagan and Christian—together presented a hostile front under Constantine, King of the Scots, and Olaf of Dublin, with Viking reinforcements from Norway. On this occasion neither life nor time was wasted in manœuvres. The fight that followed is recorded for us in an Icelandic saga and an English poem. According to the saga-man, Athelstan challenged his foes to meet him in a pitched battle, and to this they blithely agreed. The English king even suggested the place where all should be put to the test. The armies, very large for those impoverished times, took up their stations as if for the Olympic Games, and much parleying accompanied the process. Tempers rose high as these masses of manhood flaunted their shields and blades at one another and flung their gibes across a narrow space; and there was presently a fierce clash between the Northumbrian and the Icelandic Vikings on the one hand and a part of the English army on the other. In this, although the Northumbrian commander fled, the English were worsted. But on the following day the real trial of strength was staged. The rival hosts paraded in all the pomp of war, and then in hearty goodwill fell on with spear, axe, and sword. All day long the battle raged.

The original victory-song on Brunanburh opens to us a view of the Anglo-Saxon mind, with its primitive imagery and wardelight. "Here Athelstan King, of earls the lord, the giver of the bracelets of the nobles, and his brother also, Edmund the Ætheling, an age-long glory won by slaughter in battle, with the edges of swords, at Brunanburh. The wall of shields they cleaved, they hewed the battle shafts with hammered weapons, the foe flinched . . . the Scottish people and the ship-fleet.

. . . The field was coloured with the warriors' blood! After that the sun on high, . . . the greatest star, glided over the earth, God's candle bright! till the noble creature hastened to her setting. There lay soldiers, many with darts struck down, Northern men over their shields shot. So were the Scotch; weary of battle, they had had their fill! They left behind them, to feast on carrion, the dusty-coated raven with horned beak, the black-coated eagle with white tail, the greedy battle-hawk, and the grey beast, the wolf in the wood."

The victory of the English was overwhelming. Constantine, "the perjured" as the victors claimed, fled back to the North, and Olaf retired with his remnants to Dublin. Thus did King Alfred's grandson, the valiant Athelstan, become one of the first sovereigns of Western Europe. He styled himself on coin and charter *Rex totius Britanniæ*.

These claims were accepted upon the Continent. His three sisters were wedded respectively to the Carolingian king, Charles the Simple, to the Capetian, Hugh the Great, and to Otto the Saxon, a future Holy Roman Emperor. He even installed a Norwegian prince, who swore allegiance and was baptised as his vassal at York. Here again one might hope that a decision in the long quarrel had been reached; yet it persisted; and when Athelstan died, two years after Brunanburh, and was succeeded by his half-brother, a youth of eighteen, the beaten forces welled up once more against him. Edmund, in the spirit of his race, held his own. He reigned only six years, but when he died in 946 he had not ceded an inch or an ell. Edmund was succeeded by his brother Edred, the youngest son of Alfred's son Edward the Elder. He too maintained the realm against all comers, and, beating them down by force of arms, seemed to have quenched for ever the rebellious fires of Northumbria.

* * *

Historians select the year 954 as the end of the first great episode in the Viking history of England. A hundred and twenty years had passed since the impact of the Vikings had smitten the Island. For forty years English Christian society had struggled for life. For eighty years five warrior kings— Alfred, Edward, Athelstan, Edmund, and Edred—defeated the invaders. The English rule was now restored, though in a form changed by the passage of time, over the whole country. Yet underneath it there had grown up, deeply rooted in the soil, a Danish settlement covering the great eastern plain, in which Danish blood and Danish customs survived under the authority of the English king.

In the brilliant and peaceful reign of Edgar all this long building had reached its culmination. The reconquest of England was accompanied step by step by a conscious administrative reconstruction which has governed the development of English institutions from that day to this. The shires were reorganised, each with its sheriff or reeve, a royal officer directly responsible to the Crown. The hundreds, subdivisions of the shire, were created, and the towns prepared for defence. An elaborate system of shire, hundred, and burgh courts maintained law and order and pursued criminals. Taxation was reassessed. Finally, with this military and political revival marched a great re-birth of monastic life and learning and the beginning of our native English literature. The movement was slow and English in origin, but advanced with great strides from the middle of the century as it came in contact with the religious revival on the Continent. The work of Dunstan, Archbishop of Canterbury, and his younger contemporaries, Oswald, Bishop of Worcester, and Æthelwold, Bishop of Winchester, was to revive the strict observance of religion within the monasteries, and thereby indirectly to reform the Episcopate as more and more monks were elected to bishoprics. Another and happy, if incidental, result was to promote learning and the production of splendid illuminated manuscripts which were much in demand in contemporary Europe. Many of these, designed for the religious instruction of the laity, were written in English. The Catholic Homilies of Ælfric, Abbot of Eynsham, mark, we are told, the first achievement of English as a literary language—the earliest vernacular to reach this eminence in the whole of Europe. From whatever point of view we regard it, the tenth century is a decisive step forward in the destinies of England. Despite the catastrophic decline of the monarchy which followed the death of Edgar, this organisation and English culture were so firmly rooted as to survive two foreign conquests in less than a century.

It must have seemed to contemporaries that with the magnificent coronation at Bath in 973, on which all coronation orders since have been based, the seal was set on the unity of the realm. Everywhere the courts are sitting regularly, in shire and borough and hundred; there is one coinage, and one system of weights and measures. The arts of building and decoration are reviving; learning begins to flourish again in the Church; there is a literary language, a King's English, which

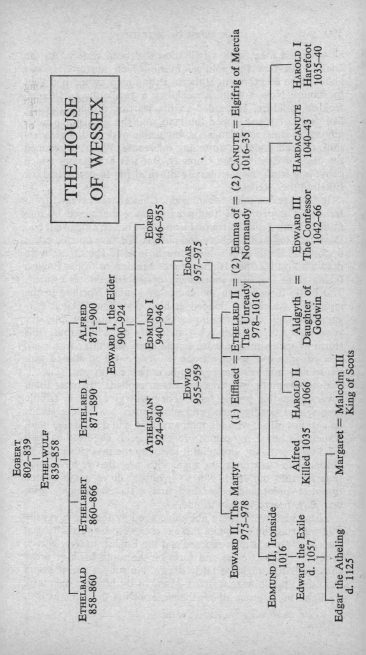

THE HOUSE
OF WESSEX

EGBERT
802–839

ETHELWULF
839–858

ETHELBALD
858–860

ETHELBERT
860–866

ETHELRED I
871–890

ALFRED
871–900

EDWARD I, the Elder
900–924

ATHELSTAN
924–940

EDMUND I
940–946

EDRED
946–955

EDWIG
955–959

EDGAR
957–975

EDWARD II, The Martyr
975–978

(1) Elfflaed = ETHELRED II = (2) Emma of = (2) CANUTE = Elgifrig of Mercia
The Unready   Normandy   1016–35
978–1016

EDMUND II, Ironside
1016

Alfred
Killed 1035

HAROLD II
1066

Aldgyth =
Daughter of
Godwin

EDWARD III
The Confessor
1042–66

HARDACANUTE
1040–43

HAROLD I
Harefoot
1035–40

Edward the Exile
d. 1057

Margaret = Malcolm III
King of Scots

Edgar the Atheling
d. 1125

all educated men write. Civilisation had been restored to the Island. But now the political fabric which nurtured it was about to be overthrown. Hitherto strong men armed had kept the house. Now a child, a weakling, a vacillator, a faithless, feckless creature, succeeded to the warrior throne. Twenty-five years of peace lapped the land, and the English, so magnificent in stress and danger, so invincible under valiant leadership, relaxed under its softening influences. We have reached the days of Ethelred the Unready. But this expression, which conveys a truth, means literally Ethelred the Ill-counselled, or Ethelred the "Redeless."

In 980 serious raids began again. Chester was ravaged from Ireland. The people of Southampton were massacred by marauders from Scandinavia or Denmark. Thanet, Cornwall, and Devon all suffered butchery and pillage. We have an epic poem upon "The Battle of Maldon," fought in 991. The Danes were drawn up on Northey Island, east of Maldon, with the English facing them from the south bank of the Blackwater estuary. The battle turned upon the causeway joining Northey to the mainland, which was flooded at high tide. The Vikings bargained in their characteristic fashion: "Send quickly rings for your safety; it is better for you to buy off with tribute this storm of spears than that we should share the bitter war. . . . We will with gold set up a truce. . . . We will go abroad with the tribute, and sail the sea, and be at peace with you." [1]

But Byrhtnoth, alderman of Essex, replied: "Hearest thou, rover, what this people saith? They will give you in tribute spears, and deadly darts, and old swords. . . . Here stands an earl not mean, with his company, who will defend this land, Æthelred's home, my prince's folk and field. The heathen shall fall in the war. Too shameful it seems to me that ye should go abroad with our tribute, unfought with, now that ye have come thus far into our land. Not so lightly shall ye come by the treasure: point and edge shall first make atonement, grim war-play, before we pay tribute." [2]

These high words were not made good by the event. As the tide was running out while these taunts were being exchanged the causeway was now exposed and the English naïvely agreed to let the Vikings cross and form on the south bank in order that the battle might be fairly drawn. No sooner had it begun than the English were worsted. Many of Byrhtnoth's men took to flight, but a group of his thanes, knowing that all was lost,

---

[1] Kendrick's *History of the Vikings*, p. 259.
[2] *Ibid.*

fought on to the death. Then followed the most shameful period of Danegeld.

We have seen that Alfred in his day had never hesitated to use money as well as arms. Ethelred used money instead of arms. He used it in ever-increasing quantities, with ever-diminishing returns. He paid as a bribe in 991 ten thousand pounds of silver, with rations for the invaders. In 994, with sixteen thousand pounds, he gained not only a brief respite, but the baptism of the raider, Olaf, thrown in as a compliment. In 1002 he bought a further truce for twenty-four thousand pounds of silver, but on this occasion he was himself to break it. In their ruin and decay the English had taken large numbers of Danish mercenaries into their service. Ethelred suspected these dangerous helpers of a plot against his life. Panic-stricken, he planned the slaughter of all Danes in the south of England, whether in his pay or living peaceably on the land. This atrocious design was executed in 1002 on St Brice's Day. Among the victims was Gunnhild, the wife of Pallig, one of the chief Vikings, and sister of Sweyn, King of Denmark. Sweyn swore implacable revenge, and for two years executed it upon the wretched Islanders. Exeter, Wilton, Norwich, and Thetford all record massacres, which show how widely the retaliation was applied. The fury of the avenger was not slaked by blood. It was baffled, but only for a space, by famine. The Danish army could no longer subsist in the ruined land, and departed in 1005 to Denmark. But the annals of 1006 show that Sweyn was back again, ravaging Kent, sacking Reading and Wallingford. At last Ethelred, for thirty-six thousand pounds of silver, the equivalent of three or four years' national income, bought another short-lived truce.

A desperate effort was now made to build a fleet. In the energy of despair which had once inflamed the Carthaginians to their last effort an immense number of vessels were constructed by the poor, broken people, starving and pillaged to the bone. The new fleet was assembled at Sandwich in 1009. "But," says the *Chronicle,* "we had not the good fortune nor the worthiness that the ship-force could be of any use to this land." Its leaders quarrelled. Some ships were sunk in the fighting; others were lost in a storm, and the rest were shamefully abandoned by the naval commanders. "And then afterwards the people who were in the ships brought them to London, and they let the whole nation's toil thus lightly pass away." There is the record of a final payment to the Vikings in 1012. This time forty-eight thousand pounds' weight of silver was exacted, and the oppressors enforced the collection by the sack of Canterbury, holding Archbishop Alphege to ransom, and finally killing him at Greenwich because he refused to coerce his flock to raise the money. The *Chronicle* states: "All these calamities fell upon us through evil counsel, because tribute was not offered to them at the right time, nor yet were they resisted; but, when they had done the most evil, then was peace made with them. And notwithstanding all this peace and tribute they went everywhere in companies, harried our wretched people, and slew them."

It is vain to recount further the catalogue of miseries. In earlier ages such horrors remain unknown because unrecorded. Just enough flickering light plays upon this infernal scene to give us the sense of its utter desolation and hopeless wretchedness and cruelty. It suffices to note that in 1013 Sweyn, accompanied by his youngest son, Canute, came again to England, subdued the Yorkshire Danes and the five boroughs in the Danelaw, was accepted as overlord of Northumbria and Danish Mercia, sacked Oxford and Winchester in a punitive foray, and, though repulsed from London, was proclaimed King of England, while Ethelred fled for refuge to the Duke of Normandy, whose sister he had married. On these triumphs Sweyn died at the beginning of 1014. There was another respite. The English turned again to Ethelred, "declaring that no lord was dearer to them than their natural lord, if he would but rule them better than he had done before."

But soon the young Danish prince, Canute, set forth to claim the English crown. At this moment the flame of Alfred's line rose again in Ethelred's son, Edmund—Edmund Ironside, as he soon was called. At twenty he was famous. Although declared a rebel by his father, and acting in complete disobedience to him, he gathered forces, and in a brilliant campaign struck a succession of heavy blows. He gained battles, he relieved London, he contended with every form of treachery; the hearts of all men went out to him. New forces sprang from the ruined land. Ethelred died, and Edmund, last hope of the English, was acclaimed King. In spite of all odds and a heavy defeat he was strong enough to make a partition of the realm, and then set himself to rally his forces for the renewal of the struggle; but in 1016, at twenty-two years of age, Edmund Ironside died, and the whole realm abandoned itself to despair.

The ecclesiastical aristocracy which played so great a part in politics dwelt long upon the prophecies of coming woe ascribed to St Dunstan. At Southampton, even while Edmund lived, the lay and spiritual chiefs of England agreed to abandon the descendants of Ethelred for ever and recognise Canute as King. All resistance, moral and military, collapsed before the Dane. The family of Ethelred was excised from the royal line, and the last sons of the house of Wessex fled into exile. The young Danish prince received this general and abject submission in a good spirit, although a number of bloody acts were required to attain and secure his position. He made good his promise to fulfil the duties of a king both in spiritual and temporal affairs to the whole country. The English magnates agreed to buy off the Danish army with a huge indemnity, and the new King, in "an oath of his soul," endorsed by his chiefs, bound himself to rule for all. Such was the compact solemnly signed by the English and Danish leaders. "The kingly house," as Ranke put it, "whose right and pre-eminence was connected with the earliest settlements, which had completed the union of the realm and delivered it from the worst distress, was at a moment of moral deterioration and disaster excluded by the spiritual and temporal chiefs, of Anglo-Saxon and Danish origin." [1]

* * *

There were three principles upon which sovereignty could be erected: conquest, which none could dispute; hereditary right, which was greatly respected; and election, which was a kind of compromise between the two. It was upon this last basis that Canute began his reign. It is possible that the early English ideal of kingship and just government in Alfred and Canute was affected by the example of Trajan. This emperor was a favourite of Pope Gregory, who had sent the first missionaries. There is evidence that stories of Trajan's virtue were read aloud in the English church service. Canute may also have studied, and certainly he reproduced, the poise of the Emperor Augustus. Everyone knows the lesson he administered to his flatterers when he sat on the seashore and forbade the tide to come in. He made a point of submitting himself to the laws whereby he ruled. He even in his military capacity subjected himself to the regulations of his own household troops. At the earliest moment he disbanded his great Danish army and trusted himself broadly to the loyalty of the humbled English. He married Emma of Normandy, the widow of Ethelred, and so forestalled any action by the Duke of Normandy on behalf of her descendants by Ethelred.

[1] History of England, vol. i, p. 25.

Canute became the ruling sovereign of the North, and was reckoned as having five or six kingdoms under him. He was already King of Denmark when he conquered England, and he made good his claim to be King of Norway. Scotland offered him its homage. The Viking power, although already undermined, still stretched across the world, ranging from Norway to North America, and through the Baltic to the East. But of all his realms Canute chose England for his home and capital. He liked, we are told, the Anglo-Saxon way of life. He wished to be considered the "successor of Edgar," whose seventeen years of peace still shone by contrast with succeeding times. He ruled according to the laws, and he made it known that these were to be administered in austere detachment from his executive authority.

He built churches, he professed high devotion to the Christian faith and to the Papal diadem. He honoured the memory of St Edmund and St Alphege, whom his fellow-countrymen had murdered, and brought their relics with pious pomp to Canterbury. From Rome, as a pilgrim, in 1027, he wrote a letter to his subjects couched in exalted and generous terms, promising to administer equal justice, and laying particular emphasis upon the payment of Church dues. His daughter was married to the Emperor Conrad's eldest son, who ultimately carried his empire across Schleswig to the banks of the Eider. These remarkable achievements, under the blessing of God and the smiles of fortune, were in large measure due to his own personal qualities. Here again we see the power of a great man to bring order out of ceaseless broils and command harmony and unity to be his servants, and how the lack of such men has to be paid for by the inestimable suffering of the many.

Some early records of Canute throw a vivid light upon his character and moods. "When he entered monasteries, and was received with great honour, he proceeded humbly; keeping his eyes fixed with a wonderful reverence on the ground, and, shedding tears copiously—nay, I may say, in rivers—he devoutly sought the intervention of the Saints. But when it came to making his royal oblations, oh! how often did he fix his weeping eyes upon the earth! How often did he beat that noble breast! What sighs he gave! How often he prayed that he might not be unworthy of clemency from on high!" [1]

But this from a saga two centuries later is in a different vein:

---

[1] From the *Encomium Emma Regina*, in Langebek, *Scriptores Rerum Danicarum* (1773).

"When King Canute and Earl Ulf had played a while the King made a false move, at which the Earl took a knight from the King; but the King set the piece again upon the board, and told the Earl to make another move; but the Earl grew angry, threw over the chess-board, stood up, and went away. The King said, 'Run away, Ulf the Fearful.' The Earl turned round at the door and said, '. . . Thou didst not call me Ulf the Fearful at Helge River, when I hastened to thy help while the Swedes were beating thee like a dog.' The Earl then went out, and went to bed. . . . The morning after, while the King was putting on his clothes, he said to his foot-boy, 'Go thou to Earl Ulf and kill him.'

"The lad went, was away a while, and then came back.

"The King said, 'Hast thou killed the Earl?'

" 'I did not kill him, for he was gone to Saint Lucius' church.'

"There was a man called Ivar White, a Norwegian by birth, who was the King's court-man and chamberlain. The King said to him, 'Go thou and kill the Earl.'

"Ivar went to the church, and in at the choir, and thrust his sword through the Earl, who died on the spot. Then Ivar went to the King, with the bloody sword in his hand.

"The King said, 'Hast thou killed the Earl?'

" 'I have killed him,' says he.

" 'Thou didst well.'

"After the Earl was killed the monks closed the church and locked the doors. When that was told the King he sent a message to the monks, ordering them to open the church and sing High Mass. They did as the King ordered; and when the King came to the church he bestowed on it great property, so that it had a large domain, by which that place was raised very high; and those lands have since always belonged to it." [1]

* * *

Meanwhile across the waters of the English Channel a new military power was growing up. The Viking settlement founded in Normandy in the early years of the tenth century had become the most vigorous military state in France. In less than a hundred years the sea-rovers had transformed themselves into a feudal society. Such records as exist are overlaid by legend. We do not even know whether Rollo, the traditional founder of the Norman state, was a Norwegian, a Dane, or a Swede. Norman history begins with the Treaty of Saint-Clair-sur-Epte, made by Rollo with Charles the Simple, King of the West

[1] From the *Heimskringla* of Snorre Sturlason.

Franks, which affirmed the suzerainty of the King of France and defined the boundaries of the Duchy of Normandy.

In Normandy a class of knights and nobles arose who held their lands in return for military service, and sublet to inferior tenants upon the same basis. The Normans, with their craving for legality and logic, framed a general scheme of society, from which there soon emerged an excellent army. Order was strenuously enforced. No one but the Duke might build castles or fortify himself. The Court or "Curia" of the Duke consisted of his household officials, of dignitaries of the Church, and of the more important tenants, who owed him not only military service but also personal attendance at Court. Here the administration was centred. Respect for the decisions and interests of the Duke was maintained throughout Normandy by the Vicomtes, who were not merely collectors of taxes from the ducal estates, but also, in effect, prefects, in close touch with the Curia, superintending districts like English counties. The Dukes of Normandy created relations with the Church which became a model for medieval Europe. They were the protectors and patrons of the monasteries in their domains. They welcomed the religious revival of the tenth century, and secured the favour and support of its leaders. But they made sure that bishops and abbots were ducal appointments.

It was from this virile and well-organised land that the future rulers of England were to come. Between the years 1028 and 1035 the Viking instincts of Duke Robert of Normandy turned him seriously to plans of invasion. His death and his failure to leave a legitimate heir suspended the project, but only for a while.

The figure of Emma, sister of Robert of Normandy, looms large in English history at this time. Ethelred had originally married her from a reasonable desire to supplement his failing armaments by a blood-tie with the most vigorous military state in Europe. Canute married her to give him a united England. Of her qualities and conduct little is known. Nevertheless few women have stood at the centre of such remarkable converging forces. In fact Emma had two husbands and two sons who were Kings of England.

In 1035 Canute died, and his empire with him. He left three sons, two by Elgiva of Northampton and one, Hardicanute, by Emma. These sons were ignorant and boorish Vikings, and many thoughts were turned to the representatives of the old West Saxon line, Alfred and Edward, sons of Ethelred and Emma, then living in exile in Normandy. The elder, Alfred, "the innocent Prince" as the chronicler calls him, hastened to England in 1036, ostensibly to visit his again-widowed mother, the ex-Queen Emma. A Wessex earl, Godwin, was the leader of the Danish party in England. He possessed great abilities and exercised the highest political influence. The venturesome Alfred was arrested and his personal attendants slaughtered. The unfortunate prince himself was blinded, and in this condition soon ended his days in the monastery at Ely. The guilt of this crime was generally ascribed to Godwin. The succession being thus simplified, Canute's sons divided the paternal inheritance. Sweyn reigned in Norway for a spell, but his two brothers who ruled England were short-lived, and within six years the throne of England was again vacant.

Godwin continued to be the leading figure in the land, and was now master of its affairs. There was still living in exile in Normandy Edward, the remaining son of Ethelred and Emma, younger brother of the ill-starred Alfred. In these days of reviving anarchy all men's minds turned to the search for some stable institution. This could only be found in monarchy, and the illustrious line of Alfred the Great possessed unequalled claims and titles. It was the Saxon monarchy which for five or six generations had provided the spearhead of resistance to the Danes. The West Saxon line was the oldest in Europe. Two generations back the house of Capet were lords of little more than Paris and the Ile de France, and the Norman dukes were Viking rovers. A sense of sanctity and awe still attached to any who could claim descent from the Great King, and beyond him to Egypt and immemorial antiquity. Godwin saw that he could consolidate his power and combine both English and Danish support by making Edward King. He bargained with the exile, threatening unless his terms were met to put a nephew of Canute on the throne. Of these the first was the restriction of Norman influence in England. Edward made no difficulty; he was welcomed home and crowned; and for the next twenty-four years, with one brief interval, England was mainly governed by Godwin and his sons. "He had been to such an extent exalted," says the *Chronicle* of Florence of Worcester, "as if he had ruled the King and all England."

Edward was a quiet, pious person without liking for war or much aptitude for administration. His Norman upbringing made him the willing though gentle agent of Norman influence, so far as Earl Godwin would allow. Norman prelates appeared in the English Church, Norman clerks in the royal household, and Norman landowners in the English shires. To

make all smooth Edward was obliged to marry Godwin's
young and handsome daughter, but we are assured by contemporary writers that this union was no more than formal.
According to tradition the King was a kindly, weak, chubby
albino. Some later writers profess to discern a latent energy
in a few of his dealings with the formidable group of Anglo-
Danish warriors that surrounded him. Nevertheless his main
interest in life was religious, and as he grew older his outlook
was increasingly that of a monk. In these harsh times he played
much the same part as Henry VI, whose nature was similar,
during the Wars of the Roses. His saintliness brought him as
the years passed by a reward in the veneration of his people,
who forgave him his weakness for the sake of his virtues.

Meanwhile the Godwin family maintained their dictatorship
under the Crown. Nepotism in those days was not merely the
favouring of a man's own family; it was almost the only way
in which a ruler could procure trustworthy lieutenants. The
family tie, though frequently failing, gave at least the assurance
of a certain identity of interest. Statistics had not been collected, but there was a general impression in these primitive
times that a man could trust his brother, or his wife's brother,
or his son, better than a stranger. We must not therefore hasten
to condemn Earl Godwin because he parcelled out the English
realm among his relations; neither must we marvel that other
ambitious magnates found a deep cause of complaint in this
distribution of power and favour. For some years a bitter intrigue was carried on between Norman and Saxo-Danish
influences at the English Court.

A crisis came in the year 1051, when the Norman party at
Court succeeded in driving Godwin into exile. During Godwin's absence William of Normandy is said to have paid an
official visit to the Confessor in England in quest of the succession to the Crown. Very likely King Edward promised that
William should be his heir. But in the following year Godwin
returned, backed by a force raised in Flanders, and with the
active help of his son Harold. Together father and son obliged
King Edward to take them back into power. Many of the
principal Norman agents in the country were expelled, and
the authority of the Godwin family was felt again throughout
the land. The territories that they directly controlled stretched
south of a line from the Wash to the Bristol Channel.

Seven months after his restoration Godwin died, in 1053.
Since Canute first raised him to eminence he had been thirty-
five years in public life. Harold, his eldest surviving son, suc-

céeded to his father's great estates. He now filled his part to the full, and for the next thirteen adventurous years was the virtual ruler of England. In spite of the antagonism of rival Anglo-Danish earls, and the opposition of the Norman elements still attached to the Confessor's Court, the Godwins, father and son, maintained their rule under what we should now call a constitutional monarchy. A brother of Harold's became Earl of Mercia, and a third son of Godwin, Tostig, who courted the Normans, and was high in the favour of King Edward, received the Earldom of Northumbria, dispossessing the earls of those regions. But there was now no unity within the house of Godwin. Harold and Tostig soon became bitter foes. All Harold's competence, vigour, and shrewdness were needed to preserve the unity of the realm. Even so, as we shall see, the rift between the brothers left the land a prey to foreign ambitions.

* * *

The condition of England at the close of the reign of Edward the Confessor was one of widespread political weakness. Illuminated manuscripts, sculpture, metalwork and architecture of much artistic merit were still produced, religious life flourished, and a basis of sound law and administration remained, but the virtues and vigour of Alfred's posterity were exhausted and the Saxon monarchy itself was in decline. A strain of feeble princes, most of whom were short-lived, had died without children. Even the descendants of the prolific Ethelred the Unready died out with strange rapidity, and at this moment only a sickly boy and his sister and the aged sovereign represented the warrior dynasty which had beaten the Vikings and reconquered the Danelaw. The great earls were becoming independent in the provinces.

Though England was still the only state in Europe with a royal treasury to which sheriffs all over the country had to account, royal control over the sheriffs had grown lax. The King lived largely upon his private estates and governed as best he could through his household. The remaining powers of the monarchy were in practice severely restricted by a little group of Anglo-Danish notables. The main basis of support for the English kings had always been this select Council, never more than sixty, who in a vague manner regarded themselves as the representatives of the whole country. It was in fact a committee of courtiers, the greater thanes, and ecclesiastics. But at this time this assembly of "wise men" in no way embodied the life of the nation. It weakened the royal executive without adding any strength of its own. Its character and quality suffered in the general decay. It tended to fall into the hands of the great families. As the central power declined a host of local chieftains disputed and intrigued in every county, pursuing private and family aims and knowing no interest but their own. Feuds and disturbances were rife. The people, too, were hampered not only by the many conflicting petty authorities, but by the deep division of custom between the Saxon and the Danish districts. Absurd anomalies and contradictions obstructed the administration of justice. The system of land-tenure varied from complete manorial conditions in Wessex to the free communities of the Danelaw in the North and East. There was no defined relation between Lordship and Land. A thane owed service to the King as a personal duty, and not in respect of lands he held. The Island had come to count for little on the Continent, and had lost the thread of its own progress. The defences, both of the coast and of the towns, were neglected. To the coming conquerors the whole system, social, moral, political, and military, seemed effete.

The figure of Edward the Confessor comes down to us faint, misty, frail. The medieval legend, carefully fostered by the Church, whose devoted servant he was, surpassed the man. The lights of Saxon England were going out, and in the gathering darkness a gentle, grey-beard prophet foretold the end. When on his death-bed Edward spoke of a time of evil that was coming upon the land his inspired mutterings struck terror into the hearers. Only Archbishop Stigand, who had been Godwin's stalwart, remained unmoved, and whispered in Harold's ear that age and sickness had robbed the monarch of his wits. Thus on January 5, 1066, ended the line of the Saxon kings. The national sentiment of the English, soon to be conquered, combined in the bitter period that lay before them with the gratitude of the Church to circle the royal memory with a halo. As the years rolled by his spirit became the object of popular worship. His shrine at Westminster was a centre of pilgrimage. Canonised in 1161, he lived for centuries in the memories of the Saxon folk. The Normans also had an interest in his fame. For them he was the King by whose wisdom the crown had been left, or so they claimed, to their Duke. Hence both sides blessed his memory, and until England appropriated St George during the Hundred Years War St Edward the Confessor was the kingdom's patron saint. St George proved undoubtedly more suitable to the Islanders' needs, moods, and character.

BOOK TWO

THE MAKING OF
THE NATION

The Norman Invasion

ENGLAND, distracted by faction and rivalry at home, had for a long time lain under rapacious glare from overseas. The Scandinavians sought to revive the empire of Canute. The Normans claimed that their Duke held his cousin Edward's promise of the throne. William of Normandy had a virile origin and a hard career. The prize was large enough for the separate ambitions of both the hungry Powers. Their simultaneous action in the opening stages was an advantage to be shared in common.

* * *

One morning Duke Robert of Normandy, the fourth descendant of Rollo, was riding towards his capital town, Falaise, when he saw Arlette, daughter of a tanner, washing linen in a stream. His love was instantly fired. He carried her to his castle, and, although already married to a lady of quality, lived with her for the rest of his days. To this romantic but irregular union there was born in 1027 a son, William, afterwards famous.

Duke Robert died when William was only seven, and in those harsh times a minor's hold upon his inheritance was precarious. The great nobles who were his guardians came one by one to violent ends, and rival ambitions stirred throughout Normandy. Were they to be ruled by a bastard? Was the grandson of a tanner to be the liege lord of the many warrior families? The taint of bastardy clung, and sank deep into William's nature. It embittered and hardened him. When, many years afterwards, he besieged the town of Alençon the citizens imprudently hung out hides upon the walls, shouting, "Hides for the tanner!" William repaid this taunt by devastating the town, and mutilating or flaying alive its chief inhabitants.

It was the declared policy of King Henry of France to recognise and preserve the minor upon the ducal throne. He became his feudal guardian and overlord. But for this the boy could hardly have survived. In 1047, when he was twenty, a formidable conspiracy was organised against him, and at the outset of the revolt he narrowly missed destruction. The confederates proposed to divide the duchy among themselves, conferring on one of their number, to whom they took an oath, the nominal title of Duke. William was hunting in the heart of the disaffected country. His seizure was planned, but his fool broke in upon him with a timely warning to fly for his life. By daybreak he had ridden forty miles, and was for the moment safe in loyal Falaise. Knowing that his own strength could not suffice, he rode on ceaselessly to appeal for help to his overlord, the King of France. This was not denied. King Henry took the field. William gathered together his loyal barons and retainers. At the Battle of Val-ès-Dunes, fought entirely on both sides by cavalry, the rebels were routed, and thenceforward, for the first time, William's position as Duke of Normandy was secure.

There was room enough within the existing social system for feuds, and in some fiefs even private wars, but when the state fell into the hands of strong overlords these were kept within bounds, which did not prevent the rapid growth of a martial society, international both in its secular and military principles. The sense of affinity to the liege lord at every stage in the hierarchy, the association of the land with fighting power, the acceptance of the Papal authority in spiritual matters, united the steel-clad knights and nobles over an ever-widening area of Europe. To the full acceptance of the universal Christian Church was added the conception of a warrior aristocracy, animated by ideas of chivalry, and knit together in a system of military service based upon the holding of land. This institution was accompanied by the rise of mail-clad cavalry to a dominant position in war, and new forces were created which could not only conquer but rule.

In no part of the feudal world was the fighting quality of the new organisation carried to a higher pitch than among the Normans. William was a master of war, and thereby gave his small duchy some of the prestige which England had enjoyed thirty years before under the firm and clear-sighted government of Canute. He and his knights now looked out upon the world with fearless and adventurous eyes. Good reasons for gazing across the Channel were added to the natural ambitions of warlike men. William, like his father, was in close touch with the Saxon Court, and had watched every move on the part of the supporters of the Anglo-Danish party, headed by Godwin and his son Harold.

Fate played startlingly into the hands of the Norman Duke. On some visit of inspection, probably in 1064, Harold was

driven by the winds on to the French coast. The Count of
Ponthieu, who held sway there, looked upon all shipwrecked
mariners and their gear as treasure-trove. He held Harold to
ransom for what he was worth, which was much. The contacts
between the Norman and English Courts were at this time
close and friendly, and Duke William asked for the release of
King Edward's thane, acting at first by civil request, and later
by armed commands. The Count of Ponthieu reluctantly
relinquished his windfall, and conducted Harold to the Norman Court. A friendship sprang up between William and
Harold. Politics apart, they liked each other well. We see
them, falcon on wrist, in sport; Harold taking the field with
William against the Bretons, or rendering skilful service in
hazardous broils. He was honoured and knighted by William.
But the Duke looked forward to his future succession to the
English crown. Here indeed was the prize to be won. Harold
had one small streak of royal blood on his mother's side; but
William, through his father, had a more pointed or at least less
cloudy claim to the Island throne. This claim he was resolved
to assert. He saw the power which Harold wielded under Edward the Confessor, and how easily he might convert it into
sovereignty if he happened to be on the spot when the Confessor died. He invited Harold to make a pact with him
whereby he himself should become King of England, and
Harold Earl of the whole splendid province of Wessex, being
assured thereof and linked to the King by marriage with
William's daughter.

All this story is told with irresistible charm in the tapestry
chronicle of the reign commonly attributed to William's wife,
Queen Matilda, but actually designed by English artists under
the guidance of his half-brother, Odo, Bishop of Bayeux. It is
of course the Norman version, and was for generations proclaimed by their historians as a full justification—and already
even in those days aggressors needed justifications—of William's invasion of England. The Saxons contended that this
was mere Norman propaganda, and there is the usual conflict
of evidence. It is probable however that Harold swore a solemn
oath to William to renounce all rights or designs upon the
English crown, and it is likely that if he had not done so he
might never have seen either crown or England again.

The feudal significance of this oath making Harold William's man was enhanced by a trick novel to those times, yet
adapted to their mentality. Under the altar or table upon which
Harold swore there was concealed a sacred relic, said by some

later writers to have been some of the bones of St Edmund. An oath thus reinforced had a triple sanctity, well recognised throughout Christendom. It was a super-oath; and the obligation, although taken unbeknown, was none the less binding upon Harold. Nevertheless it cannot be said that the bargain between the two men was unreasonable, and Harold probably at the time saw good prospects in it for himself.

By this time William had consolidated his position at home. He had destroyed the revolting armies of his rivals and ambitious relations, he had stabilised his western frontier against Brittany, and in the south-west he had conquered Maine from the most powerful of the ruling houses of Northern France, the Angevins. He had forced the powers in Paris who had protected his youth to respect his manhood; and by his marriage with Matilda, daughter of the Count of Flanders, he had acquired a useful ally on his eastern flank.

Meanwhile Harold, liberated, was conducting the government of England with genuine acceptance and increasing success. At length, in January 1066, Edward the Confessor died, absolved, we trust, from such worldly sins as he had been tempted to commit. With his dying breath, in spite of his alleged promise to William, he is supposed to have commended Harold, his young, valiant counsellor and guide, as the best choice for the crown which the Witan, or Council could make. At any rate, Harold, at the beginning of the fateful year 1066, was blithely accepted by London, the Midlands, and the South, and crowned King with all solemnity in Westminster Abbey.

This event opened again the gates of war. There had been a precedent in France of a non-royal personage, Hugh Capet, becoming King; but this had been strongly resented by the nobility, whose pride, common ideas, and sentiments were increasingly giving the law to Western Europe. Every aspiring thane who heard the news of Harold's elevation was conscious of an affront, and also of the wide ranges open to ability and the sword. Moreover, the entire structure of the feudal world rested upon the sanctity of oaths. Against the breakers of oaths the censures both of chivalry and the Church were combined with blasting force. It was a further misfortune for Harold that Stigand, the Archbishop of Canterbury, had himself received the pallium from a schismatic Pope. Rome therefore could not recognise Harold as King.

At this very moment the Almighty, reaching down from His heavenly sphere, made an ambiguous gesture. The tailed comet or "hairy star" which appeared at the time of Harold's coronation is now identified by astronomers as Halley's Comet, which had previously heralded the Nativity of Our Lord; and it is evident that this example of divine economy in the movements for mundane purposes of celestial bodies might have been turned by deft interpretation to Harold's advantage. But the conquerors have told the tale, and in their eyes this portent conveyed to men the approaching downfall of a sacrilegious upstart.

Two rival projects of invasion were speedily prepared. The first was from Scandinavia. The successors of Canute in Norway determined to revive their traditions of English sovereignty. An expedition was already being organised when Tostig, Harold's exiled and revengeful half-brother, ousted from his Earldom of Northumbria, arrived with full accounts of the crisis in the Island and of the weak state of the defences. King Harold Hardrada set forth to conquer the English crown. He sailed at first to the Orkneys, gathering recruits from the Scottish isles and from the Isle of Man. With Tostig he wended towards the north-east coast of England with a large fleet and army in the late summer of 1066.

Harold of England was thus faced with a double invasion from the north-east and from the south. In September 1066 he heard that a Norwegian fleet, with Hardrada and Tostig on board, had sailed up the Humber, beaten the local levies under Earls Edwin and Morcar, and encamped near York at Stamford Bridge. He now showed the fighting qualities he possessed. The news reached him in London, where he was waiting to see which invasion would strike him first, and where. At the head of his Danish household troops he hastened northwards up the Roman road to York, calling out the local levies as he went. His rapidity of movement took the Northern invaders completely by surprise. Within five days of the defeat of Edwin and Morcar Harold reached York, and the same day marched to confront the Norwegian army ten miles from the city.

The battle began. The Englishmen charged, but at first the Norsemen, though without their armour, kept their battle array. After a while, deceived by what proved to be a feint, the common ruse of those days, they opened up their shield rampart and advanced from all sides. This was the moment for which Harold had waited. The greatest crash of weapons arose. Hardrada was hit by an arrow in the throat, and Tostig, assuming the command, took his stand by the banner "Landravager." In this pause Harold offered his brother peace, and also quarter to all Norsemen who were still alive; but "the

Norsemen called out all of them together that they would rather fall, one across the other, than accept of quarter from the Englishmen." [1] Harold's valiant house-carls, themselves of Viking blood, charged home, and with a war shout the battle began again. At this moment a force left on board ship arrived to succour the invaders. They, unlike their comrades, were clad in proof, but, breathless and exhausted from their hurried march, they cast aside their ring-mail, threw in their lot with their hard-pressed friends, and nearly all were killed The victorious Harold buried Hardrada in the seven feet of English earth he had scornfully promised him, but he spared his son Olaf and let him go in peace with his surviving adherents. Tostig paid for his restless malice with his life. Though the Battle of Stamford Bridge has been overshadowed by Hastings it has a claim to be regarded as one of the decisive contests of English history. Never again was a Scandinavian army able seriously to threaten the power of an English king or the unity of the realm.

At the moment of victory news reached the King from the South that "William the Bastard" had landed at Pevensey.

* * *

William the Conqueror's invasion of England was planned like a business enterprise. The resources of Normandy were obviously unequal to the task; but the Duke's name was famous throughout the feudal world, and the idea of seizing and dividing England commended itself to the martial nobility of many lands. The barons of Normandy at the Council of Lillebonne refused to countenance the enterprise officially. It was the Duke's venture, and not that of Normandy. But the bulk of them hastened to subscribe their quota of knights and ships. Brittany sent a large contingent. It must be remembered that some of the best stocks from Roman Britain had found refuge there, establishing a strong blood strain which had preserved a continuity with the Classic Age and with the British race. But all France was deeply interested. Mercenaries came from Flanders, and even from beyond the Alps; Normans from South Italy and Spain, nobles and knights, answered the advertisement. The shares in this enterprise were represented by knights or ships, and it was plainly engaged that the lands of the slaughtered English would be divided in proportion to the contributions, subject of course to a bonus for good work in the field. During the summer of 1066 this great gathering of

[1] From the *Heimskringla Saga*, by Snorre Sturlason.

audacious buccaneers, land-hungry, war-hungry, assembled in a merry company around St Valery, at the mouth of the Somme. Ships had been built in all the French ports from the spring onwards, and by the beginning of August nearly seven hundred vessels and about seven thousand men, of whom the majority were persons of rank and quality, were ready to follow the renowned Duke and share the lands and wealth of England.

But the winds were contrary. For six whole weeks there was no day when the south wind blew. The heterogeneous army, bound by no tie of feudal allegiance, patriotism, or moral theme, began to bicker and grumble. Only William's repute as a managing director and the rich pillage to be expected held them together. At length extreme measures had to be taken with the weather. The bones of St Edmund were brought from the church of St Valery and carried with military and religious pomp along the seashore. This proved effective, for the very next day the wind changed, not indeed to the south, but to the south-west. William thought this sufficient, and gave the signal. The whole fleet put to sea, with all their stores, weapons, coats of mail, and great numbers of horses. Special arrangements were made to keep the fleet together, the rendezvous being at the mouth of the Somme, and the Duke by night having a lamp of special brilliancy upon his masthead. The next morning all steered towards the English coast. The Duke, who had a faster vessel, soon found himself alone in mid-Channel. He hove to and breakfasted with his staff "as if he had been in his own hall." Wine was not lacking, and after the meal he expressed himself in enthusiastic terms upon his great undertaking and the prizes and profit it would bring to all engaged therein.

On September 28 the fleet hove in sight, and all came safely to anchor in Pevensey Bay. There was no opposition to the landing. The local "fyrd" had been called out this year four times already to watch the coast, and having, in true English style, come to the conclusion that the danger was past because it had not yet arrived had gone back to their homes. William landed, as the tale goes, and fell flat on his face as he stepped out of the boat. "See," he said, turning the omen into a favourable channel, "I have taken England with both my hands." He occupied himself with organising his army, raiding for supplies in Sussex, and building some defensive works for the protection of his fleet and base. Thus a fortnight passed.

Meanwhile Harold and his house-carls, sadly depleted by

the slaughter of Stamford Bridge, jingled down Watling Street on their ponies, marching night and day to London. They covered the two hundred miles in seven days. In London the King gathered all the forces he could, and most of the principal persons in Wessex and Kent hastened to join his standard, bringing their retainers and local militia with them. Remaining only five days in London, Harold marched out towards Pevensey, and in the evening of October 13 took up his position upon the slope of a hill which barred the direct march upon the capital.

The military opinion of those as of these days has criticised his staking all upon an immediate battle. The loyalty of the Northern earls, Edwin and Morcar, was doubtful. They were hastening south with a substantial reinforcement, but he could not be sure which side they would join. In the event they "withdrew themselves from the conflict." Some have suggested that he should have used the tactics which eleven hundred years before Cassivellaunus had employed against Cæsar. But these critics overlook the fact that whereas the Roman army consisted only of infantry, and the British only of charioteers and horsemen, Duke William's was essentially a cavalry force assisted by archers, while Harold had nothing but foot-soldiers who used horses only as transport. It is one thing for mounted forces to hover round and harry an infantry army, and the opposite for bands of foot-soldiers to use these tactics against cavalry. King Harold had great confidence in his redoubtable axe-men, and it was in good heart that he formed his shield-wall on the morning of October 14. There is a great dispute about the numbers engaged. Some modern authorities suppose the battle was fought by five or six thousand Norman knights and men-at-arms, with a few thousand archers, against eight to ten thousand axe- and spear-men, and the numbers on both sides may have been fewer. However it may be, at the first streak of dawn William set out from his camp at Pevensey, resolved to put all to the test; and Harold, eight miles away, awaited him in resolute array.

As the battle began Ivo Taillefer, the minstrel knight who had claimed the right to make the first attack, advanced up the hill on horseback, throwing his lance and sword into the air and catching them before the astonished English. He then charged deep into the English ranks, and was slain. The cavalry charges of William's mail-clad knights, cumbersome in manœuvre, beat in vain upon the dense, ordered masses of the English. Neither the arrow hail nor the assaults of the horsemen could prevail against them. William's left wing of cavalry was thrown into disorder, and retreated rapidly down the hill. On this the troops on Harold's right, who were mainly the local "fyrd," broke their ranks in eager pursuit. William, in the centre, turned his disciplined squadrons upon them and cut them to pieces. The Normans then re-formed their ranks and began a second series of charges upon the English masses, subjecting them in the intervals to severe archery. It has often been remarked that this part of the action resembles the afternoon at Waterloo, when Ney's cavalry exhausted themselves upon the British squares, torn by artillery in the intervals. In both cases the tortured infantry stood unbroken. Never, it was said, had the Norman knights met foot-soldiers of this stubbornness. They were utterly unable to break through the shield-walls, and they suffered serious losses from deft blows of the axe-men, or from javelins, or clubs hurled from the ranks behind. But the arrow showers took a cruel toll. So closely were the English wedged that the wounded could not be removed, and the dead scarcely found room in which to sink upon the ground.

The autumn afternoon was far spent before any result had been achieved, and it was then that William adopted the time-honoured ruse of a feigned retreat. He had seen how readily Harold's right had quitted their positions in pursuit after the first repulse of the Normans. He now organised a sham retreat in apparent disorder, while keeping a powerful force in his own hands. The house-carls around Harold preserved their discipline and kept their ranks, but the sense of relief to the less trained forces after these hours of combat was such that seeing their enemy in flight proved irresistible. They surged forward on the impulse of victory, and when half-way down the hill were savagely slaughtered by William's horsemen. There remained, as the dusk grew, only the valiant bodyguard who fought round the King and his standard. His brothers, Gyrth and Leofwine, had already been killed. William now directed his archers to shoot high into the air, so that the arrows would fall behind the shield-wall, and one of these pierced Harold in the right eye, inflicting a mortal wound. He fell at the foot of the royal standard, unconquerable except by death, which does not count in honour. The hard-fought battle was now decided. The last formed body of troops was broken, though by no means overwhelmed. They withdrew into the woods behind, and William, who had fought in the foremost ranks and had three horses killed under him, could claim the victory. Nevertheless the pursuit was heavily checked. There is a sudden deep ditch on the reverse slope of the hill of Hastings, into which large numbers of Norman horsemen fell, and in which they were butchered by the infuriated English lurking in the wood.

The dead king's naked body, wrapped only in a robe of purple, was hidden among the rocks of the bay. His mother in vain offered the weight of the body in gold for permission to bury him in holy ground. The Norman Duke's answer was that Harold would be more fittingly laid upon the Saxon shore which he had given his life to defend. The body was later transferred to Waltham Abbey, which he had founded. Although here the English once again accepted conquest and bowed in a new destiny, yet ever must the name of Harold be honoured in the Island for which he and his famous house-carls fought indomitably to the end.

BOOK TWO · CHAPTER TEN

William the Conqueror

THE invading army had camped upon the battlefield. Duke William knew that his work was but begun. For more than a year he had been directly planning to invade England and claim the English throne. Now he had, within a month of landing, annihilated the only organised Saxon army and killed his rival. But the internal cleavages which had riven the Island in recent years added new dangers to the task of conquest. The very disunity which had made assault successful made subjugation lengthy. Saxon lords in the North and in the West might carry on endless local struggles and cut communications with the Continent. Cautiously the advance began upon London.

William was a prime exponent of the doctrine, so well known in this civilised age as "frightfulness" [1]—of mass terrorism through the spectacle of bloody and merciless examples. Now, with a compact force of Normans, French, and Bretons, he advanced through Kent upon the capital, and at first no

[1] Written early in 1939.

native came to his camp to do him homage. The people of
Romney had killed a band of Norman knights. Vengeance
fell upon them. The news spread through the country, and the
folk flocked "like flies settling on a wound" to make their submission and avoid a similar fate. The tale of these events bit
deep into the hearts of the people.

When William arrived near London he marched round the
city by a circuitous route, isolating it by a belt of cruel desolation. From Southwark he moved to Wallingford, and thence
through the Chilterns to Berkhamsted, where the leading
Saxon notables and clergy came meekly to his tent to offer him
the crown. On Christmas Day Aldred, Archbishop of York,
crowned him King of England at Westminster. He rapidly
established his power over all England south of the Humber.
Within two years of the conquest Duchess Matilda, who ruled
Normandy in William's absence, came across the sea to her
coronation at Westminster on Whit Sunday 1068, and later in
the year a son, Henry, symbol and portent of dynastic stability,
was born on English soil.

The North still remained under its Saxon lords, Edwin and
Morcar, unsubdued and defiant. The King gathered an army
and marched towards them. The track of William in the North
was marked for generations upon the countryside and in the
memories of the survivors and their descendants. From coast
to coast the whole region was laid desolate, and hunted men
took refuge in the wooded valleys of Yorkshire, to die of
famine and exposure, or to sell themselves into slavery for
food. For long years after tales were told of the "waste" and
of the rotting bodies of the famine-stricken by the roadside. At
Christmas 1069 William wintered at York, and, the feasting
over, continued the man-hunt. Only one town in England had
not yet been subjected to the Conqueror's will—Chester.
Across England in the depth of the winter of 1070 he marched
his army. The town surrendered at the summons, and submitted to the building of a castle.

England north of the Humber was now in Norman control.
The great Earldom of Richmond was created, possessing broad
estates in Yorkshire and in the adjacent counties as well. The
Bishopric of Durham was reorganised, with wide powers of
local government. It was now clear that Normandy had the
force and spirit to absorb all Saxon England; but whether
William would retain the whole of his conquests unchallenged
from without was not settled till his closing years. The period
of English subjugation was hazardous. For at least twenty

years after the invasion the Normans were an army camped in a hostile country, holding the population down by the castles at key points. The Saxon resistance died hard. Legends and chroniclers have painted for us the last stand of Hereward the Wake in the broad wastes of the fens round Ely. Not until five years after Hastings, in 1071, was Hereward put down. In his cause had fallen many of the Saxon thanage, the only class from whose ranks new leaders could spring. The building of Ely Castle symbolised the end of their order.

Other internal oppositions arose. In 1075 a serious revolt of disaffected Norman knights broke out in the Midlands, East Anglia and on the Welsh border, and one surviving Saxon leader, Waltheof, who had made his peace with William, joined them. The King in Normandy must hasten back to crush the rebels. The Saxon population supported the Conqueror against chaos. The "fyrd" took the field. Vengeance was reserved for Waltheof alone, and his execution upon a hill outside Winchester is told in moving scenes by the Saxon-hearted monkish chroniclers of the time. Medieval legend ascribed the fate of William in his later years to the guilt of this execution. It marked also the final submission of England. Norman castles guarded the towns, Norman lords held the land, and Norman churches protected men's souls. All England had a master, the conquest was complete, and the work of reconstruction began.

Woe to the conquered! Here were the Normans entrenched on English soil, masters of the land and the fullness thereof. An armed warrior from Anjou or Maine or Brittany, or even from beyond the Alps and the Pyrenees, took possession of manor and county, according to his rank and prowess, and set to work to make himself secure. Everywhere castles arose. These were not at first the massive stone structures of a later century; they were simply fortified military posts consisting of an earthen rampart and a stockade, and a central keep made of logs. From these strongpoints horsemen sallied forth to rule and exploit the neighbourhood; above them all, at the summit, sat William, active and ruthless, delighting in his work, requiring punctual service from his adherents, and paying good spoil to all who did their duty.

In their early days the Normans borrowed no manners and few customs from the Islanders. The only culture was French. Surviving Saxon notables sent their sons to the monasteries of France for education. The English repeated the experience of the Ancient Britons; all who could learnt French, as formerly the contemporaries of Boadicea had learnt Latin. At first the conquerors, who despised the uncouth English as louts and boors, ruled by the force of sharpened steel. But very soon in true Norman fashion they intermarried with the free population and identified themselves with their English past.

William's work in England is the more remarkable from the fact that all the time as Duke of Normandy he was involved in endless intrigues and conflicts with the King of France. Though England was a more valuable possession than Normandy, William and his sons were always more closely interested in their continental lands. The French kings, for their part, placed in the forefront of their policy the weakening of these Dukes of Normandy, now grown so powerful, and whose frontiers were little more than twenty miles from Paris. Hence arose a struggle that was solved only when King John lost Normandy in 1203. Meanwhile, years passed. Queen Matilda was a capable regent at Rouen, but plagued by the turbulence of her sons. The eldest, Robert, a Crusading knight, reckless and spendthrift, with his father's love of fighting and adventure but without his ruthless genius or solid practical aims, resented William's persistent hold on life and impatiently claimed his Norman inheritance. Many a time the father was called across the Channel to chastise rebellious towns and forestall the conspiracies of his son with the French Court. Robert, driven from his father's lands, found refuge in King Philip's castle of Gerberoi. William marched implacably upon him. Beneath the walls two men, visor down, met in single combat, father and son. Robert wounded his father in the hand and unhorsed him, and would indeed have killed him but for a timely rescue by an Englishman, one Tokig of Wallingford, who remounted the overthrown conqueror. Both were sobered by this chance encounter, and for a time there was reconciliation.

Matilda died, and with increasing years William became fiercer in mood. Stung to fury by the forays of the French, he crossed the frontier, spreading fire and ruin till he reached the gate of Mantes. His Normans surprised the town, and amid the horrors of the sack fire broke out. As William rode through the streets his horse stumbled among the burning ashes and he was thrown against the pommel of the saddle. He was carried in agony to the priory of St Gervase at Rouen. There, high above the town, he lay, through the summer heat of 1087, fighting his grievous injury. When death drew near his sons William and Henry came to him. William, whose one virtue had been filial fidelity, was named to succeed the Conqueror in England. The graceless Robert would rule in Normandy at last. For the youngest, Henry, there was nothing but five thousand pounds of silver, and the prophecy that he would one day reign over a united Anglo-Norman nation. This proved no empty blessing.

Fear fell upon the Conqueror's subjects when it was known that he was dying. What troubles would follow the end of a strong ruler? On Thursday, September 9, 1087, as the early bells of Rouen Cathedral echoed over the hills, William and his authority died. The caitiff attendants stripped the body and plundered the chamber where he lay. The clergy of Rouen bore him to the church of St Stephen at Caen, which he had founded. Even his final journey was disturbed. In the graveyard one Ascelin cried out that his father had been deprived by the dead Duke of this plot of ground, and before all the concourse demanded justice from the startled priests. For the price of sixty shillings the Conqueror came thus humbly to his grave. But his work lived. Says the chronicler:

"He was a very stern and violent man, so that no one dared do anything contrary to his will. He had earls in his fetters, who acted against his will. He expelled bishops from their sees, and abbots from their abbacies, and put thanes in prison, and finally he did not spare his own brother, who was called Odo; he was a very powerful bishop in Normandy and was the foremost man next the king, and had an earldom in England. He [the King] put him in prison. Amongst other things the good security he made in this country is not to be forgotten—so that any honest man could travel over his kingdom without injury with his bosom full of gold: and no one dared strike another, however much wrong he had done him. And if any man had intercourse with a woman against her will, he was forthwith castrated.

"He ruled over England, and by his cunning it was so investigated that there was not one hide of land in England that he did not know who owned it, and what it was worth, and then set it down in his record. Wales was in his power, and he built castles there, and he entirely controlled that race. In the same way, he also subdued Scotland to himself, because of his great strength. The land of Normandy was his by natural inheritance, and he ruled over the county called Maine: and if he could have lived two years more, he would have conquered Ireland by his prudence and without any weapons. Certainly in his time people had much oppression and very many injuries."

At this point the chronicler breaks into verse:

He had castles built
And poor men hard oppressed.
The king was so very stark
And deprived his underlings of many a mark
Of gold and more hundreds of pounds of silver,
That he took by weight and with great injustice
From his people with little need for such a deed.
Into avarice did he fall
And loved greediness above all,
He made great protection for the game
And imposed laws for the same.
That who so slew hart or hind
Should be made blind.

He preserved the harts and boars
And loved the stags as much
As if he were their father . . .[1]

* * *

The Normans introduced into England their system of land tenure based upon military service. A military caste was imposed from above. A revolution not only in warfare, but also in the upper reaches of society, had taken place. William aimed first at securing an effective and compact army, and the terms of knight-service and the quota of men due from each of his greater subjects interested him more than the social relationships prevailing on the lands they held. The Normans, a small minority, had destroyed the Saxon governing class and had thrust an alien domination upon England. But the mass of the inhabitants were only indirectly affected by the change, and the feudal superstructure was for many years as unsure as it was impressive. There were interminable controversies among the new masters of the country about the titles to their lands, and how these fitted the customs and laws of Anglo-Saxon England. The bishoprics and abbeys were especially loud in their complaints, and royal legates repeatedly summoned great assemblies of the shire courts to settle these disputes. Finally, in 1086 a vast sworn inquiry was made into the whole wealth of the King's feudal vassals, from whom he derived a large part of his own income. The inquest or description, as it was called, was carried through with a degree of minuteness and regularity unique in that age and unequalled for centuries after. The history of many an English village begins with an entry in Domesday Book. The result of this famous survey

[1] *Anglo-Saxon Chronicle*, in *English Historical Documents*, vol. ii. (Eyre and Spottiswoode, 1953.)

showed that the underlying structure of England and its peasant life were little changed by the shock of the invasion.

But the holding of the great Domesday inquest marks a crisis. The Norman garrison in England was threatened from abroad by other claimants. The rulers of Scandinavia still yearned for the Island once the west of their empire. They had supported the rising in the North in 1069, and again in 1085, they threatened to intervene with greater vigour. A fleet was fitted out, and though it never sailed, because its leader was murdered, William took precautions. It became necessary that all feudal controversies arising out of the Conquest should be speedily settled, and it was under the shadow of this menace that Domesday Book was compiled. In 1086 William called together at Salisbury "all the land-holding men of any account throughout England whosoever men they were." The King had need of an assurance of loyalty from all his feudal tenants of substance, and this substantial body bound itself together by oath and fealty to his person.

The Norman achievement in England was not merely military in character. Although knight-service governed the holding of property and produced a new aristocracy, much was preserved of Saxon England. The Normans were administrators and lawyers rather than legislators. Their centre of government was the royal Curia, the final court of appeal and the instrument of supervision; here were preserved and developed the financial and secretarial methods of the Anglo-Saxon kingdom. The whole system of Saxon local government, also of immense usefulness for the future—the counties, the sheriffs, and the courts—survived, and through this the King maintained his widespread contacts with the country. In fact the Conqueror himself by these means collected the information for Domesday. Not only the courts, but also the dues and taxes such as Danegeld, were preserved for the sake of the Norman revenues. The local militia raised by the counties survived the Conquest, and proved serviceable to William and his successors. Thus in the future government of England both Norman and Saxon institutions were unconsciously but profoundly blended.

In some respects all this was a sudden acceleration of the drift toward the manorial system, a process which had already gone a long way in Anglo-Saxon England, and certainly in Wessex. But even in Wessex the idea still persisted that the tie of lord and man was primarily personal, so that a free man could go from one lord to another and transfer his land with him. The essence of Norman feudalism, on the other hand, was that the land remained under the lord, whatever the man might do. Thus the landed pyramid rose up tier by tier to the King, until every acre in the country could be registered as held of somebody by some form of service. But besides the services which the man owed to the lord in arms there was the service of attending the courts of the hundred and the county, which were—apart from various exemptions—courts of the King, administering old customary law. The survival of the hundred, the county court and the sheriff makes the great difference between English and Continental feudalism. In England the King is everywhere—in Northumberland as in Middlesex; a crime anywhere is a breach of his peace; if he wants to know anything he tells his officer, the sheriff, to impanel a jury and find out, or, in later days, to send some respectable persons to Westminster and tell him. But perhaps when they got to Westminster they told him that he was badly advised, and that they would not pay any taxes till he mended his ways. Far ahead we see the seventeenth-century constitutional issue. There were in Norman days no great mercantile towns in England, except London. If William had not preserved the counties and hundreds as living and active units, there would have been no body of resistance or counter-poise to the central Government, save in the great baronial families.

In the Norman settlement lay the germ of a constitutional opposition, with the effect if not the design of controlling the Government, not breaking it up. The seat of this potential opposition was found in the counties, among the smaller nobility and their untitled descendants, Justices of the Peace and knights of the shire. They were naturally for the Crown and a quiet life. Hence after centuries they rallied to the Tudor sovereigns; and in another age to the Parliament against the Crown itself. Whatever else changed they were always *there*. And the reason why they were there is that William found the old West Saxon organisation, which they alone could administer, exceedingly convenient. He did not mean to be treated as he had treated the King of France. He had seen, and profited by seeing, the mischief of a country divided into great provinces. The little provinces of England, with the King's officers at the head of each, gave him exactly the balance of power he needed for all purposes of law and finance, but were at the same time incapable of rebelling as units. The old English nobility disappeared after the Battle of Hastings. But all over Domesday Book the opinion of what we should later call the gentry of the shire is quoted as decisive. This is the class—people of some consideration in the neighbourhood, with leisure to go to the sheriff's court and thereafter to Westminster. Out of this in the process of time the Pyms and Hampdens arose.

The Conquest was the supreme achievement of the Norman race. It linked the history of England anew to Europe, and prevented for ever a drift into the narrower orbit of a Scandinavian empire. Henceforward English history marched with that of races and lands south of the Channel.

* * *

The effect of the Conquest on the Church was no less broad and enlivening. The bishoprics and abbeys and other high posts, were now as a matter of course given to Normans, and insular customs supplanted by the newest fashions from abroad. The age of the Conquest coincided with the many-sided reforms of the Church and advances in Papal power initiated by Hildebrand who became Pope as Gregory VII in 1073. Under its new leaders England was brought into the van of this movement. New abbeys sprang up all over the country which attested the piety of the conquerors, though few of the new houses attained to the wealth or standing of the older foundations. These monasteries and bishoprics were the chief centres of religion and learning until after a century they were gradually eclipsed by the rise of the universities. But the new Churchmen were even less disposed than the nobles to draw any deep line across history at the Norman Conquest. Slowly but surely the Frenchmen came to venerate the old English saints and English shrines, and the continuity of religious life with the age of Dunstan was maintained. Under Lanfranc and Anselm, successively Archbishops of Canterbury, the Church was ruled by two of the greatest men of the age, and through them derived incalculable benefits.

In his expedition of 1066 William had received the full support of the Pope, and his standards were blessed by orthodoxy. He was known to be a zealous ecclesiastical reformer, and the Saxon Church was thought to be insular and obstinate. Peter's Pence had not been regularly paid since the Danish invasions. Stigand, blessed only by the schismatic Benedict IX, held both Winchester and Canterbury in plurality. In face of such abuses William stood forth, the faithful son of the Church. Once the secular conquest had been made secure he turned to the religious sphere. The key appointment was the

Archbishopric of Canterbury. In 1070 the Saxon Stigand was deposed and succeeded by Lanfranc. A Lombard of high administrative ability, Lanfranc had been trained in the famous North Italian schools and at the Norman Abbey of Bec, of which he became Abbot, and he rapidly infused new life into the English Church. In a series of councils such as had not been held in England since the days of Theodore organisation and discipline were reformed. Older sees were transplanted from villages to towns—Crediton to Exeter, and Selsey to Chichester. New episcopal seats were established, and by 1087 the masons were at work on seven new cathedrals. At the same time the monastic movement, which had sprung from the Abbey of Cluny, began to spread in England. The English Church was rescued by the Conquest from the backwater in which it had languished, and came once again into contact with the wider European life of the Christian Church and its heritage of learning.

The spirit of the long-vanished Roman Empire, revived by the Catholic Church, returned once more to our Island, bringing with it three dominant ideas. First, a Europe in which nationalism or even the conception of nationality had no place, but where one general theme of conduct and law united the triumphant martial classes upon a plane far above race. Secondly, the idea of monarchy, in the sense that Kings were the expression of the class hierarchy over which they presided and the arbiters of its frequently conflicting interests. Thirdly, there stood triumphant the Catholic Church, combining in a strange fashion Roman imperialism and Christian ethics, pervaded by the social and military system of the age, jealous for its own interests and authority, but still preserving all that was left of learning and art.

BOOK TWO · CHAPTER ELEVEN

Growth Amid Turmoil

THE first generation after the Norman Conquest formed a period when the victorious army and caste were settling themselves upon the lands they had gained, and forcing Saxon England, where the tie between a man and his lord was mainly personal, into the feudal pattern, where it primarily rested on landholding. Under William the Conqueror this process had been harsh and thorough. Under his son William, dubbed Rufus, the Red, it was not less harsh, but also capricious. Moreover, the accession of the Conqueror's second surviving son to the throne of England did not pass without dispute. William I's decision to divide his English from his Norman lands brought new troubles in its train. The greater barons possessed property on both sides of the Channel. They therefore now owed feudal allegiance to two sovereign lords, and not unnaturally they sought to play one against the other. Both Duke Robert and William II were dissatisfied with the division, and their brotherly ties did not mitigate their covetous desires. During the thirteen years of the reign of William the Anglo-Norman realms were vexed by fratricidal strife and successive baronial revolts. The Saxon inhabitants of England, fearful of a relapse into the chaos of pre-Conquest days, stood by the King against all rebels. The "fyrd" obeyed every summons, and supported him in the field as it had his father in 1075. Thus he was able finally to bring Cumberland and Westmorland into the kingdom. The feckless Robert, who had plagued the Conqueror so long, eventually departed in a fit of gallantry on the First Crusade, leaving Normandy pawned to Rufus for the loan of 10,000 marks.

* * *

The Crusading spirit had for some time stirred the minds of men all over western Europe. The Christian kingdoms of Spain had led the way with their holy wars against the Arabs. Now, towards the end of the eleventh century, a new enemy of Christendom appeared fifteen hundred miles to the east. The Seljuk Turks were pressing hard upon the Byzantine Empire in Asia Minor, and harassing devout pilgrims from Europe through Syria to the Holy Land. The Byzantine Emperor appealed to the West for help, and in 1095 Pope Urban II, who had long dreamt of recovering Jerusalem for Christendom, called on the chivalry of Europe to take the Cross. The response was immediate, overwhelming, and at first disastrous. An itinerant monk named Peter the Hermit took up the cry to arms. So powerful was his preaching that in 1096 an enthusiastic but undisciplined train of twenty thousand men, most of them peasants unskilled in war, set off from Cologne for the East under his leadership. Few of them ever reached the Holy Land. After marching through Hungary and the Balkans, the majority perished by Turkish arrows amid the mountains of Asia Minor.

The so-called "People's Crusade" thus collapsed. But by now the magnates of Europe had rallied to the Cause. Four armies, each numbering perhaps ten thousand men, and led by some of the greatest nobles of the age, among them Godfrey de Bouillon, converged on Constantinople from France, Germany, Italy and the Low Countries. The Byzantine Emperor was embarrassed. He had hoped for manageable mercenaries as reinforcements from the West. Instead, he found camped around his capital four powerful and ambitious hosts.

The march of the Crusaders through his dominions into the Turkish-held lands was marred by intrigue and by grievous disputes. But there was hard fighting too. A way was hacked through Asia Minor; and Antioch, once a great bastion of the Christian faith, which the Turks had taken, was besieged and captured in 1098. The Crusaders were cheered and succoured by the arrival off the Syrian coast of a fleet manned by Englishmen and commanded by an English prince, Edgar the Atheling, great-nephew of Edward the Confessor. Thus by a strange turn of fortune the displaced heir of the Saxon royal line joined hands with Robert of Normandy, the displaced heir of William the Conqueror.

Aided by divisions among the Turkish princes and by jealousy between the Turks and the Sultans of Egypt the Crusaders pressed forward. On June 7, 1099, they reached their long-sought goal and encamped about Jerusalem, then in Egyptian hands. On July 14 the City fell to their assault. Godfrey de Bouillon, refusing to wear a crown in Christ's Holy City, was acclaimed ruler, with the title "Defender of the Holy Sepulchre." Victory was made secure by the defeat at the Battle of Ascalon of a relieving army from Egypt. Many of the principal Crusaders thereupon went home, but for nearly a century a mixed international body of knights, all commonly called Franks, ruled over a string of Christian principalities in Palestine and along the coast of Syria. Western Christendom, so long the victim of invaders, had at last struck back and won its first great footing in the Eastern world.

* * *

At home Rufus's extortions and violent methods had provoked the baronage throughout his reign. In August 1100 he was mysteriously shot through the head by an arrow while hunting in the New Forest, leaving a memory of shameless exactions and infamous morals, but also a submissive realm to his successor. The main progress in his reign was financial; but the new feudal monarchy was also more firmly established, and in territory its sway was wider than at Rufus's accession. The Norman lords whom the Conqueror had settled upon the Welsh Marches had fastened a lasting grip upon Southern Wales. The Northern counties had been finally brought under Norman control, and a military frontier drawn against the Scots. While the rough hands of Rufus chafed and bruised the feudal relationship, they had also enforced the rights of a feudal king.

Prince Henry, the youngest of the royal brothers, had been a member of the fatal hunting party in the New Forest. There is no proof that he was implicated in the death of his brother, but he certainly wasted no time in mourning. He made straight for the royal treasury at Winchester, and gained possession of it after sharp argument with its custodians. Evidently he represented a strong movement of opinion among the leading classes, and he had a policy of his own. For a layman his scholarship deserved the title of Beauclerc which the custom of his day accorded him. He set the precedent, which his successor followed, of proclaiming a charter upon his accession. By this he sought to conciliate those powerful forces in Church and State which had been alienated by the rapacity and tactlessness of his predecessor. He guaranteed that the rights of the baronage and the Church should be respected. At the same time, having seen the value of Saxon loyalty in the reigns of his father and his brother, he promised the conquered race good justice and the laws of Edward the Confessor. He knew that the friction caused by the separation of Normandy from England was by no means soothed. Duke Robert was already on his way back from his Crusade with his mortgage to redeem. The barons on both sides of the Channel would profit from fraternal strife to drive hard bargains in their own interests. Henry's desire to base himself in part at least upon the Saxon population of England led him, much to the suspicion of the Norman barons, to make a marriage with Matilda, niece of the last surviving Saxon claimant to the English throne and descendant of the old English line of Kings. The barons, mollified by the charter, accepted this decisive step. The ceaseless gigantic process of intermarriage received the highest sanction.

Henry was now ready to face Robert whenever he should return. In September 1100 this event occurred. Immediately the familiar incidents of feudal rebellion were renewed in England, and for the next six years the King had to fight to make good his title under his father's will. The great house of Montgomery formed the head of the opposition in England. By a series of persevering sieges the family's strongholds fell one by one, and Henry at length destroyed their power and annexed their estates to the Crown. But the root evil lay in Normandy, and in 1105, having consolidated his position in England, Henry crossed the Channel. In September 1106 the most important battle since Hastings was fought at Tenchebrai. King Henry's victory was complete. Duke Robert was carried to his perpetual prison in England. Normandy acknowledged Henry's authority, and the control of Anglo-Norman policy passed from Rouen to London. The Saxons, who had fought heartily for Henry, regarded this battle as their military revenge for Hastings. By this new comradeship with the Crown, as well as by the royal marriage with Matilda, they felt themselves relieved from some at least of the pangs of being conquered. The shame was gone; the penalties could be endured. Through these two far-reaching factors a certain broad measure of unity was re-established in the Island.

* * *

There was now no challenged succession. The King of England's authority was established on both sides of the Channel. The Saxon people had proved their loyalty and the more powerful barons had been cowed. Foreign dangers having also been repelled, Henry was free for the time being to devote himself to internal government and to strengthening the power of the Crown throughout the land. He sought to invest the Anglo-Norman kingship with new and powerful attributes. There survived in medieval Europe a tradition of kingship more exalted than that of feudal overlord. The king was not merely the apex of the feudal pyramid, but the anointed Vicegerent of God upon earth. The collapse of the Roman Empire had not entirely destroyed this Roman conception of sovereignty, and Henry now set himself to inject this idea of kingship into the Anglo-Norman State; and in so doing he could not help reviving, whether consciously or not, the English conception of the King as the keeper of the peace and guardian of the people.

The centre of government, the Curia Regis, was an ill-defined body consisting of those tenants-in-chief whose feudal duty it was to attend when summoned, and those personal servants of the monarch who could be used for Government service as well as for their household duties. Henry realised that royal servants who were members of the minor baronage, if formed into a permanent nucleus, would act as a brake upon the turbulence of the greater feudatories. Here were the first beginnings, tentative, modest, but insinuating, of a civil administrative machinery, which within its limits was more efficient and persistent than anything yet known. These officials soon developed a vested interest of their own. Families like the Clintons and the Bassetts, whom the King, as the chronicler put it, had "raised from the dust to do him service," entrenched themselves in the household offices, and created what was in fact an official class.

The power of any Government depends ultimately upon its finances. It was therefore in the business of gathering and administering the revenue that this novel feature first became apparent. There was no distinction in feudal society between the private and public resources of the Crown. The King in feudal theory was only the greatest of the landowners in the State. The sheriffs of counties collected not only the taxes and fines accruing to the Crown, but also the income from the royal estates, and they were responsible, when they appeared yearly at the royal treasury, for the exact payment of what was due from each of their counties. Henry's officials created a special organ to deal with the sheriffs and the business the sheriffs transacted. This was the Exchequer, still regarded simply as the Curia meeting for financial purposes, but gradually acquiring a life of its own. It took its name from the chequered boards used for greater ease of calculation in Roman numerals, and its methods included the keeping of written records, among them the important documents called the Pipe Rolls because they were kept rolled up in the shape of a pipe. Thus the King gained a surer grip over the finances of the realm, and the earliest specialised department of royal administration was born. Its offspring still survives.

Henry took care that the sheriffs of the counties were brought under an increasingly strict control, and several commissions were appointed during the reign to revise their personnel. In troublous times the office of sheriff tended to fall into the hands of powerful barons and to become hereditary. The King saw to it that whenever possible his own men held these key positions. One of the most fertile sources of revenue arose from the fines imposed by the courts upon delinquents. The barons realised this as soon as the King, and their manorial courts provided them with important incomes, which could at once be turned into armed retainers. Within their domains they enjoyed a jurisdiction over nearly all laymen. But in the county courts and in the courts of the hundreds the Crown had at its disposal the old Saxon system of justice. These time-honoured institutions could well be used to rival the feudal courts of the baronage. Henry therefore revised and regularised the holding of the county courts, and made all men see that throughout the land there was a system of royal justice. King's officers—judges, as they became—in their occasional circuits administered this justice, and the very nature of their function brought them often into clash not only with humble suitors and malefactors, but with proud military magnates.

The King entered into a nation-wide competition with the baronage upon who could best deserve the rich spoils of the law. Through his control of the sheriffs he bound together the monarchy and the old Saxon system of local justice. The Conqueror had set the example when in the Domesday survey he combined the Continental system of getting information by means of bodies of men sworn to tell the truth with the English organisation by shire and hundred. His son for other purposes continued and intensified the process, sending officials constantly from his household through the kingdom, and convening the county courts to inquire into the claims of the royal revenue and to hear cases in which the Crown was interested. From these local inquiries by royal officials there were to spring far-reaching consequences in the reign of Henry II. The chroniclers spoke well of Henry I. "Good man he was," they declared, "and there was great awe of him.-In his days no man dared to harm another." They bestowed upon him the title "Lion of Justice," and none has sought to rob him of it.

We must regard his reign as a period when the central Government, by adroit and sharp accountancy and clerking, established in a more precise form the structure and resources of the State. In the process the feudatory chiefs upon whom the local government of the land depended were angered. Thus, as the years wore on the stresses grew between the royal authority and the feudal leaders. The King's hand, though it lay heavy upon all, became increasingly a protection of the people against the injustice and caprice of the local rulers. Examples there were of admirable baronial administration, for there was a light in Norman eyes which shone above the squalid pillage and appetites of earlier ages. A country held down and exploited by feudal nobles was none the less the constant victim of local oppression. We see therefore the beginning of an attachment to the King or central Government on the part of the people, which invested the Crown with a new source of strength, sometimes forthcoming and sometimes estranged, but always to be gathered, especially after periods of weakness and disorder, by a strong and righteous ruler.

* * *

The Anglo-Norman State was now powerful. Henry was lord of England, Normandy, and Maine. In 1109 his only legitimate daughter, Maud, was betrothed to Henry V, Holy Roman Emperor and King of Germany. On the other hand, the reunion of England and Normandy after Tenchebrai had stirred the hostility of France. The early twelfth century saw the revival of a capital authority at Paris. With the accession of Louis VI the real strength of the French monarchy begins. It was essential for the safety of France that the unity of the Anglo-Norman State should be finally ruptured. The Duke of Normandy was technically the feudal subject of the King of France, and the existence of the son of captive Duke Robert provided the French King with innumerable pretexts for interference and offered to discontented Norman barons perennial opportunity. These Norman commitments forced Henry in the later years of his reign to intervene in the politics of Northern France. His position in Normandy was continually threatened by the claims of Robert's son, William Clito, who until his death in 1128 was backed by Louis, and also by the neighbouring state of Anjou, which disputed King Henry's rights in Maine. A wearing warfare darkened the later years of the reign. From the military point of view Henry was easily able to hold his own against any army the French could put into the field.

What may be judged malignant fortune now intervened. The King had a son, his heir apparent, successor indisputable. On this young man of seventeen many hopes and assurances were founded. In the winter of 1120 he was coming back from a visit to France in the royal yacht called the *White Ship*. Off the coast of Normandy the vessel struck a rock and all but one were drowned. The prince had indeed been embarked in a boat. He returned to rescue his sister. In this crisis the principle of equality asserted itself with such violence that at the ship's side so many leaped into the boat that it sank. Two men remained afloat, the ship's butcher and a knight. "Where is the Prince?" asked the knight above the waves. "All are drowned," replied the butcher. "Then," said the knight, "all is lost for England," and threw up his hands. The butcher came safe to

shore with the tale. None dared tell it to the King. When at last
he heard the tidings "he never smiled again." This was more
than the agony of parental grief for an only son. It portended
the breakdown of a system and prospect upon the consolida-
tion of which the whole life's work of Henry stood. The spectre
of a disputed succession glared again upon England. The forces
of anarchy grew, and every noble in his castle balanced his
chances upon who would succeed to the Crown.

There were two claimants, each of whom had a fair share of
right. The King had a daughter, Matilda, or Maud as the English called her, but although there was no Salic Law in the
Norman code this clanking, jangling aristocracy, mailed and
spurred, did not take kindly to the idea of a woman's rule.
Against her stood the claim of Stephen, son of the Conqueror's
daughter Adela. Stephen of Blois, no inconsiderable figure on
the Continent, with great estates in England added, was, after
his elder brother had waived his claim, the rightful male heir.
The feudal system lived entirely through the spirit of sworn
allegiance. Throughout Christendom the accusation of violating
an oath was almost mortal. Only great victories could atone
and absolve. But here was a dilemma which every man could
settle for himself according to his interests and ambitions.
Split—utter, honest, total!

King Henry in the grey close of his life set himself to fill the
void with his daughter Maud as female king. He spent his remaining years in trying to establish a kind of "pragmatic sanction" for a family succession which would spare his widespread
domains from civil war. At the age of eight Maud had been
betrothed to the Holy Roman Emperor. In 1125, five years
after the *White Ship* sank, he died, and at twenty-two she was a
widow and an Empress. We have many records of this remarkable princess, of whom it was said "she had the nature of
a man in the frame of a woman." Fierce, proud, hard, cynical,
living for politics above all other passions, however turbulent,
she was fitted to bear her part in any war and be the mother of
one of the greatest English kings.

Upon this daughter, after mature consideration, Henry
founded all his hopes. On two separate occasions he called his
murmuring barons together and solemnly swore them to stand
by Maud. Subsequently, in order to enhance her unifying authority, and to protect Normandy from the claims of Anjou
after his death, he married her to the Count of Anjou, thus
linking the interests of the most powerful state in Northern
France with the family and natural succession in England. The

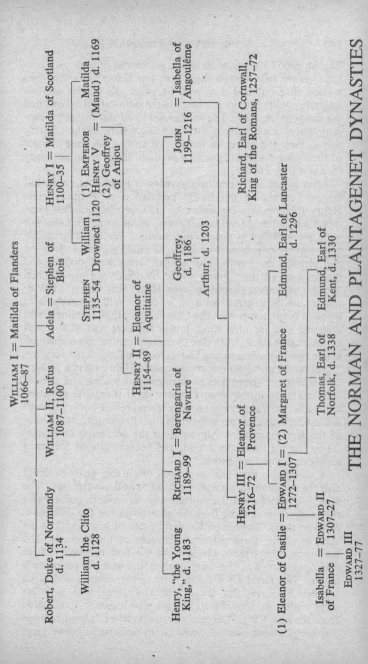

THE NORMAN AND PLANTAGENET DYNASTIES

English mood has never in later ages barred queens, and perhaps queens have served them best. But here at this time was a deep division, and a quarrel in which all parties and all interests could take sides. The gathered political arrays awaited the death of the King. The whole interest of the baronage, supported at this juncture by the balancing weight of the Church, was to limit the power of the Crown and regain their control of their own districts. Now in a division of the royal authority they saw their chance.

After giving the Island thirty years of peace and order and largely reconciling the Saxon population to Norman rule, Henry I expired on December 1, 1135, in the confident hope that his daughter Maud would carry on his work. But she was with her husband in Anjou and Stephen was the first on the spot. Swiftly returning from Blois, he made his way to London and claimed the crown. The secular forces were divided and the decision of the Church would be decisive. Here Stephen had the advantage that his brother Henry was Bishop of Winchester, with a great voice in council. With Henry's help Stephen made terms with the Church, and, thus sustained, was crowned and anointed King. It was however part of the tacit compact that he should relax the severe central control which in the two preceding reigns had so much offended the nobility.

There was an additional complication. Henry I had a bastard son, Robert of Gloucester, a distinguished soldier and a powerful magnate in the West Country, who is usually regarded as one of the rare examples of a disinterested baron. Robert did not rate his chances sufficiently high to compete with either of the legitimate heirs. Almost from the beginning he loyally supported his half-sister Maud, and became one of Stephen's most determined opponents.

A succession established on such disputable grounds could only be maintained unchallenged by skilful sovereignty. The more we reflect upon the shortcomings of modern government the readier we shall be to make allowances for the difficulties of these times. Stephen in the early years of his reign lost the support of the three essential elements of his strength. The baronage, except those favoured by the new monarchy, were sure that this was the long-awaited moment to press their claims. The novel Civil Service, the great officials all linked together by family ties, armed with knowledge, with penmanship, trained to administration, now also began to stand aside from the new King. And many prelates were offended because Stephen violated clerical privilege by imprisoning the great administrative family of Roger, Bishop of Salisbury, whom he suspected of being about to change sides. Thus he had much of the Church against him too. There were grievous discontents among the high, the middle, and the low.

"When the traitors perceived," in the words of the *Anglo-Saxon Chronicle*, that King Stephen was "a mild man and soft and good and *did no justice*, then did they all manner of horrors. They had done homage to him and sworn oaths, but they held no faith." [1]

King David of Scotland, persuaded of the English decay, crossed the Border and laid claim to Northumbria. The Archbishop of York advanced against him, with the support of the mass of the Northern counties. He displayed the standards of St Peter of York, St John of Beverley, and St Wilfred of Ripon, and in a murderous battle at Northallerton, henceforward known as the Battle of the Standard, repulsed and slaughtered the invaders. This reverse, far from discouraging the malcontents, was the prelude to civil war. In 1139 Maud, freed from entanglements that had kept her in France, entered the kingdom to claim her rights. As Stephen had done, she found her chief support in the Church. The men who had governed England under Henry I, antagonised by Stephen's weakness towards the barons, joined his enemies. In 1141 a more or less general rebellion broke out against his rule, and he himself was taken prisoner at the Battle of Lincoln. The Bishop of Winchester, Stephen's own brother and hitherto his main supporter, now went over to Maud's side. For nearly a year Maud, uncrowned, was in control of England. The Londoners after some trial liked her even less than Stephen. Rising in fury, they drove her out of the capital. She fought on indomitably. But the strain upon the system had been too great. The Island dissolved into confused civil war. During the six years that followed there was neither law nor peace in large parts of the country.

* * *

The civil war developed into the first successful baronial reaction against the centralising policy of the kings. Stephen, faced with powerful rivals, had failed to preserve the rights of the Crown. The royal revenues decreased, royal control of administration lapsed; much of the machinery itself passed for a time out of use. Baronial jurisdiction reasserted its control; baronial castles overawed the people. It seemed that a divided succession had wrecked the work of the Norman kings.

[1] Douglas, *Age of the Normans*, p. 161.

The sufferings of the Fen Country, where there was a particularly ferocious orgy of destruction during the anarchy, are grimly described in the *Anglo-Saxon Chronicle* by a monk of Peterborough.

"Every powerful man made his castles and held them against the King, . . . and when the castles were made they filled them with devils and evil men. Then they seized those men who they supposed had any possessions, both by night and day, men and women, and put them to prison for their gold and silver, and tortured them with unspeakable tortures. . . . Many thousands they killed with hunger. I neither can nor may tell all the horrors and all the tortures that they did to the wretched men of this land. And it lasted the nineteen winters while Stephen was King; and ever it was worse. They laid gelds [taxes] on the villages from time to time and called it 'Tenserie'; when the wretched men had no more to give they robbed and burnt all the villages, so that you might go a whole day's journey and you would never find a man in a village or land being tilled. Then was corn dear, and meat and cheese and butter, because there was none in the land. Wretched men starved of hunger; some went seeking alms who at one time were rich men; others fled out of the land. . . . Wheresoever men tilled the earth bare no corn, for the land was all ruined by such deeds; and they said that Christ and his saints were asleep."

Another writer, a monk of Winchester, writes in very similar terms of the disasters that came upon his part of England: "With some men the love of country was turned to loathing and bitterness, and they preferred to migrate to distant regions. Others, in the hope of protection, built lowly huts of wattle-work round about the churches, and so passed their lives in fear and anguish. Some for want of food fed upon strange and forbidden meats—the flesh of dogs and horses; others relieved their hunger by devouring unwashed and uncooked herbs and roots. In all the shires a part of the inhabitants wasted away and died in herds from the stress of famine, while others with their wives and children went dismally into a self-inflicted exile. You might behold villages of famous names standing empty, because the country people, male and female, young and old, had left them; fields whitened with the harvest as the year [1143] verged upon autumn, but the cultivators had perished by famine and the ensuing pestilence." [1]

These horrors may not have been typical of the country as a whole. Over large parts of England fighting was sporadic and

[1] Translated from *Gesta Stephani*, ed. Howlett, p. 99.

local in character. It was the central southern counties that bore the brunt of civil war. But these commotions bit deep into the consciousness of the people. It was realised how vital an institution a strong monarchy was for the security of life and property. No better reasons for monarchy could have been found than were forced upon all minds by the events of Stephen's reign. Men looked back with yearning to the efficient government of Henry I. But a greater than he was at hand.

* * *

In 1147 Robert of Gloucester died and the leadership of Maud's party devolved upon her son. Henry Plantagenet was born to empire. His grandfather Fulk had made of the Angevin lands, Anjou, Touraine, and Maine, a principality unsurpassed in France and in resources more than the equal of Normandy. Fulk died in 1143, King of Jerusalem, leaving two sons to succeed him on that precarious throne, and a third, Geoffrey, as heir to his French dominions. Geoffrey's marriage with Maud had united the Norman and Angévin lands, and the child of this marriage was from his birth in 1133 recognised as the "master of many peoples." To contemporaries he was best known as Henry Fitz-Empress; but he carried into English history the emblem of his house, the broom, the *Planta Genesta*, which later generations were to make the name of this great dynasty, the Plantagenets. He embodied all their ability, all their energy, and not a little of that passionate, ruthless ferocity which, it was whispered, came to the house of Anjou from no mortal source, but from a union with Satan himself.

When scarcely fifteen, in 1147, Henry had actively championed his claim to the English throne on English soil. His small band of followers was then defeated by Stephen's forces, and he took refuge in Normandy. The Empress Maud gave up her slender hopes of success in the following year and joined her son in the duchy. Nineteen years of life remained before her, but she never set foot in England again. Works of piety, natural to the times, filled many of her days. But during the years that followed Henry's triumph she played an important political part as regent in Normandy and in his hereditary Angevin dominions. During her interventions in England in quest of the crown the charge of arrogance was often levelled against her; but in her older age she proved a sagacious counsellor to her son.

Henry was involved in a further attempt against England in 1149, but the campaign projected on his behalf by the King of Scots and the Earl of Chester came to nothing. For a few years of comparative peace King Stephen was left in uneasy possession. In the meantime Henry was invested by his parents in 1150 as Duke of Normandy. The next year his father's death made him also Count of Anjou, Touraine, and Maine. In his high feudal capacity Henry repaired to Paris to render homage to his lord the King of France, of which country he already possessed, by the accepted law of the age, a large part.

Louis VII was a French Edward the Confessor; he practised with faithful simplicity the law of Christ. All his days were spent in devotion, and his nights in vigil or penance. When he left his own chapel he would delay the whole Court by waiting till the humblest person present had preceded him. These pious and exemplary habits did not endear him to his queen. Eleanor of Aquitaine was in her own right a reigning princess, with the warmth of the South in her veins. She had already complained that she had "married a monk and not a king" when this square-shouldered, ruddy youth, with his "countenance of fire," sprightly talk, and overflowing energy, suddenly presented himself before her husband as his most splendid vassal. Eleanor did not waste words in coming to à decision. The Papacy bowed to strong will in the high feudal chiefs, and Eleanor obtained a divorce from Louis VII in 1152 on the nominal grounds of consanguinity. But what staggered the French Court and opened the eyes of its prayerful King was the sudden marriage of Eleanor to Henry two months later. Thus half of France passed out of royal control into the hands of Henry. Rarely have passion and policy flowed so buoyantly together. The marriage was one of the most brilliant political strokes of the age. Henry afterwards admitted his designs, and accepted the admiration of Europe for their audacity. He was nineteen and she was probably thirty; and, uniting their immense domains, they made common cause against all comers. To Louis VII were vouchsafed the consolations of the spirit; but even these were jarred upon by the problems of government.

War in all quarters lay before the royal pair. The joining to Normandy and Anjou of Poitou, Saintonge, Périgord, the Limousin, the Angoumois, and Gascony, with claims of suzerainty over Auvergne and Toulouse, fascinated and convulsed the feudal Christian world. Everywhere men shook their heads over this concentration of power, this spectacle of so many races and states, sundered from each other by long feuds or divergent interests, now suddenly flung together by the hot blood of a love intrigue. From all sides the potentates confronted the upstart. The King of France, who certainly had every conceivable cause of complaint; King Stephen of England, who disputed Henry's title to the Norman duchy, though without force to intervene across the Channel; the Count of Champagne; the Count of Perche; and Henry's own brother, Geoffrey—all spontaneously, and with good reason, fell upon him.

A month after the marriage these foes converged upon Normandy. But the youthful Duke Henry beat them back, ruptured and broken. The Norman army proved once again its fighting quality. Before he was twenty Henry had cleared Normandy of rebels and pacified Anjou. He turned forthwith to England. It was a valiant figure that landed in January 1153, and from all over England, distracted by civil wars, hearts and eyes turned towards him. Merlin had prophesied a deliverer; had he not in his veins blood that ran back to William the Conqueror, and beyond him, through his grandmother Matilda, wife of Henry I, to Cedric and the long-vanished Anglo-Saxon line? A wild surge of hope greeted him from the tormented Islanders, and when he knelt after his landing in the first church he found "to pray for a space, in the manner of soldiers," the priest pronounced the wish of the nation in the words, "Behold there cometh the Lord, the Ruler, and the kingdom is in his hand."

There followed battles: Malmesbury, where the sleet, especially directed by Almighty God, beat upon the faces of his foes; Wallingford, where King Stephen by divine interposition fell three times from his horse before going into action. Glamour, terror, success, attended this youthful, puissant warrior, who had not only his sword, but his title-deeds. The baronage saw their interest favoured by a stalemate; they wanted neither a victorious Stephen nor a triumphant Henry. The weaker the King the stronger the nobles A treaty was concluded at Winchester in 1153 whereby Stephen made Henry his adopted son and his appointed heir. "In the business of the kingdom," promised Stephen, "I will work by the counsel of the Duke; but in the whole realm of England, as well in the Duke's part as my own, I will exercise royal justice." On this Henry did homage and made all the formal submissions, and when a year later Stephen died he was acclaimed and crowned King of England with more general hope and rejoicing than had ever uplifted any monarch in England since the days of Alfred the Great.

Henry Plantagenet

THE accession of Henry II began one of the most pregnant and decisive reigns in English history. The new sovereign ruled an empire, and, as his subjects boasted, his warrant ran "from the Arctic Ocean to the Pyrenees." England to him was but one—the most solid though perhaps the least attractive—of his provinces. But he gave to England that effectual element of external control which, as in the days of William of Orange, was indispensable to the growth of national unity. He was accepted by English and Norman as the ruler of both races and the whole country. The memories of Hastings were confounded in his person, and after the hideous anarchy of civil war and robber barons all due attention was paid to his commands. Thus, though a Frenchman, with foreign speech and foreign modes, he shaped our country in a fashion of which the outline remains to the present day.

After a hundred years of being the encampment of an invading army and the battleground of its quarrelsome officers and their descendants England became finally and for all time a coherent kingdom, based upon Christianity and upon that Latin civilisation which recalled the message of ancient Rome. Henry Plantagenet first brought England, Scotland, and Ireland into a certain common relationship; he re-established the system of royal government which his grandfather, Henry I, had prematurely erected. He relaid the foundations of a central power, based upon the exchequer and the judiciary, which was ultimately to supersede the feudal system of William the Conqueror. The King gathered up and cherished the Anglo-Saxon tradition of self-government under royal command in shire and borough; he developed and made permanent "assizes" as they survive to-day. It is to him we owe the enduring fact that the English-speaking race all over the world is governed by the English Common Law rather than by the Roman. By his Constitutions of Clarendon he sought to fix the relationship of Church and State and to force the Church in its temporal character to submit itself to the life and law of the nation. In this endeavour he had, after a deadly struggle, to retreat, and it was left to Henry VIII, though centuries later, to avenge his predecessor by destroying the shrine of St Thomas at Canterbury.

THE
POSSESSIONS
OF HENRY II

SCOTLAND

ULSTER
LEITRIM
MEATH
MUNSTER
Dublin
LEINSTER
PRINCIPALITY
OF WALES
THE LORDS
MARCHER

ENGLAND

NORTH
SEA

THE HOLY
ROMAN EMPIRE

London

ENGLISH CHANNEL

NORMANDY

Paris

BRITTANY

MAINE
Le Mans

FRANCE

ANJOU
TOURAINE

POITOU

AQUITAINE

Boundary of lands under
direct rule of Henry II
Lands owing him Suzerainty
Boundary of lands inherited
from his father

MILES
0   50   100   150   200

Bordeaux

FRANCE

GASCONY
Toulouse

CASTILE
NAVARRE

A vivid picture is painted of this gifted and, for a while, enviable man: square, thick-set, bull-necked, with powerful arms and coarse, rough hands; his legs bandy from endless riding; a large, round head and closely cropped red hair; a freckled face; a voice harsh and cracked. Intense love of the chase; other loves, which the Church deplored and Queen Eleanor resented; frugality in food and dress; days entirely concerned with public business; travel unceasing; moods various. It was said that he was always gentle and calm in times of urgent peril, but became bad-tempered and capricious when the pressure relaxed. "He was more tender to dead soldiers than to the living, and found far more sorrow in the loss of those who were slain than comfort in the love of those who remained." He journeyed hotfoot around his many dominions, arriving unexpectedly in England when he was thought to be in the South of France. He carried with him in his tours of each province wains loaded with ponderous rolls which represented the office files of to-day. His Court and train gasped and panted behind him. Sometimes, when he had appointed an early start, he was sleeping till noon, with all the wagons and pack-horses awaiting him fully laden. Sometimes he would be off hours before the time he had fixed, leaving everyone to catch up as best they could. Everything was stirred and moulded by him in England, as also in his other much greater estates, which he patrolled with tireless attention.

But this twelfth-century monarch, with his lusts and sports, his hates and his schemes, was no materialist; he was the Lord's Anointed, he commanded, with the Archbishop of Canterbury —"those two strong steers that drew the plough of England" —the whole allegiance of his subjects. The offices of religion, the fear of eternal damnation, the hope of even greater realms beyond the grave, accompanied him from hour to hour. At times he was smitten with remorse and engulfed in repentance. He drew all possible delights and satisfactions from this world and the next. He is portrayed to us in convulsions both of spiritual exaltation and abasement. This was no secluded monarch: the kings of those days were as accessible to all classes as a modern President of the United States. People broke in upon him at all hours with business, with tidings, with gossip, with visions, with complaints. Talk rang high in the King's presence and to His Majesty's face among the nobles and courtiers, and the jester, invaluable monitor, castigated all impartially with unstinted licence.

Few mortals have led so full a life as Henry II or have drunk so deeply of the cups of triumph and sorrow. In later life he fell out with Eleanor. When she was over fifty and he but forty-two he is said to have fallen in love with "Fair Rosamond," a damosel of high degree and transcendent beauty, and generations have enjoyed the romantic tragedy of Queen Eleanor penetrating the protecting maze at Woodstock by the clue of a silken thread and offering her hapless supplanter the hard choice between the dagger and the poisoned cup. Tiresome investigators have undermined this excellent tale, but it certainly should find its place in any history worthy of the name.

Such was the man who succeeded to the troubled and divided inheritance of Stephen. Already before his accession to the English throne Henry had fought the first of his many wars to defend his Continental inheritance. Ever since the emergence of the strong Norman power in North-West France, a hundred years before, the French monarchy had struggled ceaselessly against the encroachments of great dukedoms and countships upon the central Government. The Dukes of Normandy, of Aquitaine, and of Brittany, the Counts of Anjou, Toulouse, Flanders, and Boulogne, although in form and law vassals of the French Crown, together with a host of other feudal tenants-in-chief, aspired to independent sovereignty, and in the eclipse of the monarchy seemed at times near to achieving their ambition. The Battle of Hastings had made the greatest French subject, the Duke of Normandy, also King of England; but Henry II's accession to the Island throne in 1154 threatened France with far graver dangers. Hitherto there had always been political relief in playing off over-mighty subjects one against another. The struggle between Anjou and Normandy in the eleventh century had rejoiced the French king, who saw two of his chief enemies at grips. But when in one hour Henry II was King of England, Duke of Normandy, Lord of Aquitaine, Brittany, Poitou, Anjou, Maine and Guienne, ruler from the Somme to the Pyrenees of more than half France, all balance of power among the feudal lords was destroyed.

Louis VII found instead of a dozen principalities, divided and jealous, one single imperial Power, whose resources far surpassed his own. He was scarcely the man to face such a combination. He had already suffered the irreparable misfortune of Eleanor's divorce, and of her joining forces and blood with his rival. By him she bore sons; by Louis only daughters. Still, some advantages remained to the French king. He managed to hold out for his lifetime against the Plantagenets; and after nearly four centuries of struggle and devastation the final victory in Europe rested with France. The Angevin Empire was indeed more impressive on the map than in reality. It was a motley, ill-knit collection of states, flung together by the chance of a single marriage, and lacked unity both of purpose and strength. The only tie between England and her Continental empire was the fact that Henry himself and some of his magnates held lands on either side of the Channel. There was no pretence of a single, central Government; no uniformity of administration or custom; no common interests or feelings of loyalty. Weak as Louis VII appeared in his struggle with the enterprising and active Henry, the tide of events flowed with the compact French monarchy, and even Louis left it more firmly established than he found it.

The main method of the French was simple. Henry had inherited vast estates; but with them also all their local and feudal discontents. Louis could no longer set the Count of Anjou against the Duke of Normandy, but he could still encourage both in Anjou and in Normandy those local feuds and petty wars which sapped the strength of the feudal potentates, in principle his vassals. Nor was the exploiting of family quarrels an unfruitful device. In the later years of his reign, the sons of Henry II, eager, turbulent, and proud, allowed themselves to be used by Louis VII and by his successor, the wily and gifted Philip Augustus, against their father.

* * *

How, we may ask, did all this affect the daily life of England and her history? A series of personal feudal struggles fought in distant lands, the quarrels of an alien ruling class, were little understood and less liked by the common folk. Yet these things long burdened their pilgrimage. For many generations their bravest and best were to fight and die by the marshes of the Loire or under the sun-baked hills of Southern France in pursuit of the dream of English dominion over French soil. For this two centuries later Englishmen triumphed at Crécy, Poitiers, and Agincourt, or starved in the terrible Limoges march of the Black Prince. For this they turned fertile France into a desert where even the most needed beasts died of thirst and hunger. Throughout the medieval history of England war with France is the interminable and often the dominant theme. It groped and scraped into every reach of English life, moulding and fretting the shape of English society and institutions.

No episode opens to us a wider window upon the politics

of the twelfth century in England than the quarrel of Henry II
with his great subject and former friend, Thomas Becket,
Archbishop of Canterbury. We have to realise the gravity of
this conflict. The military State in feudal Christendom bowed
to the Church in things spiritual; it never accepted the idea of
the transference of secular power to priestly authority. But the
Church, enriched continually by the bequests of hardy barons,
anxious in the death agony about their life beyond the grave,
became the greatest landlord and capitalist in the community.
Rome used its ghostly arts upon the superstitions of almost
all the actors in the drama. The power of the State was held
in constant challenge by this potent interest. Questions of
doctrine might well have been resolved, but how was the government of the country to be carried on under two conflicting
powers, each possessed of immense claims upon limited national resources? This conflict was not confined to England. It
was the root question of the European world, as it then existed.

Under William the Conqueror schism had been avoided in
England by tact and compromise. Under Lanfranc the Church
worked with the Crown, and each power reinforced the other
against the turbulent barons or the oppressed commonalty.
But now a great personality stood at the summit of the religious
hierarchy, Thomas Becket, who had been the King's friend.
He had been his Chancellor, or, as Ranke first remarked, "to
use a somewhat equivalent expression, his most trusted Cabinet
Minister." He had in both home and foreign affairs loyally
served his master. He had re-organised the imposition of
scutage, a tax that allowed money to commute personal service in arms and thus eventually pierced the feudal system to its
core. He had played his part in the acquisition of Brittany. The
King felt sure that in Becket he had his own man—no mere
servant, but a faithful comrade and colleague in the common
endeavour. It was by the King's direct influence and personal
effort that Becket was elected Archbishop.

From that moment all his gifts and impulses ran in another
channel. Something like the transformation which carried
Henry V from a rollicking prince to the august hero-King overnight was now witnessed in Becket. His private life had always
been both pious and correct. He had of course been immersed
in political affairs; nor was it as a sombre figure behind the
throne. But whereas hitherto as a courtier and a prince he had
rivalled all in magnificence and pomp, taking his part in the
vivid pageant of the times, he now sought by extreme austeri-
ties to gather around himself the fame and honour of a saint.

Becket pursued the same methods and ambitions in the ecclesiastical as previously he had done in the political sphere; and in both he excelled. He now championed the Church against the Crown in every aspect of their innumerable interleaving functions. He clothed this aggressive process with those universal ideas of the Catholic Church and the Papal authority which far transcended the bounds of our Island, covering Europe and reaching out into the mysterious and the sublime. After a tour upon the Continent and a conclave with the religious dignitaries of France and Italy he returned to England imbued with the resolve to establish the independence of the Church hierarchy on the State as represented by the King. Thus he opened the conflict which the wise Lanfranc had throughout his life striven to avoid. At this time the mood in England was ripe for strife upon this issue.

In a loose and undefined way Saxon England had foreshadowed the theory to which the Elizabethan reformers long afterwards returned. Both thought of the monarch as appointed by God, not only to rule the State, but to protect and guide the Church. In the eleventh century however the Papacy had been reinvigorated under Hildebrand, who became Pope Gregory VII in 1073, and his successors. Rome now began to make claims which were hardly compatible with the traditional notions of the mixed sovereignty of the King in all matters temporal and spiritual. The Gregorian movement held that the government of the Church ought to be in the hands of the clergy, under the supervision of the Pope. According to this view, the King was a mere layman whose one religious function was obedience to the hierarchy. The Church was a body apart, with its own allegiance and its own laws. By the reign of Henry II the bishop was not only a spiritual officer; he was a great landowner, the secular equal of earls; he could put forces in the field; he could excommunicate his enemies, who might be the King's friends. Who, then, was to appoint the bishop? And, when once appointed, to whom, if the Pope commanded one thing and the King another, did he owe his duty? If the King and his counsellors agreed upon a law contrary to the law of the Church, to which authority was obedience due? Thus there came about the great conflict between Empire and Papacy symbolised in the question of Investiture, of which the dispute between Henry II and Becket is the insular counterpart.

The struggle between Henry II and Becket is confused by the technical details over which it was fought. There was however good reason why the quarrel should have been engaged upon incidents of administration rather than upon the main principles which were at stake. The Crown resented the claim of the Church to interfere in the State; but in the Middle Ages no king dared to challenge the Church outright, or, much as he might hope to limit its influence, thought of a decisive breach. It was not till the sixteenth century that an English king in conflict with the Papacy dared to repudiate the authority of Rome and nakedly declare the State supreme, even in spiritual matters. In the twelfth century the only practicable course was compromise. But the Church at this time was in no mood for a bargain. In every country the secular power took up the challenge; but it was hard to meet, and in Central Europe at least the struggle ended only in the exhaustion of both Empire and Papacy.

The Church in England, like the baronage, had gained greatly in power since the days of William the Conqueror and his faithful Archbishop Lanfranc. Stephen in his straits had made sweeping concessions to the Church, whose political influence then reached its zenith. These concessions, Henry felt, compromised his royal rights. He schemed to regain what had been lost, and as the first step in 1162 appointed his trusted servant Becket to be Archbishop of Canterbury, believing he would thus secure the acquiescence of the Episcopacy. In fact he provided the Church with a leader of unequalled vigour and obstinacy. He ignored or missed the ominous signs of the change in Becket's attitude, and proceeded to his second step, the publication in 1164 of the Constitutions of Clarendon. In these Henry claimed, not without considerable truth, to be re-stating the customs of the kingdom as they had been before the anarchy of Stephen's reign. He sought to retrace thirty years and to annul the effects of Stephen's surrender. But Becket resisted. He regarded Stephen's yieldings as irrevocable gains by the Church. He refused to let them lapse. He declared that the Constitutions of Clarendon did not represent the relations between Church and Crown. When, in October 1164, he was summoned to appear before the Great Council and explain his conduct he haughtily denied the King's authority and placed himself under the protection of the Pope and God.

Thus he ruptured that unity which had hitherto been deemed vital in the English realm, and in fact declared war with ghostly weapons upon the King. Stiff in defiance, Becket took refuge on the Continent, where the same conflict was already distracting both Germany and Italy. The whole thought of the ruling classes in England was shaken by this grievous dispute. It endured for six years, during which the Archbishop of Canterbury remained in his French exile. Only in 1170 was an apparent reconciliation brought about between him and the King at Fréteval, in Touraine. Each side appeared to waive its claims in principle. The King did not mention his rights and customs. The Archbishop was not called upon to give an oath. He was promised a safe return and full possession of his see. King and Primate met for the last time in the summer of 1170 at Chaumont. "My lord," said Thomas at the end, "my heart tells me that I part from you as one whom you shall see no more in this life." "Do you hold me as a traitor?" asked the King. "That be far from thee, my lord," replied the Archbishop; but he returned to Canterbury resolved to seek from the Pope unlimited powers of excommunication wherewith to discipline his ecclesiastical forces. "The more potent and fierce the prince is," he wrote, "the stronger stick and harder chain is needed to bind him and keep him in order." "I go to England," he said, "whether to peace or to destruction I know not; but God has decreed what fate awaits me."

Meanwhile, in Becket's absence, Henry had resolved to secure the peaceful accession of his son, the young Henry, by having him crowned in his own lifetime. The ceremony had been performed by the Archbishop of York, assisted by a number of other clerics. This action was bitterly resented by Becket as an infringement of a cherished right of his see. After the Fréteval agreement Henry supposed that bygones were to be bygones. But Becket had other views.

His welcome home after the years of exile was astonishing. At Canterbury the monks received him as an angel of God. "I am come to die among you," he said in his sermon, and again, "In this church there are martyrs, and God will soon increase their number." He made a triumphal progress through London, scattering alms to the beseeching and exalted people. Then hotfoot he proceeded to renew his excommunication of the clergy who had taken part in the crowning of young Henry. These unfortunate priests and prelates travelled in a bunch to the King, who was in Normandy. They told a tale not only of an ecclesiastical challenge, but of actual revolt and usurpation. They said that the Archbishop was ready "to tear the crown from the young King's head."

Henry Plantagenet, first of all his line, with all the fire of his nature, received these tidings when surrounded by his knights and nobles. He was transported with passion. "What a pack of fools and cowards," he cried, "I have nourished in my house, that not one of them will avenge me of this turbulent priest!" Another version says "of this upstart clerk." A council was immediately summoned to devise measures for reasserting the royal authority. In the main they shared the King's anger. Second thoughts prevailed. With all the stresses that existed in that fierce and ardent society, it was not possible that the realm could support a fearful conflict between the two sides of life represented by Church and State.

But meanwhile another train of action was in process. Four Knights had heard the King's bitter words spoken in the full circle. They travelled fast to the coast. They crossed the Channel. They called for horses and rode to Canterbury. There on December 29, 1170, they found the Archbishop in the cathedral. The scene and the tragedy are famous. He confronted them with Cross and mitre, fearless and resolute in warlike action, a master of the histrionic arts. After haggard parleys they fell upon him, cut him down with their swords, and left him bleeding like Julius Cæsar, with a score of wounds to cry for vengeance.

This tragedy was fatal to the King. The murder of one of the foremost of God's servants, like the breaking of a feudal oath, struck at the heart of the age. All England was filled with terror. They acclaimed the dead Archbishop as a martyr; and immediately it appeared that his relics healed incurable diseases, and robes that he had worn by their mere touch relieved minor ailments. Here indeed was a crime, vast and inexpiable. When Henry heard the appalling news he was prostrated with grief and fear. All the elaborate process of law which he had sought to set on foot against this rival power was brushed aside by a brutal, bloody act; and though he had never dreamed that such a deed would be done there were his own hot words, spoken before so many witnesses, to fasten on him, for that age at least, the guilt of murder, and, still worse, sacrilege.

The immediately following years were spent in trying to recover what he had lost by a great parade of atonement for his guilt. He made pilgrimages to the shrine of the murdered Archbishop. He subjected himself to public penances. On several anniversaries, stripped to the waist and kneeling humbly, he submitted to be scourged by the triumphant monks. We may however suppose that the corporal chastisement, which apparently from the contemporary pictures was administered with birch rods, was mainly symbolic. Under this display of contrition and submission the King laboured perseveringly to regain the rights of State. By the Compromise of Avranches in 1172 he made his peace with the Papacy on comparatively easy terms. To many deep-delving historians it seems that in fact, though not in form, he had by the end of his life re-established the main principles of the Constitutions of Clarendon, which are after all in harmony with what the English nation or any virile and rational race would mean to have as their law. Certainly the Papacy supported him in his troubles with his sons. The knights, it is affirmed, regained their salvation in the holy wars. But Becket's sombre sacrifice had not been in vain. Until the Reformation the Church retained the system of ecclesiastical courts independent of the royal authority, and the right of appeal to Rome, two of the major points upon which Becket had defied the King.

It is a proof of the quality of the age that these fierce contentions, shaking the souls of men, should have been so rigorously and yet so evenly fought out. In modern conflicts and revolutions in some great states bishops and archbishops have been sent by droves to concentration camps, or pistolled in the nape of the neck in the well-warmed, brilliantly lighted corridor of a prison. What claim have we to vaunt a superior civilisation to Henry II's times? We are sunk in a barbarism all the deeper because it is tolerated by moral lethargy and covered with a veneer of scientific conveniences.[1]

* * *

Eighteen years of life lay before the King after Becket's death. In a sense, they were years of glory. All Europe marvelled at the extent of Henry's domains, to which in 1171 he had added the Lordship of Ireland. Through the marriages of his daughters he was linked with the Norman King of Sicily, the King of Castile, and Henry the Lion of Saxony, who was a most powerful prince in Germany. Diplomatic agents spread his influence in the Lombard cities of northern Italy. Both Emperor and Pope invited him in the name of Christ and all Europe to lead a new Crusade and to be King of Jerusalem. Indeed, after the Holy Roman Emperor, Frederick Barbarossa, Henry stood next in Christendom. It was suspected by his contemporaries that his aim was to win for himself a kingdom in Italy and even to wear the imperial crown.

Yet Henry knew well that his splendour was personal in origin, tenuous and transient in quality; and he had also deep clouding family sorrows. During these years he was confronted

[1] Written in 1938.

with no less than four rebellions by his sons. For the three eldest he had provided glittering titles; Henry held Normandy, Maine and Anjou; Richard was given Aquitaine, and to Geoffrey went Brittany. These boys were typical sprigs of the Angevin stock. They wanted power as well as titles, and they bore their father no respect. Urged on by their mother, Queen Eleanor, who now lived in Poitiers apart from her husband, between 1173 and 1186 they rose in revolt in various combinations. On each occasion they could count on the active support of the watchful King of France. Henry treated his ungrateful children with generosity, but he had no illusions. The royal chamber at Westminster at this time was adorned with paintings done at the King's command. One represented four eaglets preying upon the parent bird, the fourth one poised at the parent's neck, ready to pick out the eyes. "The four eaglets," the King is reported to have said, "are my four sons who cease not to persecute me even unto death. The youngest of them, whom I now embrace with so much affection will sometime in the end insult me more grievously and more dangerously than any of the others."

So it was to be. John, whom he had striven to provide with an inheritance equal to that of his brothers, joined the final plot against him. In 1188 Richard, his eldest surviving son, after the death of young Henry, was making war upon him in conjunction with King Philip of France. Already desperately ill, Henry was defeated at Le Mans and recoiled to Normandy. When he saw in the list of conspirators against him the name of his son John, upon whom his affection had strangely rested, he abandoned the struggle with life. "Let things go as they will," he gasped. "Shame, shame on a conquered King." So saying, this hard, violent, brilliant and lonely man expired at Chinon on July 6, 1189. The pious were taught to regard this melancholy end as the further chastisement of God upon the murderer of Thomas Becket. Such is the bitter taste of worldly power. Such are the correctives of glory.

The English Common Law

THE Plantagenets were rough masters, and the temper of the age was violent. It was the violence however of vigour, not of decadence. England has had greater soldier-kings and subtler diplomatists than Henry II, but no man has left a deeper mark upon our laws and institutions. His strange outbursts of frenzied energy did not exhaust themselves in politics, war, and the chase. Like his Norman predecessors and his sons, Henry II possessed an instinct for the problems of government and law, and it is here that his achievement lies. The names of his battles have vanished with their dust, but his fame will live with the English Constitution and the English Common Law.

This great King was fortunate in his moment. William I and Henry I had brought to England or preserved there all those instruments through which their successor was to work. They themselves could move but slowly and with caution. The land must settle itself to its new rules and rulers. In 1154 however Henry of Anjou had come to a country which nearly twenty years of anarchy had prepared for the acceptance of a strong hand at the centre. Himself a Frenchman, the ruler of more than half France, he brought to his task the qualities of vision, wide experience, and a strength that did not scruple to stoop to cunning. The disasters of Stephen's reign determined Henry not only to curb baronial independence and regain the ground lost by his predecessor, but to go much further. In place of a multitude of manorial courts where local magnates dispensed justice whose quality and character varied with the customs and temper of the neighbourhood, he planned a system of royal courts which would administer a law common to all England and all men.

The policy was not without peril. The King was wise enough to avoid a direct assault, for he knew, as the Conqueror had known, that to lay a finger upon the sanctity of customary rights would provoke disaster. Faced with this barrier, Henry shrewdly opposed custom to custom and cloaked innovation in the respected garb of conservatism. He was careful to respect existing forms. His plan was to stretch old principles to take on new meanings. In an unwritten Constitution the limits of the King's traditional rights were vaguely defined. This opened a shrewd line of advance. For centuries before the Conquest, Church and King had been the enemies of seigneurial anarchy, but there had been no question of swiftly extending the Crown's jurisdiction. Fastening upon the elastic Saxon concept of the King's Peace, Henry used it to draw all criminal cases into his courts. Every man had his own Peace, which it was a crime to break, and the more important the man the graver the breach. The King's Peace was the most important of all, and those who broke it could be tried in the King's court. But the King's Peace was limited, and often embraced only offences committed in the King's presence or on the King's highway or land. When the King died his Peace died with him and men might do as they willed. Cautiously and quietly Henry began to claim that the King's Peace extended over all England, and that no matter where it was broken offenders should be tried in the King's courts. Civil cases he attracted by straining a different principle, the old right of the King's court to hear appeals in cases where justice had been refused and to protect men in possession of their lands. He did not brandish what he was about; the changes that he made were introduced gradually and without legislation, so that at first they were hardly perceived. Rarely is it possible to state the date at which any innovation was made; yet at the King's death a clever man might have looked back and seen how much had been altered in the thirty-five years that Henry II had sat on the English throne.

But if Henry was to pose as a conservative in' the legal sphere he must be consistent. Compulsion could play little part in his programme; it had to be the first principle of his policy to attract cases to his courts rather than to compel them. A bait was needed with which to draw litigants to the royal courts; the King must offer them better justice than they could have at the hands of their lords. Henry accordingly threw open to litigants in the royal courts a startling new procedure—trial by jury. *Regale quoddam beneficium,* a contemporary called it—a royal boon; and the description illuminates both the origin of the jury and the part it played in the triumph of the Common Law. Henry did not invent the jury; he put it to a new purpose. The idea of the jury is the one great contribution of the Franks to the English legal system, for, unknown in this country before the Conquest, the germ of it lies far back in the practice of the Carolingian kings. In origin the jury was a royal instrument of administrative convenience: the King had the right to summon a body of men to bear witness under oath about the truth of any question concerning the royal interest. It was through this early form of jury that William the Conqueror had determined the Crown rights in the great Domesday survey. The genius of Henry II, perceiving new possibilities in such a procedure, turned to regular use in the courts an instrument which so far had only been used for administrative purposes.

Only the King had the right to summon a jury. Henry accordingly did not grant it to private courts, but restricted it to those who sought justice before the royal judges. It was an astute move. Until this time both civil and criminal cases had been decided through the oath, the ordeal, or the duel. The court would order one of the litigants to muster a body of men who would swear to the justice of his cause and whom it was hoped God would punish if they swore falsely; or condemn him, under the supervision of a priest, to carry a red-hot iron, or eat a morsel of bread, or be plunged in a pool of water. If the iron did not burn or the bread choke or the water reject him so that he could not sink, then Divine Providence was adjudged to have granted a visible sign that the victim was innocent. The duel, or trial by battle, was a Norman innovation based on the modern theory that the God of Battles will strengthen the arm of the righteous, and was at one time much favoured for deciding disputes about land. Monasteries and other substantial landowners took the precaution however of assisting the Almighty by retaining professional champions to protect their property and their rights. All this left small room for debate on points of law. In a more rational age men were beginning to distrust such antics, and indeed the Church refused to sanction the ordeal during the same year that Magna Carta was sealed. Thus trial by jury quickly gained favour. But the old processes were long in dying. If a defendant preferred to take his case before God man could not forbid him, and the ordeal therefore was not abolished outright. Hence a later age was to know the horrors of the *peine forte et dure*—the compulsion of the accused by slow pressure to death to agree to put himself before a jury. Time swept this away; yet so late as 1818 a litigant nonplussed the judges by an appeal to trial by battle and compelled Parliament to abolish this ancient procedure.

The jury of Henry II was not the jury that we know. There were various forms of it; but in all there was this essential difference: the jurymen were witnesses as well as judges of the facts. Good men and true were picked, not yet for their impartiality, but because they were the men most likely to know the truth. The modern jury which knows nothing about the case till it is proved in court was slow in coming. The process is obscure. A jury summoned to Westminster from distant parts might be reluctant to come. The way was long, the roads unsafe, and perhaps only three or four would arrive. The court could not wait. An adjournment would be costly. To avoid delay and expense the parties might agree to rely on a jury *de circumstantibus,* a jury of bystanders. The few jurors who knew the truth of the matter would tell their tale to the bystanders, and then the whole body would deliver their verdict. In time the jurors with local knowledge would cease to be jurors at all and become witnesses, giving their evidence in open court to a jury entirely composed of bystanders. Such, we may guess, or something like it, was what happened. Very gradually, as the laws of evidence developed, the change came. By the fifteenth century it was under way; yet the old idea lingered, and even under the Tudor kings jurymen might be tried for perjury if they gave a wrongful verdict.

The jury system has come to stand for all we mean by English justice, because so long as a case has to be scrutinised by twelve honest men, defendant and plaintiff alike have a safeguard from arbitrary perversion of the law. It is this which distinguishes the law administered in English courts from Continental legal systems based on Roman law. Thus amidst the great process of centralisation the old principle was preserved, and endures to this day, that law flows from the people, and is not given by the King.

These methods gave good justice. Trial by jury became popular. Professional judges removed from local prejudice, whose outlook ranged above the interested or ignorant lord or his steward, armed with the King's power to summon juries, secured swifter decisions, and a strong authority to enforce them. Henry accordingly had to build up almost from nothing a complete system of royal courts, capable of absorbing a great rush of new work. The instrument to which he turned was the royal Council, the organ through which all manner of governmental business was already regularly carried out. It was to be the common parent of Chancery and Exchequer, of Parliament, of the Common Law courts and those Courts of Prerogative on which the Tudors and Stuarts relied. At the outset of Henry II's reign, it dealt almost indiscriminately with every kind of administrative business. On the judicial side the Court of the Exchequer, which tried cases affecting the royal revenue, was beginning to take shape; but in the main the Council in this aspect was scarcely more than the King's feudal court, where he did justice, like any other lord, among his vassals. Under Henry II all this was changed. The functions of the King's justices became more and more specialised. During the reigns of his sons the Council began to divide into two great courts, the King's Bench and the Common Pleas. They did not become fully separate till a century later. Thereafter, with the Court of the Exchequer, they formed the backbone of the Common Law system down to the nineteenth century. In addition, travelling justices—justices "in eyre"—were from time to time appointed to hear all manner of business in the shires, whose courts were thus drawn into the orbit of royal justice.

But all this was only a first step. Henry also had to provide means whereby the litigant, eager for royal justice, could remove his case out of the court of his lord into the King's court. The device which Henry used was the royal writ. At all costs baronial rights must be formally respected; but by straining the traditional rights of the Crown it was possible to claim that particular types of case fell within the King's province. Upon this principle Henry evolved a number of set formulæ, or writs, each fitted to a certain type of case; and any man who could by some fiction fit his own case to the wording of one of the royal writs might claim the King's justice. The wording of writs was rigid, but at this date new forms of writ might still be given. For about eighty years they increased in number, and with each new form a fresh blow was struck at the feudal courts. It was not until de Montfort's revolt against the third Henry in the thirteenth century that the multiplication of writs was checked and the number fixed at something under two hundred. This system then endured for six hundred years. However the times might change, society had to adapt itself to that unbending framework. Inevitably English law became weighted with archaisms and legal fictions. The whole course of a case might depend on the writ with which it was begun, for every writ had its special procedure, mode of trial, and eventual remedy. Thus the Saxon spirit of formalism survived. Henry II had only been able to break down the primitive methods of the early courts by fastening upon the law a procedure which became no less rigid. Yet, cumbersome though it was, the writ system gave to English law a conservative spirit which guarded and preserved its continuity from that time on in an unbroken line.

* * *

It is a maxim of English law that legal memory begins with the accession of Richard I in 1189. The date was set for a technical reason by a statute of Edward I. It could scarcely have been more appropriately chosen however, for with the close of the reign of Henry II we are on the threshold of a new epoch in the history of English law. With the establishment of a system of royal courts, giving the same justice all over the country, the old diversity of local law was rapidly broken down, and a law common to the whole land and to all men soon took its place. A modern lawyer, transported to the England of Henry's predecessor, would find himself in strange surroundings; with the system that Henry bequeathed to his son he would feel almost at home. That is the measure of the great King's achievement. He had laid the foundations of the English Common Law, upon which succeeding generations would build. Changes in the design would arise, but its main outlines were not to be altered.

It was in these fateful and formative years that the English-speaking peoples began to devise methods of determining legal disputes which survive in substance to this day. A man can only be accused of a civil or criminal offence which is clearly defined and known to the law. The judge is an umpire. He adjudicates on such evidence as the parties choose to produce. Witnesses must testify in public and on oath. They are examined and cross-examined, not by the judge, but by the litigants themselves or their legally qualified and privately hired representatives. The truth of their testimony is weighed not by the judge but by twelve good men and true, and it is only when this jury has determined the facts that the judge is empowered to impose sentence, punishment, or penalty according to law. All might seem very obvious, even a platitude, until one contemplates the alternative system which still dominates a large portion of the world. Under Roman law, and systems derived from it, a trial in those turbulent centuries, and in some countries even to-day, is often an inquisition. The judge makes his own investigation into the civil wrong or the public crime, and such investigation is largely uncontrolled. The suspect can be interrogated in private. He must answer all questions put to him. His right to be represented by a legal adviser is restricted. The witnesses against him can testify in secret and in his absence. And only when these processes have been accomplished is the accusation or charge against him formulated and published. Thus often arises secret intimidation, enforced confessions, torture, and blackmailed pleas of guilty.

These sinister dangers were extinguished from the Common Law of England more than six centuries ago. By the time Henry II's great-grandson, Edward I had died English criminal and civil procedure had settled into a mould and tradition which in the mass govern the English-speaking peoples to-day. In all claims and disputes, whether they concerned the grazing lands of the Middle West, the oilfields of California, the sheep-runs and gold-mines of Australia, or the territorial rights of the Maoris, these rules have obtained, at any rate in theory, according to the procedure and mode of trial evolved by the English Common Law.

Nor was this confined to how trials were conducted. The law that was applied to such multitudinous problems, some familiar, others novel, was in substance the Common Law of England. The law concerning murder, theft, the ownership of land, and the liberty of the individual was all transported, to-gether with much else, to the New World, and, though often modified to suit the conditions and temper of the times, de-scends in unbroken line from that which governed the lives and fortunes of twelfth-century Englishmen.

Most of it was then unwritten, and in England much still remains so. The English statutes, for example, still contain no definition of the crime of murder, for this, like much other law, rested on the unwritten custom of the land as declared by the inhabitants and interpreted, developed, and applied by the judges. Lawyers could only ascertain it by studying re-ports and records of ancient decisions. For this they had al-ready in this early age made their own arrangements. A century after Henry's death they began to group themselves into pro-fessional communities in London, the Inns of Court, half colleges, half law-schools, but predominantly secular, for the presence of clerics learned in the laws of Rome and the Canon Law of the Roman Church was not encouraged, and here they produced annual laws reports, or "Year Books," as they were then called, whose authority was recognised by the judges, and which continued in almost unbroken succession for nearly three centuries. In all this time however only one man at-tempted a general and comprehensive statement of the Eng-lish Common Law. About the year 1250 a Judge of Assize named Henry of Bracton produced a book of nearly nine hundred pages entitled *A Tract on the Laws and Customs of England*. Nothing like it was achieved for several hundred years, but Bracton's method set an example, since followed throughout the English-speaking world, not so much of stating the Common Law as of explaining and commenting on it, and thus encouraging and helping later lawyers and judges to develop and expand it. Digests and codes imposed in the Roman manner by an omnipotent state on a subject people were alien to the spirit and tradition of England. The law was already there, in the customs of the land, and it was only a matter of discovering it by diligent study and comparison of recorded decisions in earlier cases, and applying it to the particular dispute before the court. In the course of time the Common Law changed. Lawyers of the reign of Henry II read into the statements of their predecessors of the tenth century meanings and principles which their authors never intended, and applied them to the novel conditions and problems of their own day. No matter. Here was a precedent. If a judge could be shown that a custom or something like it had been recognised and acted upon in an earlier and similar case he would be more ready, if it accorded with his sense of what was just and with the current feelings of the community, to follow it in the dispute before him. This slow but continuous growth of what is popularly known as "case law" ultimately achieved much the same freedoms and rights for the individual as are enshrined in other countries by written instruments such as the Declarations of the Rights of Man and the spacious and splendid provisions of the American Declaration of Independence and constitutional guarantees of civil rights. But English justice advanced very cautiously. Even the framers of Magna Carta did not attempt to lay down new law or proclaim any broad general principles. This was because both sovereign and subject were in practice bound by the Common Law, and the liberties of Englishmen rested not on any enactment of the State, but on immemorial slow-growing custom declared by juries of free men who gave their verdicts case by case in open court.

Cœur de Lion

THE Christian kingdom founded at Jerusalem after the First Crusade had stood precariously for a century, guarded by the military orders of the Knights Templars and Hospitallers. Its continued existence was largely due to the disunity that prevailed among the Moslem lands surrounding it. At length the rise of a great national leader of the Turks, or Saracens, united the Moslem power. In 1169 Saladin became Vizier of Egypt. Shortly afterwards he proclaimed himself Sultan. By origin he was a Kurd, and by culture a Damascene. Soon his power was stretching out into Syria, encircling the Crusaders' principalities on the Levantine coast. He took Damascus in 1174 and Aleppo in 1183. In their anxieties at these gathering dangers the Christian community in Jerusalem, and Guy of Lusignan, the King, offered the threatened crown first to Philip of France and then to Henry II, and made the West ring with cries for help. But the quarrels of the Western princes prevented effective measures being taken in time. In 1186 Saladin in his turn proclaimed a Holy War. He promised his warlike hordes booty and adventure in this world and bliss eternal in the next, and advanced upon Jerusalem. The Christian army of occupation which took the field against him, perhaps ten thousand strong, was caught at a disadvantage in the thirsty desert and cut to pieces by greatly superior numbers at Hattin. The King, the Grand Master of the Templars, and many of the greatest nobles were taken prisoners. In October 1187 Jerusalem surrendered, and thereafter all Palestine and Syria, except Tyre, Antioch, and Tripoli, fell again into Moslem hands.

The shock of these events resounded throughout Europe. The Pope shared the general horror of the Christian West. His legates traversed the Courts enjoining peace among Christians and war against the infidel. The sovereigns of the three greatest nations of the West responded to the call, and an intense movement stirred the chivalry of England, France, and Germany. Pictures were shown of the Holy Sepulchre defiled by the horses of the Saracen cavalry. Not only the gentle folk but to some extent all classes were swept by deep emotion. Not without sorrow, as the literature of those times shows, did

many of the young Crusaders leave home and loved ones for
a journey into the dangers of the distant and the unknown.
The magnetism of war and adventure mingled with a deep
counterpart of sacrifice and mysticism which lights the age
and its efforts with the charm of true romance. In Germany
the solemn Diet of Mainz "swore the expedition" to the Holy
Land. The Kings of France and England agreed upon a joint
Crusade, without however ceasing their immediate strife. To
the religious appeal was added the spur of the tax-gatherer.
The "Saladin tithe" was levied upon all who did not take the
Cross. On the other hand, forgiveness of taxes and a stay in
the payment of debts were granted to all Crusaders. The
strongest armies ever yet sent to the East were raised. Germany marshalled a large array round the standard of Frederick Barbarossa. A Scandinavian fleet bore twelve thousand
Norsemen through the Straits of Gibraltar. Thus did armoured
Europe precipitate itself upon Asia. Meanwhile the first of
the rescuers, Conrad of Montferrat, who, hastening from Constantinople, had saved Tyre, was already besieging Acre.

In the midst of these surgings Henry II died in sorrow and
disaster. He made no attempt to prescribe the succession, and
it passed naturally to Richard. The new King affected little
grief at the death of a father against whom he was in arms.
He knelt beside his bier no longer than would have been necessary to recite the Lord's Prayer, and turned at once to the
duties of his realm. In spite of many harsh qualities, men saw
in him a magnanimity which has added lustre to his military
renown. At the outset of his reign he gave an outstanding
example. During his rebellion against his father he had pressed
hard upon Henry II's rout at Le Mans in the very forefront of
the cavalry without even wearing his mail. In the rearguard of
the beaten army stood Henry's faithful warrior, William the
Marshal. He confronted Richard and had him at his mercy.
"Spare me!" cried Richard in his disadvantage; so the Marshal
turned his lance against the prince's horse and killed it, saying
with scorn, "I will not slay you. The Devil may slay you." This
was humiliation and insult worse than death. It was not therefore without anxiety that the Marshal and his friends awaited
their treatment at the hands of the sovereign to whom their
loyalties must now be transferred. But King Richard rose at
once above the past. He spoke with dignity and detachment
of the grim incident so fresh and smarting in his mind. He
confirmed his father's true servant in all his offices and
honours, and sent him to England to act in his name. He gave

him in marriage the rich Crown heiress of Pembroke, and at a stroke the Marshal became one of the most powerful of English barons. Indeed it was noted that the King's favour lighted upon those who had stood loyally by his father against him, even to the detriment of those who had been his own fellow-rebels.

* * *

Richard, with all his characteristic virtues and faults cast in a heroic mould, is one of the most fascinating medieval figures. He has been described as the creature and embodiment of the age of chivalry. In those days the lion was much admired in heraldry, and more than one king sought to link himself with its repute. When Richard's contemporaries called him "Cœur de Lion" they paid a lasting compliment to the king of beasts. Little did the English people owe him for his services, and heavily did they pay for his adventures. He was in England only twice for a few short months in his ten years' reign; yet his memory has always stirred English hearts, and seems to present throughout the centuries the pattern of the fighting man. In all deeds of prowess as well as in large schemes of war Richard shone. He was tall and delicately shaped; strong in nerve and sinew, and most dexterous in arms. He rejoiced in personal combat, and regarded his opponents without malice as necessary agents in his fame. He loved war, not so much for the sake of glory or political ends, but as other men love science and poetry, for the excitement of the struggle and the glow of victory. By this his whole temperament was toned; and, united with the highest qualities of the military commander, love of war called forth all the powers of his mind and body.

Although a man of blood and violence, Richard was too impetuous to be either treacherous or habitually cruel. He was as ready to forgive as he was hasty to offend; he was openhanded and munificent to profusion; in war circumspect in design and skilful in execution; in politics a child, lacking in subtlety and experience. His political alliances were formed upon his likes and dislikes; his political schemes had neither unity nor clearness of purpose. The advantages gained for him by military genius were flung away through diplomatic ineptitude. When on the journey to the East Messina in Sicily was won by his arms he was easily persuaded to share with his polished, faithless ally, Philip Augustus, fruits of a victory which more wisely used might have foiled the French king's artful schemes. The rich and tenable acquisition of Cyprus was cast away even more easily than it was won. His life was one magnificent parade, which, when ended, left only an empty plain.

The King's heart was set upon the new Crusade. This task seemed made for him. It appealed to every need of his nature. To rescue the Holy Land from the pollution of the infidel, to charge as a king at the head of knightly squadrons in a cause at once glorious to man and especially acceptable to God, was a completely satisfying inspiration. The English would greatly have liked their King to look after their affairs, to give them peace and order, to nourish their growing prosperity, and to do justice throughout the land. But they understood that the Crusade was a high and sacred enterprise, and the Church taught them that in unseen ways it would bring a blessing upon them. Richard was crowned with peculiar state, by a ceremonial which, elaborating the most ancient forms and traditions of the Island monarchy, is still in all essentials observed to-day. Thereafter the King, for the sake of Christ's sepulchre, virtually put the realm up for sale. Money he must have at all costs for his campaign in far-off Palestine. He sold and re-sold every office in the State. He made new and revolutionarily heavy demands for taxation. He called for "scutage," or the commutation of military service for a money payment, and later re-introduced "carucage," a levy on every hundred acres of land. Thus he filled his chests for the Holy War.

Confiding the government to two Justiciars, William Longchamp, Bishop of Ely, and Hugh Puiset, Bishop of Durham, under the supervision of the one trustworthy member of his family, his mother, the old Queen, Eleanor of Aquitaine, he started for the wars in the summer of 1190. He had promised Philip of France to marry his sister Alice, about whom, except for her looks, the tales were none too good. Philip claimed that Richard had tried to seduce her, and there was bad feeling between the monarchs. However that may be, after Richard had marched across France and sailed to Sicily, where he rested for the winter, his mother brought out to him Berengaria, daughter of the King of Navarre, whom he had known and admired, and now resolved to marry. It was fitting that the "Lion-heart" should marry for love and not for policy, but the rejection of Alice prevented a tie between the Kings of France and England which had been deemed essential to their comradeship in the Crusade. Philip was little soothed

for the affront by a compensation of ten thousand marks. The
quarrels of England and France were not so lightly set aside,
and jealousies and bickerings distressed the winter sojourn of
the two allies in Sicily.

Meanwhile Frederick Barbarossa had led his German host
from Regensburg in May 1189 through Hungary to Constantinople. As soon as the frontiers of the Byzantine Empire
were reached difficulties arose. The successors of Constantine
still ruled over an extensive realm in Balkan Europe and in
Asia Minor. The Emperor Isaac II at this time had allied himself with Saladin, and it was only under the threat of a Crusade against these Greek schismatics that by the end of March
1190 the Germans were allowed a free passage across the
Bosphorus to the Asiatic shore. Barbarossa marched through
Asia Minor and reached Cilicia. Here this veteran of the
Second Crusade, of forty years before, was drowned in the
river Calycadnus, either through his horse slipping at the ford
or through the imprudence of bathing after dining. Some of
his troops turned back, many died of plague at Antioch, and
of his great army, the flower of Germany, barely a thousand,
under his son, reached the Crusaders' camp before Acre in
October 1190. But these kept tryst. The Anglo-French armies
did not quit Sicily till the spring of 1191. Philip sailed direct
to Acre. Richard paused in Cyprus. He quarrelled with the
local Greek ruler, declared that an insult had been offered to
his betrothed, conquered the island, and there wedded Berengaria. It was not until June 8, 1191, that he arrived with
powerful forces before Acre.

The glamours of chivalry illumine the tale of the Third
Crusade. All the chief princes of Europe were now in line
around the doomed stronghold of Saladin, rivalling each other
in prowess and jealousy. The sanctity of their cause was no
bar to their quarrels and intrigues. King Richard dominated
the scene. Fighting always in the most dangerous places,
striking down the strongest foes, he negotiated all the time
with Saladin. An agreement was in fact almost reached. To
save his garrison Saladin offered to surrender his Christian
captives, to pay a large indemnity, and to give up the cross,
captured by him in Jerusalem, on which Christ—though this
after twelve hundred years was not certain—had suffered. But
the negotiations failed, and Richard in his fury massacred in
cold blood the two thousand Turkish hostages who had been
delivered as guarantees. Within five weeks of his arrival he
brought the two years' siege to a successful conclusion.

By the time Acre fell King Richard's glory as a warrior and also his skill as a general were the talk of all nations. But the quarrels of the allies paralysed the campaign. Guy of Lusignan, the exiled King of Jerusalem, was disputing with Conrad of Montferrat for the crown. Richard took the one side and Philip the other. A compromise was arranged, but immediately the French king returned home to prosecute his designs in Flanders and to intrigue with Prince John against his absent brother. Duke Leopold of Austria, whom Richard had personally insulted, also took his departure. In these circumstances the Crusading army, ably led by Richard, in spite of the victory at Arsuf, where many thousand infidels were slain, could do no more than reach an eminence which commanded a distant view of the Holy City. The King veiled his eyes, not bearing to look upon the city he could not enter. He resolved to retreat to the coast. In the next year, 1192, he captured Jaffa. Once again the distant prospect of Jerusalem alone rewarded the achievements of the Crusaders, and once again they fell back frustrated.

By now the news from England was so alarming that the King felt it imperative to return home. He renewed his negotiations with Saladin, even offering his sister Joanna in marriage to Saladin's brother as the cement of a lasting peace. In the hard fighting the Saracens had won the respect of their martial foes. A peace or truce for three years was at length effected, by which the coastal towns were divided and the Holy Sepulchre opened as a place of pilgrimage to small parties of Crusaders. It was as tourists only that they reached their goal. The hard struggle between Guy and Conrad for the Kingdom of Jerusalem settled itself, for Conrad, at the moment when his claims had at length been recognised by Richard, was murdered by the assassins belonging to a Moslem sect ruled by "the Old Man of the Mountain." Guy, despairing of regaining his inheritance, purchased Cyprus from the English king. He settled there, and founded a dynasty which, aided by the military orders of knighthood, was to maintain itself against the Turks for nearly four hundred years.

Early in 1193 the King set out for home. Wrecked in the Adriatic, he sought to make his way through Germany in disguise, but his enemy the Duke of Austria was soon upon his track. He was arrested, and held prisoner in a castle. So valuable a prize was not suffered to remain in the Duke's hands. The Emperor himself demanded the famous captive. For many months his prison was a secret of the Imperial

Court, but, as a pretty legend tells us, Blondel, Richard's faithful minstrel, went from castle to castle striking the chords which the King loved best, and at last was rewarded by an answer from Richard's own harp.

* * *

William Longchamp, Bishop of Ely, and, with magnificent pluralism, Papal Legate, Chancellor, and Justiciar, had addressed himself with fidelity and zeal to the task of governing England, entrusted to him by Richard in 1189. Emulating the splendour of a monarch, he moved about the country with a pompous retinue, and very soon drew upon himself the envy and then the active hatred of the whole nobility. As the King's faithful servant he saw that the chief danger lay in the over-mighty position of Prince John. The indulgence of Richard had allowed his brother to form a state within a state. John held the shires of Derby, Nottingham, Somerset, Dorset, Devon, and Cornwall; the Earldom of Gloucester, with wide lands in South Wales; the honours of Lancaster, Wallingford, Eye, and Peverel. For the revenues which John drew from these lands he rendered no account to the Exchequer. Their sheriffs were responsible to him alone; their judicial business was transacted by his servants, their writs issued by his chancery and in his name. The royal officers and judges dared not enter John's shires. Bishop Longchamp determined to resist this dual system of government. His personal ostentation and arrogant airs had already multiplied his difficulties. Socially of humble origin, and by race a foreigner, he antagonised the other members of the Council, and provoked them to side with John, who knew well how to turn all this to his profit.

In the summer of 1191 there was open conflict between the two parties, and Longchamp marched against a revolt of John's adherents in the North Midlands. This was a serious crisis. Fortunately however the King, far off in the Levant, had sent home Walter de Coutances, the Archbishop of Rouen, to watch the royal interests. The Archbishop formed a third party, loyal to the King, offended by Longchamp, but unwilling to support John; and presently he succeeded to Longchamp's position when the latter fled from England in October. The return of Philip Augustus from the Crusade in this same autumn brought new opportunities to John's ambition. The French king saw in Richard's absence the chance of breaking up the Angevin power and driving the English out of France. In John he found a willing partner. It was agreed between them that Philip Augustus should attack Normandy, while John raised a revolt in England.

Early in 1193, at a moment already full of peril, the grave news reached England that the King was prisoner "somewhere in Germany." There was general and well-founded consternation among the loyal bulk of his subjects. John declared that Richard was dead, appeared in arms, and claimed the crown. That England was held for Richard in his long absence against all these powerful and subtle forces is a proof of the loyalties of the feudal age. A deep sense of his heroic character and sacred mission commanded the allegiance of a large number of resolute, independent people whose names are unknown to history. The Church never flinched; Walter de Coutances of Rouen stood firm; the Queen-Mother with septuagenarian vigour stood by her eldest son; these dominated the Council, and the Council held the country. The coasts were guarded against an impending French invasion. John's forces melted. In April the strain was relieved by the arrival of authoritative news that Richard was alive. Prince John put the best face he could upon it and stole away to France.

* * *

The Holy Roman Emperor demanded the prodigious ransom of 150,000 marks, twice the annual revenue of the English Crown. One hundred thousand was to be ready in London before the King was liberated. Richard approved and the English Council agreed. Meanwhile Philip and John were active on the other side. They offered the Emperor 80,000 marks to keep the English king under lock and key till Michaelmas 1194, or 1500 marks a month for each month he was kept, or 150,000 marks to deliver him into their hands. But the Emperor felt that his blackmailing honour was engaged to Richard, with whom he had, perhaps precipitately, settled the figure. Once Philip knew that the Emperor would not go back upon his bargain he sent John his notorious message: "Have a care—the Devil is unloosed."

It remained to collect the ransom. The charge staggered the kingdom. Yet nothing was more sacred than the feudal obligation to ransom the liege lord, above all when he enjoyed the sanctity of a Crusader. The Justiciar, the Archbishops, and Queen Eleanor addressed themselves to their grievous task. The Church faced its duty. It was lawful to sacrifice even the most holy ornaments of the cathedrals for the ransom of a Christian lost in the Holy War. From all the lands a new "scutage" was taken. All laymen had to give a quarter of their movables. The Church lands bore an equal burden; they gave their plate and treasure, and three of the monastic orders yielded unresistingly a year's wool crop. Prince John of course set an example in collecting these taxes throughout his shires. His agents dwelt upon the sacred duty of all to pay, and he kept the proceeds of their faith and loyalty for himself. Three separate attempts were made to gather the money, and although England and Normandy, taxed to the limit, could not scrape together the whole of the 150,000 marks required, the Emperor, satisfied that he could get no more, resolved to set his captive at liberty.

At the end of 1193 the stipulated first instalment was paid, and at the beginning of February 1194 Richard Cœur de Lion was released from bondage. He picked his way, we may be assured, with care across Europe, avoiding his French domains, and on March 16 arrived again in London among citizens impoverished but still rejoiced to see him and proud of his fame. He found John again in open rebellion, having seized castles and raised forces with French aid. The new Justiciar and the Council were already acting against the traitor prince, and Richard lent the weight of his strong right arm as well as the majesty of his name to the repression of the revolt. John fled once more to France. The King was recrowned in London with even more elaborate ceremony than before. As he was now plainly at war with Philip Augustus, his first, last, and only measures of government were to raise money and gather knights. These processes well started, he crossed the Channel to defend his French possessions. He never set foot in England again. But the Islanders owed him no grudge. All had been done as was right and due.

The mere arrival of the mighty warrior in France was enough to restore the frontiers and to throw King Philip and his forces upon an almost abject defensive. John sought pardon from the brother and liege lord he had so foully wronged. He did not sue in vain. With the full knowledge that if John had had his way he would still be a captive in a German castle, dethroned, or best of all dead—with all the long story of perfidy and unnatural malice in his mind, Cœur de Lion pardoned John, embraced him in fraternal love, and restored him to some of his estates, except certain fortresses which the barest prudence obliged him to reserve. This gesture was admired for its grandeur, though not perhaps for its wisdom, by the whole society, lay and spiritual, of Christendom.

* * *

The five remaining years of Richard's reign were spent in defending his French domains and raising money for that purpose from England. Once again the country was ruled by a deputy, this time Hubert Walter, a man bred in the traditions of Henry II's official household as the right-hand man of Ranulf of Glanville; no feudal amateur, but a professional administrator by training and experience. Hubert Walter was now Archbishop of Canterbury, and Richard's Justiciar. He was to become King John's Chancellor. Thus for ten years he was the kingdom's chief Minister. He had been extremely useful to Richard on the Crusade, on which he had accompanied him, and had been prominent in the organisation of the ransom. With determination, knowledge, and deft touch he developed the system of strong centralised government devised by Henry II. Hubert Walter stands out as one of the great medieval administrators. The royal authority was reasserted in the North; commissions of inquiry dealt with unfinished judicial and financial business; other commissions, with the help of local juries, carried out exhaustive inquiries into royal rights and the administration of justice. A new machinery for keeping the peace was devised, to which the origin of the Justices of the Peace can be traced, and the office of Coroner now emerged clearly for the first time. As head of the Exchequer, Walter of Coutances, Archbishop of Rouen, attempted the revision of taxation and of the existing military system. New assessments of land were begun, weights and measures standardised, and the frauds of cloth-workers and dealers purged or curbed. New concessions, involving the precious privilege of local self-government, were granted to London and the principal towns. Throughout the length and breadth of the land the machinery of government was made to work easily and quietly. If there was discontent at the taxes few dared to voice it. One man, a demagogue, "William of the Beard," uttered sentiments which would in similar circumstances readily occur to modern politicians. He was hanged.

Although Richard was an absentee King whose causes and virtues had proved a drain and disappointment to his subjects, his realm had not suffered so much as it would have seemed. The intrigues of the nobles and the treacheries of Prince John had been restrained by an impersonal Government ruling with the force and in the name of high and also well-grounded principles. The system of administration devised by Henry II—the Civil Service as we may call it—had stood the test, and, undisturbed by royal interventions, consolidated itself, to the

general convenience and advantage. It was proved that the
King, to whom all allegiance had been rendered, was no longer
the sole guarantee for law and order. There were other sureties
upon which in addition the English nation could rely.

In France the war with Philip proceeded in a curious fashion. The negotiations were unceasing. Every year there was a
truce, which every year was broken as the weather and general
convenience permitted. Richard, studying the strategic defence
of Normandy, saw in a high crag which rises at the bend of the
Seine by Andelys the key to Rouen. Although inhibited by the
truce from fortifying it, and regardless of an interdict launched
against him by the bishop of the diocese, the King set himself
during 1196 to build the most perfect fortress which his experience could devise. He called it Château Gaillard, or "Saucy
Castle," and "my fair child"; and as it rose with all its outworks, bridges, and water-defences into the immense triple-
walled stone structure which still scowls upon the roofs of
Andelys he rejoiced that it was beyond question the strongest
fortress in the world. "If its walls were iron," said Philip in his
wrath, "I would take it." "If they were of butter," retorted
Richard, "I would hold it." But fate was to give Philip the last
word.

In 1197 the skirmishing and parleying, truce-making and
truce-breaking, which had become habitual were slashed by a
fierce event. Something like a battle was fought, and Richard
drove the King of France and his army in headlong rout
through the streets of Gisors, where the solemn oaths of the
Third Crusade had been sworn barely ten years before by the
Kings of France and England.

In 1199, when the difficulties of raising revenue for the endless war were at their height, good news was brought to King
Richard. It was said there had been dug up near the castle of
Chaluz, on the lands of one of his vassals, a treasure of wonderful quality; a group of golden images of an emperor, his
wife, sons, and daughters, seated round a table, also of gold,
had been unearthed. The King claimed this treasure as lord
paramount. The lord of Chaluz resisted the demand, and the
King laid siege to his small, weak castle. On the third day, as
he rode daringly near the wall, confident in his hard-tried luck,
a bolt from a crossbow struck him in the left shoulder by the
neck. The wound, already deep, was aggravated by the necessary cutting out of the arrow-head. Gangrene set in, and Cœur
de Lion knew that he must pay a soldier's debt. He prepared
for death with fortitude and calm, and in accordance with the

principles he had followed. He arranged his affairs; he divided his personal belongings among his friends or bequeathed them to charity. He sent for his mother, the redoubtable Eleanor, who was at hand. He declared John to be his heir, and made all present swear fealty to him. He ordered the archer who had shot the fatal bolt, and who was now a prisoner, to be brought before him. He pardoned him, and made him a gift of money. For seven years he had not confessed for fear of being compelled to be reconciled to Philip, but now he received the offices of the Church with sincere and exemplary piety, and died in the forty-second year of his age on April 6, 1199, worthy, by the consent of all men, to sit with King Arthur and Roland and other heroes of martial romance at some Eternal Round Table, which we trust the Creator of the Universe in His comprehension will not have forgotten to provide.

The archer was flayed alive.

BOOK TWO · CHAPTER FIFTEEN

Magna Carta

THE character of the prince who now ascended the throne of England and became lord of Normandy, Anjou, Touraine, and Maine, claimant to Brittany and heir to Queen Eleanor's Aquitaine, was already well known. Richard had embodied the virtues which men admire in the lion, but there is no animal in nature that combines the contradictory qualities of John. He united the ruthlessness of a hardened warrior with the craft and subtlety of a Machiavellian. Although from time to time he gave way to furious rages, in which "his eyes darted fire and his countenance became livid," his cruelties were conceived and executed with a cold, inhuman intelligence. Monkish chroniclers have emphasised his violence, greed, malice, treachery, and lust. But other records show that he was often judicious, always extremely capable, and on occasions even generous. He possessed an original and inquiring mind, and to the end of his life treasured his library of books. In him the restless energy of the Plantagenet race was raised to a furious

pitch of instability. A French writer,[1] it is true, has tried to
throw the sombre cloak of madness over his moral deformities,
but a study of his actions shows John gifted with a deep and
persistent sagacity, of patience and artifice, and with an un-
shakable resolve, which he fulfilled, to maintain himself upon
the throne while the breath was in his body. The difficulties
with which he contended, on the whole with remarkable success, deserve cool and attentive study. Moreover, when the
long tally is added it will be seen that the British nation and
the English-speaking world owe far more to the vices of John
than to the labours of virtuous sovereigns; for it was through
the union of many forces against him that the most famous
milestone of our rights and freedom was in fact set up.

Although Richard had declared John to be King there were
two views upon the succession. Geoffrey, his elder brother,
had left behind him a son, Arthur, Prince of Brittany. It was
already possible to hold that this grandson of Henry II of an
elder branch had a prior right against John, and that is now
the law of primogeniture. William the Marshal put the point
before the Archbishop of Canterbury, but they both decided
that John had the right. Queen Eleanor stood by her son
against the grandson, whose mother she had never liked. John
was accepted without demur in England. In the French provinces however the opposite view prevailed. Brittany in particular adopted Arthur. The King of France and all French
interests thought themselves well served by a disputed succession and the espousal of a minor's cause. Those who had
supported Richard against his father, and John against Richard, found it logical to support Arthur against John. Moreover, John's irreverence on high State occasions gave offence
to the Church. An evil omen sprang at the outset from his
levity. When in Rouen he was handed the symbolic lance of
the Dukes of Normandy he turned to make some jocular re-
mark to his attendant courtiers and let the weapon fall to the
ground.

With the accession of John there emerges plainly in the
northern French provinces a sense of unity with one another
and with the kingdom of France; at the same time on this
side of the Channel the English baronage became ever more
inclined to insular and even nationalistic ideas. Ties with the
Continent were weakening through the gradual division of
honours and appanages in England and Normandy between
different branches of Anglo-Norman families. Moreover, the

[1] *Taine.*

growing brilliance of the French Court and royal power in the late twelfth century was a powerful magnet which drew Continental loyalties to Paris. King John found himself compelled to fight at even greater odds than his predecessors for his possessions on the Continent. He was also opposed by an increasing resistance to taxation for that purpose in England. In his coronation sermon the Archbishop is said to have mentioned that the English monarchy was in essence elective rather than hereditary. If, as was generally held, continuity with Edward the Confessor and the Anglo-Saxon kings was to be respected, many good precedents, Alfred the Great among them, could be cited for the doctrine. If the Archbishop preached in this sense there is no doubt he did so with John's full consent. But the principle of picking and choosing among the royal personages by no means weakened the claims of Arthur in regions where his sovereignty was desired.

From the first John feared Arthur. He had been in Brittany and at Arthur's Court when the news of Richard's death reached him. He had made good haste out of so dangerous an area. Arthur was received at Le Mans with enthusiasm. He did homage to Philip for Anjou, Maine, and Touraine. John's strength lay only in Aquitaine and in Normandy. The war and negotiations continued in the fitful style of the preceding reign, but without the prestige of Cœur de Lion on the side of the English Crown. In 1202 Philip, as John's overlord in respect of certain territories, issued a summons in due form citing John before his Court to answer charges made against him by the barons of Poitou. John replied that he was not amenable to such a process. Philip answered that he was summoned as Count of Poitou. John declared that the King of England could not submit himself to such a trial. Philip rejoined that the King of France could not lose his rights over a vassal because that vassal happened to acquire another dignity. All legal expedients being exhausted, John, who was not even promised safe-conduct for his return, refused to attend the Court, and was accordingly sentenced to be deprived of all the lands which he held in France because of his failure of service to his overlord. Thus armed with a legal right recognised by the jurists of the period, Philip invaded Normandy in the summer of 1202, capturing many towns with practically no resistance. The French king knighted Arthur, invested him with all the fiefs of which John had been deprived, except Normandy and Guienne, and betrothed him to his daughter Mary. Arthur was now sixteen.

When we reflect that the French provinces counted just as much with the Plantagenet kings as the whole realm of England it is obvious that a more virtuous man than John would be incensed at such treatment, and its consequences. His pent-up feelings roused in him an energy unexpected by his foes.

Arthur, hearing that his grandmother Eleanor was at the castle of Mirebeau in Poitou with a scanty escort, surrounded the castle, stormed the outworks, and was about to gain custody of this important and hostile old Queen. Eleanor contrived in the nick of time to send word to John, who was at Le Mans. Her son with ample forces covered the eighty miles between them in forty-eight hours, surprised Arthur and the besiegers at daybreak, and, as he declared, "by the favour of God" got the lot. Arthur and all who stood with him, Hugh Lusignan and a cluster of barons who had revolted, two hundred knights or more, fell at a stroke into John's power, and his mother was delivered from her dangerous plight.

Arthur was imprisoned at Falaise and then at Rouen. No one doubted that he lay in mortal peril. All those barons of Brittany who were still loyal to John asked that the Prince should be released, and on John's refusal went into immediate rebellion. John felt that he would never be safe so long as Arthur lived. This was certainly true. The havoc of disunity that was being wrought throughout the French provinces by the French king using Arthur as a pawn might well have weighed with a better man than John. Arthur, caught in open fight besieging his own grandmother, was a prisoner of war. The horrid crime of murder has often been committed for reasons of state upon lesser temptations than now assailed this exceptionally violent king. No one knows what happened to Arthur. An impenetrable veil descends upon the tragedy of Rouen. The officer commanding the fortress, one Hubert de Burgh, of whom more and better hereafter, gave out that upon the King's order he had delivered his prisoner at Easter 1203 to the hands of agents sent by John to castrate him, and that Arthur had died of the shock. This explanation by no means allayed the ill-feeling aroused in Brittany and elsewhere. Hubert then declared that Arthur was still alive, and John stated that he was glad his orders had been disobeyed. However it may be, Arthur was never seen again. That he was murdered by John's orders was not disputed at the time nor afterwards, though the question whether or not he was mutilated or blinded beforehand remains unanswered.

Although high nobles and common people in large numbers

were in those times frequently put to death without trial and for reasons of hate or policy, the murder by a king of an equal confirmed the bad impression which all the world had formed of John. Moreover, the odious crime did not prevent but rather hastened the loss of Normandy.

Arthur had been removed, but John failed to profit by his crime. For Arthur was no more than Philip Augustus's tool, and his disappearance left unchanged the iron purpose of the French king. Against this persistency Richard had roused men's devotion, but John's nature inspired none. Brittany and the central provinces of the Angevin Empire revolted. Philip had come to terms with each province, and at Easter 1203 he made a voyage down the Loire to Saumur. A deep wedge had already been driven between the northern and the southern halves of John's Continental possessions. Having encircled Normandy, Philip prepared to strike at the stronghold of the Angevin power. John, awake to his danger, poured in treasure and supplies to strengthen his defences. The military position was not yet desperate, and if John had not at the end of 1203 after a series of savage but ineffectual raids precipitately quitted Normandy he might, drawing supplies from England, have held the duchy indefinitely. But, as Philip took fortress after fortress in Central Normandy, John's nerve failed, and the Normans, not unwilling to find an excuse for surrender, made English indifference their justification. In March 1204 Richard's "fair child," the frowning Château Gaillard, fell, and the road to Rouen lay open. Three months later the capital itself was taken, and Normandy finally became French.

No English tears need have been shed over this loss. The Angevin Empire at its peak had no real unity. Time and geography lay on the side of the French. The separation proved as much in the interest of England as of France. It rid the Island of a dangerous, costly distraction and entanglement, turned its thought and energies to its own affairs, and above all left a ruling class of alien origin with no interest henceforth that was not English or at least insular. These consolations did not however dawn on John's contemporaries, who saw only disastrous and humiliating defeat, and blamed a King already distrusted by the people and at variance with the nobility.

* * *

The very success of Henry II in re-establishing order and creating an efficient central administration had left new difficulties for those who came after him. Henry II had created an instrument so powerful that it needed careful handling. He had restored order only at the cost of offending privilege. His fiscal arrangements were original, and drastic in their thoroughness. His work had infringed feudal custom at many points. All this had been accepted because of the King's tactful management and in the reaction from anarchy. Richard I, again, had left England in the hands of able administrators, and the odium of their strict government and financial ingenuity fell on them directly, and stopped short of the King, radiant in the halo of a Crusader and fortunate in his absence. John was at hand to bear the brunt in person.

John, like William Rufus, pressed to logical limits the tendencies of his father's system. There were arrears in the payment of scutage from Richard's reign, and more money was needed to fight the French King, Philip Augustus. But a division had opened in the baronage. The English barons of John's reign had become distinct from his Norman feudatories and not many families now held lands on both sides of the Channel. Even King Richard had met with refusals from his English nobles to fight abroad. Disputes about foreign service and payment of scutage lay at the root of the baronial agitation. By systematic abuse of his feudal prerogatives John drove the baronage to violent resistance. English society was steadily developing. Class interests had assumed sharper definition. Many barons regarded attendance or suit at Court as an opportunity for exerting influence rather than for rendering dutiful service. The sense of Church unity grew among the clergy, and corporate feeling in the municipalities. All these classes were needed by the new centralised Government; but John preferred to emphasise the more ruthless aspects of the royal power.

The year 1205 brought a crisis. The loss of Normandy was followed by the death of John's mother, Eleanor, to whose influence he had owed much of his position on the mainland. The death of Hubert Walter, who for the last ten years had controlled the whole machinery of administration, deprived him of the only statesman whose advice he respected and whose authority stood between the Crown and the nation. It also reopened the thorny question of who should elect the Archbishop of Canterbury.

The Papal throne at this time was occupied by Innocent III, one of the greatest of the medieval Popes, renowned for his statecraft and diplomacy, and intent on raising to its height the temporal power of the Church. The dispute between John and the monastery of Canterbury over the election to the Archbishopric offered Innocent the very chance he sought for asserting Papal authority in England. Setting aside the candidates both of the Crown and of the Canterbury clergy, he caused Stephen Langton to be selected with great pomp and solemnity at Rome in December 1206. King John, confident of sufficient influence in the Papal Court to secure the election of his own candidate, had imprudently acknowledged the validity of the Papal decision beforehand. It was with pardonable anger that he learned how neatly Innocent had introduced a third and successful candidate, whose qualifications were unimpeachable. Stephen Langton was an English cardinal of the highest character, and one of the most famous doctors of the Paris schools. In his wrath, and without measuring the strength of his opponents, the King proceeded to levy a bloodless war upon the Church. Innocent III and Stephen Langton were not men to be browbeaten into surrender, and they possessed in an age of faith more powerful weapons than any secular monarch. When John began to persecute the clergy and seize Church lands the Pope retaliated by laying all England under an interdict. For more than six years the bells were silent, the doors of the churches were closed against the devout; the dead must be buried in unconsecrated ground and without the last communion. Many of John's subjects were assured of damnation for themselves or their loved ones on this account alone.

When John hardened his heart to the interdict and redoubled the attacks upon Church property, the Pope, in 1209, took the supreme step of excommunication. The King's subjects were thereby absolved from their allegiance; his enemies received the blessing of the Church and were sanctified as Crusaders. But John was stubborn and unabashed. Interdict and excommunication brought no ghostly terrors to his soul. Indeed they aggravated the violence of his measures to a point which his contemporaries could only attribute to insanity. The royal administration, never more efficient, found little difficulty in coping with the fiscal and legal problems presented to it or in maintaining order. The interdict, if a menace, was also an opportunity for which John's plans were well matured. The ecclesiastical property of clerics who fled abroad was seized as forfeit by the Crown; and as more and more bishoprics and abbeys fell vacant their revenues were exploited by royal custodians. Thus the Exchequer overflowed with the spoils. But for the combination of the Church quarrel with stresses of mundane politics, the Crown might have established a position not reached till the days of Henry VIII.

After the loss of Normandy John had embarked upon a series of grandiose schemes for a Continental alliance against Philip Augustus. He found allies in the Emperor Otto IV and the Counts of Toulouse and Flanders; but his breach with the Church hastened a far more formidable league between the King of France and the Papacy, and in 1213 he had to choose between submission and a French invasion, backed by all the military and spiritual resources which Innocent III could set in motion. The King's insecurity at home forced him to bow to the threat, and Innocent rejoiced in victory upon his own terms.

John however was not at the end of his devices, and by a stroke of cunning choice enough to be called political genius he turned defeat into something very like triumph. If he could not prevail he would submit; if he submitted he would repent; if he repented there must be no limits to his contrition. At all costs he must break the closing circle of his foes. He spread before Innocent III the lure of temporal sovereignty which he knew that the Pontiff could never resist. He offered to make England a fief of the Papacy, and to do homage to the Pope as his feudal lord. Innocent leapt at this addition to his worldly dignities. He forgave the penitent King; he took him and the realm of England under his especial protection. He accepted the sovereignty of England from the hands of John, and returned it to him as his vassal with his blessing.

This turned the tables upon John's secular enemies. He was now the darling of the Church. Philip Augustus, who at heavy expense had gathered his armies to invade England as a Crusader for his own purposes, thought himself ill-used by the sudden tergiversation of his spiritual ally. He was indignant, and not at all inclined to relinquish the prey he had so long held in view. The barons also found meagre comfort in this transformation. Their grievances remained unredressed, their anger unappeased. Even in the English Church there was a keen division. The English Episcopacy saw themselves now carried into a subjection to Rome far beyond what their piety or interests required, and utterly at variance with the tradition in which they had been reared. Obedience to the Supreme Pontiff was a sacred duty, but it could be carried into excessive interpretations. Stephen Langton himself, the Pope's elect, was as good an Englishman as he was a Churchman. He foresaw the unbridled exploitation by Rome of the patronage of the

English Church and the wholesale engrossment of its benefices by Italian nominees. He became almost immediately an opposing force to the Pope. King John, who had lain at Dover, quaking but calculating, may have laughed while he pulled all these strings and threw his enemies into confusion.

Both John and Innocent persevered in their new partnership, and the disaffected barons drew together under the leadership of Stephen Langton. The war with the French king was continued, and John's demands in money and service kept the barons' anger hot. In 1214 an English expedition which John had led to Poitou failed. In Northern France the army led by his nephew, Otto of Saxony, and by the Earl of Salisbury, was defeated by King Philip at Bouvines. This battle destroyed in a day the whole Continental combination on which John's hopes had been based. Here again was the opportunity of the King's domestic enemies. They formed plans to restrain the rule of a despotic and defeated King, and openly threatened revolt unless their terms were accepted. Left to themselves, they might have ruined their cause by rancorous opposition and selfish demands, but Archbishop Langton, anxious for a just peace, exercised a moderating influence upon them. Nor could John, as a Papal vassal, openly disregard Langton's advice.

But John had still one final resource. Encouraged by the Pope, he took the vows of a Crusader and invoked sentence of excommunication upon his opponents. This was not denied him. The conditions of 1213 were now entirely reversed. The barons, who had thought to be Crusaders against an excommunicated King, were now under the ban themselves. But this agile use of the Papal thunders had robbed them of some of their virtues as a deterrent. The barons, encouraged by the King's defeat abroad, persisted in their demands in spite of the Papal Bull. A great party in the Church stood with them. In vain did John manœuvre, by the offer to grant freedom of election to the Church, to separate the clergy from the barons. Armed revolt seemed the only solution. Although in the final scene of the struggle the Archbishop showed himself unwilling to go to the extreme of civil war, it was he who persuaded the barons to base their demands upon respect for ancient custom and law, and who gave them some principle to fight for besides their own class interests. After forty years' experience of the administrative system established by Henry II the men who now confronted John had advanced beyond the magnates of King Stephen's time. They had learned to think intelligently and constructively. In place of the King's arbitrary despotism they proposed, not the withering anarchy of feudal separatism, but a system of checks and balances which would accord the monarchy its necessary strength, but would prevent its perversion by a tyrant or a fool. The leaders of the barons in 1215 groped in the dim light towards a fundamental principle. Government must henceforward mean something more than the arbitrary rule of any man, and custom and the law must stand even above the King. It was this idea, perhaps only half understood, that gave unity and force to the barons' opposition and made the Charter which they now demanded imperishable.

On a Monday morning in June, between Staines and Windsor, the barons and Churchmen began to collect on the great meadow at Runnymede. An uneasy hush fell on them from time to time. Many had failed to keep their tryst; and the bold few who had come knew that the King would never forgive this humiliation. He would hunt them down when he could, and the laymen at least were staking their lives in the cause they served. They had arranged a little throne for the King and a tent. The handful of resolute men had drawn up, it seems, a short document on parchment. Their retainers and the groups and squadrons of horsemen in sullen steel kept at some distance and well in the background. For was not armed rebellion against the Crown the supreme feudal crime? Then events followed rapidly. A small cavalcade appeared from the direction of Windsor. Gradually men made out the faces of the King, the Papal Legate, the Archbishop of Canterbury, and several bishops. They dismounted without ceremony. Someone, probably the Archbishop, stated briefly the terms that were suggested. The King declared at once that he agreed. He said the details should be arranged immediately in his chancery. The original "Articles of the Barons" on which Magna Carta is based exist to-day in the British Museum. They were sealed in a quiet, short scene, which has become one of the most famous in our history, on June 15, 1215. Afterwards the King returned to Windsor. Four days later, probably, the Charter itself was probably engrossed. In future ages it was to be used as the foundation of principles and systems of government of which neither King John nor his nobles dreamed.

* * *

At the beginning of the year 1216 there had seemed to be every chance that John would still defeat the baronial opposition and wipe out the humiliation of Runnymede. Yet before the summer was out the King was dead, and the Charter survived the denunciation of the Pope and the arbitrament of war. In the next hundred years it was reissued thirty-eight times, at first with a few substantial alterations, but retaining its original characteristics. Little more was heard of the Charter until the seventeenth century. After more than two hundred years a Parliamentary Opposition struggling to check the encroachments of the Stuarts upon the liberty of the subject rediscovered it and made of it a rallying cry against oppression. Thus was created the glorious legend of the "Charter of an Englishman's liberties."

If we set aside the rhetorical praise which has been so freely lavished upon the Charter, and study the document itself, we may find it rather surprising reading. It is in a form resembling a legal contract, and consists of sixty-one clauses, each dealing either with the details of feudal administration and custom or with elaborate provisions for securing the enforcement of the promises which it embodies. It is entirely lacking in any spacious statement of the principles of democratic government or the rights of man. It is not a declaration of constitutional doctrine, but a practical document to remedy current abuses in the feudal system. In the forefront stand the questions of scutage, of feudal reliefs and of wardship. The word "freeman" was a technical feudal term, and it is doubtful whether it included even the richer merchants, far less the bondmen or humbler classes who make up the bulk of a nation. It implies on the King's part a promise of good government for the future, but the terms of the promise are restricted to the observance of the customary privileges and interests of the baronial class. The barons on their part were compelled to make some provision for their tenants, the limits forced on John being vaguely applied to the tenants-in-chief as well; but they did as little as they safely and decently could. The villeins, in so far as they were protected, received such solicitous attention as befitted valuable chattels attached to the manor and not as free citizens of the realm.

The thirteenth century was to be a great age of Parliamentary development and experiment, yet there is no mention in Magna Carta of Parliament or representation of any but the baronial class. The great watchwords of the future here find no place. The actual Charter is a redress of feudal grievances extorted from an unwilling king by a discontented ruling class insisting on its privileges, and it ignored some of the most important matters which the King and baronage had to settle, such as the terms of military service.

Magna Carta must not however be dismissed lightly, in the words of a modern writer, as "a monument of class selfishness." Even in its own day men of all ranks above the status of villeins had an interest in securing that the tenure of land should be secure from arbitrary encroachment. Moreover, the greatest magnate might hold, and often did hold, besides his estate in chief, parcels of land under the most diverse tenures, by knight service, by the privileges of "socage," or as a tenant at will. Therefore in securing themselves the barons of Runnymede were in fact establishing the rights of the whole landed class, great and small—the simple knight with two hundred acres, the farmer or small yeoman with sixty. And there is evidence that their action was so understood throughout the country. In 1218 an official endeavoured to upset by writ a judgment given in the county court of Lincolnshire. The victim was a great landowner, but the whole county rallied to his cause and to the "liberty sworn and granted," stating in their protest that they acted "with him, and for him, and for ourselves, and the community of the whole realm."

If the thirteenth-century magnates understood little and cared less for popular liberties or Parliamentary democracy, they had all the same laid hold of a principle which was to be of prime importance for the future development of English society and English institutions. Throughout the document it is implied that here is a law which is above the King and which even he must not break. This reaffirmation of a supreme law and its expression in a general charter is the great work of Magna Carta; and this alone justifies the respect in which men have held it. The reign of Henry II, according to the most respected authorities, initiates the rule of law. But the work as yet was incomplete: the Crown was still above the law; the legal system which Henry had created could become, as John showed, an instrument of oppression.

Now for the first time the King himself is bound by the law. The root principle was destined to survive across the generations and rise paramount long after the feudal background of 1215 had faded in the past. The Charter became in the process of time an enduring witness that the power of the Crown was not absolute.

The facts embodied in it and the circumstances giving rise to them were buried or misunderstood. The underlying idea of the sovereignty of law, long existent in feudal custom, was raised by it into a doctrine for the national State. And when in subsequent ages the State, swollen with its own authority, has attempted to ride roughshod over the rights or liberties of the subject it is to this doctrine that appeal has again and again been made, and never, as yet, without success.

BOOK TWO · CHAPTER SIXTEEN

On the Anvil

KING JOHN died in the toils; but he died at bay. The misgovernment of his reign had brought against him what seemed to be an overwhelming combination. He was at war with the English barons who had forced him to grant the Charter. They had invited Louis, son of the implacable Philip, King of France, into the country to be their liege lord, and with him came foreign troops and hardy adventurers. The insurgent barons north of the Humber had the support of Alexander, King of Scots; in the West the rebellion was sustained by Llewellyn, the powerful Prince of North Wales. The towns were mainly against the King; London was vehemently hostile. The Cinque Ports were in enemy hands. Winchester, Worcester, and Carlisle, separated by the great distances of those times, were united in opposition to the Crown.

On the other hand, the recreant King had sacrificed the status of the realm to purchase the unswerving aid of the Papacy. A strong body of mercenaries, the only regular troops in the kingdom, were in John's pay. Some of the greatest warrior-nobles, the venerable William the Marshal, and the famous, romantic Ranulf, Earl of Chester, with a strong following of the aristocracy, adhered to his cause. The mass of the people, bewildered by this new quarrel of their masters, on the whole inclined to the King against the barons, and certainly against the invading foreigners. Their part was only to suffer at the hands of both sides. Thus the forces were evenly balanced; everything threatened a long, stubborn civil war and a return to the anarchy of Stephen and Maud. John himself, after a lifetime of subtleties and double-dealing, of illegal devices and sharp, unexpected twists of religious policy, showed himself possessed, in the last months of his life, of a warlike energy and resource which astonished friend and foe. It was at this moment that he died of dysentery, aggravated by fatigue and too much food and drink. Shakespeare has limned his final agony:

> And none of you will bid the winter come
> To thrust his icy fingers in my maw. . . .
> I beg cold comfort, and you are so strait
> And so ungrateful, you deny me that.

The death of the King in this convulsion of strife changed the conditions of the conflict without ending it. The rival interests and factions that were afoot had many purposes beyond the better government of England. Louis was in the Island, and fighting. Many had plighted him their faith, already once forsworn. The rebel lords were deeply involved with their Scottish and Welsh allies; none was in the humour for peace. Yet the sole reason and justification for revolt died with John. Henry, a child of nine, was the undoubted heir to all the rights and loyalties of his grandfather's wide empire. He was the rightful King of England. Upon what grounds could the oppressions of the father be visited upon his innocent son? A page of history had been violently turned; the new parchment was blank and clear. All parties were profoundly sensible of these considerations. Nevertheless John for the moment was missed by those whose lives and fortunes were devoted to the national cause. William the Marshal acted with honesty and decision. Had he failed in his duty to the Crown the strong centralised monarchy which Henry II had created, and upon which the growing civilisation of the realm depended, might have degenerated into a heptarchy of feudal princes, or even worse. The Papal Legate, sure of the unchanging policy of Rome, aided William the Marshal. The boy King was crowned at Gloucester and began his reign of fifty-six years on October 28, 1216. He was anointed by the Legate, and in default of the diadem which John had lost in crossing the Wash a plain gold circlet was placed upon his brow. This was to prove no inadequate symbol of his rule.

William the Marshal, aged seventy, reluctantly undertook what we should now call the Regency. He joined to himself the Earl of Chester, who might well have been his rival but did not press his claims, and Hubert de Burgh, John's faithful servant. The wisdom and the weakness of the new Government were alike revealed in the reissue of the Charter, which had been too rashly quashed by the Pope in 1215. The religious character of the King's party had become predominant. The Royalists wore white crosses, the Church preached a virtual Crusade, and the chiefs of the opposing faction were excommunicated. "At a time," said Henry in after-years to Bishop Grosseteste, "when we were orphan and minor, when our subjects were not only alienated from us, but were organised against us, it was our mother, the Roman Church, which brought this realm once more under our authority, which consecrated us King, crowned us and placed us on the throne."

It was a reign of turmoil and distress and yet the forces of progress moved doggedly forward. Redhot iron was smitten on the anvil, and the hammer-blows forged a metal more tense than had yet been seen. In this period the common people, with their Anglo-Saxon tradition of ancient rights and law running back to remote antiquity, lay suffering under the armoured feet of the nobility and of the royal mercenaries, reinforced in the main by the power of the Church. But the people's masters were disunited; not only did their jealousies and ambitions and their taste for war keep them at variance, but several rending fissures were opening among them. They were divided into parties; they were cross-cut obliquely by a strong nationalism. It is an age of impulse and experiment, not controlled by any general political theory.

* * *

The confusion and monotony of the barons' warfare, against each other, or against the King, sometimes with the Church, more often against the Church, have repelled many readers of history. But the fact is that King Henry III survived all his troubles and left England enjoying a prosperity and peace unknown when he was a child. The cruel war and anarchy lay only upon the surface; underneath, unformulated and largely unrealised by the hard-pressed actors, coursed all the tides which were to flow in Europe five hundred years later; and almost all the capital decisions which are demanded of the modern world were rife in this medieval society. From out of the conflict there rise the figures of heroes, both warriors and statesmen, from whose tribulations we are separated by long ages, but whose work and outlook unite them to us, as if we read their acts and words in the morning newspaper.

We must examine some of these figures at close quarters.

Stephen Langton, the great Archbishop, was the indomitable,
unwearying, builder of the rights of Englishmen against royal,
baronial, and even ecclesiastical pretensions. He stood against
King John; he stood against the Pope. Both cast upon him at
times their utmost displeasure, short of taking his life. Here is
a man who worked for the unity of Christendom through the
Catholic Church; but also for the interests of England against
the Papacy. Here is a faithful servant of the Crown, but at
the same time a champion of the Charter, and all it meant, and
still means. A commanding central figure, practical, resource-
ful, shifting from side to side as evils forced him, but quite
unchanging and unchangeable in his broad, wise, brave, work-
aday, liberal purpose. Here was, if not an architect of our
Constitution, at least a punctual and unfailing Clerk of the
Works.

The second personality which emerges from the restless
scene is Hubert de Burgh. Shakespeare, whose magic finger
touches in succession most of the peaks of English history and
lights them with the sunrise so that all can see them standing
out above the mountainous disorder, has brought Hubert to
our ken. Here is a soldier and a politician, armed with the
practical wisdom which familiarity with courts and camps,
with high authorities, ecclesiastical and armoured, may infuse
into a man's conduct, and even nature. John's Justiciar, identified with the crimes and the follies of the reign, was yet
known to all men as their constant resolute opponent. Under
the Marshal, who was himself a star of European chivalry,
Hubert was an outstanding leader of resistance to the rebellion against the monarchy. At the same time, above the warring factions, he was a solid champion of the rights of England.
The Island should not be ravaged by greedy nobles, nor pillaged by foreign adventurers, nor mutilated unduly even for
the high interests of the Papacy, which so often were the interests of Christendom itself.

The rebellion of the barons was quelled by fights on land
and sea. At Lincoln the King's party had gained a fantastic
but none the less decisive victory. In the streets of Lincoln,
during a whole day, we are told that four hundred royal
knights jostled and belaboured six hundred of the baronial
party. Only three were killed in the combat. Contemporary
opinion declined to accord the name of battle to this brawl.
It was called "the Fair of Lincoln." It is difficult to form a
picture of what happened. One must suppose that the knights
had upon the average at least eight or ten stalwart retainers

each, and that the almost invulnerable, chain-mailed monsters waddled about in the throng, chasing away or cutting down the unarmoured folk, and welting each other when they met, hard, but perhaps not too hard. On this basis there were intricate manœuvres and stratagems, turnings of flanks, takings in rear, entry through privy ports by local treachery, odd confrontations; all kinds of devices. But in the upshot the Royalists outwitted and out-walloped the insurgents. Accidents will happen in the best regulated faction fights, and one of the leading rebel barons, Thomas, Count of Perche, had the misfortune to be killed by a sword-thrust which penetrated his visor and sank deep into his brain. But for almost all the rest of the armoured crew it was a joyous adventure. The vengeance of the victors was wreaked mainly upon their rivals' retainers and upon the civil population, who were plundered and slaughtered on a considerable scale.

"The Fair of Lincoln" gave the infant Henry III a victory on land, and de Burgh's sea-victory off Dover against French reinforcements for Louis cut the revolt from its Continental root. Negotiations proceeded continually amid the broils. They were strenuously disputed, and meanwhile each side devastated the estates of the opposing party, to the intense misery of their inhabitants. Hubert, supported by Archbishop Langton and the Papal Legate, never lost his hold upon the Charter, although this was the nominal bond of union of their opponents. There were unavoidable stresses between the devout English Royalists and the interests of the universal Church, as interpreted by the Pope. These stresses did not however take a physical form. Compromises were reached, not only between Crown and barons, but in the ecclesiastical sphere, between England and Rome.

After a year of fighting, Louis of France was compelled to leave the country in 1217, his hopes utterly dashed. The Great Charter was now re-issued for the second time in order to show that the Government meant its word. In 1219 the old victorious Marshal died, and Hubert ruled the land for twelve years. He was a stern ruler. When Fawkes de Breauté, who had been the chief mercenary of John and William the Marshal during all these recent tumults, grew overmighty and attempted to disturb the new-found peace of the land, Hubert determined to expel him. On taking Fawkes's stronghold of Bedford Castle in 1224, after two months' siege, Hubert hanged in front of its walls the twenty-four surviving knights who had commanded the garrison. In the following year, as a sign of pacification, the Great Charter was again re-issued in what was substantially its final form. Thus it became an unchallenged part of English law and tradition. But for the turbulent years of Henry III's minority, it might have mouldered in the archives of history as a merely partisan document.

No long administration is immune from mistakes and every statesman must from time to time make concessions to wrongheaded superior powers. But Hubert throughout his tenure stood for the policy of doing the least possible to recover the King's French domains. This he carried out not only by counsel, but by paralysing action, and by organising ignominious flight before the enemy when battle seemed otherwise unavoidable. He hampered the preparation for fresh war; he stood firm against the incursions of foreign favourites and adventurers. He resisted the Papacy in its efforts to draw money at all costs out of England for its large European schemes. He maintained order, and as the King grew up he restrained the Court party which was forming about him from making inroads upon the Charter. His was entirely the English point of view.

At last in 1229 he had exhausted his goodwill and fortune and fate was upon him. The King, now twenty-two years of age, crowned and acting, arrived at Portsmouth with a large army raised by the utmost exercise of his feudal power to defend those estates in France which after the loss of Normandy still pertained to the English Crown. Hubert could not control this, but the transporting of the expedition lay apparently in his department. The King found no ships, or few, awaiting him; no supplies, no money, for his oversea venture. He flew into a rage. Although usually mild, affable, scholarly and artistic, he drew his sword and rushed upon the Justiciar, reproaching him with having betrayed his trust and being bribed by France. It certainly was a very unpleasant and awkward situation, the Army wishing to fight abroad, and the Navy and the Treasury unable or unwilling to carry them thither. The quarrel was smoothed down; the King recovered his temper; the expedition sailed in the following year and Hubert retained his place. But not for long. In 1232 he was driven from power by a small palace clique. Threatened in his life, he took sanctuary at Brentwood. He was dragged from this asylum, but the common, humble blacksmith who was ordered to put the fetters on him declared he would die any death rather than do so; and he is said to have used the words which historians have deemed to be the true monument of

Hubert de Burgh: "Is he not that most faithful Hubert who so often saved England from the devastation of foreigners and restored England to England?"

* * *

During John's reign one of the most cruel tragedies of world history had run its course in Southern France. In the domains of Raymond VI, Count of Toulouse, there had grown up during several generations a heresy, sombre and austere in theory, but genial in practice. The Albigenses, or Cathares, "the Purified," as they were called, dismissed altogether from the human mind the resurrection of the body, Purgatory, and Hell. In their view life on earth in the flesh was the work of Satan. The material phase would soon pass and the soul, freed from its accursed encumbrance, would be resumed in eternal bliss into the Godhead. The "Perfects" of this cult practised chastity and abstinence, and professed in principle a sincere wish for death; but the mass of the population, relieved from the oppression of supernatural terror, developed, we are assured, in the delicious climate of those regions, easy morals and merry character. The thrilling sensation of being raised above the vicissitudes of this world and at the same time freed from the menaces of the next produced a great happiness in these regions, in which all classes joined, and from it sprang culture of manners and fervour of conviction.

This casting off of all spiritual chains was, naturally, unwelcome to the Papacy. The whole moral scheme of the Western world was based, albeit precariously, upon Original Sin, Redemption by Grace, and a Hell of infinite torment and duration, which could only be avoided through the ministrations of the clergy. It was some time before the Papacy realised the deadliness and the magnitude of the novel sin which was spreading in what we now call Southern France. Once the gravity of the challenge was understood it superseded even the rescue of the Holy Sepulchre from the infidel. In 1209 a Crusade for a different purpose was set on foot, and all temporal forces at the disposal of Rome were directed upon the Albigenses, under the leadership of Philip of France. At this time the burning of heretics and other undesirables, which had been practised sporadically in France, received the formal sanction of law. The process of blotting out the new heresy by the most atrocious cruelties which the human mind can conceive occupied nearly a generation. The heretics, led by the "Perfects," fought like tigers, regarding death as a final release from the curse of the body. But the work was thoroughly done. The Albigensian heresy was burned out at the stake. Only poor, hungry folk in the forests and mountains, which happily abound in these parts, still harboured those doubts about approaching damnation upon which so much of the discipline and responsibility of human beings and the authority and upkeep of the Church depended.

Of all the leaders in this Crusade none surpassed a certain Simon de Montfort, "a minor lord of the Paris region." He rose to commanding control in this war, and was acclaimed the effective leader. He was made Viscount of Béziers and Carcassonne "at the instance of the barons of God's army, the legates and the priests present." This capable, merciless man accomplished the bloody task, and when he fell at the siege of Toulouse he left behind him a son who bore his name, succeeded to his high station among the nobility of the age, and became associated with an idea which has made him for ever famous.

* * *

De Burgh's conduct had been far from blameless, but his fall had been deliberately engineered by men whose object was not to reform administration but to gain power. The leader of this intrigue was his former rival Peter des Roches, the Bishop of Winchester. Des Roches himself kept in the background, but at the Christmas Council of 1232 nearly every post of consequence in the administration was conferred upon his friends, most of them, like him, Poitevins. More was involved in the defeat of de Burgh than the triumph of des Roches and his party. De Burgh was the last of the great Justiciars who had wielded plenary and at times almost sovereign power. Henceforward the Household offices like the Wardrobe, largely dependent upon the royal will and favour, began to overshadow the great "national" offices, like the Justiciarship, filled by the baronial magnates. As they came to be occupied increasingly by foreign intruders, Poitevins, Savoyards, Provençals, the national feeling of the baronage became violently hostile. Under the leadership of Richard the Marshal, a second son of the great William, the barons began to growl against the foreigners. Des Roches retorted that the King had need of foreigners to protect him against the treachery of his natural subjects; and large numbers of Poitevin and Breton mercenaries were brought over to sustain this view. But the struggle was short. In alliance with Prince Llewellyn the young Marshal drove the King among the Welsh marches, sacked Shrewsbury, and harried des Roches's lands. In the spring of 1234 Henry was forced to accept terms, and, although the Marshal was killed in April, the new Archbishop, Edmund Rich, insisted on the fulfilment of the treaty. The Poitevin officials were dismissed, des Roches found it convenient to go on a journey to Italy, and de Burgh was honourably restored to his lands and possessions.

The Poitevins were the first of the long succession of foreign favourites whom Henry III gathered round him in the middle years of his reign. Hatred of the aliens, who dominated the King, monopolised the offices, and made scandalous profits out of a country to whose national interests they were completely indifferent, became the theme of baronial opposition. The King's affection was reserved for those who flattered his vanity and ministered to his caprices. He developed a love for extravagant splendour, and naturally preferred to his morose barons the brilliant adventurers of Poitou and Provence. The culture of medieval Provence, the home of the troubadours and the creed of chivalry, fascinated Henry. In 1236 he married Eleanor, the daughter of Raymond of Provence. With Eleanor came her numerous and needy kinsmen, chief among them her four uncles. A new wave of foreigners descended upon the profitable wardships, marriages, escheats, and benefices, which the disgusted baronage regarded as their own. The King delighted to shower gifts upon his charming relations, and the responsibility for all the evils of his reign was laid upon their shoulders. It is the irony of history that not the least unpopular was this same Simon de Montfort, son of the repressor of the Albigenses.

An even more copious source of discontent in England was the influence of the Papacy over the grateful and pious King. Pope Gregory IX, at desperate grips with the Holy Roman Emperor Frederick II, made ever greater demands for money, and his Legate, Otto, took an interest in English Church Reform. Otto's demand in 1240 for one-fifth of the clergy's rents and movables raised a storm. The rectors of Berkshire published a manifesto denying the right of Rome to tax the English Church, and urging that the Pope, like other bishops, should "live of his own." Nevertheless, early in 1241 Otto returned to Rome with a great treasure; and the Pope rewarded the loyalty of the Italian clergy by granting them the next three hundred vacant English benefices. The election of Innocent IV in 1243 led to renewed demands. In that year the

Papal envoy forbade bishops in England to appoint to benefices until the long list of Papal nominees had been exhausted. Robert Grosseteste, scholar, scientist, and saint, a former Master of the Oxford Schools and since 1235 Bishop of Lincoln, led the English clergy in evasion or refusal of Papal demands. He became their champion. Although he still believed that the Pope was absolute, he heralded the attacks which Wyclif was more than a century later to make upon the exactions and corruption of the Roman Court.

The Church, writhing under Papal exaction, and the baronage, offended by Court encroachments, were united in hatred of foreigners. A crisis came in 1244, when a baronial commission was appointed to fix the terms of a money grant to the King. The barons insisted that the Justiciar, Chancellor, and Treasurer, besides certain judges, should be elected by the Great Council, on which they were strongly represented. Four of the King's Council were to be similarly elected, with power to summon the Great Council. The King turned in his distress to the already mulcted Church, but his appeal was rejected through the influence of Grosseteste. In 1247 the voracious Poitevins encouraged the King in despotic ideas of government. To their appetites were now added those of the King's three half-brothers, the Lusignans, the sons of John's Queen, Isabella, by her second marriage. Henry adopted a new tone. "Servants do not judge their master," he said in 1248. "Vassals do not judge their prince or bind him by conditions. They should put themselves at his disposal and be submissive to his will." Such language procured no money; and money was the pinch. Henry was forced to sell plate and jewels and give new privileges or new grants of old rights to those who would buy them. Salaries were unpaid, forced gifts extracted; the forest courts were exploited and extortion condoned. In 1252 the King, on the pretext of a Crusade, demanded a tithe of ecclesiastical rents and property for three years. On Grosseteste's advice the clergy refused this grant, because the King would not on his part confirm Magna Carta. Next year Grosseteste died, indomitable to the last against both Papal and royal exactions.

Meanwhile Henry had secretly accepted greater Continental obligations. The death of the Holy Roman Emperor Frederick in 1250 revived at Rome the old plan of uniting Sicily, over which he had ruled, to the Papal dominions. In 1254 Henry III accepted the Papal offer of the Sicilian Crown for his younger son Edmund. This was a foolish step, and the conditions attached to the gift raised it to the very height of folly. The English King was to provide an army, and he stood surety for a mass of Papal debts amounting to the vast sum in those days of about £90,000. When the King's acceptance of the Papal offer became known a storm of indignation broke over his head. Both the Great Council and the clergy refused financial aid. As if this were not enough, at the Imperial election of 1257 the King's brother, Richard of Cornwall, offered himself as Emperor, and Henry spent lavishly to secure his election. The final stroke was the King's complete failure to check the successes of Llewellyn, who in 1256 had swept the English out of Wales and intrigued to overthrow the English faction in Scotland. Despised, discredited, and frightened, without money or men, the King faced an angered and powerful opposition.

* * *

In the last years of Grosseteste's life he had come to hope great things of his friend, Simon de Montfort. Simon had married the King's sister and had inherited the Earldom of Leicester. He had been governor of the English lands in Gascony for four years. Strong and energetic, he had aroused the jealousy and opposition of the King's favourites; and as a result of their intrigues he had been brought to trial in 1252. The commission acquitted him; but in return for a sum of money from the King he unwillingly agreed to vacate his office. Friendship between him and the King was at an end; on the one side was contempt, on the other suspicion. In this way, from an unexpected quarter, appeared the leader whom the baronial and national opposition had long lacked.

There were many greater notables in England, and his relationship to the King was aspersed by the charge that he had seduced his bride before he married her. None the less there he stood with five resolute sons, an alien leader, who was to become the brain and driving force of the English aristocracy. Behind him gradually ranged themselves most of the great feudal chiefs, the whole strength of London as a corporate entity, all the lower clergy, and the goodwill of the nation. A letter of a Court official, written in July 1258, has been preserved. The King, so it says, had yielded to what he felt was overwhelming pressure. A commission for reform of government was set up; it was agreed that "public offices should only be occupied by the English," and that "the emissaries of Rome and the foreign merchants and bankers should be reduced to their proper station." Grants of land to foreigners, the position of the King's Household, the custody of the fortresses, were all called in question. "The barons," writes our civil servant, "have a great and difficult task which cannot be carried out easily or quickly. They are proceeding . . . *ferociter*. May the results be good!"

BOOK TWO · CHAPTER SEVENTEEN

The Mother of Parliaments

THE later years of Henry III's troubled reign were momentous in their consequences for the growth of English institutions. This may perhaps be called the seed-time of our Parliamentary system, though few participants in the sowing could have foreseen the results that were eventually to be achieved. The commission for reform set about its work seriously, and in 1258 its proposals were embodied in the Provisions of Oxford, supplemented and extended in 1259 by the Provisions of Westminster. This baronial movement represented something deeper than dislike of alien counsellors. For the two sets of Provisions, taken together, represent a considerable shift of interest from the standpoint of Magna Carta. The Great Charter was mainly concerned to define various points of law, whereas the Provisions of Oxford deal with the overriding question of by whose advice and through what officials royal government should be carried on. Many of the clauses of the Provisions of Westminster moreover mark a limitation of baronial rather than of royal jurisdiction. The fruits of Henry II's work were now to be seen; the nation was growing stronger, more self-conscious and self-confident. The notable increase in judicial activity throughout the country, the more frequent visits of the judges and officials—all of them dependent upon local co-operation—educated the country knights in political responsibility and administration. This process, which shaped the future of English institutions, had its first effects in the thirteenth century.

The staple of the barons' demand was that the King in future should govern by a Council of Fifteen, to be elected by four persons, two from the baronial party and two from the

royal. It is significant that the King's proclamation accepting
the arrangement in English as well as French is the first public
document to be issued in both languages since the time of
William the Conqueror. For a spell this Council, animated and
controlled by Simon de Montfort governed the land. They
held each other in proper check, sharing among themselves the
greater executive offices and entrusting the actual administration to "lesser men," as was then widely thought to be desirable. The magnates, once their own class interests were
guarded, and their rights—which up to a certain point were
the rights of the nation—were secure, did not wish to put the
levers of power in the hands of one or two of their number.
This idea of a Cabinet of politicians, chosen from the patrici-
ate, with their highly trained functionaries of no political status
operating under them, had in it a long vitality and many resur-
rections.

It is about this time that the word "Parlement"—Parliament—began to be current. In 1086 William the Conqueror
had "deep speech" with his wise men before launching the
Domesday inquiry. In Latin this would have appeared as *col-
loquium;* and "colloquy" is the common name in the twelfth
century for the consultations between the King and his magnates. The occasional colloquy "on great affairs of the Kingdom" can at this point be called a Parliament. But more often
the word means the permanent Council of officials and judges
which sat at Westminster to receive petitions, redress grievances, and generally regulate the course of the law. By the
thirteenth century Parliament establishes itself as the name of
two quite different, though united, institutions.

If we translate their functions into modern terms we may
say that the first of these assemblies deals with policy, the second with legislation and administration. The debate on the
Address at the beginning of a session is very like a colloquy,
while the proceedings of "Parliament" have their analogue in
the committee stage of a Bill. In the reign of Henry III, and
even of Edward I, it was by no means a foregone conclusion
that the two assemblies would be amalgamated. Rather did it
look as if the English Constitution would develop as did the
French Constitution, with a King in Council as the real Government, with the magnates reduced to a mere nobility, and
"Parlement" only a clearinghouse for legal business. Our history did not take this course. In the first place the magnates
during the century that followed succeeded in mastering the
Council and identifying their interests with it. Secondly, the

English counties had a life of their own, and their representatives at Westminster were to exercise increasing influence. But without the powerful impulse of Simon de Montfort these forces might not have combined to shape a durable legislative assembly.

* * *

The King, the Court party, and the immense foreign interests associated therewith had no intention of submitting indefinitely to the thraldom of the Provisions. Every preparation was made to recover the lost ground. In 1259 the King returned with hopes of foreign aid from Paris, where he had been to sign a treaty of peace with the French. His son Edward was already the rising star of all who wished to see a strong monarchy. Supporters of this cause appeared among the poor and turbulent elements in London and the towns. The enthusiasm of the revolution—for it was nothing less— had not been satisfied by a baronial victory. Ideas were afoot which would not readily be put to sleep. It is the merit of Simon de Montfort that he did not rest content with a victory by the barons over the Crown. He turned at once upon the barons themselves. If the King should be curbed, so also must they in their own spheres show respect for the general interest. Upon these issues the claims of the middle classes, who had played a great part in carrying the barons to supremacy, could not be disregarded. The "apprentice" or bachelor knights, who may be taken as voicing the wishes of the country gentry, formed a virile association of their own entitled "the Community of the Bachelors of England." Simon de Montfort became their champion. Very soon he began to rebuke great lords for abuse of their privileges. He wished to extend to the baronial estates the reforms already undertaken in the royal administration. He addressed himself pointedly to Richard, Earl of Gloucester, who ruled wide estates in the South-West and in South Wales. He procured an ordinance from the Council making it plain that the great lords were under the royal authority, which was again—though this he did not stress—under the Council. Here was dictatorship in a new form. It was a dictatorship of the Commonwealth, but, as so often happens to these bold ideas, it expressed itself inevitably through a man and a leader. These developments split the baronial party from end to end; and the King and his valiant son Edward, striking in with all their own resources upon their divided opponents, felt they might put the matter to the proof.

At Easter in 1261 Henry, freed by the Pope from his oath to accept the Provisions of Oxford and Westminster, deposed the officials and Ministers appointed by the barons. There were now two Governments with conflicting titles, each interfering with the other. The barons summoned the representatives of the shires to meet them at St Albans; the King summoned them to Windsor. Both parties competed for popular support. The barons commanded greater sympathy in the country, and only Gloucester's opposition to de Montfort held them back from sharp action. After the death of Gloucester in July 1262 the baronial party rallied to de Montfort's drastic policy. Civil war broke out, and Simon and his sons, all of whom played vigorous parts, a moiety of barons, the middle class, so far as it had emerged, and powerful allies in Wales together faced in redoubtable array the challenge of the Crown.

Simon de Montfort was a general as well as a politician. Nothing in his upbringing or circumstances would naturally have suggested to him the course he took. It is ungratefully asserted that he had no real conception of the ultimate meaning of his actions. Certainly he builded better than he knew. By September 1263 a reaction against him had become visible: he had succeeded only too well. Edward played upon the discontent among the barons, appealed to their feudal and selfish interest, fomented their jealousy of de Montfort, and so built up a strong royalist party. At the end of the year de Montfort had to agree to arbitration by Louis IX, the French king. The decision went against him. Loyal to his monarchial rank, the King of France defended the prerogative of the King of England and declared the Provisions to be illegal. As Louis was accepted as a saint in his own lifetime this was serious. Already however the rival parties had taken up arms. In the civil war that followed the feudal party more or less supported the King. The people, especially the towns, and the party of ecclesiastical reform, especially the Franciscans, rallied to de Montfort. New controls were improvised in many towns to defeat the royalist sympathies of the municipal oligarchies. In the summer of 1264 de Montfort once again came South to relieve the pressure which Henry and Edward were exerting on the Cinque Ports.

The King and Prince Edward met him in Sussex with a superior power. At Lewes a fierce battle was fought. In some ways it was a forerunner of Edgehill. Edward, like Rupert four hundred years later, conquered all before him, pursued incontinently, and returned to the battlefield only to find that all was lost. Simon had, with much craft and experience of war, laid a trap to which the peculiar conditions of the ground lent themselves, whereby when his centre had been pierced his two wings of armoured cavalry fell upon the royal main body from both flanks and crushed all resistance. He was accustomed at this time owing to a fall from his horse to be carried with the army in a sumptuous and brightly decorated litter, like the coach of an eighteenth-century general. In this he placed two or three hostages for their greater security, and set it among the Welsh in the centre, together with many banners and emblems suggesting his presence. Prince Edward, in his charge, captured this trophy, and killed the unlucky hostages from his own party who were found therein. But meanwhile the King and all his Court and principal supporters were taken prisoners by de Montfort, and the energetic prince returned only to share their plight.

Simon de Montfort was now in every respect master of England, and if he had proceeded in the brutal manner of modern times in several European countries by the wholesale slaughter of all who were in his power he might long have remained so. In those days however, for all their cruelty in individual cases, nothing was pushed to the last extreme. The influences that counted with men in contest for power at the peril of their lives were by no means only brutal. Force, though potent, was not sovereign. Simon made a treaty with the captive King and the beaten party, whereby the rights of the Crown were in theory respected, though in practice the King and his son were to be subjected to strict controls. The general balance of the realm was preserved, and it is clear from Simon's action not only that he felt the power of the opposing forces, but that he aimed at their ultimate unification. He saw himself, with the King in his hands, able to use the authority of the Crown to control the baronage and create the far broader and better political system which, whether he aimed at it or not, must have automatically followed from his success. Thus he ruled the land, with the feeble King and the proud Prince Edward prisoners in his hands. This opens the third and final stage in his career.

* * *

All the barons, whatever party they had chosen, saw themselves confronted with an even greater menace than that from which they had used Simon to deliver them. The combination of Simon's genius and energy with the inherent powers of a

Plantagenet monarchy and the support of the middle classes, already so truculent, was a menace to their class privileges far more intimate and searching than the misgovernment of John or the foreign encumbrances of Henry III. Throughout these struggles of lasting significance the English barony never deviated from their own self-interest. At Runnymede they had served national freedom when they thought they were defending their own privilege. They had now no doubt that Simon was its enemy. He was certainly a despot, with a king in his wallet and the forces of social revolution at his back. The barons formed a hard confederacy among themselves, and with all the forces of the Court not in Simon's hands schemed night and day to overthrow him.

For the moment de Montfort was content that the necessary steps should be taken by a council of nine who controlled expenditure and appointed officials. Any long-term settlement could be left until the Parliament which he had summoned for 1265. The Earl's autocratic position was not popular, yet the country was in such a state of confusion that circumstances seemed to justify it. In the North and along the Welsh Marches the opposition was still strong and reckless; in France the Queen and the earls Hugh Bigod and Warenne intrigued for support; the Papacy backed the King. De Montfort kept command of the Narrow Seas by raising a fleet in the Cinque Ports and openly encouraging privateering. In the West however he lost the support of Gilbert de Clare, Earl of Gloucester and the son of his former rival Richard de Clare. Without openly joining the royalists Clare conspired with them and revived his father's quarrel with de Montfort. Summoned to the Parliament of 1265, he replied by accusing the Earl of appropriating for himself and his sons the revenues of the Crown and the confiscated property of the opposition nobles. There was some truth in these accusations, but Clare's main objection appears to have been that he did not share the spoils.

In January 1265 a Parliament met in London to which Simon summoned representatives both from the shires and from the towns. Its purpose was to give an appearance of legality to the revolutionary settlement, and this, under the guidance of de Montfort, it proceeded to do. Its importance lay however more in its character as a representative assembly than in its work. The constitutional significance which was once attached to it as the first representative Parliament in our history is somewhat discounted by modern opinion. The practical reason for summoning the strong popular element was de Montfort's desire to weight the Parliament with his own supporters: among the magnates only five earls and eighteen barons received writs of summons. Again he fell back upon the support of the country gentry and the burgesses against the hostility or indifference of the magnates. In this lay his message and his tactics.

The Parliament dutifully approved of de Montfort's actions and accepted his settlement embodied in the Provisions. But Clare's withdrawal to the West could only mean the renewal of war. King Henry III abode docilely in Simon's control, and was treated all the time with profound personal respect. Prince Edward enjoyed a liberty which could only have been founded upon his parole not to escape. However, as the baronial storm gathered and many divisions occurred in Simon's party, and all the difficulties of government brought inevitable unpopularity in their train, he went out hunting one day with a few friends, and forgot to return as in honour bound. He galloped away through the woodland, first after the stag and then in quest of larger game. He at once became the active organising head of the most powerful elements in English life, to all of which the destruction of Simon de Montfort and his unheard-of innovations had become the supreme object. By promising to uphold the Charters, to remedy grievances and to expel the foreigners, Edward succeeded in uniting the baronial party and in cutting away the ground from under de Montfort's feet. The Earl now appeared as no more than the leader of a personal faction, and his alliance with Llewellyn, by which he recognised the claims of the Welsh prince to territory and independence, compromised his reputation. Out-manœuvred politically by Edward, he had also placed himself at a serious military disadvantage. While Edward and the Marcher barons, as they were called, held the Severn valley de Montfort was penned in, his retreat to the east cut off, and his forces driven back into South Wales. At the beginning of August he made another attempt to cross the river and to join the forces which his son, Simon, was bringing up from the south-east. He succeeded in passing by a ford near Worcester, but his son's forces were trapped by Edward near Kenilworth and routed. Unaware of this disaster, the Earl was caught in turn at Evesham; and here on August 4 the final battle took place.

It was fought in the rain and half-darkness of a sudden storm. The Welsh broke before Edward's heavy horse, and the small group around de Montfort were left to fight desperately until sheer weight of numbers overwhelmed them.

De Montfort died a hero on the field. The Marchers massacred large numbers of fugitives and prisoners and mutilated the bodies of the dead. The old King, a pathetic figure, who had been carried by the Earl in all his wanderings, was wounded by his son's followers, and only escaped death by revealing his identity with the cry, "Slay me not! I am Henry of Winchester, your King."

* * *

The great Earl was dead, but his movement lived widespread and deep throughout the nation. The ruthless, haphazard granting away of the confiscated lands after Evesham provoked the bitter opposition of the disinherited. In isolated centres at Kenilworth, Axholme, and Ely the followers of de Montfort held out, and pillaged the countryside in sullen despair. The Government was too weak to reduce them. The whole country suffered from confusion and unrest. The common folk did not conceal their partisanship for de Montfort's cause, and rebels and outlaws beset the roads and forests. Foreign merchants were forbidden in the King's name to come to England because their safety could not be guaranteed. A reversion to feudal independence and consequent anarchy appeared imminent. In these troubles Pope Clement IV and his Legate Ottobon enjoined moderation; and after a six-months unsuccessful siege of Kenilworth Edward realised that this was the only policy. There was strong opposition from those who had benefited from the confiscations. The Earl of Gloucester had been bitterly disillusioned by Edward's repudiation of his promises of reform. Early in 1267 he demanded the expulsion of the aliens and the re-enactment of the Provisions. To enforce his demands he entered London with general acceptance. His action and the influence of the Legate secured pardon and good terms for the disinherited on the compromise principle of "No disinheritance, but repurchase." Late in 1267 the justices were sent out through the country to apply these terms equitably. The records testify to the widespread nature of the disturbances and to the fact that locally the rebellion had been directed against the officials, that it had been supported by the lower clergy, with not a few abbots and priors, and that a considerable number of the country gentry not bound to the baronial side by feudal ties had supported de Montfort.

In the last years of his life, with de Montfort dead and Edward away on Crusade, the feeble King enjoyed comparative peace. More than half a century before, at the age of nine, he had succeeded to the troubled inheritance of his father in the midst of civil war. At times it had seemed as if he would also die in the midst of civil war. At last however the storms were over: he could turn back to the things of beauty that interested him far more than political struggles. The new Abbey of Westminster, a masterpiece of Gothic architecture, was now dedicated; its consecration had long been the dearest object of Henry III's life. And here in the last weeks of 1272 he was buried.

The quiet of these last few years should not lead us to suppose that de Montfort's struggle and the civil war had been in vain. Among the common people he was for many years worshipped as a saint, and miracles were worked at his tomb. Their support could do nothing for him at Evesham, but he had been their friend, he had inspired the hope that he could end or mend the suffering and oppression of the poor; for this they remembered him when they had forgotten his faults. Though a prince among administrators, he suffered as a politician from over-confidence and impatience. He trampled upon vested interests, broke with all traditions, did violence to all forms, and needlessly created suspicion and distrust. Yet de Montfort had lighted a fire never to be quenched in English history. Already in 1267 the Statute of Marlborough had re-enacted the chief of the Provisions of Westminster. Not less important was his influence upon his nephew, Edward, the new King, who was to draw deeply upon the ideas of the man he had slain. In this way de Montfort's purposes survived both the field of Evesham and the reaction which succeeded it, and in Edward I the great Earl found his true heir.

BOOK TWO · CHAPTER EIGHTEEN

King Edward I

FEW princes had received so thorough an education in the art of rulership as Edward I when at the age of thirty-three his father's death brought him to the crown. He was an experienced leader and a skilful general. He had carried his father on his shoulders; he had grappled with Simon de Montfort, and, while sharing many of his views, had destroyed him. He had learned the art of war by tasting defeat. When at any time in the closing years of King Henry III he could have taken control he had preferred a filial and constitutional patience, all the more remarkable when his own love of order and reform is contrasted with his father's indolence and incapacity and the general misgovernment of the realm.

Of elegant build and lofty stature, a head and shoulders above the height of the ordinary man, with hair always abundant, which, changing from yellow in childhood to black in manhood and snow-white in age, marked the measured progress of his life, his proud brow and regular features were marred only by the drooping left eyelid which had been characteristic of his father. If he stammered he was also eloquent. There is much talk of his limbs. His sinewy, muscular arms were those of a swordsman; his long legs gave him a grip of the saddle, and the nickname of "Longshanks." The Dominican chronicler Nicholas Trivet, by whom these traits are recorded, tells us that the King delighted in war and tournaments, and especially in hawking and hunting. When he chased the stag he did not leave his quarry to the hounds, nor even to the hunting spear; he galloped at breakneck speed to cut the unhappy beast to the ground.

All this was typical of his reign. He presents us with qualities which are a mixture of the administrative capacity of Henry II and the personal prowess and magnanimity of Cœur de Lion. No English king more fully lived up to the maxim he chose for himself: "To each his own." He was animated by a passionate regard for justice and law, as he interpreted them, and for the rights of all groups within the community. Injuries and hostility roused, even to his last breath, a passionate torrent of resistance. But submission, or a generous act, on many occasions earned a swift response and laid the foundation of future friendship.

Edward was in Sicily when his father died, but the greatest magnates in the realm, before the tomb had closed upon the corpse of Henry III, acclaimed him King, with the assent of all men. It was two years before he returned to England for his coronation. In his accession the hereditary and elective principles flowed into a common channel, none asking which was the stronger. His conflicts with Simon de Montfort and the baronage had taught him the need for the monarchy to stand on a national footing. If Simon in his distresses had called in

the middle class to aid him alike against Crown and arrogant
nobles, the new King of his own free will would use this force
in its proper place from the outset. Proportion is the keynote
of his greatest years. He saw in the proud, turbulent baronage
and a rapacious Church checks upon the royal authority; but
he also recognised them as oppressors of the mass of his subjects; and it was by taking into account to a larger extent than
had occurred before the interests of the middle class, and the
needs of the people as a whole, that he succeeded in producing
a broad, well-ordered foundation upon which an active monarchy could function in the general interest. Thus inspired, he
sought a national kingship, an extension of his mastery
throughout the British Isles, and a preponderant influence in
the councils of Europe.

His administrative reforms in England were not such as to
give satisfaction to any one of the strong contending forces,
but rather to do justice to the whole. If the King resented the
fetters which the Charter had imposed upon his grandfather, if
he desired to control the growing opulence and claims of the
Church, he did not himself assume the recaptured powers, but
reposed them upon a broader foundation. When in his conflicts with the recent past he took away privileges which the
Church and the baronage had gained he acted always in what
was acknowledged to be the interest of the whole community.
Throughout all his legislation, however varied its problems,
there runs a common purpose: "We must find out what is ours
and due to us, and others what is theirs and due to them."

Here was a time of setting in order. The reign is memorable,
not for the erection of great new landmarks, but because the
beneficial tendencies of the three preceding reigns were extracted from error and confusion and organised and consolidated in a permanent structure. The framework and policies
of the nation, which we have seen shaping themselves with
many fluctuations, now set and hardened into a form which,
surviving the tragedies of the Black Death, the Hundred Years
War with France, and the Wars of the Roses, endured for the
remainder of the Middle Age, and some of them for longer.
In this period we see a knightly and bourgeois stage of society
increasingly replacing pure feudalism. The organs of government, land tenure, the military and financial systems, the relations of Church and State, all reach definitions which last
nearly till the Tudors.

* * *

The first eighteen years of the reign witnessed an outburst of legislative activity for which there was to be no parallel for centuries. Nearly every year was marked by an important statute. Few of these were original, most were conservative in tone, but their cumulative effect was revolutionary. Edward relied upon his Chancellor, Robert Burnell, Bishop of Bath and Wells, a man of humble birth, who had risen through the royal chancery and household to his bishopric, and until his death in 1292 remained the King's principal adviser. Burnell's whole life had been spent in the service of the Crown; all his policy was devoted to the increase of its power at the expense of feudal privilege and influence. He had not been Chancellor for more than three weeks, after Edward's return to England in 1274, before a searching inquiry into the local administration was begun. Armed with a list of forty questions, commissioners were sent throughout the land to ask what were the rights and possessions of the King, what encroachments had been made upon them, which officials were negligent or corrupt, which sheriffs "for prayer, price, or favour" concealed felonies, neglected their duties, were harsh or bribed. Similar inquests had been made before; none was so thorough or so fertile. "Masterful, but not tyrannical," the King's policy was to respect all rights and overthrow all usurpations.

The First Statute of Westminster in the Parliament of 1275 dealt with the administrative abuses exposed by the commissioners. The Statute of Gloucester in 1278 directed the justices to inquire by writs of *Quo Warranto* into the rights of feudal magnates to administer the law by their own courts and officials within their demesnes, and ordained that those rights should be strictly defined. The main usefulness of the inquiry was to remind the great feudalists that they had duties as well as rights. In 1279 the Statute of Mortmain, *De Religiosis,* forbade gifts of land to be made to the Church, though the practice was allowed to continue under royal licence. In 1285 the Statute of Winchester attacked local disorder, and in the same year was issued the Second Statute of Westminster, *De Donis Conditionalibus,* which strengthened the system of entailed estates. The Third Statute of Westminster, *Quia Emptores,* dealt with land held, not upon condition, but in fee simple. Land held on these terms might be freely alienated, but it was stipulated for the future that the buyer must hold his purchase not from the seller, but from the seller's lord, and by the same feudal services and customs as were attached to the land before the sale. It thus called a halt to the growth of sub-infeudation, and was greatly to the advantage of the Crown, as overlord, whose direct tenants now increased in number.

The purpose of this famous series of laws was essentially conservative, and for a time their enforcement was efficient. But economic pressures were wreaking great changes in the propertied life of England scarcely less deep-cutting than those which had taken place in the political sphere. Land gradually ceased to be the moral sanction upon which national society and defence were based. It became by successive steps a commodity, which could in principle, like wool or mutton, be bought and sold, and which under certain restrictions could be either transferred to new owners by gift or testament or even settled under conditions of entail on future lives which were to be the foundation of a new aristocracy.

Of course only a comparatively small proportion of the land of England came into this active if rude market; but enough of a hitherto solid element was fluid to make a deep stir. In those days, when the greatest princes were pitifully starved in cash, there was already in England one spring of credit bubbling feebly. The Jews had unseen and noiselessly lodged themselves in the social fabric of that fierce age. They were there and they were not there; and from time to time they could be most helpful to high personages in urgent need of money; and to none more than to a king who did not desire to sue Parliament for it. The spectacle of land which could be acquired on rare but definite occasions by anyone with money led the English Jews into a course of shocking imprudence. Land began to pass into the hand of Israel, either by direct sale or more often by mortgage. Enough land came into the market to make both processes advantageous. In a couple of decades the erstwhile feudal lords were conscious that they had parted permanently for fleeting lucre with a portion of the English soil large enough to be noticed.

For some time past there had been growing a wrathful reaction. Small landowners oppressed by mortgages, spendthrift nobles who had made bad bargains, were united in their complaints. Italian moneylenders were now coming into the country, who could be just as useful in times of need to the King as the Jews. Edward saw himself able to conciliate powerful elements and escape from awkward debts, by the simple and well-trodden path of anti-Semitism. The propaganda of ritual murder and other dark tales, the commonplaces of our enlightened age, were at once invoked with general acclaim. The Jews, held up to universal hatred, were pillaged, maltreated, and finally expelled the realm. Exception was made for certain physicians without whose skill persons of consequence might have lacked due attention. Once again the sorrowful, wandering race, stripped to the skin, must seek asylum and begin afresh. To Spain or North Africa the melancholy caravan, now so familiar, must move on. Not until four centuries had elapsed was Oliver Cromwell by furtive contracts with a moneyed Israelite to open again the coasts of England to the enterprise of the Jewish race. It was left to a Calvinist dictator to remove the ban which a Catholic king had imposed. The bankers of Florence and Siena, who had taken the place of the Jews, were in their turn under Edward I's grandson to taste the equities of Christendom.

* * *

Side by side with the large statutory achievements of the reign the King maintained a ceaseless process of administrative reform. His personal inspections were indefatigable. He travelled continually about his domain, holding at every centre strict inquiry into abuses of all kinds, and correcting the excesses of local magnates with a sharp pen and a strong hand. Legality, often pushed into pedantic interpretations, was a weapon upon which he was ever ready to lay his hands. In every direction by tireless perseverance he cleansed the domestic government of the realm, and ousted private interests from spheres which belonged not only to himself but to his people.

Edward I was remarkable among medieval kings for the seriousness with which he regarded the work of administration and good government. It was natural therefore that he should place more reliance upon expert professional help than upon what has been neatly termed "the amateurish assistance of great feudalists staggering under the weight of their own dignity." By the end of the thirteenth century three departments of specialised administration were already at work. One was the Exchequer, established at Westminster, where most of the revenue was received and the accounts kept. The second was the Chancery, a general secretariat responsible for the writing and drafting of innumerable royal charters, writs, and letters. The third was the Wardrobe, with its separate secretariat, the Privy Seal, attached to the ever-moving royal household, and combining financial and secretarial functions, which might range from financing a Continental war to buying a pennyworth of pepper for the royal cook. Burnell was a typical product of the incipient Civil Service. His place after his death was taken by an Exchequer official, Walter Langton, the Treasurer, who, like Burnell, looked upon his see of Lichfield as a reward for skilful service rather than a spiritual office.

Though the most orthodox of Churchmen, Edward I did not escape conflict with the Church. Anxious though he was to pay his dues to God, he had a far livelier sense than his father of what was due to Cæsar, and circumstances more than once forced him to protest. The leader of the Church party was John Pecham, a Franciscan friar, Archbishop of Canterbury from 1279 to 1292. With great courage and skill Pecham defended what he regarded as the just rights of the Church and its independence against the Crown. At the provincial Council held at Reading in 1279 he issued a number of pronouncements which angered the King. One was a canon against plurality of clerical offices, which struck at the principal royal method of rewarding the growing Civil Service. Another was the order that a copy of the Charter, which Edward had sworn to uphold, should be publicly posted in every cathedral and collegiate church. All who produced royal writs to stop cases in ecclesiastical courts and all who violated Magna Carta were threatened with excommunication.

Pecham bowed to Edward's anger and waited his time. In 1281, when another provincial Council was summoned to Lambeth, the King, suspecting mischief, issued writs to its members forbidding them to "hold counsel concerning matters which appertain to our crown, or touch our person, our state, or the state of our Council." Pecham was undeterred. He revived almost verbatim the principal legislation of the Reading Council, prefaced it with an explicit assertion of ecclesiastical liberty, and a month later wrote a remarkable letter to the King, defending his action. "By no human constitution," he wrote, "not even by an oath, can we be bound to ignore laws which rest undoubtedly upon divine authority." "A fine letter" was the marginal comment of an admiring clerk who copied it into the Archbishop's register.

Pecham's action might well have precipitated a crisis comparable to the quarrel between Becket and Henry II, but Edward seems to have quietly ignored the challenge. Royal writs of prohibition continued to be issued. Yet moderation was observed, and in 1286 by a famous writ Edward wisely ordered his itinerant justices to act circumspectly in matters of ecclesiastical jurisdiction, and listed the kinds of case which should be left to Church courts. The dispute thus postponed was to outlive both Archbishop and King.

* * *

At the beginning of the reign relations between England and France were governed by the Treaty of Paris, which the baronial party had concluded in 1259. For more than thirty years peace reigned between the two countries, though often with an undercurrent of hostility. The disputes about the execution of the terms of the treaty and the quarrels between English, Gascon, and French sailors in the Channel, culminating in a great sea-fight off Saint-Mahé in 1293, need never have led to a renewal of war, had not the presence of the English in the South of France been a standing challenge to the pride of the French and a bar to their national integrity. Even when Philip the Fair, the French king, began to seek opportunities of provocation Edward was long-suffering and patient in his attempts to reach a compromise. Finally however the Parlement of Paris declared the Duchy of Gascony forfeit. Philip asked for the token surrender of the principal Gascon fortresses, as a recognition of his legal powers as overlord. Edward complied. But once Philip was in possession he refused to give them up again. Edward now realised that he must either fight or lose his French possessions.

By 1294 the great King had changed much from his early buoyant manhood. After the long stormy years of sustaining his father he had reigned himself for nearly a quarter of a century. Meanwhile his world had changed about him; he had lost his beloved wife Eleanor of Castile, his mother, Eleanor of Provence, and his two eldest infant sons. Burnell was now dead. Wales and Scotland presented grave problems; opposition was beginning to make itself heard and felt. Alone, perplexed and ageing, the King had to face an endless succession of difficulties.

In June 1294 he explained the grounds of the quarrel with the French to what is already called "a Parliament" of magnates in London. His decision to go to war was accepted with approval, as has often been the case in more regularly constituted assemblies.

The war itself had no important features. There were campaigns in Gascony, a good deal of coastal raiding in the Channel, and a prolonged siege by the English of Bordeaux. Any enthusiasm which had been expressed at the outset wore off speedily under the inevitable increases of taxation. All wool and leather, the staple items of the English export trade, were impounded, and could only be redeemed by the payment of a customs duty of 40s. on the sack instead of the half-mark (6s. 8d.) laid down by the Parliament of 1275. In September the clergy, to their great indignation, were ordered to contribute one-half of their revenues. The Dean of St Paul's, who attempted to voice their protests in the King's own terrifying presence, fell down in a fit and died. In November Parliament granted a heavy tax upon all movable property. As the collection proceeded a bitter and sullen discontent spread among all classes. In the winter of 1294 the Welsh revolted, and when the King had suppressed them he returned to find that Scotland had allied itself with France. From 1296 onward war with Scotland was either smouldering or flaring.

After October 1297 the French war degenerated into a series of truces which lasted until 1303. Such conditions involved expense little less than actual fighting. These were years of severe strain, both at home and abroad, and especially with Scotland. Although the King did not hesitate to recall recurrent Parliaments to Westminster and explained the whole situation to them, he did not obtain the support which he needed. Parliament was reluctant to grant the new taxes demanded of it.

The position of the clergy was made more difficult by the publication in 1296 of the Papal Bull *Clericis Laicos,* which forbade the payment of extraordinary taxation without Papal authority. At the autumn Parliament at Bury St Edmunds the clergy, under the leadership of Robert Winchelsea, the new Primate, decided after some hesitation that they were unable to make any contribution. Edward in his anger outlawed them and declared their lay fiefs forfeit. The Archbishop retaliated by threatening with excommunication any who should disobey the Papal Bull. For a time passion ran high, but eventually a calmer mood prevailed. By the following summer the quarrel was allayed, and the Pope by a new Bull, *Etsi de Statu,* had withdrawn his extreme claims.

Edward was the more prepared to come to terms with the Church because opposition had already broken out in another quarter. He proposed to the barons at Salisbury that a number of them should serve in Gascony while he conducted a campaign in Flanders. This was ill received. Humphrey de Bohun, Earl of Hereford and Constable of England, together with the Marshal, Roger Bigod, Earl of Norfolk, declared that their hereditary offices could only be exercised in the King's company. Such excuses deceived nobody. Both the Earls had personal grudges against the King, and—much more important —they voiced the resentment felt by a large number of the barons who for the past twenty years had steadily seen the authority of the Crown increased to their own detriment. The time was ripe for a revival of the baronial opposition which a generation before had defied Edward's father.

For the moment the King ignored the challenge. He pressed forward with his preparations for war, appointed deputies in place of Hereford and Norfolk, and in August sailed for Flanders. The opposition saw in his absence their long-awaited opportunity. They demanded the confirmation of those two instruments, Magna Carta and its extension, the Charter of the Forest, which were the final version of the terms extorted from John, together with six additional articles. By these no tallage or aid was to be imposed in future except with the consent of the community of the realm; corn, wool, and the like must not be impounded against the will of their owners; the clergy and laity of the realm must recover their ancient liberties; the two Earls and their supporters were not to be penalised for their refusal to serve in Gascony; the prelates were to read the Charter aloud in their cathedrals, and to excommunicate all who neglected it. In the autumn the two Earls, backed by armed forces, appeared in London and demanded the acceptance of these proposals. The Regency, unable to resist, submitted. The articles were confirmed, and in November at Ghent the King ratified them reserving however certain financial rights of the Crown.

These were large and surprising concessions. Both King and opposition attached great importance to them, and the King was suspected, perhaps with justice, of trying to withdraw from the promises he had given. Several times the baronial party publicly drew attention to these promises before Parliament, and finally in February 1301 the King was driven by the threats and arguments of a Parliament at Lincoln to grant a new confirmation of both charters and certain further articles in solemn form.

By this crisis and its manner of resolution, two principles had been established from which important consequences flowed. One was that the King had no right to despatch the feudal host wherever he might choose. This limitation sounded the death-knell of the feudal levy, and inexorably led in the following century to the rise of indentured armies serving for pay. The second point of principle now recognised was that the King could not plead "urgent necessity" as a reason for imposing taxation without consent. Other English monarchs as late as the seventeenth century were to make the attempt. But by Edward's failure a precedent had been set up, and a long stride had been taken towards the dependence of the Crown upon Parliamentary grants.

Edward to a greater extent than any of his predecessors had shown himself prepared to govern in the national interest and with some regard for constitutional form. It was thus ironical, and to the King exasperating, that he found the principles he had emphasised applied against himself. The baronial party had not resorted to war; they had acted through the constitutional machinery the King himself had taken so much pains to create. Thereby they had shifted their ground: they spoke no longer as the representatives of the feudal aristocracy, but as the leaders of a national opposition. So the Crown was once again committed solemnly and publicly to the principles of Magna Carta, and the concession was made all the more valuable because remedies of actual recent abuses of the royal prerogative powers had been added to the original charters. Here was a real constitutional advance.

* * *

In their fatal preoccupation with their possessions in France the English kings had neglected the work of extending their rule within the Island of Great Britain. There had been fitful interference both in Wales and Scotland, but the task of keeping the frontiers safe had fallen mainly upon the shoulders of the local Marcher lords. As soon as the Treaty of Paris had brought a generation's respite from Continental adventures it was possible to turn to the urgent problems of internal security. Edward I was the first of the English kings to put the whole weight of the Crown's resources behind the effort of national expansion in the West and North, and to him is due the conquest of the independent areas of Wales and the securing of the Western frontier. He took the first great step towards the unification of the Island. He sought to conquer where the Romans, the Saxons, and the Normans all in their turn had failed. The mountain fastnesses of Wales nursed a hardy and unsubdued race which, under the grandson of the great Llewellyn, had in the previous reign once again made a deep dint upon the politics of England. Edward, as his father's lieutenant, had experience of the Welsh. He had encountered them in war, with questionable success. At the same time he had seen, with disapproving eye, the truculence of the barons of the Welsh Marches, the Mortimers, the Bohuns, and in the South the Clares, with the Gloucester estates, who exploited their military privileges against the interests alike of the Welsh and English people. All assertions of Welsh independence were a vexation to Edward; but scarcely less obnoxious was a system of guarding the frontiers of England by a confederacy of robber barons who had more than once presumed to challenge the authority of the Crown. He resolved, in the name of justice and progress, to subdue the unconquered refuge of petty princes and wild mountaineers in which barbaric freedom had dwelt since remote antiquity, and at the same time to curb the privileges of the Marcher lords.

Edward I, utilising all the local resources which the barons of the Welsh Marches had developed in the chronic strife of many generations, conquered Wales in several years of persistent warfare, coldly and carefully devised, by land and sea. The forces he employed were mainly Welsh levies in his pay, reinforced by regular troops from Gascony and by one of the last appearances of the feudal levy; but above all it was by the terror of winter campaigns that he broke the power of the valiant Ancient Britons. By Edward's Statute of Wales the independent principality came to an end. The land of Llewellyn's Wales was transferred entirely to the King's dominions and organised into the shires of Anglesey, Carnarvon, Merioneth, Cardigan and Camarthen. The king's son Edward, born in Carnarvon, was proclaimed the first English Prince of Wales.

The Welsh wars of Edward reveal to us the process by which the military system of England was transformed from the age-long Saxon and feudal basis of occasional service to that of paid regular troops. We have seen how Alfred the Great suffered repeatedly from the expiry of the period for which the "fyrd" could be called out. Four hundred years had passed, and Norman feudalism still conformed to this basic principle. But how were campaigns to be conducted winter and summer for fifteen months at a time by such methods? How were Continental expeditions to be launched and pursued? Thus for several reigns the principle of scutage had been agreeable alike to barons who did not wish to serve and to sovereigns who preferred a money payment with which to hire full-time soldiers. In the Welsh wars both systems are seen simultaneously at work, but the old is fading. Instead of liege service Governments now required trustworthy mercenaries, and for this purpose money was the solvent.

At the same time a counter-revolution in the balance of warfare was afoot. The mailed cavalry which from the fifth century had eclipsed the ordered ranks of the legion were wearing out their long day. A new type of infantry raised from the common people began to prove its dominating quality. This infantry operated, not by club or sword or spear, or even by hand-flung missiles, but by an archery which, after a long development, concealed from Europe, was very soon to make an astonishing entrance upon the military scene and gain a dramatic ascendancy upon the battlefields of the Continent. Here was a prize taken by the conquerors from their victims. In South Wales the practice of drawing the long-bow had already attained an astonishing efficiency, of which one of the Marcher lords has left a record. One of his knights had been hit by an arrow which pierced not only the skirts of his mailed shirt, but his mailed breeches, his thigh, and the wood of his saddle, and finally struck deep into his horse's flank. This was a new fact in the history of war, which is also a part of the history of civilisation, deserving to be mentioned with the triumph of bronze over flint, or iron over bronze. For the first time infantry possessed a weapon which could penetrate the armour of the clanking age, and which in range and rate of fire was superior to any method ever used before, or ever used again until the coming of the modern rifle. The War Office has among its records a treatise written during the peace after Waterloo by a general officer of long experience in the Napoleonic wars recommending that muskets should be discarded in favour of the long-bow on account of its superior accuracy, rapid discharge, and effective range.

Thus the Welsh war, from two separate points of departure, destroyed the physical basis of feudalism, which had already, in its moral aspect, been outsped and outclassed by the extension and refinement of administration. Even when the conquest was completed the process of holding down the subdued regions required methods which were beyond the compass of feudal barons. Castles of stone, with many elaborations, had indeed long played a conspicuous part in the armoured age. But now the extent of the towered walls must be enlarged not only to contain more numerous garrisons, but to withstand great siege engines, such as trebuchets and mangonels, which had recently been greatly improved, and to hinder attackers from approaching to the foot of the inner walls. Now, moreover, not merely troops of steel-clad warriors will ride forth, spreading random terror in the countryside, but disciplined bodies of infantry, possessing the new power of long-range action, will be led by regular commanders upon a plan prescribed by a central command.

* * *

The great quarrel of Edward's reign was with Scotland. For long years the two kingdoms had dwelt in amity. In the year 1286 Alexander III of Scotland, riding his horse over a cliff in the darkness, left as his heir Margaret his granddaughter, known as the Maid of Norway. The Scottish magnates had been persuaded to recognise this princess of fourteen as his successor. Now the bright project arose that the Maid of Norway should at the same moment succeed to the Scottish throne and marry Edward, the King's son. Thus would be achieved a union of royal families by which the antagonism of England and Scotland might be laid to rest. We can measure the sagacity of the age by the acceptance of this plan. Practically all the ruling forces in England and Scotland were agreed upon it. It was a dream, and it passed as a dream. The Maid of Norway embarked in 1290 upon stormy seas only to die before reaching land, and Scotland was bequeathed the problem of a disputed succession, in the decision of which the English interest must be a heavy factor. The Scottish nobility were allied at many points with the English royal family, and from a dozen claimants, some of them bastards, two men stood clearly forth, John Balliol and Robert Bruce. Bruce asserted his aged father's closeness in relationship to the common royal ancestor; Balliol, a more distant descendant, the rights of primogeniture. But partisanship was evenly balanced.

Since the days of Henry II the English monarchy had intermittently claimed an overlordship of Scotland, based on the still earlier acknowledgment of Saxon overlordship by Scottish kings. King Edward, whose legal abilities were renowned, had already arbitrated in similar circumstances between Aragon and Anjou. He now imposed himself with considerable acceptance as arbitrator in the Scottish succession. Since the alternatives were the splitting of Scotland into rival kingships or a civil war to decide the matter, the Scots were induced to seek Edward's judgment; and he, pursuing all the time a path of strict legality, consented to the task only upon the prior condition of the reaffirmation of his overlordship, betokened by the surrender of certain Scottish castles. The English King discharged his function as arbitrator with extreme propriety. He rejected the temptation presented to him by Scottish baronial intrigues of destroying the integrity of Scotland. He pronounced in 1292 in favour of John Balliol. Later judgments have in no wise impugned the correctness of his decision. But, having regard to the deep division in Scotland, and the strong elements which adhered to the Bruce claim, John Balliol inevitably became not merely his choice, but his puppet. So thought King Edward I, and plumed himself upon a just and at the same time highly profitable decision. He had confirmed his overlordship of Scotland. He had nominated its king, who stood himself in his own land upon a narrow margin. But the national feeling of Scotland was pent up behind these barriers of legal affirmation. In their distress the Scottish baronage accepted King Edward's award, but they also furnished the new King John with an authoritative council of twelve great lords to overawe him and look after the rights of Scotland. Thus King Edward saw with disgust that all his fair-seeming success left him still confronted with the integrity of Scottish nationhood, with an independent and not a subject Government, and with a hostile rather than a submissive nation.

At this very moment the same argument of overlordship was pressed upon him by the formidable French king, Philip IV. Here Edward was the vassal, proudly defending feudal interests, and the French suzerain had the lawful advantage. Moreover, if England was stronger than Scotland, France was in armed power superior to England. This double conflict imposed a strain upon the financial and military resources of the English monarchy which it could by no means meet. The rest of Edward's reign was spent in a twofold struggle North and South, for the sake of which he had to tax his subjects beyond all endurance. He journeyed energetically to and fro between Flanders and the Scottish Lowlands. He racked the land for money. Nothing else mattered; and the embryonic Parliamentary system profited vastly by the repeated concessions he made in the hope of carrying opinion with him. He confirmed the bulk of the reforms wrung from John. With some exceptions among the great lords, the nation was with him in both of his external efforts, but though time and again it complied with his demands it was not reconciled to the crushing burden. Thus we see the wise law-giver, the thrifty scrutineer of English finances, the administrative reformer, forced to drive his people beyond their strength, and in this process to rouse oppositions which darkened his life and clouded his fame.

To resist Edward the Scots allied themselves with the French. Since Edward was at war with France he regarded this as an act of hostility. He summoned Balliol to meet him at Berwick. The Scottish nobles refused to allow their king to go, and from this moment war began. Edward struck with ruthless severity. He advanced on Berwick. The city, then the great emporium of Northern trade, was unprepared, after a hundred years of peace, to resist attack. Palisades were hurriedly raised, the citizens seized such weapons as were at hand. The English army, with hardly any loss, trampled down these improvised defences, and Berwick was delivered to a sack and slaughter which shocked even those barbaric times. Thousands were slain. The most determined resistance came from thirty Flemish merchants who held their depot, called the Red Hall, until it was burnt down. Berwick sank in a few hours from one of the active centres of European commerce to the minor seaport which exists to-day.

This act of terror quelled the resistance of the ruling classes in Scotland. Perth, Stirling, Edinburgh, yielded themselves to the King's march. Here we see how Edward I anticipated the teachings of Machiavelli; for to the frightfulness of Berwick succeeded a most gracious, forgiving spirit which welcomed and made easy submission in every form. Balliol surrendered his throne and Scotland was brought under English administration. But, as in Wales, the conqueror introduced not only an alien rule, but law and order, all of which were equally unpopular. The governing classes of Scotland had conspicuously failed, and Edward might flatter himself that all was over. It was only beginning. It has often been said that Joan of Arc first raised the standard of nationalism in the Western world. But over a century before she appeared an outlaw knight, William Wallace, arising from the recesses of South-West Scotland which had been his refuge, embodied, commanded, and led to victory the Scottish nation. Edward, warring in France with piebald fortune, was forced to listen to tales of ceaseless inroads and forays against his royal peace in Scotland, hitherto deemed so sure. Wallace had behind him the spirit of a race as stern and as resolute as any bred among men. He added military gifts of a high order. Out of an unorganised mass of valiant fighting men he forged, in spite of cruel poverty and primitive administration, a stubborn, indomitable army, ready to fight at any odds and mock defeat. The structure of this army is curious. Every four men had a fifth man as leader; every nine men a tenth; every nineteen men a twentieth, and so on to every thousand; and it was agreed that the penalty for disobedience to the leader of any unit was death. Thus from the ground does freedom raise itself unconquerable.

Warenne, Earl of Surrey, was Edward's commander in the North. When the depredations of the Scottish rebels had become intolerable he advanced at the head of strong forces upon Stirling. At Stirling Bridge, near the Abbey of Cambuskenneth, in September 1297, he found himself in the presence of Wallace's army. Many Scotsmen were in the English service. One of these warned him of the dangers of trying to deploy beyond the long, narrow bridge and causeway which spanned the river. This knight pleaded calculations worthy of a modern staff officer. It would take eleven hours to move the army across the bridge, and what would happen, he asked, if the vanguard were attacked before the passage was completed? He spoke of a ford higher up, by which at least a flanking force could cross. But Earl Warenne would have none of these things. Wallace watched with measuring eye the accumulation of the English troops across the bridge, and at the right moment hurled his full force upon them, seized the bridgehead, and slaughtered the vanguard of five thousand men. Warenne evacuated the greater part of Scotland. His fortress garrisons were reduced one after the other. The English could barely hold the line of the Tweed.

It was beyond the compass of King Edward's resources to wage war with France and face the hideous struggle with Scotland at the same time. He sought at all costs to concentrate on the peril nearest home. He entered upon a long series of negotiations with the French King which were covered by truces repeatedly renewed, and reached a final Treaty of Paris in 1303. Though the formal peace was delayed for some years, it was in fact sealed in 1294 by the arrangement of a marriage between Edward and Philip's sister, the young Princess Margaret, and also by the betrothal of Edward's son and heir, Edward of Carnarvon, to Philip's daughter Isabella. This dual alliance of blood brought the French war to an effective close in 1297, although through Papal complications neither the peace nor the King's marriage was finally and formally confirmed until 1299. By these diplomatic arrangements Edward from the end of 1297 onwards was able to concentrate his strength against the Scots.

Wallace was now the ruler of Scotland, and the war was without truce or mercy. A hated English official, a tax-gatherer, had fallen at the bridge. His skin, cut into suitable strips, covered Wallace's sword-belt for the future. Edward, forced to quit his campaign in France, hastened to the scene of disaster, and with the whole feudal levy of England advanced against the Scots. The Battle of Falkirk in 1298, which he conducted in person, bears a sharp contrast to Stirling Bridge. Wallace, now at the head of stronger powers, accepted battle in a withdrawn defensive position. He had few cavalry and few archers; but his confidence lay in the solid "schiltrons" (or circles) of spearmen, who were invincible except by actual physical destruction. The armoured cavalry of the English vanguard were hurled back with severe losses from the spear-points. But Edward, bringing up his Welsh archers in the intervals between horsemen of the second line, concentrated a hail of arrows upon particular points in the Scottish schiltrons, so that there were more dead and wounded than living men in these places. Into the gaps and over the carcasses the knighthood of England forced their way. Once the Scottish order was broken the spearmen were quickly massacred. The slaughter ended only in the depths of the woods, and Wallace and the Scottish army were once again fugitives, hunted as rebels, starving, suffering the worst of human privations, but still in arms.

The Scots were unconquerable foes. It was not until 1305 that Wallace was captured, tried with full ceremonial in Westminster Hall, and hanged, drawn, and quartered at Tyburn. But the Scottish war was one in which, as a chronicler said, "every winter undid every summer's work." Wallace was to pass the torch to Robert Bruce.

*   *   *

In the closing years of Edward's life he appears as a lonely and wrathful old man. A new generation had grown up around him with whom he had slight acquaintance and less sympathy. Queen Margaret was young enough to be his daughter, and sided often with her step-children against their father. Few dared to oppose the old King, but he had little love or respect in his family circle.

With Robert Bruce, grandson of the claimant of 1290, who had won his way partly by right of birth, but also by hard measures, the war in Scotland flared again. He met the chief Scotsman who represented the English interest in the solemn sanctuary of the church in the Border town of Dumfries. The two leaders were closeted together. Presently Bruce emerged alone, and said to his followers, "I doubt me I have killed the Red Comyn." Whereat his chief supporter, muttering "I'se mak' siccar!" re-entered the sacred edifice. A new champion of this grand Northern race had thus appeared in arms. King Edward was old, but his will-power was unbroken. When the news came south to Winchester, where he held his Court, that Bruce had been crowned at Scone his fury was terrible to behold. He launched a campaign in the summer of 1306 in which Bruce was defeated and driven to take refuge on Rathlin island, off the coast of Antrim. Here, according to the tale, Bruce was heartened by the persistent efforts of the most celebrated spider known to history. Next spring he returned to Scotland. Edward was now too ill to march or ride. Like the Emperor Severus a thousand years before, he was carried in a litter against this stern people, and like him he died upon the road. His last thoughts were on Scotland and on the Holy Land. He conjured his son to carry his bones in the van of the army which should finally bring Scotland to obedience, and to send his heart to Palestine with a band of a hundred knights to help recover the Sacred City. Neither wish was fulfilled by his futile and unworthy heir.

* * *

Edward I was the last great figure in the formative period of English law. His statutes, which settled questions of public order, assigned limits to the powers of the seigneurial courts, and restrained the sprawling and luxurious growth of judge-made law, laid down principles that remained fundamental to the law of property until the mid-nineteenth century. By these great enactments necessary bounds were fixed to the freedom of the Common Law which, without conflicting with its basic principles or breaking with the past, imparted to it its final form.

In the constitutional sphere the work of Edward I was not less durable. He had made Parliament—that is to say, certain selected magnates and representatives of the shires and boroughs—the associate of the Crown, in place of the old Court of Tenants-in-Chief. By the end of his reign this conception had been established. At first it lacked substance; only gradually did it take on flesh and blood. But between the beginning and the end of Edward's reign the decisive impulse was given. At the beginning anything or nothing might have come out of the experiments of his father's troubled time. By the end it was fairly settled in the customs and traditions of England that "sovereignty," to use a term which Edward would hardly have understood, would henceforward reside not in the Crown only, nor in the Crown and Council of the Barons, but in the Crown in Parliament.

Dark constitutional problems loomed in the future. The boundary between the powers of Parliament and those of the Crown was as yet very vaguely drawn. A statute, it was quickly accepted, was a law enacted by the King in Parliament, and could only be repealed with the consent of Parliament itself. But Parliament was still in its infancy. The initiative in the work of government still rested with the King, and necessarily he retained many powers whose limits were undefined. Did royal ordinances, made in the Privy Council on the King's sole authority, have the validity of law? Could the King in particular cases override a statute on the plea of public or royal expediency? In a clash between the powers of King and Parliament who was to say on which side right lay? Inevitably, as Parliament grew to a fuller stature, these questions would be asked; but for a final answer they were to wait until Stuart kings sat on the English throne.

Nevertheless the foundations of a strong national monarchy for a United Kingdom and of a Parliamentary Constitution had been laid. Their continuous development and success depended upon the King's immediate successor. Idle weaklings, dreamers, and adventurous boys disrupted the nascent unity of the Island. Long years of civil war, and despotism in reaction from anarchy, marred and delayed the development of its institutions. But when the traveller gazes upon the plain marble tomb at Westminster on which is inscribed, "Here lies Edward I, the Hammer of the Scots. Keep troth," he stands before the resting-place of a master-builder of British life, character, and fame.

BOOK TWO · CHAPTER NINETEEN

Bannockburn

EDWARD II's reign may fairly be regarded as a melancholy appendix to his father's and the prelude to his son's. The force and fame which Edward I had gathered in his youth and prime cast their shield over the decline of his later years. We have seen him in his strength; we must see him in his weakness. Men do not live for ever, and in his final phase the bold warrior who had struck down Simon de Montfort, who had reduced the Welsh to obedience, and even discipline, who was "the Hammer of the Scots," who had laid the foundations of Parliament, who had earned the proud title of "the English Justinian" by his laws, was fighting a losing battle with a singularly narrow, embittered, and increasingly class-conscious nobility. This battle old age and death forced him to confide to his embarrassed son, who proved incapable of winning it.

A strong, capable King had with difficulty upborne the load. He was succeeded by a perverted weakling, of whom some amiable traits are recorded. Marlowe in his tragedy puts in his mouth at the moment of his death some fine lines:

> Tell Isabel the Queen I looked not thus
> When for her sake I ran at tilt in France,
> And there unhorsed the Duke of Cleremont.

Of this tribute history did not deprive the unfortunate King; but the available records say little of war or tournaments and dwell rather upon Edward's interest in thatching and ditching and other serviceable arts. He was addicted to rowing, swimming, and baths. He carried his friendship for his advisers beyond dignity and decency. This was a reign which by its weakness contributed in the long run to English strength. The ruler was gone, the rod was broken, and the forces of English nationhood, already alive and conscious under the old King, resumed their march at a quicker and more vehement step. In default of a dominating Parliamentary institution, the Curia Regis, as we have seen, seemed to be the centre from which the business of government could be controlled. On the death of Edward I the barons succeeded in gaining control of this mixed body of powerful magnates and competent Household officials. They set up a committee called "the Lords Ordainers," who represented the baronial and ecclesiastical interests of the State. Scotland and France remained the external problems confronting these new masters of government, but their first anger was directed upon the favourite of the King. Piers Gaveston, a young, handsome Gascon, enjoyed his fullest confidence. His decisions made or marred. There was a temper which would submit to the rule of a King, but would not tolerate the pretensions of his personal cronies. The barons' party attacked Piers Gaveston. Edward and his

favourite tried to stave off opposition by harrying the Scots.
They failed, and in 1311 Gaveston was exiled to Flanders.
Thence he was so imprudent as to return, in defiance of the
Lords Ordainers. Compelling him to take refuge in the North,
they pursued him, not so much by war as by a process of
establishing their authority, occupying castles, controlling the
courts, and giving to the armed forces orders which were
obeyed. Besieged in the castle of Scarborough, Gaveston made
terms with his foes. His life was to be spared; and on this they
took him under guard. But other nobles, led by the Earl of
Warwick, one of the foremost Ordainers, who had not been
present at the agreement of Scarborough, violated these conditions. They overpowered the escort, seized the favourite at
Deddington in Oxfordshire, and hewed off his head on Black-
low Hill, near Warwick.

   In spite of these successes by the Ordainers royal power remained formidable. Edward was still in control of Government, although he was under their restraint. Troubles in
France and war in Scotland confronted him. To wipe out his
setbacks at home he resolved upon the conquest of the Northern kingdom. A general levy of the whole power of England
was set on foot to beat the Scots. A great army crossed the
Tweed in the summer of 1314. Twenty-five thousand men,
hard to gather, harder still to feed in those days, with at least
three thousand armoured knights and men-at-arms, moved
against the Scottish host under the nominal but none the less
baffling command of Edward II. The new champion of Scotland, Robert the Bruce, now faced the vengeance of England.
The Scottish army, of perhaps ten thousand men, was composed, as at Falkirk, mainly of the hard, unyielding spearmen
who feared nought and, once set in position, had to be killed.
But Bruce had pondered deeply upon the impotence of pikemen, however faithful, if exposed to the alternations of an
arrow shower and an armoured charge. He therefore, with a
foresight and skill which proves his military quality, took
three precautions. First, he chose a position where his flanks
were secured by impenetrable woods; secondly, he dug upon
his front a large number of small round holes or "pottes,"
afterwards to be imitated by the archers at Crécy, and covered
them with branches and turfs as a trap for charging cavalry;
thirdly, he kept in his own hand his small but highly trained
force of mounted knights to break up any attempt at planting
archers upon his flank to derange his schiltrons. These disposi-
tions made, he awaited the English onslaught.

The English army was so large that it took three days to close up from rear to front. The ground available for deployment was little more than two thousand yards. While the host was massing itself opposite the Scottish position an incident took place. An English knight, Henry de Bohun, pushed his way forward at the head of a force of Welsh infantry to try by a surprise move to relieve Stirling Castle which was in English hands. Bruce arrived just in time to throw himself and some of his men between them and the castle walls. Bohun charged him in single combat. Bruce, though not mounted on his heavy war-horse, awaited his onset upon a well-trained hack, and, striking aside the English lance with his battle-axe, slew Bohun at a single blow before the eyes of all.

On the morning of June 24 the English advanced, and a dense wave of steel-clad horsemen descended the slope, splashed and scrambled through the Bannock Burn, and charged uphill upon the schiltrons. Though much disordered by the "pottes," they came to deadly grip with the Scottish spearmen. "And when the two hosts so came together and the great steeds of the knights dashed into the Scottish pikes as into a thick wood there rose a great and horrible crash from rending lances and dying horses, and there they stood locked together for a space." As neither side would withdraw the struggle was prolonged and covered the whole front. The strong corps of archers could not intervene. When they shot their arrows into the air, as William had done at Hastings, they hit more of their own men than of the Scottish infantry. At length a detachment of archers was brought round the Scottish left flank. But for this Bruce had made effective provision. His small cavalry force charged them with the utmost promptitude, and drove them back into the great mass waiting to engage, and now already showing signs of disorder. Continuous reinforcements streamed forward towards the English fighting line. Confusion steadily increased. At length the appearance on the hills to the English right of the camp-followers of Bruce's army, waving flags and raising loud cries, was sufficient to induce a general retreat, which the King himself, with his numerous personal guards, was not slow to head. The retreat speedily became a rout. The Scottish schiltrons hurled themselves forward down the slope, inflicting immense carnage upon the English even before they could re-cross the Bannock Burn. No more grievous slaughter of English chivalry ever took place in a single day. Even Towton in the Wars of the Roses was less destructive. The Scots claimed to have slain or captured thirty thousand men, more than the whole English army, but their feat in virtually destroying an army of cavalry and archers mainly by the agency of spearmen must nevertheless be deemed a prodigy of war.

* * *

In the long story of a nation we often see that capable rulers by their very virtues sow the seeds of future evil and weak or degenerate princes open the pathway of progress. At this time the unending struggle for power had entered upon new ground. We have traced the ever-growing influence, and at times authority, of the permanent officials of the royal Household. This became more noticeable, and therefore more obnoxious, when the sovereign was evidently in their hands, or not capable of overtopping them in policy or personality. The feudal baronage had striven successfully against kings. They now saw in the royal officials agents who stood in their way, yet at the same time were obviously indispensable to the widening aspects of national life. They could no more contemplate the abolition of these officials than their ancestors the destruction of the monarchy. The whole tendency of their movement was therefore in this generation to acquire control of an invaluable machine. They sought to achieve in the fourteenth century that power of choosing, or at least of supervising, the appointments to the key offices of the Household which the Whig nobility under the house of Hanover actually won.

The Lords Ordainers, as we have seen, had control of the Curia Regis; but they soon found that many of the essentials of power still eluded their grasp. In those days the King was expected to rule as well as to reign. The King's sign manual, the seal affixed to a document, a writ or warrant issued by a particular officer, were the facts upon which the courts pronounced, soldiers marched, and executioners discharged their functions. One of the main charges brought against Edward II at his deposition was that he had failed in his task of government. From early in his reign he left too much to his Household officials. To the Lords Ordainers it appeared that the high control of government had withdrawn itself from the Curia Regis, into an inner citadel described as "the King's Wardrobe." There was the King, in his Wardrobe, with his favourites and indispensable functionaries, settling a variety of matters from the purchase of the royal hose to the waging of a Continental war. Outside this select, secluded circle the rugged, arrogant, virile barons prowled morosely. The process was exasperating; like climbing a hill where always a new summit appears. Nor must we suppose that such experiences were reserved for this distant age alone. It is the nature of supreme executive power to withdraw itself into the smallest compass; and without such contraction there is no executive power. But when this exclusionary process was tainted by unnatural vice and stained by shameful defeat in the field it was clear that those who beat upon the doors had found a prosperous occasion, especially since many of the Ordainers had prudently absented themselves from the Bannockburn campaign and could thus place all the blame for its disastrous outcome upon the King.

The forces were not unequally balanced. To do violence to the sacred person of the King was an awful crime. The Church by its whole structure and tradition depended upon him. A haughty, self-interested aristocracy must remember that in most parts of the country the common people, among whom bills and bows were plentiful, had looked since the days of the Conqueror to the Crown as their protector against baronial oppression. Above all, law and custom weighed heavily with all classes, rich and poor alike, when every district had a life of its own and very few lights burned after sundown. The barons might have a blasting case against the King at Westminster, but if he appeared in Shropshire or Westmorland with his handful of guards and the royal insignia he could tell his own tale, and men, both knight and archer, would rally to him.

In this equipoise Parliament became of serious importance to the contending interests. Here at least was the only place where the case for or against the conduct of the central executive could be tried before something that resembled, however imperfectly, the nation. Thus we see in this ill-starred reign both sides operating in and through Parliament, and in this process enhancing its power. Parliament was called together no fewer than twenty-five times under King Edward II. It had no share in the initiation or control of policy. It was of course distracted by royal and baronial intrigue. Many of its knights and burgesses were but the creatures of one faction or the other. Nevertheless it could be made to throw its weight in a decisive manner from time to time. This therefore was a period highly favourable to the growth of forces in the realm which were to become inherently different in character from either the Crown or the barons.

Thomas of Lancaster, nephew to Edward I, was the fore-front of the baronial opposition. Little is known to his credit. He had long been engaged in treasonable practices with the Scots. As leader of the barons he had pursued Gaveston to his death, and, although not actually responsible for the treachery which led to his execution, he bore henceforward upon his shoulders the deepest hate of which Edward II's nature was capable. Into the hands of Thomas and his fellow Ordainers Edward was now thrown by the disaster of Bannockburn, and Thomas for a while became the most important man in the land. Within a few years however the moderates among the Ordainers became so disgusted with Lancaster's incompetence and with the weakness into which the process of Government had sunk that they joined with the royalists to edge him from power. The victory of this middle party, headed by the Earl of Pembroke, did not please the King. Aiming to be more effi-cient than Lancaster, Pembroke and his friends tried to en-force the Ordinances more effectively, and carried out a great reform of the royal Household.

Edward, for his part, began to build up a royalist party, at the head of which were the Despensers, father and son, both named Hugh. These belonged to the nobility, and their power lay on the Welsh border. By a fortunate marriage with the noble house of Clare, and by the favour of the King, they rose precariously amid the jealousies of the English baronage to the main direction of affairs. Against both of them the hatreds grew, because of their self-seeking and the King's infatuation with the younger man. They were especially unpopular among the Marcher lords, who were disturbed by their restless am-bitions in South Wales. In 1321 the Welsh Marcher lords and the Lancastrian party joined hands with intent to procure the exile of the Despensers. Edward soon recalled them, and for once showed energy and resolution. By speed of movement he defeated first the Marcher lords and then the Northern barons under Lancaster at Boroughbridge in Yorkshire in the next year. Lancaster was beheaded by the King. But by some per-versity of popular sentiment miracles were reported at his grave, and his execution was adjudged by many of his contem-poraries to have made him a martyr to royal oppression.

The Despensers and their King now seemed to have attained a height of power. But a tragedy with every feature of classical ruthlessness was to follow. One of the chief Marcher lords, Roger Mortimer, though captured by the King, contrived to escape to France. In 1324 Charles IV of France took advantage of a dispute in Gascony to seize the duchy, except for a coastal strip. Edward's wife, Isabella, "the she-wolf of France," who was disgusted by his passion for Hugh Despenser, suggested that she should go over to France to negotiate with her brother Charles about the restoration of Gascony. There she became the lover and confederate of the exiled Mortimer. She now hit on the stroke of having her son, Prince Edward, sent over from England to do homage for Gascony. As soon as the fourteen-year-old prince, who as heir to the throne could be used to legitimise opposition to King Edward, was in her possession she and Mortimer staged an invasion of England at the head of a large band of exiles. So unpopular and precarious was Edward's Government that Isabella's triumph was swift and complete, and she and Mortimer were emboldened to depose him. The end was a holocaust. In the furious rage which in these days led all who swayed the Government of England to a bloody fate the Despensers were seized and hanged. For the King a more terrible death was reserved. He was imprisoned in Berkeley Castle, and there by hideous methods, which left no mark upon his skin, was slaughtered. His screams as his bowels were burnt out by red-hot irons passed into his body were heard outside the prison walls, and awoke grim echoes which were long unstilled.

BOOK TWO · CHAPTER TWENTY

Scotland and Ireland

THE failures of the reign of Edward II had permanent effects on the unity of the British Isles. Bannockburn ended the possibility of uniting the English and Scottish Crowns by force. Across the Irish Sea the dream of a consolidated Anglo-Norman Ireland also proved vain. Centuries could scarcely break down the barrier that the ruthless Scottish wars had raised between North and South Britain. From Edward I's onslaught on Berwick, in 1296, the armed struggle had raged for twenty-seven years. It was not until 1323 that Robert the Bruce at last obliged Edward II to come to terms. Even then

Bruce was not formally recognised as King of Scots. This title, and full independence for his country, he gained by the Treaty of Northampton signed in 1328 after Edward's murder. A year later the saviour of Scotland was dead.

One of the most famous stories of medieval chivalry tells how Sir James, the "Black" Douglas, for twenty years the faithful sword-arm of the Bruce, took his master's heart to be buried in the Holy Land, and how, touching at a Spanish port, he responded to a sudden call of chivalry and joined the hard-pressed Christians in battle with the Moors. Charging the heathen host, he threw far into the *mêlée* the silver casket containing the heart of Bruce. "Forward, brave heart, as thou wert wont. Douglas will follow thee or die!" He was killed in the moment of victory. So Froissart tells the story in prose and Aytoun in stirring verse, and so, in every generation, Scottish children have been thrilled by the story of "the Good Lord James."

While the Bruce had lived his great prestige, and the loyalty of his lieutenants, served as a substitute for the institutions and traditions that united England. His death left the throne to his son, David II, a child of six, and there ensued one of those disastrous minorities that were the curse of Scotland. The authority of the Scottish kings had often been challenged by the great magnates of the Lowlands and by the Highland chiefs. To this source of weakness were now added others The kin of the "Red" Comyn, never forgiving his assassination by Bruce, were always ready to lend themselves to civil strife. And the barons who had supported the cause of Balliol, and lost their Scottish lands to the followers of Bruce, constantly dreamt of regaining them with English help. David II reigned for forty-two years, but no less than eighteen of them were spent outside his kingdom. For a long spell during the wars of his Regents with the Balliol factions he was a refugee in France. On his return he showed none of his father's talents. Loyalty to France led him to invade England. In 1346, the year of Crécy, he was defeated and captured at Neville's Cross in County Durham. Eleven years of imprisonment followed before he was ransomed for a sum that sorely taxed Scotland. David II was succeeded by his nephew Robert the High Steward, first king of a line destined to melancholy fame.

For many generations the Stuarts, as they came euphoniously to be called, had held the hereditary office from which they took their name. Their claim to the throne was legitimate but they failed to command the undivided loyalty of the Scots.

The first two Stuarts, Robert II and Robert III, were both
elderly men of no marked strength of character. The affairs of
the kingdom rested largely in the hands of the magnates,
whether assembled in the King's Council or dispersed about
their estates. For the rest of the fourteenth century, and
throughout most of the fifteenth, Scotland was too deeply divided to threaten England, or be of much help to her old ally
France. A united England, free from French wars, might have
taken advantage of the situation, but by the mid-fifteenth century England was herself tormented by the Wars of the Roses.

Union of the Crowns was the obvious and natural solution.
But after the English attempts, spread over several reigns, had
failed to impose union by force, the re-invigorated pride of
Scotland offered an insurmountable obstacle. Hatred of the
English was the mark of a good Scot. Though discontented
nobles might accept English help and English pay, the common people were resolute in their refusal to bow to English
rule in any form. The memory of Bannockburn kept a series
of notable defeats at the hands of the English from breeding
despair or thought of surrender.

It is convenient to pursue Scottish history further at this
stage. Destiny was adverse to the House of Stuart. Dogged by
calamity, they could not create enduring institutions comparable to those by whose aid the great Plantagenets tamed English feudalism. King Robert III sent his son later James I to be
schooled in France. Off Flamborough Head in 1406 he was
captured by the English, and taken prisoner to London. He
was twelve years old. In the following month, King Robert
died, and for eighteen years Scotland had no monarch. The
English government was at last prepared to let King James I
be ransomed and return to his country. Captivity had not
daunted James. He had conceived a justifiable admiration for
the English monarch's position and powers, and on his arrival
in Scotland he asserted his sovereignty with vigour. During his
effective reign of thirteen years he ruthlessly disciplined the
Scottish baronage. It was not an experience they enjoyed.
James put down his cousins of the House of Albany, whose
family had been regents during his absence. He quelled the
pretensions to independence of the powerful Lord of the Isles,
who controlled much of the Northern mainland as well as the
Hebrides. All this was accompanied by executions and widespread confiscations of great estates. At length a party of infuriated lords decided on revenge; in 1437 they found the opportunity to slay James by the sword. So died, and before his

task had been accomplished, one of the most forceful of Scottish kings.

The throne once more descended to a child, James II, aged seven. After the inevitable tumults of his minority the boy grew into a popular and vigorous ruler. He had need of his gifts for the "Black" Douglases, descendants of Bruce's faithful knight, had now become over-mighty subjects and constituted a heavy menace to the Crown. Enriched by estates confiscated from Balliol supporters, they were the masters of South-West Scotland. Large territories in the East were held by their kin, the "Red" Douglases, and they also made agile use of their alliances with the clans and confederacies of the North. Moreover, they had a claim, acceptable in the eyes of some, to the throne itself.

For more than a century the Douglases had been among the foremost champions of Scotland; one of them had been the hero of the Battle of Otterburn, celebrated in the ballad of Chevy Chase. Their continual intrigues, both at home and at the English court, with which they were in touch, incensed the young and high-spirited King. In 1452, when he had not long turned twenty-one, James invited the "Black" Douglas to Stirling. Under a safe-conduct he came; and there the King himself in passion stabbed him with his own hand. The King's attendants finished his life. But to cut down the chief of the Douglases was not to stamp out the family. James found himself sorely beset by the Douglas's younger brother and by his kin. Only in 1455 did he finally succeed, by burning their castles and ravaging their lands, in driving the leading Douglases over the Border. In England they survived for many years to vex the House of Stuart with plots and conspiracies, abetted by the English Crown.

James II was now at the height of his power, but fortune seldom favoured the House of Stuart for very long. Taking advantage of the English civil wars, James in 1460 set siege to the castle of Roxburgh, a fortress that had remained in English hands. One of his special interests was cannon and firepower. While inspecting one of his primitive siege-guns, the piece exploded, and he was killed by a flying fragment. James II was then in his thirtieth year. For the fourth time in little more than a century a minor inherited the Scottish Crown. James III was a boy of nine. As he grew up, he showed some amiable qualities; he enjoyed music and took an interest in architecture. But he failed to inherit the capacity for rule displayed by his two predecessors. His reign, which lasted into Tudor times, was much occupied by civil wars and disorders, and its most notable achievement was the rounding off of Scotland's territories by the acquisition, in lieu of a dowry, of Orkney and Shetland from the King of Denmark whose daughter James married.

* * *

The disunity of the kingdom, fostered by English policy and perpetuated by the tragedies that befell the Scottish sovereigns, was not the only source of Scotland's weakness. The land was divided, in race, in speech, and in culture. The rift between Highlands and Lowlands was more than a geographical distinction. The Lowlands formed part of the feudal world, and, except in the South-West, in Galloway, English was spoken. The Highlands preserved a social order much older than feudalism. In the Lowlands the King of Scots was a feudal magnate, in the Highlands he was the chief of a loose federation of clans. He had, it is true, the notable advantage of blood kinship both with the new Anglo-Norman nobility and with the ancient Celtic kings. The Bruces were undoubted descendants of the family of the first King of Scots in the ninth century, Kenneth MacAlpin, as well as of Alfred the Great; the Stuarts claimed, with some plausibility, to be the descendants of Macbeth's contemporary, Banquo. The lustre of a divine antiquity illumined princes whose pedigree ran back into the Celtic twilight of Irish heroic legend. For all Scots, Lowland and Highland alike, the royal house had a sanctity which commanded reverence through periods when obedience and even loyalty were lacking; and much was excused those in whom royal blood ran.

But reverence was not an effective instrument of government. The Scottish Estates did not create the means of fusion of classes that were provided by the English Parliament. In law and fact feudal authority remained far stronger than in England. The King's justice was excluded from a great part of Scottish life, and many of his judges were ineffective competitors with the feudal system. There was no equivalent of the Justice of the Peace or of the Plantagenet Justices in Eyre.

Over much of the kingdom feudal justice itself fought a doubtful battle with the more ancient clan law. The Highland chiefs might formally owe their lands and power to the Crown and be classified as feudal tenants-in-chief, but their real authority rested on the allegiance of their clansmen. Some clan chiefs, like the great house of Gordon, in the Highlands, were also feudal magnates in the neighbouring Lowlands. In the West, the rising house of Campbell played either rôle as it suited them. They were to exercise great influence in the years to come.

Meanwhile the Scots peasant farmer and the thrifty burgess, throughout these two hundred years of political strife, pursued their ways and built up the country's real strength, in spite of the numerous disputes among their lords and masters. The Church devoted itself to its healing mission, and many good bishops and divines adorn the annals of medieval Scotland. In the fifteenth century three Scots universities were founded, St Andrew's, Glasgow and Aberdeen—one more than England had until the nineteenth century.

* * *

Historians of the English-speaking peoples have been baffled by medieval Ireland. Here in the westernmost of the British Isles dwelt one of the oldest Christian communities in Europe. It was distinguished by missionary endeavours and monkish scholarship while England was still a battlefield for heathen Germanic invaders. Until the twelfth century however Ireland had never developed the binding feudal institutions of state that were gradually evolving elsewhere. A loose federation of Gaelic-speaking rural principalities was dominated by a small group of clan patriarchs who called themselves "kings." Over all lay the shadowy authority of the High King of Tara, which was not a capital city but a sacred hill surmounted by earthworks of great antiquity. Until about the year 1000 the High King was generally a member of the powerful northern family of O'Neill. The High Kings exercised no real central authority, except as the final arbiters of genealogical disputes, and there were no towns of Irish founding from which government power could radiate.

When the long, sorrowful story began of English intervention in Ireland, the country had already endured the shock and torment of Scandinavian invasion. But although impoverished by the ravages of the Norsemen, and its accepted order of things greatly disturbed, Ireland was not remade. It was the Norsemen who built the first towns—Dublin, Waterford, Limerick and Cork. The High Kingship had been in dispute since the great Brian Boru, much lamented in song, had broken the O'Neill succession, only himself to be killed in his victory over the Danes at Clontarf in 1014. A century and a half later, one of his disputing successors, the King of Leinster, took refuge at the court of Henry II in Aquitaine. He secured permission to raise help for his cause from among Henry's Anglo-Norman knights. It was a fateful decision for Ireland. In 1169 there arrived in the country the first progenitors of the Anglo-Norman ascendancy.

Led by Richard de Clare, Earl of Pembroke and known as "Strongbow," the invaders were as much Welsh as Norman; and with their French-speaking leaders came the Welsh rank and file. Even to-day some of the commonest Irish names suggest a Welsh ancestry. Others of the leaders were of Flemish origin. But all represented the high, feudal society that ruled over Western Europe, and whose conquests already ranged from Wales to Syria. Irish military methods were no match for the newcomers, and "Strongbow," marrying the daughter of the King of Leinster, might perhaps have set up a new feudal kingdom in Ireland, as had been done by William the Conqueror in England, by Roger in Sicily, and by the Crusading chiefs in the Levant. But "Strongbow" was doubtful both of his own strength and of the attitude of his vigilant superior, Henry II. So the conquests were proffered to the King, and Henry briefly visited this fresh addition to his dominions in 1171 in order to receive the submission of his new vassals. The reviving power of the Papacy had long been offended by the traditional independence of the Irish Church. By Papal Bull in 1155 the overlordship of Ireland had been granted to the English king. The Pope at the time was Adrian IV, an Englishman and the only Englishman ever to be Pope. Here were foundations both spiritual and practical. But the Lord of England and of the greater part of France had little time for Irish problems. He left the affairs of the island to the Norman adventurers, the "Conquistadores" as they have been called. It was a pattern often to be repeated.

The century that followed Henry II's visit marked the height of Anglo-Norman expansion. More than half the country was by now directly subjected to the knightly invaders. Among them was Gerald of Windsor, ancestor of the Fitz-gerald family, the branches of which, as Earls of Kildare and Lords of much else, were for long to control large tracts of southern and central Ireland. There was also William de Burgh, brother of the great English Justiciar, and ancestor of the Earls of Ulster; and Theobald Walter, King John's butler, founder of the powerful Butler family of Ormond which took their name from his official calling. But there was no organised colonisation and settlement. English authority was accepted in the Norse towns on the Southern and Eastern coasts, and the King's writ ran over a varying area of country surrounding Dublin. This hinterland of the capital was significantly known as "The Pale," which might be defined as a defended enclosure. Immediately outside lay the big feudal lordships, and beyond these were the "wild" unconquered Irish of the west. Two races dwelt in uneasy balance, and the division between them was sharpened when a Parliament of Ireland evolved towards the end of the thirteenth century. From this body the native Irish were excluded; it was a Parliament in Ireland of the English only.

* * *

Within a few generations of the coming of the Anglo-Normans, however, the Irish chieftains began to recover from the shock of new methods of warfare. They hired mercenaries to help them, originally in large part recruited from the Norse-Celtic stock of the Scottish western isles. These were the terrible "galloglasses," named from the Irish words for "foreign henchmen." Supported by these ferocious axe-bearers, the clan chiefs regained for the Gaelic-speaking peoples wide regions of Ireland, and might have won more, had they not incessantly quarrelled among themselves.

Meanwhile a change of spirit had overtaken many of the Anglo-Norman Irish barons. These great feudatories were constantly tempted by the independent rôle of the Gaelic clan chief that was theirs for the taking. They could in turn be subjects of the English King or petty kings themselves, like their new allies, with whom they were frequently united by marriage. Their stock was seldom reinforced from England, except by English lords who wedded Irish heiresses, and then became absentee landlords. Gradually however a group of Anglo-Irish nobles grew up, largely assimilated to their adopted land, and as impatient as their Gaelic peasants of rule from London.

If English kings had regularly visited Ireland, or regularly appointed royal princes as resident lieutenants the ties between the two countries might have been closely and honourably woven together. As it was, when the English King was strong, English laws generally made headway; otherwise a loose Celtic anarchy prevailed. King John, in his furious fitful energy, twice went to Ireland and twice brought the quarrelsome Norman barons and Irish chiefs under his suzerainty. Although Edward I never landed in Ireland, English authority was in the

ascendant. Thereafter, the Gaels revived. The shining example
of Scotland was not lost upon them. The brother of the victor
of Bannockburn, Edward Bruce, was called in by his relations
among the Irish chiefs with an army of Scottish veterans. He
was crowned King of Ireland in 1316, but after a temporary
triumph and in spite of the aid of his brother was defeated
and slain at Dundalk.

Thus Ireland did not break loose from the English crown
and gain independence under a Scottish dynasty. But the victory of English arms did not mean a victory for English law,
custom or speech. The Gaelic reaction gathered force. In
Ulster the O'Neills gradually won the mastery of Tyrone. In
Ulster and Connaught the feudal trappings were openly discarded when the line of the de Burgh Earls of Ulster ended in
1333 with a girl. According to feudal law, she succeeded to
the whole inheritance, and was the King's ward to be married
at his choice. In fact she was married to Edward III's second
son, Lionel of Clarence. But in Celtic law women could not
succeed to the chieftainship. The leading male members of the
cadet branches of the de Burgh family accordingly "went
Irish," snatched what they could of the inheritance and assumed the clan names of Burke or, after their founder, Mac-
William. They openly defied the Government in Ulster and
Connaught; in the Western province both French and Irish
were spoken but not English, and English authority vanished
from these outer parts.

To preserve the English character of the Pale and of its surrounding Anglo-Norman lordships, a Parliament was summoned in the middle of the fourteenth century. Its purpose
was to prevent the English from "going Irish" and to compel
men of Irish race in the English-held parts of Ireland to conform to English ways. But its enactments had little effect. In
the Pale the old Norman settlers clung to their privileged
position and opposed all attempts by the representatives of the
Crown to bring the "mere Irish" under the protection of English laws and institutions. Most of Ireland by now lay outside
the Pale, either under native chiefs who had practically no
dealings with the representatives of the English kings, or controlled by Norman dynasts such as the two branches of the
Fitzgeralds, who were earls or clan chiefs, as suited them best.
English authority stifled the creation of either a native or a
"Norman" centre of authority, and the absentee "Lord of
Ireland" in London could not provide a substitute, nor even
prevent his own colonists from intermingling with the popu-

lation. By Tudor times anarchic Ireland lay open to recon-quest, and to the tribulations of re-imposing English royal authority was to be added from Henry VIII's Reformation onwards the fateful divisions of religious belief.

BOOK TWO · CHAPTER TWENTY-ONE

The Long-Bow

IT SEEMED that the strong blood of Edward I had but slumbered in his degenerate son, for in Edward III England once more found leadership equal to her steadily growing strength. Beneath the squalid surface of Edward II's reign there had none the less proceeded in England a marked growth of national strength and prosperity. The feuds and vengeances of the nobility, the foppish vices of a weak King, had been confined to a very limited circle. The English people stood at this time possessed of a commanding weapon, the qualities of which were utterly unsuspected abroad. The long-bow, handled by the well-trained archer class, brought into the field a yeoman type of soldier with whom there was nothing on the Continent to compare. An English army now rested itself equally upon the armoured knighthood and the archers.

The power of the long-bow and the skill of the bowmen had developed to a point where even the finest mail was no certain protection. At two hundred and fifty yards the arrow hail produced effects never reached again by infantry missiles at such a range until the American civil war. The skilled archer was a professional soldier, earning and deserving high pay. He went to war often on a pony, but always with a considerable trans-port for his comfort and his arrows. He carried with him a heavy iron-pointed stake, which, planted in the ground, afforded a deadly obstacle to charging horses. Behind this shelter a company of archers in open order could deliver a discharge of arrows so rapid, continuous, and penetrating as to annihilate the cavalry attack. Moreover, in all skirmishing and patrolling the trained archer brought his man down at

ranges which had never before been considered dangerous in
the whole history of war. Of all this the Continent, and particularly France, our nearest neighbour, was ignorant. In
France the armoured knight and his men-at-arms had long
exploited their ascendancy in war. The foot-soldiers who accompanied their armies were regarded as the lowest type of
auxiliary. A military caste had imposed itself upon society in
virtue of physical and technical assertions which the coming
of the long-bow must disprove. The protracted wars of the
two Edwards in the mountains of Wales and Scotland had
taught the English many hard lessons, and although European
warriors had from time to time shared in them they had
neither discerned nor imparted the slumbering secret of the
new army. It was with a sense of unmeasured superiority that
the English looked out upon Europe towards the middle of
the fourteenth century.

The reign of King Edward III passed through several distinct phases. In the first he was a minor, and the land was
ruled by his mother and her lover, Roger Mortimer. This Government, founded upon unnatural murder and representing
only a faction in the nobility, was condemned to weakness at
home and abroad. Its rule of nearly four years was marked by
concession and surrender both in France and in Scotland. For
this policy many plausible arguments of peace and prudence
might be advanced. The guilty couple paid their way by successive abandonments of English interests. A treaty with
France in March 1327 condemned England to pay a war indemnity, and restricted the English possessions to a strip of
land running from Saintes in Saintonge and Bordeaux to
Bayonne, and to a defenceless enclave in the interior of Gascony. In May 1328 the "Shameful Treaty of Northampton,"
as it was called at the time, recognised Bruce as King north of
the Tweed, and implied the abandonment of all the claims of
Edward I in Scotland.

The anger which these events excited was widespread. The
régime might however have maintained itself for some time
but for Mortimer's quarrel with the barons. After the fall of
the Despensers Mortimer had taken care to put himself in the
advantageous position they had occupied on the Welsh border,
where he could exercise the special powers of government
appropriate to the Marches. This and his exorbitant authority
drew upon him the jealousies of the barons he had so lately
led. His desire to make his position permanent led him to seek
from a Parliament convened in October at Salisbury the title

of Earl of March, in addition to the office he already held of Justice of Wales for life. Mortimer attended, backed by his armed retainers. But it then appeared that many of the leading nobles were absent, and among them Henry, Earl of Lancaster, son of the executed Thomas and cousin of the King, who held a counter-meeting in London. From Salisbury Mortimer, taking with him the young King, set forth in 1328 to ravage the lands of Lancaster, and in the disorders which followed he succeeded in checking the revolt.

It was plain that the barons themselves were too much divided to overthrow an odious but ruthless Government. But Mortimer made an overweening mistake. In 1330 the King's uncle, the Earl of Kent, was deceived into thinking that Edward II was still alive. Kent made an ineffective attempt to restore him to liberty, and was executed in March of that year. This event convinced Henry of Lancaster and other magnates that it might be their turn to suffer next at Mortimer's hands. They decided to get their blow in first by joining Edward III. All eyes were therefore turned to the young King. When seventeen in 1329 he had been married to Philippa of Hainault. In June 1330 a son was born to him; he felt himself now a grown man who must do his duty by the realm. But effective power still rested with Mortimer and the Queen-Mother. In October Parliament sat at Nottingham. Mortimer and Isabella, guarded by ample force, were lodged in the castle. It is clear that very careful thought and preparation had marked the plans by which the King should assert his rights. Were he to succeed, Parliament was at hand to acclaim him. Mortimer and Isabella did not know the secrets of the castle. An underground passage led into its heart. Through this on an October night a small band of resolute men entered, surprised Mortimer in his chamber, which as usual was next to the Queen's, and, dragging them both along the subterranean way, delivered them to the King's officers. Mortimer, conducted to London, was brought before the peers, accused of the murder in Berkeley Castle and other crimes, and, after condemnation by the lords, hanged on November 29. Isabella was consigned by her son to perpetual captivity. Three thousand pounds a year was provided for her maintenance at Castle Rising, in Norfolk, and Edward made it his practice to pay her a periodic visit. She died nearly thirty years later.

Upon these grim preliminaries the long and famous reign began.

* * *

The guiding spirit of the new King was to revive the policy, assert the claims, and restore the glories of his grandfather. The quarrel with Scotland was resumed. Since Bannockburn Robert Bruce had reigned unchallenged in the North. His triumph had been followed inevitably by the ruin and expulsion of the adherents of the opposite Scottish party. Edward, the son of John Balliol, the nominee of Edward I, had become a refugee at the English Court, which extended them the same kind of patronage afterwards vouchsafed by Louis XIV to the Jacobite exiles. No schism so violent as that between Bruce and Balliol could fail to produce rankling injuries. Large elements in Scotland, after Bruce's death in 1329, looked to a reversal of fortune, and the exiles, or "disinherited," as they were termed, maintained a ceaseless intrigue in their own country and a constant pressure upon the English Government. In 1332 an endeavour was made to regain Scotland. Edward Balliol rallied his adherents and, with the secret support of Edward III, sailed from Ravenspur to Kinghorn in Fife. Advancing on Perth, he met and defeated the infant David's Regent at Dupplin Moor. Balliol received the submission of many Scottish magnates, and was crowned at Scone.

Henceforward fortune failed him. Within two months he and his supporters were driven into England. Edward III was now able to make what terms he liked with the beaten Balliol. He was recognised by Balliol as his overlord and promised the town and shire of Berwick. In 1333 therefore Edward III advanced to besiege Berwick, and routed the Scots at Halidon Hill. Here was a battle very different in character from Bannockburn. The power of the archers was allowed to play its part, the schiltrons were broken, and the exiled party reestablished for a while their authority in their native land. There was a price to pay. Balliol, as we have seen, had to cede to the English King the whole of South-Eastern Scotland. In exacting this concession Edward III had overshot the mark; he had damned Balliol's cause in the eyes of all Scots. Meanwhile the descendants and followers of Robert Bruce took refuge in France. The contacts between Scotland and France, and the constant aid given by the French Court to the Scottish enemies of England, roused a deep antagonism. Thus the war in Scotland pointed the path to Flanders.

Here a new set of grievances formed a substantial basis for a conflict. The loss of all the French possessions, except Gascony, and the constant bickering on the Gascon frontiers, had been endured perforce since the days of John. Successive English kings had done homage in Paris for domains of which they had in large part long since been deprived. But in 1328 the death of Charles IV without a direct heir opened a further issue. Philip of Valois assumed the royal power and demanded homage from Edward, who made difficulties. King Edward III, in his mother's right—if indeed the female line was valid— had a remote claim to the throne of France. This claim, by and with the assent and advice of the Lords Spiritual and Temporal, and of the Commons of England, he was later to advance in support of his campaigns.

The youthful Edward was less drawn to domestic politics than to foreign adventure and the chase. He was conscious moreover from the first of the advantage to be gained by diverting the restless energies of his nobles from internal intrigues and rivalries to the unifying purpose of a foreign war. This was also in harmony with the temper of his people. The wars of John and Henry III on the mainland disclose a perpetual struggle between the King and his nobles and subjects to obtain men and money. European adventure was regarded as a matter mainly of interest to a prince concerned with his foreign possessions or claims. Now we see the picture of the Estates of the Realm becoming themselves ardently desirous of foreign conquests. Edward III did not have to wring support from his Parliament for an expedition to France. On the contrary, nobles, merchants, and citizens vied with one another in pressing the Crown to act.

The dynastic and territorial disputes were reinforced by a less sentimental but none the less powerful motive, which made its appeal to many members of the Houses of Parliament. The wool trade with the Low Countries was the staple of English exports, and almost the sole form of wealth which rose above the resources of agriculture. The Flemish towns had attained a high economic development, based upon the art of weaving cloth, which they had brought to remarkable perfection. They depended for their prosperity upon the wool of England. But the aristocracy under the Counts of Flanders nursed French sympathies which recked little of the material well-being of the burghers, regarding them as dangerous and subversive folk whose growth in wealth and power conflicted with feudal ascendancy. There was therefore for many years a complete divergence—economic, social, and political—between the Flemish towns and the nobility of the Netherlands. The former looked to England, the latter to France. Repeated obstructions were placed by the Counts of Flanders upon the wool trade, and each aroused the anger of those concerned on both sides of the narrow sea. The mercantile element in the English Parliament, already inflamed by running sea-fights with the French in the Channel, pleaded vehemently for action.

In 1336 Edward was moved to retaliate in a decisive manner. He decreed an embargo on all exports of English wool, thus producing a furious crisis in the Netherlands. The townspeople rose against the feudal aristocracy, and under Van Artevelde, a war-like merchant of Ghent, gained control, after a struggle of much severity, over a large part of the country. The victorious burghers, threatened by aristocratic and French revenge, looked to England for aid, and their appeals met with a hearty and deeply interested response. Thus all streams of profit and ambition flowed into a common channel at a moment when the flood-waters of conscious military strength ran high, and in 1337, when Edward repudiated his grudging homage to Philip VI, the Hundred Years War began. It was never to be concluded; no general peace treaty was signed, and not until the Peace of Amiens in 1802, when France was a Republic and the French Royal heir a refugee within these isles, did the English sovereign formally renounce his claims to the throne of the Valois and the Bourbons.

* * *

Edward slowly assembled the expeditionary army of England. This was not a feudal levy, but a paid force of picked men. Its backbone consisted of indentured warriors, recruited where and how their captains pleased. In consequence, far less than the legal quota of unreliable militia needed to be drawn from every shire. Both knights and archers embodied the flower of the nation, and the men who gathered in the Cinque Ports formed one of the most formidable and efficient invading armies history had yet seen. These preparations were well known in France; and the whole strength of the monarchy was bent to resist them.

Philip VI looked first to the sea. For many years there had been a warfare of privateers, and bitter hatred ruled between the maritime populations on both sides of the Channel. All the resources of the French marine were strained to produce a fleet; even hired Genoese galleys appeared in the French harbours. In Normandy plans were mooted for a counter-invasion which should repeat the exploits of William the Conqueror. But Edward had not neglected his sea-power. His interest in the Navy won him from Parliament early in his

reign the title of "King of the Sea." He was able to marshal a
fleet equal in vessels and superior in men. A great sea battle
was necessary before the transport of the English army to
France and its maintenance there was feasible. In the summer
of 1340 the hostile navies met off Sluys, and a struggle of nine
hours ensued. "This battle," says Froissart, "was right furious
and horrible, for battles by sea are more dangerous and fiercer
than battles by land, for at sea there is no retreat or fleeing;
there is no remedy but to fight and abide the fortune." The
French admirals had been ordered, under pain of death, to
prevent the invasion, and both sides fought well; but the
French fleet was decisively beaten and the command of the
Channel passed into the hands of the invading Power. The
seas being now open, the army crossed to France. At Cadzand
the landing was opposed. Large bodies of Genoese cross-bowmen and men-at-arms awaited the disembarkation. But the
English archers, shooting from the ships at long range, cleared
the shores and covered the invading troops.

Joined with the revolted Flemings, Edward's numbers were
greatly augmented, and this combined force, which may have
exceeded twenty thousand, undertook the first Anglo-Flemish
siege of Tournai. The city was stubbornly defended, and as
the grip of famine tightened upon the garrison the horrible
spectacle was presented of the "useless mouths" being driven
forth into No Man's Land to perish by inches without pity or
relief. But the capture of this fortress was beyond Edward's
resources in money and supplies. The power of the archers
did not extend to stone walls; the first campaign of what was a
great European war yielded no results, and a prolonged truce
supervened.

This truce was imposed upon the combatants through lack
of money, and carried with it no reconciliation. On the contrary, both sides pursued their quarrel in secondary ways. The
French wreaked their vengeance on the burghers of the
Netherlands, whom they crushed utterly, and Van Artevelde
met his death in a popular tumult at Ghent. The English retaliated as best they could. There was a disputed succession in
Brittany, which they fomented with substantial aids. The
chronic warfare on the frontiers of Gascony continued. Both
sides looked forward to a new trial of strength. Well-trained
men, eager to fight, there were in plenty, but to maintain them
in the field required funds, which to us seem pitifully small,
but without which all was stopped. How could these resources
be obtained? The Jews had been exploited, pillaged, and ex-

pelled in 1290. The Florentine bankers, who had found the money for the first invasion, had been ruined by royal default. The main effort, not only of the Court but of Parliament, was to secure the modest sums of ready money without which knights could not ride nor archers draw their bows. But here a fertile source was at hand. The wealthier and best-organised commercial interest in England was the wool trade, eager to profit from war. A monopoly of wool merchants was created, bound to export only through a particular town to be prescribed by the King from time to time in accordance with his needs and judgment. This system, which was called the Staple, gave the King a convenient and flexible control. By taxing the wool exports which passed through his hands at the Staple port he was assured of an important revenue independent of Parliament. Moreover, the wool merchants who held the monopoly formed a corporation interested in the war, dependent on the King, and capable of lending him money in return for considerate treatment. This development was not welcomed by Parliament, where the smaller wool merchants were increasingly represented. They complained of the favour shown to the monopolists of the Staple, and they also pointed to the menace to Parliamentary power involved in the King's independent resources.

By the spring of 1346 Parliament had at length brought itself to the point of facing the taxation necessary to finance a new invasion. The army was reconstituted, more efficiently than before, its old elements were refreshed with carefully chosen levies. In one wave 2,400 cavalry, twelve thousand archers, and other infantry sailed, and landed unopposed at St Vaast in Normandy on July 12, 1346. Their object this time was no less than the capture of Paris by a sudden dash. The secret was well kept; even the English army itself believed it was going to Gascony. The French could not for some time collect forces sufficient to arrest the inroad. Caen fell, and Edward advanced, burning and laying waste the country, to the very walls of Paris. But by this time the whole power of the French monarchy had gathered against him. A huge force which comprised all the chivalry of France and was probably three times as big as Edward's army assembled in the neighbourhood of St Denis. Against such opposition, added to the walls of a fortified city, Edward's resources could not attempt to prevail. King Philip grimly invited him to choose upon which bank of the Seine he would fight a pitched battle.

The thrust had failed and retreat imposed itself upon the

army. The challenger was forced to quit the lists at a pace which covered sixty miles in four days. The French army moved on a parallel line to the southward and denied the Seine valley to the retreating English. They must now make for the Somme, and hope to cross between Amiens and the sea. Our generation has become familiar with this stretch of the river, which flows through broad morasses, in those days quite undrained and passable only by lengthy causeways and bridges. All these were broken or held by the levies of Picardy. Four separate attempts to find a passage failed. The vanguard of the French main army was already at Amiens. Edward and the English host, which had tried so audacious, even fool-hardy, a spring, now seemed penned in a triangle between the Somme, the seashore, and the French mass. No means had been found to bring the fleet and its transports to any suitable harbour. To cross the Somme near the mouth was a desperate enterprise. The ford was very lengthy, and the tides, violent and treacherous, offered only a few precarious hours in any day.

Moreover, the passage was defended by strong forces popularly estimated to have been upwards of twelve thousand men. "The king of England," says Froissart, "did not sleep much that night, but, rising at midnight, ordered his trumpet to sound. Very soon everything was ready; and, the baggage being loaded, they set out about daybreak, and rode on until they came to the ford at sunrise: but the tide was at that time so full they could not cross." By the afternoon, at the ebb, the enemy's strength was manifest. But since to pause was to perish the King ordered his marshals to plunge into the water and fight their way across. The French resistance was spirited. The knighthood of Picardy rode out and encountered the English on the treacherous sands in the rising waters. "They appeared to be as fond of tilting in the water as upon dry land." By hard fighting, under conditions most deadly to men encased in mail, the passage was forced. At the landing the Genoese cross-bowmen inflicted losses and delayed the deployment until the long-bow asserted its mastery. Thus did King Edward's army escape.

Philip, at the head of a host between thirty and forty thousand strong, was hard upon the track. He had every hope of bringing the insolent Islanders to bay with their backs to the river, or catching them in transit. When he learned that they were already over he called a council of war. His generals advised that, since the tide was now in, there was no choice but to ascend to Abbeville and cross by the bridge which the French held there. To Abbeville they accordingly moved, and lay there for the night.

Edward and his army were intensely convinced of the narrowness of their deliverance. That night they rejoiced; the countryside was full of food; the King gathered his chiefs to supper and afterwards to prayer. But it was certain that they could not gain the coast without a battle. No other resolve was open than to fight at enormous odds. The King and the Prince of Wales, afterwards famous as the Black Prince, received all the offices of religion, and Edward prayed that the impending battle should at least leave him unstripped of honour. With the daylight he marshalled about eleven thousand men in three divisions. Mounted upon a small palfrey, with a white wand in his hand, with his splendid surcoat of crimson and gold above his armour, he rode along the ranks, "encouraging and entreating the army that they would guard his honour and defend his right." "He spoke this so sweetly and with such a cheerful countenance that all who had been dispirited were directly comforted by seeing and hearing him. . . . They ate and drank at their ease . . . and seated themselves on the ground, placing their helmets and bows before them, that they might be the fresher when their enemies should arrive." Their position on the open rolling downs enjoyed few advantages, but the forest of Crécy on their flanks afforded protection and the means of a final stand.

King Philip at sunrise on this same Saturday, August 26, 1346, heard Mass in the monastery of Abbeville, and his whole army, gigantic for those times, rolled forward in their long pursuit. Four knights were sent forth to reconnoitre. About midday the King, having arrived with large masses on the farther bank of the Somme, received their reports. The English were in battle array and meant to fight. He gave the sage counsel to halt for the day, bring up the rear, form the battleline, and attack on the morrow. These orders were carried by famous chiefs to all parts of the army. But the thought of leaving, even for a day, this hated foe, who had for so many marches fled before overwhelming forces, and was now compelled to come to grips, was unendurable to the French army. What surety had they that the morrow might not see their enemies decamped and the field bare? It became impossible to control the forward movement. All the roads and tracks from Abbeville to Crécy were black and glittering with the marching columns. King Philip's orders were obeyed by some, rejected by most. While many great bodies halted obediently, still larger masses poured forward, forcing their way through the stationary or withdrawing troops, and at about five in the afternoon came face to face with the English army lying in full view on the broad slopes of Crécy. Here they stopped.

King Philip, arriving on the scene, was carried away by the ardour of the throng around him. The sun was already low; nevertheless all were determined to engage. There was a corps of six thousand Genoese cross-bowmen in the van of the army. These were ordered to make their way through the masses of horsemen, and with their missiles break up the hostile array in preparation for the cavalry attacks. The Genoese had marched eighteen miles in full battle order with their heavy weapons and store of bolts. Fatigued, they made it plain that they were in no condition to do much that day. But the Count d'Alençon, who had covered the distance on horseback, did not accept this remonstrance kindly. "This is what one gets," he exclaimed, "by employing such scoundrels, who fall off when there is anything for them to do." Forward the Genoese! At this moment, while the cross-bowmen were threading their way to the front under many scornful glances, dark clouds swept across the sun and a short, drenching storm beat upon the hosts. A large flight of crows flew cawing through the air above the French in gloomy presage. The storm, after wetting the bow-strings of the Genoese, passed as quickly as it had come, and the setting sun shone brightly in their eyes and on the backs of the English. This, like the crows, was adverse, but it was more material. The Genoese, drawing out their array, gave a loud shout, advanced a few steps, shouted again, and a third time advanced, "hooted," and discharged their bolts. Unbroken silence had wrapped the English lines, but at this the archers, six or seven thousand strong, ranged on both flanks in "portcullis" formation, who had hitherto stood motionless, advanced one step, drew their bows to the ear, and came into action. They "shot their arrows with such force and quickness," says Froissart, "that it seemed as if it snowed."

The effect upon the Genoese was annihilating; at a range which their own weapons could not attain they were in a few minutes killed by thousands. The ground was covered with feathered corpses. Reeling before this blast of missile destruction, the like of which had not been known in war, the survivors recoiled in rout upon the eager ranks of the French

chivalry and men-at-arms, which stood just out of arrow-shot.
"Kill me those scoundrels," cried King Philip in fury, "for
they stop up our road without any reason." Whereupon the
front line of the French cavalry rode among the retreating
Genoese, cutting them down with their swords. In doing so
they came within the deadly distance. The arrow snowstorm
beat upon them, piercing their mail and smiting horse and
man. Valiant squadrons from behind rode forward into the
welter, and upon all fell the arrow hail, making the horses
caper, and strewing the field with richly dressed warriors. A
hideous disorder reigned. And now Welsh and Cornish light
infantry, slipping through the chequered ranks of the archers,
came forward with their long knives and, "falling upon earls,
barons, knights, and squires, slew many, at which the King of
England was afterwards exasperated." Many a fine ransom
was cast away in those improvident moments.

In this slaughter fell King Philip's ally, the blind King of
Bohemia, who bade his knights fasten their bridles to his in
order that he might strike a blow with his own hand. Thus
entwined, he charged forward in the press. Man and horse
they fell, and the next day their bodies were found still linked.
His son, Prince Charles of Luxembourg, who as Emperor-
elect of the Holy Roman Empire signed his name as King of
the Romans, was more prudent, and, seeing how matters lay,
departed with his following by an unnoticed route. The main
attack of the French now developed. The Count d'Alençon
and the Count of Flanders led heavy cavalry charges upon the
English line. Evading the archers as far as possible, they
sought the men-at-arms, and French, German, and Savoyard
squadrons actually reached the Prince of Wales's division. The
enemy's numbers were so great that those who fought about
the Prince sent to the windmill, whence King Edward directed
the battle, for reinforcements. But the King would not part
with his reserves, saying, "Let the boy win his spurs"—which
in fact he did.

Another incident was much regarded. One of Sir John of
Hainault's knights, mounted upon a black horse, the gift that
day of King Philip, escaping the arrows, actually rode right
through the English lines. Such was their discipline that not a
man stirred to harm him, and, riding round the rear, he returned eventually to the French army. Continuous cavalry
charges were launched upon the English front, until utter
darkness fell upon the field. And all through the night fresh
troops of brave men, resolved not to quit the field without

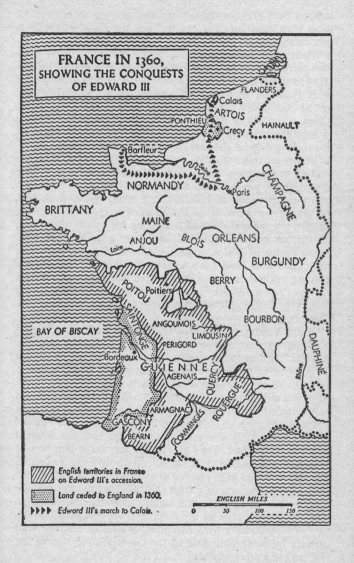

**FRANCE IN 1360,
SHOWING THE CONQUESTS
OF EDWARD III**

FLANDERS

Calais
ARTOIS
PONTHIEU
HAINAULT
Crecy

Barfleur

Seine
CHAMPAGNE

NORMANDY
Paris

BRITTANY

MAINE

ANJOU
BLOIS
ORLEANS

Loire

BURGUNDY

POITOU
Poitiers
BERRY

BAY OF BISCAY
SAINTONGE
ANGOUMOIS
BOURBON
LIMOUSIN
PERIGORD

Bordeaux
G U I E N N E
AGENAIS
QUERCY

Rhône
DAUPHINÉ

ARMAGNAC
ROUERGUE
GASCONY
COMMINGES
BEARN

///// English territories in France
on Edward III's accession.

····· Land ceded to England in 1360.

▷▷▷▷ Edward III's march to Calais.

ENGLISH MILES

0   50   100   150

striking their blow, struggled forward, groping their way. All these were slain, for "No quarter" was the mood of the English, though by no means the wish of their King.

When night had fallen Philip found himself with no more than sixty knights in hand. He was slightly wounded by one arrow, and his horse had been shot under him by another. Sir John Hainault, mounting him again, seized his bridle and forced him from the field upon the well-known principle which, according to Froissart, he exactly expounded, of living to fight another day. The King had but five barons with him on reaching Amiens the next morning.

"When on this Saturday night the English heard no more hooting or shouting, nor any more crying out to particular lords, or their banners, they looked upon the field as their own and their enemies as beaten. They made great fires, and lighted torches because of the obscurity of the night. King Edward who all that day had not put on his helmet, then came down from his post, and, with his whole battalion, advanced to the Prince of Wales, whom he embraced in his arms and kissed, and said, 'Sweet son, God give you good perseverance. You are my son, for most loyally have you acquitted yourself this day. You are worthy to be a sovereign.' The Prince bowed down very low, and humbled himself, giving all honour to the King his father."

On the Sunday morning fog enshrouded the battlefield, and the King sent a strong force of five hundred lancers and two thousand archers to learn what lay upon his front. These met the columns of the French rear, still marching up from Rouen to Beauvais in ignorance of the defeat, and fell upon them. After this engagement the bodies of 1,542 knights and esquires were counted on the field. Later this force met with the troops of the Archbishop of Rouen and the Grand Prior of France, who were similarly unaware of the event, and were routed with much slaughter. They also found very large numbers of stragglers and wandering knights, and "put to the sword all they met." "It has been assured to me for fact," says Froissart, "that of foot-soldiers, sent from the cities, towns, and municipalities, there were slain, this Sunday morning, four times as many as in the battle of the Saturday." This astounding victory of Crécy ranks with Blenheim, Waterloo, and the final advance in the last summer of the Great War as one of the four supreme achievements.[1]

* * *

[1] Written in 1939.

Edward III marched through Montreuil and Blangy to Boulogne, passed through the forest of Hardelot, and opened the siege of Calais. Calais presented itself to English eyes as the hive of that swarm of privateers who were the endless curse of the Channel. Here on the nearest point of the Continent England had long felt a festering sore. Calais was what Dunkirk was to become three centuries later. The siege lasted for nearly a year. Every new art of war was practised by land; the bombards flung cannon-balls against the ramparts with terrifying noise. By sea elaborate barriers of piles stopped the French light craft, which sought to evade the sea blockade by creeping along the coast. All reliefs by sea and land failed. But the effort of maintaining the siege strained the resources of the King to an extent we can hardly conceive. When the winter came his soldiers demanded to go home, and the fleet was on the verge of mutiny. In England everyone complained, and Parliament was morose in demeanour and reluctant in supply. The King and his army lived in their hutments, and he never recrossed the Channel to his kingdom. Machiavelli has profoundly observed that every fortress should be victualled for a year, and this precaution has covered almost every case in history.

Moreover, the siege had hardly begun when King David of Scotland, in fulfilment of the alliance with France, led his army across the Border. But the danger was foreseen, and at Neville's Cross, just west of the city of Durham, the English won a hard-fought battle. The Scottish King himself was captured, and imprisoned in the Tower. He remained there, as we have seen, for ten years until released under the Treaty of Berwick for an enormous ransom. This decisive victory removed the Scottish danger for a generation, but more than once, before and after Flodden, the French alliance was to bring disaster to this small and audacious nation.

Calais held out for eleven months, and yet this did not suffice. Famine at length left no choice to the besieged. They sued for terms. The King was so embittered that when at his demand six of the noblest citizens presented themselves in their shirts, barefoot, emaciated, he was for cutting off their heads. The warnings of his advisers that his fame would suffer in history by so cruel a deed left him obdurate. But Queen Philippa, great with child, who had followed him to the war, fell down before him in an edifying, and perhaps prearranged, tableau of Mercy pleading with Justice. So the burghers of Calais who had devoted themselves to save their people were spared, and even kindly treated. Calais, then, was the fruit, and the sole territorial fruit so far, of the exertions, prodigious in quality, of the whole power of England in the war with France. But Crécy had a longer tale to tell.

BOOK TWO · CHAPTER TWENTY-TWO

The Black Death

WHILE feats of arms and strong endeavours held the English mind a far more deadly foe was marching across the continents to their doom. Christendom has no catastrophe equal to the Black Death. Vague tales are told of awful events in China and of multitudes of corpses spreading their curse afar. The plague entered Europe through the Crimea, and in the course of twenty years destroyed at least one-third of its entire population. The privations of the people, resulting from ceaseless baronial and dynastic wars, presented an easy conquest to disease. The records in England tell more by their silence than by the shocking figures which confront us wherever records were kept. We read of lawsuits where all parties died before the cases could be heard; of monasteries where half the inmates perished; of dioceses where the surviving clergy could scarcely perform the last offices for their flocks and for their brethren; of the Goldsmiths' Company, which had four Masters in a year. These are detailed indications. But far more convincing is the gap which opens in all the local annals of the nation. A whole generation is slashed through by a hideous severance.

The character of the pestilence was appalling. The disease itself, with its frightful symptoms, the swift onset, the blotches, the hardening of the glands under the armpit or in the groin, these swellings which no poultice could resolve, these tumours which, when lanced, gave no relief, the horde of virulent carbuncles which followed the dread harbingers of death, the delirium, the insanity which attended its triumph, the blank spaces which opened on all sides in human society, stunned and for a time destroyed the life and faith of the world. This affliction, added to all the severities of the Middle

Ages, .was more than the human spirit could endure. The Church, smitten like the rest in body, was wounded grievously in spiritual power. If a God of mercy ruled the world, what sort of rule was this? Such was the challenging thought which swept upon the survivors. Weird sects sprang into existence, and plague-haunted cities saw the gruesome procession of flagellants, each lashing his forerunner to a dismal dirge, and ghoulish practices glare at us from the broken annals. It seemed to be the death-rattle of the race.

But at length the plague abated its force. The tumours yielded to fomentations. Recoveries became more frequent; the resistant faculties of life revived. The will to live triumphed. The scourge passed, and a European population, too small for its clothes, heirs to much that had been prepared by more numerous hands, assuaging its griefs in their universality, turned with unconquerable hope to the day and to the morrow.

Philosophers might suggest that there was no need for the use of the destructive mechanism of plague to procure the changes deemed necessary among men. A more scientific reagent was at hand. Gunpowder, which we have seen used in the puny bombards which, according to some authorities, Edward had fired at Crécy and against Calais, was soon decisively to establish itself as a practical factor in war and in human affairs based on war. If cannon had not been invented the English mastery of the long-bow might have carried them even farther in their Continental domination. We know no reason why the yeoman archer should not have established a class position similar in authority to that of the armoured knights, but upon a far broader foundation.

The early fifteenth century was to see the end of the rule of the armoured men. Breastplates and backplates might long be worn as safeguards to life, but no longer as the instrument and symbol of power. If the archers faded it was not because they could not master chivalry; a more convenient agency was at hand which speedily became the common property of all nations. Amid jarring booms and billowing smoke which frequently caused more alarm to friends than foes, but none the less arrested all attention, a system which had ruled and also guided Christendom for five hundred years, which had in its day been the instrument of an immense advance in human government and stature, fell into ruins which were painfully carted away to make room for new building.

* * *

The calamity which fell upon mankind reduced their numbers and darkened their existence without abating their quarrels. The war between England and France continued in a broken fashion, and the Black Prince, the most renowned warrior in Europe, became a freebooter. Grave reasons of State had been adduced for Edward's invasion of France in 1338, but the character of the Black Prince's forays in Aquitaine can vaunt no such excuses. Nevertheless they produced a brilliant military episode.

In 1355 King Edward obtained from Parliament substantial grants for the renewal of active war. An ambitious strategy was adopted. The Black Prince would advance northward from the English territories of Gascony and Aquitaine towards the Loire. His younger brother, John of Gaunt, Duke of Lancaster, struck in from Brittany. The two forces were to join for a main decision. But all this miscarried, and the Black Prince found himself, with forces shrunk to about four thousand men, of whom however nearly a half were the dreaded archers, forced to retire with growing urgency before the advance of a French royal army twenty thousand strong. So grim were his straits that he proposed, as an accommodation, that he and the army should be allowed to escape to England. These terms were rejected by the French, who once again saw their deeply hated foe in their grasp. At Poitiers the Prince was brought to bay. Even on the morning of his victory his vanguard was already marching southwards in retreat. But King John of France was resolved to avenge Crécy and finish the war at a stroke. Forced against all reason and all odds to fight, the haggard band of English marauders who had carried pillage and arson far and wide were drawn up in array and position chosen by consummate insight. The flanks were secured by forests; the archers lined a hedgerow and commanded the only practicable passage.

Ten years had passed since Crécy, and French chivalry and high command alike had brooded upon the tyranny of that event. They had been forced to accept the fact that horses could not face the arrow storm. King Edward had won with an army entirely dismounted. The confusion wrought by English archery in a charging line of horses collapsing or driven mad through pain was, they realised, fatal to the old forms of warfare. King John was certain that all must attack on foot, and he trusted to overwhelming numbers. But the great merit of the Black Prince is that he did not rest upon the lessons of the past or prepare himself to repeat the triumphs of a former battle. He understood that the masses of mail-clad footmen who now advanced upon him in such towering numbers would not be stopped as easily as the horses. Archery alone, however good the target, would not save him. He must try the battle of manœuvre and counter-attack. He therefore did the opposite to what military convention, based upon the then known facts, would have pronounced right.

The French nobility left their horses in the rear. The Black Prince had all his knights mounted. A deadly toll was taken by the archers upon the whole front. The French chivalry, encumbered by their mail, plodded ponderously forward amid vineyards and scrub. Many fell before the arrows, but the arrows would not have been enough at the crisis. It was the English spear and axe men who charged in the old style upon ranks disordered by their fatigue of movement and the accidents of the ground. At the same time, in admirable concert, a strong detachment of mounted knights, riding round the French left flank, struck in upon the harassed and already disordered attack. The result was a slaughter as large and a victory as complete as Crécy, but with even larger gains. The whole French army was driven into ruin. King John and the flower of his nobility were captured or slain. The pillage of the field could not be gathered by the victors; they were already overburdened with the loot of four provinces. The Black Prince, whose record is dinked by many cruel acts of war, showed himself a paladin of the age when, in spite of the weariness and stresses of the desperate battle, he treated the captured monarch with all the ceremony of his rank, seated him in his own chair in the camp, and served him in person with such fare as was procurable. Thus by genius, valour, and chivalry he presents himself in a posture which history has not failed to salute.

King John was carried to London. Like King David of Scotland before him, he was placed in the Tower, and upon this personal trophy, in May 1360, the Treaty of Brétigny was signed. By this England acquired, in addition to her old possession of Gascony, the whole of Henry II's possessions in Aquitaine in full sovereignty, Edward I's inheritance of Ponthieu, and the famous port and city of Calais, which last was held for nearly two hundred years. A ransom was fixed for King John at three million gold crowns, an equivalent of £500,000 sterling. This was eight times the annual revenue of the English Crown in time of peace.

At Crécy France had been beaten on horseback; at Poitiers

she was beaten on foot. These two terrible experiments against the English bit deep into French thought. A sense of hopelessness overwhelmed the French Court and army. How could these people be beaten or withstood? A similar phase of despair had swept across Europe a century earlier after the menacing battles of the Mongol invasions. But, as has been wisely observed, the trees do not grow up to the sky. For a long spell the French avoided battles; they became as careful in fighting the England of King Edward III as in the days of Marlborough they fought the England of Queen Anne. But a great French hero appeared in Bertrand du Guesclin, who, like Fabius Cunctator against Hannibal, by refusing battle and acting through sieges and surprises, rallied the factor of time to the home side. The triumph and the exhaustion of England were simultaneously complete. It was proved that the French army could not beat the English, and at the same time that England could not conquer France. The main effort of Edward III, though crowned with all the military laurels, had failed.

* * *

The years of the war with France are important in the history of Parliament. The need for money drove the Crown and its officials to summoning it frequently. This led to rapid and important developments. One of the main functions of the representatives of the shires and boroughs was to petition for the redress of grievances, local and national, and to draw the attention of the King and his Council to urgent matters. The stress of war forced the Government to take notice of these petitions of the Commons of England, and during the reign of Edward III the procedure of collective petition, which had started under Edward II, made progress. The fact that the Commons now petitioned as a body in a formal way, and asked, as they did in 1327, that these petitions should be transformed into Parliamentary statutes, distinguishes the lower House from the rest of Parliament. Under Edward I the Commons were not an essential element in a Parliament, but under Edward III they assumed a position distinct, vital, and permanent. They had their own clerk, who drafted their petitions and their rejoinders to the Crown's replies. The separation of the Houses now appears. The Lords had come to regard themselves not only as the natural counsellors of the Crown, but as enjoying the right of separate consultation within the framework of Parliament itself. In 1343 the prelates and magnates met in the White Chamber at Westminster, and the knights and burgesses adjourned to the Painted Chamber to discuss the business of the day. Here, in this Parliament, for the first time, the figure of a Speaker emerged. He was not on this occasion a Member of the House, and for some time to come the Commons generally spoke through an appointed deputation. But by the end of the reign the rôle of the Speaker was recognised, and the Crown became anxious to secure its own nominees for this important and prominent office.

The concessions made by Edward III to the Commons mark a decisive stage. He consented that all aids should be granted only in Parliament. He accepted the formal drafts of the Commons' collective petitions as the preliminary bases for future statutes, and by the time of his death it was recognised that the Commons had assumed a leading part in the granting of taxes and the presentation of petitions. Naturally the Commons stood in awe of the Crown. There was no long tradition of authority behind them. The assertions of the royal prerogative in the days of Edward I still echoed in their minds, and there was no suggestion that either they or Parliament as a whole had any right of control or interference in matters of administration and government. They were summoned to endorse political settlements reached often by violence, to vote money and to voice grievances. But the permanent acceptance of Parliament as an essential part of the machinery of government and of the Commons as its vital foundation is the lasting work of the fourteenth century.

Against Papal agents feeling was strong. The interventions of Rome in the days of John, the submissiveness of Henry III to the Church, the exactions of the Papal tax-collectors, the weight of clerical influence within the Household and the Council, all contributed to the growing criticism and dislike of the Church of England. The reign of Edward III brought the climax of this mood. The war with France had stimulated and embittered national sentiment, which resented the influence of an external institution whose great days were already passing. Moreover, this declining power had perforce abandoned its sacred traditional seat in Rome, and was now installed under French influence in enemy territory at Avignon. During these years Parliament passed statutes forbidding appeals to be carried to the Papal Curia for matters cognisable in the royal courts and restricting its power to make appointments in the Church of England. It is true that these statutes were only fitfully enforced, as dictated by diplomatic demands, but the drain of the war left little money for Rome, and the

Papal tax-collectors gleaned the country to little avail during the greater part of the reign.

The renewal in 1369 of serious fighting in Aquitaine found England exhausted and disillusioned. The clergy claimed exemption from taxation, though not always successfully, and they could often flaunt their wealth in the teeth of poverty and economic dislocation. Churchmen were ousting the nobility from public office and anti-clerical feeling grew in Parliament. The King was old and failing, and a resurgence of baronial power was due. John of Gaunt set himself to redress the balance in favour of the Lords by a carefully planned political campaign against the Church. Ready to his hand lay an unexpected weapon. In the University of Oxford, the national centre of theological study and learning, criticism of Papal pretensions and power raised its voice. The arguments for reform set forth by a distinguished Oxford scholar named Wyclif attracted attention. Wyclif was indignant at the corruption of the Church, and saw in its proud hierarchy and absolute claims a distortion of the true principles of Christianity. He declared that dominion over men's souls had never been delegated to mortals. The King, as the Vicar of God in things temporal, was as much bound by his office to curb the material lavishness of the clergy as the clergy to direct the spiritual life of the King. Though Pope and King was each in his sphere supreme, every Christian held not "in chief" of them, but rather of God. The final appeal was to Heaven, not to Rome.

Wyclif's doctrine could not remain the speculations of a harmless schoolman. Its application to the existing facts of Church and State opened deep rifts. It involved reducing the powers of the Church temporal in order to purify the Church spiritual. John of Gaunt was interested in the first, Wyclif in the second. The Church was opposed to both. Gaunt and Wyclif in the beginning each hoped to use the other for his special aim. In 1377 they entered into alliance. Gaunt busied himself in packing the new Parliament, and Wyclif lent moral support by "running about from church to church preaching against abuses." But counter-forces were also aroused. Wyclif's hopes of Church reform were soon involved in class and party prejudices, and Gaunt by his alliance with the revolutionary theologian consolidated the vested interest of the Episcopate against himself. Thus both suffered from their union. The bishops, recognising in Wyclif Gaunt's most dangerous supporter, arraigned him on charges of heresy at St Paul's.

Gaunt, coming to his aid, encountered the hostility of the London mob. The ill-matched partnership fell to pieces and Wyclif ceased to count in high politics.

It was at this same point that his enduring influence began. He resolved to appeal to the people. Church abuses and his own reforming doctrines had attracted many young students around him. He organised his followers into bands of poor preachers, who, like those of Wesley in a later century, spread the doctrines of poverty and holiness for the clergy throughout the countryside. He wrote English tracts, of which the most famous was *The Wicket*, which were passed from hand to hand. Finally, with his students he took the tremendous step of having the Bible translated into English.

"Cristen men and wymmen, olde and yonge, shulden studie fast in the Newe Testament, for it is of ful autorite, and opyn to undirstonding of simple men, as to the poyntis that be moost nedeful to salvacioun. . . . Each place of holy writ, both opyn and derk, techith mekenes and charite; and therfore he that kepith mekenes and charite hath the trewe undirstondyng and perfectioun of al holi writ. . . . Therefore no simple man of wit be aferd unmesurabli to studie in the text of holy writ . . . and no clerk be proude of the verrey undirstondyng of holy writ, for why undirstonding of hooly writ with outen charite that kepith Goddis [be]heestis, makith a man depper dampned . . . and pride and covetise of clerkis is cause of her blindnes and eresie, and priveth them fro verrey undirstondyng of holy writ."

The spirit of early Christianity now revived the English countryside with a keen, refreshing breeze after the weariness of sultry days. But the new vision opened to rich and poor alike profoundly disturbed the decaying society to which it was vouchsafed. The powers of Church and State were soon to realise their danger.

* * *

The long reign had reached its dusk. The glories of Crécy and Poitiers had faded. The warlike King, whose ruling passions were power and fame, who had been willing to barter many prerogatives for which his ancestors had striven in order to obtain money for foreign adventure, was now in old age a debtor to time and fortune. Harsh were the suits they laid against him. He saw the wide conquests which his sword and his son had made in France melt like snow at Easter. A few coastal towns alone attested the splendour of victories long to be cherished in the memories of the Island race. Queen Philippa, his loving wife, had died of plague in 1369. Even before her death the old King had fallen under the consoling thrall of Alice Perrers, a lady of indifferent extraction, but of remarkable wit and capacity, untrammelled by scruple or by prudence. The spectacle of the famous King in his sixties, infatuated by an illicit love, jarred upon the haggard yet touchy temper of the times. Here was something less romantic than the courtly love that had been symbolised in 1348 by the founding of the Order of the Garter. Nobles and people alike would not extend to the mistress of the King's old age the benefits of the commanding motto of the Order, *Honi soit qui mal y pense*. Alice not only enriched herself with the spoils of favour, and decked herself in some at least of the jewels of Queen Philippa, but played high politics with lively zest. She even took her seat with the judges on the bench trying cases in which she was concerned. The movement of the nobility and the Commons was therefore united against her.

The King, at length worn down by war, business, and pleasure, subsided into senility. He had reached the allotted span. He celebrated the jubilee of his reign. The last decade was disparaging to his repute. Apart from Alice, he concentrated his remaining hopes upon the Black Prince; but this great soldier, renowned throughout Europe, was also brought low by the fatigues of war, and was sinking fast in health. In 1376 the Black Prince expired, leaving a son not ten years old as heir apparent to the throne. King Edward III's large share of life narrowed sharply at its end. Mortally stricken, he retired to Sheen Lodge, where Alice, after the modern fashion, encouraged him to dwell on tournaments, the chase, and wide plans when he should recover. But hostile chroniclers have it that when the stupor preceding death engulfed the King she took the rings from his fingers and other movable property in the house and departed for some time to extreme privacy. We have not heard her tale, but her reappearance in somewhat buoyant situations in the new reign seems to show that she had one to tell. All accounts, alas! confirm that King Edward died deserted by all, and that only the charity of a local priest procured him the protection and warrant of the Church in his final expedition.

The Black Prince's son was recognised as King by general assent on the very day his grandfather died, no question of election being raised, and the crown of England passed to a minor.

BOOK THREE

THE END OF THE FEUDAL AGE

King Richard II and
the Social Revolt

JOHN OF GAUNT, Duke of Lancaster, younger brother of the Black Prince, uncle of the King, was head of the Council of Regency and ruled the land. Both the impact and the shadow of the Black Death dominated the scene. A new fluidity swept English society. The pang of almost mortal injury still throbbed, but with it crept a feeling that there was for the moment more room in the land. A multitude of vacant places had been filled, and many men in all classes had the sense of unexpected promotion and enlargement about them. A community had been profoundly deranged, reduced in collective strength, but often individually lifted.

The belief that the English were invincible and supreme in war, that nothing could stand before their arms, was ingrained. The elation of Crécy and Poitiers survived the loss of all material gains in France. The assurance of being able to meet the French or the Scots at any time upon the battlefield overrode inquiries about the upshot of the war. Few recognised the difference between winning battles and making lasting conquests. Parliament in its youth was eager for war, improvident in preparation, and resentful in paying for it. While the war continued the Crown was expected to produce dazzling results, and at the same time was censured for the burden of taxation and annoyance to the realm. A peace approached inexorably which would in no way correspond to the sensation of overwhelming victory in which the English indulged themselves. This ugly prospect came to Richard II as a prominent part of his inheritance.

In the economic and social sphere there arose a vast tumult. The Black Death had struck a world already in movement. Ever since the Crown had introduced the custom of employing wage-earning soldiers instead of the feudal levy the landed tie had been dissolving. Why should not the noble or knight follow the example of his liege lord? Covenants in which a small landowner undertook to serve a powerful neighbour, "except against the King," became common. The restriction would not always be observed. The old bonds of mutual loyalty were disappearing, and in their place grew private armies, the hired defenders of property, the sure precursors of anarchy.

In medieval England the lords of the manors had often based their prosperity on a serf peasantry, whose status and duties were enjoined by long custom and enforced by manorial courts. Around each manor a closely bound and self-sufficient community revolved. Although there had been more movement of labour and interchange of goods in the thirteenth and early fourteenth centuries than was formerly supposed, development had been relatively slow and the break-up of the village community gradual. The time had now come when the compartments of society and toil could no longer preserve their structure. The convulsion of the Black Death violently accelerated this deep and rending process. Nearly one-third of the population being suddenly dead, a large part of the land passed out of cultivation. The survivors turned their ploughs to the richest soils and quartered their flocks and herds on the fairest pastures. Many landowners abandoned ploughs and enclosed, often by encroachment, the best grazing. At this time, when wealth-getting seemed easier and both prices and profits ran high, the available labour was reduced by nearly a half. Small-holdings were deserted, and many manors were denuded of the peasantry who had served them from time immemorial. Ploughmen and labourers found themselves in high demand, and were competed for on all sides. They in their turn sought to better themselves, or at least to keep their living equal with the rising prices. The poet Langland gives an unsympathetic but interesting picture in *Piers Plowman:*

> Labourers that have no land, to live on but their hands,
> Deigned not to dine a day, on night-old wortes.
> May no penny ale him pay, nor a piece of bacon,
> But it be fresh flesh or fish, fried or baked,
> And that chaud and plus-chaud, for chilling of their maw,
> But he be highly-hired, else will he chide.

But their masters saw matters differently. They repulsed fiercely demands for increased wages; they revived ancient claims to forced or tied labour. The pedigrees of villagers were scrutinised with a care hitherto only bestowed upon persons of quality. The villeins who were declared serfs were at least free from new claims. Assertions of long-lapsed authority, however good in law, were violently resisted by the country

folk. They formed unions of labourers to guard their interests.
There were escapes of villeins from the estates, like those of
the slaves from the Southern states of America in the 1850's.
Some landlords in their embarrassment offered to commute
the labour services they claimed and to procure obedience by
granting leases to small-holders. On some manors the serfs
were enfranchised in a body and a class of free tenants came
into being. But this feature was rare. The greatest of all landlords was the Church. On the whole the Spiritual Power stood
up successfully against the assault of this part of its flock.
When a landlord was driven, as was the Abbot of Battle, on
the manor of Hutton, to lease vacant holdings this was done
on the shortest terms, which at the first tactical opportunity
were reduced to a yearly basis. A similar attempt in eighteenth-
century France to revive obsolete feudal claims aroused the
spirit of revolution.

The turmoil through which all England passed affected the
daily life of the mass of the people in a manner not seen again
in our social history till the Industrial Revolution of the nineteenth century. Here was a case in which a Parliament based
upon property could have a decided opinion. In England,
as in France, the Crown had more than once in the past in-
terfered with the local regulation of wages, but the Statute of
Labourers (1351) was the first important attempt to fix wages
and prices for the country as a whole. In the aggravated conditions following the pestilence Parliament sought to enforce
these laws as fully as it dared. "Justices of labour," drawn
from the rural middle classes and with fixed salaries, were
appointed to try offenders. Between 1351 and 1377 nine
thousand cases of breach of contract were tried before the
Common Pleas. In many parts the commissioners, who were
active and biased, were attacked by the inhabitants. Unrest
spread wide and deep.

Still, on the morrow of the plague there was an undoubted
well-being among the survivors. Revolts do not break out in
countries depressed by starvation. Says Froissart, "The peasants' rebellion was caused and incited by the great ease and
plenty in which the meaner folk of England lived." The people were not without the means of protesting against injustice,
nor without the voice to express their discontent. Among the
lower clergy the clerks with small benefices had been severely
smitten by the Black Death. In East Anglia alone eight hundred priests had died. The survivors found that their stipends
remained unaltered in a world of rising prices, and that the

higher clergy were completely indifferent to this problem of
the ecclesiastical proletarian. For this atonement was to be
exacted. The episcopal manors were marked places of attack
in the rising. At the fairs, on market-day, agitators, especially
among the friars, collected and stirred crowds. Langland
voiced the indignation of the established order against these
Christian communists:

> They preach men of Plato and prove it by Seneca
> That all things under heaven ought to be in common:
> And yet he lies, as I live, that to the unlearned so preacheth.

Many vehement agitators, among whom John Ball is the
best known, gave forth a stream of subversive doctrine. The
country was full of broken soldiers, disbanded from the war,
and all knew about the long-bow and its power to kill nobles,
however exalted and well armed. The preaching of revolutionary ideas was widespread, and a popular ballad expressed the
response of the masses:

> When Adam delved, and Eve span,
> Who was then a gentleman?

This was a novel question for the fourteenth century, and
awkward at any time. The rigid, time-enforced framework of
medieval England trembled to its foundations.

These conditions were by no means confined to the Island.
Across the Channel a radical and democratic movement, with
talk much akin to that of our own time, was afoot. All this
rolled forward in England to the terrifying rebellion of 1381.
It was a social upheaval, spontaneous and widespread, arising
in various parts of the country from the same causes, and
united by the same sentiments. That all this movement was the
direct consequence of the Black Death is proved by the fact
that the revolt was most fierce in those very districts of Kent
and the East Midlands where the death-rate had been highest
and the derangement of custom the most violent. It was a cry
of pain and anger from a generation shaken out of submissiveness by changes in their lot, which gave rise alike to new hope
and new injustice.

* * *

Throughout the summer of 1381 there was a general ferment. Beneath it all lay organisation. Agents moved round the
villages of Central England, in touch with a "Great Society"

which was said to meet in London. In May violence broke out in Essex. It was started by an attempt to make a second and more stringent collection of the poll-tax which had been levied in the previous year. The turbulent elements in London took fire, and a band under one Thomas Faringdon marched off to join the rebels. Walworth, the mayor, faced a strong municipal opposition which was in sympathy and contact with the rising. In Kent, after an attack on Lesnes Abbey, the peasants marched through Rochester and Maidstone, burning manorial and taxation records on their way. At Maidstone they released the agitator John Ball from the episcopal prison, and were joined by a military adventurer with gifts and experience of leadership, Wat Tyler.

The royal Council was bewildered and inactive. Early in June the main body of rebels from Essex and Kent moved on London. Here they found support. John Horn, fishmonger, invited them to enter; the alderman in charge of London Bridge did nothing to defend it, and Aldgate was opened treacherously to a band of Essex rioters. For three days the city was in confusion. Foreigners were murdered; two members of the Council, Simon Sudbury, the Archbishop of Canterbury and Chancellor, and Sir Robert Hales, the Treasurer, were dragged from the Tower and beheaded on Tower Hill; the Savoy palace of John of Gaunt was burnt; Lambeth and Southwark were sacked. This was the time for paying off old scores. Faringdon had drawn up proscription lists, and the extortionate financier Richard Lyons was killed. All this has a modern ring. But the loyal citizen body rallied round the mayor, and at Smithfield the King faced the rebel leaders. Among the insurgents there seems to have been a general loyalty to the sovereign. Their demands were reasonable but disconcerting. They asked for the repeal of oppressive statutes, for the abolition of villeinage, and for the division of Church property. In particular they asserted that no man ought to be a serf or do labour services to a *seigneur,* but pay fourpence an acre a year for his land and not have to serve any man against his will, but only by agreement. While the parley was going on Tyler was first wounded by Mayor Walworth and then smitten to death by one of the King's squires. As the rebel leader rolled off his horse, dead in the sight of the great assembly, the young King met the crisis by riding forward alone with the cry, "I will be your leader. You shall have from me all you seek. Only follow me to the fields outside." But the death of Tyler proved a signal for the wave of reaction. The leaderless bands wandered home and spread a vulgar lawlessness through their counties. They were pursued by reconstructed authority. Vengeance was wreaked.

The rising had spread throughout the South-West. There were riots in Bridgewater, Winchester, and Salisbury. In Hertfordshire the peasants rose against the powerful and hated Abbey of St Albans, and marched on London under Jack Straw. There was a general revolt in Cambridgeshire, accompanied by burning of rolls and attacks on episcopal manors. The Abbey of Ramsey, in Huntingdonshire, was attacked, though the burghers of Huntingdon shut their gates against the rioters. In Norfolk and Suffolk, where the peasants were richer and more independent, the irritation against legal villeinage was stronger. The Abbey of Bury St Edmunds was a prominent object of hatred, and the Flemish woollen-craftsmen were murdered in Lynn. Waves of revolt rippled on as far north as Yorkshire and Cheshire, and to the west in Wiltshire and Somerset.

But after Tyler's death the resistance of the ruling classes was organised. Letters were sent out from Chancery to the royal officials commanding the restoration of order, and justices under Chief Justice Tresilian gave swift judgment upon insurgents. The King, who accompanied Tresilian on the punitive circuit, pressed for the observance of legal forms in the punishment of rebels. The warlike Bishop le Despenser, of Norwich, used armed force in the Eastern Counties in defence of Church property, and a veritable battle was fought at North Walsham. Nevertheless the reaction was, according to modern examples, very restrained. Not more than a hundred and fifty executions are recorded in the rolls. There was nothing like the savagery we have seen in many parts of Europe in our own times. Law re-established ruled by law. Even in this furious class reaction no men were hanged except after trial by jury. In January 1382 a general amnesty, suggested by Parliament, was proclaimed. But the victory of property was won, and there followed the unanimous annulment of all concessions and a bold attempt to re-create intact the manorial system of the early part of the century. Yet for generations the upper classes lived in fear of a popular rising and the labourers continued to combine. Servile labour ceased to be the basis of the system. The legal aspect of serfdom became of little importance, and the development of commutation went on, speaking broadly, at an accelerated pace after 1349. Such were the more enduring legacies of the Black Death. The revolt, which to the historian is but a sudden flash of revealing light on medieval conditions among the poorer classes, struck with lasting awe the imagination of its contemporaries. It left a hard core of bitterness among the peasantry, and called forth a vigorous and watchful resistance from authority. Henceforth a fixed desire for the division of ecclesiastical property was conceived. The spread of Lollardy after the revolt drew upon it the hostility of the intimidated victors. Wyclif's "poor preachers" bore the stigma of having fomented the troubles, and their persecution was the revenge of a shaken system.

In the charged, sullen atmosphere of the England of the 1380's Wyclif's doctrines gathered wide momentum. But, faced by social revolution, English society was in no mood for Church reform. All subversive doctrines fell under censure, and although Wyclif was not directly responsible or accused of seditious preaching the result was disastrous to his cause. The landed classes gave silent assent to the ultimate suppression of the preacher by the Church. This descended swiftly and effectively. Wyclif's old opponent, Courtenay, had become Archbishop after Sudbury's murder. He found Wyclif's friends in control of Oxford. He acted with speed. The doctrines of the reformer were officially condemned. The bishops were instructed to arrest all unlicensed preachers, and the Archbishop himself rapidly became the head of a system of Church discipline; and this, with the active support of the State in Lancastrian days, eventually enabled the Church to recover from the attack of the laity. In 1382 Courtenay descended upon Oxford and held a convocation where Christ Church now stands. The chief Lollards were sharply summoned to recant. The Chancellor's protest of university privilege was brushed aside. Hard censure fell upon Wyclif's followers. They blenched and bowed. Wyclif found himself alone. His attack on Church doctrine as distinct from Church privilege had lost him the support of Gaunt. His popular preachers and the first beginnings of Bible-reading could not build a solid party against the dominant social forces.

Wyclif appealed to the conscience of his age. Baffled, though not silenced, in England, his inspiration stirred a distant and little-known land, and thence disturbed Europe. Students from Prague had come to Oxford, and carried his doctrines, and indeed the manuscripts of his writings, to Bohemia. From this sprang the movement by which the fame of John Huss eclipsed that of his English master and evoked the enduring national consciousness of the Czech people.

By his frontal attack on the Church's absolute authority over men in this world, by his implication of the supremacy of the individual conscience, and by his challenge to ecclesiastical dogma Wyclif had called down upon himself the thunderbolts of repression. But his protest had led to the first of the Oxford Movements. The cause, lost in his day, impelled the tide of the Reformation. Lollardy, as the Wyclif Movement came to be called, was driven beneath the surface. The Church, strengthening its temporal position by alliance with the State, brazenly repelled the first assault; but its spiritual authority bore henceforward the scars and enfeeblement resulting from the conflict.

Fuller, the seventeenth-century writer, wrote of Wyclif's preachers, "These men were sentinels against an army ot enemies until God sent Luther to relieve them." In Oxford Wyclifite tradition lingered in Bible study until the Reformation, to be revived by Colet's lectures of 1497–98. In the country Lollardy became identified with political sedition, though this was not what Wyclif had taught. Its ecclesiastical opponents were eager to make the charge, and the passionate, sometimes ignorant, invective of the Lollard preachers, often laymen, supplied a wealth of evidence. Cruel days lay ahead. The political tradition was to be burned out in the misery of Sir John Oldcastle's rebellion under Henry V. But a vital element of resistance to the formation of a militant and triumphant Church survived in the English people. A principle had been implanted in English hearts which shaped the destiny of the race. Wyclif's failure in his own day was total, and the ray of his star faded in the light of the Reformation dawn. "Wyclif," wrote Milton in *Areopagitica,* "was a man who wanted, to render his learning consummate, nothing but his living in a happier age."

The stubborn wish for practical freedom was not broken in England, and the status and temper of the people stand in favourable contrast to the exhausted passivity of the French peasant, bludgeoned to submission by war, famine, and the brutal suppressions of the Jacquerie.

"It is cowardise and lack of hartes and corage," wrote Sir John Fortescue, the eminent jurist of Henry VI's reign, "that kepeth the Frenchmen from rysyng, and not povertye; which corage no Frenche man hath like to the English man. It hath ben often seen in Englond that iij or iv thefes, for povertie, hath sett upon vij or viij true men, and robbyd them al. But it had not been seen in Fraunce, that vij or viij thefes have ben hardy to robbe iij or iv true men. Wherefor it is right seid that few Frenchmen be hangyd for robbery, for that they have no hertys to do so terryble an acte. There be therefor mo men hangyd in Englnd, in a yere, for robberye and manslaughter, than ther be hangid in Fraunce for such cause of crime in vij yers."

* * *

The King was now growing up. His keen instincts and precocious abilities were sharpened by all that he had seen and done. In the crisis of the Peasants' Revolt the brunt of many things had fallen upon him, and by his personal action he had saved the situation on a memorable occasion. It was the King's Court and the royal judges who had restored order when the feudal class had lost their nerve. Yet the King consented to a prolonged tutelage. John of Gaunt, Viceroy of Aquitaine, quitted the realm to pursue abroad interests which included claims to the kingdom of Castile. He left behind him his son, Henry, a vigorous and capable youth, to take charge of his English estates and interests.

It was not till he was twenty that Richard determined to be complete master of his Council, and in particular to escape from the control of his uncles. No King had been treated in such a way before. His grandfather had been obeyed when he was eighteen. Richard at sixteen had played decisive parts. His Household and the Court around it were deeply interested in his assumption of power. This circle comprised the brains of the Government, and the high Civil Service. Its chiefs were the Chancellor, Michael de la Pole, Chief Justice Tresilian, and Alexander Neville, Archbishop of York. Behind them Simon Burley, Richard's tutor and close intimate, was probably the guide. A group of younger nobles threw in their fortunes with the Court. Of these the head was Robert de Vere, Earl of Oxford, who now played a part resembling that of Gaveston under Edward II, and in one aspect foreshadowed that of Strafford in a future generation. The King, the fountain of honour, spread his favours among his adherents, and de Vere was soon created Duke of Ireland. This was plainly a political challenge to the magnates of the Council. Ireland was a reservoir of men and supplies, beyond the control of Parliament and the nobility, which could be used for the mastery of England.

The accumulation of Household and Government offices by the clique around the King and his effeminate favourite af-

fronted the feudal party, and to some extent the national
spirit. As so often happens, the opposition found in foreign
affairs a vehicle of attack. Lack of money, fear of asking for
it, and above all no military leadership, had led the Court to
pacific courses. The nobility were at one with the Parliament
in decrying the unmartial Chancellor Pole and the lush hedon-
ism of the Court. "They were," they jeered, "rather knights
of Venus than of Bellona." War must be waged with France;
and on this theme in 1386 a coherent front was formed against
the Crown. Parliament was led to appoint a commission of
five Ministers and nine lords, of whom the former Councillors
of Regency were the chiefs. The Court bent before the storm
of Pole's impeachment. A purge of the Civil Service, supposed
to be the source alike of the King's errors and of his strength,
was instituted; and we may note that Geoffrey Chaucer, his
equerry, but famous for other reasons, lost his two posts in the
Customs.

When the commissioners presently compelled the King to
dismiss his personal friends Richard in deep distress withdrew
from London. In North Wales he consorted with the new
Duke of Ireland, at York with Archbishop Neville, and at
Nottingham with Chief Justice Tresilian. He sought to marshal
his forces for civil war at the very same spot where Charles I
would one day unfurl the royal standard. Irish levies, Welsh
pikemen, and above all Cheshire archers from his own earldom,
were gathering to form an army. Upon this basis of force
Tresilian and four other royal judges pronounced that the
pressure put upon him by the Lords Appellant, as they were
now styled, and the Parliament was contrary to the laws and
Constitution of England. This judgment, the legal soundness
of which is undoubted, was followed by a bloody reprisal.
The King's uncle, Gloucester, together with other heads of the
baronial oligarchy, denounced the Chief Justice and those who
had acted with him, including de Vere and the other royal advisers, as traitors to the realm. The King—he was but twenty
—had based himself too bluntly upon his royal authority. The
lords of the Council were still able to command the support of
Parliament. They resorted to arms. Gloucester, with an armed
power, approached London. Richard, arriving there first, was
welcomed by the people. They displayed his red and white
colours, and showed attachment to his person, but they were
not prepared to fight the advancing baronial army. In Westminster Hall the three principal Lords Appellant, Gloucester,
Arundel, and Warwick, with an escort outside of three hun-

dred horsemen, bullied the King into submission. He could do
no more than secure the escape of his supporters.

De Vere retired to Chester and raised an armed force to
secure the royal rights. With this, in December 1387, he
marched towards London. But now appeared in arms the
Lords Appellant, and also Gaunt's son Henry. At Radcot
Bridge, in Oxfordshire, Henry and they defeated and broke
de Vere. The favourite fled overseas. The King was now at the
mercy of the proud faction which had usurped the rights of
the monarchy. They disputed long among themselves whether
or not he should be deposed and killed. The older men were
for the extreme course; the younger restrained them. Richard
was brutally threatened with the fate of his great-grandfather,
Edward II. So severe was the discussion that only two of the
Lords Appellant consented to remain with him for supper. It
was Henry, the young military victor, who pleaded for moderation, possibly because his father's claim to the throne would
have been overridden by the substitution of Gloucester for
Richard.

The Lords Appellant, divided as they were, shrank from
deposing and killing the King; but they drew the line at
nothing else. They forced him to yield at every point. Cruel
was the vengeance that they wreaked upon the upstart nobility
of his circle and his legal adherents. The Estates of the Realm
were summoned to give countenance to the new régime. On
the appointed day the five Lords Appellant, in golden clothes,
entered Westminster Hall arm-in-arm. "The Merciless Parliament" opened its session. The most obnoxious opponents were
the royal judges, headed by Tresilian. He had promulgated at
Nottingham the doctrine of the Royal Supremacy, with its
courts and lawyers, over the nobles who held Parliament in
their hand. To this a solemn answer was now made, which,
though, as so often before, it asserted the fact of feudal power,
also proclaimed the principle of Parliamentary control. The
fact vanished in the turbulence of those days, but the principle
echoed down into the seventeenth century.

Chief Justice Tresilian and four of the other judges responsible for the Nottingham declaration were hanged, drawn,
and quartered at Tyburn. The royal tutor, Burley, was not
spared. The victory of the old nobility was complete. Only the
person of the King was respected, and that by the narrowest
of margins. Richard, forced not only to submit but to assent to
the slaughter of his friends, buried himself as low as he could
in retirement.

We must suppose that this treatment produced a marked impression upon his mind. It falls to the lot of few mortals to endure such ordeals. He brooded upon his wrongs, and also upon his past mistakes. He saw in the triumphant lords men who would be tyrants not only over the King but over the people. He laid his plans for revenge and for his own rights with far more craft than before. For a year there was a sinister lull.

* * *

On May 3, 1389, Richard took action which none of them had foreseen. Taking his seat at the Council, he asked blandly to be told how old he was. On being answered that he was three-and-twenty he declared that he had certainly come of age, and that he would no longer submit to restrictions upon his rights which none of his subjects would endure. He would manage the realm himself; he would choose his own advisers; he would be King indeed. This stroke had no doubt been prepared with the uncanny and abnormal cleverness which marked many of Richard's schemes. It was immediately successful. Bishop Thomas, the Earl of Arundel's brother, and later Archbishop of Canterbury, surrendered the Great Seal at his demand. Bishop Gilbert quitted the Treasury, and the King's sympathisers, William of Wykeham and Thomas Brantingham, were restored to their posts as Chancellor and Treasurer. King's nominees were added to those of the Appellants on the judicial bench. Letters from the King to the sheriffs announced that he had assumed the government, and the news was accepted by the public with an unexpected measure of welcome.

Richard used his victory with prudence and mercy. In October 1389 John of Gaunt returned from Spain, and his son, Henry, now a leading personage, was reconciled to the King. The terrible combination of 1388 had dissolved. The machinery of royal government, triumphant over faction, resumed its sway, and for the next eight years Richard governed England in the guise of a constitutional and popular King.

This was an age in which the masses were totally excluded from power, and when the ruling classes, including the new middle class, even in their most deadly quarrels, always united to keep them down. Richard has been judged and his record declared by the socially powerful elements which overthrew him; but their verdict upon his character can only be accepted under reserve. That he sought to subvert and annul the constitutional rights which the rivalries of factions and of Church and baronage had unconsciously but resolutely built up cannot be denied; but whether this was for purposes of personal satisfaction or in the hope of fulfilling the pledge which he had made in the crisis of the Peasants' Revolt, "I will be your leader," is a question not to be incontinently brushed aside. It is true that to one deputation of rebels in 1381 he had testily replied, "Villeins ye are still, and villeins ye shall remain," adding that pledges made under duress went for nothing. Yet by letters patent he freed many peasants from their feudal bonds. He had solemnly promised the abolition of serfdom. He had proposed it to Parliament. He had been overruled. He had a long memory for injuries. Perhaps also it extended to his obligations.

The patience and skill with which Richard accomplished his revenge are most striking. For eight years he tolerated the presence of Arundel and Gloucester, not, as before, as the governors of the country, but still in high positions. There were moments when his passion flared. In 1394, when Arundel was late for the funeral of the Queen, Anne of Bohemia, and the whole procession was delayed, he snatched a steward's wand, struck him in the face and drew blood. The clergy raised a cry that the Church of Westminster had been polluted. Men raked up an old prophecy that God's punishment for the murder of Thomas à Becket would not be exacted from the nation until blood was shed in that sacred nave. Yet after a few weeks we see the King apparently reconciled to Arundel and all proceeding under a glittering mask.

While the lords were at variance the King sought to strengthen himself by gathering Irish resources. In 1394 he went with all the formality of a Royal Progress to Ireland, and for this purpose created an army dependent upon himself, which was to be useful later in overawing opposition in England. When he returned his plans for subduing both the baronage and the Estates to his authority were far advanced. To free himself from the burden of war, which would make him directly dependent upon the favours of Parliament, he made a settlement with France. After the death of his first wife, Anne, he had married in 1396 the child Isabelle, daughter of Charles VI of France. Upon this a truce or pact of amity and non-aggression for thirty years was concluded. A secret clause laid down that if Richard were in future to be menaced by any of his subjects the King of France would come to his aid. Although the terms of peace were the subject of complaint the

King gained immensely by his liberation from the obligation of making a war, which he could only sustain by becoming the beggar and drudge of Parliament. So hard had the Estates pressed the royal power, now goading it on and now complaining of results, that we have the unique spectacle of a Plantagenet king lying down and refusing to pull the wagon farther over such stony roads. But this did not spring from lack of mental courage or from narrowness of outlook. It was a necessary feature in the King's far-reaching designs. He wished beyond doubt to gain absolute power over the nobility and Parliament. Whether he also purposed to use this dictatorship in the interests of the humble masses of his subjects is one of the mysteries, but also the legend, long linked with his name. His temperament, the ups and downs of his spirits, his sudden outbursts, the almost superhuman refinements of his calculations, have all been abundantly paraded as the causes of his ruin. But the common people thought he was their friend. He would, they imagined, had he the power, deliver them from the hard oppression of their masters, and long did they cherish his memory.

*　*　*

The Irish expedition had been the first stage towards the establishment of a despotism; the alliance with France was the second. The King next devoted himself to the construction of a compact, efficient Court party. Both Gaunt and his son and Mowbray, Earl of Norfolk, one of the former Appellants, were now rallied to his side, partly in loyalty to him and partly in hostility to Arundel and Gloucester. New men were brought into the Household. Sir John Bushy and Sir Henry Greene represented local county interests and were unquestioning servants of the Crown. Drawn from the Parliamentary class, the inevitable arbiter of the feuds between Crown and aristocracy, they secured to the King the influence necessary to enable him to face the Estates of the Realm. In January 1397 the Estates were summoned to Westminster, where under deft and at the same time resolute management they showed all due submission. Thus assured, Richard decided at last to strike.

Arundel and Gloucester, though now somewhat in the shade, must have considered themselves protected by time and much friendly intercourse from the consequences of what they had done in 1388. Much had happened since then, and Chief Justice Tresilian, the tutor Burley, and other victims of that blood-bath seemed distant memories. It was with amazement that they saw the King advancing upon them in cold hatred rarely surpassed among men. Arundel and some others of his associates were declared traitors and accorded only the courtesy of decapitation. Warwick was exiled to the Isle of Man. Gloucester, arrested and taken to Calais, was there murdered by Richard's agents; and this deed, not being covered by constitutional forms, bred in its turn new retributions. A stigma rested henceforward on the King similar to that which had marked John after the murder of Arthur. But for the moment he was supreme as no King of all England had been before, and still his wrath was unassuaged.

Parliament was called only to legalise these events. It was found to be so packed and so minded that there was nothing they would not do for the King. Never has there been such a Parliament. With ardour pushed to suicidal lengths, it suspended almost every constitutional right and privilege gained in the preceding century. It raised the monarchy upon a foundation more absolute than even William the Conqueror, war-leader of his freebooting lieutenants, had claimed. All that had been won by the nation through the crimes of John and the degeneracy of Edward II, all that had been conceded or established by the two great Edwards, was relinquished. And the Parliament, having done its work with this destructive thoroughness, ended by consigning its unfinished business to the care of a committee of eighteen persons. As soon as Parliament had dispersed Richard had the record altered by inserting words that greatly enlarged the scope of the committee's work. If his object was not to do away with Parliament, it was at least to reduce it to the rôle it had played in the early days of Edward I, when it had been in fact as well as in name the "King's Parliament."

The relations between Gaunt's son, Henry, the King's cousin and contemporary, passed through drama into tragedy. Henry believed himself to have saved the King from being deposed and murdered by Gloucester, Arundel, and Warwick in the crisis of 1388. Very likely this was true. Since then he had dwelt in familiarity and friendship with Richard; he represented a different element from the old nobility who had challenged the Crown. These two young men had lived their lives in fair comradeship; the one was King, the other, as son of John of Gaunt, stood near the throne and nearer to the succession.

A quarrel arose between Henry and Thomas Mowbray,

now Duke of Norfolk. Riding back from Brentford to London, Mowbray voiced his uneasiness. The King, he said, had never forgiven Radcot Bridge nor the former Appellant party, to which he and his companion had both belonged. They would be the next victims. Henry accused Mowbray of treasonable language. Conflicting reports of what had been said were laid before Parliament. Each, when challenged, gave the lie to the other. Trial by battle appeared the correct solution. The famous scene took place in September 1398. The lists were drawn; the English world assembled; the champions presented themselves; but the King, exasperating the spectators of all classes who had gathered in high expectation to see the sport, cast down his wardour, forbade the combat, and exiled Mowbray for life and Henry for a decade. Both lords obeyed the royal commands. Mowbray soon died; but Henry, astounded by what he deemed ingratitude and injustice, lived and schemed in France.

* * *

The year which followed was an unveiled despotism, and Richard, so patient till his vengeance was accomplished, showed restlessness and perplexity, profusion and inconsequence, in his function. Escorted by his faithful archers from Cheshire, he sped about the kingdom beguiling the weeks with feasts and tournaments, while the administration was left to minor officials at Westminster or Ministers who felt they were neither trusted nor consulted. Financial stringency followed royal extravagance, and forced loans and heavier taxes angered the merchants and country gentry.

During 1398 there were many in the nation who awoke to the fact that a servile Parliament had in a few weeks suspended many of the fundamental rights and liberties of the realm. Hitherto for some time they had had no quarrel with the King. They now saw him revealed as a despot. Not only the old nobility, who in the former crisis had been defeated, but all the gentry and merchant classes, were aghast at the triumph of absolute rule. Nor did their wrath arise from love of constitutional practices alone. They feared, perhaps with many reasons not known to us, that the King, now master, would rule over their heads, resting himself upon the submissive shoulders of the mass of the people. They felt again the terror of the social revolution which they had tasted so recently in the Peasants' Revolt. A solid amalgamation of interest, temper, and action united all the classes which had raised or found themselves above the common level. Here was a King, now absolute, who would, as they muttered, let loose the mob upon them.

In February of 1399 died old John of Gaunt, "time-honoured Lancaster." Henry, in exile, succeeded to vast domains, not only in Lancashire and the north but scattered all over England. Richard, pressed for money, could not refrain from a technical legal seizure of the Lancaster estates in spite of his promises; he declared his cousin disinherited. This challenged the position of every property-holder. And forthwith, by a fatal misjudgment of his strength and of what was stirring in the land, the King set forth in May upon a punitive expedition, which was long overdue, to assert the royal authority in Ireland. He left behind him a disordered administration, deprived of troops, and a land violently incensed against him. News of the King's departure was carried to Henry. The moment had come; the coast was clear, and the man did not tarry. In July Henry of Lancaster, as he had now become, landed in Yorkshire, declaring that he had only come to claim his lawful rights as heir to his venerated father. He was immediately surrounded by adherents, particularly from the Lancaster estates, and the all powerful Northern Lords led by the Earl of Northumberland. The course of his revolt followed exactly that of Isabella and Mortimer against Edward II seventy-two years before. From York Henry marched across England, amid general acclamation, to Bristol, and just as Isabella had hanged Hugh Despenser upon its battlements, so now did Henry of Lancaster exact the capital forfeit from William Scrope, Earl of Wiltshire, Bushy, and Greene, King Richard's Ministers and representatives.

It took some time for the news of Henry's apparition and all that followed so swiftly from it to reach King Richard in the depths of Ireland. He hastened back, though baffled by stormy seas. Having landed in England on July 27, he made a rapid three weeks' march through North Wales in an attempt to gather forces. What he saw convinced him that all was over. The whole structure of his power, so patiently and subtly built up, had vanished as if by enchantment. The Welsh, who would have stood by him, could not face the advancing power of what was now all England. At Flint Castle he submitted to Henry, into whose hands the whole administration had now passed. He rode through London as a captive in his train. He was lodged in the Tower. His abdication was extorted; his death had become inevitable. The last of all

English kings whose hereditary right was indisputable disappeared for ever beneath the portcullis of Pontefract Castle. Henry, by and with the consent of the Estates of the Realm and the Lords Spiritual and Temporal, ascended the throne as Henry IV, and thereby opened a chapter of history destined to be fatal to the medieval baronage. Although Henry's lineage afforded good grounds for his election to the Crown, and his own qualities, and still more those of his son, confirmed this decision, a higher right in blood was to descend through the house of Mortimer to the house of York, and from this after a long interval the Wars of the Roses broke out upon England.

* * *

The character of Richard II and his place in the regard of history remain an enigma. That he possessed qualities of a high order, both for design and action, is evident. That he was almost from childhood confronted with measureless difficulties and wrongful oppressions against which he repeatedly made head is also plain. The injuries and cruelties which he suffered at the hands of his uncle Gloucester and the high nobility may perhaps be the key to understanding him. Some historians have felt that he was prepared not only to exploit Parliamentary and legal manœuvres against the governing classes, but perhaps even that he would use social forces then and for many generations utterly submerged. At any rate, the people for their part long cherished some such notion of him. These unhappy folk, already to be numbered by the million, looked to Richard with hopes destined to be frustrated for centuries. All through the reign of Henry IV the conception they had formed of Richard was idealised. He was deemed, whether rightly or wrongly, a martyr to the causes of the weak and poor. Statutes were passed declaring it high treason even to spread the rumour that he was still alive.

We have no right in this modern age to rob him of this shaft of sunlight which rests upon his harassed, hunted life. There is however no dispute that in his nature fantastic error and true instinct succeeded each other with baffling rapidity. He was capable of more than human cunning and patience, and also of foolishness which a simpleton would have shunned. He fought four deadly duels with feudal aristocratic society. In 1386 he was overcome; in 1389 he was victorious; in 1397-98 he was supreme; in 1399 he was destroyed.

The Usurpation of
Henry Bolingbroke

ALL power and authority fell to King Henry IV, and all who had run risks to place him on the throne combined to secure his right, and their own lives. But the opposite theme endured with strange persistency. The Court of France deemed Henry a usurper. His right in blood was not valid while Richard lived, nor even afterwards when the lineage was scrutinised. But other rights existed. The right of conquest, on which he was inclined to base himself, was discarded by him upon good advice. But the fact that he was acclaimed by the Estates summoned in Richard's name, added to a near right by birth, afforded a broad though challenged foundation for his reign. Many agreeable qualities stand to his credit. All historians concur that he was manly, capable, and naturally merciful. The beginning of his reign was disturbed by the tolerance and lenity which he showed to the defeated party. He who had benefited most from the violent spasm and twist of fortune which had overthrown Richard was the least vindictive against Richard's adherents. He had been near the centre of all the stresses of the late reign; he had been wronged and ill-used; yet he showed a strong repugnance to harsh reprisals. In the hour of his accession he was still the bold knight, surprisingly moderate in success, averse from bloodshed, affianced to growing constitutional ideas, and always dreaming of ending his life as a Crusader. But the sullen, turbulent march of events frustrated his tolerant inclinations and eventually soured his generous nature.

From the outset Henry depended upon Parliament to make good by its weight the defects in his title, and rested on the theory of the elective, limited kingship rather than on that of absolute monarchy. He was therefore alike by mood and need a constitutional King. Great words were used at his accession. "This honourable realm of England, the most abundant angle of riches in the whole world," said Archbishop Arundel, "has been reduced to destruction by the counsels of children and widows. Now God has sent a man, knowing and discreet, for governance, who by the aid of God will be governed and counselled by the wise and ancient of his realm."

"The affairs of the kingdom lie upon us," said the Archbishop. Henry would not act by his own will nor of his own "voluntary purpose or singular opinion, but by common advice, counsel, and consent." Here we see a memorable advance in practice. Parliament itself must not however be deemed a fountain of wisdom and virtue. The instrument had no sure base. It could be packed or swayed. Many of the Parliaments of this period were dubbed with epithets: "the Good Parliament," "the Mad Parliament," "the Merciless Parliament," were fresh in memory. Moreover, the stakes in the game of power played by the great nobles were far beyond what ordinary men or magnates would risk. Who could tell that some sudden baronial exploit might not overset the whole structure upon which they stood? As each change of power had been attended by capital vengeance upon the vanquished there arose in the Commons a very solid and enduring desire to let the great lords cut each other's throats if they were so minded. Therefore the Commons, while acting with vigour, preferred to base themselves upon petition rather than resolution, thus throwing the responsibility definitely upon the most exalted ruling class.

Seeking further protection, they appealed to the King not to judge of any matter from their debates or from the part taken in them by various Members, but rather to await the collective decision of the House. They strongly pressed the doctrine of "grievances before supply," and although Henry refused to accept this claim he was kept so short of money that in practice it was largely conceded. During this time therefore Parliamentary power over finance was greatly strengthened. Not only did the Estates supply the money by voting the taxes, but they began to follow its expenditure, and to require and to receive accounts from the high officers of the State. Nothing like this had been tolerated by any of the Kings before. They had always condemned it as a presumptuous inroad upon their prerogative. These great advances in the polity of England were the characteristics of Lancastrian rule, and followed naturally from the need the house of Lancaster had to buttress its title by public opinion and constitutional authority. Thus Parliament in this early epoch appears to have gained ground never held again till the seventeenth century.

But although the spiritual and lay Estates had seemed not only to choose the sovereign but even to prescribe the succession to the Crown, and the history of these years furnished precedents which Stuart lawyers carefully studied, the actual power of Parliament at this time must not be overstated. The usurpation of Henry IV, the establishment of the rival house in the person of Edward IV, the ousting of Edward V by his uncle, were all acts of feudal violence and rebellion, covered up by declaratory statutes. Parliament was not the author, or even the powerful agent, in these changes, but only the apprehensive registrar of these results of martial and baronial struggles. Elections were not free: the pocket borough was as common in the fifteenth as in the eighteenth century, and Parliament was but the tool and seal of any successful party in the State. It had none the less been declared upon Parliamentary authority, although at Henry's instance, that the crown should pass to the King's eldest son, and to his male issue after him. Thus what had been the English usage was overridden by excluding an elder line dependent on a female link. This did not formally ban succession in the female line, but such was for a long time the practical effect.

On one issue indeed, half social, half religious, King and Parliament were heartily agreed. The Lollards' advocacy of a Church purified by being relieved of all worldly goods did not command the assent of the clergy. They resisted with wrath and vigour. Lollardy had bitten deep into the minds not only of the poorer citizens but of the minor gentry throughout the country. It was in essence a challenge first to the Church and then to the wealthy. The Lollards now sought to win the lay nobility by pointing out how readily the vast treasure of the Church might provide the money for Continental war. But this appeal fell upon deaf ears. The lords saw that their own estates stood on no better title than those of the Church. They therefore joined with the clergy in defence of their property. Very severe laws were now enacted against the Lollards. The King declared, in full agreement with the Estates, that he would destroy heresies with all his strength. In 1401 a terrible statute, *De Heretico Comburendo,* condemned relapsed heretics to be burnt alive, and left the judgment solely to the Church, requiring sheriffs to execute it without allowing an appeal to the Crown. Thus did orthodoxy and property make common cause and march together.

* * *

But the Estates of the Realm considered that their chief immediate safeguard lay in the blotting out of the eclipsed faction. They were the hottest against Richard and those who had been faithful to him. Henry might have been able to stem this tide of cowardly retribution but for a sinister series of events. He and most of his Court fell violently ill through something they had eaten, and poison was suspected. The Welsh, already discontented, under the leadership of Owen Glendower, presently espoused Richard's cause. The slowness of communication had enabled one set of forces to sweep the country while the opposite had hardly realised what was happening. Now they in their turn began to move. Five of the six former Lords Appellant, finding themselves in the shade, formed with friends of Richard II a plot to seize the usurping prince at Windsor. Recovered from his mysterious sickness, riding alone by dangerous roads, Henry evaded their trap. But armed risings appeared in several parts of the country. The severity with which these were quelled mounted to the summit of government. The populace in places joined with the Government forces. The townsfolk at Cirencester beheaded Lord Lumley and the Earls of Kent and Salisbury, the last a Lollard. The conspiracy received no genuine support. All the mercy of Henry's temper could not moderate the prosecutions enforced by those who shared his risks. Indeed in a year his popularity was almost destroyed by what was held to be his weakness in dealing with rebellion and attempted murder. Yet we must understand that he was a braver, stronger man than these cruel personages below him.

The unsuccessful revolt, the civil war which had begun for Richard after his fall, was fatal to the former King. A sanctity dwelt about his person, and all the ceremonial and constitutional procedure which enthroned his successor could not rob him of it. As he lay in Pontefract Castle he was the object of many sympathies both from his adherents and from the suppressed masses. And this chafed and gnawed the party in power. Richard's death was announced in February 1400. Whether he was starved, or, as the Government suggested, went on hunger strike, or whether more direct methods were used, is unknowable. The walls of Pontefract have kept their secret. But far and wide throughout England spread the tale that he had escaped, and that in concealment he awaited his hour to bring the common people of the time to the enjoyment of their own.

All this welled up against Henry of Bolingbroke. He faced continual murder plots. The trouble with the Welsh deepened into a national insurrection. Owen Glendower, who was a remarkable man, of considerable education, carried on a war which was the constant background of English affairs till

1409. The King was also forced to fight continually against the Scots. After six years of this harassment we are told that his natural magnanimity was worn out, and that he yielded himself to the temper of his supporters and of his Parliament in cruel deeds. It may well be so.

His most serious conflict was with the Percys. These lords of the Northern Marches, the old Earl of Northumberland and his fiery son Hotspur, had for nearly three years carried on the defence of England against the Scots unaided and almost entirely at their own expense. They also held important areas for the King in North Wales. They could no longer bear the burden. They demanded a settlement of the account. The Earl presented a bill for £60,000. The King, in bitter poverty, could offer but £40,000. Behind this was a longer tale. The Percys had played a great part in placing Henry on the throne. But Edmund Mortimer, Hotspur's brother-in-law, had joined Glendower in rebellion, and the family were now under suspicion. They held a great independent power, and an antagonism was perhaps inevitable. Hotspur raised the standard of revolt. But at Shrewsbury on July 21, 1403, Henry overcame and slew him in a small, fierce battle. The old Earl, who was marching to his aid, was forced to submit, and pardon was freely extended to him. Parliament was at pains to absolve him from all charges of treason and rebellion and declared him guilty of trespass alone. This clemency was no doubt due to the necessities of the Border and to lack of any other means of defending it against the Scots. The Earl therefore addressed himself to this task, which secured his position at the head of strong forces.

But two years later, with his son's death at heart, he rebelled again, and this time the conspiracy was far-reaching. Archbishop Scrope of York and Thomas Mowbray, Earl of Nottingham, were his principal confederates. The programme of the rebellion was reform, and all personal issues were avoided. Once again Henry marched north, and once again he was successful. Northumberland was driven across the Border, where for some years he remained a menace. Scrope and Mowbray fell into the hands of the King's officers, and Henry, in spite of the appeals of the Archbishop of Canterbury, allowed them to be beheaded after a summary trial. Scrope's execution caused a profound shock throughout the land, and many compared it with the murder of Thomas Becket. At the same time the King's health failed. He was said to be smitten with leprosy, and this was attributed to the wrath of God. The diagnosis at least was incorrect. He had a disfiguring affection of the skin, and a disease of the heart, marked by fainting fits and trances. He was physically a broken man. Henceforward his reign was a struggle against death as well as life.

He still managed to triumph in the Welsh war, and Owen Glendower was forced back into his mountains. But Parliament took all advantages from the King's necessities. Henry saw safety only in surrender. He yielded himself and his burdens to the Estates with the constitutional deference of a modern sovereign. They pressed him hard, and in all the ways most intimately galling. Foreigners, not even excepting the Queen's two daughters, were to be expelled. A Council must be nominated by the King which included the Parliamentary leaders. The accounts of Government expenses were subjected to a Parliamentary audit. The King's own Household was combed and remodelled by unfriendly hands. The new Council demanded even fuller powers. The King pledged himself to govern only by their advice. By these submissions Henry became the least of kings. But he had transferred an intolerable task to others. They had the odium and the toil. They were increasingly unworthy of the trust.

*　*　*

A new figure now came upon the scene. Henry's eldest son, the Prince of Wales, showed already an extraordinary force and quality. He had led the charge against Hotspur at Shrewsbury. He had gained successes in Wales. It was only after the virtual defeat of Glendower that Prince Henry was free to turn to large political intrigue. As his father's health declined he was everywhere drawn into State business. He accepted all duties, and sought only for more. Pressed by his adherents, principally his half-uncles, the three Beaufort brothers, to take over the Government from the failing hands of an invalid, he headed a demand that the King should abdicate in his favour. But Henry of Bolingbroke, though tottering, repulsed the proposal with violent indignation. There was a stern confrontation of father and son at Westminster in 1411. The King's partisans appeared to be the more numerous or more resolute. The Prince withdrew abashed. He was removed from the presidency of the Council and his adherents were dismissed from office. He hid his head in retirement. His opponents even charged him with embezzling the pay of the Calais garrison. From this he cleared himself decisively. But there can be no doubt that the dying sovereign still gripped convulsively the reins of power. Misgovernment and decrepitude remained for a while successfully enthroned. In 1412, when the King could no longer walk and scarcely ride, he was with difficulty dissuaded by his Council from attempting to command the troops in Aquitaine. He lingered through the winter, talked of a Crusade, summoned Parliament in February, but could do no business with it. In March, when praying in Westminster Abbey, he had a prolonged fit, from which he rallied only to die in the Jerusalem Chamber on March 20, 1413.

Thus the life and reign of King Henry IV exhibit to us another instance of the vanities of ambition and the harsh guerdon which rewards its success. He had had wrongs to avenge and a cause to champion. He had hardly dared at first to aim at the crown, but he had played the final stake to gain it. He had found it less pleasing when possessed. Not only physically but morally he sank under its weight. His years of triumph were his years of care and sorrow. But none can say he had not reason and justice behind his actions, or that he was not accepted by the country at large. Upon his death a new personality, built upon a grand historic scale, long hungry for power, ascended without dispute the throne not only of England, but very soon of almost all Western Christendom.

BOOK THREE · CHAPTER TWENTY-FIVE

The Empire of Henry V

A GLEAM of splendour falls across the dark, troubled story of medieval England. Henry V was King at twenty-six. He felt, as his father had never done, sure of his title. He had spent his youth in camp and Council; he had for five or six years intermittently conducted the government of the kingdom during his father's decline. The romantic stories of his riotous youth and sudden conversion to gravity and virtue when charged with the supreme responsibility must not be pressed too far. It may well be true that "he was in his youth a diligent follower of idle practices, much given to instruments of music, and fired with the torches of Venus herself." But if he had thus yielded to the vehement ebullitions of his nature this was no more than a pastime, for always since boyhood he had been held in the grasp of grave business.

In the surging realm, with its ailing King, bitter factions, and deep social and moral unrest, all men had for some time looked to him; and succeeding generations have seldom doubted that according to the standards of his day he was all that a king should be. His face, we are told, was oval, with a long, straight nose, ruddy complexion, dark, smooth hair, and bright eyes, mild as a dove's when unprovoked, but lion-like in wrath; his frame was slender, yet well-knit, strong and active. His disposition was orthodox, chivalrous and just. He came to the throne at a moment when England was wearied of feuds and brawl and yearned for unity and fame. He led the nation away from internal discord to foreign conquest; and he had the dream, and perhaps the prospect, of leading all Western Europe into the high championship of a Crusade. Council and Parliament alike showed themselves suddenly bent on war with France. As was even then usual in England, they wrapped this up in phrases of opposite import. The lords knew well, they said, "that the King will attempt nothing that is not to the glory of God, and will eschew the shedding of Christian blood; if he goes to war the cause will be the renewal of his rights, not his own wilfulness." Bishop Beaufort opened the session of 1414 with a sermon upon "Strive for the truth unto death" and the exhortation "While we have time, let us do good to all men." This was understood to mean the speedy invasion of France.

The Commons were thereupon liberal with supply. The King on his part declared that no law should be passed without their assent. A wave of reconciliation swept the land. The King declared a general pardon. He sought to assuage the past. He negotiated with the Scots for the release of Hotspur's son, and reinstated him in the Earldom of Northumberland. He brought the body, or reputed body, of Richard II to London, and re-interred it in Westminster Abbey, with pageantry and solemn ceremonial. A plot formed against him on the eve of his setting out for the wars was suppressed, by all appearance with ease and national approval, and with only a handful of executions. In particular he spared his cousin, the young Edmund Mortimer, Earl of March, who had been named as the rival King, through whose family much that was merciless was to follow later.

During the whole of 1414 Henry V was absorbed in war-like preparations by land and sea. He reorganised the Fleet.

Instead of mainly taking over and arming private ships, as was
the custom, he, like Alfred, built many vessels for the Royal
Navy. He had at least six "great ships," with about fifteen hundred smaller consorts. The expeditionary army was picked and
trained with special care. In spite of the more general resort to
fighting on foot, which had been compelled by the long-bow,
six thousand archers, of whom half were mounted infantry,
were the bulk and staple of the army, together with two thousand five hundred noble, knightly, or otherwise substantial
warriors in armour, each with his two or three attendants and
aides.

In 1407 Louis, Duke of Orleans, the decisive power at the
Court of the witless French King, Charles VI, had been murdered at the instigation of the Duke of Burgundy, and the strife
of the two parties which divided France became violent and
mortal. To this the late King of England had owed the comparative relief from foreign menace which eased the closing
years of his reign. At Henry V's accession the Orleanists had
gained the preponderance in France, and unfurled the Ori-
flamme against the Duke of Burgundy. Henry naturally allied
himself with the weaker party, the Burgundians, who, in their
distress, were prepared to acknowledge him as King of France.
When he led the power of England across the Channel in con-
tinuation of the long revenge of history for Duke William's
expedition he could count upon the support of a large part of
what is now the French people. The English army of about ten
thousand fighting men sailed to France on August 11, 1415,
in a fleet of small ships, and landed without opposition at the
mouth of the Seine. Harfleur was besieged and taken by the
middle of September. The King was foremost in prowess:

> Once more unto the breach, dear friends, once more;
> Or close the wall up with our English dead.

In this mood he now invited the Dauphin to end the war by
single combat. The challenge was declined. The attrition of the
siege, and disease, which levied its unceasing toll on these
medieval camps, had already wrought havoc in the English
expedition. The main power of France was now in the field.
The Council of War, on October 5, advised returning home by
sea.

But the King, leaving a garrison in Harfleur, and sending
home several thousand sick and wounded, resolved, with about
a thousand knights and men-at-arms and four thousand archers, to traverse the French coast in a hundred-mile march to his

fortress at Calais, where his ships were to await him. All the circumstances of this decision show that his design was to tempt the enemy to battle. This was not denied him. Marching by Fécamp and Dieppe, he had intended to cross the Somme at the tidal ford, Blanchetaque, which his great-grandfather had passed before Crécy. Falsely informed that the passage would be opposed, he moved by Abbeville; but here the bridge was broken down. He had to ascend the Somme to above Amiens by Boves and Corbie, and could only cross at the ford of Béthencourt. All these names are well known to our generation. On October 20 he camped near Péronne. He was now deeply plunged into France. It was the turn of the Dauphin to offer the grim courtesies of chivalric war. The French heralds came to the English camp and inquired, for mutual convenience, by which route His Majesty would desire to proceed. "Our path lies straight to Calais," was Henry's answer. This was not telling them much, for he had no other choice. The French army, which was already interposing itself, by a right-handed movement across his front fell back before his advance-guard behind the Canche river. Henry, moving by Albert, Frévent, and Blangy, learned that they were before him in apparently overwhelming numbers. He must now cut his way through, perish, or surrender. When one of his officers, Sir Walter Hungerford, deplored the fact "that they had not but one ten thousand of those men in England that do no work today," the King rebuked him and revived his spirits in a speech to which Shakespeare has given an immortal form:

> If we are marked to die, we are enough
> To do our country loss; and if to live,
> The fewer men, the greater share of honour.

"Wot you not," he actually said, "that the Lord with these few can overthrow the pride of the French?" [1] He and the "few" lay for the night at the village of Maisoncelles, maintaining utter silence and the strictest discipline. The French headquarters were at Agincourt, and it is said that they kept high revel and diced for the captives they should take.

The English victory of Crécy was gained against great odds upon the defensive. Poitiers was a counter-stroke. Agincourt ranks as the most heroic of all the land battles England has ever fought. It was a vehement assault. The French, whose numbers have been estimated at about twenty thousand, were drawn up in three lines of battle, of which a proportion re-

[1] *Gesta Henrici V*, English Historical Society, ed. B. Williams.

mained mounted. With justifiable confidence they awaited the attack of less than a third their number, who, far from home and many marches from the sea, must win or die. Mounted upon a small grey horse, with a richly jewelled crown upon his helmet, and wearing his royal surcoat of leopards and lilies, the King drew up his array. The archers were disposed in six wedge-shaped formations, each supported by a body of men-at-arms. At the last moment Henry sought to avoid so desperate a battle. Heralds passed to and fro. He offered to yield Harfleur and all his prisoners in return for an open road to Calais. The French prince replied that he must renounce the crown of France. On this he resolved to dare the last extremity. The whole English army, even the King himself, dismounted and sent their horses to the rear; and shortly after eleven o'clock on St Crispin's Day, October 25, he gave the order, "In the name of Almighty God and of Saint George, Avaunt Banner in the best time of the year, and Saint George this day be thine help." The archers kissed the soil in reconciliation to God, and, crying loudly, "Hurrah! Hurrah! Saint George and Merrie England!" advanced to within three hundred yards of the heavy masses in their front. They planted their stakes and loosed their arrows.

The French were once again unduly crowded upon the field. They stood in three dense lines, and neither their cross-bowmen nor their battery of cannon could fire effectively. Under the' arrow storm they in their turn moved forward down the slope, plodding heavily through a ploughed field already trampled into a quagmire. Still at thirty deep they felt sure of breaking the line. But once again the long-bow destroyed all before it. Horse and foot alike went down; a long heap of armoured dead and wounded lay upon the ground, over which the reinforcements struggled bravely, but in vain. In this grand moment the archers slung their bows, and, sword in hand, fell upon the reeling squadrons and disordered masses. Then the Duke of Alençon rolled forward with the whole second line, and a stubborn hand-to-hand struggle ensued, in which the French prince struck down with his own sword Humphrey of Gloucester. The King rushed to his brother's rescue, and was smitten to the ground by a tremendous stroke; but in spite of the odds Alençon was killed, and the French second line was beaten hand to hand by the English chivalry and yeomen. It recoiled like the first, leaving large numbers of unwounded and still larger numbers of wounded prisoners in the assailants' hands.

Now occurred a terrible episode. The French third line, still

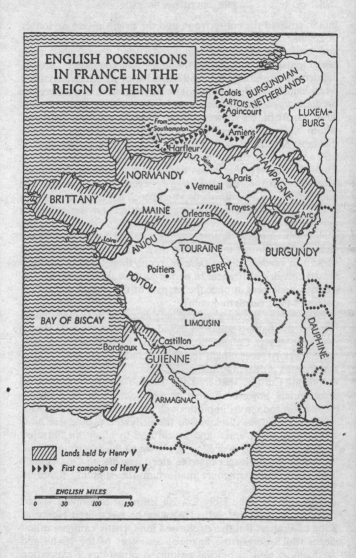

ENGLISH POSSESSIONS
IN FRANCE IN THE
REIGN OF HENRY V

Calais
BURGUNDIAN
ARTOIS
NETHERLANDS
Agincourt
LUXEM-
BURG

From
Southampton
Amiens

Harfleur
Seine
CHAMPAGNE

NORMANDY
Paris

Verneuil

BRITTANY
Troyes
Arc

MAINE
Orleans

ANJOU
TOURAINE
BURGUNDY

Loire
BERRY

Poitiers

POITOU

BAY OF BISCAY

DAUPHINÉ

LIMOUSIN

Castillon

Bordeaux
GUIENNE

Garonne

ARMAGNAC

Lands held by Henry V

First campaign of Henry V

ENGLISH MILES

0   30   100   150

intact, covered the entire front, and the English were no longer in regular array. At this moment the French camp-followers and peasantry, who had wandered round the English rear, broke pillaging into the camp and stole the King's crown, wardrobe, and Great Seal. The King, believing himself attacked from behind, while a superior force still remained unbroken on his front, issued the dread order to slaughter the prisoners. Then perished the flower of the French nobility, many of whom had yielded themselves to easy hopes of ransom. Only the most illustrious were spared. The desperate character of this act, and of the moment, supplies what defence can be found for its ferocity. It was not in fact a necessary recourse. The alarm in the rear was soon relieved; but not before the massacre was almost finished. The French third line quitted the field without attempting to renew the battle in any serious manner. Henry, who had declared at daybreak, "For me this day shall never England ransom pay," [1] now saw his path to Calais clear before him. But far more than that: he had decisively broken in open battle at odds of more than three to one the armed chivalry of France. In two or at most three hours he had trodden underfoot at once the corpses of the slain and the will-power of the French monarchy.

After asking the name of the neighbouring castle and ordering that the battle should be called Agincourt after it, Henry made his way to Calais, short of food, but unmolested by the still superior forces which the French had set on foot. Within five months of leaving England he returned to London, having, before all Europe, shattered the French power by a feat of arms which, however it may be tested, must be held unsurpassed. He rode in triumph through the streets of London with spoils and captives displayed to the delighted people. He himself wore a plain dress, and he refused to allow his "bruised helmet and bended sword" to be shown to the admiring crowd, "lest they should forget that the glory was due to God alone." The victory of Agincourt made him the supreme figure in Europe.

When in 1416 the Holy Roman Emperor Sigismund visited London in an effort to effect a peace he recognised Henry as King of France. But there followed long, costly campaigns and sieges which outran the financial resources of the Island and gradually cooled its martial ardour. A much larger expedition crossed the Channel in 1417. After a hard, long siege Caen was taken; and one by one every French stronghold in Nor-

[1] *Chronicles of London*, ed. C. L. Kingsford, p. 119.

mandy was reduced in successive years. After hideous massacres in Paris, led by the Burgundians, hot-headed supporters of the Dauphin murdered the Duke of Burgundy at Montereau in 1419, and by this deed sealed the alliance of Burgundy with England. Orleanist France was utterly defeated, not only in battle, but in the war. In May 1420, by the Treaty of Troyes, Charles VI recognised Henry as heir to the French kingdom upon his death and as Regent during his life. The English King undertook to govern with the aid of a Council of Frenchmen, and to preserve all ancient customs. Normandy was to be his in full sovereignty, but on his accession to the French throne would be reunited to France. He was accorded the title "King of England and Heir of France." To implement and consolidate these triumphs he married Charles's daughter Catherine, a comely princess, who bore him a son long to reign over impending English miseries.

"It was," says Ranke, "a very extraordinary position which Henry V now occupied. The two great kingdoms, each of which by itself has earlier or later claimed to sway the world, were (without being fused into one) to remain united for ever under him and his successors. . . . Burgundy was bound to him by ties of blood and by hostility to a common foe." [1] He induced Queen Johanna of Naples to adopt his eldest brother as her son and heir. The King of Castile and the heir of Portugal were descended from his father's sisters. Soon after his death the youngest of his brothers, Humphrey of Gloucester, married Jacqueline of Holland and Hainault, who possessed other lands as well. "The pedigrees of Southern and Western Europe alike met in the house of Lancaster, the head of which thus seemed to be the common head of all." It seemed to need only a Crusade, a high, sacred common cause against the advancing Ottoman power, to anneal the bonds which might have united, for a space at least, all Europe under an Englishman. The renewal of strife between England and France consumed powerful contingents which could have been used in defending Christendom against the Turkish menace.

This was the boldest bid the Island ever made in Europe. Henry V was no feudal sovereign of the old type with a class interest which overrode social and territorial barriers. He was entirely national in his outlook: he was the first King to use the English language in his letters and his messages home from the front; his triumphs were gained by English troops; his policy was sustained by a Parliament that could claim to speak for

[1] *History of England*, vol. i, p. 84.

the English people. For it was the union of the country gentry and the rising middle class of the towns, working with the common lawyers, that gave the English Parliament thus early a character and a destiny that the States-General of France and the Cortes of Castile were not to know. Henry stood, and with him his country, at the summit of the world. He was himself endowed with the highest attributes of manhood. "No sovereign," says Stubbs, "who ever reigned has won from contemporary writers such a singular unison of praise. He was religious, pure in life, temperate, liberal, careful, and yet splendid, merciful, truthful, and honourable; 'discreet in word, provident in counsel, prudent in judgment, modest in look, magnanimous in act'; a brilliant soldier, a sound diplomatist, an able organiser and consolidator of all forces at his command; the restorer of the English Navy, the founder of our military, international, and maritime law. A true Englishman, with all the greatnesses and none of the glaring faults of his Plantagenet ancestors."

Ruthless he could also be on occasion, but the Chroniclers prefer to speak of his generosity and of how he made it a rule of his life to treat all men with consideration. He disdained in State business evasive or cryptic answers. "It is impossible" or "It shall be done" were the characteristic decisions which he gave. He was more deeply loved by his subjects of all classes than any King has been in England. Under him the English armies gained an ascendancy which for centuries was never seen again.

* * *

But glory was, as always, dearly bought. The imposing Empire of Henry V was hollow and false. Where Henry II had failed his successor could not win. When Henry V revived the English claims to France he opened the greatest tragedy in our medieval history. Agincourt was a glittering victory, but the wasteful and useless campaigns that followed more than outweighed its military and moral value, and the miserable, destroying century that ensued casts its black shadow upon Henry's heroic triumph.

And there is also a sad underside to the brilliant life of England in these years. If Henry V united the nation against France he set it also upon the Lollards. We can see that the Lollards were regarded not only as heretics, but as what we should now call Christian Communists. They had secured as their leader Sir John Oldcastle, a warrior of renown. They threatened nothing less than a revolution in faith and property.

Upon them all domestic hatreds were turned by a devout and credulous age. It seemed frightful beyond words that they should declare that the Host lifted in the Mass was a dead thing, "less than a toad or a spider." Hostility was whetted by their policy of plundering the Church. Nor did the constancy of these martyrs to their convictions allay the public rage. As early as 1410 we have a strange, horrible scene, in which Henry, then Prince of Wales, was present at the execution of John Badby, a tailor of Worcestershire. He offered him a free pardon if he would recant. Badby refused and the faggots were lighted, but his piteous groans gave the Prince hope that he might still be converted. He ordered the fire to be extinguished, and again tempted the tortured victim with life, liberty, and a pension if he would but retract. But the tailor, with unconquerable constancy, called upon them to do their worst; and was burnt to ashes, while the spectators marvelled alike at the Prince's merciful nature and the tailor's firm religious principles. Oldcastle, who, after a feeble insurrection in 1414, fled to the hills of Herefordshire, was captured at length, and suffered in his turn. These fearful obsessions weighed upon the age, and Henry, while King of the world, was but one of its slaves. This degradation lies about him and his times, and our contacts with his personal nobleness and prowess, though imperishable, are marred.

Fortune, which had bestowed upon the King all that could be dreamed of, could not afford to risk her handiwork in a long life. In the full tide of power and success he died at the end of August 1422 of a malady contracted in the field, probably dysentery, against which the medicine of those times could not make head. When he received the Sacrament and heard the penitential psalms, at the words "Build thou the walls of Jerusalem" he spoke, saying, "Good Lord, thou knowest that my intent has been and yet is, if I might live, to re-edify the walls of Jerusalem." This was his dying thought. He died with his work unfinished. He had once more committed his country to the murderous dynastic war with France. He had been the instrument of the religious and social persecution of the Lollards. Perhaps if he had lived the normal span his power might have become the servant of his virtues and produced the harmonies and tolerances which mankind so often seeks in vain. But Death drew his scythe across these prospects. The gleaming King, cut off untimely, went to his tomb amid the lamentations of his people, and the crown passed to his son, an infant nine months old.

Joan of Arc

A BABY was King of England, and two months later, on the death of Charles VI, was proclaimed without dispute the King of France. Bedford and Gloucester, his uncles, became Protectors, and with a Council comprising the heads of the most powerful families attempted to sustain the work of Henry V. A peculiar sanctity enshrined the hero's son, and the glory of Agincourt played radiantly around his cradle. Nurses, teachers, and presently noble guardians, carefully chosen for the boy's education and welfare, were authorised to use "reasonable chastisement" when required. But this was little needed, for the child had a mild, virtuous, honest, and merciful nature. His piety knew no bounds, and was, with hunting and a taste for literature, the stay and comfort of his long, ignominious, and terrifying pilgrimage. Through his father he inherited the physical weakness of the house of Lancaster, and through his mother the mental infirmities of Charles VI. He was feeble alike in body and mind, unwise and unstable in his judgments, profuse beyond his means to his friends, uncalculating against his enemies, so tender-hearted that it was even said he would let common thieves and murderers live, yet forced to bear the load of innumerable political executions. Flung about like a shuttlecock between the rival factions; presiding as a helpless puppet over the progressive decay of English society and power; hovering bewildered on the skirts of great battles; three times taken prisoner on the field; now paraded with all kingly pomp before Parliaments, armies, and crowds, now led in mockery through the streets, now a captive, now a homeless fugitive, hiding, hunted, hungry; afflicted from time to time by phases of total or partial idiocy, he endured in the fullest measure for nearly fifty years the extreme miseries of human existence, until the hand of murder dispatched him to a world which he was sure would be better, and could hardly have been worse than that he had known. Yet with all his shame of failure and incompetence, and the disasters these helped to bring upon his country, the English people recognised his goodness of heart and rightly ascribed to him the quality of holiness. They never lost their love for him; and in many parts of the country wherever the house of Lancaster was stubbornly defended he was venerated both as saint and martyr.

* * *

At the time of the great King's death the ascendancy of the English arms in France was established. In his brother, John, Duke of Bedford, who went to France as Regent and Commander-in-Chief, a successor of the highest military quality was found. The alliance with Burgundy, carrying with it the allegiance and the sympathies of Paris, persisted. The death, in October 1422, of the French king, who had signed the Treaty of Troyes, while it admitted the English infant to the kingship of France, nevertheless exposed his title to a more serious challenge. South of the Loire, except of course in Gascony, the Dauphin ruled and was now to reign. The war continued bitterly. Nothing could stand against the English archers. Many sieges and much ravaging distressed the countryside. In 1423 the Scots and French under the Earl of Buchan defeated the English at Beaugé, but three other considerable actions ended in English victories. At Cravant, in August 1423, the French found themselves aided by a strong Scottish contingent. These Scotsmen were animated by a hatred of the English which stood out above the ordinary feuds. But the English archers, with their Burgundian allies, shot most of them down. At Verneuil a year later this decision was repeated. Buchan, who had been made Constable of France after Beaugé, had induced his father-in-law, the Earl of Douglas, to bring over a new Scots army and to become Constable himself. The French, having had some success, were inclined to retire behind the Loire, but the rage of the Scots, of whom there were no fewer than five thousand under Douglas, Constable of Scotland, was uncontrollable. They forced a battle, and were nearly all destroyed by the arrow storm. Douglas, Buchan, and other Scottish chieftains fell upon the field, and so grievous was the slaughter of their followers that it was never again possible to form in these wars a separate Scottish brigade.

The English attempt to conquer all vast France with a few thousand archers led by warrior nobles, with hardly any money from home, and little food to be found in the ruined regions, reached its climax in the triumph of Verneuil. There seemed to the French to be no discoverable way to contend against these rugged, lusty, violent Islanders, with their archery, their flexible tactics, and their audacity, born of victories great and small under varying conditions and at almost any odds. Even five years later at the "Battle of the Herrings," gained in February 1429 by Sir John Falstaff, odds of six to one could not prevail. A convoy of four hundred wagons was bringing to the front the herrings indispensable to the English army during Lent.

They were suddenly attacked on the road. But they formed their wagons into what we should now call a laager; the archers stood between and upon them, and at ranges greater than the muskets of Marlborough, Frederick the Great, or Napoleon could ever attain broke the whole assault. Yet the Dauphin, soon to be King Charles VII, stood for France, and everywhere, even in the subjugated provinces, a dull, deep sense of nationality, stirring not only in gentlefolk, but in all who could rise above the submerged classes, centred upon him.

At this time the loves and the acquisitiveness of the Duke of Gloucester, who in Bedford's absence in France became Protector of the English child-King, drove a wedge between England and Burgundy. Jacqueline, Princess of Hainault, Holland, and Zeeland, and heir to these provinces, a woman of remarkable spirit, at the high tide of her nature had been married for reasons of Burgundian policy to the Duke of Brabant, a sickly lout fifteen years of age. She revolted from this infliction, took refuge in England, and appealed to Gloucester for protection. This was accorded in full measure. Gloucester resolved to marry her, enjoy her company, and acquire her inheritance. Some form of divorce was obtained for Jacqueline from the Anti-Pope Benedict XIII, and the marriage took place early in 1423. This questionable romance gave deep offence to the Duke of Burgundy, whose major interests in the Low Countries were injured. Philip of Burgundy saw the world vindictively from his own standpoint. Hitherto his wrath against the treacherous murderers of his father had made him the Dauphin's relentless foe. But this English intrigue gave him a countervailing cause of personal malice, and when Gloucester in State correspondence accused him of falsehood, and in company with Jacqueline descended with a considerable force upon Hainault and Holland, his attachment to English interests became profoundly deranged. Although both Bedford in France and the English Council at home completely disclaimed Gloucester's action, and were prodigal in their efforts to repair the damage, and the Pope was moved by Philip of Burgundy to be tardy in the necessary annulments, the rift between England and Burgundy dates from this event. During these years also the Duke of Brittany detached himself from the English interest and hearkened to the appeals and offers of the French King. By the Treaty of Saumur in October 1425 he obtained the supreme direction of the war against the English. Although no results came to either side from his command the confederacy against France was weakened, and opportunity, faint, fleeting, was offered to the stricken land. The defects of the Dauphin, the exhaustion of the French monarchy, and the disorder and misery of the realm had however reached a pitch where all hung in the balance.

* * *

There now appeared upon the ravaged scene an Angel of Deliverance, the noblest patriot of France, the most splendid of her heroes, the most beloved of her saints, the most inspiring of all her memories, the peasant Maid, the ever-shining, ever-glorious Joan of Arc. In the poor, remote hamlet of Domrémy, on the fringe of the Vosges Forest, she served at the inn. She rode the horses of travellers, bareback, to water. She wandered on Sundays into the woods, where there were shrines, and a legend that some day from these oaks would arise one to save France. In the fields where she tended her sheep the saints of God, who grieved for France, rose before her in visions. St Michael himself appointed her, by right divine, to command the armies of liberation. Joan shrank at first from the awful duty, but when he returned attended by St Margaret and St Catherine, patronesses of the village church, she obeyed their command. There welled in the heart of the Maid a pity for the realm of France, sublime, perhaps miraculous, certainly invincible.

Like Mahomet, she found the most stubborn obstacle in her own family. Her father was scandalised that she should wish to ride in male attire among rough soldiers. How indeed could she procure horses and armour? How could she gain access to the King? But the saints no doubt felt bound to set her fair upon her course. She convinced Baudricourt, governor of the neighbouring town, that she was inspired. He recommended her to a Court ready to clutch at straws. She made a perilous journey across France. She was conducted to the King's presence in the immense stone pile of Chinon. There, among the nobles and courtiers in the great hall, under the flaring torches, she at once picked out the King, who had purposely mingled with the crowd. "Most noble Lord Dauphin," she said, "I am Joan the Maid, sent on the part of God to aid you and the kingdom, and by His order I announce that you will be crowned in the city of Rheims." The aspersion that he was a bastard had always troubled Charles, and when the Maid picked him out among the crowd he was profoundly moved. Alone with him, she spoke of State secrets which she must either have learned from the saints or from other high authority. She asked for an ancient sword which she had never seen, but which she described minutely before it was found. She fascinated the royal circle. When they set her astride on horseback in martial guise it was seen that she could ride. As she couched her lance the spectators were swept with delight.

Policy now, if not earlier, came to play a part. The supernatural character of the Maid's mission was spread abroad. To make sure that she was sent by Heaven and not from elsewhere, she was examined by a committee of theologians, by the Parlement of Poitiers, and by the whole Royal Council. She was declared a virgin of good intent, inspired by God. Indeed, her answers were of such a quality that the theory has been put forward that she had for some time been carefully nurtured, and trained for her mission. This at least would be a reasonable explanation of the known facts.

Orleans in 1429 lay under the extremities of siege. A few thousand English, abandoned by the Burgundians, were slowly reducing the city by an incomplete blockade. Their self-confidence and prestige hardened them to pursue the attack of a fortress deep in hostile territory, whose garrison was four times their number. They had built lines of redoubts, within which they felt themselves secure. The Maid now claimed to lead a convoy to the rescue. In armour plain and without ornament, she rode at the head of the troops. She restored their spirits; she broke the spell of English dominance. She captivated not only the rough soldiery but their hard-bitten leaders. Her plan was simple. She would march straight into Orleans between the strongest forts. But the experienced captain, Dunois, a bastard of the late Duke of Orleans, had not proposed to lead his convoy by this dangerous route. As the Maid did not know the map he embarked his supplies in boats, and brought her by other ways into the besieged town almost alone. She was received with rapture. But the convoy, beaten back by adverse winds, was forced after all to come in by the way she had prescribed; and in fact it marched for a whole day between the redoubts of the English while they gaped at it dumbfounded.

The report of a supernatural visitant sent by God to save France, which inspired the French, clouded the minds and froze the energies of the English. The sense of awe, and even of fear, robbed them of their assurance. Dunois returned to Paris, leaving the Maid in Orleans. Upon her invocation the spirit of victory changed sides, and the French began an offensive which never rested till the English invaders were driven out of France. She called for an immediate onslaught upon the besiegers, and herself led the storming parties against them. Wounded by an arrow, she plucked it out and returned to the charge. She mounted the scaling-ladders and was hurled half stunned into the ditch. Prostrate on the ground, she commanded new efforts. "Forward, fellow-countrymen!" she cried. "God has delivered them into our hands." One by one the English forts fell and their garrisons were slain. The Earl of Suffolk was captured, the siege broken, and Orleans saved. The English retired in good order, and the Maid prudently restrained the citizens from pursuing them into the open country.

Joan now was head indeed of the French army; it was dangerous even to dispute her decisions. The contingents from Orleans would obey none but her. She fought in fresh encounters; she led the assault upon Jargeau, thus opening the Loire above Orleans. In June 1429 she marched with the army that gained the victory of Patay. She told Charles he must march on Rheims to be crowned upon the throne of his ancestors. The idea seemed fantastic: Rheims lay deep in enemy country. But under her spell he obeyed, and everywhere the towns opened their gates before them and the people crowded to his aid. With all the pomp of victory and faith, with the most sacred ceremonies of ancient days, Charles was crowned at Rheims. By his side stood the Maid, resplendent, with her banner proclaiming the Will of God. If this was not a miracle it ought to be.

Joan now became conscious that her mission was exhausted; her "voices" were silent; she asked to be allowed to go home to her sheep and the horses of the inn. But all adjured her to remain. The French captains who conducted the actual operations, though restive under her military interference, were deeply conscious of her value to the cause. The Court was timid and engaged in negotiations with the Duke of Burgundy. A half-hearted attack was made upon Paris. Joan advanced to the forefront and strove to compel victory. She was severely wounded and the leaders ordered the retreat. When she recovered she again sought release. They gave her the rank and revenue of an earl.

But the attitude both of the Court and the Church was changing towards Joan. Up to this point she had championed the Orleanist cause. After her "twenty victories" the full character of her mission appeared. It became clear that she served God rather than the Church, and France rather than the Orleans party. Indeed, the whole conception of France seems to have sprung and radiated from her. Thus the powerful particularist interests which had hitherto supported her were estranged. Meanwhile she planned to regain Paris for France. When in May 1430 the town of Compiègne revolted against the decision of the King that it should yield to the English, Joan with only six hundred men attempted its succour. She had no doubt that the enterprise was desperate. It took the form of a cavalry sortie across the long causeway over the river. The enemy, at first surprised, rallied, and a panic among the French ensued. Joan, undaunted, was bridled from the field by her friends. She still fought with the rearguard across the causeway. The two sides were intermingled. The fortress itself was imperilled. Its cannon could not fire upon the confused *mêlée*. Flavy, the governor whose duty it was to save the town, felt obliged to pull up the drawbridge in her face and leave her to the Burgundians.

She was sold to the rejoicing English for a moderate sum. To Bedford and his army she was a witch, a sorceress, a harlot, a foul imp of black magic, at all costs to be destroyed. But it was not easy to frame a charge; she was a prisoner of war, and many conventions among the warring aristocrats protected her. The spiritual arm was therefore invoked. The Bishop of Beauvais, the learned doctors of Paris, pursued her for heresy. She underwent prolonged inquisition. The gravamen was that by refusing to disown her "voices" she was defying the judgment and authority of the Church. For a whole year her fate hung in the balance, while careless, ungrateful Charles lifted not a finger to save her. There is no record of any ransom being offered. Joan had recanted under endless pressure, and had been accorded all the mercy of perpetual imprisonment on bread and water. But in her cell the inexorable saints appeared to her again. Entrapping priests set her armour and man's clothes before her; with renewed exaltation she put them on. From that moment she was declared a relapsed heretic and condemned to the fire. Amid an immense concourse she was dragged to the stake in the market-place of Rouen. High upon the pyramid of faggots the flames rose towards her, and the smoke of doom wreathed and curled. She raised a cross made of firewood, and her last word was "Jesus!" History has recorded the comment of an English soldier who witnessed the scene. "We are lost," he said. "We have burnt a saint." All this proved true.

Joan was a being so uplifted from the ordinary run of mankind that she finds no equal in a thousand years. The records of her trial present us with facts alive to-day through all the mists of time. Out of her own mouth can she be judged in each generation. She embodied the natural goodness and valour of the human race in unexampled perfection. Unconquerable courage, infinite compassion, the virtue of the simple, the wisdom of the just, shone forth in her. She glorifies as she freed the soil from which she sprang. All soldiers should read her story and ponder on the words and deeds of the true warrior, who in one single year, though untaught in technical arts, reveals in every situation the key of victory.

Joan of Arc perished on May 29, 1431, and thereafter the tides of war flowed remorselessly against the English. The boy Henry was crowned in Paris in December amid chilly throngs. The whole spirit of the country was against the English claim. Burgundy became definitely hostile in 1435. Bedford died, and was succeeded by lesser captains. The opposing Captain-in-Chief, Dunois, instead of leading French chivalry to frontal attacks upon the English archer array, acted by manœuvre and surprise. The French gained a series of battles. Here they caught the English men-at-arms on one side of the river while their archers were on the other; there by a cannonade they forced a disjointed English attack. The French artillery now became the finest in the world. Seven hundred engineers, under the brothers Bureau, used a heavy battering-train of twenty-two inches calibre, firing gigantic stone balls against the numberless castles which the English still held. Places which in the days of Henry V could be reduced only by famine now fell in a few days to smashing bombardment. All Northern France, except Calais, was reconquered. Even Guienne, dowry of Eleanor of Aquitaine, for three hundred years a loyal, contented fief of the English Crown, was overrun. It is remarkable however that this province almost immediately revolted against France, called upon the English to return, and had to be subdued anew. The Council of competing noble factions in England was incapable of providing effective succour. The valiant Talbot, Earl of Shrewsbury, was killed with most of his English in his foolhardy battle of Castillon in 1453. The surviving English made terms to sail home from La Rochelle. By the end of that year, through force or negotiation, the English had been driven off the Continent. Of all their conquests they held henceforward only the bridgehead of Calais, to garrison which cost nearly a third of the revenue granted by Parliament to the Crown.

York and Lancaster

A S Henry VI grew up his virtues and simpleness became equally apparent. He was not entirely docile. In 1431 when he was ten years old Warwick, his preceptor, reported that he was "grown in years, in stature of his person, and also in conceit and knowledge of his royal estate, the which causes him to grudge any chastising." He had spoken "of divers matters not behoveful." The Council had in his childhood made a great show of him, brought him to ceremonies, and crowned him with solemnity both in London and Paris. As time passed they became naturally inclined to keep him under stricter control. His consequence was maintained by the rivalry of the nobles, and by the unbounded hopes of the nation. A body of knights and squires had for some years been appointed to dwell with him and be his servants. As the disastrous years in France unfolded he was pressed continually to assert himself. At fifteen he was already regularly attending Council meetings. He was allowed to exercise a measure of prerogative both in pardons and rewards. When the Council differed it was agreed he should decide. He often played the part of mediator by compromise. Before he was eighteen he had absorbed himself in the foundation of his colleges at Eton and at Cambridge. He was thought by the high nobles to take a precocious and unhealthy interest in public affairs which neither his wisdom nor experience could sustain. He showed a feebleness of mind and spirit and a gentleness of nature which were little suited to the fierce rivalries of a martial age. Opinion and also interests were divided upon him. Flattering accounts of his remarkable intelligence were matched by other equally biased tales that he was an idiot almost incapable of distinguishing between right and wrong. Modern historians confirm the less complimentary view. At the hour when a strong king alone could re-create the balance between the nation and the nobility, when all demanded the restraint of faction at home and the waging of victorious war without undue expense abroad, the throne was known to be occupied by a devout simpleton suited alike by his qualities and defects to be a puppet.

These were evil days for England. The Crown was beggarly,

the nobles rich. The people were unhappy and unrestful rather than unprosperous. The religious issues of an earlier century were now dominated by more practical politics. The empire so swiftly gained upon the Continent was being cast away by an incompetent and self-enriching oligarchy, and the revenues which might have sent irresistible armies to beat the French were engrossed by the Church.

The princes of the house of Lancaster disputed among themselves. After Bedford's death in 1435 the tension grew between Gloucester and the Beauforts. Cardinal Beaufort, Bishop of Winchester, and one of the legitimised sons of John of Gaunt's third union, was himself the richest man in England, and a prime master of such contributions as the Church thought it prudent to make to the State. From his private fortune, upon pledges which could only be redeemed in gold, he constantly provided the Court, and often the Council, with ready money. Leaning always to the King, meddling little with the ill-starred conduct of affairs, the Beauforts, with whom must be counted William de la Pole, Earl of Suffolk, maintained by peaceful arts and critical detachment an influence to which the martial elements were often forced to defer. The force of this faction was in 1441 turned in malice upon the Duke of Gloucester. He was now wedded, after the invalidation of his marriage with his wife Jacqueline, to the fair Eleanor Cobham, who had long been his mistress. As the weakest point in his array she was singled out for attack, and was accused with much elaboration of lending herself to the black arts. She had made, it was alleged, a wax figure of the King, and had exposed it from time to time to heat, which wasted it away. Her object, according to her accusers, was to cause the King's life to waste away too. She was declared guilty. Barefoot, in penitential garb, she was made to walk for three days through the London streets, and then consigned to perpetual imprisonment with reasonable maintenance. Her alleged accomplices were put to death. This was of course a trial of strength between the parties and a very real pang and injury to Gloucester.

The loss of France, as it sank in year by year, provoked a deep, sullen rage throughout the land. This passion stirred not only the nobility, but the archer class with their admiring friends in every village. A strong sense of wounded national pride spread among the people. Where were the glories of Crécy and Poitiers? Where were the fruits of famous Agincourt? All were squandered, or indeed betrayed, by those who had profited from the overthrow and murder of good King Richard. There were not lacking agitators and preachers, priestly and lay, who prepared a national and social upheaval by reminding folks that the true line of succession had been changed by violence. All this was an undercurrent, but none the less potent. It was a background, shadowy but dominant. Exactly how these forces worked is unknown; but slowly, ceaselessly, there grew in the land, not only among the nobility and gentry, strong parties which presently assumed both shape and organisation.

At twenty-three it was high time that King Henry should marry. Each of the Lancastrian factions was anxious to provide him with a queen; but Cardinal Beaufort and his brothers, with their ally, Suffolk, whose ancestors, the de la Poles of Hull, had founded their fortunes upon trade, prevailed over the Duke of Gloucester, weakened as he was by maladministration and ill-success. Suffolk was sent to France to arrange a further truce, and it was implied in his mission that he should treat for a marriage between the King of England and Margaret of Anjou, niece of the King of France. This remarkable woman added to rare beauty and charm a masterly intellect and a dauntless spirit. Like Joan the Maid, though without her inspiration or her cause, she knew how to make men fight. Even from the seclusion of her family her qualities became well known. Was she not then the mate for this feeble-minded King? Would she not give him the force that he lacked? And would not those who placed her at his side secure a large and sure future for themselves?

Suffolk was well aware of the delicacy and danger of his mission. He produced from the King and the lords an assurance that if he acted to the best of his ability he should not be punished for ill consequences, and that any errors proved against him should be pardoned in advance. Thus fortified he addressed himself to his task with a zeal which proved fatal to him. The father of Margaret, René of Anjou, was not only cousin of the French King, his favourite and his Prime Minister, but in his own right King of Jerusalem and of Sicily. These magnificent titles were not sustained by practical enjoyments. Jerusalem was in the hands of the Turks, he did not own a square yard in Sicily, and half his patrimony of Anjou and Maine was for years held by the English army. Suffolk was enthralled by Margaret. He made the match; and in his eagerness, by a secret article, agreed without formal authority that Maine should be the reward of France. So strong was the basic power of Gloucester's faction, so sharp was the antagonism against France, so loud were the whispers that England had been betrayed in her wars, that the clause was guarded as a deadly secret. The marriage was solemnised in 1445 with such splendour as the age could afford. Suffolk was made a marquis, and several of his relations were ennobled. The King was radiantly happy, the Queen faithfully grateful. Both Houses of Parliament recorded their thanks to Suffolk for his public achievement. But the secret slumbered uneasily, and as the sense of defeat at the hands of France spread through everwidening circles its inevitable disclosure boded a mortal danger.

During the six years following the condemnation of his wife Eleanor in 1441 Gloucester had been living in retirement, amusing himself with collecting books. His enemies at this grave juncture resolved upon his final overthrow. Suffolk and Edmund Beaufort, nephew of the Cardinal, supported by the Dukes of Somerset and Buckingham, with the Queen in their midst and the King in their charge, arrested Gloucester when he came to a Parliament summoned at St Edmondsbury, where an adequate royal force had been secretly assembled. Seventeen days later Gloucester's corpse was displayed, so that all could see there was no wound upon it. But the manner of Edward II's death was too well known for this proof to be accepted. It was generally believed, though wrongly, that Gloucester had been murdered by the express direction of Suffolk and Edmund Beaufort. It has however been suggested that his death was induced by choler and amazement at the ruin of his fortunes.

It soon appeared that immense forces of retribution were on foot. When in 1448 the secret article for the cession of Maine became public through its occupation by the French anger was expressed on all sides. England had paid a province, it was said, for a princess without a dowry; traitors had cast away much in the field, and given up the rest by intrigue. At the root of the fearful civil war soon to rend the Island there lay this national grief and wrath at the ruin of empire. All other discontents fused themselves with this. The house of Lancaster had usurped the throne, had ruined the finances, had sold the conquests, and now had stained their hands with foul murder. From these charges all men held the King absolved alike by his good heart and silly head. But henceforward the house of York increasingly becomes a rival party within the State.

Edmund Beaufort, now Duke of Somerset, became commander of the army in France. Suffolk remained at home to face a gathering vengeance. The Navy was disaffected. Bishop Moleyns, Keeper of the Privy Seal, sent to Portsmouth to pay what could be paid to the Fleet, was abused by the sailors as a traitor to the country, and murdered in a riot of the troops about to reinforce Somerset in France. The officer commanding the fortresses which were to be ceded to France had refused to deliver them. The French armies advanced and took with a strong hand all that was now denied. Suffolk was impeached. The King and Margaret strove, as in honour bound, to save him. Straining his prerogative, Henry burked the proceedings by sending him in 1450 into a five years' exile. We now see an instance of the fearful state of indiscipline into which England was drifting. When the banished Duke was crossing the Channel with his attendants and treasure in two small vessels, the *Nicholas of the Tower*, the largest warship in the Royal Navy, bore down upon him and carried him on board. He was received by the captain with the ominous words "Welcome, traitor," and two days later he was lowered into a boat and beheaded by six strokes of a rusty sword. It is a revealing sign of the times that a royal ship should seize and execute a royal Minister who was travelling under the King's special protection.

In June and July a rising took place in Kent, which the Lancastrians claimed to bear the marks of Yorkist support. Jack Cade, a soldier of capacity and bad character, home from the wars, gathered several thousand men, all summoned in due form by the constables of the districts, and marched on London. He was admitted to the city, but on his executing Lord Say, the Treasurer, in Cheapside, after a mob trial, the magistrates and citizens turned against him, his followers dispersed under terms of pardon, and he himself was pursued and killed. This success restored for the moment the authority of the Government, and Henry enjoyed a brief interlude in which he devoted himself anew to his colleges at Eton and Cambridge, and to Margaret, who had gained his love and obedience.

As the process of expelling the English from France continued fortresses fell, towns and districts were lost, and their garrisons for the most part came home. The speed of this disaster contributed powerfully to shock English opinion and to shake not only the position of individual Ministers but the very foundations of the Lancastrian dynasty. With incredible folly and bad faith the English broke the truce at Fougères in March 1449. By August 1450 the whole of Normandy was lost. By August 1451 the whole of Gascony, English for three centuries, had been lost as well, and of all the conquests of Henry V which had taken England eleven years of toil and blood to win only Calais remained. Edmund Beaufort, the King's commander, friend, and Lancastrian cousin, bore the blame for unbroken defeat, and this reacted on the King himself. England became full of what we should call "ex-Service men," who did not know why they had been beaten, but were sure they had been mishandled and had fought in vain. The nobles, in the increasing disorder, were glad to gather these hardened fighters to their local defence. All the great houses kept bands of armed retainers, sometimes almost amounting to private armies. They gave them pay or land, or both, and uniforms or liveries bearing the family crest. The Earl of Warwick, perhaps the greatest landowner, who aspired to a leading part in politics, had thousands of dependants who ate what was called "his bread," and of these a large proportion were organised troops proud to display the badge of the Bear and the Ragged Staff. Other magnates emulated this example according to their means. Cash and ambition ruled and the land sank rapidly towards anarchy. The King was a helpless creature, respected, even beloved, but no prop for any man. Parliament, both Lords and Commons, was little more than a clearing-house for the rivalries of nobles.

A statute of 1429 had fixed the county franchise at the forty-shilling freeholder. It is hard to realise that this arbitrarily contracted franchise ruled in England for four hundred years, and that all the wars and quarrels, the decision of the greatest causes, the grandest events at home and abroad, proceeded upon this basis until the Reform Bill of 1832. In the preamble to this Act it was alleged that the participation in elections of too great a number of people "of little substance or worth" had led to homicides, riots, assaults, and feuds. So was a backward but enduring step taken in Parliamentary representation. Yet never for centuries had the privilege of Parliament stood so high. Never for centuries was it more blatantly exploited.

The force of law was appropriated by intrigue. Baronial violence used or defied legal forms with growing impunity. The Constitution was turned against the public. No man was safe in life or lands, or even in his humblest right, except through the protection of his local chief. The celebrated

Paston Letters show that England, enormously advanced as it was in comprehension, character, and civilisation, was relapsing from peace and security into barbaric confusion. The roads were insecure. The King's writ was denied or perverted. The royal judges were flouted or bribed. The rights of sovereignty were stated in the highest terms, but the King was a weak and handled fool. The powers of Parliament could be turned this way and that according as the factions gripped it. Yet the suffering, toiling, unconquerable community had moved far from the days of Stephen and Maud, of Henry II and Thomas à Becket, and of King John and the barons. There was a highly complex society, still growing in spite of evils in many regions. The poverty of the Executive, the difficulties of communication, and the popular strength in bills and bows all helped to hold it in balance. There was a public opinion. There was a collective moral sense. There were venerated customs. Above all there was a national spirit.

* * *

It was upon this community that the agonies of the Wars of the Roses were now to fall. We must not underrate either the great issues which led to the struggle or the conscious, intense, prolonged efforts made to avert it. The need of all men and their active desire was for a strong and capable Government. Some thought this could only be obtained by aiding the lawful, established régime. Others had been for a long time secretly contending that a usurpation had been imposed upon them which had now become incompetent. The claims and hopes of the opposition to the house of Lancaster were embodied in Richard, Duke of York. According to established usage he had a prior right to the crown. York was the son of Richard, Earl of Cambridge, and grandson of Edmund, Duke of York, a younger brother of John of Gaunt. As the great-grandson of Edward III he was the only other person besides Henry VI with an unbroken male descent from Edward III, but in the female line he had also a superior claim through his descent from Gaunt's elder brother, Lionel of Clarence. By the Act of 1407 the Beauforts—Gaunt's legitimised bastards—had been barred from the succession. If Henry VI should succeed in annulling the Act of 1407 then Edmund Beaufort (Somerset) would have a better good male claim with York. It was this that York feared. York had taken Gloucester's place as first Prince of the Blood. After Gloucester's death there survived no male of the legitimate house of Lancaster save Henry VI.

Around York and beneath him there gathered an immense party of discontent, which drove him hesitantly to demand a place in the Government, and eventually. through Queen Margaret's increasing hostility, the throne itself.

A Yorkist network grew up in all parts of the country, but mainly in the South and West of England. in Kent, in London, and in Wales. It was significant that Jack Cade, at the head of the Kentish insurgents, had pretended to the name of Mortimer. It was widely believed that the Yorkists, as they began to style themselves, had procured the murder of Bishop Moleyns at Portsmouth, and of Suffolk on the high seas. Blood had thus already flowed between the houses of Lancaster and York.

In these conditions the character of Richard of York deserves close study. He was a virtuous, law-respecting, slow-moving, and highly competent prince. Every office entrusted to him by the Lancastrian régime had been ably and faithfully discharged. He had given good service. He would have been content with the government of Calais and what was left of France, but being deprived of this for the sake of Somerset he accepted the government of Ireland. Not only did he subdue part of that island, but in the very process he won the goodwill of the Irish people. Thus we see on the one side a weak King with a defective title in the hands of personages discredited by national disaster, and now with blood-guilt upon them, and on the other an upright and wise administrator supported by a nation-wide party and with some superior title to the crown.

Anyone who studies the argument which now tore the realm will see how easily honest men could convince themselves of either cause. When King Henry VI realised that his right to the throne was impugned he was mildly astonished. "Since my cradle, for forty years," he said, "I have been King. My father was King; his father was King. You have all sworn fealty to me on many occasions, as your fathers swore it to my father." But the other side declared that oaths not based on truth were void, that wrong must be righted, that successful usurpation gained no sanctity by time, that the foundation of the monarchy could only rest upon law and justice, that to recognise a dynasty of interlopers was to invite rebellion whenever occasion served, and thus dissolve the very frame of English society; and, finally, that if expediency were to rule, who could compare the wretched half-wit King, under whom all was going to ruin, with a prince who had proved himself a soldier and a statesman of the highest temper and quality?

All England was divided between these two conceptions. Although the Yorkists predominated in the rich South, and the Lancastrians were supreme in the warlike North, there were many interlacements and overlaps. While the townsfolk and the mass of the people, upon the whole, abstained from active warfare in this struggle of the upper classes and their armed retainers, and some thought "the fewer nobles the better," their own opinion was also profoundly divided. They venerated the piety and goodness of the King; they also admired the virtues and moderation of the Duke of York. The attitude and feeling of the public, in all parts and at all times, weighed heavily with both contending factions. Thus Europe witnessed the amazing spectacle of nearly thirty years of ferocious war, conducted with hardly the sack of a single town, and with the mass of the common people little affected and the functions of local government very largely maintained.

* * *

In 1450 the ferment of discontent and rivalries drew the Duke of York into his first overt act. He quitted his government in Ireland and landed unbidden in Wales. During the Parliamentary session of the following year a member of the Commons, one Young, boldly proposed that the Duke of York should be declared heir to the throne. This demand was formidable, not only for its backing, but for its good sense. The King had now been married for six years and had no child. The repute in which he stood made it seem unlikely that he would have any. Ought he not, men asked at this time, to designate his successor? If not York, whom then? It could only be Somerset or another representative of the Beaufort line. One can see how shrewdly this thrust was made. But the King, animated certainly by Margaret, repulsed it with unwonted vigour. He refused to abandon his hope of progeny, and, as soon as the Parliament had dispersed, sent the presumptuous Member to the Tower. At this time, also, he broke with the Duke of York, who retired to his castle at Ludlow, on the borders of Wales.

Disgusted by the Government's failure to restore order and justice at home, and to prevent military disasters in France, York became more and more convinced that the Beaufort party, which dominated the weak-willed King, must be driven from power. Prayers and protests had failed; there remained the resort to arms. Accordingly, on February 3, 1452, York sent an address to the citizens of Shrewsbury, accusing Somer-

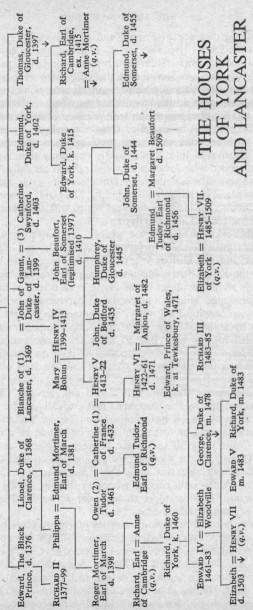

THE HOUSES
OF YORK
AND LANCASTER

set of the disgrace in France and of "labouring continually about the King's Highness for my undoing, and to corrupt my blood and to disinherit me and my heirs and such persons as be about me . . Seeing that the said Duke ever prevaileth and ruleth about the King's person, and advises him so ill that the land is likely to be destroyed, I may full conclude to proceed in all haste against him with the help of my kinsmen and friends." On this he marched from Shrewsbury towards London, with an army of several thousand men, including artillery. He moved into Kent, plainly expecting that those who had marched with Jack Cade would rally to his cause. The response was disappointing. London closed its gates against his emissaries. The King was carried by Margaret, Somerset, and the Lancastrian interests to Blackheath, with a superior force. Civil war seemed about to begin.

But York felt himself the weaker. He was constitutionally averse from violence. Norfolk was on his side, and other great nobles, but the Earl of Warwick, twenty-four years old, was with the King. Every effort was made to prevent bloodshed. Parleys were unending. In the event York dispersed his forces and presented himself unarmed and bareheaded before King Henry, protesting his loyalty, but demanding redress. His life hung by a thread. Few about the King's person would have scrupled to slay him. But all knew the consequences. York stood for a cause; he was supported by the Commons; half the nation was behind him; his youthful son, the Earl of March, had a second army on foot on the Welsh border. York declared himself "the King's liegeman and servant." Since he was supported by the Commons and evidently at the head of a great party, the King promised that "a sad and substantial Council" should be formed of which he should be a member. The Court had still to choose between Somerset and York. The Queen, always working with Somerset, decided the issue in his favour. He was appointed Constable of Calais, garrisoned by the only regular troops in the pay of the Crown, and was in fact for more than a year at the head of affairs both in France and at home.

Then in quick succession a series of grave events occurred. The disasters culminated in France. Talbot's attempt to reconquer Gascony failed; he was defeated at Castillon in July 1453, and Bordeaux fell in October. Somerset, the chief commander, bore the burden of defeat. In this situation the King went mad. He had gone down to Wiltshire to spend July and August. Suddenly his memory failed. He recognised no one, not even the Queen. He could eat and drink, but his speech was childish or incoherent. He could not walk. For another fifteen months he remained entirely without comprehension. Afterwards, when he recovered, he declared he remembered nothing. The pious Henry had been withdrawn from the worry of existence to an island of merciful oblivion. His body gaped and drivelled over the bristling realm.

When these terrible facts became known Queen Margaret aspired to be Protector. But the adverse forces were too strong for the Lancastrian party to make the challenge. Moreover, she had another preoccupation. On October 13 she gave birth to a son. How far this event was expected is not clear, but, as long afterwards with James II, it inevitably hardened the hearts of all men. It seemed to shut out for ever the Yorkist claim. Hitherto neither side had been inclined to go to extremes. If Lancaster ruled during the life of Henry, York would succeed at his death, and both sides could accommodate themselves to this natural and lawful process. Now it seemed there would be a Lancastrian ascendancy for ever.

The insanity of the King defeated Somerset: he could no longer withstand York. Norfolk, one of York's supporters, presented a petition against him to the Council, and in December 1453 he was committed to the Tower. The strength of York's position bore him to the Protectorate. He moved by Parliamentary means and with great moderation, but he was not to be withstood. He obtained full control of the Executive, and enjoyed the support of both Houses of Parliament. He had not long to show his qualities, but an immediate improvement in the administration was recognised. He set to work with cool vigour to suppress livery and maintenance and to restore order on the roads and throughout the land. He did not hesitate to imprison several of his own most prominent adherents, among them the Earl of Devonshire, for levying a private war. If he refrained from bringing Somerset, who was still imprisoned, to trial, this was only from mercy. His party were astounded at his tolerance. When the Government was in his hands, when his future was marred by the new heir to the Crown, when his power or his life might be destroyed at any moment by the King's recovery, he kept absolute faith with right and justice. Here then is his monument and justification. He stands before history as a patriot ready to risk his life to protect good government, but unwilling to raise his hand against the State in any personal interest.

Surprises continued. When it was generally believed that

Henry's line was extinct he had produced an heir. When he seemed to have sunk into permanent imbecility he suddenly recovered. At Christmas 1454 he regained all his faculties. He inquired whether he had been asleep and what had happened meanwhile. Margaret showed him his son, and told him she had named him Edward. Hitherto he had looked with dull eyes upon the infant. Every effort to rouse him had been in vain. Now he was as good as he had ever been. He held up his hands and thanked God, and, according to the Paston Letters, he said he "never knew till that time, nor wist not what was said to him, nor wist where he had been while he had been sick, till now." He sent his almoner to Canterbury with a thank-offering, and declared himself "in charity with all the world," remarking that he "only wished the lords were too."

BOOK THREE • CHAPTER TWENTY-EIGHT

The Wars of the Roses

IN the spring of 1455 the Red Rose of Lancaster bloomed again. York ceased legally to be Protector from the moment that the King's mental recovery was known; he made no effort to retain the power. Queen Margaret took the helm. Somerset was not only released but restored to his key position. York's government of Calais, which had been conferred upon him for seven years, was handed back to his rival. He was no longer invited to the King's Council board; and when a Great Council of peers was convened at Leicester he feared that he was summoned only to be tried. He retired to Sandal, in Yorkshire, and, being joined by the Earls of Warwick and Salisbury, together with a large company of nobles, strongly attended, he denounced Somerset as the man who, having lost Normandy and Guienne, was now about to ruin the whole kingdom. York's lords agreed upon a resort to arms. With three thousand men they marched south. At the same time the Duke of Norfolk appeared at the head of several thousand men, and Shrewsbury and Sir Thomas Stanley of a few thousands more. All these forces moved towards London, with St Albans as their point of concentration. The King, the Queen,

Somerset, and the Court and Lancastrian party, with their power, which numbered less than three thousand men, moved to Watford to meet them.

St Albans was an open town. The ancient, powerful monastery there had prevented the citizens from "girding themselves about with a great wall," lest they should become presumptuous. For this reason it was a convenient rendezvous. The King's army got there first, and the royal standard was unfurled in St Peter's Street and Hollowell Street. York, Salisbury, and Warwick did not wait for the heavy reinforcements that were approaching them. They saw that their forces had the advantage and that hours counted. This time there was a fight. It was a collision rather than a battle; but it was none the less decisive. Lord Clifford held for the King the barrier across the street, which York attacked with archery and cannon; but Warwick, circling the town, came in upon him from behind, slew him, and put the royal troops to flight. Somerset was killed "fighting for a cause which was more his own than the King's." The Duke of Buckingham and his son were wounded by arrows; Somerset's son, the Earl of Dorset, was captured sorely wounded and carried home in a cart. The King himself was slightly wounded by an arrow. He did not fly, but took refuge in a tradesman's house in the main street. There presently the Duke of York came to him, and, falling upon his knees, assured him of his fealty and devotion. Not more than three hundred men perished in this clash at St Albans, but these included an extraordinary proportion of the nobles on the King's side. The rank and file were encouraged to spare one another; the leaders fought to the death. The bodies of Somerset and Clifford lay naked in the street for many hours, none daring to bury them. The Yorkist triumph was complete. They had now got the King in their hands. Somerset was dead. Margaret and her child had taken sanctuary. The victors declared their devotion to the royal person and rejoiced that he was rid of evil counsellors. Upon this Parliament was immediately summoned in the King's name.

Historians have shrunk from the Wars of the Roses, and most of those who have catalogued their events have left us only a melancholy and disjointed picture. We are however in the presence of the most ferocious and implacable quarrel of which there is factual record. The individual actors were bred by generations of privilege and war, into which the feudal theme had brought its peculiar sense of honour, and to which the Papacy contributed such spiritual sanction as emerged from its rivalries and intrigues. It was a conflict in which personal hatreds reached their maximum, and from which mass effects were happily excluded. There must have been many similar convulsions in the human story. None however has been preserved with characters at once so worldly and so expensively chiselled.

Needless causes of confusion may be avoided. Towns must not be confused with titles. The mortal struggle of York and Lancaster did not imply any antagonism between the two well-known English counties. York was in fact the stronghold of the Lancastrians, and the Yorkists founded their strength upon the Midlands and the south of England. The ups and downs of fortune were so numerous and startling, the family feuds so complicated, the impact of national feeling in moments of crisis so difficult to measure, that it has been the fashion to disparage this period. Only Shakespeare, basing himself largely upon Hall's *Chronicle,* has portrayed its savage yet heroic lineaments. He does not attempt to draw conclusions, and for dramatic purposes telescopes events and campaigns. Let us now set forth the facts as they occurred.

* * *

St Albans was the first shedding of blood in strife. The Yorkists gained possession of the King. But soon we see the inherent power of Lancaster. They had the majority of the nobles on their side, and the majesty of the Crown. In a few months they were as strong as ever. Continual trials of strength were made. There were risings in the country and grim assemblies of Parliament. Legality, constitutionalism, and reverence for the Crown were countered, but not yet overthrown, by turbulent and bloody episodes. The four years from 1456 to 1459 were a period of uneasy truce. All seemed conscious of the peril to themselves and to their order. But Fate lay heavy upon them. There were intense efforts at reconciliation. The spectacle was displayed to the Londoners of the King being escorted to Westminster by a procession in which the Duke of York and Queen Margaret walked side by side, followed by the Yorkist and Lancastrian lords, the most opposed in pairs. Solemn pledges of amity were exchanged; the Sacrament was taken in common by all the leaders; all sought peace where there was no peace. Even when a kind of settlement was reached in London it was upset by violence in the North. In 1459 fighting broke out again. A gathering near Worcester of armed Yorkists in arms dispersed in the presence of the royal army and their chiefs scattered. York returned to Ireland, and Warwick to his captaincy of Calais, in which he had succeeded Somerset.

War began in earnest in July 1460. York was still in Ireland; but the Yorkist lords under Warwick, holding bases in Wales and at Calais, with all their connections and partisans, supported by the Papal Legate and some of the bishops, and, on the whole, by the Commons, confronted the Lancastrians and the Crown at Northampton. Henry VI stood entrenched, and new cannon guarded his line. But when the Yorkists attacked, Lord Grey of Ruthven, who commanded a wing, deserted him and helped the Yorkists over the breastworks. The royal forces fled in panic. King Henry VI remained in his tent, "sitting alone and solitary." The victors presented themselves to him, bowing to the ground. As after St Albans, they carried him again to London, and, having him in their power once more, ruled in his name. The so-called compromise in which all the Estates of the Realm concurred was then attempted. "The Duke of York," says Gregory's *Chronicle* "kept King Harry at Westminster by force and strength, till at last the King, for fear of death, granted him the Crown, for a man that hath but little wit will soon be afeared of death." Henry was to be King for life; York was to conduct the government and succeed him at his death. All who sought a quiet life for the nation hailed this arrangement. But the settlement defied the fact that Queen Margaret, with her son, the Prince of Wales, was at liberty at Harlech Castle, in Wales. The King in bondage had disinherited his own son. The Queen fought on.

With her army of the North and of North Wales Margaret advanced to assert the birthright of her son. The Duke of York, disdaining to remain in the security of Sandal Castle until his whole strength was gathered, marched against her. At Wakefield on December 30, 1460, the first considerable battle of the war was fought. The Lancastrians, with superior forces, caught the Yorkists by surprise, when many were foraging, and a frightful rout and massacre ensued. Here there was no question of sparing the common men; many hundreds were slaughtered; but the brunt fell upon the chiefs. No quarter was given. The Duke of York was killed; his son, the Earl of Rutland, eighteen years old, was flying, but the new Lord Clifford remembering St Albans, slaughtered him with joy, exclaiming, "By God's blood, thy father slew mine; and so will I do thee, and all thy kin." Henceforward this was the rule of the war. The old Earl of Salisbury, caught during the

night, was beheaded immediately by Lord Exeter, a natural
son of the Duke of Buckingham. Margaret's hand has been
discerned in this severity. The heads of the three Yorkist
nobles were exposed over the gates and walls of York. The
great Duke's head, with a paper crown, grinned upon the land-
scape, summoning the avengers.

Hitherto the struggle had been between mature, comfortable magnates, deeply involved in State affairs and trying hard
to preserve some limits. Now a new generation took charge.
There was a new Lord Clifford, a new Duke of Somerset,
above all a new Duke of York, all in the twenties, sword in
hand, with fathers to avenge and England as the prize. When
York's son, hitherto Earl of March, learned that his father's
cause had devolved upon him he did not shrink. He fell upon
the Earl of Wiltshire and the Welsh Lancastrians, and on
February 2, 1461, at the Battle of Mortimer's Cross, near
Hereford, he beat and broke them up. He made haste to repay
the cruelties of Wakefield. "No quarter" was again the word.
Among those executed after the battle was Owen Tudor, a
harmless notable, who, with the axe and block before him,
hardly believed that he would be beheaded until the collar of
his red doublet was ripped off. His son Jasper lived, as will be
seen, to carry on the quarrel.

The victorious Yorkists under their young Duke now
marched to help the Earl of Warwick, who had returned from
Calais and was being hard pressed in London; but Queen
Margaret forestalled him, and on February 17, at the second
Battle of St Albans, she inflicted upon Warwick a bloody
defeat. Warwick, who was at this time the real leader of
the Yorkist party, with many troops raised abroad and with
the latest firearms and his own feudal forces, had carried the
captive King with him and claimed to be acting in his name.
But Margaret's onset took him by surprise. "Their prickers
[scouts] came not home to bring tidings how nigh the Queen
was, save one came and said that she was nine mile off."
Warwick and Norfolk escaped; half their army was slaughtered. King Henry had been carted to the scene. There, beneath a large tree, he watched what happened with legitimate
and presently unconcealed satisfaction. Two knights of high
renown in the French war, one the redoubtable Sir Thomas
Kyriel, had been appointed as his warders and guardians.
Above all they were to make sure no harm came to him. They
therefore remained with him under his tree, and all were surrounded by the victorious army. Among the many captains

ENGLAND AND WALES
DURING THE
WARS OF THE ROSES

SCOTLAND

Berwick
Norham
Hedgley Moor ✕
Bamborough
Dunstanburgh
Alnwick
Newcastle
Hexham ✕
Durham

Battlefields marked ✕

Middleham

York
Clitheroe ✕ Towton
Wakefield ✕
Sandal Castle
Ravenspur

Holt
Harlech
Shrewsbury
Bosworth ✕
Nottingham
✕ Losecoat Field
WALES
Ludlow
Coventry
Mortimers Cross ✕
Northampton
Worcester ✕
Milford Haven
Edgecot ✕ Stony Stratford
Tewkesbury
Dunstable
Watford ✕ St. Albans
London ✕ Barnet

Cerne Abbey

Dartmouth

of consequence whom Margaret put to death in cold blood
the next morning these two cases needed special consideration.
King Henry said he had asked them to bide with him and that
they had done so for his own safety. Queen Margaret produced her son Edward, now seven years old, to whose disinheritance the King had perforce consented, and asked this
child, already precociously fierce, to pronounce. "Fair son,
with what death shall these two knights die whom you see
there?" "Their heads should be cut off" was the ready answer.
As Kyriel was being led away to his doom he exclaimed, "May
the wrath of God fall on those who have taught a child to
speak such words." Thus was pity banished from all hearts,
and death or vengeance was the cry.

* * *

Margaret now had her husband safe back in her hands, and
with him the full authority of the Crown. The road to London was open, but she did not choose to advance upon it. The
fierce hordes she had brought from the North had already
disgraced themselves by their ravages far and wide along their
line of march. They had roused against them the fury of the
countryside. The King's friends said, "They deemed that the
Northern men would have been too cruel in robbing if they
had come to London." The city was, upon the whole, steadfast
in the Yorkist cause, but it was also said, "If the King and
Queen had come with their army to London they would have
had all things as they wished." We cannot judge the circumstances fully. Edward of York was marching with the triumphant army of Mortimer's Cross night and day to reach
London. Warwick had joined him in Oxfordshire with the
survivors of St Albans. Perhaps King Henry pleaded that the
capital should not become a battlefield, but at any rate Margaret and her advisers did not dare to make it so. Flushed with
victory, laden with spoil, reunited with the King, the Lancastrians retired through Dunstable to the North, and thus
disguised the fact that their Scottish mercenaries were already
joggling home with all that they could carry. According to
Holinshed, "The Queen, having little trust in Essex, less in
Kent, and least of all in London, . . . departed from St Albans into the North Country, where the foundation of her
strength and refuge only rested."

This was the turning-point in the struggle. Nine days after
the second Battle of St Albans Edward of York entered London. The citizens, who might have submitted to Margaret and

the King, now hailed the Yorkists with enthusiasm. They thanked God and said, "Let us walk in a new vineyard, and let us make a gay garden in the month of March, with this fair white rose and herb, the Earl of March." [1] It was a vineyard amid thorns. The pretence of acting in the King's name could serve no longer. The Yorkists had become without disguise traitors and rebels against the Crown. But the mood of the youthful warrior who had triumphed and butchered at Mortimer's Cross recked little of this charge. As he saw it, his father had been ruined and killed through respect for the majesty of Henry VI. He and his friends would palter no longer with such conceptions. Forthwith he claimed the crown; and such was the feeling of London and the strength of his army, now upon the spot, that he was able to make good show of public authority for his act. He declared himself King, and on March 4, 1461, was proclaimed at Westminster with such formalities as were possible. Henceforward he declared that the other side were guilty of treason, and that he would enforce upon them every penalty.

These assertions must now be made good, and King Edward IV marched north to settle once and for all with King Henry VI. Near York the Queen, with the whole power of Lancaster, confronted him not far from Tadcaster, by the villages of Saxton and Towton. Some accounts declare that a hundred thousand men were on the field, the Yorkists having forty and the Lancastrians sixty thousand; but later authorities greatly reduce these figures.

On March 28 the Yorkist advance-guard was beaten back at Ferry Bridge by the young Lord Clifford, and Warwick himself was wounded; but as heavier forces arrived the bridge was carried, Clifford was slain, and the Yorkist army passed over. The next day one of the most ruthless battles on English soil was fought. The Lancastrians held a good position on rising ground, their right flank being protected by the flooded stream of the Cock, in many places unfordable. Although Edward's army was not complete and the Duke of Norfolk's wing was still approaching, he resolved to attack. The battle began in a blinding snowstorm, which drove in the faces of the Lancastrians. Under this cover clumps of Yorkist spearmen moved up the slope. The wind gave superior range to the archery of the attack and the Lancastrian shafts fell short, while they themselves suffered heavily. Under this pressure the decision was taken to advance downhill upon the foe. For six hours

[1] Gregory's *Chronicle*.

the two sides grappled furiously, with varying success. At the height of the battle Warwick is said to have dismounted and slain his horse to prove to his men he would not quit them alive. But all hung in the balance until late in the afternoon, when the arrival of the Duke of Norfolk's corps upon the exposed flank of the Lancastrians drove the whole mass into retreat, which soon became a rout.

Now the Cock beck, hitherto a friend, became an enemy. The bridge towards Tadcaster was blocked with fugitives. Many thousands of men, heavily armoured, plunged into the swollen stream, and were drowned in such numbers that hideous bridges were formed of the corpses and some escaped thereby. The pursuit was carried on far into the night. Margaret and her son escaped to York, where King Henry had been observing the rites of Palm Sunday. Gathering him up, the imperious Queen set out with her child and a cluster of spears for the Northern border. The bodies of several thousand Englishmen lay upon the field. Edward, writing to his mother, conceals his own losses, but claims that twenty-eight thousand Lancastrian dead had been counted. It is certain that the flower of the Lancastrian nobility and knighthood fell upon the field. For all prisoners there was but death. The Earl of Devonshire and "the bastard of Exeter" alone were spared, and only for a day. When Edward reached the town of York his first task was to remove the heads of his father and others of Margaret's victims and to replace them with those of his noblest captives. Three months later, on June 28, he was crowned King at Westminster, and the Yorkist triumph seemed complete. It was followed by wholesale proscriptions and confiscations. Parliament in November 1461 passed an Act of Attainder which, surpassing all previous severities, lapped a hundred and thirty-three notable persons in its withering sweep. Not only the throne but one-third of the estates in England changed hands. It was measure for measure.

* * *

After Towton the Lancastrian cause was sustained by the unconquerable will of Queen Margaret. Never has her tenacity and rarely have her vicissitudes been surpassed in any woman. Apart from the sullen power of Lancaster in the North, she had the friendly regard of two countries, Scotland and France. Both had felt the heavy arm of England in former reigns; both rejoiced at its present division and weakness. The hatred of the Scots for the English still excited by its bitterness the wonder of foreigners. When Louis XI succeeded his father, Charles VII, in 1461, the year of Towton, he found his country almost a desert, horrible to see. The fields were untilled; the villages were clusters of ruined hovels. Amid the ruins, the weeds and brushwood—to use a term which recurs —of what were formerly cultivated and fertile fields there dwelt a race of peasants reduced to the conditions and roused to the ferocity of wolves. All this was the result of the English invasion. Therefore it was a prime aim of Scottish and French policy, always moving hand-in-hand, to foster the internal strife of England and to sustain the weaker party there.

Margaret, as Queen of England and Princess of France, was an outstanding personage in the West of Europe. Her qualities of courage and combativeness, her commanding, persuasive personality, her fury against those who had driven her and her husband from the throne, produced from this one woman's will-power a long series of desperate, forlorn struggles after the main event had been decided, and after the lapse of years for one brief spell reversed it. English national interests did not enter her mind. She had paid her way with Scotland by the surrender of Berwick. She clinched her bargain with Louis XI by mortgaging Calais to him for 20,000 gold livres.

In 1462 Margaret, after much personal appeal to the Courts of France, Burgundy, and Scotland, found herself able to land with a power, and whether by treachery or weakness the three strongest Northern castles, Bamburgh, Alnwick, and Dunstanburgh, opened their gates to her. Louis XI had lent her the services of a fine soldier, Pierre de Brézé, who under her spell spent his large fortune in her cause. In the winter of 1462 therefore King Edward gathered his Yorkist powers, and, carrying his new train of artillery by sea to Newcastle, began the sieges of these lost strongholds. The King himself lay stricken with measles at Durham, and Lord Warwick conducted the operations. The heavy cannon, each with its pet name, played havoc with the masonry of the castles. So vigorously were the sieges conducted that even Christmas leave was forbidden. Margaret, from Berwick, in vain attempted the relief of Alnwick. All three fortresses fell in a month.

The behaviour of Edward at this moment constitutes a solid defence for his character. This voluptuous young King, sure of his position, now showed a clemency unheard of in the Wars of the Roses. Not only did he pardon the Lancastrian nobles who were caught in the fortresses, but he made solemn pacts with them and took them into his full confidence. The

Duke of Somerset and Sir Ralph Percy, on swearing allegiance, were not merely allowed to go free, but restored to their estates. Percy was even given the guardianship of two of the castles. Somerset, son of the great Minister slaughtered in the first Battle of St Albans, was admitted to even higher favour. Having made his peace, he was given a high command and a place in the inner councils of the royal army. In this new position at first he gave shrewd military advice, and was granted special pensions by the King.

Edward's magnanimity and forgiveness were ill repaid. When Margaret returned with fresh succours from France and Scotland in 1463 Percy opened the gates of Bamburgh to the Scots, and Alnwick was betrayed about the same time by a soured Yorkist officer, Sir Ralph Grey. Meanwhile Queen Margaret, with King Henry in her hands, herself besieged the castle of Norham, on the Tweed, near Berwick. Once again Edward and the Yorkists took the field, and the redoubtable new artillery, at that time esteemed as much among the leading nations as atomic weapons are to-day, was carried to the North. The great guns blew chunks off the castles. Margaret fled to France, while Henry buried himself amid the valleys and the pious foundations of Cumberland. This was the final parting of King Henry VI and his Queen—Queen she was. Margaret took the Prince with her on her travels. These were remarkable. With the Duke of Exeter, six knights, and her faithful Pierre de Brézé she landed at Sluys, and appealed to the renowned chivalry of the house of Burgundy. She came "without royal habit or estate"; she and her seven waiting-women had only the clothes they were wearing. Brézé paid for their food. Nevertheless she was treated even in this adverse Court with royal honours. Philip, Duke of Burgundy, was aged; his son Charles was surnamed "the Bold." The ambassadors of England were active. Margaret got nothing from Burgundy except the gifts and courtesies which old-time hospitality would afford to "a dame in distress." It is however from these contacts that our knowledge of Margaret's adventures is derived.

Chastellain, the Burgundian chronicler, recorded her tales. Thus only has history heard how she, King Henry, and her son had lived for five days without bread, upon a herring each day between them. At Mass once the Queen found herself without even a penny for the offertory. She asked a Scottish archer near by to lend her something. "Somewhat stiffly and regretfully" he drew a groat from his purse. At the latest disaster at Norham, recounted the Queen, she had been captured by plundering Yorkist soldiers, robbed, and brought before the captain to be beheaded. Only a quarrel of her captors over the spoil delayed her execution. But there stood a Yorkist squire, and to him she turned, "speaking pitifully." "Madam," he said, "mount behind me, and Monseigneur the Prince in front, and I will save you or die, seeing that death is more likely to come to me than not." Three-a-back they plunged into the forest, Margaret in terror for her son's life, on which her cause depended. The Yorkist squire now rode off. The forest was a known haunt of bandits, and mother and son crouched in its recesses. Soon there appeared a man of hideous and horrible aspect, with obvious intention to kill and rob. But once more Margaret, by her personal force, prevailed. She said who she was, and confided her son, the heir to the throne, to the brigand's honour. The robber was faithful to his charge. The Queen and the Prince at last both reached the shelter of the fugitive King.

* * *

Edward's clemency had been betrayed by Percy, but he did not withdraw his confidence from Somerset. The King was a man capable of the most bloody deeds when compelled, as he thought, by necessity, and at the same time eager to practise not only magnanimity, but open-hearted confidence. The confidence he showed to Somerset must have led him into deadly perils. This third Duke was during the beginning of 1463 high in the King's favour. "And the King made full much of him, in so much he lodged with the King in his own bed many nights, and sometimes rode a-hunting behind the King, the King having about him not passing six horse at the most, and yet three were of the Duke's men of Somerset."

When in the autumn of 1463 he went to the North, Somerset and two hundred of his own men were his bodyguard. At Northampton, where bitter memories of the battle lingered, the townsfolk were first astounded and then infuriated to see this bearer of an accursed name in company with their Yorkist sovereign. Only King Edward's personal exertions saved his new-found follower from being torn to pieces. After this he found it necessary to provide other employment for Somerset and his escort. Somerset was sent to Holt Castle, in Denbighshire. The brawl at Northampton we must suppose convinced him that even the King could not protect him from his Yorkist foes. At Christmas 1463 Somerset deserted Edward and returned to the Lancastrian side. The names of these great nobles were magnets in their own territories. The unstable Duke had hoped to gain possession of Newcastle, and many of his adherents on the report that he was in the neighbourhood came out to him; but he was driven away, and they were caught and beheaded.

Again the banner of Lancaster was raised. Somerset joined King Henry. Alnwick and Bamburgh still held out. Norham and Skipton had been captured, but now Warwick's brother Montagu with a substantial army was in the field. On April 25, 1464, at Hedgeley Moor, near Alnwick, he broke and destroyed the Lancastrian revolt. The leaders perished on the field, or afterwards on the block. Sir Ralph Percy fought to the death, and used the expression, remarkable for one who had accepted pardon and even office from King Edward, "I have saved the bird in my bosom." What was this "bird"? It was the cause of Lancaster, which might be dissembled or even betrayed under duress, but still remained, when occasion served, the lodestar of its adherents. There were many who had this bird in their bosoms, but could never have coined Percy's grand phrase or stooped to his baseness.

Edward's experiment of mercy in this quarrel was now at an end, and the former rigours were renewed in their extreme degree. Somerset, defeated with a small following at Hexham on May 15, 1464, was beheaded the next morning. Before the month was out in every Yorkish camp Lancastrian nobles and knights by dozens and half-dozens were put to death. There was nothing for it but to still these unquiet spirits. John Tiptoft, Earl of Worcester, Constable of England, versed in the civil war, and with Italian experience, presided over drumhead courts-martial, and by adding needless cruelties to his severities justified a vengeance one day to be exacted.

Meanwhile the diplomacy of the English Crown had effected a fifteen years' truce with the King of Scotland, and was potent both at the Courts of France and Burgundy. Margaret remained helpless at Bar-le-Duc. Poor King Henry was at length tracked down near Clitheroe, in Lancashire, and conveyed to London. This time there was no ceremonial entry. With his feet tied by leather thongs to the stirrups, and with a straw hat on his head, the futile but saintly figure around whom such storms had beaten was led three times round the pillory, and finally hustled to the Tower, whose gates closed on him, yet not—this time—for ever.

With the fall of Alnwick only one fortress in the whole

kingdom still resisted. The castle of Harlech, on the western sea, alone flaunted the Red Rose. Harlech stood a siege of seven years. When it surrendered in 1468 there were found to be but fifty effective men in the garrison. With two exceptions, they were admitted to mercy. Among them was a child of twelve, who had survived the rigours of the long blockade. He was the nephew of Jasper, the grandson of Owen Tudor, and the future founder of the Tudor dynasty and system of government. His name was Richmond, later to become King Henry VII.

BOOK THREE · CHAPTER TWENTY-NINE

The Adventures of Edward IV

KING EDWARD IV had made good his right to the Crown upon the field. He was a soldier and a man of action; in the teeth of danger his quality was at its highest. In war nothing daunted or wearied him. Long marches, hazardous decisions, the marshalling of armies, the conduct of battles, seemed his natural sphere. The worse things got the better he became. But the opposite was also true. He was at this time a fighting man and little more, and when the fighting stopped he had no serious zest for sovereignty. The land was fair; the blood of youth coursed in his veins; all his blood debts were paid; with ease and goodwill he sheathed his sharp sword. It had won him his crown; now to enjoy life.

The successes of these difficult years had been gained for King Edward by the Neville family. Warwick or Montagu, now Earl of Northumberland, with George Neville, Archbishop of York, had the whole machinery of government in their hands. The King had been present only at some of the actions. He could even be reproached for his misguided clemency, which had opened up again the distresses of civil war. His magnanimity had been at length sternly repressed by his counsellors and generals. In the first part of his reign England was therefore ruled by the two brothers, Warwick and Northumberland. They believed they had put the King on the throne, and meant him to remain there while they governed.

The King did not quarrel with this. In all his reign he never fought but when he was forced; then he was magnificent. History has scolded this prince of twenty-two for not possessing immediately the statecraft and addiction to business for which his office called. Edward united contrasting characters. He loved peace; he shone in war. But he loved peace for its indulgences rather than its dignity. His pursuit of women, in which he found no obstacles, combined with hunting, feasting, and drinking to fill his life. Were these not the rightful prizes of victory? Let Warwick and Northumberland and other anxious lords carry the burden of State, and let the King be merry. For a while this suited all parties. The victors divided the spoil; the King had his amusements, and his lords their power and policy.

Thus some years slipped by, while the King, although gripping from time to time the reins of authority, led in the main his life of pleasure. His mood towards men and women is described in the well-chosen words by the staid Hume:

"During the present interval of peace, he lived in the most familiar and sociable manner with his subjects, particularly with the Londoners; and the beauty of his person, as well as the gallantry of his address, which, even unassisted by his royal dignity, would have rendered him acceptable to the fair, facilitated all his applications for their favour. This easy and pleasurable course of life augmented every day his popularity among all ranks of men. He was the peculiar favourite of the young and gay of both sexes. The disposition of the English, little addicted to jealousy, kept them from taking umbrage at these liberties. And his indulgence in amusements, while it gratified his inclination, was thus become, without design, a means of supporting and securing his Government." After these comparatively mild censures the historian proceeds to deplore the weakness and imprudence which led the King to stray from the broad, sunlit glades of royal libertinage on to the perilous precipices of romance and marriage.

One day the King a-hunting was carried far by the chase. He rested for the night at a castle. In this castle a lady of quality, niece of the owner, had found shelter. Elizabeth Woodville, or Wydvil, was the widow of a Lancastrian knight, Sir John Grey, "in Margaret's battle at St Albans slain." Her mother, Jacquetta of Luxemburg, had been the youthful wife of the famous John, Duke of Bedford, and after his death she had married his steward, Sir Richard Woodville, later created Earl Rivers. This condescension so far below her station caused offence to the aristocracy. She was fined £1,000 as a deterrent to others. Nevertheless she lived happily ever after, and bore her husband no fewer than thirteen children, of whom Elizabeth was one. There was high as well as ordinary blood in Elizabeth's veins; but she was an austere woman, upright, fearless, chaste and fruitful. She and her two sons were all under the ban of the attainder which disinherited the adherents of Lancaster. The chance of obtaining royal mercy could not be missed. The widow bowed in humble petition before the youthful conqueror, and, like the tanner's daughter of Falaise, made at first glance the sovereign her slave. Shakespeare's account, though somewhat crude, does not err in substance. The Lady Elizabeth observed the strictest self-restraint, which only enhanced the passion of the King. He gave her all his love, and when he found her obdurate he besought her to share his crown. He spurned the counsels of prudence and worldly wisdom. Why conquer in battles, why be a king, if not to gain one's heart's desire? But he was well aware of the dangers of his choice. His marriage in 1464 with Elizabeth Woodville was a secret guarded in deadly earnest. The statesmen at the head of the Government, while they smiled at what seemed an amorous frolic, never dreamed it was a solemn union, which must shake the land to its depths.

* * *

Warwick's plans for the King's future had been different. Isabella of the house of Spain, or preferably a French princess, were brides who might greatly forward the interests of England. A royal marriage in those days might be a bond of peace between neighbouring states or the means of successful war. Warwick used grave arguments and pressed the King to decide. Edward seemed strangely hesitant, and dwelt upon his objections until the Minister, who was also his master, became impatient. Then at last the truth was revealed: he had for five months been married to Elizabeth Woodville. Here then was the occasion which sundered him from the valiant King-maker, fourteen years older, but also in the prime of life. Warwick had deep roots in England, and his popularity, whetted by the lavish hospitality which he offered to all classes upon his many great estates, was unbounded. The Londoners looked to him. He held the power. But no one knew better than he that there slept in Edward a tremendous warrior, skilful, ruthless, and capable when roused of attempting and of doing all.

The King too, for his part, began to take more interest in

affairs. Queen Elizabeth had five brothers, seven sisters, and two sons. By royal decree he raised them to high rank, or married them into the greatest families. He went so far as to marry his wife's fourth brother, at twenty, to the Dowager Duchess of Norfolk, aged eighty. Eight new peerages came into existence in the Queen's family: her father, five brothers-in-law, her son, and her brother Anthony. This was generally thought excessive. It must be remembered that at this time there were but sixty peers, of whom not more than fifty could ever be got to Parliament on one occasion. All these potentates were held in a tight and nicely calculated system. The arrival of a new nobility who had done nothing notable in the war and now surrounded the indolent King was not merely offensive, but politically dangerous to Warwick and his proud associates.

But the clash came over foreign policy. In this sad generation England, lately the master, had become the sport of neighbouring states. Her titled refugees, from one faction or the other, beset the Courts of Western Europe. The Duke of Burgundy had been shocked to learn one morning that a Duke of Exeter and several other high English nobles were actually begging their bread at the tail of one of his progresses. Ashamed to see such a slight upon his class, he provided them with modest dwellings and allowances. Similar charities were performed by Louis XI to the unhappy descendants of the victors of Agincourt. Margaret with her retinue of shadows was welcomed in her pauper stateliness both in Burgundy and in France. At any moment either Power, now become formidable as England had waned, might support the exiled faction in good earnest and pay back the debts of fifty years before by an invasion of England. It was the policy of Warwick and his connection to make friends with France, by far the stronger Power, and thus obtain effectual security. In this mood they hoped to make a French match for the King's sister. Edward took the opposite line. With the instinct which afterwards ruled our Island for so many centuries, he sought to base English policy upon the second strongest state in Western Europe. He could no doubt argue that to be the ally of France was to be in the power of France, but to be joined with Burgundy was to have the means of correcting if not of controlling French action. Amid his revelries and other hunting he nursed a conqueror's spirit. Never should England become a vassal state; instead of being divided by her neighbours, she would herself, by dividing them, maintain a balance. At this time these politics were new; but the stresses they wrought in the small but vehement world of English government can be readily understood nowadays.

The King therefore, to Warwick's chagrin and alarm, in 1468 married his sister Margaret to Charles the Bold, who had in 1467 succeeded as Duke of Burgundy. Thus not only did these great lords, who at the constant peril of their lives and by all their vast resources had placed him on the throne, suffer slights and material losses by the creation of a new nobility, but they had besides to stomach a foreign policy which they believed would be fatal to England, to the Yorkist party, and to themselves. What help could Burgundy give if France, joined to the house of Lancaster, invaded England? What would happen to them, their great estates, and all who depended upon them, in such a catastrophe? The quarrel between the King and Warwick, as head of the Nevilles, was not therefore petty, or even, as has often been suggested, entirely personal.

The offended chiefs took deep counsel together. Edward continued to enjoy his life with his Queen, and now and again, with others. His attention in public matters was occupied mainly with Lancastrian plots and movements, but underneath and behind him a far graver menace was preparing. The Nevilles were at length ready to try conclusions with him. Warwick's plan was singular in its skill. He had gained the King's brother, Clarence, to his side by whispering that but for this upstart brood of the Woodvilles he might succeed Edward as King. As bond it was secretly agreed that Clarence should marry Warwick's daughter Isabella.

When all was ready Warwick struck. A rising took place in the North. Thousands of men in Yorkshire under the leadership of various young lords complained in arms about taxation. The "thrave," a levy paid since the days of Athelstan, became suddenly obnoxious. But other grievances were urged, particularly that the King was swayed by "favourites." At the same time in London the House of Commons petitioned against lax and profuse administration. The King was now forced to go to the North. Except his small bodyguard he had no troops of his own, but he called upon his nobles to bring out their men. He advanced in July to Nottingham, and there awaited the Earls of Pembroke and Devon, both new creations of his own, who had marshalled the levies of Wales and the West. As soon as the King had been enticed northwards by the rebellion Warwick and Clarence, who had hitherto crouched at Calais, came to England with the Calais garrison.

Warwick published a manifesto supporting the Northern rebels, "the King's true subjects" as he termed them, and urged them "with piteous lamentations to be the means to our Sovereign Lord the King of remedy and reformation." Warwick was joined by many thousands of Kentish men and was received with great respect in London. But before he and Clarence could bring their forces against the King's rear the event was decided. The Northern rebels, under "Robin of Redesdale," intercepted Pembroke and Devon, and at Edgcott, near Banbury, defeated them with a merciless slaughter, a hundred and sixty-eight knights, squires, and gentlemen either falling in the fight or being executed thereafter. Both Pembroke and later Devon were beheaded.

The King, trying to rally his scattered forces at Olney, in Buckinghamshire, found himself in the power of his great nobles. His brother, Richard of Gloucester, known to legend as "Crookback" because of his alleged deformity, seemed his only friend. At first he attempted to rally Warwick and Clarence to their duty, but in the course of conversation he was made to realise that he was their captive. With bows and ceremonies they explained that his future reign must be in accordance with their advice. He was conveyed to Warwick's castle at Middleham, and there kept in honourable but real restraint under the surveillance of the Archbishop of York. At this moment therefore Warwick the King-maker had actually the two rival Kings, Henry VI and Edward IV, both his prisoners, one in the Tower and the other at Middleham. This was a remarkable achievement for any subject. To make the lesson even plainer, Lord Rivers, the Queen's father, and John Woodville, her brother, were arrested and executed at Kenilworth without any pretence of trial. Thus did the older nobility deal with the new.

But the relations between Warwick and the King did not admit of such simple solutions. Warwick had struck with suddenness, and for a while no one realised what had happened. As the truth became known the Yorkist nobility viewed with astonishment and anger the detention of their brave, victorious sovereign, and the Lancastrians everywhere raised their heads in the hopes of profiting by the Yorkist feud. The King found it convenient in his turn to dissemble. He professed himself convinced that Warwick and Clarence were right. He undertook to amend his ways, and after he had signed free pardons to all who had been in arms against him he was liberated. Thus was a settlement reached between Warwick and the Crown.

King Edward was soon again at the head of forces, defeating
Lancastrian rebels and executing their leaders, while Warwick
and all his powerful connections returned to their posts, proclaimed their allegiance, and apparently enjoyed royal favour.
But all this was on the surface.

* * *

In March 1470, under the pretence of suppressing a rebellion in Lincolnshire, the King called his forces to arms. At
Losecoat Field he defeated the insurgents, who promptly fled;
and in the series of executions which had now become customary after every engagement he obtained a confession from
Sir Robert Welles which accused both Warwick and Clarence
of treason. The evidence is fairly convincing; for at this
moment they were conspiring against Edward, and shortly
afterwards refused to obey his express order to join him. The
King, with troops fresh from victory, turned on them all of a
sudden. He marched against them, and they fled, astounded
that their own methods should be retorted upon themselves.
They sought safety in Warwick's base at Calais; but Lord Wenlock, whom he had left as his deputy, refused to admit them.
Even after they had bombarded the sea-front he made it a
positive favour to send a few flagons of wine to Clarence's
bride, who, on board ship, had just given birth to a son. The
King-maker found himself by one sharp twist of fortune deprived of almost every resource he had counted upon as sure.
He in his turn presented himself at the French Court as a
suppliant.

But this was the best luck Louis XI had ever known. He
must have rubbed his hands in the same glee as when he visited
his former Minister, Cardinal Jean Balue, whom he kept imprisoned in an iron cage at Chinon because he had conspired
with Charles the Bold. Two years earlier Edward as the ally of
Burgundy had threatened him with war. Now here in France
were the leaders of both the parties that had disputed England
for so long. Margaret was dwelling in her father's Anjou.
Warwick, friend of France, vanquished in his own country,
had arrived at Honfleur. With gusto the stern, cynical, hard-
pressed Louis set himself to the task of reconciling and combining these opposite forces. At Angers he confronted Margaret and her son, now a fine youth of seventeen, with Warwick
and Clarence, and proposed brutally to them that they should
join together with his support to overthrow Edward. At first
both parties recoiled. Nor can we wonder. A river of blood

flowed between them. All that they had fought for during these cruel years was defaced by their union. Warwick and Margaret had slain with deliberation each other's dearest friends and kin. She had beheaded his father Salisbury, slain his uncle York and his cousin Rutland. He for his part had executed the two Somersets, father and son, the Earl of Wiltshire, and many of her devoted adherents. The common people who had fallen in their quarrel, they were uncounted. In 1459 Margaret had declared Warwick attainted, a terrible outlawry. In 1460 he had branded her son as bastard or changeling. They had done each other the gravest human injuries. But they had one bond in common. They hated Edward and they wanted to win. They were the champions of a generation which could not accept defeat. And here, as indeed for a time it proved, appeared the means of speedy triumph.

Warwick had a fleet, commanded by his nephew, the bastard of Fauconberg. He had the sailors in all the seaports of the south coast. He knew he had but to go or send his summons to large parts of England for the people to take arms at his command. Margaret represented the beaten, disinherited, proscribed house of Lancaster, stubborn as ever. They agreed to forgive and unite. They took solemn oaths at Angers upon a fragment of the Holy Cross, which luckily was available. The confederacy was sealed by the betrothal of Margaret's son, the Prince of Wales, to Warwick's younger daughter, Anne. No one can blame Queen Margaret because in the ruin of her cause she reluctantly forgave injuries and welcomed the Kingmaker's invaluable help. She had never swerved from her faith. But for Warwick the transaction was unnatural, cynical and brutal.

Moreover, he overlooked the effect on Clarence of the new marriage he had arranged for his daughter Anne. A son born of this union would have had a great hope of uniting torn, tormented England. It was reasonable to expect the birth of an heir to these prospects. But Clarence had been swayed in his desertion of his brother by thoughts of the crown, and although he was now named as the next in succession after Margaret's son the value of his chance was no longer high. Edward had been staggered by his brother's conduct. He did not however allow his personal resentment to influence his action. A lady in attendance upon the new Duchess of Clarence proved to be a discreet and accomplished emissary of the King. She conveyed to Clarence soon after he fled from England that he had only to rejoin his brother for all to be pardoned and forgotten. The new agreement between Warwick and Margaret decided Clarence to avail himself of this fraternal offer, but not immediately. He must have been a great dissembler; for Warwick was no more able to forecast his actions in the future than his brother had been in the past.

King Edward was by now alarmed and vigilant, but he could scarcely foresee how many of his supporters would betray him. Warwick repeated the process he had used a year before. Fitzhugh, his cousin, started a new insurrection in Yorkshire. Edward gathered some forces and, making little of the affair, marched against the rebels. Warned by Charles of Burgundy, he even expressed his wish that Warwick would land. He seems to have been entirely confident. But never was there a more swift undeception. Warwick and Clarence landed at Dartmouth in September 1470. Kent and other southern counties rose in his behalf. Warwick marched to London. He brought the miserable Henry VI from his prison in the Tower, placed a crown on his head, paraded him through the capital, and seated him upon the throne.

At Nottingham Edward received alarming news. The major part of his kingdom seemed to have turned against him. Suddenly he learned that while the Northern rebels were moving down upon him and cutting him from his Welsh succours, and while Warwick was moving northward with strong forces, Northumberland, Warwick's brother, hitherto faithful, had made his men throw up their caps for King Henry. When Edward heard of Northumberland's desertion, and also of rapid movements to secure his person, he deemed it his sole hope to fly beyond the seas. He had but one refuge—the Court of Burgundy; and with a handful of followers he cast himself upon his brother-in-law. Charles the Bold was also cautious. He had to consider the imminent danger of an attack by England and France united. Until he was sure that this was inevitable he temporised with his royal refugee relation. But when it became clear that the policy of Warwick was undoubtedly to make war upon him in conjunction with Louis XI he defended himself by an obvious manœuvre. He furnished King Edward with about twelve hundred trustworthy Flemish and German soldiers and the necessary ships and money for a descent. These forces were collected secretly in the island of Walcheren.

* * *

Meanwhile the King-maker ruled England, and it seemed that he might long continue to do so. He had King Henry VI a puppet in his hand. The unhappy man, a breathing ruin sitting like a sack upon the throne, with a crown on his head and a sceptre in his hand, received the fickle caresses of Fortune with the same mild endurance which he had shown to her malignities. Statutes were passed in his name which annihilated all the disinheritances and attainders of the Yorkist Parliament. A third of the land of England returned to its old possessors. The banished nobles or the heirs of the slain returned from poverty and exile to their ancient seats. Meanwhile all preparations were made for a combined attack by England and France on Burgundy, and war became imminent.

But while these violent transformations were comprehensible to the actors, and the drama proceeded with apparent success, the solid bulk of England on both sides was incapable of following such too-quick movements and reconciliations. Almost the whole population stood wherever it had stood before. Their leaders might have made new combinations, but ordinary men could not believe that the antagonism of the Red and the White Rose was ended. It needed but another shock to produce an entirely different scene. It is significant that, although repeatedly urged by Warwick to join him and her husband, King Henry, in London, and although possessed of effective forces, Margaret remained in France, and kept her son with her.

In March 1471 Edward landed with his small expedition at Ravenspur, a port in Yorkshire now washed away by the North Sea, but then still famous for the descent of Henry of Bolingbroke in 1399. The King, fighting for his life, was, as usual, at his best. York shut its gates in his face, but, like Bolingbroke, he declared he had only come to claim his private estates, and bade his troops declare themselves for King Henry VI. Accepted and nourished on these terms, he set forth on his march to London. Northumberland, with four times his numbers, approached to intercept him. Edward, by extraordinary marches, manœuvred past him. All Yorkist lords and adherents in the districts through which he passed joined his army. At Warwick he was strong enough to proclaim himself King again. The King-maker, disconcerted by the turn of events, sent repeated imperative requests to Margaret to come at once, and at Coventry stationed himself in King Edward's path. Meanwhile his brother Northumberland followed Edward southward, only two marches behind. In this dire strait Edward had a resource unsuspected by Warwick. He knew Clarence was his man. Clarence was moving from Gloucestershire with considerable forces, ostensibly to join Warwick; but Edward, slipping round Warwick's flank, as he had out-marched and out-witted Northumberland, placed himself between Warwick and London, and in the exact position where Clarence could make his junction with him.

Both sides now concentrated all their strength, and again large armies were seen in England. Edward entered London, and was cordially received by the bewildered citizens. Henry VI, who had actually been made to ride about the streets at the head of six hundred horsemen, was relieved from these exertions and taken back to his prison in the Tower. The decisive battle impended on the North Road, and at Barnet on April 14, 1471, Edward and the Yorkists faced Warwick and the house of Neville, with the new Duke of Somerset, second son of Edmund Beaufort, and important Lancastrian allies.

Throughout England no one could see clearly what was happening, and the Battle of Barnet, which resolved their doubts, was itself fought in a fog. The lines of battle overlapped; Warwick's right turned Edward's left flank, and *vice versa*. The King-maker, stung perhaps by imputations upon his physical courage, fought on foot. The new Lord Oxford, a prominent Lancastrian, whose father had been beheaded earlier in the reign, commanding the overlapping Lancastrian left, found himself successful in his charge, but lost in the mist. Little knowing that the whole of King Edward's rear was open to his attack, he tried to regain his own lines and arrived in the rear of Somerset's centre. The badge of a star and rays on his banners was mistaken by Warwick's troops for the sun and rays of King Edward. Warwick's archers loosed upon him. The mistake was discovered, but in those days of treason and changing sides it only led to another blunder. It was assumed that he had deserted. The cry of treason ran through Warwick's hosts. Oxford, in his uncertainty, rode off into the gloom. Somerset, on the other flank, had already been routed. Warwick, with the right wing, was attacked by the King and the main Yorkist power. Here indeed it was not worth while to ask for mercy. Warwick, outnumbered, his ranks broken, sought to reach his horse. He would have been wise in spite of taunts to have followed his usual custom of mounting again on the battle-day after walking along the lines; for had he escaped this zigzag story might have ended at the opposite point. But north of the town near which the main struggle was fought the King-maker, just as he was about to reach the necessary horse, was overtaken by the Yorkists and battered to death. He had been the foremost champion of the Yorkist cause. He had served King Edward well. He had received ill-usage from the youth he had placed and sustained upon the throne. By his depraved abandonment of all the causes for which he had sent so many men to their doom he had deserved death; and for his virtues, which were distinguished, it was fitting that it should come to him in honourable guise.

* * *

On the very day of Barnet Margaret at last landed in England. Somerset, the fourth Duke, with his father and his elder brother to avenge, fresh from the disaster at Barnet, met her and became her military commander. On learning that Warwick was slain and his army beaten and dispersed the hitherto indomitable Queen had her hour of despair. Sheltering in Cerne Abbey, near Weymouth, her thought was to return to France; but now her son, the Prince of Wales, nearly eighteen, in whose veins flowed the blood of Henry V, was for fighting for the crown or death. Margaret rallied her spirits and appeared once again unbroken by her life of disaster. Her only hope was to reach the Welsh border, where strong traditional Lancastrian forces were already in arms. The King-maker aberration had been excised. The struggle was once again between Lancaster and York. Edward, near London, held interior lines. He strove to cut Margaret off from Wales. Both armies marched incessantly. In their final march each covered forty miles in a single day. The Lancastrians succeeded in reaching the goal first, but only with their troops in a state of extreme exhaustion. Edward, close behind, pressed on, and on May 3 brought them to battle at Tewkesbury.

This battle was simple in its character. The two sides faced each other in the usual formation of three sectors, right, centre, and left. Somerset commanded Margaret's left, Lord Wenlock and the Prince of Wales the centre, and Devon her right. King Edward exercised a more general command. The Lancastrian position was strong; "in front of their field were so evil lanes, and deep dykes, so many hedges, trees, and bushes, that it was right hard to approach them here and come to hands." [1] Apparently the Lancastrian plan was to await the attack which the Yorkists were eager to deliver. However, Somerset saw an opportunity for using one of the "evil lanes" to pierce the Yorkist centre, and, either without consulting the other generals or in disagreement with them, he charged forward and

[1] *The Arrival of Edward IV.*

gained a momentary success. But King Edward had foreseen his weakness in this quarter. He manfully withstood the irruption upon his main body, and two hundred spears he had thrown out wide as a flank guard fell upon Somerset at a decisive moment and from a deadly angle. The Lancastrians' wing recoiled in disorder. The Yorkists advanced all along the line. In their turn they fell upon their enemies' now unguarded flank, and the last army of the house of Lancaster broke into ruin. Somerset the Fourth evidently felt that he had not been supported at the critical moment. Before flying from the field he dashed out Wenlock's brains with his mace. This protest, while throwing a gleam upon the story of the battle, did not affect the result.

The Lancastrians were scattered or destroyed. Somerset and many other notables who thought themselves safe in sanctuary were dragged forth and decapitated. Margaret was captured. The Prince of Wales, fighting valiantly, was slain on the field, according to one chronicler, crying in vain for succour to his brother-in-law, the treacherous Clarence. Margaret was kept for a show, and also because women, especially when they happened to be queens, were not slaughtered in this fierce age.

Richard of Gloucester hastened to London. He had a task to do at the Tower. As long as the Prince of Wales lived King Henry's life had been safe, but with the death of the last hope of Lancaster his fate was sealed. On the night of May 21 the Duke of Gloucester visited the Tower with full authority from the King, where he probably supervised the murder of the melancholy spectator who had been the centre of fifty years of cruel contention.

When King Edward and his victorious army entered London, always their partisan, especially at such moments, the triumph of the Yorkist cause was complete.

> Once more we sit in England's royal throne,
> Re-purchas'd with the blood of enemies:
> What valiant foemen like to autumn's corn,
> Have we mow'd down, in tops of all their pride!
> Three Dukes of Somerset, threefold renown'd
> For hardy and undoubted champions;
> Two Cliffords, as the father and the son,
> And two Northumberlands: two braver men
> Ne'er spurr'd their coursers at the trumpet's sound;
> With them, the two brave bears, Warwick and Montagu,
> That in their chains fetter'd the kingly lion,
> And made the forest tremble when they roar'd.

Thus have we swept suspicion from our seat,
And made our footstool of security.
Come hither, Bess, and let me kiss my boy.
Young Ned, for thee thine uncles and myself
Have in our armours watch'd the winter's night;
Went all a-foot in summer's scalding heat,
That thou might'st repossess the crown in peace;
And of our labours thou shalt reap the gain.

* * *

The rest of the reign of Edward IV may be told briefly. The King was now supreme. His foes and his patrons alike were dead. He was now a matured and disillusioned statesman. He had every means of remaining complete master of the realm while leading a jolly life. Even from the beginning of his reign he had been chary of calling Parliaments. They made trouble; but if money were needed they had to be called. Therefore the cry in those days which sobered all sovereigns was, "The King should live of his own." But this doctrine took no account of the increasing scope of government. How could the King from his paternal estates, together with certain tolls and tithes, fifteenths, and a few odd poundages, and the accidents of people dying intestate or without adult heirs, or treasure-trove and the like, maintain from these snips an administration equal to the requirements of an expanding society? Still less on this basis could full-blooded wars be waged against France as was expected. It was difficult indeed even to defend the Scottish Border. One had to make use of the warlike nobility of the North, whose hereditary profession was to keep the Marches. Money —above all, ready money. There was the hobble which cramped the medieval kings; and even now it counts somewhat.

Edward was resolved to have as little to do with Parliament as possible, and even as a boy of twenty in the stress of war he tried hard and faithfully to "live of his own." Now that he was victorious and unchallenged, he set himself to practise the utmost economy in everything except his personal expenses, and to avoid any policy of adventure abroad which might drive him to beg from Parliament. He had a new source of revenue in the estates of the attainted Lancastrians. The Crown had gained from the Wars of the Roses. Many were the new possessions which yielded their annual fruit. Thus so long as there was peace the King could pay his way. But the nobility and the nation sought more. They wanted to reconquer France. They mourned the loss of the French provinces. They looked back across their own miseries to the glories of Agincourt, Poitiers, and Crécy. The King, the proved warrior, was expected to produce results in this sphere. It was his intention to do the least possible. He had never liked war, and had had enough of it. Nevertheless he obtained from the Parliament considerable grants for a war in alliance with Burgundy against France.

In 1475 he invaded France, but advanced only as far as Picquigny, near Amiens. There he parleyed. Louis XI had the same outlook. He too saw that kings might grow strong and safe in peace, and would be the prey and tool of their subjects in war. The two kings sought peace and found it. Louis XI offered Edward IV a lump sum of 75,000 crowns, and a yearly tribute of 50,000. This was almost enough to balance the royal budget and make him independent of Parliament. Edward closed on the bargain, and signed the treaty of Picquigny. But Charles the Bold, his ally of Burgundy, took it amiss. At Péronne, in full assembly, with all the English captains gathered, he declared that he had been shamefully betrayed by his ally. A most painful impression was created; but the King put up with it. He went back home and drew for seven successive years this substantial payment for not harrying France, and at the same time he pocketed most of the moneys which Parliament had voted for harrying her.

At this date the interest of these transactions centres mainly upon the character of Edward IV, and we can see that though he had to strive through fierce deeds and slaughter to his throne he was at heart a Little-Englander and a lover of ease. It by no means follows that his policy was injurious to the realm. A long peace was needed for recovery from the horrible civil war. The French Government saw in him with terror all the qualities of Henry V. They paid heavily to hold them in abeyance. This suited the King. He made his administration live thriftily, and on his death he was the first King since Henry II to leave not debts but a fortune. He laboured to contain national pride within the smallest limits, but meanwhile he let the nation grow strong again. He who above all others was thought to be the spear-point became a pad; but at that time a good pad. It may well be, as has been written, that "his indolence and gaiety were mere veils beneath which Edward shrouded profound political ability." [1]

There came a day when he had to call Parliament together. This was not however to ask them for money. What with confiscations, the French tribute, and the profits of his private

[1] J. R. Green.

trading ventures, he could still make his way. His quarrel was with his brother Clarence. Although the compact made between these brothers before Barnet and Tewkesbury had been strictly kept, Edward never trusted Clarence again. Nothing could burn out from his mind the sense that Clarence was a traitor who had betrayed his cause and his family at one decisive moment and had been rebought at another. Clarence for his part knew that the wound although skinned over was unhealed; but he was a magnificent prince, and he sprawled buoyantly over the land. He flouted the King, defying the royal courts; he executed capital sentences upon persons who had offended him in private matters, and felt himself secure. He may have discovered the secret of Edward's alleged pre-contract of marriage with Eleanor Butler which Richard of Gloucester was later to use in justifying his usurpation. Certainly if Edward's marriage to Elizabeth Woodville were to be proved invalid for this reason Clarence was the next legitimate heir, and a source of danger to the King. When in January 1478 Edward's patience was exhausted he called the Parliament with no other business but to condemn Clarence. He adduced a formidable catalogue of crimes and affronts to the Throne, constituting treason. The Parliament, as might be expected, accepted the King's view. By a Bill of Attainder they adjudged Clarence worthy of death, left the execution in the hands of the King, and went home relieved at not having been asked to pay any more taxes.

Clarence was already in the Tower. How he died is much disputed. Some say the King gave him his choice of deaths. Certainly Edward did not intend to have a grisly public spectacle. According to Shakespeare the Duke was drowned in a butt of Malmsey wine. This was certainly the popular legend believed by the sixteenth century. Why should it not be true? At any rate no one has attempted to prove any different tale. "False, fleeting, perjured Clarence" passed out of the world astonished that his brother should have so long a memory and take things so seriously.

Other fortunes had attended Richard of Gloucester. Shortly after the death of Henry VI he got himself married to Anne, daughter of the dead King-maker and co-heiress to the vast Warwick estates. This union excited no enthusiasm; for Anne had been betrothed, if not indeed actually married, to the young Prince Edward, killed at Tewkesbury. Important interests were however combined.

Queen Elizabeth over the course of years had produced not

only five daughters, but two fine boys, who were growing up. In 1483 one was twelve and the other nine. The succession to the Crown seemed plain and secure. The King himself was only forty. In another ten years the Yorkist triumph would have become permanent. But here Fate intervened, and with solemn hand reminded the pleasure-loving Edward that his account was closed. His main thought was set on securing the crown to his son, the unfledged Edward V; but in April 1483 death came so suddenly upon him that he had no time to take the necessary precautions. Although always devoted to Queen Elizabeth, he had lived promiscuously all his life. She was in the Midlands, when, after only ten days' illness, this strong King was cut down in his prime. The historians assure us that this was the penalty of debauchery. It may well have been appendicitis, an explanation as yet unknown. He died unprepared except by the Church, and his faithful brother Richard saw himself suddenly confronted with an entirely new view of his future.

BOOK THREE · CHAPTER THIRTY

Richard III

THE King died so suddenly that all were caught by surprise. A tense crisis instantly arose. After Barnet and Tewkesbury the old nobility had had to swallow with such grace as they could muster the return of the surviving Woodvilles to the sunlight of power and favour. But throughout England the Queen's relations were viewed with resentment or disdain, while the King made merry with his beautiful, charming mistress, Jane Shore. Now death dissolved the royal authority by which alone so questionable a structure could be sustained. His eldest son, Edward, dwelt at Ludlow, on the Welsh border, under the care of his uncle, the second Lord Rivers. A Protectorate was inevitable. There could be no doubt about the Protector. Richard of Gloucester, the King's faithful brother, renowned in war, grave and competent in administration, enriched by Warwick's inheritance and many other great estates, in possession of all the chief military offices, stood forth without compare, and had been nominated by the late King himself. Around him gathered most of the old nobility. They viewed with general distaste the idea of a King whose grandfather, though a knight, had been a mere steward to one of their own order. They deplored a minority and thereafter the rule of an unproved, inexperienced boy-King. They were however bound by their oaths and by the succession in the Yorkist line that their own swords had established.

One thing at least they would not brook: Queen Elizabeth and her low-born relations should no longer have the ascendancy. On the other hand, Lord Rivers at Ludlow, with numerous adherents and family supporters, had possession of the new King. For three weeks both parties eyed one another and parleyed. It was agreed in April that the King should be crowned at the earliest moment, but that he should come to London attended by not more than two thousand horsemen. Accordingly this cavalcade, headed by Lord Rivers and his nephew, Grey, rode southward through Shrewsbury and Northampton. They had reached Stony Stratford when they learned that Gloucester and his ally, the Duke of Buckingham, coming to London from Yorkshire, were only ten miles behind them. They turned back to Northampton to greet the two Dukes, apparently suspecting no evil. Richard received them amicably; they dined together. But with the morning there was a change.

When he awoke Rivers found the doors of the inn locked. He asked the reason for this precaution. Gloucester and Buckingham met him with scowling gaze and accused him of "trying to set distance" between the King and them. He and Grey were immediately made prisoners. Richard then rode with his power to Stony Stratford, arrested the commanders of the two thousand horse, forced his way to the young King, and told him he had discovered a design on the part of Lord Rivers and others to seize the Government and oppress the old nobility. On this declaration Edward V took the only positive action recorded of his reign. He wept. Well he might.

The next morning Duke Richard presented himself again to Edward. He embraced him as an uncle; he bowed to him as a subject. He announced himself as Protector. He dismissed the two thousand horsemen to their homes; their services would not be needed. To London then! To the coronation! Thus this melancholy procession set out.

The Queen, who was already in London, had no illusions. She took sanctuary at once with her other children at Westminster, making a hole through the wall between the church and the palace to transport such personal belongings as she could gather.

The report that the King was in duress caused a commotion in the capital. "He was to be sent, no man wist whither, to be done with God wot what." [1] But Lord Hastings reassured the Council that all was well and that any disturbance would only delay the coronation, upon which the peace of the realm depended. The Archbishop of York, who was also Chancellor, tried to reassure the Queen. "Be of good cheer, madam," he said, "for if they crown any other than your son whom they now have with them, we shall on the morrow crown his brother whom you have with you here." He even gave her the Great Seal as a kind of guarantee. He was not in any plot, but only an old fool playing for safety first and peace at any price. Presently, frightened at what he had done, he managed to get the Great Seal back.

The King arrived in London only on May 4, and the coronation, which had been fixed for that date, was necessarily postponed. He was lodged at the Bishop of London's palace, where he received the fealty of all the lords, spiritual and temporal. But the Protector and his friends felt that it was hardly becoming that he should be the guest of an ecclesiastic, and when the Queen's friends suggested that he might reside at the Hospital of the Knights of St John in Clerkenwell Richard argued that it would be more fitting to the royal dignity to dwell in one of his own castles and on his own ground. The Tower was a residence not only commodious but at the same time safe from any popular disorder. To this decision the lords of the Council gave united assent, it not being either easy or safe for the minority to disagree. With much ceremony and protestations of devotion the child of twelve was conducted to the Tower, and its gates closed behind him.

London was in a ferment, and the magnates gathered there gazed upon each other in doubt and fear. The next step in the tragedy concerned Lord Hastings. He had played a leading part in the closing years of Edward IV. After the King's death he had been strong against the Woodvilles; but he was the first to detach himself from Richard's proceedings. It did not suit him, nor some of the other magnates, that all power should rapidly be accumulating in Richard's hands. He began to be friendly with the Queen's party, still in the sanctuary of Westminster Abbey. Of what happened next all we really know is

[1] More.

that Hastings was abruptly arrested in council at the Tower on June 13 and beheaded without trial on the same day. Sir Thomas More late in the next reign wrote his celebrated history. His book was based of course on information given him under the new and strongly established régime. His object seems to have been less to compose a factual narrative than a moralistic drama. In it Richard is evil incarnate, and Henry Tudor, the deliverer of the kingdom, all sweetness and light. The opposite view would have been treason. Not only is every possible crime attributed by More to Richard, and some impossible ones, but he is presented as a physical monster, crookbacked and withered of arm. No one in his lifetime seems to have remarked these deformities, but they are now very familiar to us through Shakespeare's play. Needless to say, as soon as the Tudor dynasty was laid to rest defenders of Richard fell to work, and they have been increasingly busy ever since.

More's tale however has priority. We have the famous scene at the Council in the Tower. It was Friday, June 13. Richard arrived in the Council chamber about nine, apparently in good humour. "My lord," he said to Bishop Morton, "you have very good strawberries in your garden at Holborn. I pray you let us have a mess of them." The Council began its business. Richard asked to be excused for a while; when he returned between ten and eleven his whole manner was changed. He frowned and glared upon the Council, and at the same time clusters of armed men gathered at the door. "What punishment do they deserve," demanded the Protector, "who conspire against the life of one so nearly related to the King as myself, and entrusted with the government of the realm?" There was general consternation. Hastings said at length that they deserved the punishment of traitors. "That sorceress my brother's wife," cried Richard, "and others with her—see how they have wasted my body with sorcery and witchcraft." So saying, he is supposed to have bared his arm and showed it to the Council, shrunk and withered as legend says it was. In furious terms he next referred to Jane Shore, with whom Hastings had formed an intimacy on the late King's death. Hastings, taken aback, replied, "Certainly if they have done so heinously they are worth a heinous punishment." "What?" cried Crookback. "Dost thou serve me with 'ifs' and 'ands'? I tell thee they have done it, and that I will make good upon thy body, traitor!" He struck the Council table with his fist, and at this signal the armed men ran in, crying "Treason!" and Hastings, Bishop Morton, and the Archbishop of York with some others were seized. Richard bade Hastings prepare for instant death. "I will not dine until I have his head." There was barely time to find a priest. Upon a log of wood which lay by chance in the Tower yard Hastings was decapitated. Terror reigned.

Richard had ordered his retainers in the North to come to London in arms under his trusted lieutenant, Sir Richard Ratcliffe. On the way south Ratcliffe collected Lords Rivers, Vaughan, Grey, and the commanders of the two thousand horse from the castles in which they were confined, and at Pomfret cut off their heads a few days after Hastings had suffered. Their executions are undisputed fact.

Meanwhile the Queen and her remaining son still sheltered in sanctuary. Richard felt that it would be more natural that the two brothers should be together under his care, and he moved the purged Council to request the Queen to give him up. The Council contemplated the use of force in the event of a refusal. Having no choice, the Queen submitted, and the little prince of nine was handed over in Westminster Hall to the Protector, who embraced him affectionately and conducted him to the Tower, which neither he nor his brother was ever to leave again. Richard's Northern bands were now approaching London in considerable numbers, many thousands being expected, and he felt strong enough to take his next step. The coronation of Edward V had been postponed several times. Now a preacher named Shaw, brother of the Lord Mayor of London, one of Richard's partisans, was engaged to preach a sermon at St Paul's Cross. Taking his text from the Book of Wisdom, "Bastard slips shall not take deep root," he impugned Edward IV's marriage with Elizabeth Woodville upon a number of grounds, including sorcery, violation of the alleged previous betrothal to Eleanor Butler, and the assertion that the ceremony had been performed in an unconsecrated place. He argued from this that Edward's children were illegitimate and that the crown rightly belonged to Richard. The suggestion was even revived that Edward IV himself had not been his father's son. Richard now appeared, accompanied by Buckingham, evidently expecting to be publicly acclaimed; but, says More, "the people were so far from crying 'King Richard!' that they stood as if turned into stones for wonder of this shameful sermon." Two days later the Duke of Buckingham tried his hand, and according to an eye-witness he was so eloquent and well rehearsed that he did not even pause to spit; but once again the people remained mute, and only some of the Duke's servants threw up their caps, crying, "King Richard!"

Nevertheless on June 25 Parliament met, and after receiving a roll declaring that the late King's marriage with Elizabeth was no marriage at all and that Edward's children were bastard it petitioned Richard to assume the crown. A deputation, headed by the Duke of Buckingham, waited on Richard, who was staying at the house of his mother, whose virtue he had aspersed. With becoming modesty Richard persistently refused; but when Buckingham assured him of their determination that the children of Edward should not rule and that if he would not serve the country they would be forced to choose some other noble he overcame his conscientious scruples at the call of public duty. The next day he was enthroned, with much ceremony. At the same time the forces which Ratcliffe had sent from the North were reviewed in Finsbury Fields. They proved to be about five thousand strong, "evil apparelled . . . in rusty harness neither defensible nor scoured." The City was relieved to find that the reports of their strength and numbers had been exaggerated.

The coronation of King Richard III was fixed for July 6, and pageants and processions diverted the uneasy public. As an act of clemency Richard released the Archbishop of York from arrest, and transferred Bishop Morton of Ely to the easier custody of Buckingham. The coronation was celebrated with all possible pomp and splendour. Particular importance was attached to the religious aspect. Archbishop Bourchier placed the crowns on the heads of the King and Queen; they were anointed with oil; they received the Sacrament in the presence of the assembly, and finally repaired to a banquet in Westminster Hall. The King now had a title acknowledged and confirmed by Parliament, and upon the theory of the bastardy of Edward's children he was also the lineal successor in blood. Thus the whole design seemed to have been accomplished. Yet from this very moment there began that marked distrust and hostility of all classes towards King Richard III which all his arts and competence could not allay. "It followed," said the chronicler Fabyan, whose book was published in 1516, "anon as this man had taken upon him, he fell in great hatred of the more part of the nobles of his realm, insomuch that such as before loved and praised him . . . now murmured and grudged against him in such wise that few or none favoured his party except it were for dread or for the great gifts they had received of him."

It is contended by the defenders of King Richard that the Tudor version of these events has prevailed. But the English people who lived at the time and learned of the events day by day formed their convictions two years before the Tudors gained power or were indeed a prominent factor. Richard III held the authority of government. He told his own story with what facilities were available, and he was spontaneously and almost universally disbelieved. Indeed, no fact stands forth more unchallengeable than that the overwhelming majority of the nation was convinced that Richard had used his power as Protector to usurp the crown and that the princes had disappeared in the Tower. It will take many ingenious books to raise this issue to the dignity of a historical controversy.

No man had done more to place Richard upon the throne than the Duke of Buckingham, and upon no one had the King bestowed greater gifts and favours. Yet during these first three months of Richard's reign Buckingham from being his chief supporter became his mortal foe. His motives are not clear. Perhaps he shrank from becoming the accomplice in what he foresaw would be the closing act of the usurpation. Perhaps he feared for his own safety, for was he not himself of royal blood? He was descended both through the Beauforts and Thomas of Woodstock from Edward III. It was believed that when the Beaufort family was legitimated by letters patent under King Richard II, confirmed by Henry IV, there had been a reservation rendering them incapable of inheriting the crown; but this reservation had not been a part of the original document, but had only been written in during the reign of Henry IV. The Duke of Buckingham, as a Beaufort on his mother's side, possessed the original letters patent under the Great Seal, confirmed in Parliament, in which no such bar was mentioned. Although he guarded this secret with all needful prudence he must now look upon himself as a potential claimant to the crown, and he must feel none the safer if Richard should so regard him. Buckingham's mind was troubled by the knowledge that all the ceremony and vigour with which Richard's ascent to the throne had been conducted did not affect the general feeling that he was a usurper. In his castle at Brecknock he began to talk moodily to his prisoner, Bishop Morton; and the Bishop, who was a master of the persuasive arts and a consummate politician, undoubtedly gained a great hold upon him.

*   *   *

Meanwhile King Richard began a progress from Oxford through the Midlands. At every city he laboured to make the best impression, righting wrongs, settling disputes, granting favours, and courting popularity. Yet he could not escape the sense that behind the displays of gratitude and loyalty which naturally surrounded him there lay an unspoken challenge to his Kingship. There was little concealment of this in the South. In London, Kent, Essex, and throughout the Home Counties feeling already ran high against him, and on all men's lips was the demand that the princes should be liberated. Richard did not as yet suspect Buckingham, who had parted from him at Gloucester, of any serious disaffection. But he was anxious for the safety of his crown. How could he maintain it while his nephews lived to provide a rallying point for any combination of hostile forces against him? So we come to the principal crime ever afterwards associated with Richard's name. His interest is plain. His character was ruthless. It is certain that the helpless children in the Tower were not seen again after the month of July 1483. Yet we are invited by some to believe that they languished in captivity, unnoticed and unrecorded, for another two years, only to be done to death by Henry Tudor.

According to Thomas More's story, Richard resolved in July to extirpate the menace to his peace and sovereignty presented by the princes. He sent a special messenger, by name John Green, to Brackenbury, the Constable of the Tower, with orders to make an end of them. Brackenbury refused to obey. "Whom should a man trust," exclaimed the King when Green returned with this report "when those who I thought would most surely serve at my command will do nothing for me?" A page who heard this outburst reminded his master that Sir James Tyrell, one of Richard's former companions in arms, was capable of anything. Tyrell was sent to London with a warrant authorising Brackenbury to deliver to him for one night all the keys of the Tower. Tyrell discharged his fell commission with all dispatch. One of the four gaolers in charge of the princes, Forest by name, was found willing, and with Dighton, Tyrell's own groom, did the deed. When the princes were asleep these two assassins pressed the pillows hard down upon their faces till they were suffocated, and their bodies were immured in some secret corner of the Tower. There is some proof that all three murderers were suitably rewarded by the King. But it was not until Henry VII's reign, when Tyrell was lying in the Tower under sentence of death for quite a separate crime, that he is alleged to have made a confession upon which, with much other circumstantial evidence, the story as we know it rests.

In the reign of Charles II, when in 1674 the staircase leading to the chapel in the White Tower was altered, the skeletons
of two young lads, whose apparent ages fitted the two princes,
were found buried under a mass of rubble. They were examined by the royal surgeon, and the antiquaries reported that
they were undoubtedly the remains of Edward V and the Duke
of York. Charles accepted this view, and the skeletons were
reburied in Henry VII's Chapel at Westminster with a Latin
inscription laying all blame upon their perfidious uncle "the
usurper of the realm." This has not prevented various writers,
among whom Horace Walpole is notable, from endeavouring
to clear Richard of the crime, or from attempting to cast it,
without any evidence beyond conjecture, upon Henry VII.
However, in our own time an exhumation has confirmed the
view of the disinterested authorities of King Charles's reign.

Buckingham had now become the centre of a conspiracy
throughout the West and South of England against the King.
He had reached a definite decision about his own claims to the
crown. He seems to have assumed from his knowledge of Richard that the princes in the Tower were either dead or doomed.
He met at this time Margaret, Countess of Richmond, survivor
of the Beaufort line, and recognised that even if the house of
York were altogether set aside both she and her son Henry
Tudor, Earl of Richmond, stood between him and the crown.
The Countess of Richmond, presuming him to be still Richard's
right-hand man, asked him to win the King's consent to a marriage between her son Henry of Richmond and one of King
Edward's daughters, Elizabeth, still in sanctuary with their
mother at Westminster. Richard would never have entertained
such a project, which was indeed the extreme opposite to his
interests. But Buckingham saw that such a marriage would
unite the claims of York and Lancaster, bridge the gulf that
had parted England for so long, and enable a tremendous front
to be immediately formed against the usurper.

The popular demand for the release of the princes was followed by a report of their death. When, how, and by whose
hand the deed had been done was not known. But as the news
spread like wildfire a kind of fury seized upon many people.
Although accustomed to the brutalities of the long civil wars,
the English people of those days still retained the faculty of
horror; and once it was excited they did not soon forget. A
modern dictator with the resources of science at his disposal
can easily lead the public on from day to day, destroying all
persistency of thought and aim, so that memory is blurred by

the multiplicity of daily news and judgment baffled by its perversion. But in the fifteenth century the murder of the two
young princes by the very man who had undertaken to protect
them was regarded as an atrocious crime, never to be forgotten or forgiven. In September Richard in his progress
reached York, and here he created his son Prince of Wales,
thus in the eyes of his enemies giving confirmation to the
darkest rumours.

All Buckingham's preparations were for a general rising on
October 18. He would gather his Welsh forces at Brecknock;
all the Southern and Western counties would take up arms;
and Henry, Earl of Richmond, with the aid of the Duke of
Brittany, would land with a force of five thousand men in
Wales. But the anger of the people at the rumoured murder of
the princes deranged this elaborate plan. In Kent, Wiltshire,
Sussex, and Devonshire there were risings ten days before the
appointed date; Henry of Richmond was forced to set sail
from Brittany in foul weather on October 12, so that his fleet
was dispersed; and when Buckingham unfurled his flag at
Brecknock the elements took sides against him too. A terrific
storm flooded the Severn valley, and he found himself penned
on the Welsh border in a district which could not supply the
needs of his army, and unable, as he had planned, to join the
rebels in Devonshire.

King Richard acted with the utmost vigour. He had an army
and he marched against rebellion. The sporadic risings in the
South were suppressed. Buckingham's forces melted away, and
he himself hid from vengeance. Richmond reached the English
coast at last with only two ships, and sailed westwards towards
Plymouth, waiting for a sign which never came. Such was the
uncertainty at Plymouth that he warily made further inquiries,
as a result of which he sailed back to Brittany. Buckingham,
with a high price on his head, was betrayed to Richard, who
lost not an hour in having him slaughtered. The usual crop of
executions followed. Order was restored throughout the land,
and the King seemed to have established himself securely
upon his throne.

He proceeded in the new year to inaugurate a series of enlightened reforms in every sphere of Government. He revived
the power of Parliament, which it had been the policy of Edward IV to reduce to nullity. He declared the practice of
raising revenue by "benevolences" illegal. Parliament again
legislated copiously after a long interval. Commerce was protected by a series of well-meant if ill-judged Acts, and a land

law was passed to regulate "uses," or, as we should now say, trusts. Attempts were made to please the clergy by confirming their privileges, endowing new religious foundations, and extending the patronage of learning. Much care was taken over the shows of heraldry and pageantry; magnanimity was shown to fallen opponents, and petitioners in distress were treated with kindness. But all counted for nothing. The hatred which Richard's crime had roused against him throughout the land remained sullen and quenchless, and no benefits bestowed, no sagacious measures adopted, no administrative successes achieved, could avail the guilty monarch.

An impulsive gentleman, one Collingbourne, formerly Sheriff of Worcester, was so much incensed against the King that he had a doggerel rhyme he had composed nailed on the door of St Paul's:

> The Catte, the Ratte, and Lovell our dogge
> Rulyth all Englande under a Hogge.

Catesby, Ratcliffe, Viscount Lovell, and Richard, whose badge was a boar, saw themselves affronted. But it was not only for this that Collingbourne suffered an agonising death at the end of a year. He was undoubtedly a rebel, actively engaged in conspiracy.

Even Richard's own soul rebelled against him. He was haunted by fears and dreams. He saw retribution awaiting him round every corner. "I have heard by creditable report," says Sir Thomas More, "of such as were secret with his chamberers, that after this abominable deed done he never had quiet in his mind, he never thought himself sure. Where he went abroad, his eyes whirled about, his body privily fenced, his hand ever on his dagger, his countenance and manner like one always ready to strike again. He took ill rest at nights, lay long waking and musing; sore wearied with care and watch, he rather slumbered than slept. Troubled with fearful dreams, suddenly sometimes started he up, leapt out of his bed and ran about the chamber. So was his restless heart continually tossed and tumbled with the tedious impression and stormy remembrance of his most abominable deed."

* * *

A terrible blow now fell upon the King. In April 1484 his only son, the Prince of Wales, died at Middleham, and his wife, Anne, the daughter of the King-maker, whose health was broken, could bear no more children. Henry Tudor, Earl of Richmond, now became obviously the rival claimant and successor to the throne. Richmond, "the nearest thing to royalty the Lancastrian party possessed," was a Welshman, whose grandfather, Owen Tudor, executed by the Yorkists in 1461, had married, if indeed he married, Henry V's widow, Catherine of France, and whose father Edmund had married the Lady Margaret Beaufort. Thus Richmond could trace his descent through his mother from Edward III, and on his father's side had French royal blood in his veins as well as a shadowy claim to descent from Cadwallader and the legendary ancient kings of Britain, including King Arthur. His life had been cast amid ceaseless trouble. For seven years of childhood he had been besieged in Harlech Castle. At the age of fourteen, on the defeat of the Lancastrians at Tewkesbury, he was forced to flee to Brittany. Thereafter exile and privation had been his lot. These trials had stamped themselves upon his character, rendering him crafty and suspicious. This, however, did not daunt a proud spirit, nor cloud a wise and commanding mind, nor cast a shadow over his countenance, which was, we are told, "smiling and amiable, especially in his communications."

All hopes in England were now turned towards Richmond, and it was apparent that the marriage which had been projected between him and Edward IV's eldest daughter Elizabeth offered a prospect of ending for ever the cruel dynastic strife of which the land was unutterably weary. After the failure of Buckingham's rebellion Richmond and his expedition had returned to Brittany. The Duke of Brittany, long friendly, again accorded shelter and subsistence to the exile and his band of perhaps five hundred Englishmen of quality. But King Richard's diplomacy was active. He offered a large sum of money for the surrender of his rival. During the illness of the Duke of Brittany the Breton Minister, Landois, was disposed to sell the valuable refugee. Richmond however, suspecting the danger, escaped in the nick of time by galloping hell for leather into France, where, in accordance with the general policy of keeping English feuds alive, he was well received by the French regent, Anne. Meanwhile the Duke of Brittany, recovering, reproved his Minister and continued to harbour the English exiles. In France Richmond was joined by the Earl of Oxford, the leading survivor of the Lancastrian party, who had escaped from ten years' incarceration and plunged once again into the old struggle. As the months passed many prominent Englishmen, both Yorkist and Lancastrian, withdrew themselves from Richard's baleful presence, and made their way to Richmond, who from this time forth stood at the head of a combination which might well unite all England.

His great hope lay in the marriage with the Princess Elizabeth. But in this quarter Richard had not been idle. Before the rebellion he had taken steps to prevent Elizabeth slipping out of sanctuary and England. In March 1484 he made proposals to the Dowager Queen, Dame Elizabeth Grey as he called her, of reconciliation. The unhappy Queen did not reject his overtures. Richard promised in a solemn deed "on his honour as a King" to provide maintenance for the ex-Queen and to marry her daughters suitably to gentlemen. This remarkable document was witnessed not only by the Lords Spiritual and Temporal, but in addition by the Lord Mayor of London and the Aldermen. In spite of the past the Queen had to trust herself to this. She quitted sanctuary. She abandoned the match for her daughter with Richmond. She and the elder princesses were received at Richard's Court and treated with exceptional distinction. At the Christmas Court at Westminster in 1484 high revels were held. It was noticed that the changes of dress provided for Dame Elizabeth Grey and her daughters were almost royal in their style and richness. The stigma of bastardy so lately inflicted upon Edward's children, and the awful secret of the Tower, were banished. Although the threat of invasion was constant, gaiety and dancing ruled the hour. "Dame Elizabeth" even wrote to her son by her first marriage, the Marquis of Dorset, in Paris, to abandon Richmond and come home to share in the new-found favour. More surprising still, Princess Elizabeth seems to have been by no means hostile to the attentions of the usurper. In March 1485 Queen Anne died, probably from natural causes. Rumours were circulating that Richard intended to marry his niece himself, in order to keep her out of Richmond's way. This incestuous union could have been achieved by Papal dispensation, but Richard disavowed all intention of it, both in Council and in public. And it is indeed hard to see how his position could have been strengthened by marrying a princess whom he had declared illegitimate. However that may be, Richmond was thereby relieved of a great anxiety.

All through the summer Richmond's expedition was preparing at the mouth of the Seine, and the exodus from England of substantial people to join him was unceasing. The suspense was wearing to Richard. He felt he was surrounded by hatred and distrust, and that none served him but from fear, or hope of favour. His dogged, indomitable nature had determined him to make for his crown the greatest of all his fights. He fixed his headquarters in a good central position at Nottingham. Commissions of muster and array were ordered to call men to arms in almost every county. Departing perforce from the precepts he had set himself in the previous year, he asked for a "benevolence," or "malevolence" as it was described, of thirty thousand pounds. He set on foot a disciplined regular force. He stationed relays of horsemen every twenty miles permanently along the great roads to bring news and carry orders with an organised swiftness hitherto unknown in England. This important development in the postal system had been inaugurated by Edward IV. At the head of his troops he ceaselessly patrolled the Midland area, endeavouring by strength to overawe and by good government to placate his sullen subjects. He set forth his cause in a vehement proclamation, denouncing ". . . one, Henry Tydder, son of Edmund Tydder, son of Owen Tydder," of bastard blood both on his father's and mother's side, who of his ambition and covetousness pretended to the crown, "to the disinheriting and destruction of all the noble and worshipful blood of his realm for ever." But this fell cold.

On August 1 Richmond embarked at Harfleur with his Englishmen, Yorkist as well as Lancastrian, and a body of French troops. A fair wind bore him down the Channel. He evaded the squadrons of "Lovell our Dogge," doubled Land's End, and landed at Milford Haven on the 7th. Kneeling, he recited the psalm *Judica me, Deus, et decerne causam meam.* He kissed the ground, signed himself with the Cross, and gave the order to advance in the name of God and St George. He had only two thousand men; but such were his assurances of support that he proclaimed Richard forthwith usurper and rebel against himself. The Welsh were gratified by the prospect of one of their race succeeding to the crown of mighty England. It had been for ages a national dream. The ancient Britons would come back into their own. Richard's principal chieftain and officer, Rhys ap Thomas, considered himself at first debarred by his oath of allegiance from aiding the invader. He had declared that no rebels should enter Wales, "except they should pass over his belly." He had however excused himself from sending his only son to Nottingham as a hostage, assuring Richard that nothing could bind him more strongly than his conscience. This now became an obstacle.

However, the Bishop of St David's offered to absolve him from his oath, and suggested that he might, if still disquieted, lay himself upon the ground before Richmond and let him actually step over his belly. A more dignified but equally satisfactory procedure was adopted. Rhys ap Thomas stood under the Molloch Bridge near Dale while Henry of Richmond walked over the top. Anything like a scandalous breach of faith was thus avoided. The Welsh gentry rallied in moderate numbers to Richmond, who displayed not only the standard of St George, but the Red Dragon of Cadwallader. With five thousand men he now moved eastwards through Shrewsbury and Stafford.

* * *

For all his post-horses it was five days before the King heard of the landing. He gathered his army and marched to meet his foe. At this moment the attitude of the Stanleys became of decisive importance. They had been entrusted by the King with the duty of intercepting the rebels should they land in the West. Sir William Stanley, with some thousands of men, made no attempt to do so. Richard thereupon summoned Lord Stanley, the head of the house, to his Court, and when that potentate declared himself "ill of the sweating sickness" he seized Lord Strange, his eldest son, to hold him answerable with his life for his father's loyalty. This did not prevent Sir William Stanley with the Cheshire levies from making friendly contact with Richmond. But Lord Stanley, hoping to save his son, maintained till the last moment an uncertain demeanour.

The city of York on this occasion stood by the Yorkist cause. The Duke of Norfolk and Percy, Earl of Northumberland, were Richard's principal adherents. "The Catte and the Ratte" had no hope of life but in their master's victory. On August 17, thus attended, the King set forth towards Leicester at the head of his army. Their ordered ranks, four abreast, with the cavalry on both flanks and the King mounted on his great white charger in the centre, made a formidable impression upon beholders. And when on Sunday, the 21st, this whole array came out of Leicester to meet Richmond near the village of Market Bosworth it was certain that a decisive battle impended on the morrow.

Appearances favoured the King. He had ten thousand disciplined men under the royal authority against Richmond's hastily gathered five thousand rebels. But at some distance from the flanks of the main army, on opposite hill-tops, stood the respective forces, mainly from Lancashire and Cheshire, of Sir William Stanley and Lord Stanley, the whole situation resembling, as has been said, four players in a game of cards. Richard, according to the Tudor historians, although confessing to a night of frightful dreams and demon-hauntings, harangued his captains in magnificent style. "Dismiss all fear. . . . Every one give but one sure stroke and the day is ours. What prevaileth a handful of men to a whole realm? As for me, I assure you this day I will triumph by glorious victory or suffer death for immortal fame." He then gave the signal for battle, and sent a message to Lord Stanley that if he did not fall on forthwith he would instantly decapitate his son. Stanley, forced to this bitter choice, answered proudly that he had other sons. The King gave orders for Strange's execution. But the officers so charged thought it prudent to hold the stroke in suspense till matters were clearer. "My lord, the enemy is past the marsh. After the battle let young Stanley die."

But even now Richmond was not sure what part Lord Stanley and his forces would play. When, after archery and cannonade, the lines were locked in battle all doubts were removed. The Earl of Northumberland, commanding Richard's left, stood idle at a distance. Lord Stanley's force joined Richmond. The King saw that all was lost, and, shouting "Treason! Treason!" hurled himself into the thickest of the fray in the desperate purpose of striking down Richmond with his own hand. He actually slew Sir William Brandon, Richmond's standard-bearer, and laid low Sir John Cheney, a warrior renowned for his bodily strength. He is said even to have reached Richmond and crossed swords with him. But at this moment Sir William Stanley's three thousand, "in coats as red as blood," fell upon the struggling Yorkists. The tides of conflict swept the principals asunder. Richmond was preserved, and the King, refusing to fly, was borne down and slaughtered as he deserved.

> One foot I will never flee, while the breath is my breast within.
> As he said, so did it he—if he lost his life he died a king.

Richard's crown, which he wore to the last, was picked out of a bush and placed upon the victor's head. The Duke of Norfolk was slain fighting bravely; his son, Lord Surrey, was taken prisoner; Ratcliffe was killed; Catesby, after being allowed to make his will, was executed on the field; and Henry Tudor became King of England. Richard's corpse, naked, and torn by wounds, was bound across a horse, with his head and long hair hanging down, bloody and hideous, and in this condition borne into Leicester for all men to see.

* * *

Bosworth Field may be taken as closing a long chapter in English history. Though risings and conspiracies continued throughout the next reign the strife of the Red and the White Rose had in the main come to an end. Neither won. A solution was reached in which the survivors of both causes could be reconciled. The marriage of Richmond with the adaptable Princess Elizabeth produced the Tudor line, in which both Yorkists and Lancastrians had a share. The revengeful ghosts of two mangled generations were laid for ever. Richard's death also ended the Plantagenet line. For over three hundred years this strong race of warrior and statesmen kings, whose gifts and vices were upon the highest scale, whose sense of authority and Empire had been persistently maintained, now vanished from the fortunes of the Island. The Plantagenets and the proud, exclusive nobility which their system evolved had torn themselves to pieces. The heads of most of the noble houses had been cut off, and their branches extirpated to the second and third generation. An oligarchy whose passions, loyalties, and crimes had for long written English history was subdued. Sprigs of female or bastard lines made disputable contacts with a departed age. As Cœur de Lion said of his house, "From the Devil we sprang and to the Devil we shall go."

At Bosworth the Wars of the Roses reached their final milestone. In the next century the subjects of the Tudors liked to consider that the Middle Ages too had come to a close in 1485, and that a new age had dawned with the accession of Henry Tudor. Modern historians prefer to point out that there are no sharp dividing lines in this period of our history, and that Henry VII carried on and consolidated much of the work of the Yorkist Kings. Certainly the prolongation of strife, waste, and insecurity in the fifteenth century had aroused in all classes an overpowering desire for strong, ordered government. The Parliamentary conception which had prevailed under the house of Lancaster had gained many frontiers of constitutional rights. These were now to pass into long abeyance. Not until the seventeenth century were the old maxims, "Grievances before supply," "Responsibility of Ministers in accordance with the public will," "The Crown the servant and not the master of the State," brought again into the light, and, as it happened, the glare of a new day. The stir of the Renaissance, the storm of the Reformation, hurled their new problems on the bewildered but also reinspired mortals of the new age upon which England entered under the guidance of the wise, sad, careful monarch who inaugurated the Tudor dictatorship as King Henry VII.

Index

Special of the Day

"You don't like French food?" Roxanne asked. Did he not *want* the job?

"I don't like French anything," Steve said.

She sat back and crossed her arms over her chest. He was kidding. He had to be. "Not even French fries?"

Steve shook his head. "They're not even French."

"All right then." Roxanne paused and looked toward the ceiling contemplatively. "French poodles."

Steve laughed, and despite herself she felt warmed by it. "Too ridiculous."

"French films?"

"Too pretentious."

Roxanne's lips curved. "How about French bread? Everybody likes French bread."

A short shake of the head. "Too crumbly."

"Hmm. French toast?"

He shrugged. "Too rich."

She raised one brow and sat forward. "French women?"

Steve's eyes grew subtly more attentive and he gave a low chuckle. "Too...scary."

"I know..." Roxanne paused, studied the challenging look he was giving her and said, "French kisses..."

By Elaine Fox

SPECIAL OF THE DAY
HOT STUFF
IF THE SLIPPER FITS
MAN AT WORK
MAYBE BABY

Elaine Fox

Special of the Day

AVON BOOKS
An Imprint of HarperCollinsPublishers

This is a work of fiction. Names, characters, places, and incidents are products of the author's imagination or are used fictitiously and are not to be construed as real. Any resemblance to actual events, locales, organizations, or persons, living or dead, is entirely coincidental.

AVON BOOKS
An Imprint of HarperCollins*Publishers*
10 East 53rd Street
New York, New York 10022-5299

Copyright © 2005 by Elaine McShulskis
ISBN: 0-06-074059-0
www.avonromance.com

First Avon Books paperback printing: March 2005

Avon Trademark Reg. U.S. Pat. Off. and in Other Countries, Marca Registrada, Hecho en U.S.A.
HarperCollins® is a registered trademark of HarperCollins Publishers Inc.

Printed in the U.S.A.

10 9 8 7 6 5 4 3 2 1

For my mother, Connie Atkins,
who spent my school years
polishing my grammar
and correcting my punctuation,
and without whom
I would never have been able
to embark on this career.

1

Bar Special
Fish House Punch—<u>expect the unexpected...</u>
Light and dark rum, brandy,
   peach brandy, lemon juice, sugar

Roxanne Rayeaux raised her hips and let out a little moan. She tilted her head back, exposing her throat, and arched her back, moving one shoulder to release the tangled locks of her long hair from beneath her.

Enveloped in darkness, surrounded by mystery, she had to admit she was nervous. Yes, very nervous.

She bit her bottom lip and reached out, palms sweating, to find the steely shaft in the dark. Cupping it with uncertain hands, she felt its length. Could she find the right spot? She hoped she wouldn't get wet.

She tried to remember the page in the book that had shown this maneuver. She was not at all sure she was in the right position; it certainly didn't *feel* like the right position. She was . . . uncomfortable.

Though she would have admitted it to no one, she had never done anything like this before.

If only she'd thought to light a candle. She could at least have made sure she wasn't lying down with a rat.

She didn't have a flashlight, not one of her lamps would fit in here, and her body blocked most of the light from the cabinet door.

She was alone under the sink with the pipes. And a more inept plumber she'd be hard pressed to find.

Steve Serrano knocked again on the oak-paneled door, then tilted his head to align an eyeball to the opening. A woman's shoe kept the door from closing completely, leaving a crack through which to see the inside of the apartment.

Nice furnishings. Some boxes. Classical music on the radio. Or no, he leaned further to the right, on the high-end CD system he could see in the corner against the exposed brick wall.

He pushed on the door and it swung wider.

"Hello?" he called.

An orange cat bolted from the couch, lit out across the room and disappeared through a door down a short hallway.

Steve stepped inside the apartment. This one was definitely nicer than his, but maybe that was because there were real oriental rugs on the hardwood floor and actual artwork hanging on the walls.

He moved into the living room and put his hands on his hips. This was one high-class woman. He'd seen the truck from his window when she'd moved in two weeks ago, but he'd never seen her. And he'd expected to. She'd just bought the restaurant downstairs in which he worked as a bartender.

He set the bottle of wine he'd brought as a welcome gift on a sleek glass-topped coffee table and moved toward the kitchen. She had to be home. Why else would her door have been ajar?

He stopped at the entry to the kitchen, his attention caught by the sight of two long jean-clad legs sticking out from beneath the sink. Above the waistband, where her shirt had hiked up, he saw the jut of a hip bone and the curve of a small waist.

He strode across the black and white tiles to look down the drain opening. There, in the dim light, glowed the pale profile of a woman.

"Hey," he greeted mildly.

She gasped, and dropped something loud and metallic beside her.

"Damn it," she hissed.

To herself, he thought, though she could have been swearing at him. Then she started to push herself out from inside the cabinet.

As she wriggled from the space he couldn't help noticing—objectively, of course—that she had a lithe, agile body, if a little on the skinny side. But when her head emerged, complete with a tangled mass of dark hair and black smudges on her forehead and cheek, his breath about left his body.

She was—again, objectively—*gorgeous*. Maybe the most gorgeous woman he'd ever seen in real life.

Even sitting on the floor, covered in dirt, a spiderweb in her hair, she looked like something out of a movie. Her dark eyes flashed above high cheekbones and her mouth was so sensually shaped he couldn't help picturing it sucking strawberries on the big screen.

He almost glanced around to see if someone was playing a joke. As if he might have stumbled into one of those homemaking reality shows, one that pitted beautiful women against average men in some kind of plumbing contest.

She ran one hand across her brow, moving locks of long hair to the side of her face. "You scared me."

"I, uh, I didn't mean to." The words came out like bricks. He'd never been struck so dumb by a pretty face. "I thought you heard me coming."

"What, over the music?" She threw a hand out toward the sound system. She was over her fright now and clearly getting angry.

"Well I was singing along." He couched this with a smile.

Slim, arched brows descended over luscious, inky eyes. "Who *are* you? And what are you doing in here?"

He motioned behind him, unable to pry his gaze from her face. "The door was open."

"And that looked like an invitation to you?" Those lips quirked in a sarcastic—*attractively* sarcastic, God help him—manner.

"Well, I thought, you know, I had this wine . . ." He looked around for it, had forgotten what he'd done with it.

She exhaled. "Listen, I'm not interested, got it? And next time, knock. Though I'd appreciate it if there wasn't a next time."

He looked back at her. She had one hand on her hip,

clutching a wrench. The other hand was slimed from nails to knuckles with trap grease. Still, she managed to look haughty.

He laughed once. Amazing how beauty could dim with the wrong personality attached to it. Words flooded back to him.

He raised his own brows. "No problem, Cinderella. I just thought you should know your door was open."

"Oh my God, the cat—"

"Took off for your bedroom. And I brought the wine as a housewarming, though with the chill in here I probably should have brought a case. I'm your neighbor from upstairs."

She didn't look abashed, exactly. It was more that she looked less combative.

"Oh. All right. Well, thanks—"

"No need to thank me." He held up one hand as if she might get effusive. "But I'll know from here on out to leave you alone. You obviously know what you're doing." He let his gaze sweep her from messy hair to greasy hands to dusty pants, a half smile on his face. "And it's none of my business if you like to leave your door open." He started for the exit. "But, for the record?" He turned before walking out of view. "I'm not interested either. Okay?"

He flashed her a smile and left.

Roxanne's cheeks flamed as she watched the door close to shoe width behind him. She'd forgotten to close the door after bringing the last box up from her car. How could she have done that? Cheeto, her cat, was a master escape artist. He must still be freaked out from the move, she thought, plucking the shoe from the door and closing it firmly.

She had just gotten the last of her things from New York that had been shipped to her rented storage unit before she'd settled on this place. Between that and hauling up the toolbox she'd bought at a yard sale to fix the sink, she'd forgotten to lock the door. Or even close it.

Seems she thought she was back in the Virginia of her youth. When you didn't have to lock your doors to keep strange men from wandering in.

She hadn't even gotten his name. Had just assumed he was some jerk who'd recognized her on the street and followed her home. It had happened before.

Still, this *was* Virginia, and not New York City. She should refrain from jumping to such conclusions. She'd lived in New York for so long she didn't know how to respond to simple Virginia neighborliness.

He probably thought she was a first-class bitch.

And maybe she was. Now.

As she passed the coffee table, her eyes strayed to the bottle of wine. She wiped her hands on her jeans, frowned at how ineffectual that was, then picked up the bottle.

A '94 Bordeaux. The guy knew his wines. She looked again at the door.

He hadn't seemed to know who she was. Evidently he wasn't one of those guys who drooled—or worse—over the *Sports Illustrated* swimsuit edition every year. She'd met some who could rattle off what year each supermodel had appeared and even describe the suit they were wearing. Which surprised her, considering that she'd always thought they were trying hard not to see the suit at all.

So she would apologize to him later if she saw him, she told herself. Not that it mattered. She didn't care what any guy's opinion of her was. She was done trying to figure out what they even thought in the first place. Men were inherently untrustworthy where women were concerned.

Okay, sure, not *all* men. Her dad was a great guy. And her high-school friend Skip. Even Marcel Girmond, her chef due to arrive from New York next week. To all of them she had trusted her heart in some way.

But she was through with romance, at least for a while. Right now she had bigger fish to fry. Or rather, eclairs to bake. She had just finished an intensive course at the Culinary Institute of America and was ready to fulfill her lifelong dream. She'd bought herself a restaurant to convert into a fancy French bistro. And Step One was about to begin.

In approximately twenty-one hours she was to meet with the staff of Charters Fish House, the failing restaurant in the ground floor of the rowhouse she'd just bought in Old Town Alexandria. Her plan was to offer jobs to any of them who cared to stay on and learn the fine art of French restaurateuring. This meant waiting tables with professionalism and aplomb, clearing tables with the subtlety of first-class servants, serving wine with the decorum of a seasoned sommelier, and generally behaving as differently as possible from the pub workers they currently were.

Roxanne was pretty sure she would lose or get rid of three quarters of the staff, but it didn't matter. She had the most important people in place. Her chef, the award-winning Marcel Girmond from New York; his sous-chef, Bertrand Noor; and her maitre d', the ostentatious Sir Nigel from Carruthers' in downtown D.C., where it was rumored the front-room staff trembled in servile awe when he issued an edict. Everyone else could be trained—or hired away from the finest restaurants in town, if need be.

Then she was going to close the place for a few weeks to remodel and re-open it as *Chez Soi*, which was a French idiom she'd always found charming that meant "to have company."

This was going to be the crowning achievement of her life, she'd decided. A life that so far had been spent making money on her looks. For the last ten years she'd worked as a model in major magazines and a few television commercials. But while the living had been good, her looks were something she had done nothing to earn and she knew full well that they would fade before long. When they did, she'd vowed, she would have something real to fall back on. She'd planned to use the money she'd socked away to start her own business.

It was a risk, sure. Nobody with a brain started a restaurant without knowing they could lose their shirt. But the restaurant business was in her blood—and it was one thing she was passionate about. She knew good cooking, she valued excellent service, and she craved a warm atmosphere.

So she would create it. The perfect restaurant. And she would prove to herself that she could make money with her brain instead of her body.

It had been sheer chance she'd been born with looks

that would sell magazines. It was going to be sheer smarts that would make her restaurant a success. Of *that* she would make certain. She would succeed if it killed her.

And it might. She was already as nervous as a wet cat at the prospect of addressing the restaurant staff tomorrow. Though she'd been raised in the restaurant business—she'd been "discovered" while working as a waitress in her parents' homey Italian restaurant in downtown D.C. when she was seventeen—she had never taken on a venture as complicated as this one would be.

She would just have to fake it.

But before that . . . she tossed the wrench in her hand and turned back to the kitchen . . . she had to finish replacing the trap under the sink. She was pouring nearly every penny she had into the restaurant and saving what was left to deal with restaurant emergencies.

Everything else, like household plumbing, had to be done by herself or not done at all.

Steve plopped his plate of cheese fries onto the bar and pushed them toward the plucky redhead across from him.

"So you say she's a bitch, huh?" the redhead said, never one to mince words.

Steve chuckled. "Now, now, Rita. I said she seemed a little tough. Tougher than she looks. So don't be fooled."

He picked up a fry, stirred it around a mound of yellow cheese before putting it in his mouth.

"Sounds to me like she's gonna fire us. Hey, Georgie,

think the new owner's gonna fire our asses?" Rita gave George, another waiter showing up for the meeting, one of her trademark devil's grins. "Rumor has it she's a bitch."

"*She?*" George slid onto a barstool and unwound a scarf from his neck. "There's your first clue right there. Hey Steve, gimme a Bloody Mary, would you? My head feels like it's wearing a mashed potato helmet."

"Told you you shouldn't have had that last kamikaze last night. How about a Coke?" Steve bent to fill a glass with ice and pushed the Coke button on the dispenser.

"You are such a sexist," Rita said, pushing a cheese fry into her mouth. "I hope she rips you a new one for dropping that case of Sam Adams last night."

"How's she going to know about that?" George fixed her with a red eye. "Unless some other gossipy female tells her, huh?"

Rita laughed and tipped her spiky red hair back as she popped in another cheese fry. "You just guaranteed it, my brain-dead friend. These fries are gross," she said to Steve.

Steve ate another. "I know. They were left over from last night. I nuked 'em."

"Eww." Rita swiveled on her chair as two more waiters arrived and sat on bar stools.

Before long the whole crew had assembled, four waiters, two waitresses, two bartenders, three busboys and two line cooks. Their numbers were down since the bar had started doing so badly. Mostly, Steve knew, because of the quality of the food. Which would explain why the main cook had yet to show. No doubt he'd already been fired.

Which was great. Because all it would take to save this place was a reliable chef, a plentiful happy hour and a little bit of advertising. He had a bunch of ideas he planned to share with their lovely new boss, once she untwisted her britches over the fact that he'd let himself into her apartment.

Steve looked at his watch. Eleven ten. She was late. That wasn't exactly the right example to set for this crew, he knew. He'd add that to his list of suggestions. Waitstaff were like children, he would tell her. You have to be nice to them, but don't let them get away with a thing.

He glanced at George, who cradled his head in his hands as if it were a delicate scientific instrument trying to get a reading off the bar top. Poor guy had worked a double yesterday and thought he needed the kamikazes to get to sleep last night. He'd obviously forgotten about today's meeting. Steve was about to cave on the Bloody Mary when the door opened and Her Highness swept in on the frigid January breeze.

Her hair was piled onto her head in a casual style with wisps running loose next to her wind-pinkened cheeks. Her dark eyes actually sparkled in the dim light of the bar.

She held a big piece of corrugated cardboard under one arm, a stack of papers in one hand and was unzipping her white ski jacket with the other.

"Hi all. I'm sorry I'm late. I just spent two and a half hours with the decorator." Her voice was slightly husky and she looked no one in the eye as she propped the cardboard against the wall and lay the papers on a table.

Too good for eye contact, Steve surmised. He wondered if she didn't have some henchman she could have sent to fire them all, if that was her intention. Personally, he hoped it wasn't. Looking for a new job did not fit into his current plans at all. He was too busy with his own project for that.

The rest of the crew just looked at her. The busboys seemed to be having trouble closing their gaping mouths. George lifted his head and Pat, one of the rowdier waiters, sat up far straighter and quieter than he probably ever had in his life

"*That,*" George hissed at Steve, canting his body across the bar toward him, "*is one hot chick.*"

Steve just raised his brows. Interestingly, she wasn't as good-looking as she'd been before she'd opened her mouth yesterday. He wondered if anyone else would feel that way after she spoke to them today.

She took off her jacket and the temperature in the room went up another ten degrees. George and Pat were now leaning forward at the sight of her tight jeans and scoop-neck shirt. Though it was not a provocative outfit, technically speaking, the clothes clung to her curves with what could only be described as tenacity.

She lay her coat over the back of a chair and glanced over the assembled crew. "Hi. My name's Roxanne Rayeaux and I'm the new owner of, uh, Charters. I'm sure you all have been wondering what my plans for the place are, since it's my understanding that it's been generally considered an unsuccessful restaurant for some time now."

People shifted in their seats. Steve could tell that comment struck them, as it did him, as an accusation—that she held them responsible for the restaurant's failing.

Steve cleared his throat. "Uh, that's not exactly true."

Her eyes met his and she gave a little start of recognition. "It's not?"

"I mean, it's true we're all curious about you. But it's not true that the place hasn't been successful. It used to be extremely successful, until a few months ago when management pulled the plug on us," Steve continued. "The chef quit, the distributors started cheating us out of the fresh stuff and we couldn't get anyone to sign a check to save our lives. So you see it was all management. With the proper support, this place is a moneymaker."

She studied him. "You're the guy who lives upstairs, aren't you?" she asked. "What's your name?"

"Steve. Steve Serrano. And I can tell you anything you need to know about this place. Including how to get it back up and running at its full potential."

He owed it to her, he thought, because she was his new boss, to tell her that she hadn't just bought a lemon, that they did all believe in the place, though its success had been compromised lately.

A faint smile crossed her lips. "That's all right, Mr. Serrano. I have a pretty good idea of what to do here. Now—"

"Do you?" He smiled. "I don't mean to tell you your business, but I mean it when I say that up until about six months ago this place was hot. The formula we have here, when adequately funded, works. Happy hours were packed, the dinner crowd was consistent, even lunches—"

"Mr. Serrano," she interrupted.

He stopped, irked by her tone. "Yes, Ms. Rayeaux?"

"What this place *was*, once upon a time, no longer matters. If you'll give me a chance, I'll tell you exactly what I'm going to do with it." She smiled tightly at him.

"Well, sure. Go ahead." He gestured with one hand for her to continue. So much for trying to help her out.

"Thank you." She turned the length of cardboard around and leaned it back against a chair. On the face of it were fabric swatches, pictures of furniture, paint samples and various other glued-on pictures that were hard to make out from behind the bar.

Steve noticed all the heads in front of him lean forward in an attempt to make out the clues, and felt the group's perplexity rise like a cloud to hover over the bar.

She lay one hand along the top of the cardboard. "As you can see, my vision is quite different from what this place has been until now. At the end of next week, I'm closing Charters to do a massive redecoration and remodel. I'm having wine caves installed and updating the bathrooms. I'm also replacing all the tables, chairs, carpeting and artwork, so that in the span of about three weeks, this place will be transformed into an upscale French bistro. We will serve only the freshest food, brilliantly prepared by Chef Girmond from La Finesse in New York, and served by a professional staff of well-trained waiters and waitresses. Which brings me to you all."

Steve's heart sank. This was worse than he'd feared.

Her dark eyes made their way down the line of employees sitting on bar stools before her. Her face was an unreadable mask, until she got to Steve, standing behind the rest of them at the bar. To him, she gave a small smile.

Was she gloating? he wondered. Could she possibly know how much he hated French food? Not to mention French chefs, French décor and French women who belittled American men with condescending smiles.

She shifted her look back to the employees. "I'm willing to offer each of you a job if you agree to be trained by the new maitre d', Sir Nigel Wallings. Some of you may know of Sir Nigel, he's been maitre d' at Carruthers, downtown, for many years and we are extremely lucky to have lured him away from that fine restaurant. You'll be paid your regular hourly wage during training, which I recognize is not much compared to what you make in tips, but you will be guaranteed a job at the end of it."

Silence dominated the room before Rita raised her hand. For a moment Steve tried to imagine Rita, who had once escorted an unruly bar patron from the restaurant by gripping him firmly by the balls, brushing bread crumbs from a linen tablecloth with a silver server.

Roxanne's gaze settled on Rita. The two of them were like fire and ice, Steve reflected.

"Yes?"

"I've heard of that Sir Nigel," Rita said, her narrow back ramrod straight. "He's supposed to be a class-A prick. I don't know anybody who's ever worked for him who could say they liked him."

Steve sighed. He was going to miss working with Rita.

For a moment, Roxanne seemed to be weighing something. Then, hands on her hips, she said, "He *is* a prick."

George and Pat tittered and the busboys shared surreptitious smiles. Despite himself, Steve felt a twinge of admiration for her candor.

"But he knows food, he knows service and he knows people. More importantly, people know *him*, and they will follow him to whatever restaurant he chooses to work for. I'm not going to hide what I'm trying to do here. I don't care about keeping whatever patrons Charters happens to have left. If we alienate every last one of them I'll be happy. I want the high rollers. And frankly, so do you. If you spend two hours waiting on a table ordering burgers, you're going to make a helluva lot less money than if you spend two hours on a table ordering sweetbreads."

"Sweet bread?" One of the busboys, Manuel, piped up. "How much you gonna be charging people for sweet *bread*?"

Steve chuckled, but he was the only one.

Roxanne's eyes scanned the group for whoever had spoken.

"Not sweet *bread*, Manuel." Steve directed his words to the wiry young busboy. "*Sweet*breads. It's a fancy way of saying 'brains.'"

"Brains!" The word popped out of Rita's mouth and she turned to Steve. "You're shittin' me."

"'Fraid not."

Roxanne looked at him in surprise.

"That's right." He grinned back at her. "The savant knows a thing or two about food."

Her lips curved into a smile. "Very good. But it's actually the thymus or pancreas of a young calf. You go to the head of the class anyway, however, for knowing sweetbreads are an organ meat."

George muttered a comment about "organ meat" that made the whole left side of the bar erupt into laughter.

Steve lifted a brow. "I would, ma'am, but I don't want my classmates to think I'm trying to be teacher's pet." To this insolence he added a wink.

She stiffened and her expression went cold. "There'll be no pets in this restaurant, Mr. Serrano, real or figurative." Her gaze dropped his like a dirty dishrag. "Here's how this is going to work. I'm going to be in the restaurant all weekend, seeing how things are currently done before closing down next week. Those of you who would like to be considered for employment at Chez Soi, please fill out one of these forms." She indicated the stack of papers on the table. "Next week, I'll be calling those of you interested in staying on."

"What do you mean you'll be seeing how things are done?" George asked. "I thought you were changing everything anyway."

"She means we'll be auditioning for our jobs, dipstick," Rita said. "Jeez, don't you listen?"

"Is that right?" Steve asked.

The dark gaze was back upon him.

"Will we be auditioning for our jobs?" he persisted.

She seemed to take a deep breath. "My plan is to watch how things are done and make notes on what needs to change. Whether that means personnel or procedure, I can't really say right now. I've never been in here when the place was open."

"It's not much different than it is now," Pat said.

"Except it's crowded now." George snickered.

Roxanne looked from one end of the group to the other. "Anybody have any other questions?"

Everyone was silent. Steve gazed around the room, wondering just what kind of remodeling she planned on doing. If she took out the right wall, he thought, looking at the place where the old staircase used to be, there was a slight chance it could result in a historical gold mine for him.

"Okay, then," she said on an exhale, straightening the papers on the table beside her.

Steve raised his hand. "Yeah, I have a question."

She lifted her chin. "Yes?"

"If you've got this fancy chef coming to run the kitchen, and this Sir Nigel character to run the front, and you're looking at us to possibly keep our jobs, what, exactly, are *you* going to do?"

Rita snorted, then quickly covered her mouth with a hand. She shot a laughing glance back at him.

Roxanne settled those black eyes on Rita, then shifted her gaze back to Steve. "That's a good question. You should know my credentials and why I'm qualified to create and run a successful restaurant. First of all, I've just spent a year at the CIA, and—"

Rita made a noise between a grunt and a scoff, jutting her chin out in disbelief. "You telling us you were *a spy*?"

Steve couldn't help but laugh. "That's the Culinary Institute of America, darlin'."

"Oh." Rita pulled her chin back but looked dubious. "She could have just *said* that."

Roxanne's expression as she looked at Rita was inscrutable but the attention did not bode well for his friend, Steve thought.

"I should have been clearer," she said icily. "In any case, I also have years of waitressing experience as well as firsthand knowledge of the business of running a restaurant, with all of its risks and rewards. I grew up working in a restaurant my parents owned in the Adams Morgan section of D.C."

"Which one?" Steve asked, if only to draw Roxanne's focus from poor Rita, whom he knew needed her job even more than he did his.

"It was a small place—family style—called Mama's." Roxanne's gaze skidded away from the group in a move that looked uncharacteristically vulnerable to him. "My father died and shortly thereafter my mother retired, so it's been gone for several years now."

"I remember Mama's," Steve murmured, trying to call up more than just the sign in his memory.

"In any case," she inhaled and looked steadily back at Rita, "I'm a pastry chef by training. So I'll be in charge of desserts."

Rita turned on her stool and looked at Steve. Just loud enough for him to hear, she said, "*Just desserts*, sounds like. Whether we deserve them or not."

2

Bar Special
Charters Sundowner—in honor of the sun setting
on the old Fish House
Brandy, lemon juice, orange juice, van der Hum

Springsteen throbbed over the sound system. *Hard to Be a Saint in the City*—an old song that Steve had long considered his anthem. The driving rhythm and souped-up bass made the blood pound ecstatically in his ears as he poured a line of lime green Jell-O shooters for George's friend Billy and two of his buddies.

It was almost like the old days in Charters, with the place packed and the energy high. The small dining room was nearly full and orders of fish and chips careened out of the kitchen as fast as the line cooks could pull them out of the deep fryer. Girls strutted their stuff and guys laughed too loud over impossible-to-hear jokes while their eyes darted with feral intent from one sexily clad female to the next.

Of course, it was all a fake. The remaining staff of the dying restaurant had called in their friends to fill the place up, begging them to make a showing so they could have a roomful of happy customers to show their new boss. God only knew what they were going to do tomorrow night. These people sure as hell wouldn't be coming back for Round Two.

Steve slid a couple of longneck Budweisers to Manuel's friends at the end of the bar and waved off their surprise.

"On the house," he said over the music.

What the hell, he thought. No sense making the busboys' friends go broke so their pals could continue making a couple bucks an hour. What were the chances Ms. Snooty-Pants was going to keep a bunch of Ecuadorians in her fancy French restaurant anyway?

"Hey, Buttcheeks!"

Steve looked over and grinned at Rita, with her sharp face and porcupine hair. "Hey, darlin'. How's the classiest woman I know doing tonight?"

"I'll be better with two whiskey sours and a scotch, straight up." She pushed a pen behind one ear and rearranged the checks in her apron pocket.

"Wouldn't we all?" Steve pulled out a couple of tumblers and set them on the bar.

"So when's Frenchy showing up?" Rita lay her elbows on the bar and leaned, giving her feet a break. "Don't tell me tomorrow because there's no fucking way my parents are coming two nights in a row."

"Your parents are here?" Steve looked out over the crowd but wouldn't have known Rita's parents if they were throwing back Jell-O shooters with George's friends. And, knowing Rita, they might be.

"Yeah, I finally told them about your passionate desire to marry me and they came to check you out." She rubbed her nose with one hand and scrunched her face. She was allergic to cigarette smoke, Steve knew. "But don't worry, Dad only brought the twelve-gauge."

"Good. For a second I was nervous."

Steve set the drinks on her tray and she disappeared into the crowd with it.

"Steve-arino!" A tall blond man emerged from the horde at the bar and reached a square hand over the teased hair of a woman drinking a margarita in front of him.

"Hey, P.B." Steve reached up and shook his friend's hand, sending the woman with the margarita an apologetic wink. "Glad you could make it."

"Wouldn't miss it, wouldn't miss it." P.B., so tall, blond and good-looking he'd been called P.B.—for Pretty Boy—since high school, looked admiringly around the room. "Hey, looks like old times in here. You guys get a new cook?"

Steve grimaced. "Worse. New owner. This is probably Charters' last gasp, my friend. Say good-bye to the world as we know it."

"What do you mean? The place is doing great, who'd mess with it?" P.B. slid onto the bar stool vacated by Margarita Girl's cohort.

Margarita Girl tapped him on the shoulder. "My friend only went to the bathroom. She's coming back."

P.B. grinned at her, melting her as only P.B. could, and patted his lap with one hand. "I'm saving a place for her."

The girl put one hand into her mass of curls and smiled flirtatiously. "I'm sure she'll appreciate your keeping it warm."

P.B. laughed and turned back to Steve with a conspiratorial look. Having girls come on to him was like a drug to P.B. He had to have a hit of it regularly to keep his high.

"Hey," a customer in front of the beer taps summoned Steve. "This beer's flat." He pushed a pint glass across the bar.

"Which one was it?" Steve asked.

The guy indicated the Bud tap. Steve opened it into a glass and tasted. Sure enough.

"Sorry, pal. What'll you have instead?"

"Bud bottle?"

"No problem."

Steve moved to the cooler and retrieved a bottle.

"Great crowd," P.B. said when Steve returned. "So maybe seeing this, the new owner'll just keep it the way it is. And bring back happy hour. Charters' happy hour was legendary."

"I know. But this, tonight, this is all a show." Steve delivered the Bud bottle, picked up a pint glass, filled it with Bass Ale from the tap and put it on the bar in front of P.B. "Most of the time these days the place is dead. Ever since Mario left to work at the place downtown and we stopped validating parking. We just called in a bunch of people to make it look good tonight for the new owner."

P.B. put a hand to one pocket and frowned. "Shit. You don't validate parking anymore?"

Steve moved down the bar to fix a martini for a young guy wearing what Steve interpreted as a stockbroker suit, then came back to his friend.

P.B. was craning his neck to look toward the kitchen. "So where is he? The new owner? I'll give him an earful about this place. Hey, you should tell him about all that history you dug up here. That stuff's great. You can't close a place with stories like that attached to it."

"Something tells me she won't care about any of that. Besides, she's not closing us. She's *reinventing* us."

"She?" P.B. was instantly intrigued.

"Yeah. 'Rox-Zilla.' The new owner. She wants to turn it into some fancy little French bistro, complete with frog legs and stuffed shirts."

"No." P.B. groaned and lay his head on the bar. Picking it up again he said, "Where's a guy gonna go to get a decent beer around here? This was one of the last great bars in town. I mean, look, you still use real pint glasses. Guess a woman wouldn't appreciate something like that, though. What'd you call her?"

"Rox-Zilla. Her name's Roxanne. Rita's been riffing on it all night. That's one of her better ones."

"Hey." Margarita Girl leaned forward and looked around P.B.'s shoulder to get his attention. "I'm a woman and I appreciate a good bar."

P.B. swiveled to her and gave her another smile. "A woman who likes a good bar?"

She nodded. Her eyes were getting glazed. Steve could tell she was succumbing to the tequila. He scooped a glass of ice, filled it with water, and put it in front of her. If she ordered another drink he'd make it weaker.

"Naawww." P.B. leaned back as if to see her more clearly, turning on the charm. "Women don't like bars. *Chicks* do. And you're a chick if I've ever seen one."

The girl, looking as if she wanted to be pleased but wasn't sure, rolled her eyes and nearly lost her balance. P.B. steadied her with a hand at the small of her back.

"What're you drinking there? Can I buy you another one? Steve, another one of those."

"Heads up," Rita called from the waitress station. " 'Shock-Rox,' coming to a theater near you."

Steve glanced from Rita to the door and saw Roxanne Rayeaux enter the fray with the aplomb of a seasoned bullfighter. She was dressed to kill, too, in a form-fitting white sweater and black jeans with boots. Her hair tumbled around her head as if styled by Vidal Sassoon himself just outside the front door and her dark eyes had the mysterious look of an Egyptian goddess.

"Holy shit," Steve heard P.B. say.

He looked over to see P.B. rise and move reverently forward, as if to greet the Pope. More power to him, Steve thought, then smiled to himself. Rox-Zilla might be the perfect challenge for his pal, who in Steve's opinion did not suffer nearly enough rejection.

"That's an evil smile," Rita said, behind him.

Steve made no effort to conceal it. "Just thinking a little character-building experience might be coming up for old P.B."

"At the hands of our fearless leader, you mean?"

"None other." Steve crossed his arms over his chest and leaned against the back counter.

* * *

Roxanne entered the smoky bar with a mixture of surprise and distaste. On the few occasions she'd visited Charters prior to buying it the place had been empty, making it easy for her to see the space and imagine her own cozy restaurant instead.

Now, however, she could barely see across the room for all the smoke, and the loud music and smell of beer made her want to turn tail and run. As she walked toward the kitchen, her shoes stuck to the floor and she was reminded unpleasantly of college frat parties. On the mirror behind the bar, scrawled in what looked like lipstick, were the words BAR SPECIAL: CHARTERS SUNDOWNER, IN HONOR OF THE SUN SETTING ON THE OLD FISH HOUSE.

She turned back to her friend Skip and made a face. This was not going to give him a very accurate idea of what she was planning to do.

Skip had been her pal since high school. A short fireplug of a guy, he didn't look like the type who'd be particularly sensitive. In fact, if anything, he looked like a Mafia thug. But something, perhaps growing up with the name "Skip," had made him unusually sensitive to the world, and he'd always been the most perceptive of all her friends. Even if he did go out of his way to tell her exactly what he thought, and usually in no uncertain terms.

"I thought you said this place was dead." He stepped close to be heard over the din.

"It is. Or it was." She looked around in some confusion, her gaze coming to rest on a drunk young man throwing pretzels at a girl near the front window.

Roxanne leaned back toward Skip. "In any case, it will be. And I'm just the one to put the bullet through its head."

"I don't know if I'd be sneering at a crowd this size." Skip's head swiveled left, then right, to illustrate his point. The place was wall-to-wall people. "Not if I owned the place. Are you sure you want to change it?"

"Skip, take a look at the floor. It's covered with peanut shells. And it smells like Sigma Nu after Fat Tuesday. You think this is the kind of place I had in mind? Come on."

She elbowed her way through the crowd until she met head-on with a tall, blond man wearing a beaming smile.

"You must be the renowned Roxanne." He was good-looking, in a Ken-doll kind of way, and had to bend close to speak over the music. So close that his breath brushed her cheek. He smelled like Binaca.

Roxanne backed up a step, suspicion crawling along her nerves. *Renowned?* He looked like just the type to have the last ten years' worth of *Sports Illustrated* indexed in his closet.

She raised her chin. "Have we met?"

"We're meeting now." He took her hand in both of his and showered her with another smile. "I'm Peter Baron. Here, let me get you a seat."

Roxanne's brows rose and she looked back at her friend Skip skeptically.

But Peter Baron was taking her in the direction she wanted to go, so she let the man lead her by the hand. She was not going to make the same mistake she made with Steve Serrano and assume the worst. She'd wait until he proved himself a snake and then take him down.

They stopped at the far end of the bar, next to the last two bar stools. A girl with big hair was being helped off one of them and into her coat by another girl.

"Do you want to go get sick first?" the helper girl asked. "That's what I did. I feel much better."

The girl with the big hair shook her head. "No, I'll be fine once I get in my car."

Roxanne stopped dead in her tracks. "Let me call you a cab, all right? You're in no shape to drive."

Both girls looked at her as if she'd offered to slap their faces. "We're fine," the first girl said. "As if it's any of your business."

"Actually, it *is* my business. This whole place is my business." Roxanne spread her hands to encompass the stinky bar. "So let me call you both a cab. I'll pay for it."

"I'll do it," the blond man—Peter—said with an indulgent smile. "Don't you worry about a thing."

"That's all right," Roxanne said. Her eyes scanned the bar. "I'll just get Steve to call—"

"It's not a problem." Peter held up a hand. Then, with gallant aplomb, he offered each drunk girl an arm. "Hey, aren't you the girl who said she knew a good bar when she saw one? I couldn't agree with you more. Look, there's a chair by the front door. Let's go sit there and wait for the cab."

Roxanne watched them go. "Who the heck *was* that?" she asked, as Rita marched up with another order.

"Who? The blond guy? That's Steve's friend P.B.," Rita said. "Two more Jaegermeisters," she called to Steve.

Roxanne and Skip sat on the two stools the girls had vacated.

"Well, that was really something," Roxanne mused, looking after the blond. "He just took care of it. Look, they're even sitting down to wait. Smiling."

"Wonder what he said to make them listen." Skip looked over his shoulder at them.

"Probably told them he's a cop," Rita offered. "That usually makes 'em listen."

Roxanne turned back to her. "He's a cop?"

"You bet. Hey, Candyass!" she yelled to Steve. "I said two Jaegermeisters. Did you hear me? Those guys threatened to drop trou if I didn't get back to them within five minutes."

"Drop *trow*?" Roxanne repeated.

"Drop their trousers," Skip supplied. "Where've you been? You're like the parent who wanders into their kids' keg party, Rox."

"Please. I'm not going to feel bad about not knowing what 'drop trou' means. And that is exactly why I have to change this place." Roxanne spun on her seat to look out over a crowd that almost looked dusty with all the smoke in the room. "I have no desire to play mom to a bunch of rowdy kids at a keg party every night."

"I doubt that's the role they'd want you to play either," Steve said, plopping two shots on Rita's tray.

Roxanne turned back to the bar. She had to admit, Steve looked pretty at home in this atmosphere. With his slightly too-long hair, his black shirt and that *play with me* grin, he was just appealing enough to have every big-haired girl in town sucking down drinks at the bar in hopes of getting a flirtatious word from him.

"Steve." Roxanne held a hand out toward her friend,

"This is my friend Skip Williams. Skip, this is Steve Serrano, the bartender."

The two shook hands.

Skip laughed. "Oh, the *bar*tender. I thought maybe he was just a privileged guest, being on that side of the bar and all."

"Very funny. I meant, well, never mind." Roxanne meant that he would probably be the bartender for Chez Soi, too, but she didn't want to give Steve that reassurance just yet. She wasn't sure why. Something about wanting to keep him off balance, she thought, instead of letting him keep *her* that way.

"So, how long you two been together?" Steve asked, picking up a rag and fisting his hand in it to dry the inside of a glass.

Roxanne blushed, grateful to the smoke for at least hiding that. "Oh, we're not—"

Skip laughed. "We're just friends. We've been friends since high school, so we know far too much about each other to ever get involved. Besides, I've got a girlfriend."

Roxanne mentally cursed herself. All Steve had to do was ask one question and he had her flustered. What was *with* that?

Steve's expression was intrigued and he cocked his head toward Roxanne. "So what do you think of your friend's new venture?"

Skip scratched the side of his face and looked dubiously around them. "I think she's nuts."

"Way to make me look good," she said in Skip's ear as Peter—the "Viking," as she had come to think of him—showed up at her elbow again.

"No need to worry." Peter settled himself against the

bar next to Roxanne with a confident smile. "The girls are safely in a cab and out of harm's way." Relieved, Roxanne smiled back at him. "Thank you so much."

"You know, Steve," Peter continued, "bartenders get sued all the time for things their drunken customers do. You ought to be careful."

Steve shot his friend an ironic look. "Thanks, buddy. I'll remember that."

Peter's face was somber. "No really. It's serious business."

"I know that, P.B., and if I could have stopped the last asshole from buying them a drink, I would have." Steve's gaze was pointed, his eyes amused.

"Oh well." Peter shrugged and hunkered himself down, one elbow on the bar. "Those girls were drunk when they got here anyway. So Roxanne, tell me about you. How did such a sweet, beautiful woman, such as yourself, come to be the owner of a place like Charters?"

Roxanne scooted her chair back a tad from the bar to include Skip in their conversation. "It's kind of you to assume that I'm sweet but I can assure you I'm not. And as for ending up the owner of Charters, I have really only bought the building. Charters just happens to be what's in it at the moment."

Steve leaned over at that. "I'm sorry, I missed that last part. Did you say you *bought* the *building*?"

Roxanne's cheeks heated. *Damn.* She had not meant to reveal that she had in fact bought the whole building, instead of just leasing the restaurant space, though she wasn't sure why. Something about keeping her past in the past. She didn't want to be known as the model who was trying to open a restaurant. Having people

come to Chez Soi with the idea of seeing her or thinking they were going to a celebrity restaurant was precisely what she *didn't* want.

But then, if nobody had recognized her yet—and it
had been a few years since her modeling heyday—
chances were they wouldn't. They would just have to
guess how she'd gotten her money, if they were so inclined.

"Yes, I did say that." She looked Steve dead in the eye
as calmly as she could, almost daring him to ask the
crass question.

But he just nodded and went back to drying glasses.
His gaze was disturbingly shrewd, though.

"So Steve says you're turning the place into a French
restaurant," Peter continued. "I think that's a *great* idea."

Steve's smile turned wry and his eyes rolled briefly
up into his head.

Roxanne's mood was restored.

"Do you really?" She turned to Peter. He was the first
person she knew to say her venture was a good idea,
and she was filled with a ridiculous gratitude. Who was
he, after all?

"Yes, really. There aren't nearly enough white-
tablecloth restaurants down here. And certainly nobody doing French the way it should be done."

"Which is . . . ?" Skip muttered next to her.

Roxanne tilted her head at Peter. "So you know
French food?"

"I love it. It's my favorite." He produced his signa-
ture smile again.

"I don't."

All eyes turned to Steve.

"You don't what? Like French food?" Roxanne asked. Did he not *want* the job?

She glanced at Skip, who shot back an I'm-not-saying-anything look. He'd already made it abundantly clear he didn't think she should be doing this.

"I don't like French anything," Steve said. His *play with me* smile was back and Roxanne wasn't sure whether he was joking or not.

She leaned forward on the bar. "Nothing?"

He acted like he was thinking, then said, "Nope. Not a thing."

She sat back and crossed her arms over her chest. He was kidding. He had to be. "Not even French fries?"

Steve shook his head. "They're not French."

"All right then." Roxanne paused and looked toward the ceiling contemplatively. "French poodles."

Steve laughed and despite herself she felt warmed by it. "Too ridiculous."

"French films?"

"Too pretentious."

"I'm with you there," Skip said.

Roxanne's lips curved. "How about French bread? Everybody likes French bread."

A short shake of the head. "Too crumby."

"Hmm. French toast?"

He shrugged. "Too rich."

She raised one brow and sat forward. "French women?"

Steve's eyes grew subtly more attentive and he gave a low chuckle. "Too . . . scary."

"I know . . ." Roxanne paused, studied the challenging look he was giving her and said, "French kisses."

* * *

Peter and Skip laughed. Steve eyed his adversary with fresh respect.

Roxanne continued to look at him, a beguiling half smile on her lips. She knew she had him.

He hesitated a fraction of a second, then returned a smile that was probably a tad less confident than usual. "You might have me there."

Roxanne sat back with a triumphant grin and glanced at Skip. "Well, then."

"I know you've got *me*." Peter put a hand lightly on her back. "Let me buy you a drink."

Roxanne turned to him and smiled. "No, let me buy *you* one. I appreciate your taking care of those girls. Did they give you a hard time?"

So much for P.B. getting a little of what was coming to him, Steve thought.

"Not a bit." P.B. was all graciousness. "And I would never let a lady buy me a drink."

Uh-oh. Maybe there was hope. Steve had been about to check in with the customers down the bar but he decided he had to wait to hear her response.

Roxanne's eyes narrowed. "You wouldn't? Isn't that a bit chauvinistic?"

Oblivious, P.B. laughed. "Absolutely not. I just would never want a woman to think I needed that kind of persuasion to . . . appreciate her."

Steve tried to stop the smile that hit his face but he couldn't do it.

Roxanne laughed. "I hate to disappoint you, Peter, but I only meant to thank you for your help. Not . . . how did you put it?"

Steve leaned in. "I believe he wanted to be persuaded to appreciate you."

P.B. shot him a look. "That's not what I said."

Roxanne put a hand on P.B.'s forearm, which lay on the bar. "Don't worry about it. I'm just teasing you. Steve, whatever he's drinking." She made a motion with her hand that told him to get whatever it was.

Steve executed a short bow—which Roxanne didn't even notice as she smiled at P.B.—and grabbed a glass. This time, Steve thought, P.B. was drinking Bud on tap.

3

Bar Special
Cuban Tango—because it only takes two...
Curacao, pineapple juice, lime juice, white rum,
  with a twist

There was no disguising it this evening, Steve thought, as he dusted the bottles behind the bar for the third time. Charters was dead and there was no reviving it. The only sign that there had been any recent life in the place was a telltale stickiness on the floor today. Something the busboys would have mopped last night, if not for the fact that by the end of the evening, even the staff was pretty much sloshed.

Except Steve. He had learned long ago that to drink on the job was to invite trouble. Big trouble. Bartending was fun, but not when you woke up every morning of your life with a hangover. At that point, the only thing scarier than that was *not* waking up with a hangover—

which was when you should know you were well on your way to alcoholism.

He had the music on low this evening, though he chose Stevie Ray Vaughan—something with some energy so he didn't risk actually drifting into a coma. There were two people having drinks in the dining room with little chance of ordering dinner. In fact, they looked like a couple discussing the particulars of a breakup.

Perfect for Charters' last night.

P.B. said he might stop by tonight, too, and Steve knew the only reason was Roxanne. P.B. had been taken by her, of course. The way he was taken by any beautiful—or even cute, or even conscious—woman who'd give him the time of day. What was surprising was Roxanne's giving him that time.

Steve exhaled slowly and started wiping down the end of the bar. Again.

He certainly wasn't one to claim he knew what women really wanted, but if P.B. was attractive to Roxanne, so be it. Best of luck to both of them. So what if she was high class and P.B. was low brow? What did it matter that he was love-'em-and-leave-'em and she was, from all appearances, hang-'em-high?

The door opened and Steve looked up, hoping for a customer. If he had to spend any more time tonight with his own thoughts he'd lose his mind.

On his way to work he'd put a letter in the mail to a publisher asking if they'd consider his book for publication. It wasn't a blockbuster or anything—just the history of a man who'd lived in this building two hundred years ago—but it had been Steve's passion for three years. He was almost finished with it, and it was time to make the ultimate move and market it.

Now all he had to do was figure out how to forget he'd sent the query so he wouldn't agonize every time his mailbox was empty.

Sure enough, three thirty-something guys who'd obviously been doing some sort of athletic activity took seats at the end of the bar. Steve took a stack of napkins over and tossed three, one by one, onto the bar in front of them.

"What can I get you guys?"

The three ordered beers, then conversed quietly among themselves, obviously not looking for entertainment from their bartender. Steve got them their drinks and went back to polishing the bar.

He looked at his watch. Five-twenty. It was going to be a long evening.

At eight o'clock—after Steve had eaten a burger, a leftover salad and a cup of ice cream one of the busboys had gotten from Ben & Jerry's, down the street—P.B. showed up. He strolled into the bar with his hair combed perfectly, his shoulders thrown back and his chest puffed out for all the world like an amorous pigeon on a city sidewalk. His bearing was so over-the-top cop that he might as well have been wearing his badge and gun belt.

He greeted Steve with an upraised hand as his eyes scanned the near-empty restaurant. The three athletes had left, to be replaced by two women nursing martinis and a burly-looking bearded man putting away gin and tonics at an alarming rate.

So he was inordinately glad to see P.B., if for no other reason than that P.B. usually revved up the conversation.

Steve smiled as he noted P.B.'s roaming eyes. "You can relax, Romeo. Roxanne's not here yet."

P.B. shook his head and sat on a bar stool. "Who? Oh, no. I was just checking the place out. Looks different empty." He smoothed a hand along one side of his hair, confirming its perfection. "Smells a little like stale beer, too."

"Last night got pretty wild. I don't think any of the busboys got around to mopping the floor, and they weren't too happy this afternoon either. What can I get you?"

P.B. looked at the taps. "Uh, Sam Adams." He paused a fraction of a second then lay his forearms on the bar and leaned forward. "Got a question for you, Steve."

Steve opened the Samuel Adams tap. "Shoot."

"What's this girl really like, huh? This Roxanne." P.B. looked so earnest Steve actually felt a little sorry for him. "And what the hell kind of name is that, anyway? 'Roxanne'? Rocks-Ann. Rock-Sand."

Steve chuckled. "It's French, Pretty Boy. Like the woman in *Cyrano*? You know that story?"

"Cyrano?"

"Yeah. You know, the guy with the big nose who's in love with the beautiful Roxanne, but it's his better-looking friend she really wants?" He slid P.B. the beer.

P.B. looked confused.

"Steve Martin made a movie of it a few years ago. He was the fireman with the big nose?"

P.B.'s brows shot up. "The one with Daryl Hannah?"

"That's the one."

"Oh yeah. And she looked good in that movie, too. She doesn't always, you know."

Steve shrugged. "Blondes aren't my thing. Anyway, that was the Cyrano story, essentially."

P.B. nodded. "Uh-huh. Okay. But do you know if this Roxanne's got a boyfriend? She's not dating that little twerp from last night, I hope."

"I don't think so." Steve took a bar towel from a heap that lay on the cold chest and started folding it. "But I don't know what else to tell you, P.B. She only just popped up on Thursday."

"I know, but . . ." P.B. looked down at his fingers, splayed on the bar top. "You *have* talked to her. You have, you know, been around her a little."

Steve nodded, wondering what to tell him.

P.B. sighed. "She *is* a hottie, though, isn't she?"

"Yeah. I suppose." Steve bit the inside of his lip thoughtfully. *If you didn't know that inside, she's as prickly as barbed wire.*

"Did she say anything about me? You know, after last night?"

"P.B., I told you, I haven't seen her. She hasn't gotten here yet." Steve took a moment to study his friend. "Look, what's going on here? Are you really that worked up about this girl? She doesn't seem all that different from the rest, if you ask me."

"Are you kidding? She's like the ultimate babe." P.B. ran a hand through his hair again, this time actually messing it up, which tweaked Steve's concern. "But I know. It's crazy to get worked up about her. It's just, she's just . . . there's something about her. She's hot, but it's like . . . she's really cool, you know?"

"A riddle wrapped in a mystery inside an enigma?"

P.B. considered this. "Yeah. Like that. She's kind of irresistible."

Steve heaved a sigh of his own. "God help the man blinded by a challenge."

This wasn't going to be nearly as fun as he'd thought. If his friend's heart was involved, then Roxanne's rejection would be hard to watch, as opposed to mildly enjoyable, just seeing P.B.'s colossal ego taken down a notch or two.

"Look, P.B., I gotta tell you. I think she's something of a hard-ass. And a woman like that, who looks like that, she can be . . ." He shrugged one shoulder. "She can be hard to get."

"Hard to get?" P.B. straightened on the stool. "Are you saying you don't think I have a chance with her? Is that what you're saying?" He looked genuinely surprised.

Steve laughed. "Hell, I don't know. Why? You think it's not possible for you to be turned down?"

P.B. took a swig of his beer, his expression suddenly shrewd. "I know what it is. You've got a thing for her too, don't you." It wasn't a question. P.B. was far too smug for that.

Steve scoffed. "Believe me, no."

P.B. slapped one palm on the bar in delight, laughing. "I love it! Hah! No need to deny it, old buddy. How could you not? It's just a natural fact." He took another swig of his beer, looking happier than he had since he'd walked through the door.

Misery not only loved company, Steve thought, it

looked for it in the most unlikely places. There was no way he was or ever would be interested in Roxanne Rayeaux.

"Tell you what," P.B. continued. "Let's make this fun. I've got a hundred bucks says I'll get her before you do. You ready to match that? Put your money where your mouth is?"

Steve rolled his eyes and put up both hands. "No way. I don't make bets like that. Especially when we both know it's not my mouth we're talking about."

"Damn right it's not. You chicken?" P.B.'s grin regained its usual cockiness. "A month ago you told me you could get any woman you wanted, you just didn't want anyone right now. So what is it really? Not so sure of your way with the ladies these days?"

Steve already missed his lovesick friend of sixty seconds ago.

"That's not exactly what I said." Wasn't anywhere close, actually, but he didn't mind P.B. thinking he'd said it.

"Come on, *wuss*. A hundred bucks to whoever gets her first." P.B. pulled out his wallet, took out some bills and placed them on the counter. "Here."

"P.B., forget it. Put your money away. I'm not playing that game."

P.B. stopped and gave him an indulgent smile. "Okay, here's what I'll do. Make it fair. I'll spot you some good words. Work on making you look good to her."

Steve's ire blossomed. He dropped the towel he was folding and crossed his arms over his chest. "And why would you do that?"

"Because . . ." P.B. held a hand out and moved it up

and down to encompass Steve's person. "Well, you know. The girls think you're a nice guy and all, but I got the whole cop thing working for me. A real, upstanding profession. You know, stability. A future. Stuff like that. Chicks love that shit." He smoothed a hand along his hair, straightening it back out.

Not only did Steve know P.B.'s hair was one of his biggest vanities, it now appeared to be an emotional barometer of sorts as well.

Steve swept the money up with one hand, folded it tight and tucked it into one of the many chinks in the brick wall behind the bar. Out of some of the other chinks around the mirror stuck such things as a Redskins pennant, a lace garter and a stack of unused bar checks.

"Great." Steve pushed the bills far enough in that they weren't visible without looking hard. "We'll just put this up here as a reminder of what a stable, upstanding professional you are."

"Don't forget about yours." P.B. directed a finger from Steve to the wall.

Steve laughed.

Rita pulled up to the waitress station. "Two Fosters, drafts." She plucked a swizzle stick from the glassful and stuck it in her mouth, chewing.

"Besides," P.B. added, settling back on his bar stool, "Roxanne seems to listen to me. I think she respects my air of authority."

Steve sputtered as he grabbed two pint glasses. "Yeah, right. That's why she refused your offer to buy her a drink. I've never seen anybody step on so many land mines when talking to a woman without getting blown to smithereens." He tipped a glass under the Fosters tap.

"You see what I'm saying?" P.B. grinned. "She liked me."

Steve shook his head. "Listen, I don't know why she didn't blow you out of the water last night. Maybe she appreciated you taking care of those girls—"

"Authority," P.B. sang.

"But in every other way I can guarantee you alienated her." Steve stopped the tap and leaned forward. "Listen to me, whatever else Roxanne Rayeaux might be, she's definitely an intelligent woman. And an intelligent woman likes to be treated as if she can tell sincerity from a load of crap. Tell you what, you want to bet so bad, I'll bet you a million bucks right now she saw half of what you said last night as the thinly disguised chauvinism it was."

"You're on."

"Good luck figuring out how to prove that," Rita said.

Steve finished filling the pints. "If you really want to date her, Pretty Boy, I suggest you start treating her as an equal, not some little lady who needs you to take care of things."

"See? That's where you're wrong." P.B. sipped his beer, unperturbed by Steve's diatribe. "That's where you get into trouble with the women you date. Women *like* to be taken care of. Even the strong ones. Maybe the strong ones most of all, because nobody thinks to do it. So when a guy comes along and treats her like her problems are his problems they love it. Too much equality makes them feel insecure. And I'll bet on that, too, my friend."

Steve glanced over at Rita, who was looking at P.B. with a penetrating, but surprisingly not hostile, gaze.

"You don't have anything to say to that, Rita?" Steve threw a hand out toward P.B. "You think women want guys like him to carry them over mud puddles and bring them flowers to solve their problems? Or do they want a real man who treats them like an equal? Like they're strong and smart enough to handle their own problems?"

Rita looked from Steve to P.B. and back again. "We want both."

Steve gaped at her.

P.B. beamed.

And Roxanne walked through the front door.

"Speak of the devil." Rita scooped up her tray of beers and moved back to the lone table in the dining room.

The first thing Roxanne did was check out the kitchen, noting the mess left from the night before and resolving to fire both line cooks. Same with the busboy who was supposed to mop the floors last night. The place stank.

She would keep whichever waiters wanted to stay, especially hoping that Rita would want to. Rita was rough around the edges but she kept up with the craziness last night and every single one of her tables was happy. Whereas George got a little too tangled up in the bar crowd to keep his from complaining.

Not that any of last night's tables were going to complain much. It was obvious from the first few minutes of observation that the staff had stocked the room with friends.

In any case, George did a serviceable job and could probably be counted on to improve with training, though Steve might have better insight on that. She wondered if the bartender would be inclined to share his opinions on the staff with her, despite their rocky introduction and apparent disagreement. His experience with the others was a lot more valuable than her two-day evaluation.

First, though, she had to see if Steve was interested in staying on.

After tonight, Charters would be closed and on Monday the decorators would begin the transformation. Over the next two weeks the waitstaff she chose would be trained.

"So Steve," Roxanne said, moving through the swinging doors from the kitchen to the bar. "Are you interested in working for Chez Soi?"

Steve turned to her and cocked his head. "Why, Ms. Rayeaux, are you offering me a job? Even despite my professed hatred for all things French?"

Roxanne slid onto the empty bar stool next to P.B. "Are you turning the job down?"

She was pretty sure he wasn't. She didn't know him well but she could already spot the look in his eye when he was teasing. Kind of a cross between devilment and laughter, even when he wasn't smiling.

"Well now . . ." Steve scratched his chin. "What are the terms? Are you giving me a raise?"

"Why would I do that?"

"So I'll stay?"

She smiled. "You'll stay. We both know you'll stay, Steve, so let's not waste time taunting each other. Terms are the same as you have now. But you'll be making more money, nonetheless. Which you probably already know."

"*If* the restaurant succeeds."

She inclined her head. "It will."

"You're pretty confident."

She crossed her legs. "I have to be." She glanced to her right and smiled. "How are you tonight, P.B.?"

"I'm just great." He leaned one arm across the back of her bar seat and gave her a significant look. "*Now.*"

Roxanne looked back at Steve, laughter welling in the back of her throat. "See? If I can make P.B. happy by just sitting down, surely I can make my restaurant a success."

One side of Steve's mouth kicked up wryly. "Yeah. P.B.'s a pretty tough sell."

Roxanne glanced at P.B. to see how he took that. He just grinned.

Steve studied her a moment. "I knew you were going to offer me the job."

She leaned back, determined to humor Steve. They were a little like oil and water, but it was important to get along, so she wouldn't let him get to her. Besides, most of the time he was just playing with her. She *thought*. "And how did you know that?"

He smiled. "Because you own the building. You fire me and I can't pay my rent. You could kick me out but that would mean more expenses. Easier to keep me on, I figure, than upset the whole equilibrium. Plus, I'm good at my job."

She smiled and tipped her head. "You are good at your job. Though you could be better. And, besides, I knew you would take me up on it."

"You did, huh? How?"

Because you're a career bartender, she thought. *And career bartenders get stuck in their jobs just like every other kind of lifer.*

She knew his type all right. Handsome, charming and going nowhere.

Right now it was fun, like playing. He could socialize, get dates, make good money, without having to challenge himself at all. But before long he'd start looking a little haggard. He'd cease being able to handle the long hours, or the after-work drinking, the way he could when he was younger, and he would feel fed up with the routine. But by then he'd have nowhere else to go. He'd have squandered his most productive years in a dead-end job and he'd be stuck in it for the rest of his life. Because who would hire a guy, who should be twenty years into a career, who'd done nothing but bartend?

Yes, she'd seen it before and she knew all the signs.

She couldn't even count the number of bartenders, waiters and waitresses she'd known who still considered the job temporary—just a stepping stone to their *real* career, whatever that might be—despite being on the job for a decade.

"I knew you'd want to stay, because you're a creature of habit, Steve Serrano." She kept her tone light and her lips smiling. "And creatures of habit hate to move. At any rate, I know you'll be good at the job I'm offering, even though your experience here is somewhat . . . ." she let her eyes scan the bar . . . "unrelated."

Steve scoffed and looked at P.B. "What'd I tell you? Hard-ass."

"Did you just call me a hard-ass?" This pleased Roxanne inordinately.

"I did. And what makes you think I'll work out at Shaaay Swahhh?" He exaggerated the French accent and extended his arms with a short bow.

"First, because of that bottle of wine you left me the other day. It's good wine. And it's *French*."

Steve straightened, chuckling. "In vino veritas."

Latin. Roxanne raised her brows. "And second, because I suspect you are a chameleon who will fit into any atmosphere. All the best bartenders are."

"So Steve-arino brought you some wine, huh?" P.B. said, obviously tired of being left out of the conversation.

Something about P.B. appealed to Roxanne. Not his looks, despite being classic and clean-cut, or his personality, which was like a TV car salesman's. It was more because he was such a caricature. At some point in his life he'd adopted the role of playboy, clearly from some seventies role model, perhaps appearing on *Love, American Style*, and he'd mastered every stereotype of the character. It was impossible not to be entertained by him.

"Yes." She turned to him. "As a housewarming gift."

P.B. snaked a smile to Steve. "Well, isn't that neighborly? You're just a stand-up guy, aren't you, Stevie?"

"That I am, my friend. That I am." He grinned and looked down the bar, checking the other customers. Nobody flagged him so he looked back at Roxanne. "I hope you liked the wine."

"I haven't opened it yet."

P.B. swooped in. "Looking for someone to share it with? I love a good French wine, myself."

"You wouldn't know a good French wine if it slapped you across the face," Steve said. "And it might."

"Sure I would."

"Name one vineyard. Hell, name one *varietal*."

P.B. turned to Roxanne. "Did you know that in addition to being a pompous ass about wine, Steve here is also a pompous ass about history? He's bored the pants off more women than I can count with that stuff."

Roxanne looked at Steve. "Seems like a handy skill for a single guy."

Steve laughed. "Unfortunately, P.B. didn't mean that literally."

"But you are a history buff?" she persisted. Roxanne considered it important to find out details about people that surprised her. Especially people who worked for her. And anything scholarly about Steve Serrano would definitely surprise her.

Steve shrugged. "A little."

"Oh come on." P.B. needled. "He's got his head in a book more often than anybody I've ever seen. It's about all he does, other than work here."

"That's me. Mr. Excitement." Steve moved off toward the other end of the bar, where the ladies finally looked ready for another round.

P.B. sat forward on his stool, closer to Roxanne. "I'll tell you, though, Roxanne. That's a beautiful name, *Roxanne*, you know that?"

He looked as if he wanted to take her by the hand, so she picked up her water glass. "Thank you."

"Were you named after the character from *Cyrano*?" he asked. "That's always been one of my favorite stories."

This surprised her. P.B., a reader? "As a matter of fact, I was, in a way. My mother never liked that story, but she did like the name." She grinned. "Personally, I liked the Steve Martin movie best."

P.B. put his chin on his hand. "There was a movie?"

"Don't tell me you read the play? By Rostand?"

"It was years ago." P.B. waved a hand nonchalantly. "Hey, I'm glad you decided to keep Steve on." He glanced toward the other end of the bar where Steve was pouring a scotch and chatting with a white-haired man. "He's a really good guy. And he needs this job."

She too glanced at Steve. "You think so? There are a lot of other bars in town and he's a *very* good bartender." It was true. If last night was any indication, he was one of the better ones she'd seen.

"Well, sure. But you know, you had it right about the creature-of-habit thing. Old Steve's been here for years. It'd take a lot out of him to start over doing something different."

Roxanne looked at P.B. Was he trying criticize his friend or did the truth just come out that way?

Steve returned to the conversation and P.B. changed the subject.

"As I was saying," P.B. sat up straighter. "Stevie does find some interesting historical stuff every once in a while in all that reading. He started out by researching this house we're in right now. And you'll never guess who used to live here."

He looked expectantly at Roxanne. She raised her brows and looked from him to Steve. "I can't imagine."

But she was pretty sure if it was somebody famous the previous owners would have used it to get more money out of her.

"None other than Thomas Jefferson!" P.B. crowed. "It was after he was president, but—"

"Hang on a minute." Steve shook his head and gave his friend a look of exasperation. "I can see the years since high school haven't honed your skills as a student any."

Roxanne had to admit, she loved the interplay between these two. They were so antagonistic it was hard to believe they were really friends. And yet they had been for years. One of those kinds of friendships only men seemed to have.

Steve fixed P.B. with the eye of an unhappy schoolteacher. "Thomas Jefferson did *not* live here. If he had, you can bet we wouldn't be sitting in a restaurant in this building. Or if we were, it would be run by the Park Service and we'd all be eating hot dogs."

P.B. looked scandalized. "But you told me—"

"I told you a *cousin* of Thomas Jefferson's lived here. Portner Jefferson Curtis. A little-known and rather morally impoverished cousin, as a matter of fact."

"And I told all those guys down at the station . . ." P.B. muttered.

"'Little-known'?" Roxanne looked to Steve, concerned. It would be just her luck for this guy to dig up something the Historical Society would be interested in. Something that could get in the way of her business plan. "I would think anyone related to Jefferson would have been somewhat known. Especially one who was doing well enough to have lived in a house this size. Surely this was considered an expensive house, even back then."

"That's actually a really good point."

She could swear he looked impressed and she wasn't sure whether that gratified or annoyed her.

"It's something of a mystery," Steve said, leaning against the bar and warming to his topic, "who actually bought this place. Some say Jefferson did, for Portner to live in. But Jefferson himself wrote shortly after Portner moved into the house to ask how he was faring and whether he might divulge the nature of the business he was engaged in. That makes some historians question whether Portner bought the place with some kind of ill-gotten gains."

"And did he?" Roxanne asked. "Surely by now everything there is to be known about this guy is known."

Steve shrugged. "Actually, no. We're not sure. Not only did Portner not divulge what business he was in when he wrote back, but he essentially told Jefferson to mind his own damn business."

Roxanne laughed. If the exchange was public enough for this bartender to know about it, it certainly wouldn't take the Historical Society by surprise. "How rude."

Steve smiled with her. "You bet. So rude it marked the end of their correspondence, as far as we can tell. And especially rude considering that in his earlier days, just after Jefferson moved back home from Washington in 1809, Portner was unemployed and pretty bad off, so Jefferson let him stay at Monticello. It was Jefferson who got him back on his feet and enabled him, one way or another, to move here, in 1810."

"That kind of makes you wonder . . ." Roxanne began, then stopped. She was never very good at history, truth be told, and she had no desire to reveal her ignorance to these two overconfident guys. Especially not when she was trying so hard to exude competence. Not that P.B. would care one way or the other. Roxanne was sure that as long as she "smiled pretty," he'd say she was just as smart as could be.

"It does make you wonder," P.B. said. "Makes me wonder, too. Mostly about having another beer, eh, Steve?" He laughed.

"Makes you wonder what?" Steve directed this to Roxanne, ignoring P.B.

Roxanne was about to answer when two big guys—construction workers?—came in and sat down on the other side of P.B., who instantly straightened on the bar stool to his full height and stretched in such a way that his chest expanded impressively.

If he up and peed on the bar he couldn't have looked any more territorial, Roxanne thought.

Steve held up his index finger to Roxanne. "Hold that thought."

She watched him go, appreciating his professionalism. Yes, he'd be a good hire. She just needed to know a little bit more about him, a little bit more about Steve Serrano, career bartender, who seemed to have hidden depths.

"Pretty interesting stuff, huh?" P.B. asked. "Maybe you can use some of that history in marketing this place. Spread a rumor that it's haunted." P.B. made a low, spooky noise and fluttered his hands out by his sides.

Roxanne considered this. "You might be right. Though it would have been better if it had been a cousin of Lafayette's who lived here."

P.B. gave her a blank look.

"Because he was French?" she prompted.

Steve was back before P.B. could reply.

"Now, what were you saying?" Steve asked.

Roxanne regretted saying anything, her thought had been such a silly one. "Well, it just made me wonder. The fact that . . . uh . . . Portner . . . ?"

Steve nodded.

"The fact that Portner was living at Monticello when Jefferson might have gone out of his way to get this place for him makes me think Portner was rude early on and Jefferson just wanted him out of his house. I mean, first of all, we're *miles* from Monticello, and second, since Portner was so disrespectful later it would make sense that he had been pretty ungrateful all along."

Steve looked at her with a contemplative smile.

"What?" she said, laughing uncomfortably. "Was that stupid? I guess I like to make things into soap operas."

"No." Steve rubbed the side of his face with a palm. "No, not at all. I'd had the very same thought. The fact is . . ." He looked from Roxanne to P.B. and back again.

"The fact is . . . ?" P.B. prompted.

Steve chuckled lightly. "Well, it makes perfect sense when coupled with something else I read recently. I had this idea that . . ." He stopped himself and took a step back from the bar. "But you're probably not interested in my boring theories."

Roxanne couldn't help being apprehensive. If he really was some kind of amateur historian bent on making this house famous—or at least historically interesting, even if just to others of his ilk—she needed to know. The Alexandria Historical Society took things like this very seriously—so seriously they could hold up entire building projects for archeological purposes. Postponing a little remodeling in a place where a famous person had resided would be far from out of the question.

"I'm definitely not bored," she said. "Come on, you can't leave us hanging here."

"Yeah, come on," P.B. said, with a look of utter insincerity.

"Okay." He leaned forward, his arms on the bar. "There was something in Jefferson's letter to the land agent who arranged for Portner to move into this house. Something about Portner being 'prone to mischief,' he believed. And for years, in historical circles, there've been rumors that Portner stole something from Jefferson that caused the rift between them."

Roxanne was filled with dread. "What was it?"

Steve grinned like he held the punch line to a scary story. "A draft of the Declaration of Independence."

"No way," P.B. said. "Are you shitting me?" Then, remembering Roxanne, he leaned toward her abjectly. "I'm so sorry."

She gave him a blank look. What was he sorry for? Could he be thinking what she was? That this would interest more than just the *amateur* historians? She couldn't afford to hold up the opening to her restaurant so a team of archeologists could climb all over it.

But P.B. merely turned back to Steve with an amended version of his question. "Are you kidding me?"

Steve shook his head, smiling like the cat that swallowed the canary. "Furthermore, speculation is that the draft was hidden here in this very house for his heirs. But he never had any children and no one else was very intent on searching the place for something that might or might not exist. It was pretty well established that Portner could be less than honest, at times."

"Shut *up*!" P.B. shouted, catching the attention of everyone at the bar. "You mean to tell me there could be an original copy of the Declaration of Frickin' Independence hidden in this building right here right now as we speak?"

Silence throughout the room greeted this outburst.

The construction workers looked at them with great interest, and even Rita and George stared in from the dining room.

Roxanne frowned, dread growing within her. "Surely not, after more than two hundred years."

Steve let his eyes scan the room. "I doubt it, too. For one thing, this place has to have been remodeled dozens of times over nearly two centuries. And for another, historians have been talking about this for decades and in the few documented searches that were made, nobody found anything. So, I'm sure there's something somewhere that refutes the possibility. But I spent most of the last month looking for evidence that the draft turned up and haven't found anything yet."

She heaved a sigh of relief. *Historians have been talking about this for decades.* So it wasn't news.

"Where do you look for this stuff?" she asked. "I've always wondered how people still discover things now that happened hundreds of years ago."

"Mostly I go to the Library of Congress. Have you ever been there?"

Roxanne shook her head.

P.B., coming out of a reverie, said, "What? Where?"

"The Library of Congress," Steve said with a conspiratorial smile at Roxanne. It was obvious to both of them P.B. was losing interest. "It's just across the river and one of the most incredible places I've ever been. You can actually look at old letters and documents and books, sometimes things that haven't been touched in years. Once you've been there, it's easy to see how not everything has been discovered yet. And maybe never will be."

"I should go," Roxanne mused.

"I'll take you sometime." Steve's eyes met hers and she caught her breath.

"Oh you don't need to do that," she said quickly, to cover a sudden and inexplicable blush.

"So," P.B. said, "how much you think a draft of the Declaration of Independence would be worth now? I mean, if it were found."

Steve blew air out of his cheeks and thought a moment. "Hell, I don't know. It would probably be sold at auction and those things can either skyrocket or tank. But I would think maybe millions, at any rate."

"*Millions*," P.B. marveled, looking as if he might just go out and buy himself one of those Declaration of Independence lottery tickets.

4

Bar Special

Tom and Jerry— for those who like to play
cat and mouse

White rum, brandy, maple sugar, allspice,
nutmeg, 1 egg, boiling water

Roxanne wrestled with taking the wine, then decided she was making too big a deal of it. She'd just take the bottle with her to Steve's apartment to ask him about the staff. It would serve as a kind of olive branch after she'd been so obnoxious the first time they met.

Her one other concern was that he would think she was asking his opinion because she didn't know what she was doing. But all she wanted was some confirmation, or denial, of the reliability of some of the servers. Like George, for example. And getting the opinion of someone who'd worked with them for years was just good business. Getting that opinion with honey—or in this case wine—instead of vinegar was also good business.

So, in the name of competent management, Roxanne closed her door firmly behind her and, with the neck of the wine bottle grasped in one sweaty hand, she proceeded up the stairs to Steve's apartment.

The moment she reached the top step his door opened. With a mental curse she stopped in her tracks. She thought she'd have a moment to compose herself outside the door and figure out what to say. Now he was leaving and she was stuck on the stairs, directly in the path of rejection.

Without noticing her, he pulled the door shut and turned his key in the deadbolt lock. A duffle bag was looped over his shoulder, out of which the handle of some sort of tool protruded.

For a split second, she contemplated fleeing. If she could have turned around and disappeared without his noticing she would have. But there was no way he wouldn't at least hear her clomping down the wooden steps and then she'd look an even bigger fool than she already did, standing silently on the top step with a bottle of wine in her hands.

Instead, she took the initiative.

"Going out?" she asked.

Startled, he turned swiftly. "Jesus. You scared the crap out of me."

He took a step forward and his eyes raked her from head to hands, landing squarely on the bottle of wine.

"Sorry." She raised the bottle with a wan smile. "Guess you don't want any of this, then."

He quirked a brow, his expression going from wary to surprised. "You bringing it back?"

She opened her mouth to reply.

"Wait, don't tell me," he said with a cock of his head. "As my boss, you can't accept gifts. Favoritism and all that."

"No, of course not." She forced a smile. "Feel free to give me as many gifts as you want. This isn't the army."

He grinned. "Oh, right. It was the boot camp that threw me."

Maybe it was being a couple steps below him but she felt at a disadvantage in more ways than she was comfortable with. She stepped up to the landing.

"It's called training, Mr. Serrano. But you can think of it as gourmet boot camp, if that'll make your martyrdom any more satisfying."

"Actually yeah, that'll help." He looked from the bottle to her face again and frowned. "So . . . what's up with the wine?"

She took a deep breath. In for a penny, in for a pound. "I just had a couple questions. Not about the wine. I was hoping you'd have time to talk about the restaurant with me." She looked down at her own hands and gave a light laugh. "And I was bringing the wine as a bribe."

He hefted the duffle bag higher on his shoulder. His expression was almost one of confusion, though what he had to be confused about was, well, confusing.

"This is a change of heart, isn't it? I gathered from the meeting last week that you didn't need or want my input." He gestured toward the wine. "Let alone that you might decide to bribe me for it."

Roxanne's cheeks warmed and she looked down at the bottle. He was being somewhat contrary, she thought. "I know what I'm doing with the restaurant. There's really no question of reverting to Charters' old, uh, strategies, so I wasn't looking for input on that. I just thought, because you know the staff so well, I'd ask your opinion about some of them."

There was a window right next to him on the landing and he leaned one hip against the sill, one thumb looped through the duffle bag's shoulder strap. Light from an outdoor streetlamp shone through his gray eyes, making his assessing gaze even more penetrating.

"You want me to rat on my coworkers?"

She lifted her chin. What was *with* him?

"Absolutely not! I would never put you or anybody else in that position." She put a hand on one hip. "You know, I don't know where you get off thinking I'm such a bad person just because I happened to buy the place where you work. Is it just because you don't like anything French? Or is it me? Because all I wanted was to know . . . was . . . you, you're . . ."

In the middle of this speech her brain finally registered his teasing look. Unfortunately it was a few seconds before she could get her mouth to stop running.

Steve chuckled and straightened from his leaning stance. He moved a couple steps toward her on the landing, his expression amused and, she thought, exasperated. "That's right. I was kidding."

"Well." She nodded once, then took a deep breath. "Well. I hope so."

Her voice sounded petulant. She wished she'd never left her apartment. Why couldn't she have deliberated another five minutes about this stupid course of action?

Another *two* minutes? He would have already been gone and this whole conversation would never have taken place.

"I was."

"Okay." She swallowed. *Keep it light*, she told herself. He was; why couldn't she? "I was just looking for a little psychology, which you bartenders are supposed to be so adept at."

Tone, Roxanne, tone. She could have smacked her own forehead. She could tell by his face that though her words had said one thing, her manner had said something else. Something derogatory.

"Yeah, we're pretty savvy at judging people," he drawled. His gaze judged her where she stood.

"Well, if it makes you at all uncomfortable to talk about your coworkers, then never mind." She paused, unsure how to end this debacle. "So where are you going?" she asked—though it sounded like she demanded—and waved a hand toward his duffle bag.

He glanced over his shoulder at it.

"Me? I'm going to a friend's house." Steve gestured for Roxanne to precede him, so she turned and headed down the stairs ahead of him. "She's got something she needs help with. Well, not help really. Just, something she wants me to look at."

Roxanne glanced back at him as they both clopped down the wooden stairs.

"In the garden?" she asked as they reached the landing.

"Garden?" They paused in front of the door to her apartment. "Why do you say that?"

She inclined her head toward the handle sticking out of his bag. "It looks like a hoe. Or something."

He laid a hand on it. "This? No. Too short to be a hoe, for one thing." They stood looking at each other a moment. "Well, gotta go. See ya."

He turned down the hall toward the last flight of stairs, then stopped. "We can talk another time, if you want, about the restaurant. And you don't need to bribe me with wine. Just let me know."

"Sure. Yeah, see you." She watched him go.

He had long legs, she noted as he walked away from her. And an easy way of carrying that bag that looked awfully heavy.

Had it just been her imagination or had he been uncomfortable when she'd asked him what he was doing? Maybe it was because he was seeing a woman, and he'd thought she might be bothered by that. Because she'd brought the wine.

Damn. She clenched one hand into a fist so that her nails bit into her palm. She should have been clearer that she was just trying to be friendly. Business friendly. The last thing she'd wanted was for him to think she was coming on to him.

She opened her apartment door and went straight to the kitchen. She set the bottle firmly on the counter, pulled open the utility drawer and dug through utensils until she found the corkscrew. Then she opened the bottle and poured herself a glass of wine.

She'd drink the whole thing, if necessary. She didn't ever want to be tempted to share it with him again. He was obviously the type who'd misunderstand. He probably thought every woman was coming on to him. Hell, maybe every woman *was* coming on to him. He was pretty cute.

But the last thing she, Roxanne Rayeaux, needed was an employee thinking she was making a pass. Because she was *not* making a pass. Or if she was, it was just a friend pass. A pass at making a friend. Instead all she'd gotten was a cocky, suspicious employee. Not to mention a neighbor who thought he'd just had to reject her.

She took a sip of the wine and let it roll around her tongue a second.

Damn again, she thought. It was excellent.

Steve hopped in his pickup truck and sat for a moment in the dark.

That was weird. Roxanne Rayeaux wanted to share a bottle of wine with him. Ostensibly to talk about the restaurant, but come on. They could talk about the restaurant any day of the week, during daylight hours, at one of the staff meetings—or rather, training sessions—she had set up. Or over lunch.

But at night? With a bottle of wine? Wheels turned in his head.

Surely she wasn't coming on to him. That just wouldn't make any sense. She thought he was an unsophisticated beer jockey. Someone beneath her social notice. He'd seen that on her face the night he'd impulsively offered to take her to the Library of Congress and she'd nearly recoiled.

He took a deep breath, fished his keys out of his

jacket pocket and started the truck. Despite the cold, the old Toyota purred quietly to life.

What would have happened if he hadn't been going out? he wondered. Suppose he'd said yes to sharing the wine with her? They'd have talked about the restaurant, maybe gotten a little loose—what with the wine and no food—and . . . what? Was she lonely? Would she have expected him to make a move of some sort? Would she have *wanted* him to make a move?

Of course, there was the fact that he didn't *want* to make a move on her. She was hot, sure. And smart, he'd give her that. But she was the type to eat men like him for breakfast. High maintenance, all the way. He'd sensed it the moment he laid eyes on her.

He didn't know her well, but he knew as surely as if she'd told him so that she required her men to live up to an unrealistic standard. And he was really not into living up to other people's standards, unrealistic or not. Not when he was just figuring out his own.

Which was why he dated women like Lia, who was expecting him. He put the car in reverse and backed out of his parking space.

Technically, he and Lia had broken up a few weeks ago, but they'd both known they'd slide back into something. Such was the nature of their relationship. Break up, take a breather, get back in touch, sleep together, stay together a few months, break up.

Only this time Steve wasn't sure he wanted to slide back. The only reason he was seeing her tonight was because she was offering him an opportunity that would be otherwise unattainable.

Lia did a lot of housesitting in the historic district

and sometimes she let him come snoop around if a place was particularly interesting. Tonight she'd called and told him to bring his metal detector, she was in a house near where a Civil War armory had stood and there would probably be, as she'd put it, *bullets galore*.

He figured it could be interesting. He'd never used the metal detector, which his mother had gotten him for Christmas and which he and Lia had joked about incessantly afterwards, but there were stories of people making some interesting finds with them. Not to mention that it would please his mother to know he'd finally unboxed it. She was always buying things to keep him interested in history, as she was sure it would eventually lead to a "real career."

His only hesitation about doing this was that Lia was not above having ulterior motives. She was lonely, he would bet. It was part of the pattern.

But he wasn't. In fact, before the last time they'd broken up, he'd spent weeks canceling dates and not calling and generally acting like the worst kind of boyfriend ever, to get her to end things.

He wasn't proud of it, but then he'd never been very good at telling women he wasn't interested.

With the exception of Roxanne Rayeaux. For some reason that had been easy.

He pulled up in front of the house where Lia was staying and cut the engine. Gathering up his bag from the backseat, he glanced up and down the street to be sure no neighbors were out walking their dog or anything to see him enter the house with a metal detector and bag of tools.

It had taken him a while to convince Lia he was responsible when it came to poking around people's historic homes. She always questioned what he got out of it. So he wanted to come *look*, what good would that do him? It wasn't as if he ever discovered anything. Even if he did, he wouldn't be able to tell anyone. How would he explain poking around someone else's house?

It was a good point. One he couldn't satisfactorily answer, not without revealing goals he'd rather keep to himself until he was sure he could achieve them.

For now, he told Lia, he just liked seeing if he was right about things. He liked to theorize about historical sites and personages, and if he could find things that confirmed his theories, it would tell him his instincts were right, his research was valid.

That was something he did a lot. Tested himself, to see if he was right. He'd make bets on people at the bar, who they were, what they did for a living, where they were from, and kept a mental tally of how often he was right (most of the time, he was pleased to note).

He rang the bell, but he was not thinking about Lia, or even the possibilities of the metal detector.

No, he was thinking about Roxanne Rayeaux and her bottle of wine. And he was wondering if he was right about her.

Roxanne didn't get through the whole bottle of wine. She didn't even get through half before falling asleep on the couch, dreaming that she and Steve were in the restaurant waiting for her ex-boyfriend, Martin. In the dream she was tense, then hysterical when one of the brick walls slumped in front of them, stray bricks tumbling across the floor and dropping from the ceiling to tear the fabric on the new chairs.

Dimly, as she drifted in and out of sleep, she knew she was focused on these subjects because of the remodeling that had just started. That, and the ongoing fear that Martin actually would show up, promising that *this* time he really *would* leave his wife for her. The wife she didn't know he had until they'd been dating close to six months.

She woke up fully after dreaming that George dropped an entire tray full of stemware—wineglasses stacked dozen upon dozen—onto the hard brick floor of a wine cave, the pyramid crashing to the ground in a symphony of shattering glass.

She jerked up on the couch and one hand went reflexively to her neck, which had crimped from her odd resting angle on the pillow. Her eyes swept the room, deducing at a painfully slow rate that it was late at night and she was here, in her apartment in Virginia, and not in her New York high rise.

As she eased herself up off the couch her eyes landed on the box she'd been unpacking before a nap seemed like a good idea. There was the reason she'd dreamed of Martin. In the box she'd found a package of condoms. Martin's condoms. He had never been without them, always so afraid of a "mistake." He'd practically begged her to go on the pill—which she couldn't do because, for her, the pill changed her body too much for modeling—and finally had bought what looked like a case of Trojans, which he left everywhere they might end up getting intimate.

He'd never understood how much that hurt her, his

mortal fear of a mistake. And after a while she'd stopped trying to explain it.

She picked up the package and moved purposefully toward the bedroom. Opening up the bedside table drawer, she thought defiantly, *Just in case*, and tossed them in.

She went back out to the living room, determined to get rid of the last couple of boxes, when she heard footsteps on the wooden stairs outside her door. An automatic hit of panic shot through her and she tiptoed to the front door to look through the peephole. The downstairs door was not open to the public, so if this was anyone but Steve, she should be ready to call the police.

Cheeto trotted up behind her, no doubt hoping to bolt out the door if she opened it. Skip said she should have named the cat Magellan, since he was such an explorer.

For a minute she hovered between standing at the door and going to retrieve the phone, finally opting to stay by the door and see who it was.

The footsteps topped the first flight, then started down the hall toward the second. For a mere moment in the warped lens of the peephole she saw Steve Serrano's profile as he walked by her door in the light of the hall's overhead bulb.

It was only a fleeting view, but she thought he looked tired and kind of mussed, as if he'd been doing something physical.

Yeah, physical, she thought, remembering that he was going to a woman's house that night. Then, unexpectedly, she was assailed by an image of him shirtless and sweaty, bending above her with that dark grin on his face. The image was so sexy and so powerful that heat rushed to her core and she put a hand to her stomach, where a whole flock of birds simultaneously took flight.

For God's sake, she told herself. *Get a grip*. It had obviously been far too long since she'd had sex.

She brushed the hair from her forehead and crept away from the door, then turned out the living-room lamp and closed herself in her bedroom. There she lay awake for precisely five minutes before falling into a hot, steamy sleep, filled with images of a lean, naked man with hair just a tad too long, doing all manner of devilish and delightful things to her.

The next morning she awoke with the cat on her head and the sheets tangled around her legs. Rarely had she spent such a restless night.

It was nine before she made it downstairs to start coffee for the trainees. Sir Nigel was coming today to teach them all about French table service and the different glasses and silverware it required.

Also, workmen were coming to install the wine caves and she wanted to be sure they had a clear path through the kitchen to bring them in.

She pushed through the swinging doors from the bar to the kitchen and headed for the coffee service. She had just scooped out some coffee and was filling the pot with water when she noticed a cold breeze on her back.

She turned, expecting to see someone coming in the back door, and froze. A second later the water overflowed the pot onto her arm and she turned back to fumble with the faucet.

After laying the carafe in the sink with a shaking

hand she turned back to the rear door, her eyes riveted on the pile of broken glass on the floor.

Slowly, she moved her gaze around the room, her brain putting the pieces together.

Someone had broken in.

Someone must have taken something.

Something must be missing.

Someone could still be here now.

Adrenaline shot through her veins, making her shake.

Last night, she'd awoken because she'd dreamed about breaking glass. But maybe it was this she had heard. Could she have heard this door breaking from her living room?

Her eyes scanned the room. Things were disturbed, little things overturned along the counters. A refrigerator had been pulled away from the wall about six inches. The freezer was not closed tightly. A trash can lay on its side, its contents strewn about the floor. Workstations had obviously been messed with—knives and whisks, side towels and clipboards were scattered helter-skelter.

She looked at the floor. Near the door to the office a floorboard had been pried up. One end was split and gnawed-looking.

What in God's name was going on? What had the intruders been doing in here?

Her mind flew immediately to the theoretical draft of the Declaration of Independence. She almost had to laugh at herself for thinking anyone would take that conversation seriously enough to break in, but it was too odd for this to happen right after that discussion.

Plus, there'd been plenty of people around when P.B. had blurted out the possibility that it existed right here in this very building.

She frowned. But to come in and scatter tools on the workstations . . . to be rooting through the trash . . . No, this had to be something else.

The mayhem didn't quite look as if whoever had broken in had been looking for something. More that they'd been trying to do damage. Could the cook have been that angry at being fired? What about the busboys she'd let go?

Her mind flew to the moment she'd woken up last night. Moments afterward she'd watched Steve go past her apartment door on the way to his. Maybe he'd noticed something when he got home. Maybe he'd seen a car pull away, or a person in the back alley. Something he might not have registered as odd last night, but that would fit with what had obviously happened here.

She strode to the office, taking care not to touch anything or trip over the displaced floorboard, and looked at the phone list. Then she grabbed the receiver and dialed his number.

He answered on the fifth ring. A low, gruff hello that sent her reeling back to the dream she'd had last night of him bare-chested and hot with arousal. She blushed as she spoke, angry with herself for being so sexually deprived that she couldn't keep her mind on a break-in, for God's sake.

"Steve, it's Roxanne."

There was a muffled sound. Then, "Huh? Oh."

"I'm sorry to wake you."

His voice became clearer. "No, it's okay. Don't worry

about it." He cleared his throat and she relaxed a tense breath. Not being irritated when awakened by a ringing phone said a lot about a person. "What's up?"

"Could you, uh, could you come down to the restaurant? Soon, I mean?" She suddenly wasn't sure calling him first was the right thing to do. She should call the police. What was wrong with her?

She could hear what sounded like him rolling over in bed and a cool mist of perspiration broke onto her forehead.

"Sure." He cleared his throat again. "Yeah, sure. Is something wrong?"

Yes, yes, *yes*! Something was wrong, *that's* why she was calling. Not to give fertilizer to her already unmanageable sexual urges.

She mentally took hold of herself. "It seems we've had a break-in. The window on the back door is broken and things in the kitchen look . . . disturbed."

"What?" His voice was crystal clear now. She imagined him sitting up straight in bed. "Somebody broke in?"

"Yes, I—"

"Stay right there. I'll be right down." The phone on the other end clattered and went dead.

She exhaled. He was awake now, she thought, as she pressed the OFF button on the phone and looked at it a moment. She should call the police. She'd need a police report for the insurance. Not to mention that she didn't want whoever did this to come back.

Had they found what they were looking for? There hadn't been any money in the place. That had been deposited yesterday morning. They hadn't even been open for business yesterday, so there was no reason to think there would be any money.

It had to have been the cook. Or the busboys. It had to have just been someone wanting to scare her, or make a point. There wasn't anything here worth stealing. Nothing that would get you any money, that you could get out the door in the dead of night, anyway. She'd like to see the thief who could steal a steam table or a walk-in freezer. If they'd been thieves who knew anything about kitchen equipment they would have stolen some of those knives, not just scattered them around the workstations.

She pulled the phone book from the desk drawer and looked up the non-emergency number for the police. After all, it wasn't as if there was a theft in progress or anything. She didn't need to call 911.

Her finger landed on the number and she'd just picked up the portable again when a noise in the kitchen caught her ear. She had just enough time to think she'd been a fool not to call 911, because the thieves could still be in the building, when Steve appeared in the office doorway.

She heaved a sigh of relief.

"Are you okay?" His face was sober, but it was his sleep-rumpled hair and disheveled clothes that caught her attention. Never had a mere bartender looked so good.

Roxanne shook her head against the thought. Lord, one sex dream and she had completely lost control. This was just Steve, she reminded herself, her inherited employee.

She looked down at the phone book. "I'm fine. A little

surprised, maybe, but fine. I was just calling the police." She held up the phone in illustration.

He came toward her and gently took it from her. "Your hands are shaking. Here, let me call P.B."

Her hands *were* shaking, she realized, just as her knees were. She sat down in the desk chair and watched him dial the phone.

"Yeah, Peter Baron," Steve said into the receiver. He gave her a grim smile.

He'd obviously come straight from bed the instant she'd called. She couldn't even tell him how grateful she was. Not that she couldn't have managed this on her own. She *could* have, and *would* have, if she hadn't thought he might know something that would help. Still, she had to admit she was glad she didn't have to do it alone. Starting this restaurant by herself was scary enough. To think someone might want to sabotage it made everything seem that much harder.

"Hey, P.B. It's Steve." He ran a hand back through his hair, making a vague, halfhearted effort to straighten it. "Listen, we've got a situation here at Charters. Someone broke in last night . . ." His eyes slid over to Roxanne and his lips turned up wryly. "She's sitting right here and she *looks* fine. Are you all right, Roxanne?"

She gave a strained laugh. She could just imagine the he-man way P.B. had put the question. "I'm fine."

"Yeah, she's fine. Hmm. I don't know." He shifted the receiver down away from his mouth and addressed her again. "Anything missing?"

She shrugged. "I'm not sure. But things have definitely been disturbed." She pointed to the floor behind him. "Look, someone even pried up one of the floorboards."

He turned to look, taking a step closer to try to peer inside. "P.B.? Yeah, things are definitely messed up, but we're not sure if anything's missing yet. What?" He looked back at Roxanne. "Was there any money taken?"

She shook her head. "It was all deposited yesterday morning. There was nothing here."

"No," he said into the phone. "Yeah, okay, good." He hung up. "He's coming right over."

She sighed. "Thank you, Steve."

He leaned one hip against the desk and looked down at her. "No problem. Hey, I know these things can be unnerving. Me? Snakes are what get to me. I can handle anything but snakes."

She shifted her eyes to his. "Snakes, huh?"

"Yeah. I don't know what it is, but they make my skin crawl." He shivered once, apparently just thinking about it, then wandered over to the pried up floorboard and squatted beside it, adding, "You got a snake problem next time, call somebody else to deal with it."

"Sure. But . . ." She raised her chin and looked at him. "I could have handled this on my own. I wasn't hoping you would 'deal with it' for me. That's not why I called you."

He issued a short laugh and gave her a look that seemed to say, *Sure you could, little lady.* "I didn't say you couldn't."

He poked a couple fingers into the age-old, lintlike insulation filling the space below the floor and stirred it around a little.

"Can't imagine they found anything in here," he murmured, wiping his hand on his jeans.

She studied him. Was he being condescending or did it just seem like it? "Listen, the reason I called is because you came home last night right about the time I think this happened."

He turned to her, his eyes widened. "What? How do you know when I came home last night?"

"Because I heard you coming up the stairs."

He stood up. "Really? How do you know it was me?"

She threw a hand out. "Well who else would it be?"

"I don't know." He looked around with exaggerated wonder. "An *intruder*, maybe?"

She shook her head. "No, smart guy, it was you. I saw you through the peephole."

At that he seemed to color. "You saw me through the peephole. Great, now I've got a spy living below me."

"I wasn't spying. How paranoid are you? You think I've got nothing better to do than wait for you to get home from your girlfriend's house? I was looking to be *sure* it was you. If it wasn't, I would have called the police, because you're the only one other than me who should be on those stairs."

"So you sit up nights guarding the stairwell by looking through the peephole?"

"Oh please. I just happened to wake up and hear you—"

"At *three o'clock in the morning*?" He looked incredulous.

"That's right." She glared at him. "What are you insinuating?"

He moved back into the office. "I've said what I was

insinuating. What are *you* insinuating? You think *I* had something to do with this?" He spread his arms wide, his face indignant.

She stood up, angry at being deliberately misunderstood. "No! I'm not accusing you of anything, Steve. I just thought you might have seen something."

"Like a broken window? You think I'd just go on to bed if I did? What kind of idiot do you think I am?"

She put her hands on her hips. "Why are you being so defensive?"

"I'm not being defensive." He crossed his arms over his chest. "I just want to know what the hell you think I did."

She rolled her eyes. "Oh, that's much better."

He just looked at her. "Look." She steeled her voice and gave him a hard look. "I woke up last night about three because I thought I heard glass breaking." There was no way on earth she was going to tell him about her dreams. "Then I heard you coming up the stairs. This morning, when I found this," she indicated the mess around them, "I thought maybe you might have seen someone in the alley, maybe a suspicious car or something. That's *all* I thought, okay?"

His expression went from belligerent to wary.

"So? *Did* you see anything?" she asked.

"No."

He didn't even think about it.

She was so mad she could spit. He was so damned secretive he couldn't even take the time to think whether or not he might have seen something suspicious last night. Either that or he thought she was so desperate for company she had stayed up late to spy on him. Either way, he wasn't very concerned about getting at the truth.

So, all right then, fine. He'd be the police's problem. She'd tell them what she just told Steve and let them take care of it.

"Forget it." She shook her head and moved past him toward the office door. When he didn't move she turned back. "Are you coming? We should probably wait in the dining room. Make sure we don't touch anything in here."

Slowly, Steve turned and followed her out the door, through the kitchen and into the dining room. When they reached the bar, the front door opened and a tall, distinguished gentleman with thinning dark hair and an ebony cane entered.

Roxanne took a deep breath and forced a smile. "Sir Nigel." She moved toward him, looking at her watch. "You're early."

"Good morning. I wanted a chance to examine the dining area before beginning," he said in his precise British accent.

He was perfectly turned out, in a three-piece suit complete with watch chain and French cuffs. She'd forgotten how tall he was, nearly six foot three, and she wondered if his cane, which he did not appear to need except as an accessory, was extra long.

Roxanne suddenly became acutely aware of her untamed hair and jeans.

He took her hand in his and bent over it with great formality. He smelled just faintly of cologne. "Lovely to see you, madamoiselle. I trust everything is in readiness for today's training."

"Well, actually . . ." She glanced over her shoulder at Steve. He lounged idly on one of the bar stools, looking like he'd just done the very thing he had: rolled out of bed. "We have a little problem this morning. Someone broke into the kitchen last night."

"Good Lord," Sir Nigel exclaimed, if saying the words in the same even tones of his clipped Oxford accent could be called exclaiming. "Was anyone hurt?"

"No, it was nothing like that. Just a little breaking and entering."

Sir Nigel's hawklike eye moved past her to spear Steve with a haughty glare. "I see you've caught the culprit. Good show. Have the authorities been called?"

Roxanne strangled half a laugh. "No. That is, yes, the police are on their way. But this is not the culprit. This . . ." She turned and held a hand out toward Steve. "Is our bartender. Steve Serrano. Steve was the bartender at Charters but he really knows what he's doing. Steve, this is Sir Nigel Wallings."

"Our bartender?" Sir Nigel said incredulously. "The bartender for our elegant little French restaurant with renowned chef Marcel Girmond—this . . . person?"

Steve didn't rise. Instead he fixed Sir Nigel with a look of thinly veiled hostility and said, "Nice to meet you, too."

Roxanne clasped her hands together in front of her and slowly exhaled. With a tight smile at no one she said, "Well, this is getting off to a great start."

5

Bar Special
Sidecar—have one when three's a crowd
Brandy, Cointreau, lemon juice, with a twist

P.B. sidled up to Steve near the bar. "So, how's she doing?" He jutted his chin in Roxanne's direction and donned a concerned expression.

Steve, still slumped on a bar stool and wishing he'd gotten more sleep, looked up and said, "She's fine. Look at her. She's her own pit bull. You don't need to worry about her."

They could see Roxanne through the kitchen doors, which were propped open, looking over the shoulder of the fingerprint guy. Steve would bet she was pointing out places he missed.

P.B. turned to him. For some reason, P.B., in his blues, always looked about twice his normal size. Maybe it was the gun.

"You seem a little pissed, big guy. What's up with that?" P.B. leaned a square hand on the bar. "The burglars didn't make off with anything of yours, did they?"

Steve shook his head, gazing at Roxanne. She thought he had something to do with this, he was sure of it. She and her pompous pal *Sir Nigel*. They were the purebreds and he was the mongrel, so it had to be him to blame for the mess on the floor.

"Let's just say I've been robbed of my dignity." Steve turned on the bar stool and reached across the bar for the bag of pretzels he knew was on top of the cold chest.

He unfolded the plastic bag, relishing the loud crunchy sound as it went a small way toward drowning out the pompous Sir Nigel's voice in the dining room, droning on about show plates and fingerbowls, *guéridons* and *réchauds*. He was accompanied by Rita, George, Pat and some French chick whose sole purpose seemed to be demonstrating the proper way to open a wine bottle.

Tomorrow, Sir Nigel had threatened, Steve was to get a lesson in Armagnacs. As if Steve needed anyone to tell him about brandies. He *lived* brandies. Hell, he *bathed* in brandies. Brandies were his *life*. He didn't need to spend an afternoon with Sir Nigel's ebony cane up his butt to serve Armagnacs to a bunch of French-restaurant-bar patrons who were probably too old to tell the difference between brandy and Listerine.

P.B. laughed and slapped him on the back. "Get over it, buddy. You never had much dignity to speak of anyway. Besides, that's what women are all about. They bust your balls just to see if you're strong enough to stand up to them."

Steve stuffed a pretzel in his mouth and looked at P.B.

"And if you are? What does that mean? You argue with them, walk away or just keep taking their shit?"

"You let their shit roll right off your back, my friend. Don't even listen to it. They don't mean it anyway. They're just exercising their control muscles. Let them spit it all out, pay them a little lip service, then forget about it."

"I can't believe you actually think that's good advice. Is that what you do, P.B.?" Steve raised a skeptical brow. "Because if you keep talking like that, you might have to turn in your male chauvinist membership card. Sounds like you let women walk all over you."

P.B. wagged a finger at him. "I let them *think* they're walking all over me. Then I do whatever I want." He dug into the pretzel bag and pulled out a handful.

Steve settled back in the stool. "I guess I have to say that's probably the right tack to take with Roxanne. She likes giving people an earful, if my experience with her is any indication."

"What do you mean?" P.B.'s eyes were suddenly alert. He almost looked like the detective he was supposed to be right now. "What's your experience with her?"

Steve chewed his pretzels and smirked. "Ooh, down boy. I didn't mean *that* kind of experience. I just meant having to try and work with her. She's tough as nails, even when she doesn't have to be."

"Hm." P.B.'s eyes trailed back to Roxanne and his mouth took on a little smile. "Fiery. I like that."

Steve grunted. "Positively searing."

"Listen, I'm going to ask her out. How do you think I should do it?"

Steve shook his head. "Very, very carefully."

"No, I mean, what should I ask her to do? You know her a little better than I do. I was thinking I'd take her out to eat or something. What do you think?"

"I think that's a great idea. Because she probably doesn't spend enough time in restaurants."

P.B. put a hand to his chin. "Good point. Hmm. Then again, maybe she'd like to check out the competition. I was thinking that new pizza place on King. You know the one?" Steve looked up at him with his first truly delighted smile of the day. "Are you serious?"

P.B. scratched the back of his neck. "Yeah. Why?"

"Pizza," Steve confirmed.

P.B. drew his chin back, defensive. "Yeah."

Steve shrugged. "Okay. I guess she might like pizza. I mean, really, who doesn't?"

"Exactly." P.B. looked at him warily. "What?"

Steve pulled another pretzel out of the bag, but hesitated before eating it. He turned his eyes from the snack to P.B. "Well, considering she's putting everything she's got into opening a top-drawer, chi-chi, you-better-own-a-tie type place, I'm thinking she might like a restaurant that doesn't rely too much on plastic knives and forks."

P.B. looked into the dining room, where Sir Nigel was demonstrating the proper way to align a white linen tablecloth.

Steve ate the pretzel.

"Yeah, maybe . . ." P.B. brooded.

"Not to mention," Steve continued, "she's not striving for the pizza market, so that wouldn't exactly be her competition."

P.B.'s tongue found the side of his mouth as he deliberated. "So, you're thinking . . . French?"

"I'm thinking *expensive*."

P.B. narrowed his eyes, thinking hard. "What's that little place on Washington Street? You know the one I mean? Isn't it French?"

"Yep. And way out of your budget, Pretty Boy."

He dropped his hands to his hips. "Hey, I make a good living."

"Oh yeah. I forgot you're the consummate, upstanding professional. The guy with a future." Steve let his eyes linger sardonically on P.B. a minute. "Then sure, that's the kind of place I'm talking about. Go for it."

P.B. tilted his head. "I know why you're being such a jerk about this."

"I'm not being a jerk."

"Sure you are." P.B.'s expression was smug. "And you're probably giving me bad advice too, just so I'll blow it with her. Well, I'm onto you, buddy. I'm taking her to the pizza place. She's probably sick to death of French."

Steve snorted. "She better not be. We haven't even opened yet."

He glanced back toward the kitchen and wondered if, after this morning, Roxanne might be hoping he'd quit. She couldn't think he was behind a break-in and still want him working for her. Hell, maybe she'd even fire him.

Roxanne strode out of the kitchen and P.B. swiftly straightened.

Steve stifled an urge to do the same. Manners be damned, they were adversaries now.

She drilled Steve with a challenging look. "Steve, I've

told Officer Stuart that you got home last night about the time I thought I heard breaking glass."

Slowly Steve pushed himself up on the stool and glanced at P.B., wondering if he noticed her accusatory tone.

"He wants to ask you some questions," she added.

Officer Stuart stepped forward. A short, stocky guy, he was obviously new and looked at P.B. as if one bad question would make P.B. fire him on the spot.

He cleared his throat and poised his pen on his tiny, spiral-topped pad. "Mr. Serrano, approximately what time did you arrive home last night?"

Steve gazed coolly at Roxanne and answered, "About three. This morning. As I'm sure my *employer* informed you."

The cop nodded and wrote on his pad.

With a last lift of her brows, Roxanne excused herself and went back to the kitchen. P.B. immediately followed.

The little cop breathed an audible sigh. "And when you arrived home, where did you park?" He studiously made notes on the pad.

Steve wondered if he was writing down the questions as well as the answers.

He sighed. "In the alley, at the back of the building. Where I always park."

"And did you see anything suspicious?" *Scratch, scratch, scratch.*

"You mean other than the guy with a grappling hook, dressed in black, wearing a ski mask and crawling up the side of the building?" He shook his head pensively. "No. No, I don't think so."

Officer Stuart stopped writing and looked eagerly

from his pad to Steve's face. "A man in a ski mask? Is that what you saw?"

Steve sat back and studied the guy until the cop actually blushed. "What do you think?"

In classic P.B.-style, Officer Stuart puffed his chest out and looked stern. "Mr. Serrano, I need you to take my questions seriously."

Steve's gaze moved into the kitchen, where P.B. was standing too close to Roxanne, speaking to her with an overly charming look on his face.

Great, that would be all he needed. Roxanne for a boss with P.B for her boyfriend. The two of them would be insufferable. And P.B. would think he owned the place.

Steve turned back to the officer just as Roxanne reemerged from the kitchen. She looked flushed and slightly flustered. Had P.B. done that to her? He tried to imagine her being girlish and flirty, really interested in P.B., and couldn't do it.

He had to admit, though, every time she came into a room he was reminded of how beautiful she was, as if his memory changed when she was absent, because he couldn't quite believe it unless she was right there in front of him. It wasn't that he desired her, he was just taken aback time and again by her presence. Perfect lips, ivory skin, ink-dark eyes and that abundance of thick shiny hair. Not to mention the way she moved. Graceful. Catlike.

He'd have been in real trouble if she'd turned out to be nice.

Right behind her, however, came P.B. and in his hands was something to startle both Steve and Officer Stuart.

With a big grin, P.B. held aloft a dead squirrel. At least Steve thought it was dead. It wasn't moving.

"Found the perp!" he announced. Two fingers gripped the squirrel's tail. He swung it from side to side.

Everyone in the dining room stopped and turned at his voice.

"Is that a squirrel?" Rita called.

P.B. turned his grin on her. "Sure is. Nothing like wildlife trapped indoors to make a helluva mess."

"I'm thinking Brunswick stew tonight, chef." George guffawed. "A Virginia classic!"

"Good Lord, Officer." Sir Nigel sniffed and turned his head partly away, keeping one wary eye on the thing. "Please remove it from the dining area expeditiously."

P.B. turned back toward the bar.

Steve looked from the squirrel to Roxanne's face. So that's what had made her flush. Good, he thought. His faith in her was restored. She hadn't seemed the type to make a fool of herself over P.B.

"We're going to have to sterilize the entire kitchen." She grimaced and threw herself on a bar stool. "Fill the entire place with boiling water."

"Is it dead?" Steve asked.

P.B. swung the animal so close to Steve's face he had to pull back to avoid being hit.

"Of course it's dead," P.B. said. "You think it'd let me do this if it wasn't?"

Steve moved sideways away from the swinging animal. "For God's sake, P.B. What are you, in fourth grade?"

"What? It's cute." P.B. backed off but swung it a little more, watching it with a boyish grin.

Steve glanced at Roxanne, who watched P.B. with a look of concern.

"So how did it die?" Steve asked. "There's not a drop of blood on it."

"Huh?" P.B. stopped the animal and dropped his arm to his side. "I don't know. Scared itself to death, I guess."

Steve laughed. "You're saying it gave itself a heart attack?"

P.B. looked at him with heavy-lidded eyes. "You want me to ask the department to autopsy it?"

"Can we just," Roxanne motioned the squirrel away, "put it in a bag or something? I don't want its fleas or whatever other parasites it might have flung all over the restaurant. We're going to have to sandblast the place as it is."

"Oh sure." P.B. was instantly contrite. "Sorry about that." He went back to the kitchen.

"So . . ." Steve looked cautiously at Roxanne. "A nocturnal squirrel."

"Hm." She nodded, not looking at him. "So it would seem."

"A nocturnal squirrel that threw itself through the back window."

She turned her eyes to his face. "I had the same thought."

He held her gaze. "Curious."

"Yes." She looked away again, nodding. "Yes."

Then, after a second, she turned a sly look on him and said, "Good thing it wasn't a snake."

"You agreed to go *out* with that guy?" Skip sounded appalled. "That big blond guy with all the teeth?"

Roxanne turned from the seafood case and laughed at him. "All the teeth?"

They were standing in the Whole Foods Market, trying to figure out what to buy. Roxanne had invited Skip and his girlfriend, Kelly, to dinner and had promised to cook. Besides, she wanted to try out a couple of desserts on them, see which they thought were the best. But Kelly couldn't make it so it was just the two of them.

Skip shook his head with dismissive disgust. "He bares his teeth a lot. He's the kind of guy who makes people think he's smiling, but he's not. He's showing dominance."

Roxanne snickered and bent over again to look more closely at the scallops.

"I like the look of these scallops. I can do them with asparagus and black truffles. Or I can do the sole. What do you think?" she asked.

Skip leaned over next to her. "I don't know. How about a burger?"

"Funny." She waved the clerk over and inquired about the sole, then ordered the scallops.

They waited while he wrapped the order.

"I don't get it, Rox, why that guy? He gave me the creeps." Skip looked at an older woman who was carefully examining four different types of cocktail sauce. "Get the *organic* kind," he leaned over and confided. "They'll think less of you here if you don't."

The woman glanced up, saw he was talking to her and her expression turned haughty.

"Really." Skip nodded. "People talk."

"Skip," Roxanne admonished, with an embarrassed smile at the woman.

The woman grabbed the organic one, turned on her heel and left.

Skip laughed. "I'm sorry. It's just that everyone here is so pretentious. Look at them, with their tiny carts and their designer vegetables."

"This place is great. You're just jealous because all you have in your neighborhood is a Safeway."

"I like hormones in my meat. Keeps me manly." Skip flexed.

"That explains *that*."

"I'm serious, Rox. I mean, it's one thing for you to lose your mind and give up the big bucks of modeling for the hardscrabble life of a restaurant owner. But to go completely nuts and start dating G.I. Joe?"

"You really think P.B.'s that bad?" She tried to remember her thought process this morning when P.B. had caught her off guard with his offer. "He's actually nice. And he's helped me twice now with difficult situations."

"Oh please. Putting a couple of girls in a cab? I could have done that."

Roxanne snorted. "But you didn't."

She grabbed a pound of organic butter and they moved toward the cheese section. This was by far Roxanne's favorite area. Huge wax-coated wheels of cheddars and Jarlesburgs and Romanos stood amidst wedges of jack, Swiss, gouda and edam. Piles of bries and camemberts vied with goat cheese of every description and fresh balls of mozzarella in plastic tubs.

It looked like a Disney-inspired Cheese World.

"And his help with the burglary was his job." Skip picked up a paper-wrapped round of Cowgirl Creamery. "He was *paid* to help you out with that, sister." He put the cheese down and studied a jar of dried fig spread. "If you ask me, the only one who's really helped you out so far is the bartender. He's the one who got up first thing in the morning to help without getting paid for it. If you give anybody a gratitude date it should be him."

"Steve? He's not even looking for a gratitude date." Roxanne scoffed, but couldn't help remembering that steamy dream, albeit with nothing but consternation now. "He's got a girlfriend, for one thing. And for another, he is *so* not my type."

"Oh, I forgot. Your type is—what, now? Married?"

Roxanne stopped dead in her tracks and glared at him.

Skip threw his hands up in immediate surrender. "Sorry. Sorry. That was below the belt. I'm sorry." He lowered his hands and picked up a bag of grated parmesan. "I just don't see this P.B. guy being any better for you than Marty What's-his-face. P.B.'s got arrogant written all over him. Is that what you want? Someone to push you around?"

"He has not once pushed me around, Skip. And besides, I'm just going out to eat with the guy. I'll probably save moving in with him for the second date."

Skip inhaled and exhaled heavily. "All right."

"Oh good God. Now you sound like my mother."

"How is your mother?"

They moved to the wine section and Roxanne picked up a bottle to read the label.

"Fine. And every bit as optimistic about my success as you are. Thank God she lives in Florida now and can't visit me with her dire predictions."

Skip raised his brows but didn't look at her. He picked up a bottle, too, then placed it in the cart. "Well, she *did* own a restaurant most of her life. She must know what she's talking about."

Roxanne turned around, one hand on the cart handle. "You know as well as I do that she *loved* owning that restaurant. You were a waiter there; you saw her. She loved the customers, the food, the day-to-day planning and delivery. She loved being in control of everyone and everything. *And* she loved complaining about it."

"That's true." Skip nodded.

"Trust me. It's not that she doesn't think it's a good thing to do. She just doesn't think *I* can do it."

She put the wine she'd chosen in the cart and started to turn around to move back down the aisle. Skip stopped her. "That's not what *I* mean, Rox. I know you *can* do it. I just don't understand why you want to. You've worked your tail off and made a boatload of money. Why not relax for a little while?"

"Because I haven't *accomplished* anything, Skip."

"What do you mean? Your face was all over everything for a while. You were in *Sports Illustrated*, for crying out loud. I *still* get more respect from the kids because I know you, by the way."

She smiled. "I'm glad it helped you. But it didn't do much for me. Beyond making money, that is. Which was nice. But still. It was just my face."

"And your body."

She rolled her eyes toward him. "Right. But I didn't *do* anything. I wasn't respected. I've told you all this before. It's important for me to succeed on my own, using my head."

"I know." He picked up a loaf of bread, sighing. "I just can't help thinking I'd like to fly all over the world having my picture taken and getting paid tons of money instead of coaching a bunch of spoiled high schoolers to throw each other around."

"Skip, you are molding young minds. Shaping people's futures. Being a role model for the leaders of tomorrow." She shot him a smirk. "And you only work nine months out of the year."

"You've got me on the last point. The other three are highly debatable."

They got in line to check out. Roxanne, in front of the cart, pulled down a *Yoga Journal* and started flipping through it. Behind the cart, Skip pushed into her gently.

She looked over.

Look, Skip mouthed, pointing in front of her.

Roxanne glanced ahead and saw the back of a tousled male head. Her stomach lurched. *Steve*.

Skip pushed on the cart again.

Roxanne looked over.

Skip mouthed something she didn't get. She shook her head, squinting at him. He mouthed it again, as incomprehensibly as the first time.

She leaned across the cart and whispered, "*Vitamins*? What are you talking about?"

Skip rolled his eyes. "No. I said *invite* him."

She pulled back and whispered indignantly, "Where?"

"To dinner," he whispered back. "Tonight. With us."

She shook her head. "No way. You're crazy." She looked away.

Skip pushed on the cart again.

"*What?*"

"You said you wanted to talk to him and you blew it the other day. Now's the perfect opportunity."

"No!"

"Come on. I'll be there to keep it from looking like a date. Besides, I want to know a little more about his toothy friend."

She gave him an admonishing look. "Then definitely no."

"If he knows you're going out with his friend, he's not going to think you're coming on to him. Besides, I'm just kidding."

She turned back to the magazine. "Good."

"No, I mean asking about G.I. Joe." He pushed on the cart again and jerked his head in Steve's direction. "Look. All he's got there is a wrap. He's having a friggin' *sandwich* for dinner. As a chef, that should offend all your sensibilities."

"I'm a pastry chef. Besides, their wraps are very good here."

"Just invite him," Skip said. "It's neighborly."

Roxanne, visions of that evening on the stairwell still vivid in her memory, shook her head. "Absolutely not." She looked back at her magazine.

Skip was silent a minute. Then Roxanne noticed the cart pressing harder and harder into her hip. She braced a foot outward and pushed back.

Skip pushed harder.

She dropped the magazine, turned and put both hands on the cart and glared at him. "What are you *doing*?" she hissed.

Skip grinned and looked just beyond her. "Oh hey. How you doing?"

Roxanne closed her eyes, then turned to look behind her. Steve had glanced back, no doubt to see what all the stage whispering was about, and Skip had caught his eye.

Roxanne put on a smile. "Hello, Steve. Fancy meeting you here."

He looked genuinely surprised—as she knew she did not—and glanced from one to the other of them. "Hey, hello." He extended a hand toward Skip, avoiding any contact with Roxanne by leaning pointedly away from her. "Skip, right?"

Skip smiled and looked smugly at Roxanne. "That's right. Good memory."

Steve straightened back up. "Trick of the trade." He shot Roxanne a small, albeit fiendish, smile. "How're you doing, boss?"

She answered with a slight nod. "Fine. You don't have to call me boss."

His smile grew. "I know."

"Whatcha got there, Steve? A wrap?" Skip asked, gazing over the basket toward his small wrapped parcel on the conveyor belt.

Steve glanced back at it a second. "Yeah. Chicken Caesar."

"Those are good," Roxanne said.

"And it looks good, but you should join us," Skip said. "We're having scallops and truffles. Roxanne's one helluva cook."

"Is she? I thought she just did desserts." Steve inched forward as the food on the conveyor belt in front of him was tallied.

"That too. In fact," Skip turned a pleasant face to Roxanne, "didn't you say you had some desserts to sample tonight? Steve's opinion would be a good one to get, too, don't you think? Especially since Kelly couldn't make it."

"Of course." Roxanne shot daggers at Skip with her eyes before turning back to Steve. "You're welcome to join us if you've got nothing better to do."

Steve glanced from Roxanne to Skip.

"Really." Skip nodded confidently, gesturing toward Roxanne. "Excellent cook. And you guys can talk about the restaurant. I won't mind."

"Ah, a working dinner." Steve sent a lazy glance to Roxanne.

"Six eighty-nine," the cashier told Steve. "Do you want plastic or paper?"

"Neither." Steve pulled out his wallet and glanced back at Roxanne. "I don't want to interrupt your—"

"Don't think twice. Roxanne and I are sick to death of each other." Skip grinned at her, while she *did* try to look pretty sick of him. "Just come on by in about half an hour."

Steve picked up his wrap and, with a wry smile, said, "All right then. Thanks."

6

Bar Special
Angel's kiss—<u>devilishly delightful</u>
Crème de cacao, heavy cream

"I can't believe you did that." Roxanne pressed the button on her car key and the automatic door locks beeped as they opened. "You shanghaied him into coming."

"Come on. I did you a favor. You said yourself you need to get on better terms with this guy and you were right." Skip ducked into the passenger side and pulled the door shut.

Roxanne got in her side. "What do you mean, I was right?"

"Well from the expression on his face when I invited him, he looked as if he thought you might be planning to serve him arsenic." Skip fastened his seat belt.

She stuck the key in the ignition, then, sighing, lay her head on the steering wheel. "Great."

She'd seen it too, that look on Steve's face. They kept

butting heads, misunderstanding each other, and she didn't know how to fix it. She hoped it was just a matter of earning his respect, but she feared it might be some prejudice he had against women owning restaurants. Young women, in particular. *Her.* Maybe he felt defensive, being her employee. Embarrassed about being older and without a career other than bartending.

Maybe he just didn't like her.

In any of those cases, Skip was probably right to have invited him, or rather, bulldozed him into coming.

"Look," Skip continued, rubbing a hand on her back comfortingly, "for all your mother's idiosyncrasies, she didn't tolerate friction among the staff, right?"

Roxanne raised her head with a laugh. "That's right. Everyone came together to curse her."

She started the car.

"So, you could do that, or you could make nice. Right now, most of your staff know Steve and are loyal to him. Not you. You need him on your side, Roxanne."

Roxanne grumbled, "Or I could fire him."

Skip patted her back one last time. "Easier to just make friends. He seems like a nice guy."

"Sure. To you. Me, he took an instant dislike to." She remembered how snotty she was to him that day he came to give her the housewarming wine. A simple misunderstanding, but he hadn't known where her attitude had come from.

"All right," she capitulated. "You're probably right. But Skip, promise me one thing."

"Anything."

"Don't tell him what I used to do for a living." She turned pleading eyes to him. "I really want to get away from that, from being looked at like that. Right now he sees me as a kind of bitchy newbie owner, and that's okay. He can still think I know what I'm doing. But if he found out I used to be a model I just know he'd lose all respect for me."

Skip studied her for a second. "All right. Laying aside that I think it's unhealthy to be ashamed of something you spent ten years making a success of, I'll honor your request. In the name of baby steps."

She quirked a smile. "Baby steps?"

"Yeah, you know. Forward movement, progress. Sometimes it can only be accomplished by taking one baby step at a time. Whatever you can handle."

She put the car in reverse and looked at him sideways. "Laying aside how condescending that sounds, I appreciate your agreement to keep mum."

Steve hadn't been sure what to expect, but it wasn't the smiling, self-deprecating woman who was in the kitchen sautéing scallops and drinking wine when he arrived.

"Can I pour you a glass of wine, Steve?" she asked when Skip ushered him into the kitchen. "I have to warn you, though, it's French."

He laughed. "I think French wine was a positive on the list of French things."

He looked around the room. She'd fixed the place up since he'd last seen it—and apparently had been successful in fixing the sink drain—because the kitchen was warm and inviting and bubbling over with delicious scents. A basket hanging from the beamed ceiling held fruits, vegetables and herbs. The counters were clean, with minimal clutter, but were lined with sophisticated-looking salt and pepper shakers, an espresso machine and what might have been a pasta maker. A long loaf of French bread lay on a cutting board near the sink and a rack with copper pots hung near the stove.

An island in the center of the kitchen held an open bottle of white Bordeaux, a wedge of brie, and plates of asparagus, mushrooms, butter and several spices, presumably to be added to the dinner dish.

Steve slid onto one of the island's bar stools. "The place is looking great."

She poured a generous dram of white wine into a large goblet and handed it to him. When he took it, he met her eyes and she smiled. A genuine smile, he thought. Less guarded than usual.

"Thanks. It's been a lot of work, but as of today the last of the boxes is gone. Not only that, the painters have finished downstairs. Now I can relax."

She held up her wineglass and he touched it with his.

"Cheers," he said. "To your new home."

She smiled, her dark eyes seeming to look all the way through him, and sipped from her glass.

He wondered what was going on. In the grocery store, he could tell that inviting him to this dinner had been Skip's idea, and Roxanne had been none too pleased about it. But now she seemed different.

Maybe she'd thought he would refuse to come. (And he would have, if Skip hadn't been so damned insistent.) Or maybe she felt awkward after practically accusing him of being behind the squirrel break-in.

Who knew? She was a riddle (wrapped in a mystery

inside an enigma, etc. etc.). Maybe it was time to sit down and talk right up front about how they could work together amicably. Or *whether* they should work together, amicably or not.

Roxanne threw a glob of butter into a hot sauté pan and directed a question over her shoulder at him. "So Steve, where are you from, originally?"

He put his wineglass down carefully on the butcher block surface. "D.C. Out Sixteenth Street."

"Really? An actual D.C. native? That's rare."

"Where are you from?" He directed the question to her but looked at Skip too. If they went to high school together they must have come from the same place.

"Right here in Alexandria." She reached behind her for the plate of mushrooms. She lifted the plate slightly in his direction. "Do you like truffles?"

"Is that what those are?"

She narrowed her eyes as she smiled, as if he was trying to pull one over on her. Fact of the matter was, he may know his alcohol but he had no idea about fancy French cooking. He'd heard of truffles and foie gras and all that, but he hadn't spent much time eating any of it.

He was about to pick up his wineglass when a huge orange cat, the same one he'd seen that first day, leaped onto his lap.

"Whoa," Steve said reflexively, moving his hand from his glass lest he knock it over. "Who's this big guy?"

Roxanne looked back over her shoulder. She laughed. "Oh, that's Cheeto. You're lucky he likes you. People he doesn't like tend to leave with shredded pant legs."

Steve scratched behind one of the cat's ears, but the

animal ducked his head, giving him a look that said he was an imbecile and doing it wrong. He lifted his hand and looked into the cat's face.

"Cheeto, huh? That's kind of an uncultured name for a French restaurant's mascot. I would think something like Paté or Fromage would have been better."

"Not for him." Roxanne slid the truffles into a bath of boiling water, then moved the scallops around a little in the sauté pan. "He's definitely a junk-food cat. Besides, Cheetos are my downfall. Horrible for your health, just deadly to any diet, but oh so irresistible."

Aha, Steve thought, a chink in her armor. She *did* have weaknesses. "So will we be seeing Cheeto Almondine on the new menu? Vichyssoise with ground-Cheeto garnish? No wait, you're desserts. Cheeto à la mode?"

Skip laughed.

Roxanne said, "Believe it or not, those all sound pretty good to me."

This drew a laugh from all of them.

He tried petting the cat again, this time stroking him from head to tail. As he did, the cat rose up, arched his back and dug his needlelike claws into Steve's legs through his jeans.

He removed his hand again. Cheeto looked back at him, eyes narrowed. They regarded each other a moment.

"So what are your plans for the bar," Steve asked, "if you don't mind my asking?"

Cheeto leaped from his lap and thudded to the floor. After a pointed yawn, he proceeded to saunter off, obviously disappointed in Steve's petting abilities.

"My plans?" Roxanne said. "You mean the decorating?"

Steve picked up his wineglass. "No. I mean the populating. Charters had a great happy hour. Brought in tons of people. People who then got hungry and stayed for dinner."

She made a light scoffing sound. "If only to sober up before getting in their cars and driving home, no doubt."

She flipped the scallops over in the pan, shook the whole thing in a circular motion, then slid them onto a plate. He had to admit, he liked the way she moved. Graceful. Practiced. Like a ballerina in the kitchen.

"Happy hours are great," Skip volunteered, pouring himself more wine. "They give people a chance to taste your food, too. It's like advertising."

"Exactly." Steve shared a companionable look with Skip. He was starting to like the guy. Maybe Roxanne wasn't all bad, if she had normal friends. And if he could get her friends on his side, then maybe he wouldn't end up yawning through nothing but predinner *kirs* night after night once the place became a haunt for people following the latest haute cuisine.

If they were that lucky.

"I'm not interested in catering to the happy-hour crowd." Roxanne threw the asparagus rather vehemently into some boiling water. "Happy-hour drinkers are people after a cheap drunk and they're not particularly discerning. Furthermore, generally speaking, people who show up for free food are not going to fork over twenty-eight bucks for *cuisses de grenouilles*."

Steve raised his brows. "What the hell is that?"

She smirked at him through her lashes. "Frog legs."

"No. Please. Tell me you're kidding."

She just laughed and continued slicing asparagus.

Steve looked at her face—so much easier to do with her eyes downcast—and realized again how stunning her features were, especially when she was smiling. She looked like someone off a magazine page. Advertising mascara or face makeup with those lush lashes set against smooth skin.

"Okay, well, frog legs aside. You don't have to serve dollar beers and hot wings for happy hour," he offered. "You could put out some showy, frou-frou stuff and lure them in with, I don't know, change-back-from-your-ten brandy night or something."

Roxanne looked up and laughed again. Perfect teeth, Steve noted. And he liked the way her lips curved into a flawless bow. Was she wearing lipstick? Or were her lips just naturally that color?

"Change-back-from-your-ten," she repeated. "I like it."

He couldn't believe this woman had agreed to go out with P.B. Steve tried to remember the face of the last girl P.B. had dated, but could only recall big hair and giant breasts.

Roxanne, on the other hand, was sleek. Both her hair and her body. She was tall, thin, and knew how to dress to accentuate her curves, as opposed to putting them up on display like a tray of hors d'oeuvres.

"I'll think about it," Roxanne said, her voice low and husky. For a second Steve had to work to remember what it was he'd last said. For another second he wished he'd said something more provocative and gotten the same response.

Skip cleared his throat. "Speaking of happy-hour crashers, what about this friend of yours: P.B.?"

Steve's eyes shot to Skip's as if the latter had been reading his thoughts. "What about him?"

"Oh Skip, please." Roxanne's expression was stern. "Don't bother Steve with that."

Skip looked at her and shrugged. "What? I'm just wondering what kind of guy he is."

Steve took another sip of wine. "He's all right. Why?"

Skip filled Steve's glass again, then his own. "Did you know he asked Roxanne out?"

Roxanne checked the asparagus.

Her back was ramrod straight and her hands moved with confidence. She took the truffles off the stove and drained them. Then did the same with the asparagus. Steam rose in the air over the sink like a ghost.

"I heard he might." Steve looked at Skip, keeping his face bland. Skip obviously didn't like the idea of Roxanne going out with P.B. He didn't need to know that Steve was disappointed in her for accepting the date, too.

"Well? Is he a good guy?" Skip asked.

Steve made a noncommittal gesture. "I think he is. But then I've never been on a date with him. He could be a total cad. Talk with his mouth full, split the check, that kind of thing."

Roxanne turned back to the island with a chuckle. She picked up her glass. "That, I can handle."

"I'm sure you could." Steve tilted his head. "What couldn't you handle?"

"Is that a rhetorical question?" She sipped her wine.

"I'll tell you," Skip said, reaching across to cut a piece

off the wedge of brie. "She doesn't handle liars very well. He doesn't have a wife tucked away somewhere, does he?" He popped the cheese in his mouth.

At that, the look Roxanne shot her friend was enough to burn holes in his face. If her friend wasn't already immune, that was, as he seemed to be. There was a story there, Steve could tell.

He shook his head slowly. "No, he doesn't have a wife. Not unless he's keeping it secret from me, too. Though it wouldn't be like him not to ask for a wedding gift."

Roxanne moved to a cabinet and pulled out a trivet. She looked as if she wanted to hurl it at Skip but she merely placed it in front of him.

"Make yourself useful and put this on the table," she said to Skip. Then, turning, she said, "Look, Steve, no offense, but I'm just going out with P.B. as a friend. He . . . well, he doesn't really seem like my type. Though he certainly seems to be a nice guy."

Steve chuckled. "How would that offend me?"

Skip got up, took the trivet and went into the dining room.

"He's your friend." She paused. "Isn't he?" She looked genuinely curious.

"Sure." Steve nodded.

"I just don't want you to think I don't like him. Or that I'm—using him or anything."

Steve lifted his brows. "*Using* P.B.?" he mused. "That would be novel."

She frowned and looked down at the cutting board. She pushed a few truffles around on it.

"Roxanne"—he leaned slightly toward her until she

lifted her eyes to his—"what goes on between you and P.B. is your business. He doesn't need me to protect him and I'm sure you don't want me chiming in about your decisions." He let that stand a minute before adding, "Me, I'm just the friendly barkeep."

"Ah yes." Skip re-entered the kitchen, his glass raised. "To the friendly bartender. You probably see romances come and go all the time."

"This is *not* a romance." Roxanne began cutting the truffles in circles.

Steve raised his glass to Skip's and smiled. "I do, that's true."

They drank, emptying their glasses.

"You any good at telling which ones will stick?" Skip poured the last drop of wine into his own glass, made a face at its demise, then got up and grabbed the second bottle.

"Sometimes. Here, let me." He took the corkscrew from Skip and opened the bottle swiftly with a soft pop. He first poured more into Roxanne's, then Skip's goblet.

Roxanne turned from the conversation to combine the scallops, truffles and asparagus on a plate. "I'm sorry, Steve, it was not my idea to put you in the middle of this. I'm sure you have no interest in what I do."

He rubbed one side of his face thoughtfully. "I wouldn't say that."

She turned to look at him, her face aglow either from the heat of the stove or from a blush.

"I'm very interested in what you do with the restaurant." He swirled the new wine in his glass, sniffed it, then took a sip. "Pretty good," he admitted. "I could get used to this part of the French atmosphere."

"What is it you want to know?" Her eyes seemed to glow, paralyzing him where he sat. "I'll tell you anything."

A shiver ran up his spine and he was again transported to some completely different situation in which she might say the exact same words.

A married man, he pondered. *How long had that gone on?*

He patted his breast pocket halfheartedly and smiled. "And here I've gone and forgotten my list of questions. Can I get back to you?"

She inclined her head. "Any time." Then she turned, took up the platter now filled with scallops, truffles and asparagus and added, "But first, dinner. Come on, into the dining room."

The dining room was really a dining area between the kitchen and living room, just as in Steve's apartment. But through the miracle of fabric and screens and lighting, not to mention a generous wooden country dining table, the place was transformed. It felt cozy and intimate.

Skip lit a series of candles on the table and a couple more on tall pedestals near the sideboard as Roxanne set out the food.

"So what did you do before buying this place?" Steve asked as they sat down around the table, arranging wineglasses, moving water glasses and picking up napkins.

Roxanne shot a quick glance at Skip, then said, "I was at the CIA for a year. I told you that, didn't I?"

"Yes, but, what did you do for a living? Acquiring this place was a pretty brave thing to do and couldn't have been cheap." He sent his eyes around the room as if to encompass the whole building.

She was silent a long minute and he looked back over at her. It might have been his imagination but her cheeks looked pink as she dished scallops onto Skip's plate.

"I, uh . . ."

"Do you mean does she have restaurant experience?" Skip interjected, picking up his knife and fork. "Because that's what I'd want to know if I were you. Who *is* this person taking over my place of employment?"

Skip looked at Roxanne and prompted her with a nod.

"Well, yes, of course you'd want to know that," she said with a light laugh. "And I have *years* of restaurant experience, trust me. My parents owned a restaurant in downtown D.C. I practically grew up in."

She held out a hand for Steve's plate.

"You mentioned that." He handed it to her. "At that first meeting. Mama's, right?"

She gave him a brilliant smile. "That's right. Did you know it?"

He watched her hands as she put his plate down on her empty one. "The name sounds familiar, but I can't really say I remember it."

She nodded, her smile fading slowly as she filled his plate. She handed it back to him. "So, have you, ah, been a bartender . . . long?"

He chuckled wryly and speared a scallop. "Too long, yes. Since college."

"So you went to college?"

His eyes shot quickly up to hers. Was that surprise in her voice? Did she think a lowly bartender wouldn't have gone to college? "Yes, in fact. UVA. History major."

Her brows rose, impressed. *Score one for Steve*, he

thought, and popped the scallop into his mouth. Perhaps he was rising in her estimation, if only a little.

As the first bite sank onto his palate, he had to stop and look down at his plate. The flavor was amazing—a rich, creamy burst of it in his mouth that was totally unexpected because of the simple look of the dish.

"This is incredible." He poked the fork at another scallop, as if making sure it was real. "What did you do to this?"

"Isn't it?" Skip said. He was focused on his plate as well.

"I wish I had gone to college," Roxanne said, almost wistfully.

Steve stopped eating. She hadn't gone to college? Now *he* felt like the snob. There was nothing wrong with her not going, of course, but he had her pegged as such a princess he was surprised she hadn't been personally escorted through Vassar or someplace.

"Never too late," was all he could think to say.

She laughed and her beauty hit him again. "I guess I've done all right without it so far. And I think I'll be a little too busy for a while now."

He gazed at her a long moment, longer than he'd intended. When she glanced back at him he dropped his gaze to his plate.

She had done all right, he thought, realizing that she hadn't answered his question about what she'd done before this. He hadn't been kidding when he'd said this building couldn't have been cheap. Throw in a business on top of that and she had to have some serious assets.

Family money? he wondered. His eyes swept her

face again, marveling at the smooth skin, the way her dark eyebrows gave the perfect tilt to her eyes.

She caught him looking at her again and his eyes darted away.

"Sorry," he said, "I don't mean to stare. I was just thinking how you could have been a model. You've got that look."

She gaped at him, clearly startled. She turned her head to Skip.

He looked back down at his plate, ashamed that he'd been reduced to saying something that sounded so much like a pickup line. "But I'm sure you've been told that before."

"Well, yes." She cleared her throat. "But I don't want to make money off my appearance. Ever. I did nothing to earn my looks."

She was so firm he felt stupid for having said anything. He wasn't even sure why he had, except that without the spoiled-rich-girl mantle he'd given her she had suddenly seemed even more stunning. *And she could be a model*, he thought, *let's face it*.

"Well, not so for me." He laughed a little too heartily. "I've worked hard for my craggy face and I use it. I think it makes the customers open up to me more."

She smiled, her voice emerging gently. "You don't have a craggy face."

He laughed again, stupidly, and ate one of the truffles. "This really is the most amazing food."

The entire meal was amazing, Steve thought. The best food he'd ever eaten, in fact. He didn't know why she was hiring a chef when she had this kind of talent herself, and he told her so.

She smiled self-deprecatingly. "If you think this is good, wait until you taste Monsieur Girmond's food. He's . . . he's a magician. He does things with food that you just have to see and taste to believe. He's an absolute artist."

She held her hands together at her heart as she said this and Steve could see the passion she had for her work. Considering it was food, it was a wonder she was so thin.

The conversation loosened up nicely throughout the meal and laughter began to flow almost as freely as the wine.

Steve found himself enjoying not just Skip's irreverent company, but Roxanne's wit as well. She seemed to have figured out the waitstaff pretty astutely, making it easy for him to offer what tidbits of information he had about each one. And he admitted to her that up till now he thought she'd made pretty prudent hiring and firing decisions.

She was surprisingly gratified by that.

"Thank you," she said warmly, "that makes me feel good. Especially when everyone's been saying how crazy I am to attempt this."

"Really?" Steve glanced at Skip.

"He's the worst one," Roxanne said sourly, sipping her wine.

"Well, don't you agree?" Skip said to Steve. "I mean, you've worked in restaurants since college, haven't you? Would *you* want to own one?"

Steve tilted his head, looking from Skip to Roxanne. "I don't know. It's not something I've ever considered."

Skip threw out a hand. "There you go."

"I don't mean it that way. I just was thinking about other stuff. Other goals."

"Like what?" Roxanne looked at him with interest.

It was his turn to be firm. If there was one thing he was sure of, it was that he didn't want to talk about his aspiration before he achieved his goal. He didn't want to be seen as some pathetic wannabe. Not by anybody, but especially not by Roxanne Rayeaux.

"Nothing I've accomplished yet," he said with a tempering smile. "But I'll let you know when I do."

His tone was obviously effective, because Roxanne didn't press. Instead she excused herself to get the desserts.

If Steve thought dinner was fantastic, dessert was a whole other story. She'd prepared several things to try out for the restaurant, so it was something of an orgy of sweets after the meal. A crème brûlée, something called a *bombe Andalouse*, a chocolate Napoleon and fresh fruit in a sabayon sauce.

"I think I've died and gone to heaven," Steve moaned, leaning back in the chair.

Roxanne brought out espressos for the three of them. "Did I kill you?" she asked with a wicked grin.

His eyes warmed on her. "You did. And what a way to go. This was the most incredible meal I've ever had. I know I keep saying that, but it's true."

Roxanne laughed and cast her eyes down to her coffee as she sat. "I'm glad you liked it. Maybe now you won't be so resistant to French food."

"I think a lot of things on that list are getting more palatable." He held up a hand to Skip. "But don't go out of your way to track down a French film."

"How about a French poodle?" Roxanne asked.

Skip put a hand to his chin and drummed his fingers along his cheek. "Hmm, I'm trying to remember what else was on that list."

"Skip." Roxanne's voice held a warning. She knew just what he was referring to; she could tell by the fiendish look he gave her.

"French toast, I think." He grinned at Roxanne and she lifted a brow. "But it's not quite time for breakfast. Yet." He glanced at his watch, then sat bolt upright in his chair. "Holy shit, is this right? Is it really midnight?"

Roxanne smirked and looked into the kitchen at the clock. Nothing like instant payback for his evil intentions. "So it is. And on a school night." She tsked.

"Oh my God, I've got to go. I have an eight a.m. P.E. class to teach." He shot out of his chair and looked around for his coat. "Rox, I'm so sorry to leave you with all these dishes."

"Don't worry." She waved a hand. She was feeling so relaxed at the moment she was even thinking she might leave them until morning, something she almost never did. "Go, get some sleep. Thank you for coming."

"Thank *you*, doll." He kissed her cheek while dragging on his jacket. "Spectacular meal, as usual." He turned to Steve, hand outstretched. "Steve, good to spend time with you. Hope to see you again."

They shook.

"Might be hard to avoid me," Steve said.

Roxanne looked at him in surprise, her cheeks heating. What did he mean by that? Had she been too nice to him? Had he seen through her to that tiny piece of her that tonight had found him attractive?

Oh God, she thought. Did he think now that maybe . . . maybe he would be having, uh, dinner here more often?

But he must have caught her expression.

"I live right upstairs," he added quickly. "And work right downstairs. Hell, I never leave the building except for special occasions."

Roxanne sighed.

Skip laughed and slapped him on the back. "Oh. For a second there I thought you meant—"

"Good night, Skip," Roxanne said firmly.

"Good night, Roxie." With a grin and a wave, he dashed through the door.

Steve looked after him, his face a study in contrasts in the candlelight. He was really quite handsome, she thought, noting the shadows at his cheekbones, the light shining through his gray eyes. She even liked the way he slumped in his chair, all casual and angled.

But Steve, here for, uh, dinner, more often?

No, she shook her head. *No.* He was an *employee*, for God's sake. Not to mention just totally inappropriate for her anyway.

She tried to picture him at the Met and knew he'd sooner hunt rattlesnakes than go to an opera. Tried to imagine him strolling through an art gallery, sipping a glass of chardonnay, and could only imagine him scoffing at the idea. *Real men do Jell-O shooters.*

No, he was not her type. She wanted a guy like Martin. Handsome, cultured, urbane.

Steve might be handsome, but he was as cultured as a dime-store pearl.

Martin, on the other hand, had had connections all over New York City, knew everyone who was anyone, had his own limo and never failed to get into the most exclusive openings.

Yes, call her shallow, but she knew what she wanted, because she'd almost had it. It was another Martin she was after.

Well, a Martin minus the wife.

"Is he going to be okay to drive?" Steve asked, looking back at her.

She forced herself back to the present and started picking up plates. She was *not* going to start thinking about Martin. "He takes the metro."

Steve rose too, and picked up glasses. "You're kidding. That's like a mile away. I should give him a ride."

That got her attention. He was completely sincere. It would never have occurred to Martin to give Skip a ride. "What a nice thought. But don't bother. He runs. You'd never catch him now."

"He *runs*?"

"Yeah. He's a fitness instructor and a coach. He prides himself on being in shape. I know it's crazy, believe me, I tell him all the time, but he regularly runs to the metro after a night out. Says it works off the night's excesses faster."

"Okay . . ."

Roxanne laughed and shook her head. "I know." She headed into the kitchen.

Steve followed. When she turned on the hot water, he took her by the shoulders and gently moved her aside.

The instant he touched her, her skin warmed and she felt like melting back into him. How long had it been since she'd been held, or even touched? A year?

Longer? Sometimes she felt starved for it, and now was one of those times.

"Let me do this," Steve said, adjusting the water temperature. Water flowed over his hands and through his fingers, making them look both graceful and hard. "You just cooked the best meal I've ever had. You are *not* doing the dishes, too."

She stepped back carefully and attempted to get a grip on her libido.

One kiss, she thought, *would be so nice. Just one hot kiss, hard arms around me. Passion. Heat. God, it would feel so nice.*

She sighed. Steve looked over at her and smiled.

But not with Steve, she told herself, moving away to one of the island bar stools. *Definitely not with Steve. The last thing you need is a one-night stand with a bartender. Or worse, a relationship with someone so different from what you want. If you want to be touched by someone, wait for your date.*

But the idea of P.B. was as appealing as trying to eat another piece of cheese. She was stuffed and tired and pleasantly hazy from the wine. And Steve was right here . . .

She pushed the leftover brie away and picked up a wineglass. She was fairly certain it was hers. She tipped the contents into her mouth and watched Steve's back.

"You're doing a pretty efficient job there, Steve. Somebody raised you right."

She could see him laugh even as she heard it, his head dipping slightly and his back moving under his shirt, but he didn't turn around. She smiled.

"I'll take that as a compliment," he said. "You see, I have hidden assets as an employee."

There, she pointed out to herself. *Right there, even he's saying he's an employee. And boss-employee relationships don't work. Especially when it happens only because the boss is horny and the employee handy.*

"So in a pinch I can use you as a dishwasher," she said, thinking, *It's a pinch now, can I use you for something else?* This thought actually made her giggle.

Steve turned around, a half smile on his face. "What's going on back there?"

She sighed and put a hand over her mouth. "I'm sorry. I seem to have had a bit too much to drink."

"Join the club." He turned back to the dishes. "Good thing I don't have to get up in the morning."

She sat in silence and watched him work for a while, alternately marshalling her fantasies and letting them run free. She felt so relaxed and happy at the moment she almost couldn't hang on to the idea that anything she did now would be wrong.

She'd gotten through a vigorous year of schooling. Made the move from New York. Broken off completely with Martin. Bought this house and started a restaurant. Or rather, almost started it. But here she was, back home with friends. She'd had a lovely evening with people who wanted nothing from her. Everything so far had worked out. She should celebrate that.

She smiled to herself and folded her arms in front of her. She was happy, she thought. What a lovely feeling that was.

Steve finished the dishes, just as she was coming to this conclusion, and he turned from the sink, wiping his hands on a dish towel.

She even had a handsome man in her kitchen. What could be better?

"I think that's it." He looked at her warmly. "I better go, too. Let you get some sleep."

"Hmm, yes." She rose from the stool as he moved into the living room.

At the door, he stopped. She stopped too, maybe a little closer than she might have a bottle of wine or two ago. Just slightly inside his personal space.

"Thanks for dinner. It was . . ." He looked down at her and she could tell he was aware of how close they were. "Amazing."

"Thanks for coming." She smiled slightly, let her eyes drift to his lips. "And for cleaning up. There's nothing like a man who cleans."

She was close enough to smell the soap he used. To hear his breathing. To feel the slight breeze of it on her cheek.

Slowly, she moved her gaze from his lips back to his eyes and saw the heat in them. Her lips curved a bit more. She would see if he did something, if he made a move. If he did . . . well, maybe just one kiss . . . a kiss didn't have to mean anything . . .

"Okay," he said softly.

She watched the pulsing of the artery in his neck, thought about how it would feel to put her lips on it.

She was incorrigible, she thought. But God, she was *hungry*.

She looked back up into his face and saw an answering hunger there. So when he bent down to kiss her cheek, she shifted her face, ever so slightly, at the last minute so he caught the corner of her mouth.

He drew slightly back, just enough for them to focus on each other's eyes, and stayed there an eternal moment. Roxanne held her breath under his assessing gaze. Then, when she couldn't take it another second, she moved forward that bare inch and touched her lips to his again.

She almost felt the *whoosh* of the genie leaving the bottle.

Steve stepped closer and put an arm around her waist, cinching her in tight to his body. She raised her hands to his shoulders and her mouth opened under his. Their tongues found each other and mated, their lips moving in synch, a dance, an age-old interplay of heat and sex and desire.

And restraint.

Steve pulled back first, his expression intense, his eyes searching.

Roxanne couldn't hold his gaze. She put a hand to her lips and tried to slow her breathing. "Thank you," she said, apropos of nothing, in a near whisper.

He hesitated a fraction of a second, then answered, "Good night."

7

Bar Special
Scotch Sling — for that unexpected injury
Scotch, soda, lemon peel

"How come you sound so muffled?" Steve's sister, Dana, asked.

"Because I have a pillow over my head." Steve pushed the pillow off and readjusted the phone receiver at his ear.

"What are you doing still in bed? It's almost noon."

He could hear Dana doing something in the background. No doubt cleaning or cooking or doing something for one of the kids. She had a husband and three children and never seemed to stop moving.

"I'm getting over one of the stupidest nights of my life," he said, with probably too much honesty. But what the heck, Dana almost always got his secrets out of him anyway, and he usually felt better after the swift shot upside the head she gave him for them.

"Oh no. What have you done now?" She was stern, but he could hear the grim smile in her voice.

"Hell, I don't know. I was stupid, that's all. There's something wrong with me. If there's something I shouldn't do, I do it."

"Oh good God, you didn't get back with Lia, did you? If you ask me, that girl is the reason you've never had a decent relationship."

Steve turned over onto his side and looked at the digital clock—11:57. "Well, I didn't ask you, but now that it's out there, why do you say that?"

Dana sighed. "Because she's there for you. You need sex, she's there. You need some kind of female companionship, she's there. She's not perfect, but she's *there*. And that satisfies you enough that you never look for anything different."

He scoffed. "That shows how much *you* know. If that were true I wouldn't have done the stupid thing last night."

"Which was . . . ?" She sounded intrigued.

It was his turn to sigh. He almost didn't know how to describe what had happened. On the one hand, it was simple. He'd *kissed* her. But on the other, it made absolutely no sense at all. For no earthly reason, without any anticipation of doing it beforehand, he'd kissed her.

What the hell had he been thinking?

From the headboard, the pillow dropped back onto his head and he let it stay. "I think I hit on my new boss."

Dana let out a burst of air. "*What?* The one P.B.'s going out with?"

Steve frowned and put his hand over his eyes. "He just has a date with her, that's all. It's not like she's his girlfriend or anything."

Still, the feeling burning his skin was shame. As unintentional as it was, he'd undercut his buddy. P.B. may be a lot of things, but he'd been a friend of Steve's for a lot of years.

Dana was still sputtering on the phone. "Oh yeah, he just has a date with her. Nothing to keep you from hitting on her. So, what—how—what did you do? How in the world did it happen?"

Steve chuckled wryly. "Well, she looked good, better than usual."

Dana inhaled sharply, in preparation for, he could tell, giving him hell.

"Just kidding," he said quickly, laughing. "She always looks fabulous, it's one of her biggest flaws. But last night she looked . . . accessible. Or something. Smiling. She has this great smile. Real first rate, when she decides to trot it out. And last night for the first time it seemed really, I don't know, easy. Uncalculated."

"So, you, what? Asked her out? Pinched her ass? What?"

"I kissed her."

"You kissed her," Dana repeated, dry as dust.

"And her friend was there," Steve continued, needing to explain, if only to make himself understand, "not when I kissed her. Before. This guy Skip. And he was funny and kind of laid back. Made us all laugh. Got rid of some of Roxanne's usual edginess."

"So, you kissed her."

"I guess I was lulled into a sense of security. Yeah, that's what it was. She made this incredible meal, we had a lot of wine."

"So . . ."

"I kissed her."

Dana laughed. "How'd she take it?"

Steve thought, remembering the moment at the door, when Roxanne had stood so close to him that he could smell her perfume, or maybe it was just her shampoo. In any case, she was *close*, with that little knowing smile. She had done it on purpose. Hadn't she?

He simply could not fathom why she would.

But, she had turned her head for his kiss, hadn't she? Turned her head at the last minute to capture his lips as he went for her cheek.

It just didn't make sense. She wouldn't do that. She was control personified. Coolness incarnate. She had the world by the balls. Didn't she?

Who knew? He sure couldn't figure her out when he was having a hard time understanding himself.

"She didn't slap me or anything, so I guess she took it okay. Hard to say. I was so surprised by it myself, I can't imagine what she was thinking." He scratched the side of his face and pushed the pillow back again. "Honestly Dana, for the life of me I can't figure out why I did it. I was leaning in to kiss her cheek as I was leaving, which was weird in itself, and then it just . . . happened."

"But, you were there for dinner? She invited you to dinner? That must have meant she was interested." She paused. "Except she's your boss. That's not good."

He grimaced. "Her friend invited me, really."

"The guy? Is he gay?"

"No. He's just one of those guys. We ran into each other at the grocery store. They were buying stuff for dinner and he said I should come. It was obviously a whim. And she didn't look too into it. I tried to get out of it but this guy Skip was pretty relentless. But then, we . . . I guess we had a good time."

Good enough that she would need—or expect—a kiss good night? No. *What had he been thinking?* But there it was. He'd accidentally kissed her, and he wasn't even a kiss-on-the-cheek kind of guy.

It was a damn fine kiss, though. Damn fine.

"I have to say, Steve,"—Dana's voice was matter-of-fact—"I think you might have taken something the wrong way. From what you've said about this woman, it doesn't sound like she'd want to carry on with someone she works with."

"We're not *carrying on*, Dana. It was a *moment*. A really strange moment." He pushed himself up in bed and leaned back on the headboard.

"You sure it wasn't just a forbidden moment? You know how you are, Steve. You always want what you think you can't have."

"Thanks for the pop psychology, Sis. Really clarifying."

"Glad you liked it."

"I'm serious. Something weird happened right at the door, as I was leaving. She was standing really close and, I don't know, I think she went for the kiss. I can't imagine why, but she did. It was like there was some kind of weird, gravitational pull or . . . or . . ."

"Destiny," Dana said dramatically.

"Yeah right. That's the word I was looking for," Steve said dryly. "And now I'm destined to get fired."

The Call Waiting beeped.

"Steve—"

"Wait. That's my other line. Hang on a sec, can you, Dana?"

"Actually no. As riveted as I am by this turn of events, I have to go get Jamie. Call me later, though, okay? I'm going to mull this over and come up with the answer."

"You do that." He pushed the flash button on the phone, finally awake and realizing it was nearly noon. He had work to do. He couldn't lie in bed all day lamenting the most stupid thing he'd done in years.

"Yeah," he said into the receiver.

"Where the hell are you?" P.B., too loud and sounding annoyed, spoke from what sounded like an echo chamber.

"Where the hell are *you*?" Steve rubbed a hand through his hair, massaging his scalp.

"I'm at the gym, where *you're* supposed to be. Remember you said you'd fill in for Larry?"

Steve closed his eyes, remembering some vague conversation about a handball game.

"Today?" Steve rubbed his eyes. He couldn't see P.B. today. P.B., who would want to talk about his date this week, with Roxanne Rayeaux.

"Yes, today, genius. Right now. Jesus, what the hell have you been doing?" The sound of tennis shoes on a wooden gym floor squeaked through the receiver.

"I, uh, overslept. Sorry, Peeb. Can't we just do it another—?"

"Oh come on, you're five minutes away. Drag your ass outa bed and get over here. It'll do you good. What'd you do last night, see Lia again?"

Steve sighed. "No, nothing like that. I'm just tired. All right, let me get my stuff together. I'll be there in ten minutes."

"Great, I'll reserve the court for another hour, if I can."

Steve hung up the phone, trying several times to set it straight in the cradle.

So now he had to go face P.B.

He wasn't a fool. He wasn't going to tell him what happened with Roxanne—especially since he was absolutely certain it wouldn't happen again. In fact, he wouldn't be surprised if Roxanne didn't want him to work there now.

Not that she'd fire him, he thought. No, she'd just pull him aside and talk to him in that low, sultry voice, making him understand that it would be better for both of them if he didn't take the job after all. Surely he could see that, couldn't he?

For some reason, he could picture the scene perfectly.

He got out of bed, his bare feet hitting the cold wood floor. He wondered if the wood floor in Roxanne's bedroom was as cold and doubted it. She probably had rugs. And comforters on the bed. Pillows, lots of pillows. Maybe a canopy. He pictured her hair spread long and lacy on a white pillowcase, those dark eyes half closed and catlike . . .

Steve swore. This was nuts. He opened a dresser

drawer, pulled out gym shorts and slammed the drawer shut. Opened another, pulled out socks and slammed it. Opened a third, grabbed a T-shirt and slammed it, just as the phone rang again.

It was Dana, from her cell phone. "I just thought of an important question."

"What's that?" He sat on the side of the bed, pushed the receiver between his cheek and shoulder, and unballed the socks with both hands.

"When you kissed her, your *boss*, you randy dog, did she kiss you back?"

Steve stopped, one sock in each hand, and let his arms drop to his sides. "Yeah," he said slowly. He took the receiver in his left hand and straightened his neck, remembering the way her lips had opened under his, the way her hands had taken the front of his shirt in a tight, unequivocal grip. "Yeah, actually, she did."

He frowned. His body had responded so powerfully, so instantly, he'd been shocked at himself. Which is when—and why—he'd stopped, as if awakened from some truly bizarre dream. One you had no idea where it came from.

And at the end—it was coming back to him now—had she really said "Thank you"? Or had he just dreamed that too? At that point his mind was so blown he couldn't trust himself to remember any of it right.

"Huh," Dana said, road noise washing white in the background.

"Yeah," Steve said, "huh."

Roxanne was thrilled Monsieur Girmond was finally arriving. Ever since she'd met him—eight years ago in his restaurant in New York—he'd been like a father to her. She had been fairly close to her own father when he was alive—the whole family, she, her sister, brother and father, had united to deal with her mother, their feared and fearless leader—but her father had never been as protective and nurturing as M. Girmond.

When she met him, she'd been lunching at La Finesse with her agent, a fast-talking, know-it-all deal-maker named Derek Gold, picking through a dressing-less salad when the chef had come to their table. Apparently he knew Derek—as all of New York City seemed to—and wanted to know why he was lunching with a beautiful girl and only buying her a salad. Roxanne explained that she was a model and had to watch what she ate, though she eyed the food around her covetously.

M. Girmond immediately declared this a crime, and vowed that the next time she came in he would prepare for her a feast fit for a queen but that would add not an ounce of weight to her peerless frame.

She'd laughed, embarrassed, and had not taken him seriously. But the next time she'd gone in, as it happened about two weeks later, again with Derek, M. Girmond prepared a salad with a light vinegar dressing, followed by sole on watercress, followed by a tiny scoop of fresh homemade sorbet. When she'd gone back to the kitchen to thank him, he'd insisted she come in at least once a week so he could keep her healthy. It was one thing to be skinny, he said, but another to be sick. He would keep her thin and glowing, he promised, if she promised to come "take his light offerings off his hands."

They had become fast friends. Roxanne had often

thought it lucky that she'd met M. Girmond when she had, before she'd been in New York too long. Before her modeling career had taken off and she'd stopped trusting anyone. If she had met him after five years instead of two, for example, she would never have gone back to the restaurant, figuring he wanted something from her she would not want to give.

Then, years later, when she told him she was giving up modeling to go to the CIA for a year, he confided that he was thinking of retiring. La Finesse was too big, New York too busy, and he missed his daughters, who now lived in D.C. Roxanne said she was thinking of going back to D.C., too, and would love to open a pastry shop. After much discussion they realized that together they could start a French restaurant that would accommodate both of their desires while remaining small enough to keep them both sane.

If she had gotten nothing else from her years in New York—and she had, of course—she was glad to have met M. Girmond.

He was coming to the restaurant at noon and they were to discuss the kitchen, the menu and the staff. She had been consulting him all along on the renovations and equipment purchasing via email and fax, and now it was time for him to put his stamp on things.

Roxanne was relieved. So much of running a restaurant lay on the chef's shoulders, and M. Girmond was experienced enough to handle this with ease. Shifting some of the burden onto him would be a welcome relief now.

She unlocked the restaurant door from the street and entered the small front foyer. It smelled like fresh paint and new varnish. She inhaled it deeply, thinking, *I've still done this right, whatever else I might have screwed up.*

She pushed the image of Steve behind the now-empty bar from her head. She had to focus. She didn't have time for adolescent hormonal reactions to men. Particularly not men on her staff.

The decorators had done a wonderful job on the small space, successfully transforming it from a gritty college-style pub to a quaint, warm restaurant. The bar gleamed in the unlit room, ambient light from the windows glancing off its surface and making the copper on the lamps hanging from the ceiling glow.

The exposed brick walls gave the place a close feeling that was warmed by the rich wood of the bar and tables and the light French country fabrics on the chairs and window treatments. Individual lamps hung over each table, and plants, low screens and a few carefully chosen metal sculptures broke the room up into separate areas where diners could eat and converse in relative privacy.

Roxanne was extremely pleased with the look.

She moved into the dining room and sat in a chair near the fireplace. It was cold, of course, but she imagined the roaring fire she would ensure was tended nightly in the winter months. She stared into its imaginary depths and thought about what she'd done last night.

Her impulse was to believe she'd made a fool of herself. For a stupid, stupid reason. But she fought that. No, she understood why she'd done what she'd done, and it certainly wasn't a crime. She was a woman nearing thirty, no longer a green girl with illusions of romance, and she had, well, needs. Physical hungers. She'd been without a man for over a year—though

Martin had shown up at the CIA one night and very nearly convinced her he was ready to commit to her—and she wanted one. It was as simple as that.

Her stupidity lay in choosing Steve. He was her employee, and getting involved with him, even just sexually, would be a distraction on the job she could not afford.

She needed to be careful. If she wanted a convenient relationship, she needed it to be separate from her job, separate from the place she'd created here. Restaurants were a small, small world when it came to relationships. Not to mention that she didn't want a relationship with Steve. She wanted someone with class and stability, someone who'd be interested in the symphony, plays at the Kennedy Center, dinner at the Willard. Someone who knew what he wanted from life and how to get it.

The bottom line was, she wanted someone who liked the same things she did, wanted to do what she liked to do. She had no idea what she and Steve would find to do together.

Other than the obvious.

A hot flash of hunger seared her as she remembered last night's kiss. They both had enjoyed doing *that*, she thought wryly.

The question was, what did she do now that she'd cracked open that can of worms? Talk to him about it? He wasn't exactly the easiest person to talk to. Most of the time he seemed to deliberately misunderstand her. But then, subtlety wasn't likely to work either.

"*Bonjour, mon ange!*" M. Girmond's voice rolled into the room like a warm breeze on a cool day.

Roxanne turned to the door and smiled, rising to her feet. "Monsieur Girmond."

He was a tall man but he gave more an impression of roundness, with a round balding head, round glasses, a wide girth and thick, sausage-fingered hands. The next most noticeable thing about him was that he was always smiling. When he ran La Finesse, people were constantly calling looking for work with him because not only was he one of the best chefs in town, he was also one of the most liked.

She walked toward him, her hands outstretched. He took them in his callused ones and they kissed both cheeks, European style.

"I'm so glad you're finally here," she said, unable to dim the smile on her face. "How is the move going? Are you all here?"

"Ah, *oui*. It goes very well, very well, *mon trésor*. And you, how are you living here back home? You feel good, *oui*? You look *magnifique*." He held one of her hands out and stepped back, as if they'd just performed a dance move, to survey her from head to foot.

"*Merci beaucoup*." She inclined her head. "The move has gone fine. I'm still adjusting, I think, to being here, but I'm all unpacked. And I'm glad I did it. It's been good to see old friends again."

She thought about last night's dinner, how relaxed she'd felt, but the memory was ruined by its ending. Would she feel so bad, she wondered, if she'd impulsively kissed someone who did not work for her?

"And this place," M. Girmond said, walking into the center of the small dining room and turning in a slow circle, *"c'est parfait! Bien joue!* I feel that I am back in Provence, in the house of my *grande-mère*. Lovely, lovely."

Roxanne clutched her hands together in front of her and scanned the room again. "Do you really like it? There were so many decisions to make, I second-guessed myself every step of the way."

"It is perfect." M. Girmond faced her again with a smile. He took her clasped hands together in his and separated her tensely entwined fingers. "No more worries, *oui*? You and I, we do this to escape such things. This is *un petit restaurant*. Simple! We will enjoy ourselves. Have fun."

Roxanne felt as if a huge weight were being lifted from her chest and she inhaled what felt like the first truly unencumbered breath she'd taken in weeks.

"I know," she said on a long exhale. "Yes, you're right. Everything is fine now that you're here."

As she looked up into his face, her eyes were caught by a shape in the front window. She shifted her gaze only to have it land on Steve's as he peeked inside.

He looked as startled as she did and she raised her hand in an awkward wave. Steve did the same, then turned quickly away. He jogged across the street and down the sidewalk, out of sight.

"Who was that?" M. Girmond asked, turning his eyes back to her face, which was much hotter than it had been before seeing Steve.

"That was our bartender. Steve Serrano." She brushed the hair from her forehead and ran her fingers through it over the top of her head, looking toward the bar. "You'll meet him soon. He also lives upstairs, on the top floor."

At M. Girmond's silence, she looked at him and saw

his brows had risen. A small, very French smile curved his lips and he stroked his chin with one thick but gentle hand.

"I see," he said slowly.

She wasn't sure if it was just her guilty conscience, but she was afraid he really did see.

"Okay—*oof*." P.B. slapped the handball with a gloved palm and crab-jumped back to the center of the court. "I've made reservations at Le Gaulois, think she'll like that?"

Steve returned the ball, forcing P.B. to the back corner and took his place in the middle. "Sure."

P.B. lumbered to the corner, hit the ball and then grunted as his shoulder hit the wall. "What do you think we should talk about? I mean . . ."

He returned Steve's volley.

". . . what's she interested in?"

Steve slammed the ball to the crease where front wall met floor and it rolled off, impossible to return. He turned a triumphant grin on P.B. "Game!"

P.B. put his hands on his hips and panted. "Damn, Serrano. For a guy who doesn't exercise, you seem mighty cool."

Steve rolled his shoulders back a couple times and dipped his head from side to side, loosening up. "I exercise. Every day, practically."

"Bullshit." P.B. leaned over, hands on his knees.

Steve jogged in place. "No shit. I run and have free weights in my apartment. Come on, one more game, Blue Boy. How you gonna catch the bad guys if you can't play three straight handball games?"

"Give me a minute." P.B. straightened. "I want to know about Roxanne."

Steve made an annoyed face. "What makes you think I know anything?"

"Well for one thing, you had dinner at her place last night." P.B. wiped his forehead with a sweatbanded wrist, his eyes tight on Steve. "I still don't understand how you finagled that."

"Gimme a break. I didn't finagle anything. I was forced into it."

P.B. wagged a finger at him. "Trying to upstage me to win that bet? It ain't gonna work, compadre."

Steve laughed cynically. "You and your bet. Okay, I'll tell you what I observed last night. She's got class. She has posters from the New York City Ballet on her walls. She plays classical music. Bach, I think, last night. She speaks some French, though it might just be menu French for all I know. She reads, has tons of books on her shelves. Ah . . ." He stretched one arm overhead and did a side bend to stay warm, thinking about Roxanne Rayeaux's apartment. He was surprised how much he could recall about it. "She's got a knack for making a room comfortable. Good design sense, I guess. Likes rich colors. Is good with plants. And, most important to you, she loosens up nicely with a bottle of wine."

He tried not to imagine Roxanne leaning into P.B. the way she had leaned into him. Tried not to picture her lips parting and P.B. taking advantage of it. Tried not to see her lithe body being swallowed up by P.B.'s big muscular one.

He jogged in place again. "Come on, let's play."

P.B. stood with one hand on his hip, watching him. "That's a lot to remember."

Steve waved a hand in his direction. "Take notes."

"No, I mean for you. You seem to have been paying pretty close attention."

Steve shrugged. "I'm an observant guy. Now come on. Your serve." He trotted to center court and bounced on the balls of his feet.

"Tell me one more thing."

Steve sighed and dropped his hands, turning. "What?"

"What did you guys talk about last night?"

"I don't know. Regular stuff. Where're you from? Where'd you go to school? What did you do before? That kind of thing. The kind of thing *you* should ask her. Be interested."

"Hey, you don't have to tell me how to *date*, big guy. I *know* how to date. I just want to know what she's interested in so I can be prepared."

"Oh, so, what, you gonna go home and listen to some Bach?"

P.B. grinned. "Got any I can borrow?"

"Yeah, right. And I'll lend you my tape of *Swan Lake*, too. Come to think of it, I do have one of those NFL tapes set to ballet music."

P.B. snorted. "I've got that one, too. That's pretty funny. Maybe she'd like that."

Steve just turned and gave him a deadpan look over his shoulder. "Come on, let's play."

"One more thing."

He turned back. "You said that a minute ago."

"I mean it this time." P.B. tossed him the ball. "You get a look at her bedroom?"

Steve crossed his arms over his chest and tried to look stern, but he couldn't help wondering if he might have been *able* to see her bedroom last night, if he'd reacted differently to the kiss. If he hadn't stopped it, if he'd said something other than "Good night."

His gut clenched.

He scowled. "No, I didn't see her bedroom. Why?"

P.B. gave him a shit-eating grin and said, "Just want to know what color flowers to bring, 'cause I'll be carrying 'em in there at the end of the night."

Steve dropped the ball and slammed it, hard, into the front wall. It went untouched by P.B. An unreturnable serve.

8

Bar Special
Rum/Brandy Flip—first one, then the other
Rum or cognac, bar syrup, nutmeg, 1 egg

Roxanne must have been crazy to have agreed to a date two days before the opening of Chez Soi. Especially a date with someone like P.B. From the first moments of the evening it was obvious he had no desire to talk about the restaurant, or indeed anything but himself. Not that Roxanne blamed him for this; she was sure the restaurant wasn't all that interesting if you weren't involved. And since it had been about all she'd had on her mind for months, she found she was something of a one-note conversationalist.

During dinner a lovely French country meal at Le Gaulois, she'd had a hard time not examining the food and pointing out how they'd cooked it, what was in it, and how Chez Soi would be either the same or different, just as good or better.

P.B. listened with patience at first, making the effort to look interested and nodding along, asking the occasional question. But after a while he'd begun to interrupt her and soon was talking pretty much nonstop about himself.

Surprisingly, Roxanne found this something of a relief. She didn't want to have to think up other things to say about her life when all she could think about was her current project—and by *project* she meant the entire move from New York and the subsequent shift in her way of thinking.

She was busy breaking old habits—like thinking about how she looked all the time and watching every little thing she ate. She was relieved to be out of the pressure cooker of the high-fashion scene, and had given up the destructive pattern of alternately fitting in and kicking Martin out of her life. Now she was concentrating hard on making new habits, healthy ones.

So letting P.B. ramble on about "life on the job" and "collaring perps" was fine with her. And he was interesting. She'd never known a cop personally before. It sounded like a world unto itself.

The only problem was, he wouldn't let the evening end. She had unfortunately started out the date tired from a long day in the kitchen with M. Girmond and overindulging at dinner had only left her sleepier. But after dinner, P.B. had insisted on taking her to Murphy's Pub, his favorite bar now that Charters was gone.

Murphy's was a lively place with lots of people and good music, and because P.B. knew almost everyone who worked there they were still able to score a seat at the bar. Though it was freezing outside, the crowd was so tight and the thermostat had been cranked up so high to compensate that after about ten minutes Roxanne had to take off her sweater.

She pulled it over her head, trying hard not to elbow anyone next to her, and shook her hair loose, glancing at P.B. just in time to see his eyes jerk up from her breasts. It startled her, the suggestiveness of his gaze.

He leaned close, his breath fanning her cheek, and grinned. "Can I help you with that?"

She brought the sweater down between them, forcing him back a few inches, and pulled her hands from the sleeves. With an impersonal smile she said, "No thanks."

He backed off. "Hey, I heard you had dinner with Steve the other night." He raised a pint glass of Guinness to his lips, his eyes steady on her.

Roxanne folded the sweater in her lap and rested her fingers against her glass of wine but did not pick it up. "I did, yes. Skip and I ran into him at Whole Foods. We saved him from a night of carry-out."

"Hah! Good old Steve and his carry-out. That's what he said." P.B.'s light eyes were on her with a small smile that made her wonder just what else Steve had told him about the evening. "He's a pretty good guy, Steve is. But we're all still waiting on him to grow up, if you know what I mean."

"We are?"

He shrugged one shoulder. "Sure. I'm pretty close to his family and I know his sister wishes he'd get a real job and settle down. For a long time now he's been, you know, pretty stuck."

Roxanne stifled a yawn. "You mean stuck in his job?"

"Yeah and, you know, in his life. He doesn't have much drive. No ambition. I tried to get him on the force once." P.B. boomed a laugh. "Said he didn't even want to attempt it. He was happy doing what he was doing."

Roxanne tried to picture Steve's lanky frame and general air of insouciance contained in a police uniform. "No, I can't really see him as a cop."

"Me neither, tell you the truth. He doesn't have the right attitude. But he needed some direction and I thought he could cut it, make it through training. Maybe make something of himself, you know?"

"You don't think he's made anything of himself?"

P.B. tilted his head and gave her a benevolent smile. "Don't get me wrong. I think Steve's a great guy. But let's face it, he could be doing something a helluva lot better than bartending. I mean, where's that gonna get him?"

Roxanne nodded, not really liking the fact that she agreed with this. Or maybe she just didn't like talking about Steve with P.B. She still hadn't talked to him about the kiss they'd shared and was feeling strange about what he must be thinking. It had only been a couple days, but she felt more and more strongly that she needed to define it for both of them as something that could not be repeated. But the two times she'd gone upstairs to knock on his door he hadn't been home.

Or he hadn't been answering.

"What about all that history he studies?" Roxanne asked. "Does he do anything with that?"

P.B. grinned. "Hell, yeah. He impresses the hell out of women at the bar. Makes him sound smart, I think."

"Surely that's not the only reason he does it. He even

goes down to the Library of Congress. He must be doing something with it."

P.B. shrugged, careless. "It's just a hobby. I mean, what's he gonna do with history, huh? It's not like he's gonna become a professor or anything."

"He could go to law school," Roxanne mused. Would that make him seem more eligible, she wondered. Was she really just all about careers?

No, she knew it was more than that. It was a guy with direction. Purpose. Somebody looking for some meaning in life.

"Yeah, right," P.B. scoffed. "Steve, a lawyer. He'd be about as cutthroat as Santa Claus."

"Santa decides who's naughty and who's nice," she pointed out.

P.B.'s eyes gleamed. "And are you naughty, Roxanne?"

Roxanne resisted the urge to roll her eyes. Instead she shifted her eyes away from him and said, "Well, all I know is Steve's making good money and he seems happy enough. Isn't that all any of us can ask? To be happy in our work?"

"Sure." He smiled at her, his eyelids half lowered. "I like the way you think, Roxanne. You're generous, you know that?" He let that statement hang a moment, while Roxanne took a sip of her wine. "And who could blame Steve for being happy? The way things were at Charters, back when it was popular, he was like a rock star. You know how the bartenders at hot spots are. He got the girls, made the bucks, partied after work and slept all day. Great life for a twenty-five-year-old. But Steve's thirty now. How's he gonna feel in five years?

Or ten? Permanently hungover, that's how. Hungover by *life*."

"Hmm." Roxanne let her eyes scan P.B.'s solid frame as he looked off down the bar. He waved to another friend—he had many here—and laughed at something they said or did. Roxanne was too tired to turn around and look.

But P.B. was right. Steve was the kind of guy with a lot of charisma, the kind that made him a social success early in life. But it took drive in addition to charisma to really get somewhere. And it took a lot of hard work.

"So what's your goal, P.B.?" she asked him, forcing herself to remember with whom she was on a date. And as dates went, she could do worse than P.B. He'd taken her out for a nice dinner.

"Me?" He looked delighted at the question. "I'm working toward detective. Then, what the hell, maybe chief. I tell you, I got a helluva lot more ideas for running that place than the current chief. He's all right, but he doesn't think, you know? I'm always thinking." He tapped a finger to his head and looked at her intently, as if she might not have understood just what he meant.

"Sure," she said, holding back another yawn as if her life depended on it. "I can tell that about you."

And she could. But she would have used the word *calculating* instead of *thinking*. Something about him struck her as very shrewd.

"So, Roxanne." He said her name in a half growl and grinned at her. "I like saying your name. Rrrrrroxanne. Roxie."

She smiled, wishing she were home in bed. Alone.

He leaned one hand on the bar beside her and let his

hip touch her legs. "I was looking in the paper and saw the National Symphony's playing some Bach in a couple weeks. Wanna go? Bach's one of my favorites."

"Really?" Roxanne couldn't hide her surprise.

"Yeah, I like all that classical stuff." He waved a hand nonchalantly but kept his eyes expectantly on her face. "Whaddya say?"

The last thing she would have guessed was that P.B. was a classical music fan. But then, ever since Martin, she'd had to doubt all her perceptions about men. And this was just more evidence of how off her instincts could be.

She straightened on the bar stool and took a deep breath in an attempt to wake up. "Well, it sounds great, but I'll have to let you know. I'm not sure how the restaurant will be doing, but it's going to keep me really busy, especially at first. These things take up a lot of time. And I mean *a lot.*"

P.B. sank down on an elbow, bringing himself even closer to her, and fingered the ends of one lock of her hair. His hand lingered close to her breast. "Aw, come on." He gave her a boyish smile. "It's just a couple hours, one evening. I'll make sure it's a night you're closed."

She was sorry now she'd told him they were only going to be open Wednesday through Saturday at first. But then she wondered why she was sorry—an evening at the symphony sounded fabulous. Just the kind of thing she'd been missing without Martin. But . . . with P.B.?

"Okay," she said, regretting it instantly.

He beamed and clutched her upper arm in one big square hand. "Great. That's great."

"But, can I let you know when it would be best?" She was desperate to backpedal. From the look on P.B.'s face it seemed he thought she'd just agreed to far more than a night at the symphony. "I just know these first few weeks are going to be hell. Exhausting hell. And speaking of that"—she looked pointedly at her watch—"I really should be going. I have so much to do tomorrow."

P.B. stroked a hand down her upper arm familiarly. "Sure, Babe. Whatever you say. I'm ready to blow this joint, too."

Roxanne felt simultaneously drawn to and repelled by the contact. Her body ached for a soft touch—she'd always been very physical in her relationships—but her desire was different from what she'd experienced the other night with Steve. Then she had felt overwhelmed with need, and blind to the consequences. With P.B., all of her senses rebelled against the idea of him touching her.

They drove the short blocks back to Roxanne's building. P.B. pulled his Chevy Suburban into the back alley and left it in the spot where Steve usually parked his truck, as well as part of the space next to it. Getting out, he looked displeased as she opened her own door and let herself out her side, just as he had earlier in the evening. And just as he had earlier in the evening, he said, "I was going to get that for you."

"That's all right." She moved toward the back door, rummaging through her purse for her keys, and turned when she reached the threshold. "Thanks so much, P.B. I had a really nice evening." She smiled and held out her hand.

P.B. looked taken aback, then covered it quickly with

a smile and took her hand, cradling it in both of his. "I was going to walk you to your door."

"This *is* my door." She laughed lightly, hoping to sound less off-putting than she knew she was being.

He paused, his expression skeptical. "So it is." He lifted her fingers to his lips and kissed them.

Involuntarily, her fingers clenched, more out of a desire to make a fist and pull away than anything else. But P.B. misunderstood and tightened his grip. He tried to draw her closer.

She resisted.

"You are . . ." He growled low in his throat and smiled as if they were playing a game. "Irresistible. *Rrroxanne*. Now come on, all I want's a hug." He pulled on her hand again companionably. "I had a nice night, too."

She was being a jerk, she thought, and let him pull her into his bearlike embrace. There was actually something somewhat comforting about it. He was big and solidly built, and he smelled clean, like laundry detergent. She patted his back with one hand, her face squished against his chest. But the hug went on just a tad too long.

And then a car's headlights lit up the alley. Roxanne pulled her head back enough to see Steve's truck round the corner from the street.

P.B. didn't let her go immediately, but leaned down and gave her a solid, closed-lip kiss on the mouth before stepping slowly back.

More than enough time, Roxanne was sure, for Steve—who was vainly looking for his parking spot—to see them and suspect that they'd been doing more than sharing one reluctant kiss.

Roxanne's face burned with humiliation. Nothing

like being caught kissing one man by the man you'd kissed just days earlier.

What in the world would Steve think of her? And what would he tell the rest of the staff? They'd been bought by a slut, that's what.

Steve pulled his truck into the half spot next to P.B.'s Suburban. The SUV dwarfed the pickup like a territorial Rottweiler standing over a friendly spaniel.

The door opened and Roxanne caught a glimpse of Steve's tousled hair in the cab light before turning to unlock the door to the building.

"I forgot, was this date night?" Steve's voice sent a shiver up her spine and she was finally glad P.B. was there, if only because he could talk to Steve and she could beat it upstairs.

She called good night to the two of them as P.B. was shaking Steve's hand and, ignoring what sounded like a protest from P.B., she trotted up the steps to her apartment.

She realized as she was sighing and closing the door behind her that she'd left her sweater in P.B.'s car, but that would just have to wait. She could get it from him when they went to the symphony. *If* they went to the symphony. Heck, she didn't really need that sweater back.

She took off her coat and hung it in the closet. The symphony. Why had she said yes? It didn't matter if her instincts were all off about men. That didn't mean she had to go out with guys she wasn't attracted to. It just meant she had to be careful of the ones she *was* attracted to.

And she had no business thinking about *men* right now anyway. She had a restaurant to open. This was it, the culmination of months of work, her lifelong ambition coming true before her very eyes. And she was putzing around with a couple of unsuitable guys who were nothing but an unwanted distraction.

She needed to focus. They were opening in two days. No doubt there'd be some kinks to work out in both the menu and the service, too, so it wouldn't run smoothly at first.

It was exciting and stressful and scary. All the things dating was, so she certainly didn't need *both*.

She started down the hall toward the bathroom, anxious to get all her makeup off and crawl into bed, into oblivion. But she couldn't stop thinking about all she needed to do. Her mind spun with excuses to get out of going out with P.B. again—too busy, too tired, menu problems, dough preparation, she couldn't get involved right now.

And when she tried to turn her mind from that it reeled over to what she should say to Steve. I was crazy? Temporary insanity? I kiss everyone like that after dinner? (Except P.B.)

She was halfway to the bathroom when someone knocked on the door.

Roxanne's stomach flipped with dread. P.B., she'd bet. Steve probably let him in and he was here for a better good-night kiss, at her *real* door.

She walked back across the living room and opened the door to see Steve, holding her sweater.

"Delivery," he said dryly, holding it out in front of him.

"Oh. Thanks." She took it from him, concentrating on smoothing the wrinkles and folding it neatly. She couldn't meet his eyes, she was so embarrassed.

"You guys have a good time?"

She glanced up, his face was bland. She had no idea what he was thinking, but she knew it couldn't be good.

"It was fine. We . . . just ate." She waved a hand to encompass everything else.

They stood in awkward silence a long minute. Was he waiting for an explanation? She knew he deserved one, but she couldn't think how to begin. It was crazy to even find herself in this situation. It was like middle school all over again—the awkwardness, the uncertainty, the boys.

"Look, about the other night," he began.

"I know. I'm so sorry about that," the words rushed out on an exhale. "It's just—"

"*You're* sorry?"

Her eyes flicked to his. He was genuinely surprised.

"Well, yes, I, uh," she said haltingly. "I shouldn't have . . . well, you know . . ."

She *had* kissed him. She remembered that. She'd turned her head when he'd obviously been going for her cheek. Then she'd leaned forward and put her lips on his again. She had done it and she had gotten what she'd asked for. Boy, had she ever.

He laughed once, then sobered. "I thought *I* shouldn't have. But then, I wasn't even sure—"

"I know. I wasn't either—"

She stopped herself. *Sure of what? Let the man finish!*

But he stopped, too, and they stood looking at each other.

"Look, do you want to come in for a minute? I, uh . . ." She leaned on the doorknob. "Maybe we should clear the air, you know? And I have part of a bottle of wine, if you'd like a glass."

He paused and she wondered if she should have just left it at whatever point it was they'd gotten to.

He glanced at his watch. "Okay, sure. I guess it's not too late."

It was close to eleven, late enough for Roxanne to be exhausted when she'd been with P.B., but she was wide awake now and ready to "clear the air," as she'd said. She tried to remember all the little speeches she'd made up in her head the day after their dinner, but recalled only "it was a mistake" and "it should never happen again." At this moment, though, those only sounded condemning, and somewhat accusatory, and she didn't want to stir the waters up any more than they already were.

She stepped back and ushered Steve in. He dropped what looked like a bookbag by the door, took off his coat and she led him into the kitchen.

"Wine? Or would you rather have tea or hot chocolate?" She glanced around the kitchen nervously, then moved to the refrigerator and opened it. "I also have some soda, I think. Ginger ale?" She peered back over her shoulder at him.

He seated himself at the kitchen island. "Tea would be great, actually."

She straightened, pushing the door shut. "Okay. I think I have herbal, if you don't want the caffeine. Or do you like regular?" She opened the cabinet next to the stove and poked around. "I don't know about you, but I can't sleep at all if I have caffeine at night."

She heard him chuckle. "Either way. I just got cold out there, talking to P.B."

At the mention of his friend, Roxanne felt humiliation return and with it her unmistakable blush. She kept her back to Steve, turned to the stove, picked up the kettle and moved to the sink. She filled it with enough water for probably ten mugs of tea, then placed it back on the stove, adjusting the flame to high.

The box of tea she'd pulled from the cabinet lay next to the stove. She picked it up and brandished it in his direction. "How about Red Zinger?"

"Fine."

She opened the box, pulled out a bag and placed it in a mug, making all moves deliberately while she tried to come up with something to say. Finally, she turned around, box of tea in hand. She leaned against the counter, her fingers fidgeting with the flap of the box.

"I don't know what you must think of me," she said breathlessly. "I was just—out there—" She extended a hand to indicate the back alley. "With P.B. But I—"

"Roxanne. That's none of my business." Steve shook his head, his eyes on the island in front of him.

"I know, I know." She pushed her hair back from her face and felt it fall in disarray. "But actually it is, in a way. I mean, a few nights ago I was kissing you and tonight . . . well, I just want you to know that I'm not playing games with you guys, no matter how it might look. I'm not even interested in P.B., not that way."

Steve looked up at her, his brows raised as if to say, *And me?* But he just murmured, "Is that right?"

"And as for, well, you, the other night, I don't even

know what happened, why that happened. But it's obvious, isn't it? I mean it's clear we can't be, uh, doing that. We *work* together. We, I, I *own* the place. I can't be . . ." She flipped a hand out in front of her and searched for words. But there weren't any. All she could think was, *I can't be screwing around with the flippin' employees*, and she knew *that* wouldn't sound right.

Steve took the words right out of her head. "You can't be fraternizing with the employees." His voice was low and rich with sarcasm.

Beside her, the water in the kettle started to stir.

Her hands gripped the counter behind him. "Well, yes. Don't you think that's true?"

His gaze was steady on her, his eyes slightly narrowed. She wished to God she knew what he was thinking. "I understand why you do."

On the burner, the kettle began to hiss.

"What does that mean? You don't think so?" She stared at him, trying to fathom what he was saying. "I mean, you don't think I should? Or rather, you do?"

He looked confused. "You should what?"

She threw a hand out. "Fraternize!"

"With me?" He put a hand to his chest. His eyes seemed to be laughing at her now, *dammit*.

The action in the kettle increased. A trickle of steam floated upward in the air next to her.

"With anyone." She swallowed. "Look, if you thought you started things the other night, then you obviously—you must have, well, *thought* of starting things. So maybe we need to agree . . ."

She turned and slapped the box back down on the counter. She was making a mess of this.

"Roxanne," he said. His voice was so calm she was sure she sounded like a neurotic idiot in comparison.

She turned around.

"I think we've gotten off to a strange start." He pushed himself around on his seat so that he was facing her more fully. "But it's obvious we've both been caught off guard by events that . . . well, maybe we consider missteps."

Her heart thrummed in her chest as she looked at him, and she willed herself for once to keep quiet to hear what he had to say.

But she couldn't help herself.

"What did you consider a misstep?" she blurted. It was one thing for her not to want to "fraternize," as he'd put it, quite another for him.

The kettle beside her was about to whistle, but she didn't want to relinquish his gaze. What, *exactly*, had he regretted? It was suddenly very important for her to know.

Steve rose and made the two strides it took to reach the stove. He stood close and with one arm reached around her to move the kettle and turn off the burner.

She glanced at the floor in an effort not to look too closely at his face, which was now practically beside hers. That's what had resulted in the kiss the other night. He'd been so close, his lips *right there*. His body, his warmth, his seductive appeal . . .

What *was* it about him?

His words low, he said, "Why don't we just stop analyzing this?"

She glanced quickly up at him, then away. "I can't. I don't know what to do."

He paused a long moment, during which time she expected him to move away again. But he didn't.

Finally, he said, "I think you can do whatever the hell you want."

She looked up, into his eyes, blue-gray and sharp. His face was calm, his cheeks brushed with the barest stubble, just enough to make him look sinful. His hair, too long, lay about his head in casual disorder, and his white Oxford shirt was unironed. He looked like every mother's nightmare. And every young girl's bad boy.

"Whatever I want," she repeated, thinking, *How the hell should I know what I want?*

But she *did* know what she wanted, she told herself. Someone like Martin, but not Martin. A non-lying Martin. Someone with whom she had something in common.

Steve's eyebrows twitched and he smiled in such a way that sent her thoughts careening wickedly, away from logic, past common sense, and straight into desire. Heat blasted through her body and she felt like the tea kettle, steam wafting out her pores.

Whatever I want.

Her body knew what that was. Even Steve seemed to know what that was. Wasn't that why he was standing here, so close to her? Giving her that look that said, *Take what you want, you idiot, or stop bothering me.*

She inhaled quickly and exhaled, realizing as she did that she was breathing as if she'd just run up the stairs. Her nerves pulsed, electrified.

Her eyes dropped from Steve's face to the open collar of his shirt. She wanted to put her lips there, on that sweet space of skin, just below the stubble. She licked her lips.

"Roxanne," Steve said, this time in a near whisper.

His hand reached out and skimmed her waist to lie warmly on her hip. With a gentle grip he pulled her toward him.

She swallowed hard and moved forward with his hand, coming up against his chest, her palms flat against his ribcage. She looked up at him, saw again that hunger in his eyes and felt her insides go molten.

She parted her lips. He lowered his head. And they kissed.

9

Bar Special
Between the Sheets—<u>happy tonight,
hungover tomorrow</u>
white rum, brandy, Cointreau, lemon juice

Okay, so he was attracted to her. And okay, so it wasn't smart.

But hell, she was a beautiful woman and her body was pressed up against his like she wanted to crawl right inside his skin.

He had stopped the kiss the other night. Out of consideration, confusion, uncertainty over whether he'd crossed the line or she had.

Well, tonight, they both had. And if she wanted it stopped, then she was going to have to do it.

The kiss started out frenzied. Her mouth was hungry on his, he answered with equal energy. Their hands groped, clutched and traveled over each other's bodies, exploring, grasping, needing closer contact.

Steve felt as if he were going to explode right out of his body. His blood sang, his senses spun, his desire was out of control.

With great effort he slowed the kiss, running his hands up her back and into the dark softness of her hair, then to the sides of her face.

She sighed against his mouth, and he teased her lips with his teeth and tongue. His hands held her head gently as he tasted her, sending her the message that he wanted to appreciate every slow sip of her.

Roxanne's mouth was rich and sweet under his, the skin of her face so soft he felt as if she were a delicacy exotic enough to have come from another world.

Her hands moved down his back and rounded over his hips. With surprising strength, she pulled him into her, his desire, hard and obvious beneath his jeans, straining toward this oblique touch.

His hands ran down her sides, found the spot at her hips where the shirt tucked into her jeans and pulled upward. His fingers found flesh and she gave a little moan. Her body melted against his.

She was smooth and hot, her torso toned and strong, taut like a bow flexed against his frame.

His hands touched her bra and moved around to cup her breasts. He groaned as he found the nipples peaked against his fingers.

Tilting his head, he trailed his lips to her neck. Just below her ear he took a soft bite and sucked as his fingers softly pinched.

She gasped and pulled him tighter, her hips moving into his.

"The bedroom?" he murmured against her ear.

He felt her nod. Slowly, he peeled himself away from her, letting his hands slide down her belly to her hips.

Her face was flushed, her dark eyes nearly black with dilated pupils. Her lips were slightly swollen from his kisses. And her expression was pure desire.

He could hardly believe she was real. The most exquisite woman he'd ever seen, hot, disheveled and glowing with passion *for him*.

Freeing his hands from her shirt, he cupped her face, then took another long sip from her mouth. She responded like a magnet, leaning into him again, her hands grabbing the belt loops on his jeans and yanking him against her.

"You know where it is." Her voice was low, husky, and she gave him a heavy-lidded smile that was so seductive it kicked him in the gut.

Taking her hand he led her down the hallway that was identical to his, turning left into the bedroom.

She followed him into the room and he closed the door behind them. They fumbled for each other in the dark, clasped hands and drew close.

Steve's hands took her shirt and pulled it up over her head. Her fingers went for his shirt buttons, but got tangled as he ducked to kiss the mound of one breast. He moved the lace of her bra downward and captured her nipple.

She made a soft sound deep in her throat and gave up on his buttons, throwing her head back as his lips pulled her nipple and his tongue played with its peak.

Her hands held his shoulders and she pulled them

both backward until he felt her lower herself on the bed. As his eyes adjusted to the dark, the light from the window illuminated the room. He could see her, a dark fluid mass on the bed, her hair spread out around her and her tender skin glowing pale in the moonlight.

He pulled his own shirt over his head and let it drop behind him. Then he leaned over and kissed her again, his hands plunging onto the mattress to snake behind her. He undid her bra with a practiced snap and pulled the straps down her arms.

Dropping the bra behind him onto the floor, he felt her hand find his crotch and cup him. Her thumb stroked his erection and he groaned. Her other hand unbuttoned his jeans and slid the zipper down.

He slid down the length of her body until he crouched at the side of the bed, his lips and hands trailing from her breasts to her belly to her thighs. He pushed his jeans off with one hand and rose again, kissing her belly button as he undid the top of her jeans.

She raised her hips and he drew her jeans down her legs and off. Beneath them, she wore a thong.

"Oh sweet Jesus." Steve's voice was hoarse, a guttural plea for control.

In the dim light of the room he could see Roxanne Rayeaux's incredible figure, naked but for the dark strings of a lacy thong. From bountiful breasts, over a taut belly to the luscious curve of her hips. He wanted those long, long legs around him now.

He rose up above her and pushed his erection against the thong's slip of fabric. His lips found her breast, first one, then the other, and she arched into him, her hands holding his head. Then he rose and took her mouth again.

She opened to him hungrily, her legs loosely circling his hips. His hardened penis in her hands, she stroked it so that he thought he'd lose his mind. Her touch was perfect, magic. He dropped his hand to the thong and slipped a finger easily around it to find the center of her heat.

She was more than ready for him. He plunged two fingers inside her and she pushed her hips up with a soft, high-pitched sound of pleasure. She was slick and soft as silk. His thumb found the spot and moved a slow circle around it.

"Oh," she said on a hot, heavy breath. "Ah." She slid her hand to the top of his penis and moved it in short rhythmic strokes.

He exhaled hard, throbbing in her hands and nearly desperate for relief. He circled his thumb faster. She writhed beneath him.

"Steve," she breathed. "I—I . . . *ahhh*. In the drawer . . ."

He paused.

"A . . . you know . . . for protection," she added in a near whisper.

"Of course." He rose, looked blankly around. "Where?"

She turned over onto her hands and knees. Steve's body tensed and throbbed at the sight of her. She leaned across the bed and opened a drawer to a small night stand. Then she sat back and handed him a condom.

"Wait a minute," he said, when she started to turn around.

Slipping the condom on, he took her hips in his hands and turned her onto her stomach, nearly coming undone again as he saw the perfect rounds of her buttocks, neatly defined by the strip of thong.

She rose onto her hands and knees and he pulled the piece of fabric away from her center, moving himself toward it.

He touched the head to her and strangled a moan. She pushed her hips back but he pulled away, teasing. She groaned. He pushed the head against her again, up and back, along her slickest spot, tormenting her silken heat as she moved her hips again. He leaned over her, bit softly at her shoulder and ran one arm around her stomach. With his other hand he kept the thong aside and positioned himself. Then, body trembling with need, he thrust deeply inside her.

She inhaled sharply and he pushed again. She arched back into him and cried, *"Yes."*

He thrust again, holding the string of the thong as if barely restraining a wild horse.

The sensation was exquisite. She was tight and hot and wet. He slid effortlessly, deeply, pleasure cascading up his spine as his eyes drank in the lithe form of her back, her tangled hair. Her tight round buttocks moved smoothly, soft and firm, toward him and away, his penis disappeared again and again into her core.

Curving around her once more, he moved his arm across her belly and his fingers again found her spot, this time swollen and primed for his touch. She made a soft sound as he touched her, his hips still thrusting against her. Then she grabbed him, her body did, down deep, and she uttered an ecstatic cry as she shuddered in his arms.

Steve exploded inside her, pulsing as if every ounce of his soul was being pumped into her body. He gasped, then moaned and, as she lay her body slowly onto the mattress, he came down on top of her, their bodies still joined.

Roxanne opened her eyes. She was in bed, facing the windows, and the clock on the bedside table read 6:57. Her body was molten relaxation on the mattress, and she'd slept as soundly as if she'd run a marathon the day before.

Lying perfectly still, she listened for the sound of Steve's breathing. Was he still here? Did she *want* him to still be here?

If he was, how did she act now? What did she *say*? She guessed it was too late to talk about what a mistake the kiss had been.

He stirred, the mattress dipped slightly, and she exhaled in surprising but undiluted relief. He hadn't left. He hadn't snuck out like a forbidden suitor who had gotten everything, the *only* thing, he'd wanted.

She closed her eyes again.

She had to talk to P.B. That was her first problem. She couldn't do this balancing act of having one guy she allowed herself to go out with and another she couldn't stop herself from touching.

Nerves tingled across her body as she remembered last night, the way Steve had touched her, the rough desperate need each of them had had for the other.

Then the complete and utter fulfillment of that need.

She was quenched to her core. If it weren't for the obvious lack of wisdom in her choice of bedmate, she would be completely, blissfully satisfied.

Steve stirred again and she turned slowly onto her back. He was pushing himself up to a sitting position on the edge of the bed. His back was long and tapered to a trim waist, one hand rubbed the back of his neck. As she moved, he looked over his shoulder at her.

His hair was a tousled mess and his cheeks bore the swath of overnight stubble. His eyes were piercing gray in the daylight, and they were smiling.

He was, quite literally, as handsome as sin.

Her lips curved cautiously as their eyes met. Heat suffused her.

"Menu run-through today, right?" His voice was warm and low. Intimate.

She liked that he'd said something mundane about their day, as if this were not a colossal mistake that needed a dramatic conversation to conclude it.

"Yes." She pushed herself up against the pillows, holding the sheets to her chest, and ran a hand through her hair to push it off her face. "Monsieur Girmond will be cooking for the staff at noon. He's probably already in the kitchen. Four apps, six entrees, four sides. I'll have three desserts."

They'd go over how each was made, the ingredients, the flavors, the sauces, the portions, so the waitstaff would be familiar with what the customers were ordering. They would also go over wine accompaniments and pronunciation of each dish—something she hoped Rita could master, as it would go a long way toward making her the best server they had. Right now she was still saying *blanquette de veau* as "blanket of view." Confusing, to say the least. And hardly appetizing.

"I'll come hungry."

For some reason Steve's words made her blush as he reached down to pick up his clothes.

"Not too hungry," she said. "We'll all be sharing."

She tucked the covers in tighter around her, wondering what to do. She watched Steve's back as he rose, admiring his body in the cold light of day. He was sinewy and strong, defined muscles covered that lanky frame and his legs were lean and powerful, runner's legs.

She wondered if in fact he was a runner. She wondered what he did with all his time when he wasn't working. She wondered who on earth he was, this man she'd just uninhibitedly made love with.

At the same time she felt as if a wall was constructed inside her chest. A wall that would not let her through to ask these questions, nor to get any more intimate than they'd been physically.

He was different from anyone she'd ever been with. More intense, less predictable. He challenged her, and though it made her feel stupid to admit it, she didn't want to be challenged. She had too much challenging stuff on her plate already.

What she needed was somebody simple and undemanding. Somebody to support her when she needed it and disappear when she didn't. Selfish, sure, but that was all she felt she could handle right now.

Steve donned his pants and picked up his shirt, now

even more wrinkled than when he'd arrived last night. He put it on without noticing and didn't tuck it in. She loved the way it looked, white against the tawny skin of his throat and chest, loose across the expanse of his shoulders and over his flat belly.

He turned to look at her, his eyes raking her from head to blanket-covered toe as he stood next to the bed.

"Damn," he said softly, with a short shake of his head. "It's hard to leave you looking like that."

She didn't know what to say. She pressed her lips together, a small smile, and looked at the covers. She should get up, too, but she didn't feel comfortable enough to be naked in front of him in the morning light. Which, considering what they'd done last night, was ridiculous.

"I'll see you at noon." She kept her voice even. She didn't know what tone to take, how to be, *who* to be. She glanced back up at him.

"You bet." His grin was cocky and before she knew it he'd knelt on the bed and planted a solid kiss on her lips.

Without thinking, her mouth opened under his and her body ignited like a gas burner to a match.

One of Steve's hands cupped her cheek, but as their tongues found each other and mated as easily as if they'd been doing it for years, it slid down her neck and over her shoulder to her breast. His fingers found the nipple under the covers and she inhaled, her body instantly turning to liquid for him.

Steve groaned and pulled back, his face intent, his eyes hot. "You are . . ." he said with a devouring look, but he didn't finish. He just smiled one last time and concluded, "See you at noon." He strode out of the room.

Roxanne's head dropped back onto the pillows as he left and she exhaled a huge, pent-up breath. Her body hummed as if she were a guitar string he'd just plucked. One note of desire singing through her, reverberating to infinity like a soprano in a cathedral.

She'd never felt so on fire with a man. She didn't know what it was he did to her, but whatever it was, it should be classified and controlled by the FDA. He was damned dangerous. And, she feared, addictive.

The *fervor*, she thought again, closing her eyes. The *vehemence* of their lovemaking had been astonishing.

She pushed the covers aside and got out of bed. Her clothes were scattered about the room, fabric shrapnel testifying to the explosion of desire that had taken place.

This was the strangest thing about modern relationships, she thought, in an effort to be objective. Not that she'd call what she and Steve had a *relationship*. But you could sleep with someone, share the most personal parts of your body, open yourself in the most physically vulnerable way to a man, and not have the foggiest idea what to say to him the next day.

It was sick, really. And sad. This kind of passion was supposed to come with love.

Wasn't it?

She snapped her jeans off the floor. If only she had fallen head over heels in love with someone when she was twenty-two. Then she could have avoided all these years of false starts and missteps, failed relationships and disappointing mistakes.

If only Martin had been all that he'd seemed. Cultured, clever, sentimental and romantic. He had made a life of passion and friendship seem possible.

Too bad he had been a liar. And too bad the lies had colored all that was good a dirty hue.

She tried to picture his face and couldn't do it. She'd spent so long blocking out his image, she could no longer make him real. All that lingered was a melancholy impression of a sandy-haired man in a tuxedo, his elegant fingers holding a wineglass.

And yet she had felt so close to him, once upon a time.

She wondered what Steve would look like in a tuxedo, and the mental picture made her stop and take a deep breath.

After a second she picked up her shirt and bra, and walked into the bathroom, dumping the clothes into the hamper. Then she turned on the water in the shower.

She had éclairs to bake, sauces to make and custards to prep. She couldn't sit around thinking about her latest male mistake. Or, okay, not mistake. At this point he was a compulsion. A physical obsession. A dangerously beguiling substance, like chocolate.

The worst part, though, was that she knew he was just a Band-Aid, a temporary substitute to sate her hunger for the real thing. Steve Serrano was a gift from the gods in bed, there was no doubt about that, but ultimately he wasn't right for her. Nor was she right for him. What she needed was someone she could fall in love with. Someone easy and uncomplicated. The guy from *Father Knows Best*, she thought. Or *Leave It to Beaver*. One of those kindly TV husbands who went through life just trying to do the right thing.

Someone fictional, she told herself with a laugh.

Someone—and this was important—who didn't need her to be June Cleaver to his Ward.

Just before she stepped into the shower, wondering if maybe it should be a cold one after Steve's scorching good-bye kiss, she pictured Steve's eyes. The sharp, intense look he sometimes gave her, the one that made her think he was seeing right through her. And her stomach did a little flip.

A flip, she thought vaguely, that had nothing to do with sex.

Steve's shower was cold, and long. He stood under it, letting the water beat down on his upturned face, until he could stand it no longer and he shut the whole thing off.

He was possessed. That was it. He'd been possessed by the devil. The devil in the dark eyes of Roxanne Rayeaux.

He couldn't stop himself last night. Could barely stop himself this morning, then wondered why he had. She had certainly been willing, he could see it in her eyes. In her devil eyes.

He dried himself roughly and got dressed. This was ridiculous. He could control himself. He wasn't going to lose it over a pretty face; he never had before.

But it was more than her face, more than her beauty, that drew him. There was something downright electric about her, something sultry and fierce and uncompromising. She had let go of her inhibitions as if she'd never had any. For weeks now he'd thought of her as the queen of control, restraint personified, but last night she had broken those bonds as if they'd been web-thin silk. At the same time she'd drawn him in as inextricably as a spider does a moth.

And God help him, he did not trust himself to resist her again.

Would he have to? he wondered. Would he have to at least pretend to try?

What did this mean?

Steve dressed, packed up his books and went to the library until eleven thirty, but it was no use. His research could not compete with the buzzing of his skin as he grappled with uncontrollable memories of the night before.

It wasn't until he remembered P.B. that he could get his physical reactions under control again. Like a bucket of cold water, Steve knew he had to tell his buddy that Roxanne was . . . what? Not available? He had no illusions that last night meant they were in some kind of relationship. They barely knew each other, for one thing. Ironically.

But he wouldn't—couldn't—let P.B. think he had some kind of chance with Roxanne while she was sleeping, or had slept, with him. Maybe it was altruistic—he truly didn't want his friend's heart broken, or even bruised—but mostly he knew it was selfish. He couldn't stand the thought of P.B. even trying to hold her hand when he, Steve, wanted to see and touch and hold so much more.

Steve packed up his notebooks and papers at quarter to twelve and headed for the restaurant. He'd be late, but he doubted everyone would get there on time anyway. And he didn't want Roxanne thinking he was too eager to see her again, a panting puppy who didn't know when to stop begging for play.

But when he arrived, the dining room had nearly the full complement of servers and cooks the restaurant now employed. George was the only one later than he was, but he was routinely late. When the restaurant was Charters, they would tell George his shift started half an hour before it really did, and he had never caught on.

The cooks, he'd never seen before—certainly not the tall rotund man with the moustache and round glasses. He assumed that this was the Monsieur Girmond Roxanne had talked so rhapsodically about.

Assisting him were two men wearing chefs' whites and black-and-white checkered pants. The three of them wore black clogs on their feet.

Sir Nigel was there as well, in his trademark three-piece suit with French cuffs and watch chain. His hair was slicked back over his balding English pate and he looked over the crew with a haughty eye. Most particularly, his gaze seemed caught on Rita.

In white shirt, black pants and long white apron, she was dressed like the other three waiters, but her spiky red hair made its trademark impertinent statement.

As Steve entered the room not wearing his white shirt and black pants all eyes turned to him.

Sir Nigel's colorless gaze swept him and his lips twitched just enough to convey displeasure.

"Sorry." Steve shrugged with a grin, his peripheral vision searching for Roxanne. "I didn't know this was a dress rehearsal."

"No matter, no matter," M. Girmond boomed, waving him in with a substantial hand. "You are the bartender, no? I saw you, through the window the other day." He indicated the front window with his head.

"Did you?" Steve strode across the room and shook the man's hand. "Steve Serrano. Good to meet you."

"Marcel Girmond, at your service." He spread his arms to encompass a table full of plates containing appetizers and laughed. "We are just now beginning. Roxanne said we are not to wait for stragglers, but now we are down to just one missing. *Oui?*"

"Yeah." Rita turned to send Steve a wink. "Just George now. Then our motley crew will be complete."

Steve took off his coat and laid it over a chair back, ignoring Sir Nigel's glare. He went to stand next to Rita.

"Lookin' good, darlin'," he said out of the corner of his mouth.

"I *know*." She looked down at herself with a pleased grin. "I'm a real professional now."

Steve smiled at her. He wasn't often surprised by people—last night notwithstanding—but he wouldn't have expected this from Rita. He thought she'd fight the fussy nature of this restaurant every step of the way, just as he had planned to. But now . . . well, now he had bigger fish to fry.

He was just settling comfortably in to the instructional nature of the program, listening to Monsieur Girmond's lilting accent, when Roxanne emerged from the kitchen. She too wore chef's whites with the black-and-white checkered pants, but with her hair in a bun and the memory of last night so fresh, Steve felt sucker-punched.

She was gorgeous no matter what she put on, and knowing what was under that primly buttoned jacket raised his blood to an instant boil. Their eyes met and as stupid as it sounded even to himself, he felt a bolt of electricity pass between them. The sensation was so strong, he colored as if the rest of the group might have perceived it.

"Steve," she said coolly. The control queen was back. "So glad you could make it."

She held a towel on which she was wiping her hands, and her eyes, after branding him with their heat, moved to the table of food Monsieur Girmond presided over.

Rita glanced up at him, a long look through her pale lashes.

Had she seen it?

To Steve's surprise, the presentation of the food was actually interesting. Girmond was so enthralled by his topic, so enthusiastic about his productions, that it was impossible not to be drawn in. Indeed, most of the staff seemed taken with the food—even George, who had shown up in time for the last bite of the appetizers.

Roxanne's desserts were likewise a big hit and she looked gratified by the effusiveness of the reactions.

As the group broke up, and Steve's eyes kept track of Roxanne as she answered questions from Rita and Pat, Sir Nigel glided over to him.

"I trust you will be appropriately attired for tomorrow's opening," he said in a voice coated with British pomposity.

"Why Nigel, I didn't know you cared," Steve said. He was thinking he should make his way over to Roxanne, figure out a way to ask her when they could see each other. Without, of course, seeming like he was worried about it. He hadn't quite worked that part out yet.

"Mr. Serrano, you don't seem to have grasped that I am your boss."

That got Steve's attention. He turned a deceptively lazy expression on the man. "Congratulations. You must be very proud."

Sir Nigel regarded him a long moment, his eyes flat, like a shark's. "You might want to think harder about the situation. I make decisions regarding your future employment here. No matter what edge you think you can gain by . . ." He stopped, cleared his throat delicately, and let his eyes drift pointedly to Roxanne. ". . . pursuing alternate means of job security. Whatever else our new owner may be, she is not one to be deeply affected by a fleeting bit of charm."

10

Bar Special
Third Rail—Danger! Touch it
 and it might just kill you
Dry vermouth, sweet vermouth, rum, orange juice

"Roxanne, baby. Glad you called." P.B.'s voice seemed too loud on the line and she pulled the phone receiver a couple inches away from her ear. "Listen, just got some news about a possible match on some fingerprints from your break-in."

"Oh. But I thought it was just the squirrel." She tapped a pencil eraser on the counter in front of her. Her kitchen was bright from the morning sun. *The hard light of a new day*, she thought. She rocked the sole of a clog on one of the bottom rungs of a stool by her kitchen island.

She'd come up from the kitchen downstairs to make this call, the obligation weighing too heavily to put it off any longer. She was already nervous about tonight's opening of the restaurant. She didn't need the prospect of this conversation taking up any more mental space too. So while her dough rested, she made a temporary escape to lower the boom on P.B.

"Sure, it probably was." P.B.'s voice was unconcerned. "But we ran the prints anyway. For all you know, you've got someone working for you with a record."

"I really doubt that."

"I know you do, honey. But it's my job to protect you, isn't it?"

Something about P.B.'s tone irked her. Was it in the nature of cops to think everyone else around them was a criminal? And did he mean he was supposed to protect *her*, in particular, as in the "little woman"?

She gritted her teeth. "A possible match. What does that mean? Do you know whose fingerprints they are?"

Her palms were sweating and she dropped the pencil.

"Not yet. Maybe later today. I thought I'd drop by your place tonight. Let you know the details."

"P.B., I'm opening the restaurant tonight. This is our first night."

Didn't he *know* this? It was all she'd talked about for weeks with anyone.

"It'll probably be slow," she added. "But I'll be busy at least until midnight anyway."

Papers shuffled in the background. "Oh yeah. The opening. That's tonight?"

She sighed. "Yes."

"Well, I'll just stop by the restaurant then."

Roxanne pictured P.B. coming into Chez Soi with his

"Roxanne-baby's" and his "honeys" in front of Steve and knew she could not handle the juxtaposition. She was torn enough as it was over the strange turn her dealings with Steve had taken. She didn't need to add to what was already an awkward threesome by having them all together in one spot.

"By the way"—P.B. covered the mouthpiece and said something to someone nearby, she could only hear muffled murmurings—"yeah, sorry. Uh, by the way, I got the symphony tickets you wanted. Hope you don't mind balcony seats."

She wanted?

She took a deep breath. First things first. "Listen, P.B., I really don't think tonight's going to be a good time to come by. Opening night, as I said. We could be busy working out kinks in the service. I know I won't have time to talk."

"Oh, well." He paused. She hoped he was digesting this as a possible rejection. "No problem. I can talk to you later. But you can always use another customer, right? I'll just shoot the shit with Steve. Maybe grab a bite to eat at the bar."

Roxanne closed her eyes, picturing the scene perfectly. P.B.'s blustering candor bumping right into Steve's quiet perception. No doubt—*no* doubt—P.B. would mention the symphony date. No doubt Steve would put together his own theory on how that had come about. No doubt she would end up looking even worse than she already did.

"P.B., I just don't think—"

"Babe, listen, sorry, I gotta go." She could hear someone talking in the background and P.B.'s answering "uh-huhs." He came back on. "Really, sorry. I'll come by tonight, let you know what's going on."

She gave it one last shot. "Not tonight, please, Peter. Let's have lunch sometime this week, okay?"

"Uh-huh. Right. Gotcha."

She breathed a sigh of relief until she realized he was talking to whoever was with him.

"Okay, Rox, see ya later," he said to her.

"Bye," she said dispiritedly, but he was already gone. She took the phone from her ear and slowly pressed the OFF button.

She just wouldn't come out of the kitchen, that was all. He could talk to Steve all he wanted and she wouldn't show. Come to think of that, though, he and Steve probably had already talked, on the phone or whatever. They were friends. Maybe Steve had told him what had happened the other night. But no, P.B. wouldn't have been so casually proprietary with her as he was just now. He probably wouldn't have been so easy about "babe"-ing her either. And he certainly wouldn't have been interested in "shooting the shit" with Steve. Not after being upstaged by him.

She got up off the stool and headed back downstairs. Realistically, it would probably be slow tonight. They had done very little advertising, just enough to let the neighborhood know they were opening up, so they'd be lucky to turn tables even once. Which meant that there would be plenty of time for her to be expected to socialize with P.B.

Well, so what, she told herself. She was the boss and P.B. was someone she'd been out with *once*. She didn't owe him anything. For that matter she didn't owe Steve anything either.

Let 'em talk, she thought cavalierly. That's what a man would think and do.

Not any man she'd want to be with, however.

They were slammed.

From the moment Sir Nigel opened the doors that night, people streamed in. Apparently word had gotten out that the three-star chef from New York's La Finesse had come to Alexandria and all the Washingtonian foodies pounced on it, exclaiming to each other how lucky and/or prescient they were to have gotten a jump on the culinary scene by being there the first night.

They were standing two deep at the bar as Steve's gaze raked the crowd, searching for the tiny blonde woman who had ordered the Amaretto sour.

"Amaretto?" a dark-suited, power-tied man of about fifty called.

Steve caught his eye and held up the drink. The man nodded, indicating the top of a blonde head at his side, hidden by the crowd.

"Seven twenty," Steve said, over the head of the white-haired gentleman on a barstool in front of him.

Without batting an eye, the suited man handed him a fifty.

Considering nobody was supposed to know the restaurant even existed yet, Steve was amazed by the sheer numbers of people here, not to mention amused by their ease with the high prices of the drinks. At Charters it had taken several hours of drinking for people to get so free with their credit cards. Here they didn't bat an eye at paying nine bucks for a martini.

And still they kept coming through the door. Even the unflappable Sir Nigel looked a little hot under the collar. Steve caught him glancing out the door to the street at one point as if there might be a bus unloading somewhere nearby.

Rita, George and Pat, expecting an easy opening night, were flying wild-eyed through the double doors from the kitchen with plates of exquisitely presented food, looking as if they were having to negotiate an obstacle course with their mother's best china on their heads.

Steve himself was kept hopping by such orders as Pink Ladies and Green Turtles, drinks he'd almost never gotten orders for at Charters that now he had to wrack his brain to remember how to make. He'd even had to look surreptitiously at the dusty bartender's manual under the register at one point to figure out what the hell a Queen's Park Swizzle was.

Catering to an older crowd was definitely different from the burger-and-beer stuff he'd been doing for Charters. Back then, the most complicated drinks he'd had to produce were six different kinds of margaritas and the latest craze in shooters, neither of which required much presentation.

Mixed in with all the crazy drink drinkers were also a host of fine-wine fanciers. Each wanted to know the years and varietals of every offering they had by the glass, not to mention "how it was." Full-bodied? Fruity? Lots of tannins?

Steve started out saying things like "robust" and "oak-y," and eventually branched out into "a little floral" for the cheaper labels to a "hint of blackberry"—or lingonberry or chocolate or whatever—for the more expensive ones.

It seemed to be working. Everyone liked what they were drinking and nobody had looked at him yet and repeated, "*Lingonberry!*"

About half past nine, P.B. pushed his way through the crowd. As usual, he was visible from the moment he walked in the door and audible shortly thereafter.

"Steve!" he called, raising a hand high. His grin was expansive and all-encompassing, benevolent to the masses around him. That, and the casual way he brushed by Sir Nigel at the door, spoke volumes about how close he thought he was to being lord of the manner.

"Hey, Peeb." Steve glanced at him as he filled a pint glass with Stella Artois, a Belgian beer they now carried. "What's up?"

P.B. shouldered between two men in suits who had their backs to each other to secure a standing spot at the bar. "I promised Rox I'd stop by. She here?"

Rox?

Steve couldn't help it, he scowled. "Of course she's here, Peeb, she's the owner, for Chrissake."

He moved down the bar to deliver the Stella, irritation crawling along his nerves like bugs. It wasn't P.B.'s fault. In fact, if there was fault involved it was all Steve's. Not P.B.'s, not Roxanne's. Steve's. He was the one who'd initiated things with Roxanne and pushed them beyond what either of them had expected.

And he was the one who had not yet spoken to his friend about it. P.B., in this instance, was just an innocent bystander to his, Steve's, lack of control.

He moved back toward P.B., taking a deep breath and marshalling his annoyance.

"What can I get for you?" he asked his friend.

P.B. grinned. "Roxanne, straight up, slightly warmed."

Steve almost laughed—cynically—at how ironic that was. She'd been warmed all right.

"Man, you shoulda seen the looks I got at Murphy's the other night," P.B. continued, laughing. "Walking in with her. Christ, I couldn't have done better if I'd brought in all the MTV Spring Break girls together. Don Flannery about pissed his pants when he saw she was with me."

"That's great," Steve said. He could just imagine P.B.'s cronies talking about her.

"You know it. My stock went *up*, brother, let me tell you." He laughed again, pounding his palm on the bar with glee. "She's by far the hottest chick I've ever brought in there—they all said so—and you know I've brought some hot ones in. She takes the cake, though."

"So? You get to see her bedroom like you predicted?" Maybe it was mean, since he knew full well the answer to the question, but P.B.'s cockiness set him off.

P.B. chuckled. "It's just a matter of time, buddy. Just a matter of time."

Steve looked at him, wishing, hopelessly, that P.B. would hear how he sounded and shut the hell up. He'd always treated his women like trophies and it seemed Roxanne was to be no exception.

"So where is she, huh?" P.B. looked around, apparently oblivious to what a crowd this size would mean to a chef. "I gotta tell her she's a star at the pub."

"She's in the back. *Cooking*," he said pointedly.

P.B. shrugged. "Tell her it's break time."

Steve scoffed. "I don't think so. Look around you, P.B., she's probably up to her eyeballs in orders right now." He glanced over the heads of the people at the bar into the bustling dining room. "We turned section one over an hour ago, so there're probably a bunch of desserts on order right now."

In fact Steve himself had seen her only a couple of times that evening, once when she'd run out of rum for something she was doing, and once when she'd come to refill the pitcher of ice water she kept back there. Both times she'd looked both elated and shell-shocked. All she could do was stare wide-eyed at Steve and shake her head in wonder.

Steve had laughed and said, "Looks like you're on your way."

To which she'd shaken her head again and said, "We all are."

But it wasn't just the amazing crowd that stuck in his mind at the moment. Like an adolescent schoolboy, what he kept running over and over in his thoughts was the moment when he'd handed her the pitcher and their hands had touched on the handle. For a second they had both frozen, prolonging the contact and looking at each other with such heat that Steve could feel it deep in his gut.

Or had it been just him?

He exhaled and wiped down the counter.

"I'll just hang out here for a while then," P.B. said. "I told her I'd be coming by, so she'll probably be out before too long looking for me."

Steve figured they'd just see about that. He threw the

bar towel down on the cold chest and took an order from the woman next to P.B. for a Cosmopolitan.

P.B. looked down the bar, then back at the shelf of liquors. "Think I'll have one of those," he added, pointing to the Queen's Park Swizzle as Steve mixed the Cosmopolitan. "What's in that?"

"Roxanne knew you were coming by?" Steve asked, unable to help himself as he slid the Cosmo to the woman.

Had Roxanne made a date with P.B.? Maybe an after-work thing? He himself had done that plenty of times, with plenty of women, but it galled him to think of Roxanne being so casual about seeing both him and P.B. Not to mention seeing them both in the same place at the same time.

"Yeah." P.B. shed his jacket and hung it over the seat back behind him. They had tall bar stools now, with cushioned seats and backs, and Steve had to admit the whole place felt more comfortable. "I was going to tell her about the fingerprint results, from the break-in."

Steve raised a skeptical brow. "Squirrels have fingerprints?"

"No, smart-ass, people do. Thought we'd gotten a live one—maybe someone working here, one of those Ecuadorans or something—but we didn't. Close, but no cigar."

"So you came by to tell her you have nothing on the break-in." Several people at the bar were looking restless but Steve couldn't let this go. "That's full-service police work."

P.B. frowned at him. "What bee got up your butt? No, I came by to see her, talk about our next date. We're going to the symphony and I just got tickets. Bach, thanks to you."

Steve felt his blood go cold. He shouldn't be surprised. She'd gone out with P.B. first. The thing between himself and her had been a spontaneous moment that had gotten out of hand, and that was all. Clearly, that was all. Still, he felt a little sick.

What had all those protestations of hers meant about only liking P.B. as a friend? About how P.B. wasn't her type? Had she felt guilty about Steve and been giving him lip service? Come to think of it, her assertions on that score could conceivably be construed as coming on to him, couldn't they?

This was stupid. Maybe he should just tell P.B. about him and Roxanne. Didn't P.B. have a right to know that his best friend was making tracks with the woman he was dating?

Then again, wasn't it Roxanne's place to tell P.B. what she was doing, seeing as how she had a date lined up with him and all?

Confused, Steve shook his head and moved down the bar to a man waving a twenty at him.

"Hey, get me a beer, will you?" P.B. said as he moved off.

Steve nodded.

This was about as uncomfortable as Steve had ever been with his friend, or anybody, come to think of it. He felt like a liar and a cheat, and he wasn't even sure it was worth it.

What was he doing this for? Why had he gone after Roxanne when he wasn't even certain that he liked her?

Well, that wasn't true. It was more that he didn't

know what she thought of him. Roxanne's feelings were a mystery, but he was not naïve enough to believe she'd fallen for him. They had some amazing physical chemistry, but whether it could be more than that remained to be seen.

He just hoped he wasn't the only one looking . . .

Roxanne wiped her brow and breathed a sigh of relief. No more tickets. Dinner service was over and the last dessert had been plated and taken to its table.

The night had been incredible, a rush to her system she had never experienced before. Chefs, cooks, waiters, busboys, dishwashers all working excellently in concert for the first time was like piecing together a motor with nothing but an instruction manual and hearing the gratifying roar when you first turn the key.

Knowing that this all boded extremely well for the future of her venture was no small part of the equation either.

The only thing marring the evening was the knowledge that P.B. was sitting at the bar and had been for the last hour, waiting for her. Rita had told her during a hurried pass through for food that he was making "a bunch of dog-in-heat noises" about seeing her and if she wanted her bartender to stay sane she ought to get out there and say hi, "or whatever."

Roxanne had thanked her as if she couldn't have cared less, then wished she could park her head in the sand and leave it there.

Now, though, she guessed she had to go out there and face the music. She wished she had someone to talk to about it. Rita, of everyone present, would probably give her the most unvarnished assessment of the situation, but she was too tight with Steve to be trusted. Not to mention that Roxanne wasn't eager to hear Rita's honest opinion of her and the awkward problem of having varying degrees of entanglement with two guys.

In the past, she'd spoken some to M. Girmond about Martin, but she didn't want him thinking she expected him to be her psychologist as well as her chef, so she wouldn't talk to him about this. Besides, he was out back with his sous-chef, both of them smoking well-deserved cigars she'd provided for them.

Roxanne pulled off her toque and pushed her hair back from her temples. She probably looked a mess, what with sweating it out in a hot kitchen at full throttle for six hours, but maybe that was best. She didn't want either one of these guys thinking she looked good. Except—

She stopped herself. She wasn't going to spend one more minute thinking about that look in Steve's eyes, or the moment when their hands had touched on the water pitcher and she'd felt as if her insides had melted all over again.

She brushed her palms down the sides of her chef's jacket, took a fortifying breath and pushed through the swinging doors to the bar.

P.B. spotted her immediately and beamed, turning on his stool with arms outstretched as if she might walk into them for a hug.

Her eyes shot immediately to Steve, who, thankfully, was serving a white-haired gentleman farther down the bar and didn't see her.

Instead of going toward P.B. she moved toward the

service bar and ducked under it to put the main bar between him and herself. To cover for this move, she grabbed a glass and filled it with ice, then water from the soda gun.

"Hey, babe. I thought you were never gonna come out of there." P.B. smiled but she sensed an edge. "Didn't anyone tell you I was here?"

She leaned back against the liquor shelf and sipped her water. "Rita told me, but I've been in the weeds for the last hour and a half. I'm *exhausted*."

"Yeah, I had a tough day, too. Not too tough to want to see you, though." He laughed jovially as if this wasn't the accusation she knew it was. "I'll always have *that* energy, believe me."

He winked at her and leaned forward on his elbows, as if trying to get closer.

She stayed back, leaning against the cabinets, her stomach contracting at the carnal appetite in his expression.

"We had an amazing night," she said, clinging to the wonderful part of the evening. "It took all of us completely by surprise, but wow. It worked! Everything worked. It was so great."

"Yeah, hey, I wasn't expecting to see a crowd here either, that's for sure." P.B. laughed again and Roxanne struggled with feeling insulted. Had he meant that the way it sounded? Because it sounded as if he was blown away that the restaurant wasn't an immediate failure.

Steve approached from the other end of the bar and Roxanne turned her eyes toward him.

His expression was cool and he was shaking his head. "I don't get this guy. All night he's drinking scotch, one after the other, the good stuff, you know. And now suddenly he's got a hankering for Chambord, if you can believe it."

"Old coot's drunk as a skunk, that's why." P.B. didn't bother to lower his voice. "Probably couldn't taste the difference at this point anyway."

Steve ignored P.B. and turned to Roxanne, standing before her a second as if awaiting her opinion on the subject.

She looked up into his face, felt that fire start low in her body and stopped breathing. His expression was grave. What had P.B. said to him?

"Excuse me, darlin'," he said in a tone similar to the one he used with Rita—though not as friendly—and stepped closer. Putting his hands lightly on her hips, he pressed her to the left.

It took her a moment—during which desire sprang onto her skin like raindrops in a thunderstorm—to realize that he was moving her aside to get to the Chambord.

She flushed hot and laughed. "Oh! Sorry." She stepped left.

But Steve's left hand lingered on her hip as he grabbed the bottle with his right, leaning so close to her she could smell his clean masculine scent. Stepping back, he let his hand slide slowly off her torso but his eyes met hers with undisguised, and clearly sensual, hunger.

He turned, took a cordial glass from the shelf and poured the Chambord.

"Another beer, P.B.?" he asked, not looking at his friend.

But Roxanne did, and what she saw was a look of calculating displeasure. Whether that was because he didn't like Steve's touching her at all, or because he saw something more in the exchange, she couldn't tell. All she knew was that she had to set P.B. straight. She had to tell him that they—she and P.B.—were *not* in a relationship and they never would be.

"Yeah." P.B. drained his glass in one gulp and pushed the empty toward Steve. Then he reached into his breast pocket and pulled out an envelope. "Hey, Rox, look what I've got here." He smiled at Roxanne and held the paper out to her.

"Be right back," Steve said and went to deliver the cordial to the white-haired man.

Roxanne pushed off the back counter and took the envelope from P.B., setting her water glass on the bar. "What is it?" she asked, not opening it.

"Tickets. To the symphony. Remember I told you?" He had on his most sincere eager-puppy-dog look.

Remember I told you not to come tonight? she wanted to retort. *Remember I said I'd be too busy to talk? Remember I told you I wanted to pick the night for the symphony?*

She sighed and flipped open the envelope, glancing inside. Sure enough, two tickets.

"It's a Wednesday but you can get someone to cover for you, right?" P.B. added.

Steve returned with P.B.'s beer and snorted at this last comment.

"What?" P.B. gave him a belligerent look.

Roxanne gave P.B. an appalled one.

"No. I can't get someone to 'cover for me.'" She shook her head.

P.B. turned back to her, his expression caught between quarrelsome and confused.

"Peter . . ." She noticed she used his real name only when she was annoyed with him, like a mother trotting out first and middle names to warn her child that he was in trouble. "I told you I needed to pick the night. I also told you I couldn't go unless it was a night I had off. Don't you see? I *own* this place. I'm the pastry chef. I have a responsibility to be here."

"Don't *you* see?" he countered, leaning forward and taking her hand before she could jerk it away. She hoped to God Steve was doing something that prevented him from seeing it. "You *do* own this place. Which means you can decide when to come in and when to take a night off. What're they gonna do, fire you?"

Ire burned in her breast and she tried to pull her hand away gently. But P.B.'s grip was tight, his expression oblivious.

"P.B., it's not a lark, what I'm doing here," she said. "I *work* here. I've put everything I have into this place. And I'm the only pastry chef I've got, so I *have* to be here if there are going to be any desserts."

P.B. looked at the bar, his fingers toying with hers, sulking. "It's only one night."

She pulled her hand forcefully from his. "No it's not. It's *my* life. This is *my* life."

P.B. looked at her. "Isn't that a little dramatic?"

Steve turned from ringing up the old man's cordial at

the register and directed a slightly smug look at Rox-anne, as if to say, *See what a moron you've attached your-self to?*

"You know I'd cover you, *Rox*," he said with a lazy grin, "if I could."

Roxanne shot him a quick mind-your-own-business look, then glared at P.B.

"We need to talk," she said firmly.

Steve raised his brows and turned back to the regis-ter, flipping through the bar checks on its deck.

"Let's go out front a minute." Roxanne ducked back under the service bar and approached P.B. "Bring your coat."

With an exaggerated look of fear directed at Steve, P.B. complied and followed her out the front door.

The frigid air hit her face, delivering equal parts of re-lief and shock. Her sweat-salted skin contracted in the icy breeze. Mostly it felt good after her hot night in the kitchen, and it cooled her desperation to set P.B. straight just enough so that she could approach it calmly.

She took a deep breath. "Listen, P.B., I am truly sorry if I led you to believe—"

"Oh, *no!*" he exclaimed, shutting her up with the ve-hemence of the words.

She looked at him in surprise as he lay one hand on his face and tipped his head back. He laughed con-temptuously, presumably at himself, and turned once in a circle.

Lowering his hand, he faced her again. "Don't tell me. Are you *blowing me off?*"

He didn't appear angry so much as appalled.

"No, not 'blowing you off,'" she countered, "just, telling you how I feel. I am in no position to start a relationship right now and I should have told you that right up front. It seems we've been operating under two different assumptions. I looked at our getting together as developing a friendship. And you . . ." She trailed off. "Well, I'm not sure you were looking at it the same way."

"Huh." It wasn't quite a laugh but his lips were quirked. "I was thinking you liked me." He paused a moment, his mouth working as if to control a sneer. Finally he said, "It's Steve, isn't it?"

She was taken aback by this—wondered again what Steve might have told him—and could come up with nothing to say other than, "What?"

He laughed harshly. "*Dammit.* I knew it. I've seen how you look at him."

She was glad for the dark and the cold. It made it easier to keep her expression composed. "Steve and I have nothing to do with this."

"Shit." P.B. ran a hand through his hair and looked at the stars. "You and *Steve. Shit.* I knew it. I knew it." He shook his head. "That *dog.* I mean it, he knew how I felt about you."

"It's not Steve," she said, but her voice lacked conviction. It felt like a lie, even if it wasn't. And she suddenly felt worse than ever for coming between these two friends.

"Oh please." His laugh was so derisive she felt stupid. As if he really did know all about what had happened.

"That bastard." P.B. shook his head some more. "Well, I'll tell you." He pointed a finger at her. "You tell Steve he wins, he can go ahead and keep that hundred bucks, but I don't like the way he competes."

"He wins? What do you mean?" She frowned. Was this some kind of masculine game talk? Or was he talking about something completely different now?

"The bet." He laughed again and smacked his forehead mockingly. "But no, of course he wouldn't tell *you* about the bet. You, of all people."

Roxanne's stomach clenched. "What bet?"

"About you, babe." He chucked her softly under the chin with a light fist. "Whoever got you first."

Roxanne felt as if he'd punched her hard in the stomach.

"That's a terrible thing to say." She squeezed the words out of a suddenly airless chest.

"Oh, you don't believe me." He nodded knowingly. "That bad, huh? Well you just go in and look in that little cubbyhole by the register. The one in the brick wall there. There's a hundred dollars in there that's got Steve's name on it now. And good luck to you, doll."

With that, he put his hands in his pockets, turned and sauntered off.

She watched him go, barely breathing, hating the indolent air of his stride. Any ounce of sympathy she had for him before was gone as surely as if it had never existed.

A bet. The two had made a juvenile, disgusting, humiliating bet. About *her*.

What had been the crowning blow? What line had she crossed that had cemented the win for Steve? When she'd kissed him? Or when she'd let him into her bed, into her body?

She turned on her heel and strode back into the restaurant. George and Rita sat at the bar, sipping beers, while Steve stood behind it drying a glass with a white bar towel.

She stalked the length of the room, ducked under the service bar and went straight for the chink in the brick wall next to the register.

"You guys get everything worked out?" Steve asked. His tone was still mocking, still superior.

She looked straight at him as she put her fingers in the hole, then closed her eyes briefly as they found something.

She pulled the folded sheets of paper out, their edges catching on the rough brick, and looked down at a roll of twenties.

Fearing she might throw up—or worse, *cry*—she tossed the twenties on the counter in front of Steve and said, "You're fired."

Then she walked, on wooden legs, straight through the kitchen and out the back door.

11

Bar Special
Gin & Bitters on the Rox— for the day after
Gin, angostura bitters, with a twist

Steve drummed his fingers on his desk and looked at
his notes. He'd gone to the library and hadn't been able
to concentrate. He'd come home, turned on the computer, and still wasn't able to concentrate.

Last week's notes lay inert on the desk beside the
keyboard, waiting for some brain other than his to piece
them together and turn them into something coherent.

He tried going through them again. Notes from Portner's will. He'd found the will a couple of weeks ago,
and it was interesting but hadn't contained anything
new. There was one intriguing line just after the part
where he left everything to his sister, in which he said,
"includes the contents under the first step as described
to my Executor." But that had been well known by historians for years.

What had been described to the Executor would probably forever remain a mystery, but the "under the first step" part had at one time led to an examination of all the staircases in the house. The search had turned up nothing, furthering the case made by most historians that if the "contents" Portner was talking about had in fact been what Jefferson termed the "fair copy" of the Declaration of Independence that Portner had been suspected of stealing—the one that included edits made by John Adams and Benjamin Franklin—then he'd unloaded it sometime before his death.

The fact that that's the one draft that did not survive to this day was the only thing keeping alive the idea that it might still be hidden in the house.

The weakness of the evidence was brought home to him last week when even the supremely indifferent P.B. had said, after hearing this story, "And that's *it*? That's all you've got to back up that stupid story you tell everyone who happens to walk into the bar? Jeez, Steve, you might as well be telling ghost stories."

Beyond the will, however, Steve could find no other clues to the document or Portner's role in it's having gone missing.

He put his notes down. He couldn't do this now. He would just get more discouraged about his book. And besides, his brain was fried. It had been fried last night.

Last night, when it had become obvious that anything between him and Roxanne was most definitely not going to work. Last night, when P.B. had blown up all three of them with one traitorous bomb.

He'd considered wringing P.B.'s neck.

Then he thought about how, if he were P.B., he'd be pretty eager to wring Steve's.

It was only when he considered how much it must have hurt Roxanne to hear P.B.'s version of the bet that he actually rose from his desk to get the portable phone to call up and lambaste P.B.

Then he thought about Roxanne and wondered if he should be calling her first. How, from her point of view, he, Steve, looked bad. Really bad.

On the other hand, it could be argued that *he* was the one wronged. After all, she hadn't *asked* him about the bet. Hadn't even asked him if it were true. And even if she was sure it was true, she hadn't given him the opportunity to explain. She'd just believed the worst, right off the bat.

On the other hand, he had to concede, a hundred dollars in a hole in the wall looked bad. Really bad.

Still, it could have been anything. She didn't know, and she didn't ask. She just didn't trust him. That was the bottom line.

On the other hand, something like that would hurt first, then seem suspicious later. Maybe.

But he'd never done anything to hurt her. She was the one who'd had an attitude about him from the start. To just walk in and fire him—in front of the staff—was emotional and unprofessional. She'd leaped to a conclusion, then stood on it like a pillar of righteousness.

On the other hand, she didn't know P.B. like he did. Maybe she believed he was sincere, an injured suitor setting her straight.

But then, if P.B. was in on the bet, that made him as guilty as Steve.

On the other hand . . .

He groaned and lay his head down on the desk. Too many hands. He couldn't figure this out. It was an ugly, messy situation that should never have come up. If he'd kept his hands to himself, he wouldn't have this problem. She'd still just be the prickly new boss.

And then there was P.B. Why had he done it? Roxanne must have been canceling the symphony date and he got bent out of shape and screwed them both. Or he got cocky and told her she was just a bet between himself and Steve. It would be just like P.B. to confront rejection with some nasty jab of his own.

Had he known how far down he was taking Steve? Had Roxanne maybe even said something about what had happened between them?

He needed to talk to her.

But he knew she wouldn't talk. Not to him. She'd made up her mind about him the moment she'd first laid eyes on him. The first day she'd said she wasn't interested.

Well, maybe *she* wasn't, but her body was. They'd proven that much.

A knock sounded at the door.

Steve's head whipped up and he spun on his desk chair, pulling a Post-it note from his forehead.

Roxanne? he thought. Here with his final paycheck or some other confirmation of his termination? The last nail for his coffin perhaps?

Or maybe—just maybe—she'd come to discuss this in a calm, rational manner.

He strode across the living room and opened the door.

Rita stood in the hall holding a bouquet of flowers.

"Rita," he said in surprise. "I didn't know you cared."

She scowled. "I don't, you idiot, these are for *her*. You owe me fourteen dollars."

"Her?" He stepped back as she pushed through the door. "Her who?"

She turned to him with a look of exasperation. "Roxanne, of course. You take them to her, you explain, and you beg for your job back."

Steve crossed his arms over his chest and gaped at her, not bothering to move from, nor close, the front door. "Explain and beg? This is your advice? Without knowing any of the particulars, you want me to *explain and beg*?"

She put the bouquet down on the coffee table and shrugged out of her coat. "Yep."

She looked even smaller out of her puffy down coat, but she put her hands on her hips and stared him down anyway.

"We both know you can be a dog with women, Steve. I'm guessing you did something stupid—like nailing the boss and then not calling her—and now you've got to suck it up to keep your job."

"And this concerns you how?" Steve reached one hand out and slammed the door closed.

"Do you know how much money I made last night?" Rita glared at him as if it were somehow his fault.

"I don't know. It couldn't have been that bad, we were swamped."

"*Bad!*" She laughed, a ruthless sound. "Bad? It was *fantastic*. The best night waitressing of my entire life. And I don't want you or anybody else fucking this up for me. If Roxanne gets ditzy or we go without a decent bartender and screw up the damn good start we made last night, that's going to affect my income. My *new* income. Which is only one night old but already I'm pretty attached to it. So you go and explain and beg to Ms. High-and-Mighty and make sure that this damn restaurant is a success so I can finally get out of that hellhole I'm living in."

Steve looked at her red face and fierce eyes and couldn't help smiling. "What makes you think she didn't nail *me*?"

Rita threw her head back and sighed. "Because you're the one who's got no sense when it comes to women."

She moved into the kitchen.

"That's not true." He followed to where she opened the refrigerator door and peered inside. "When have I ever been stupid about women?"

Rita scoffed and craned her neck sideways. "You got any soda?"

"No. And answer the question."

She rolled her eyes toward him. "What about Lia? On-again, off-again, come-when-you're-called Lia? I wouldn't call that a good example of being smart about women."

He shrugged. "It's easy."

She pulled out a piece of pumpkin pie on a paper plate wrapped in plastic. "Can I eat this?"

"I wish you would. It's been in there since Christmas."

She made a face and slid it back onto the refrigerator shelf.

"Besides," she continued, opening up the vegetable

bin, "Roxanne's totally out of your league. I mean, look at her. She's a beauty queen with a shitload of money. You're just a guy with a nice smile."

"Gee, thanks."

She made a compromising movement with her head and added grudgingly, "I also hear you're pretty good in bed."

"What?"

She shrugged. "Girls talk."

She bent forward and disappeared behind the refrigerator door.

Despite himself, Steve's heart rate accelerated. "*Roxanne* told you that?"

Rita's head popped back up, an orange in her hand and her expression gleeful. She pushed the door shut. "Would Roxanne *know*?"

Damn.

"No—"

She raised her brows skeptically.

"—comment."

"Hah!" She leaned against the counter. "Okay, don't tell me. But whether she went slumming or not, you have to admit you are now in the position of having to apologize for whatever it is she thinks you did."

"I don't have to admit that. And what do you mean by 'slumming'?"

She grinned. "No comment."

"Look, I'll admit she's pretty. And she does seem to have some money. But what does that mean? That she can walk all over people? That she can be excused for thinking the worst of everyone? Even after lowering herself to—to *fraternize* with one of us?"

Rita, with her fingernails in the skin of the orange, raised her eyes to his, their green depths alight. "Holy shit, Serrano. You have no boundaries at all. You *did* nail her, didn't you?"

Her smile was straight from the devil.

Steve exhaled and ran a hand through his hair. "I didn't say that."

She widened her eyes innocently. "Oh yeah, right. Officially, sure. Gotcha." She pulled back the skin of the orange and the scent filled the kitchen air. "So what'd she fire you for, exactly?"

He studied her a second. Then he moved to the counter by the sink and pushed himself up onto it, resting his feet on a partly opened drawer beneath. "Okay, listen to this. You know how P.B. is."

Rita snorted and rolled her eyes, nodding.

"One night he was talking all kinds of trash about Roxanne and . . ." He filled her in on the genesis of the bet. "So I took the money just to shut him up," he finished. "Not to mention that it was fun to deprive him of a hundred bucks for a while. But I was *not* taking him up on the damn bet. Anybody who knows me knows I wouldn't make a bet like that. Hell, I'd forgotten all about it."

Rita narrowed her eyes and put another section of orange into her mouth.

Steve looked at her incredulously. Didn't Rita know that? How bad of a reputation did he have?

"I do know that about you," she said finally.

Steve exhaled.

"But *she* doesn't," she added. "Roxanne. Probably, I mean."

Another knock came from the front door.

Steve and Rita looked at each other.

"Think it's her?" Rita stage-whispered.

"Couldn't say." But his pulse quickened as he pushed off the counter and jogged to the foyer.

Opening the door, Steve couldn't have been more surprised to see the rotund figure of Monsieur Girmond. Even Roxanne would have been less startling.

"Steve. Ah, good. You are home," he said in a curiously hushed voice. His smile, however, was broad. "May I come in?"

Steve stepped back and extended a hand into the apartment. "Sure. Why are you whispering?" He peered out into the hall as the large man stepped past him.

Girmond shook his head, answering in a normal tone as soon as he entered the living room. "No reasons. Just a little frog in my throat."

Steve gestured for Girmond to follow him. "Come on into the kitchen. Rita's here, too."

"Rita?" Girmond stroked his moustache quizzically. "Waitress? Red hair?"

"Ah, yes. *Mon petit chou.*" He grinned and looked around the living room. "This is just exactly like Roxanne's apartment, no?"

Steve glanced around his barely decorated space, remembering the cozy atmosphere of Roxanne's.

"Not just exactly. But similar," he said, leading the way into the kitchen.

Rita was throwing the orange peel into the trash when they walked in. "Oh. Hi." She looked from Girmond to Steve with obvious curiosity.

"*Mademoiselle.*" Girmond gave a short bow and

turned back to Steve. "You are wondering why I am here."

"I have to say I am." Steve stepped toward the refrigerator. "Can I get you something to drink?"

Girmond looked around the kitchen with the critical eye of a chef, no doubt seeing the derelict, half-clean space of a non-cook. "Always the bartender, eh, Steve? No, thank you. I am here to speak with you about your job at the restaurant. May I speak freely?" He inclined his head toward Rita. "Pardon me, *mademoiselle*."

She shrugged. "You're pardoned."

Steve leaned back against the counter. "Go ahead. Rita knows most of my problems anyway."

He wondered how much say Girmond had about the running of the restaurant and guessed he had quite a bit, considering that without him there would *be* no restaurant.

Girmond nodded curtly. "Excellent. I have come to ask you to reconsider leaving your job. We need you, obviously, as we have no other bartender. And I believe you would maybe rather not look for new employment?"

Steve frowned. "I don't think it's me who needs to reconsider. I didn't quit, I was fired."

The older man held his hands behind his back and made a small, deferential bow. "Of course. I know that. Still, I ask you to come back."

Steve looked at him, perplexed. "What do you propose? That I tell Roxanne I don't accept her offer to be fired?"

Girmond's face was confident and he laughed. "Do not fear. She will want you back, as well."

"She will?"

"She is a passionate woman, our Roxanne. Sometimes led more by her emotions than is, ah, prudent." He gave a Gallic shrug. "But such is the nature of women, eh? They bring spirit to this world of ours."

Steve glanced at Rita, who was looking torn between insult and flattery.

He turned back to Girmond. "You seem to be forgetting something. She's also the owner of the restaurant. If she fires me, I gotta believe I'm gone."

Girmond inclined his head. "I intend to talk with her."

Steve looked at the floor. "Look, Mr. Girmond, I'm sure you have her best interests at heart, but generally speaking she seems to know what she wants. And what she doesn't."

Girmond chuckled. "Does she?"

Steve looked up. What did he mean by that?

"She is upset with you," Girmond said. "For what reason, I know not. She was not forthcoming with me."

"Hah! Join the club." Steve smiled to soften the edge on his words.

Girmond held up a meaty hand. "But to me it was a heated moment. She was inflamed, not thinking clearly. All I would like to know from you is, if she were to agree, would you take your job back?"

The man acted as if he knew he had some influence on her, Steve thought. Not only that, Steve could sense in the way he talked, the quiet sureness and humor of his expression, that Girmond knew Roxanne better than any of them had realized. Even if that weren't true, however, as the chef, the premier draw of the restaurant, chances were he could demand Steve be re-hired and Roxanne would cave.

Besides, God knew they'd need a bartender tonight, if last night was any indication.

"I don't know . . ." The devil in him didn't want to capitulate so easily. "If she's going to be this hotheaded I'm not sure she's the ideal employer."

Steve could feel Rita gaping beside him.

"For God's sake, Steve," she said. "Just tell him you'll take the job back. You know you will anyway."

He looked at her. "Do I? I was rather unfairly terminated, I think." He turned back to Girmond. "No offense, but your friend is a distrustful, suspicious woman with a heart of stone."

Girmond frowned and stroked his moustache. "She has some trouble trusting, for good reason. She should not be punished for this. She is a very beautiful woman, *monsieur*, and she deserves a second chance."

Steve folded his arms over his chest. "Beauty's only skin deep. Coldness goes all the way through."

Rita sighed. "Oh brother."

"She needs to stop jumping to conclusions about me," Steve added. "She's done that since the first time we met."

Girmond gave him a look that cut right through his bullshit. "Roxanne is perhaps reserved, and fearful of getting hurt. The unperceptive man," he enunciated this pointedly, "might see this as cold." The Gallic shrug again. *Nothing he could do about stupid people*, it seemed to say.

Steve's eyes narrowed. So the old guy had some manipulation in him. He'd have to remember that.

"All right," Steve said. "I'll come back. If she asks. But tell her she needs to stop thinking the worst of me."

Girmond smiled, eyes twinkling. "I will tell her to strive to look beyond the obvious."

Roxanne gritted her teeth and punched down her dough, dumping it out on the table into a mound of flour. She coughed as the cloud that ensued enveloped her.

She didn't want to see him. Didn't want to talk to him. Didn't want to have anything to do with his ugly little world. He belonged in a bar like Charters—smoky, dirty, scented with stale beer and filled with other juvenile minds—not in her radiant temple of gastronomic pleasure.

Steve was beneath her, she told herself, devoid of common human decency and sentiment. Anybody who could place a bet on emotion, on passion, was a degenerate of the worst sort. He did not deserve her notice.

At least Martin, for all his flaws, respected the passion that was between them. He hadn't belittled it by turning it into a . . . a *conquest*.

Or had he? Maybe hooking up with a young woman who graced the covers of magazines was a kind of triumph for him over what he'd always termed "the stagnation" of his marriage.

She shook her head. She didn't need to impugn anyone else with Steve's falseness. And she certainly didn't need to be thinking about Martin in any context. Though she had to wonder how in the *world* she'd managed to learn nothing from Martin's treachery. She'd trusted Steve when she should have been at her most vigilant. After learning how selfish men could be, she had turned around and trusted another liar, all the while believing her only problem with him was their lack of common interests. What a fool she was.

She punched her dough again and began rolling it out.

She would just stay here in the kitchen. She didn't need to see Steve. If she needed more water, she could send a busboy.

No.

No, it wasn't incumbent upon *her* to hide from *him*. Let him be the one worried about seeing her. Let him be anxious about what to say now that she'd discovered his true character.

He was just lucky M. Girmond was able to convince her that having a lying, philandering bartender was better than having no bartender at all. Business first, he'd said. And that would be her motto from here on out.

Business first.

"No, no, no!" she heard M. Girmond say to one of the assistants—the garde-manger—behind her. "You treat asparagus like a *flower*, do you understand me? You do not lay it in a tub full of water to soak like a baby. You stand it *up*, like a flower!"

"But before I always—"

"I do not care about before. Before means nothing to me. *Rien!* Before you did not work for a place that respected the food, or they would have stood the asparagus up."

"Like a flower . . ."

"*Exactement.* Now, about the fish. It should be stored in the same position in which it swims, *oui*?"

Roxanne smiled to herself. She couldn't help but feel confident with M. Girmond in the kitchen. He was a master, a perfectionist, with an attention to detail unrivalled in culinary circles. And she knew, even if tonight was as busy as last night, and tomorrow night as busy as tonight, that that attention to detail wouldn't waver in the slightest.

She turned from her dough and began working on the custard filling.

Roxanne's strategy for dealing with Steve worked and didn't work. She succeeded in not seeing him all night, but she also succeeded in not leaving the kitchen. The crowd was in fact the same as the previous night's, and while that elated her, it also ran her ragged.

Sir Nigel came back at one point early in the evening to report, with what constituted a smile on his face, that reservations for Friday night had been filled.

Booked! she thought, her stomach sailing with excitement. Open two days and she was already booked solid one weekend night.

She wished she had a moment to call Skip. Even though he'd been negative about her plan to open this restaurant she knew he'd be pleased for her. As he had said, he didn't *want* her to fail; he was just afraid she would.

It didn't look like that would happen now, she thought with a deep, quiet joy. Everything was coming together perfectly. And with that thought she pulled a perfect raspberry soufflé out of the oven.

The kitchen was quiet, she was wiping down her counter, and M. Girmond was packing up for the evening. Out front, most of the waitstaff was gone, but she could still hear the vacuum being run in the dining room. George, probably. It was his night to close.

"Well, my dear. It is another night of adventure, *n'est pas*?" M. Girmond stopped behind her and gave her shoulders a squeeze with his big warm hands. "You should be so proud of yourself, *mon ange*."

She smiled and dropped her head as he kneaded her aching muscles. "I'm proud of *you*, mostly. It's because of you that everyone came. But I am proud of the way the employees all came together and worked so well. Who would have thought there would be so few glitches?"

He patted her back. "There is time for glitches. But here we are getting our feet in the door. Problems later . . ." He put his hands up, nonchalantly. "We will deal with them."

She smiled, tired down to her very bones. "No, no. No problems. I won't allow it."

M. Girmond laughed, his hearty, comforting laugh. "We cannot hope that there will never be problems, *ma puce*. We can only aspire to dealing with them well."

"Spoken like a true Zen master."

M. Girmond laughed again, patted her once more on the back, then wished her good night. "Go to sleep soon!" he called as he went out the back door.

Roxanne locked the door behind him, then turned out the lights. She pushed through the swinging doors to the dining room, which was dark. Everyone had finished, cleaned up and gone home. The only light was from the bar, where soft spotlights on the bottles gave them a jewel-like glow.

She sighed and sat in one of the bar chairs, looking out over the dining room. Street lamps from the sidewalk outside lit the tables by the front window, gleaming off the glasses and silverware laid out for tomorrow's service. Some of the tables were bare, waiting for clean dishes to be set out, but for now the place looked quiet and ready for another day. Everything was under control.

Her restaurant was a success.

She let the thought wash over her. A calm such as she had never known settled within her. Even the fiasco with Steve seemed small compared to all that was right. Besides, Steve was still here.

Not that it mattered that he was still here. Mostly it just meant that she hadn't screwed up so badly that she was without a bartender. That was all.

She should go to bed, she thought. She was too tired to be thinking these thoughts. But she was too tired to get up off the chair, too. She thought briefly about laying her head down right here, but knew she'd only wake up in an hour with a stiff neck wondering where she was.

She hoisted herself out of the chair and stopped abruptly.

Had she heard something?

She stopped breathing. It sounded again. Someone working at the lock on the front door.

Her heart immediately started hammering in her chest. What if last time there really *had* been an intruder and it was not just the squirrel? What if he had come back to finish the job? At a million thoughts a minute, she had already constructed the scene of her demise when whoever was at the door succeeded in getting it open.

She gasped. The door swung wide. She stood frozen as a hand hit the switch for the light over the maitre d' station.

She squinted in the light. It was Steve. And he was apparently as startled to see her as she was to see him.

"Jesus," he breathed, after visibly jumping when he saw her. "You scared the shit out of me."

She took a deep, wavering breath. "What are you doing here?"

Her tone was imperious. She knew because she made it that way. And Steve obviously picked up on it.

"I forgot my backpack." He gave her a cool look as he walked around the bar. "Don't worry. I'll be out of your hair in a minute."

She didn't say anything, just watched him lift the hinged door of the service bar and root around in the lower cabinets for his bag.

"So what are you waiting for?" He pulled the bag out and looped it over his shoulder. "Got a hot date?"

Roxanne brushed her palms down her sides, her posture impeccable. "I could ask the same of you."

"You could. But *I* would answer. There's the difference." He closed the service bar quietly behind him.

"What does that mean?"

"It means . . ." He stopped before her and tilted his head. "That if I'd heard a story about you, I would ask you about it before flying off the handle."

"Would you?" she said, her tone reflecting that she didn't believe it for an instant.

"I would."

"I did something different." She crossed her arms over her chest and forced herself to hold his gaze, though it did all kinds of syrupy things to her insides. "I consulted the evidence, and in doing so found confirmation of the whole sordid story."

"And by evidence you're referring to . . . ?"

"The money, of course."

"Ah, of course." He nodded his head. "For women, money always talks, that's for sure."

"And men are so impervious to money."

"Some men."

"I wouldn't bet on that," she replied with a chuckle.

He stood quiet for a moment, studying her. She fought the urge to squirm under his regard.

"Roxanne, listen, I'm only going to say this once—"

"Is that a threat? Because I don't feel very afraid."

His brows lowered. "I had nothing to do with that bet, other than taking P.B.'s money to shut him up."

"Which apparently didn't work." She gave him a mock-sympathetic look.

He took a frustrated breath. "I just want you to understand that I did not bet on you. On us. On—you know. I didn't bet that I could *get* you."

"And yet, you did."

"No I didn't! Oh, you mean . . . I didn't plan on that. I didn't plan on anything that evening. Surely you know that."

"And now we both regret it. But look on the bright side. *You* won a hundred dollars."

He shook his head. "I'm not keeping that. I told you, it was never a bet."

"So P.B.'s getting his money back?" She laughed cynically, spreading her arms wide. "All this and change back?"

"Roxanne . . ."

She shook her head, nerves shaking from her head to her feet. "I think I should get it."

"You—what?"

She held out a hand. "The money. You should at least split it with me."

Steve gave an incredulous laugh. "You want the money?"

"Half of it. I want to get a new lock for my door."

The smile was still half on his face. "That only works if you don't open it yourself."

Her eyes were steady on his. "I don't think that'll be a problem anymore."

He laughed again, shaking his head, and plopped his backpack on the bar. Unzipping an outer pocket he said, "I'd rather you have this than P.B. anyway."

He held out the roll of bills to her.

She stepped toward him, took the roll and counted the twenties, five of them.

"Thank you." She pushed them into her pocket. "Now we're even. So from now on if you'll keep your mind on the job and your pants zipped, we won't have any problems."

She turned away.

Steve's hand took her upper arm and turned her back to face him. "Excuse me?" he said. "If *I'll* keep *my* pants zipped? Can we just jump back in time a little bit and remember who kissed whom first that night at your apartment?"

He dropped his hand.

"*You* apologized for that." Heat rose in her cheeks but she didn't care. He was off balance now.

"As did *you*." He glared at her. "And if you're honest with yourself you'll remember that I did not exactly have to force myself on you the other night. You were right there with me. Right there," he repeated, stepping closer, "*with me.*"

She stared back at him, her chin lifted and her heart beating wildly. He was close to her, his eyes fiery, and God help her, she felt a wave of desire wash over her.

Something flickered in his eyes, and after a second a slight smile curved his lips. "Don't pretend you didn't feel anything. Don't pretend you don't feel anything right now, Roxanne."

She inhaled slowly to brace herself and said, cool as she could, "How much do you have on *this* encounter? Huh, Steve? Another hundred?"

"Consider this a gentleman's bet," he said. "With you."

She laughed. "Control yourself, Serrano. I don't like betting on the same horse twice. Besides, your charm has a limited life span."

His eyes were soft now, enticing, and somehow they compelled her to stay where she stood.

"I know that," he said, his voice low.

He stood close, too close for her to draw an even breath, and he reached a hand up to touch her cheek.

The contact zinged through her and she felt that now-familiar melting at her core that signaled her body's unequivocal desire.

"But something tells me it hasn't worn off yet." With that, he took her chin in his hand and laid a kiss on her lips.

Despite herself, her mouth opened under his. Their tongues met. Heat flared within her and the kiss deepened.

He wanted her too, she could feel it in his mouth, his tongue, his lips. Could feel it in the heat coming off of his body, in the way he stood rigid, unwilling to touch her beyond his fingers on her chin.

Just as she was willing to throw the whole damn fight out the window, just as she raised her hand to touch his body, he pulled back.

She stood before him, on fire, but unable to move.

Dead serious, pulse beating hard in his neck, he let his fingers trail her cheek as he dropped his hand.

"I'm not the only one who can't control himself," he said and stepped back. With one shake of his head, he added, "Don't kid yourself, Roxanne."

12

Dessert Special of the Day
Bombe Chez Soi—what you least expect
Strawberry ice mold filled with vanilla mousse,
   surrounded by sliced fresh strawberries

Steve hunched over his notebook, open books spread
on the table around him in the hush of the Library of
Congress. He scratched out one sentence on the pad in
front of him, then another, then sat back.

Portner Jefferson Curtis was proving to be an inadequate distraction from Roxanne Rayeaux.

He should call Lia, he thought. That was the kind of
distraction he needed. Flesh and blood. Not musty old
papers and unprovable theories.

Of course, with Lia he'd also get guilt and remorse,
additional proof that she and Steve had absolutely
nothing in common.

He scratched his forehead, then rubbed his palm
against it.

He didn't want Lia, couldn't even quite remember what was appealing about Lia, with Roxanne taking over his mind. All he could think about was Roxanne's thick, glossy hair cascading through his fingers. Her hot, soft skin, pale in the moonlight next to his. Her lithe body as eager and hungry as his, pressing, shifting, winding around him like a cloud of erotic energy— or an impossibly seductive serpent.

His body began to tighten and he leaned forward again, staring at the portrait of Portner in the dusty book in front of him.

Thin, pointed face. Slick black hair. Beady, unscrupulous eyes. The man's face screamed *thief*.

Steve was as certain he'd stolen the "fair copy" of the Declaration of Independence as if he'd known him personally. And he probably did know him better than he knew most modern-day people. He'd read the man's letters, examined his will, studied his history, lived in his house.

Steve sighed.

The worst part was, it wasn't just Roxanne's body that made her so irresistible to his thoughts. She was completely unpredictable. He never knew what she was going to say or do.

Lia, he could predict like the sequence of the old *Mousetrap* game. Say this and that falls, do this thing and you end up in that trap, make her mad and the whole thing comes tumbling down.

Roxanne was just the opposite. Do something you think will earn you a slap across the face and you end up having the night of your life. Challenge her in a way that would make other women explode and she throws it right back at you.

He couldn't have been more stunned, or more impressed, when she said she deserved P.B.'s bet money. He chuckled even now just thinking about it.

"Mr. Serrano?" A rumpled man of about fifty with glasses on the end of his nose stood next to him with a cardboard box.

"Yes?" Steve sat up, feeling as if he'd been caught talking to himself. He used the opportunity to stretch elaborately, and his back muscles screamed in protest.

"We came across another box of letters you might be interested in." The man smelled heavily of body odor as he leaned over to put it on Steve's table. "There are at least a couple letters that other people wrote to Jefferson, but there might be one in here from the cousin you're looking for."

Steve's eyes shifted to the box. It looked like something that might come out of his mother's attic. Fatigue washed over him. How many boxes like this had he prowled through? How many times had he thought *here* was going to be the evidence he was looking for?

"Thanks," he said, mustering a smile. "Thanks very much."

The man nodded and went back to his desk.

Steve stood up and ran a finger along one edge of the box to remove a spiderweb. He tried to remind himself that this *could* be the very box that would contain what he most needed, despite his being tired and discouraged. He even tried to tell himself he could find something else, just as good, to give merit to all his time spent studying this degenerate Jefferson cousin.

But he didn't believe it.

Still, he reached a hand in and gently pulled forth a sheaf of folded parchment. Slowly, he laid the letters out on the table, one by one, searching for the hand-writing he'd come to know so well . . .

"And it'll be delivered this afternoon?" she asked, hold-ing the phone between her ear and shoulder as she put her wallet with her credit cards in it back into her purse. "Yes, just put them in a box. That's great, thank you."

She hung up the phone and smiled. Roxanne: 1, Steve: 0.

After locking the apartment door behind her, Rox-anne trotted down the stairs to the restaurant, her kitchen clogs galloping on the wooden treads like a herd of horses.

She felt good. No, more than good. She felt like the world was her oyster. Something about that kiss had set her free. Or maybe it was the moments leading up to it. When she'd realized this was not something to ag-onize about, but maybe something she could have a lit-tle fun with.

The bottom line was, she was in control.

Strange, she knew, considering she was most defi-nitely *out* of control when Steve kissed her—at least physically. But there it was.

It helped that she believed him about the bet. She'd seen enough of both Steve and P.B. to know who was probably telling the truth and which scenario was more likely. So she was able to shed the ugly fear that she'd been the object of some sick joke between them.

Not that that meant she was eager to be involved with either one. Quite the contrary. It just meant she and Steve could probably get back to some semblance of a decent working relationship.

The best thing—the thing that really kept her spirits buoyed—was that the restaurant was doing well, far better than expected. Her life in New York was becoming a distant memory and—most of all—she was barely thinking about Martin, at least not with any sort of longing. When she left him over a year ago to go to culinary school, she thought he'd be in her thoughts forever. A constant ache of failure, of love lost.

Now the only reason he was even a blip on her radar was as a cautionary tale. A lesson.

Instead she was excited by her work. By her whole new life. And even by the way she was dealing with her mistakes.

She let herself into the restaurant, taking a good long minute in the dining room to appreciate the warm colors, the welcoming French country prints, the coziness of the brick walls. Winter sun poured through the front window, making the whole place feel like a little oasis of spring, even though it was twenty degrees and as windy as a Chicago city street outside.

Maybe someday she'd have to open for lunches. The place was just too charming in daylight to be empty.

With a smile she moseyed back to the kitchen, where she was greeted by gleaming chrome and the fresh smell of a meticulously clean room.

She was going to make *le délice de Montecito* for dessert tonight. A special cake made with chocolate and meringue and Amaretto. Her favorite part, however, was the French butter cream.

As she got out the ingredients, she noticed a cold draft on her feet. Trepidation oozed up her spine as she remembered the last time she felt an indoor breeze—when the back door had been broken into—and she looked toward that exit now.

Shut and locked tight, the windows intact. She glanced around the room. Nothing seemed amiss.

She kept working. But every now and then another draft would eddy around her ankles and creep up her pants legs. Was it just because she wore clogs that she felt it more on her heels? Or was the breeze coming from someplace low, some vent gone awry?

She squatted and put her hands near the mats covering the floor. There was definitely a draft. She tried to follow it toward the back door, but it was coming from across the room.

From, she discovered as she hobbled low across the floor, the basement door.

She put her hand by the crack at the base of the door and felt the frigid air wafting through it.

She stood up. This wasn't normal, was it? Surely it wasn't *that* cold out, that the basement would let fly a frosty breeze.

The office was the next door over and she entered it to get her keys. Normally the keys to the basement, the freezer (which they never locked, but *could*, if they wanted to), and the middle drawer of the desk hung on a nail protruding from the door trim.

That nail was empty.

She narrowed her eyes and stepped back out of the office. Turning to the basement door, she put a hand on the knob and paused. Should she call someone before going downstairs?

No. She didn't want to call Steve. She'd done that last time and regretted it. And she certainly didn't want to call P.B. She could call Skip, but he was at school and wouldn't be able to come over until later. She could call the police and ask for someone other than P.B., but it wasn't as if she knew something was wrong. Right now it was just a case of missing keys, and you didn't call the cops for that.

She turned the knob. The door opened.

Maybe she'd gone down here earlier and just forgotten to lock up again. Or maybe M. Girmond had put something down here and accidentally pocketed the keys. They had talked about using the basement for additional dry goods storage.

She flipped the light switch and was glad to see the bare bulb come on. It wasn't particularly bright, but it was better than nothing.

She trod carefully down the stairs, taking each step as if it might collapse under her weight, her eyes slowly adjusting to the dim light. The breeze grew and the temperature dropped the farther she descended.

When she neared the bottom she saw a huge hole dug in the hard dirt floor of the cellar, just at the base of the stairs. She stepped around it and looked inside. It was empty. Nothing but chopped up dirt and clay.

She turned in a circle. It took her eyes a moment to fully adjust to the contrast of outside light and cellar darkness, mixed with the dim glow of the bare light-bulb, but when they did, what she saw was destruction.

At the opposite end of the cellar, daylight shone through the split boards of the trapdoor to the alley, il-luminating a space strewn with broken wood, scat-tered bricks and cracked mortar.

This was not the work of any squirrel. She doubted even a bear could do this.

One side of the brick foundation had been picked at here and there, as if someone had taken several large pieces out of the jigsaw puzzle that made up the wall. The bricks that had occupied those spaces lay scattered on the dirt floor.

At the far end, broken boards lay in haphazard piles and the cotton-candy trailings of fiberglass insulation blew in the breeze.

Roxanne put a hand to her throat, felt her heart pounding in the arteries there. For a moment she thought she might throw up.

The abandoned cellar entrance from the alley had been boarded up and nailed shut, she happened to know. Not only that, but the space beneath the trapdoor had been stuffed with that pink fiberglass insulation.

She would bet anything most of that insulation was now swirling around the back alley in the wind.

And at the bottom of the trapdoor stairs, too, was a hole. Not quite as large or as deep as the other, but still a hole.

But . . . if someone had broken in through the outside entrance, why were the keys missing?

The answer came to her immediately.

To break in again.

She heard a slight sound behind her and jumped, whirling toward the dark end of the room. She saw nothing, then spotted a piece of the paper that had covered the insulation listing in the breeze.

She had to call the police.

She jumped over the hole at the bottom of the kitchen steps and took the stairs two at a time, started to slam the door at the top but realized she shouldn't touch anything. She wondered what they would get fingerprints off of in the basement, what with all the broken wood and brick. Would brick hold a fingerprint? The back cellar entrance looked like someone had taken an axe to it. Who would do such a thing?

And why hadn't she heard it?

Because she'd been exhausted. She'd slept like the dead last night.

She sat down at her desk chair in the office and dialed 911. No messing around this time. Maybe they'd send someone other than P.B., but even if they didn't, she needed the cops. Someone was obviously looking for something and unless they'd gotten it out of one of those holes they would probably be back.

Naturally they sent P.B.

Roxanne could only shake her head as she saw his squad car pull up in front of the restaurant and his square blond head appear over the door.

He parked right in front, of course, with the lights on so as to draw as much attention to the scene as possible, it seemed.

She walked slowly to the front door and pulled it open.

She didn't know what she expected, but it wasn't the same old overly friendly P.B. he'd always been.

"Hey, Roxanne," he said with that trademark rise of one big square hand. "Hear you had another encounter with a squirrel."

He laughed at his own joke as his little partner—Officer Stuart?—got out of the passenger-side door.

She shook her head. "Unless this squirrel was the size of a gorilla, I don't think that's what we're dealing with."

"Well, we'll check it out for you."

He arrived at her side and gave her shoulder a squeeze with one hand. It was a companionable gesture, making her feel slightly guilty for all the awful thoughts she'd had about him since learning of the bet.

His next words, however, erased any pity she might have felt.

"I know you girls get all in a tizzy about your things getting messed up or not looking the way they should, so we'll just see if there was an actual intruder this time." He gestured toward his partner. "Stu, you wanna take the squad car around back? I'll meet you there. C'mon, Rox, let's take a look at what this giant squirrel did."

She rolled her eyes as she turned toward the door, resenting the feel of his meaty paw on the small of her back. How could she ever have accepted a date with this guy? Had he just hidden all this condescending crap?

Maybe so. And maybe he didn't feel like he had to hide it anymore . . .

That made her feel better, and she was happy to lead him down the basement steps to the destruction no wildlife creature could have wreaked.

"Holy shit," P.B. said, his tone reverential, as he stepped over the hole in the dirt. He strode into the room, bending to look at a cracked brick, then moved close to the wall to examine one of the patchwork holes.

He pulled a flashlight from his belt and shone it on the mud exposed behind the wall, looking all around the edges, and even prodding some of the bricks with a pen.

"This is bad. Any worse and I'd say you should get someone in here to look at this foundation."

She closed her eyes. *Damn.* "It's that bad? You think it's, it's been compromised?"

P.B. shrugged. "Nah. It's probably okay. But it sure as hell is a mess."

"What do you think they were looking for?" She caught herself wringing her hands in a very "tizzy-like" way and dropped them to her sides.

"Hey!" Officer Stuart yelled from the broken cellar door at the far end of the room. "I found an old padlock out here, maybe something from the door? And a sliver of metal, like maybe a broken tool or something."

"Bag it up, Stu," P.B. called, walking over to look into the hole by the trap door.

Roxanne started toward P.B. to see what he was looking at so intently, but at the sound of her movement he turned and held a hand out. "Hold it right there."

She jumped, her heart rate accelerating with another surge of adrenaline. It had been surging since she'd found the break-in.

"What? What is it?" She looked upward as if the

foundation had already started giving way and she was about to be crushed by three stories of eighteenth-century townhouse.

P.B. looked annoyed. "I don't want you kicking this stuff around. We gotta look at everything. Where it sits, how it fell, everything." He strode toward her, seemingly heedless of where he put his big bootheels.

Roxanne flushed and nearly made some churlish retort, when he said in a more hushed tone, "Let's go upstairs. I want to ask you something." He glanced over his shoulder, intimating he didn't want Officer Stuart to hear what he was going to say.

Roxanne turned and went up the stairs, P.B. right behind her. In fact, he was so close behind, she felt a little self-conscious about where her rear end was in relation to his eyes.

When they reached the kitchen, P.B. took her arm and pulled her away from the back door. Her back against the wall near the office, he stood very close. Too close for comfort.

"Do you know where Steve was last night?" His eyes were flat and intent, a cop's eyes.

Heat poured into her cheeks. "He was here. Until we closed, obviously." Then she remembered. "And just afterward. He came back when I was locking up because he forgot his backpack."

P.B.'s brows rose. "He came back," he repeated significantly.

She nodded. "Because he forgot his backpack."

P.B.'s head moved in the barest nod. "Uh-huh."

She frowned. "Why? What are you saying?"

"Did he know you were going to be here when he came back?"

"I don't know." Did P.B. think *Steve* had something to do with this? That was ridiculous. Surely he wasn't saying that. "It was late," she added, "but it wasn't that much later than I usually leave."

Though Steve had nearly jumped out of his skin when he'd seen her.

"You say he came back for the backpack?"

"Yes. I saw him get it." Her heart was beating fast, as if she herself were being accused of something.

"The one he keeps under the bar?"

"Yes."

"The one that's *always* under the bar?" he said again.

She narrowed her eyes. If she could have backed away from him, she would have, but he had her against the wall and was standing so close she would have had to push him away.

"What are you saying, P.B.?"

At this he crossed his arms over his chest and turned away, one hand stroking his chin as he thought, as if he fancied himself some kind of Sherlock Holmes.

She took the opportunity to draw a relieved breath.

"Tell me." He turned back to her. "Has Steve talked any more about his *research*? You know, all that stuff about Thomas Jefferson and the draft of the Declaration of Independence?"

She shook her head. "No. He hasn't said a word about that since that one night."

"He hasn't said a word," P.B. repeated slowly, as if that, too, were significant. "Not a word?"

"Well, no. But we don't talk history a lot."

P.B. raised one brow and she knew immediately what he was thinking. "No, I don't imagine you do much talking." He let that sit a beat, then added, "About history."

"Look, P.B., I'm not sure what you're insinuating, but you can't possibly think Steve had anything to do with this."

"Can't I?"

Roxanne's mouth dropped open.

"Look, Roxanne, he talks to me about it all the time. I'm telling you, Steve's obsessed. It's got to be him."

Roxanne stared at him in disbelief. "You can't be serious."

"Hey, I know it's a terrible thing to say." P.B.'s face took on a concerned expression. "But Steve hasn't been himself lately. He's been worried about the fact that he's not going anywhere, that he doesn't have a career, a future, you know. Same stuff you and I talked about the night I took you out. For a while there he even thought he might have to leave this job. You gotta know I hate to say it. But I think he might be getting desperate."

"So desperate he'd start digging in the basement walls for some mythical document?" She nearly laughed. "He'd have to be an idiot!"

"What do you mean?" P.B. demanded. "You heard him talk about that draft. There's *evidence*—history, theories, whatever. There's good reason to believe something's hidden in this house. Why wouldn't he try to find it? It's worth a shitload of money."

"Because it's ridiculous. If nobody's found it yet, after all the years this house has been lived in, worked in, remodeled—well, it's crazy."

"I think you'd better take another look at your basement."

She took a deep breath. "Besides, what about this: Steve doesn't *have* to break in to look around the basement. The last thing he'd have to do is take an axe to the cellar door, for God's sake. He's got keys. He can walk down there whenever he wants."

P.B. gave her what could only be called a pitying look. "But, honey," he said slowly, as if to an inquisitive first grader, "then it wouldn't look like a break-in. The man's not stupid. If it's an inside job, you make it look like an outside job."

Roxanne's cheeks burned. He was right, of course. You wouldn't start tearing up the basement and not make it look like a break-in.

"Was anything else missing?" he asked. "Even if he did know enough to make it look like an outside job, Steve's an amateur, he probably wouldn't think to swipe a thing or two to throw us cops off the scent."

"I—I haven't looked around," she said desperately, knowing in her heart that nothing else was missing. The kitchen had been immaculate this morning. Just the way it had been left the night before.

"Uh-huh." P.B. nodded, looking at her knowingly.

"P.B., I simply don't believe—"

"Hey." Steve pushed through the swinging doors to the kitchen and Roxanne jumped enough to bump her head against the wall behind her.

"Hey, big guy," P.B. said, too heartily, in Roxanne's opinion. "What's going on?"

Steve looked from P.B. to Roxanne. "That's just what I was going to ask."

"We were just about to call you. Where you been?" P.B. asked, still grinning like a used-car salesman and sounding like a radio announcer.

Again he looked from P.B. to Roxanne. "At the library. And you wouldn't believe what I found. It's just what I've been—"

"The *library*," P.B. repeated, looking at Roxanne.

Steve stopped. "What's going on here?"

Roxanne looked at Steve. "Steve, there's been another break-in. In the basement—"

P.B. put a hand out, his arm blocking Roxanne's chest as if she were about to step into a street teeming with traffic. "I'll handle this."

"*Handle* this?" Steve repeated.

"I'm the one who should explain," P.B. amended, puffing out his chest a little. "I've just finished examining the damage. She might even need to call in an engineer to check the foundation."

"The foundation!" Steve was obviously disconcerted. "What'd they do, detonate a bomb?"

To Roxanne, it was obvious Steve had no idea what was going on.

Or did she just *want* to think that?

She shook her head. P.B. was throwing out a theory. He didn't have any facts. That it was a theory that implicated a friend who had just betrayed him with a woman he'd wanted to date said it all.

"Come on," P.B. said to Steve, "I'll show you the damage. But you gotta be careful. Don't forget it's a crime scene. You can't be touching or moving anything."

"Come off it, P.B.," Steve said tiredly, stepping past Roxanne, with a quick glance at her. "Just show me what happened."

Before they got to the basement door, however, Officer Stuart knocked on the back door.

"You got a key for that?" P.B. said, directing an officious finger from Roxanne to the back door, even though she'd already started across the kitchen to unlock it.

She pulled the door open and let him in.

"I found this." Officer Stuart looked triumphant as he held one black glove aloft in his hand.

"No, that's mine," Steve said, shaking his head. "I've been looking for it. It must have dropped out of my pocket when I got out of the truck the other night."

He strode across the room toward the officer, hand out.

Behind his back, P.B. gave Roxanne a sad but meaningful look.

"'Fraid not, sir," Officer Stuart said, lowering the glove to his side. "Everything I find out here today is evidence."

13

Dessert Special of the Day
Apple Fig Turnover—<u>because turnabout's
   fair play</u>
Apples and figs sauteed in sweet butter
   with vanilla and cognac in puff pastry

Steve looked suspiciously from Officer Stuart to Roxanne to P.B.

"So you're saying I can't get my glove back until you figure out who broke in?" he asked.

P.B. scowled and glanced away. Then he jerked his head in the direction of the basement door and said, "C'mon. Let me show you this."

Steve's eyes met Roxanne's and she shrugged her brows. "I've got work to do," she said, turning away.

He watched her back, then followed P.B. down the basement steps.

The moment he and P.B. reached the cellar and

Steve's eyes adjusted to the light, P.B. turned to him and said, "You know I oughta punch you in the face, you dog. You could have at least told me you were going after Roxanne."

Steve stopped, glad P.B. had brought the matter up directly but distracted by the presence of a large hole at the base of the stairs. He knew why that hole was there, but who else would?

He tried to focus on P.B. "From the way you took that damn bet so seriously I figured you thought I was. Besides, it was something that just happened, kind of by accident. I wasn't trying to go behind your back."

P.B. shook his head. "Well, you could have told me you were *successful* anyway. Now what am I gonna do with these damn symphony tickets? Nobody I know's gonna wanna go listen to that shit."

Steve chuckled and after a second P.B. joined him.

Steve studied the hole, then cast his gaze around the basement. Chinks of wall were missing, which made no historical sense, but another hole at the bottom of the unused stairs to the outside trapdoor caught his eye. Those steps were too recent to be of interest to any historian, but the only logical reason to dig there was the historical one.

"This is some kind of mess, huh?" Steve said. "What do you think they were doing down here?"

P.B. shrugged. "Who knows? Maybe looking for drug money."

Steve had nothing to say to that. It didn't seem likely, but sounded like a typical cop suspicion.

He looked hard at P.B.

P.B. noticed the look. "What?"

Steve hesitated. "You shouldn't have told her about that bet, Peeb. She didn't deserve to have her feelings hurt like that."

P.B. shrugged and kicked a broken brick across the dirt floor. "I know. I feel a little bad about that. But still, she was stepping out on me. You know, in a way."

Which is why she told you she didn't want to go to the damn symphony, Steve thought, but he didn't say it. It was enough that P.B. admitted to feeling some guilt.

"So . . ." Steve moved back across the cellar toward P.B., holding out a hand. "Should we let bygones be bygones and all that?"

P.B. laughed and slap-grabbed Steve's hand. "Done. It'd take more than just some chick to undo our friendship, right? Hell, I've known you longer than I've known anybody, except my parents."

"And they *have* to keep in touch with you," Steve said with a grin.

It took P.B. a minute, then he punched Steve in the arm. "So tell me about what you found at the library. You seemed pretty stoked when you came in. Good news?"

Steve couldn't help smiling. It had to be a conscious decision but he let go of his anger toward P.B. Hanging onto it would have been a little like kicking a dog, then being mad at it for biting you. "The best."

In the interest of laying this rocky patch between them to rest, Steve told him about what amounted to his best day of research yet. Because today, he had found what he'd been looking for. A letter from Portner Jefferson Curtis to a Mr. Stanhope in May 1826, following up an apparent face-to-face meeting, further clarifying the terms of his will to include an object that "has been kept under lock and key," and would be kept "likewise sequestered until such time as the Notable Author, Mr. Jefferson, who is known to be ailing, has left this earthly plane, or I have done so."

Furthermore, he stated that this object "has been seen by none other than" himself for years, and that it was hidden, "quite cleverly", within his abode until such time as Mr. Stanhope had need of executing Portner's will.

This letter might have been enough to prove Steve's theory—or at least fuel it for the purposes of his book—but with the object in question undefined, Steve dug further. In a batch of letters he'd copied some months ago, Steve, remembering the name Stanhope, found a letter from June 1826 from one Mortimer Stanhope to Portner Jefferson Curtis of Alexandria, Virginia, declaring that Portner would be best advised to place what he suspected was "a document of significant historical merit" with the appropriate authorities at the Department of State. The Department of State was created by the Constitution and was supposed to keep "the custody and charge of all records, books and papers" of importance to the new Republic.

If that didn't strongly suggest that Portner's "object" could very well be Jefferson's "fair copy," Steve didn't know what would.

In addition, Stanhope wondered why Portner would want to keep something that could not "morally have been acquired, and therefore could not be honorably displayed nor employed for any profitable purpose."

Not only did this imply that the document in question had been stolen, but it also seemed to confirm that the draft was still in Portner's possession when he died less than a year after receipt of Mr. Stanhope's letter, and only three months after Jefferson himself had died.

It also confirmed that the draft had at one time been hidden somewhere within this very house. Meaning there was at least a chance that it was still here, in some form or other—most probably in a pile of decomposing parchment.

P.B. listened to this story in silence, feigning, Steve was certain, what little interest showed on his face. At the end of Steve's monologue, P.B. frowned, nodded, said, "Cool," then said he had to go.

Steve could only chuckle at himself. He was so excited about his find he'd had to tell *somebody*. That it was the last person on earth who would be interested served him right. He should choose his audiences more wisely.

The two of them left the basement and headed in their separate directions.

Roxanne was not in the kitchen when Steve passed through it again, though judging by her workspace she was obviously in the middle of something, and he wondered if she was avoiding him or P.B. Probably both, he thought, though she could hardly avoid him for long. He'd be back at work in a few short hours.

Climbing the three flights of stairs to his apartment, Steve thought about the hole at the bottom of the steps in the basement. Was it just coincidence that it was "under the first step" of both cellar staircases? He didn't see how it could be. But how many people knew about that will who didn't also know that the steps had already been investigated? Including, Steve believed, the cellar stairs, and not so very long ago either. Within the last fifty years, he was fairly certain.

Of course, there'd also been a hole at the bottom of the trapdoor stairs, which, as any decent historian knew, were built in the late 1800s, long after Portner's death, when the house had been owned by a grain merchant and the basement used for storage. So maybe the holes were for something else.

Steve reached the top of the staircase and turned left toward his apartment door, where he was greeted by the sight of a large cardboard box. On top of the box, written with a black marker in block letters was his name and address.

There was no return address. There was not even a postmark or any postage.

Steve fished his keys out of his pocket and slid one into the door lock, looking askance at the carton. When he got the door open, he pushed the box inside with one foot and put his backpack on the floor. He took off his coat, then dragged the box into the living room to examine it.

The cardboard had obviously been ripped open at some point and taped back up. But after a minute of trying to wriggle his fingers under the new packing tape, he still couldn't open it. He went to the kitchen to get a knife, wondering if he should call Homeland Security and report a suspicious package.

Could this have anything to do with the break-in? Some message the intruders left behind?

But that was ridiculous. For one thing, the box would have been here this morning, and he certainly wouldn't have missed it when he left for the library.

Or would he have? He'd been pretty distracted most of the day. Up until he'd found Portner's letter, in fact.

He stuck the knife under one flap and cut through the tape. First one side, then the other, then across the top. Then he pulled back the flaps.

With an *oof* as if he'd been punched in the stomach, he dropped the flaps and jerked away.

He stepped back so fast he tripped over his backpack and landed flat on his ass against the coffee table.

Heart pounding wildly in his chest, he took a deep breath.

They couldn't be real.

He sat on the floor, watching the box with wary eyes, waiting for one of them to poke its pointy head out the top and come slithering over the side. The rest of them would follow and before he knew it—

This was stupid. They couldn't possibly be real.

He stood up and shook off his fear as if an imaginary audience were watching. Then he reached out the hand containing the knife. His palms were wet and sweat prickled along his scalp. With the tip of the blade, he pulled the cardboard flap back again.

From as far a distance as possible, he peered into the box. Then he exhaled, sagging in relief, despite the imaginary audience.

They were fake.

It was a box full of fake snakes. Who in God's name would *do* this? How many people knew he hated snakes?

That was easy. Everyone, Steve thought. He wasn't shy about his phobia, figuring the more people who knew, the less likely it would be he'd end up in a situation with snakes.

He kicked the carton and they jiggled like they were alive. He felt a little sick to his stomach. There had to be hundreds of them. Big, small, fat, thick, black, green, brown and speckled. He kicked the box again and watched them quiver.

Then he noticed the envelope.

He hated to admit it even to himself, but with his adrenaline still pumping he didn't even like reaching into the box to retrieve the envelope, despite knowing they were fake.

What if some smart aleck had put one real one into the mix?

That's what he would have done, if he were trying to scare the shit out of someone.

He plucked out the envelope with two fingers and backed away to sit on the couch. With the knife, he sliced the top and pulled out the note.

It was one white sheet of paper, folded in half, upon which was written:

Don't mess with things you can't handle.

—R.

Roxanne?

Roxanne had done this?

A chuckle started low in his gut. Then it rose until it was an outright laugh.

He could kill her, he thought. She'd given him the scare of a decade. And yet he had to laugh. It was so perfect. He couldn't remember the last time his heart had pounded that fast from fright.

He shook his head in wonder. *Unpredictable*. And he thought he'd liked that. He chuckled again.

If he could handle a box full of snakes, he could certainly handle Roxanne Rayeaux, he thought with a smile.

He dropped the note to his lap and gazed at the carton of serpents. A fitting gift in so many ways . . . one that deserved an appropriate thank you.

So what, he speculated with a small evil smile, would scare her?

Roxanne barely got her prep work done on time, what with the confusion accompanying the break-in, but by the time the restaurant opened she was equipped to handle the crowd.

She couldn't say she felt particularly safe knowing the police—specifically, P.B.—were on the case, but she had at least come to the conclusion that whoever was doing this was intent on something other than money. For some reason that made it more bearable.

Rita pushed through the double doors. "Roxanne, Steve needs you at the bar."

It was early, so she hadn't any desserts going out yet. But this was the night the reservation book was full and she was anticipating another hectic evening.

"What does he want?"

"I don't know. Got something on his mind, though." She pushed back out the doors with a trayful of appetizers.

Roxanne could swear Rita was smirking.

Wiping her hands on her apron, Roxanne followed her through the swinging doors and stopped, caught by unexpected laughter at the sight of Steve behind the bar.

He wore a long, green rubber snake on his head like a turban, and another around his waist like a belt. He was talking to an older, white-haired man at the bar—a guy who was here a lot, she noticed—who seemed to be admiring the outfit, based on Steve's pirouette to show off the hat.

In the middle of his spin he saw Roxanne and stopped, spreading his hands wide.

"I see you received my gift." She leaned on the service bar, unable to quell her smile. "And decided to . . . wear it to work?"

"Hey, the ladies love me in rubber." He grinned.

Despite herself, she guffawed.

"And there's more where this came from." He took the turban off and put it under one arm like a helmet. "I took a bunch of these babies to the shoe repair guy down the street. Always wanted me a pair of snakeskin boots," he said, the last in a pretty good imitation of John Wayne.

"I'm glad you like them so much. I have to say, I wasn't sure how they'd be received."

He sauntered toward her, his eyes laughing and his lips quirked in a half smile she found decidedly seductive, and put the turban on one side of the bar. Then he leaned over and put his elbows on the service bar across from her. Leaning over as they both were, his face was close to hers. Her folded hands were near enough to touch his and a zip of desire coursed through her center at the thought of doing it.

The devil was still in his smile when he asked, "What *ever* inspired you to give me such a gift, darlin'?"

His voice was low with proximity, his eyes captivating. She could see the smile playing on his lips and wondered what he'd do if she inched forward and planted hers on them.

Actually, she knew exactly what he'd do, and she knew that it was something she would be foolish to invite again. Much as she liked to think about it.

She tilted her head and spoke in her best Southern drawl. "It was like this, sugar. I had a hundred dollars just burnin' a big ol' hole in my li'l ol' pocket. So when I saw these charmin' fellas in the shop window, I just knew I had to get 'em for you."

He laughed, a low, sexy laugh that she felt clear through her body.

"So I guess I got that hundred dollars back, after all," he said.

She let her gaze linger on his. "Guess you did."

"Miss Roxanne, might I have a word?" The nasal tone and precise diction could belong to no one other than Sir Nigel, who was suddenly standing just next to her right hip.

She hadn't even noticed him approach.

She straightened. "Certainly, Sir Nigel. What is it?"

The tall man cast a disdainful glance at Steve, who stood up with a look of exaggerated affront.

"Excuse me, I have many important duties to attend," Steve said, with a bow at Roxanne.

"I've just had word," Sir Nigel said with some urgency tingeing his voice, "from an associate of mine at the *Washington Post* that Chez Soi is being discussed for an imminent review."

"By the *Post*?" Roxanne asked, pulse thrumming. "When?"

"He couldn't tell me, precisely. I don't believe he knew, to be honest, but he wanted to give me the 'heads up.'" Sir Nigel used the phrase stiffly, making Roxanne smile.

"That's fantastic. But—God. That means we really have to be on our toes. We haven't even had time to work out all the new-business kinks yet. Have you told Monsieur Girmond?"

Sir Nigel drew himself up imperiously. "Of course not. My duty was to inform you before anyone else. I shall apprise him instantly if you so desire."

Roxanne knew full well that wasn't the only reason he hadn't told the chef. Sir Nigel and M. Girmond had no conflict that she could sense, but they circled each other with wary politeness whenever interaction was called for. It could be just the age-old front-of-the-house/back-of-the-house contention, but she wasn't sure.

"Don't worry about it. I'll tell him." Roxanne thought for a moment. "Sir Nigel, I know who the *Post*'s reviewer is, but not by sight. Is there any way we can find out what he looks like? It would be nice if we could know when he was here. Not that we'd cook any differently, of course, but we'd know to treat him with V.I.P. status."

"Of course," Sir Nigel agreed with a smug smile. "Which is why it's fortunate that I do indeed know what Mr. Richards looks like. I will be able to alert the crew the moment he steps through the door."

Roxanne beamed up at the man. He might be pompous and he might keep the waitstaff on their toes by being both annoying and frightening, but the man was a treasure.

He gave her a short bow.

"Oh, Sir Nigel, you are the *best*." She reached up and gave him a quick hug, finding his tall frame surprisingly bony underneath his three-piece suit. She could swear she saw him blush.

"It is part of my job, madam."

"And you are doing it excellently. Thank you."

He gave her another short bow when George blew by waving a check. "Got a soufflé order."

"Okay. Gotta go. I'll tell Monsieur Girmond," she said to Sir Nigel. With a quick glance over her shoulder at Steve, she pushed back through the swinging doors to the kitchen, fairly aglow with the knowledge that Steve had been looking at her, too.

The following Monday, Roxanne returned from the grocery store—lugging four plastic bags in two aching hands up the tall flight of stairs and vowing to look into elevator costs—to find two boxes next to her door.

She looked around as if someone might be watching her, then stopped trying to contain her smile. After placing her groceries on the floor, she opened the apartment door.

The cat greeted her with an attempt to get out, and as Roxanne pushed him back inside with a foot he yowled and wound around her feet.

"I know," she said, picking up the bags to bring them to the kitchen island. "I just got you some food, and darting out the door isn't going to get you any. You can just quit your bitchin'."

She quickly put away the frozen items, then opened a can of cat food and filled Cheeto's dish.

She went back to look at the boxes. They were plain brown cardboard with no writing and the flaps were folded together over-under, so they wouldn't spring open.

She nudged one, jerking slightly as it was much lighter than she'd anticipated. She dragged each of them into the apartment. Taped to one was an envelope with the letter R on it. Still smiling, she opened the note.

In a strong, slanted masculine hand was written:

I had to think: What is she afraid of . . . ?

Steve's writing, she thought, looking at the sharply crossed *t*'s and flourish-less loops. She should probably have it analyzed, figure out if this guy was all he seemed. And not all she feared.

Roxanne put the note down and eyed the boxes warily. Unless Steve was curled up inside one, she didn't think any of her greatest fears could be contained in a cardboard box, or even two.

Just as she was about to slit the tape on one with a fingernail, the phone rang. She hunted for the portable, finally finding it wedged between two cushions on the couch.

"Hello?" she said breathlessly, catching it on the last ring before the answering machine would pick up.

Skip laughed in her ear. "Oh my, I didn't interrupt anything good, did I?"

"I can't even imagine what you mean by that," she said primly.

He sighed. "I'm afraid that's probably true these days."

She put one hand on her hip. "What's that supposed to mean?"

"Only that a girl like you is not supposed to be burying herself in her work."

"Oh no, not that old rant. So what's a girl like me supposed to be doing, huh?" She walked back to the dining room and the boxes, giving one a little shake with one hand. It sounded like a bunch of wadded-up paper.

"If you have to ask . . ."

She laughed. "A lot you know, Skip. I am right now about to open a large, very curious gift from . . . hang onto your hat . . . a *man*."

Silence greeted this announcement.

"Skip?"

"Oh no." His voice was somber. "Tell me it's not from Martin. Please tell me he's not up to his old tricks. Or if he is, that you're not going to fall for it again."

"Oh, Skip." She laughed ruefully. "Did I really put you through so much, talking about him all the time?"

"*Me*? It's *you* I'm worried about. That guy's given you emotional whiplash more times than I like to count. Don't even open it, Rox. I mean it. Just write 'Return to Sender' on it and throw it right back in the mailbox."

"Relax. It's not from Martin." She smiled again. "And it's way too big to fit in the mailbox."

"Not from Martin?" He perked up instantly. "Who's it from?"

"Steve. Steve Serrano. You remember the guy—"

"Oh come off it, Rox. I remember the guy. Mr. Charming from dinner. Why's he buying you a gift? You getting some on the side and not telling me about it?"

Roxanne actually blushed. Good thing she was on the phone. "Mr. Charming, eh? I'll have to tell him you said so."

"You didn't answer the question." Skip's voice was increasingly intrigued.

"It's not really a gift. That is, I doubt it's . . . well . . . anyway, I bought *him* something last week because I was mad at him because . . ." She remembered the kiss he gave her that night in the restaurant. It had felt so . . . intimate. "Well, it's too long a story to get into here, but I gave him a bunch of rubber snakes and I think this is his, uh, revenge."

Skip paused. "You—what? You bought him rubber snakes?"

"He's afraid of snakes."

"Ah."

"And he says in his note to me on these boxes that he had to think about what *I* was afraid of."

"You guys are trying to scare each other?"

"Uh, kind of." Maybe they already *did* scare each other. Maybe this was just some kind of weird, elaborate foreplay. Could it be foreplay if they'd already had sex?

"So, what is it?" Skip's voice brought her back.

She bit her lip. "I don't know. I haven't opened the boxes yet." "Box*es*? There's more than one?"

"There're two."

"Well, open them! I want to know how good this guy

is. Let's see, what's Roxanne afraid of? Failure? Maybe it's a box full of bad restaurant reviews."

"Very funny. Don't you have a class or something?"

"It's lunchtime. Besides, I'm not missing this. Open them and tell me what's in them."

"Okay, I'm opening one."

She pulled on the flaps of the top one and, with a cardboard squeak, they unwove themselves. Spotting what was inside, she laughed out loud.

"What?" Skip demanded. "What's in it? Tell me!"

"Ch—ch—ch—" She couldn't stop laughing.

"Roxanne."

She pulled on the flaps of the other box and encountered more of the same.

"Cheetos!" she finally shrieked. "Oh my God. This is amazing. He got me a hundred dollars' worth of Cheetos!"

14

Dessert Special of the Day
Chocolate Decadence— <u>for people with
  no self-control</u>
Chocolate bombe filled with chocolate mousse,
  topped with chocolate hazelnut cream
  and surrounded by mini chocolate truffles

"So what's the shelf life on these things?" Skip asked, looking at the mound of Cheetos bags on her floor. There were thirty-eight of them. They'd counted.

Roxanne sat with her feet up on the table, an open bag in her lap and the fingers of her right hand completely orange.

She lifted the bag and looked. "The 'Best By' date is November of this year." She looked at the pile, nodding. "That oughta be about right."

Skip looked at her. "You are *not* going to eat all of

these." He picked up a bag. "Look at this—have you read the label? *Ten* grams of fat per ounce—"

"Skip, Skip, Skip," she said, shaking her head. "You don't understand, I'm not one of your wrestlers. I'm a pastry chef. I'm *supposed* to be fat. If I'm not fat, people will think my food's no good."

He gave her a deadpan look. "Rox, you never leave the kitchen as it is. Who's going to know you're not fat enough?"

She popped another Cheeto into her mouth.

"Your tongue is orange," Skip said, going into the kitchen. "Does beer go with Cheetos?"

"Everything goes with Cheetos. Bring me one, too, please."

He came back into the dining room with two open beers and a roll of paper towels. He ran off about four of them and handed the wad to Roxanne. "Here, you're going to need these. Or are you just planning to shower after your snack?"

She grinned. "Pull up a bag and sit down." At his wince she laughed. "Are my teeth orange too?"

"This is sick." Skip plucked a bag from the table and tore it open. "I've never seen you so happy."

She finished a big swig from the beer and ran her tongue over her teeth. "It's incredible. I've never felt so guiltless." She grimaced at him. "Better?"

He examined her teeth. "All clean. Once again, beer solves the problem."

She laughed. "I guess Steve got this wrong, huh?"

"What's that?"

"Well, he was hoping to *scare* me with something. Do

I look scared to you?" She placed a Cheeto between her teeth and closed her eyes, blissful.

Skip looked down at the bag in his hands. "He's scared *me* with them. And I'm becoming a little afraid of you." He looked at her sideways. "Are these things addictive? How many of these bags have you eaten?"

She waved a Cheeto in the air nonchalantly. "Five or six. So how do you think I should respond? Or should I respond at all? I mean, this is fun and all, but I don't want this guy getting any ideas."

Any more *ideas*, she amended silently.

Skip looked at her, his expression dry. "Trust me, after you eat all these, he won't be getting any ideas."

She laughed and popped another puff. "I'm serious. What should I do?"

He poked his nose in the bag and sniffed. "Send him your Jenny Craig bill."

She smacked her lips.

Gingerly, he pulled out a cheese puff and, after studying it, put it in his mouth.

"Oh," he said, closing his eyes. "Oh my God. I'm back in Joey Fannini's wood-paneled basement, listening to Cheap Trick." He opened his eyes. "This is amazing. I haven't had one of these since I was a kid. It's like time travel in a bag."

She nodded. "I know. Aren't they good? I don't think I've had more than one or two at a time for at least fifteen years."

A knocked sounded on the door.

Skip and Roxanne looked at each other.

"Mr. Charming?" Skip mouthed, eyes wide, grin maniacal.

Roxanne chuckled and got up to answer the door. With two relatively un-orange fingers she turned the knob and pulled it open.

Steve's face split immediately into a smile and he started laughing. "I see you got my gift."

She put the bag behind her back. "What makes you say that?"

He lifted a hand and brushed gently at her cheek. Roxanne's pulse jumped as if she'd been electrocuted.

"You've got an orange streak on your face," he said, pulling his hand back and shoving it into his pocket.

"Is that the devil at the door?" Skip came out from the dining room and held out his hand to Steve. "Hey, good to see you."

"Skip." Steve shook his hand, then looked down at the orange crumbs on his palm.

Skip brushed his hand on his jeans. "Sorry about that. I hope you know you're going to be personally responsible for the enormity of one formerly attractive pastry chef."

Steve's brows rose. "So I see."

"Apparently she's not afraid of Cheetos anymore. Not since she quit—"

"Skip!" Roxanne turned on him suddenly, knowing just where he was going with that statement. "Why don't you *go into the kitchen* . . ." She searched for a task.

"And get Steve a beer?" Skip provided. "Can you come in for a beer, Steve? I think we've got a few munchies lying around."

"No, I don't want to interrupt." Steve shook his head and backed up a step, one hand up. "I just wanted to be sure you got the, the, uh . . ."—he gestured toward the bag in Roxanne's hand—". . . packages."

"It's no interruption," Roxanne said. "Come on in."

They heard the clink of glass against glass and then the thunk of a bottle landing on the counter.

"Besides," Skip called from the kitchen, "the beer's already open."

Steve gave her an ironic look. "Skip wins again. One of these days *you're* going to invite me over. I promise to decline, if that's what it'll take."

She crunched the bag closed in one fist and cocked her head at him. "Maybe Skip's are the only invitations you accept."

Steve strolled through the door, leaning close to her as he passed, saying, "Try me."

Their eyes met and Roxanne's body temperature sky-rocketed. Steve gave her a quick wink and continued on toward the kitchen, while Roxanne wiped the back of her hand across her forehead. Lord, she thought, was the guy on fire? Every time she stood near him she heated up like bread in a toaster.

She was drunk on Cheetos, that was it. It wasn't that she was unable to be within two feet of Steve Serrano without thinking about sex. She was just high on partially hydrogenated soybean oil.

She followed him into the kitchen, placing her bag of Cheetos carefully on the dining room table as she passed it.

"You didn't get yourself a bag," she said to Steve,

who sat on the stool by the kitchen island as casually as if he lived there. "I'm afraid you can't stay at this party without paying homage to the guest of honor." She inclined her head back toward the pile of Cheeto bags.

Steve laughed. "Not me. I don't touch that stuff. My body is a temple."

"Oh please," she said, "I saw you stuff that temple with a plate full of cheese fries not so very long ago."

They all laughed and settled in with their beers. Before long, talk turned to the break-in.

"It seems to me they're bent on destruction," Skip said. "Maybe it's somebody trying to scare you off, out of the business."

"Someone like you?" she asked. "You're the only one who's been completely against it from the start."

Skip's expression was hurt. "No I haven't. I've just wanted you to be happy. And we all know restaurateurs aren't happy. They're just crazy."

"Oh Skip, I know." She leaned across the couch—where they had migrated during the course of conversation—and squeezed his hand. "Of course I don't think it's you behind the break-ins. I'm thinking maybe it's somebody who lived here before and left something behind."

From the armchair, Steve gave her a dubious look. "Somebody who left something buried in the basement floor? Or behind a brick foundation that hasn't been disturbed for centuries?"

Roxanne turned to him. "Can you tell that? Can you tell the brick hasn't been disturbed?"

He shrugged one shoulder. "Most of the time, yes. If

the mortar's different, the pattern is broken, the bricks are not all the same age, you can tell someone's done some patchwork. But the wall where they were digging around . . ." He shook his head. "I don't know what's going on with that."

"Maybe they think there's some kind of buried treasure," Skip volunteered, with a kidlike grin.

"There is!" Roxanne said excitedly. "We thought of that, didn't we, Steve?" She looked over at Steve. "The Declaration of Independence, right?"

Skip scoffed. "The Declaration of Independence is in your basement?"

"Just a draft." At Steve's dark look she added, "Maybe. Steve, tell him the story."

Steve related the short version, finishing with, "But that would be ridiculous. Anybody who knew enough to be looking for that draft wouldn't just start digging around somebody else's basement. They're historians, academics. They'd have maps and documents and theories about where to search. They'd know the places that had *already* been searched. And they'd know to look for things like patterns in the brick."

"So you really don't think it has anything to do with that?" Roxanne asked, disappointed. She'd been hoping her intruder would turn out to be some nerdy guy in glasses with a history book in one hand and a shovel in the other. Not some drug-crazed former tenant as P.B. had suggested. Or Steve, as P.B. had ended up insisting.

The idea of Steve destroying her property in search of his theoretical draft was ludicrous, but like the circumstances of the bet between him and P.B., there was enough ambiguity in the facts to leave room for doubt.

And doubt about men was what Roxanne specialized in these days.

Still, would Steve be able to discuss this so casually now if he were the one looking around? Of course not.

Steve gave it another moment of thought. "It's doubtful. But if it's not that, I'll be damned if I know what they *are* looking for."

"It seems obvious they're looking for something, though," Roxanne mused, "doesn't it? Remember how in the first break-in one of the kitchen floorboards had been pried up?"

"I thought the squirrel did that," Skip said.

Steve laughed and Roxanne's eyes shot to his.

"You didn't believe that?" she asked.

"You *did*?" he countered.

She picked at the label of her beer with a fingernail. "It's obvious now, of course, that the first was an actual break-in. But I have to confess, for a long time I was really hoping it was just that squirrel."

"The one that hurled itself through the back window." Steve was smiling at her but it was a gentle smile, a teasing one.

"That never made sense to me either," Skip said.

"I chose to ignore that part of the equation," Roxanne admitted. "Besides, I figured if it was good enough for the police . . ."

Steve's expression darkened and Roxanne kicked herself for bringing up—even indirectly—P.B.

After a bit more discussion, Skip stood up. "All right,

kids. Tonight, I'm hitting the hay early. No more midnight Mondays for me."

They all stood up and Skip said his good-nights, then he trotted down the stairs.

Roxanne and Steve stood at the door, silent until Skip's footsteps stopped and the outside door slammed.

Roxanne was pretty sure Steve was going to leave too, but since he hadn't said anything she pushed the door shut and turned her back against it, looking up at him.

"I guess I should go, too," he said.

Roxanne nodded, one hand on the doorknob behind her without turning it. "Big day tomorrow?"

He laughed wryly and put his hands in his pockets. "Just the library. Again. That's how I usually spend my days."

"At the Library of Congress?" she asked.

He nodded.

"You're that into the history thing, huh? Are you taking a class or something?"

He shook his head. "No, I just like investigating things. I've been interested in Portner for some time now. He's kind of a fascinating character."

"So you're just doing it for fun?"

He shrugged. "Keeps the librarians busy and me off the streets."

"They should start paying you," she teased.

"I wish someone would." Then, at her look, he added, "For the library work, I mean, the research. You pay me just fine, boss."

He smiled and her stomach turned to jelly. *Boss*, she repeated to herself. *Remember that.*

"I knew what you meant." Slowly, she pushed herself away from the door and pulled it open.

She had to let him leave, she told herself. But, maybe it was the beers on nothing but a Cheeto-laden stomach, she couldn't quite remember just why this relationship was so wrong. So she owned the place—didn't most people meet the people they dated at work? So what if she was the boss? It wasn't like she would let the personal aspect get in the way of the professional.

Well, she thought, her reaction to news of that awful bet springing to mind, *not again, anyway*.

Remembering the bet only increased her resolve, however. She shouldn't trust him. If they got involved and later he did something that hurt her she would kick herself for not paying attention to the signs. And what bigger red flags could there be than that he might have made a bet about getting her in bed and there was a chance he was behind a series of break-ins at her restaurant?

And she was considering trusting him? Was she crazy?

Then again, if she just assumed she couldn't trust him and didn't let her heart become involved . . . what would be possible then?

Steve stepped through the door as she stared at the floor. It was silly but she was afraid that if she looked at him she might do something stupid. Like throw herself at him.

"Thanks for, uh, dinner," Steve said, amusement in his voice. "It wasn't quite as good as last time, but I guess that's because I provided this meal."

Roxanne laughed. "I'll cook you something better next time."

She looked at him quickly, nerves buzzing with implications she was both dying and afraid to make.

"That is," she added, "if Skip invites you over again anytime soon."

He was standing in the hall, looking as reluctant to leave as she was reluctant to let him. His hands were shoved in his jeans pockets and his eyes, though laughing at her joke, were uncertain.

Desire washed over her. He wanted to stay, she was sure she could see it. He wanted her again . . . as much as she wanted him again?

"Steve," she said, not sure what she intended to say next.

Their eyes met and she stopped breathing.

"Yes, Roxanne?" His voice was quiet and seemed to whisper along her nerves.

She stepped into the hall and put her fingers around one of his wrists, where his hand disappeared into his pocket. His hand came out and she took it in hers, looking at it.

They were strong hands, sculpted, somehow refined-looking. She imagined him at the Library of Congress, writing away as he researched whatever it was he researched.

His fingers curled around hers.

She looked up at him, stepping closer until their bodies almost touched.

She took a deep, tremulous breath, knowing she wasn't going to back away. Though her brain told her she was being stupid, self-indulgent, her body would not obey her commands to stop desiring this man.

"Do you think this is a mistake?" she asked him.

His eyes dropped to their clasped hands and his other came out of his pocket to snake around her waist. Pulling her gently but firmly into him, he brought his gaze to hers.

"I don't know," he said.

He looked so sincere. So serious and yet so uncertain, she wanted to take his face in her hands and tell him not to worry, it didn't matter.

But . . . she was the one who was worried, wasn't she?

"Are you afraid that it is?" she asked.

He shook his head slightly, a small laugh escaping. "If it is, it's the best damn mistake I've ever made."

That made her blush and she looked down briefly.

"How about you?" he asked softly. "Afraid?"

She shrugged one shoulder, then looked up at him. "Life is scary."

"Only if you live it," he said. With that he bent his head and kissed her.

Their lips met tenderly, experimentally. Soft kisses that followed one after the other. Roxanne's hands rose up his chest, and his clasped behind her back, keeping her close.

His embrace felt so warm, so fragile and sweet, she was almost taken off guard when his head tilted to drop kisses along her jawline and her breathing accelerated. His lips moved down to that spot below her ear and sucked lightly, sending shivers shooting through her body in all directions.

She gasped lightly, arching her neck, and that impulse, that overpowering thing within her, took over. It was a wave of longing, a physical demand that she knew she couldn't resist—didn't *want* to resist—an impelling force that turned her insides to lava and made her passion volcanic.

He moved against her, his desire hardening between them, and she pressed her hips against it. Her hands dropped to his waistband and she grasped two belt loops in her fingers to pull him closer, circling her hips into his just enough to massage that hardness.

He made a sound low in his throat. His hands held her buttocks and stilled her against him.

They stood a moment, breathing hard in the hallway, under the dim overhead bulb. Steve dropped his head to her shoulder, seeming to think about the next move.

Was he asking himself if it was a good idea to continue? she wondered. Had she read him completely wrong? Maybe he was regretting stopping by. Maybe he thought it would be wiser to stop it right here. Should she tell him she's sorry and let him go home?

He sighed. "Am I going to have to wait for Skip to invite me in again?"

Laughter bubbled up from inside her, relief cascading out of her lungs.

She took his hand again and turned, leading him back into her apartment. As she started down the hallway toward the bedroom he stopped her.

"Wait." He pulled her back toward the living room, turning out the light as he did, then turned her in his arms as if waltzing.

She smiled quizzically, thinking he wanted to dance.

But when he circled nearer the sofa, he lowered her as if in a dip, onto the cushions.

"I want you to think of me every time you sit on this couch." He lowered himself on top of her and kissed her, hard, his mouth devouring, his hands weaving through her hair to cradle her head.

Their hips met and circled together, their hands reached and sought each other's body, pulling up shirts and searching for skin amidst the fabric.

Steve's hands pushed her shirt aside, his long fingers finding the peaked nipple of one breast through the fabric of her bra. With a gentle pinch, he sent desire coursing through her.

Her hands fumbled for his jeans, undid his belt buckle, then popped open the button. She unzipped his fly and felt his hardness through the thin cotton of his boxers.

Steve's lips took the peak of one breast as his hands reached the top of her jeans.

Roxanne's hand found the opening in his boxers and Steve gasped as her fingers found flesh. She caressed the velvety softness of his skin and his hands stopped as if he were paralyzed above her.

"Just a second," he said, standing to pull off his jeans.

Roxanne sat up and watched him, saw him pull his own shirt over his head to reveal that defined, muscular chest, saw him push the boxers down to reveal the straining hard evidence of his desire.

Naked, he looked down on her like a warrior regarding his prize. His gray eyes were direct and glittery in the darkened apartment.

She pushed herself up to stand before him, then turned and moved toward the bedroom, unclasping her bra and slipping it off as she walked.

"Wait right there," she said in a husky voice.

Once in the bedroom, she opened up the bedside table drawer, pulled out a condom, then moved back to the living room, her eyes meeting his as she walked slowly across the room, unbuttoning her jeans.

She reached the floor lamp and turned the dimmer so that the barest candle of light shone. Then she pushed her jeans past her hips and stepped out of them.

"Oh my God," he breathed, then grinned at her. "Another thong."

She smiled her best slow smile and took one side of the thong, twisting it in her finger. Then she pulled it down, her eyes never leaving his. She could see him pulse with the effort of control, and his eyes burned into hers. She pulled off the thong and walked the rest of the way toward him, twirling it on one finger.

She dropped it on the floor by the coffee table and cupped his penis with her hands, then moved her fingers up and over it. Her eyes were still on his as she lowered herself to her knees, and took the long shaft into her mouth.

Steve shuddered and swore, his eyes closing as she took him in. His hands held her head, his fingers diving into her hair as she moved back and forth, holding his length in her mouth and moving her tongue to increase his pleasure.

He moaned and pushed his hips gently into her, his hands holding her head. "Oh God," he muttered. "Ah . . ."

He was nearly out of control, she could feel him trembling with the effort, and she was the one pushing him toward the brink. She controlled his every sensation, directed every reaction, anticipated every involuntary response he made. *She* did it.

She held him captive.

When he was on the verge of losing it, he pulled her up and took her mouth with his, his tongue plunging into her. She answered with a kiss just as hungry and wound one leg around his hip. He grabbed it, pulled her upward and she wrapped the other around him too. Then he lowered himself onto the couch, sitting with her on his lap.

Knees on the cushions, she rose and held his penis gently as she unfurled the condom onto it. Then she guided him toward her with one hand, lowering down, then pulling up just long enough to look into his eyes.

"Say my name," she whispered.

He looked at her a long moment, his eyes intense enough to see right through her.

"Roxanne," he said finally, in a voice as hot and sweet as toasted honey.

She pushed him inside of her.

The sensation was brilliant.

He exhaled sharply, and his eyes seemed to look inward a moment before boring back into hers.

She pushed herself onto the shaft again and her eyes closed halfway with pleasure. He was so hard he filled her and she rose slowly, not wanting it to end too quickly.

His palm was hot as he took her breast and held it for his mouth to find the nipple. Closing his lips around it, he sucked, pulling hard, but she didn't care. She wanted it harder, wanted him to brand her with his lips. She lowered herself on him again, felt him deep within her, then rose. Her body clenched around him and he groaned.

Then he rose up, holding her impaled against him and lay her back on the couch.

"You've been in charge long enough." His eyes sparkled like the devil's own as he rose above her.

Then he thrust into her deep and she gasped with pleasure. He thrust again, then again, seeming to get deeper and harder with each plunge and chills raced up and down her spine. Her legs held his hips and she countered his every thrust as his penis coursed up and over her most sensitive spot again and again.

She cried out his name as she came. His eyes met hers and she could swear they held the light of more than just desire. Or maybe it was just her, bathed in the sensations of love as her body dissolved into starlight.

He pushed into her one final time, and with an uninhibited sound of release he came into her.

She held him as tight as she could then, with her arms, her legs, and her body, until they both melted into the cushions.

15

Dessert Special of the Day
Génoise, Crème au Beurre avec
 Langues de Chat—
<u>because you shouldn't put real Cheetos</u>
 <u>in a dessert</u>
Light butter cake with buttercream frosting
 and cats' tongues—pencil-shaped strips
 made of sugar, butter and vanilla

The restaurant was crazy. Just when Roxanne thought she'd surely seen the end of the boom of being the new kid on the block, another round of reservations would come in, filling up Friday and Saturday before they even opened on Wednesday.

A few things had gone wrong. The freezer had burned out (the one piece of equipment from Charters she'd counted on not having to replace) and they had to offer a world of unusual specials to use the food before she could get the new one in. On the plus side, business had been so good she had enough money to be able to get a new one, but it cleaned her out.

Then M. Girmond's sous-chef of twelve years had quit because of a sudden opportunity to head his own kitchen, and the replacement had yet to be found who would live up to Girmond's standards. In addition, she had to watch her normally buoyant and enthusiastic chef grow increasingly short-tempered without his right-hand man, which affected the entire kitchen staff and annoyed the hell out of the waitstaff.

For Roxanne, however, it was all a blur. She was cooking more, faster and better than she'd ever done in her life, while trying to manage accounts and keep the staff happy and productive. Before starting the restaurant, she had thought her biggest worry would be making ends meet despite slow business for the first few months. Now she thought running at capacity might kill them.

The synchronized waltz in the kitchen she had reveled in those first few heady nights had become more of a pinball game with the constant nightly pressure. The new sous-chef—Ralph, available on short notice—bumped into everyone, the dishwasher had been deported; her seafood purveyor had become unreliable—bringing grouper when she ordered sole, clams when she ordered mussels; and the bakery down the street was going out of business, meaning she now had to get up at the crack of dawn to make bread until another supplier of suitable quality could be found.

Nights, after leaving the crazy, hot atmosphere of the restaurant, she would crawl into bed exhausted. On Monday and Tuesday, when they were closed, she tried to catch up with her prep work and get ahead on the bread-making as much as she could.

A few times Steve had come down for dinner, and had stayed the night, at least until she got up before dawn to make the bread.

Those nights were crazy too, in their own way, but energizing. Their chemistry was incredible, but Roxanne wondered what was really going on between them. They talked, but never about themselves, about what was happening between them. And between being so tired and getting up so early, their time always seemed short. Too, too short.

Even aside from the doubts she had about her own judgment—she'd been crazy about Martin at first, too, though their chemistry hadn't been anywhere near as good—she worried about the fact that she and Steve worked together, and slept together, but rarely did anything else other than occasionally eat together.

Had she somehow signed up for a purely sexual relationship? Is this what she got for caving in completely to her desires before establishing some kind of friendship with Steve?

But then, she thought, they *were* friends, weren't they? Just friends who couldn't talk about the elephant that sat between them—the relationship.

They certainly had some fun at work, before the evenings became chaos. But when it came to seeing each other alone, they came together like shipwreck victims grasping at the lone life raft—and went off to-gether like a flare, only to fade quickly after their mo-ment of fire.

Maybe they were both just too damned tired for any-thing else, she thought, realizing that she was every bit as guilty as Steve was of dropping immediately off to sleep on the nights he was there.

"I don't know," she told Skip on the phone, after con-fessing what was going on. "It seems to be enough for him. And maybe it's all I can handle, too."

"That doesn't sound very romantic," Skip said.

"No, but . . . I just don't know."

"That's about the fiftieth time you've said that. What are you really worried about?"

For the umpteenth time she searched her heart, focus-ing on that feeling of dread deep in her chest. "I don't—" She stopped herself. "I guess I'm worried about being wrong. Being fooled. Like I was with Martin."

"I think you'd notice a wife and kids traipsing up those stairs," Skip had said, with an attempt at laughter.

Roxanne shook her head. "It's that bet. Or no, not the bet, really—I believe him about that. But it's like I was left with the feeling of mistrust after that—even though I *do* trust him now—and it won't go away. I mean, this is a guy whose best friend said to me he thought Steve could be guilty of a crime. A crime *against* me. Shouldn't I be taking that into consideration?"

"First of all, do you really think Steve wouldn't tell you if he found that draft he's been talking about? It's not like he's kept it a secret or anything," countered Skip.

"No, but if he's the one behind the break-ins, what

does that mean? Breaking and entering isn't exactly legal, even if he did plan to tell me what he found. But if he was planning to tell me about finding the draft, why wouldn't he tell me about looking for it? And why would he do *so* much damage? And if he wasn't going to tell me about finding the draft, then he was basically planning on stealing it from this house, and therefore from me."

"Hold on. Hold on. I'm getting confused." Skip inhaled loudly over the phone. "If the draft is found in your house, it would be yours?"

"I don't know, and frankly I don't really care. That's not the point." Roxanne put a hand to her forehead and squeezed. This whole situation was giving her a headache. "The point is, if Steve is digging around and making it look like a break-in, it means he's lying to me, probably because he's afraid the draft *might* be mine if he finds it on my property."

"Well, yeah, I guess that would be a pretty big breach of trust. But that just doesn't sound like Steve to me," Skip said.

"I know, but you and I barely know the guy. And if P.B. could think him capable of it . . ."

"P.B.?" Skip scoffed. "He was *bitter*, Rox, come on. I wouldn't believe a thing that guy said."

"But . . . it's the only theory about these break-ins that makes sense."

Skip laughed. "The only theory that makes sense is some guy looking for a draft of the Declaration of Independence in your basement? That's pretty pathetic. And I'm sorry, but a cop shouldn't be going around whispering suspicions about people without any real grounds for having them."

She sighed. "You're probably right but . . . maybe he *does* have grounds. Maybe he knows something about Steve that we don't. And maybe he was hoping I would say something to Steve so Steve would stop doing it and he wouldn't have to arrest his buddy."

"Or maybe he made it all up to get back at both of you."

"Maybe . . ." Roxanne felt the weight of the world descend on her shoulders. "Or maybe it doesn't matter who's doing what or lying about whom. Maybe I shouldn't be sleeping with a guy I could suspect of destroying my property."

And that, Roxanne thought, was the bottom line.

Even Skip had nothing to say to that.

It was a Thursday night and Roxanne was especially tired, wondering if maybe she was coming down with something, when halfway through the evening Sir Nigel edged uncomfortably into the kitchen, looking around like a kid who'd been summoned to the principal's office for the first time.

She looked up, surprised to see him. He almost never came through the swinging doors to the kitchen, as if pretending this part of the restaurant did not really exist was an essential part of his job.

"Sir Nigel," she said, scooping raspberry sauce out of a bowl and into a small pitcher with a spatula. "What can I do for you?"

"*He's here,*" Sir Nigel hissed.

She drew a blank. "I'm sorry?"

"He's *here*," he said again, big eyes directed toward the dining room. "Frederick Richards. Reviewer from the *Washington Post*."

Roxanne's heart leaped out of her chest directly into her throat. "Oh my God. Should we tell Monsieur Girmond? We should tell Monsieur Girmond." She wiped her hands on the towel at her waist and turned to look at Girmond. "Should we tell him?" She looked back at Sir Nigel.

"Of *course*." He made a motion as if pushing her. "Richards has just been seated by the fireplace, number twenty-four. I'll let you know what he orders."

"Make sure Rita waits on him," Roxanne directed, turning toward Girmond, then spinning back. "But don't tell her who he is."

Sir Nigel gave a curt nod and pushed back out the swinging doors, like a swimmer heading for the surface and air.

Roxanne moved swiftly toward M. Girmond. Just as she was about to reach him, the new sous-chef (who was admittedly annoying, simultaneously obsequious and arrogant) stepped on her foot and dropped a bowl of mussels.

"Watch it," he growled, before realizing who he was speaking to. "Oh, sorry, so sorry, Miss Rayeaux. My fault. Entirely. I should have been aware of you walking through my station."

She waved a hand and continued to M. Girmond as Ralph bent to the floor to pick up the mussels. She arrived at Girmond's elbow as he sliced a duck terrine with smooth, confident knife strokes.

"He's here," she said low, not wanting to alarm the

rest of the kitchen. "The reviewer from the *Post*. He's at twenty-four, Rita will be waiting on him."

M. Girmond nodded once, quickly. "Thank you for telling me, *ma biche*."

She smiled and squeezed his upper arm with one hand. "I know we'll do great."

He winked at her, then turned to Ralph, who still squatted on the floor, and said, "Where is the sauce, eh? The orange-ginger, for the terrine."

"I—yes, it's right here," he started to stand, then spotted another mussel and bent again. "If you had only let me know—"

"I called for it three minutes ago! Get up!" Girmond gestured with his knife. "You must pay attention, monsieur. It is all about attention."

Roxanne slipped back to her station. A minute later she heard the crash of a pan hitting the floor and turned in time to see Ralph dancing around as if he'd burned himself.

M. Girmond was yelling something, and Ralph was yelling something else, and for some reason two of the busboys were running in circles.

She raced over. "What in the world's going on?"

"I've just seen—Oh my God, what was it? A *rat*?" Ralph was near shrieking. "It had to be a *rat*. *Jesus Christ*, I've never seen one so huge!"

"*C'est de la merde.*"

Roxanne was shocked. She'd never heard M. Girmond swear before and she was pretty sure he'd just said the French equivalent of *bullshit*.

Girmond turned on Ralph fiercely. "There are no rats

in my kitchen. My kitchen is spotless. Get ahold of yourself."

"I'm telling you, it was right there." Ralph threw a hand toward the floor, where a sticky glaze now oozed underneath the overturned pan. "It made me drop the pan. All my sauce! *They* saw it!" He pointed to two bus-boys, prowling near the garde-manger station like hunters.

"Calm down, *salaud*," Girmond boomed, his voice so loud Roxanne was afraid the customers might hear him. She hoped none of them had heard his French, be-cause M. Girmond had just called Ralph a bastard. "I don't care if it was a horse you saw, get me the sauce!"

"Monsieur Girmond!" she pleaded.

He swung to her, nearly decapitating a busboy with his elbow.

"*Il est un idiot! Un crétin!*" He threw out his hands in exasperation. "Look at him, he wears my sauce. This dish is getting *cold*!" He turned to his beautiful duck terrine.

"*There!*" Ralph screamed, hurling a finger outward and knocking over the bowl of mussels he'd just gath-ered from the floor.

"Number five, order up!" one of the line cooks said. Then, "*Shit!*"

Roxanne spun and saw a flash of orange, with a large piece of grouper in its mouth.

Her heart stopped as he leaped to the counter and headed toward the red-hot stove.

"Cheeto!" she yelled. "Not on the stove! Get him away from the stove!"

Rafe, the line cook, was nearest. Just as Cheeto was about to reach the burners, the cook swept an arm out and across, propelling the cat, along with several dishes and entrees in various states of assembly, sideways and onto the floor.

Roxanne exhaled and dashed toward the cat, but she slipped on the sauce that covered the floor and had to grab the sous-chef's workstation. Before going all the way down, she managed to steady herself.

Cheeto had made it to the pastry station and was trotting over its floured surface, eyes alert, tail high, the grouper still in his mouth.

Was it really him? She narrowed her eyes. There were black patches along his side that gave her pause. But what were the odds of another orange cat showing up in the kitchen?

From the pastry station, the cat leapt nimbly to the service counter and glanced at her. She lunged for him, ready to kill, and he took off for the swinging doors. But just as he reached them, Rita pushed through yelling, "I need the Paté de Campagne with the Canapés Micheline for the V.I.P. at twenty-four."

Cheeto screeched—a nearly human sound—as the door caught him broadside, and he dropped the grouper. He scooted toward the dishwashing station, Manuel in hot pursuit.

Rita stepped on the grouper and slipped, dropping her tray as she hit the floor with a curse.

Manuel, the busboy, threw himself at the cat but missed, colliding with Ralph's legs and making him drop a knife he'd picked up for God knew what reason.

Manuel screamed as the blade caught him across the fingers. Blood spurted instantly along his knuckles.

"Oh my God," Roxanne said, grabbing the cleanest towel within reach and heading for the busboy.

Cheeto leaped up onto the workstation of the only person in the place he recognized other than Roxanne, who was clearly going to punish him: M. Girmond.

Unfortunately, M. Girmond was plating a blanquette of veal, which went flying when Cheeto's front paws hit the edge of the plate.

"What is this animal doing here?" he bellowed.

"What the hell is going on in here?"

Roxanne turned, wild-eyed, to see Steve standing inside the swinging doors.

"People are starting to—holy shit," he said, taking in the mayhem around him.

Rita was rubbing her back and reading off orders to one of the line cooks. Manuel was dragging himself off the floor with Roxanne's help, clutching a bloody towel around his hand. And Ralph was scurrying around, bitching as loud as he could, wiping up sauce with one hand and picking up mussels from the floor like errant marbles with the other.

"There is *cat hair* in my consommé!" M. Girmond roared.

"Oh my God," Roxanne moaned again, her head on the table. "I am so, so sorry."

Around her were seated M. Girmond, Ralph and Rita. Sir Nigel and Steve stood on opposite sides of the table, Sir Nigel with his arms crossed, Steve leaning against the back of a chair.

The evening had been a disaster. They'd had to send George to the hospital with the bleeding Manuel, because he was the only one with a car who could be spared. Several dinners were ruined and had to be started over from scratch—causing a backup that they never recovered from—and cat hair had indeed been found in several dishes, one of which had gone out to a customer and had been returned, with a terse "No, I do not want it replaced."

M. Girmond was humiliated and furious.

Ralph couldn't stop excusing himself and explaining how none of it was his fault.

Rita kept rubbing her lower back, convincing Steve—and no doubt Roxanne—that a Worker's Comp claim was in the offing. And all he could do was watch Roxanne's misery in silence, unable to come up with one reassuring thing to say that he thought would mean anything. The night truly had been a disaster.

The review, it seemed fair to say, was probably going to be negative. Though they'd given him V.I.P. status, Frederick Richards had ordered several things they had to tell him were out, since the cat had ruined the base stock and the soup, and the sauce for one of the most popular items had waxed the kitchen floor. The reviewer had also had to wait an inordinate amount of time for his food, since the place was packed and both the kitchen and waitstaff had become short-handed.

"How did the cat even get *in* there?" Roxanne asked, raising her head enough to prop it up with her hands. "He was locked in my apartment." She straightened suddenly, a look of alarm on her face, and turned to Steve. "You don't think someone broke into my apartment, do you? And left the door open? How else would Cheeto have gotten out?"

Steve shook his head, having already had that same thought. "I already checked the place out, when I put the cat back. Besides, even if he'd been let out by burglars, he couldn't have gotten into the kitchen from the upstairs hall. He'd have had to go out one of the outside doors and come back in one of the restaurant doors."

"Then how did he *get* there?" She sounded angry at him, but Steve knew she was just upset. He also knew she considered this her fault, since it was her cat. But of course it wasn't her fault. It wasn't anybody's fault, though he would have loved to have been able to pin it on the irritating Ralph somehow. Steve just wasn't sure how to convey to her that it was an accident, pure and simple. Just saying it didn't seem like enough.

Steve exhaled. "Listen, Roxanne, this isn't such a tragedy. The place was still packed tonight, most people loved their food and the reservation book is still full for the weekend. So you get one bad review. Big deal. The fact that people are lining up to get in to this place ought to be more important."

"The people *did* love their food, didn't they?" M. Girmond echoed.

"And there, Mr. Serrano," intoned Sir Nigel, "is exposed the extent of your ignorance. Having the majority of your experience in what could only be termed a 'beer joint,' you obviously have no idea how the real culinary world works. A bad review from a reputable publication could be devastating for future receipts."

M. Girmond made a pained sound and took off his

glasses, pinching the bridge of his nose with two large fingers.

Steve gave Sir Nigel an exasperated look. "That's a big help, Nigel. I'm sure that makes us *all* feel better. Thanks for backing me up."

"I will not 'back up,' as you say, a false statement." Sir Nigel sniffed. "Reality must be faced."

"I'm with Steve on this one," Rita piped up. "We ran our asses off tonight. We did the best we could and most people were happy with the food, even if they did have to wait a little while for it. So what if some fancy-ass reviewer didn't like his paté?"

"He did not like the paté?" M. Girmond cried.

"I had nothing to do with the paté," Ralph said.

Rita glanced worriedly at M. Girmond and wound a finger around one of the long dangly earrings she wore. "I don't know if he didn't like it. He just didn't finish it. But maybe that's because the other appetizers arrived first and he was the last to get his. He didn't want to hold up the entrees."

Roxanne moaned and put her head back on the table. "Oh God. This is all my fault. I am so, so very sorry."

Steve wanted to shake her. She needed to take this as the mere pothole it was. They weren't going to go under because of one bad night, or even—Sir Nigel be damned—one bad review.

"Or maybe he just didn't want to fill up on the appetizer," Rita added, her expression increasingly anxious. "He had a little bit of everything, from soup to nuts. He had to save room."

"I didn't serve him any nuts," Ralph said. "Do we really serve nuts?"

"You know," Rita continued, spearing Sir Nigel with an irritated glance, "if I'd actually known who the hell the guy was, maybe I could have done something different. I don't know why you didn't tell me."

"That's my fault, too," Roxanne said. "I didn't want you to get nervous. And you, all of you, worked so hard. I just—just—"

"Look," Steve tried again, "this isn't the end of the world here. We did huge business tonight. Huge. So we had a problem with the cat. Maybe we could call the *Post* and explain to the guy—"

Sir Nigel's snort cut him off. "Oh yes. *Excellent* idea, Mr. Serrano. Let's call Mr. Richards and explain that there was an *animal* in the kitchen during dinner service. That will do us a world of good."

Steve shot him an angry look. "It was an accident, for Christ's sake. Half the evening was an accident. We've been favorably reviewed by every person who's come through those doors until tonight. And tonight was a fluke."

"An unfortunately timed fluke," Sir Nigel said dourly. "And you, Mr. Serrano, do not help things by sousing customers at the bar. Do you know how that looks to the diners waiting for tables?"

"What the hell are you talking about now?" Steve's back was ramrod straight as he turned again to Sir Nigel. Could the guy possibly think his dire pronouncements were helping? Steve was almost ready to crawl across the table and grab him by his prissy little vest lapels.

"That older gentleman you serve shots to every night until he can barely stand up." Sir Nigel's face was pinched with disapproval. "Do you really think we need a whiskey-swilling drunkard—"

"Ew, whiskey. I never drink whiskey," Ralph said.

"The white-haired guy?" Steve couldn't believe it. Nigel was really getting low now, to lay this at his feet. "Hey, he doesn't harm anybody. And he pays his tab. *And* he drinks thirty-year-old single-malt scotch. Do you know how much that costs? It's one of the most expensive drinks we have."

"So you're making very nice tips," Sir Nigel concluded. "And the fact that you have to pour him into a cab every evening doesn't concern you?"

"Actually, the fact that he's *here* every evening is what concerns me. And he frequently eats dinner at the bar. He's one of our best customers, if you want to know the truth. And I don't *pour* him into the cab. He's old. He doesn't drive after he's had a couple."

Sir Nigel's lips compressed into a disapproving line. "He *is* old. He should probably not be drinking at all. He could die at that bar and then where would we be?"

Steve laughed at the absurdity. "Now you're worried customers are actually going to *die* here? Don't you think that's going a little overboard?"

"Steve!" Roxanne's voice got his attention. "Sir Nigel. *Please.* This is ridiculous." She took a deep breath, put both palms on the table and pushed herself to her feet. "Steve's right," she said.

"Hah!" Steve shot a triumphant, if immature, look at Sir Nigel.

"But Sir Nigel's point is well taken." She sent Steve a quelling glance. "The bottom line is, we had a bad night. We were due for one, actually. We'd been lucky up to now. The fact that it was when the reviewer was here is unfortunate, but there's nothing we can do about that now." She looked at each of them. "You all did an outstanding job tonight, and I want you to know how lucky I feel to have each of you on the staff. Thank you. And George and Manuel, too. George called me from the hospital a little while ago. Manuel just needed a few stitches. He'll be back to work in a few days."

"I've never had stitches," Ralph said. "I've never even broken a bone."

"I've got George's tip money," Rita said, reaching into her apron pocket.

Roxanne shook her head. "You keep it, Rita. You worked nearly the entire room this evening and kept up better than anybody could ever have expected you to. I'll compensate George."

Rita started to beam, then realized the mood was still somber and simply said, "Thanks."

"Now I think we should all go to bed," she finished with a sigh. "I know I'm exhausted. You all must be, too. And once again, this was nobody's fault but mine. I'm very sorry all your hard work had to be compromised by this."

"It was not your fault, *mon ange*," M. Girmond said.

Murmurs of agreement rose from the rest of the group as they got up to leave.

Girmond stood and took her shoulders in his hands. "It was a terrible evening, but we will live to fight another day, *eh, ma biche*?"

He kissed her on the forehead, then turned to join

the rest of the crew in heading for the exits. All of them moved slowly as if weighted down by the events of the evening. All except Sir Nigel, that was, who appeared to feel his stature grow in the presence of a disaster that was entirely blamable on persons other than himself.

"See you all tomorrow," Roxanne called as they filed out of the dining room. "Thank you!"

Responses in kind drifted back.

Roxanne turned to Steve and their eyes met. She looked so sad and tired he wanted to gather her up in his arms and hold her. But there was something in her posture, a defensiveness, that stopped him.

"Shall I come up?" he asked quietly, with a quick glance at the departing employees.

She looked down at the floor and he had his answer. She wanted no comfort from him. He was more of a plaything, he surmised. Not someone who could offer her any kind of real solace.

"I think I just need to sleep," she said, looking back up at him. "I'm just so—"

"I understand," he said, more curtly than he'd intended. He didn't want to hear whatever excuses she felt she had to make for not wanting to be with him. It was clear that unless she was in a sensual mood there was no place for him in her life. "I've got a few things I should do here anyway, before tomorrow."

She lifted her brows, surprised. "Really? Anything I can help with?"

He shook his head. "No. You go on to bed. I can see you're exhausted."

She smiled wanly and, with a long last look, confirming their unspoken policy that they make no physical contact in the restaurant, she went toward the kitchen and the back door that would take her to her apartment.

Steve continued to stand in the dining room, feeling emptiness down to the core of his being. Had that really been the brush-off he'd felt it was? Had this been a turning point? A moment when they both realized the limitations of their relationship?

Because he had to admit, at least to himself, that if this really was just a sexual thing, he couldn't sustain it. He wanted more, he thought, his mind veering away from what that meant, exactly.

He simply wanted more.

16

Bar Special

Stinger—<u>it sneaks up on you</u>
white crème de menthe, cognac, over cracked ice

Steve couldn't sleep. He rolled onto his back and stared up at the ceiling, arms behind his head.

He should talk to her. Tell her—no, *ask* her how she felt. About him. Ask her if what they had was enough for her. Or if she thought something was . . . missing.

He grabbed the pillow from under his head and put it over his face. He had turned into Lia. Or Joanne. Or Corinne. Or any one of a dozen other women who used to ask him how *he* felt, when all he felt was a physical connection. He'd always thought that if you had to ask, you had to know the answer wasn't going to be good.

Was this some kind of cosmic payback? He'd finally met a woman he couldn't get enough of and she only wanted him for sex. It was a cruel irony, made worse by the fact that he had, in the beginning, actually tried to resist her. Hell, he'd even thought that she wasn't all that beautiful, what with how stuffy and prickly and high maintenance she was.

But none of that turned out to be true. She wasn't stuffy, she was shy. She may have been prickly at first, but it was defensive.

And she was about as low maintenance as they came. Ending up, as it happened, *too* low maintenance. She didn't need anything from him.

It was all so obvious now.

Steve threw off the covers and swung his legs over the side of the bed. He needed to do something, occupy his mind with something else. He got up, slipped on some jeans and a sweatshirt and pulled on his shoes.

He'd go down and investigate the kitchen. There was no way that cat had come through three doors to get into the kitchen—somehow getting out of the apartment, then outside, then inside the restaurant. He had to have come through the inside somehow. If nothing else, Steve could ensure that a disaster like tonight never happened again.

He crept down the stairs quietly, then let himself in the back door of the restaurant. Once in the kitchen he turned on the lights, squinting in the brightness and marveling at how clean and shiny everything looked, when just a few hours ago chaos had reigned.

His eyes scanned the walls and the ceiling above the stove, the workstations, around past the door to the dining room, over the office door, to the wall of refrigerators and the new freezer, to the back door again.

No obvious holes or gaps in the old tin ceiling. The walls looked solid enough.

The cat had been a mess when he'd grabbed him to take him back upstairs, squirming and fighting when Steve had first picked him up, desperate to get back to all that food that was now all over the floor. So Steve had ample time to notice that the animal was covered with dirt and flour and some kind of sticky sauce. It even had a flake of fish caught in one whisker. But it was the black streaks along the cat's sides that had him intrigued. It was soot, Steve was certain, but where had it come from?

He thought about his own apartment, how there was a mantel with no fireplace, just a hole for an old fashioned coal stove, probably used in the late 1800s to early 1900s. In his kitchen, too, he knew there was one of those holes behind the counter on the back wall, and at the roofline you could see the old chimney. No doubt a flue came all the way down to the first floor.

He looked at the new freezer in its alcove near the back door. It protruded into the kitchen a little farther than the old one had—it was a bigger and more efficient model—at about the same spot where his counter covered the stove hole upstairs.

Eyes raking down the stainless steel exterior, he smiled. There were wheels on this freezer, probably to make it easier to service. The last one had taken four burly guys to get out the back door, and even then it had cracked the back threshold.

Rolling up his sleeves, he grabbed hold of one side and rolled the thing out slowly from the wall.

Sure enough, behind the appliance was a stove hole partially covered by a round tin, the kind with spring-like metal pieces to hold it in place, just like in his apartment. Clearly, something had pushed the tin aside and Steve would bet anything it had been the cat.

He squeezed around the freezer and pulled the tin covering off, finding several cat hairs clinging to the side. He tried to peer in the hole but it was too dark. He thought about calling up through it, to see if Roxanne could hear him, but of course that would scare her to death. He smiled grimly at the thought that maybe he could practice a little subconscious conditioning.

Steve is the most handsome man you've ever seen. The smartest, wittiest, most . . . whatever, he couldn't even come up with anything that seemed remotely true.

Readjusting the wire clasps in back of the cover, he pushed it back into place, then thought he should do something more permanent than that. Maybe nail it shut, though he should nail the one in Roxanne's apartment first, so the cat didn't crawl in only to get stuck at the bottom. Or better yet, the whole thing could be covered over by a piece of plywood, unless whoever retrofitted the place had run plumbing up through the flue, as was common.

His eyes trailed around what was probably the original fireplace and what would therefore be brick but was now covered with plaster. The wall ran almost three feet beyond where the fireplace would have ended, to the back wall of the building. So if someone had run plumbing and/or electrical, they could have housed it in that three-foot space and not in the chimney.

He tapped the wall beside the fireplace. It sounded hollow. At floor level, there was a slight gap where the toe molding had been eaten away by some insect or small animal, and he wriggled two fingers under it.

The covering was boarded ribbing, as was typical for the late nineteenth century, that had been plastered over to match the chimney camouflage. He pulled gently and it gapped slightly. Curious, and knowing this area would never show, he pulled a little harder. A small shower of plaster rained down on his hand and a crack ran up the wall.

He stopped, reluctant to cause any more damage than necessary.

Still, his curiosity was piqued. He should ask Roxanne if she'd mind if he looked in here. Aside from being a possible escape route for her curiously exploratory cat, it could contain interesting historical details.

He pulled on the panel again and tried to look in. Too dark. He needed a flashlight.

His right hand holding the plaster-covered wood, he tried to slide his left hand through the crack to see what he could feel, anticipating all manner of spiders or maybe even a dead mouse or two.

Webs, for sure. He flicked what was probably a dead roach aside, then felt . . . nothing. About three inches back there was a space where the floor ended. He ran his fingers over the edge of the floor. It was smooth and rounded.

He pushed his hand farther into the space and felt nothing. No pipes, no wires, just the edge of the floor. He pushed his hand in up to his wrist and let his fingers drop. The tips barely brushed another piece of wood about eight inches below floor level.

Steve caught his breath, as his fingers backed up and found what could be a riser, just below the lip of the floor. His pulse accelerated as he considered that this cavity could possibly have contained an old staircase, one that went *down*. He pictured the basement and knew there was no staircase on this end. If there were, it would have blocked the outside cellar entrance, the one that had been broken into and was now boarded up.

When had that entrance been installed? Late 1800s? He tried to remember the exact year, and thought it had been something like 1868 or 1870, fairly soon after the end of the Civil War. So if there had been a staircase here, they would have had to take it out to make room for the trap door entrance.

Under the first step . . . he remembered, blood thrumming through his veins.

Steve could picture the words written in Portner's spidery scrawl.

Includes the contents under the first step as described to my Executor . . .

Steve's lungs felt near to bursting and he exhaled, realizing as he did that he'd stopped breathing. This could be the spot, he thought. No wonder all those earlier excavations had found nothing in the old staircases. There was a *back* stair. One that nobody had considered or knew existed for probably a hundred and fifty years.

Elation flooded his veins like oxygen and he tried to temper it. He could be wrong. It could be anything. An old pantry or dumbwaiter. Maybe even an early-twentieth-century trash chute. If there had been a back staircase, surely someone would have known about it, or at least suspected.

Then again, this place had always been privately owned . . . And the theories about the fair copy—

known mostly in academic circles—had never truly been believed.

Steve examined the plaster covering the old fireplace and the wall beside it. He picked at a piece with one fingernail near where it had cracked. A couple coats of paint were obvious, as was an old layer of wallpaper.

This space had been covered over a long time, there was no doubt about it.

This could, he thought, fighting heart palpitations, be *it*.

Roxanne tiptoed down the stairs. Steve hadn't answered her knock on his door. He was probably as exhausted as she was, only without the neurotic inability to fall asleep that she had.

Lying in bed telling herself she needed to deal with her troubles alone had not, after a couple hours, made any sense to her. She knew she would feel better with Steve beside her, just holding her and assuring her that she was not alone, that her fear that she would lose her business was not justified. It *was* just one review, after all. She had to be jumping to the worst conclusions.

That Steve could make her feel better was something she was sure of. She had just been so sure she was going to dissolve into tears the moment she left the restaurant that she felt she had to turn him away earlier. She was too afraid to let him see her that way.

Thinking about it, though, as she lay alone in her bed, she knew in her heart of hearts that he would understand. In fact, of all the people in the world he would probably understand the best. After all, he was nearly as involved in this restaurant as she was.

How silly she'd been to think they had nothing in common, she reflected. They lived in the same building, worked in the same restaurant, dealt with the same people day in and day out—the plain truth was, she had more in common with Steve than she'd ever had in common with Martin.

All this time she had thought she wanted someone cultured and urbane, but she understood now how completely superficial that was. Steve seemed to understand her, and he certainly seemed to care. He made her laugh and, best of all, they had *fun* together.

What did it matter that he wasn't a patron of the arts or a season ticket holder at the Kennedy Center? Who cared that he probably hadn't worn a tuxedo since his high-school prom? If he could hold her in the middle of the night and allay her fears, he was a man she knew she could fall in love with.

But right now it was too late. He was asleep and she had to lie in her bed alone, with nothing to do but go over and over all that had gone wrong that night.

She reached the landing for her apartment and her eye caught on a patch of light outside the window. She leaned toward the glass.

In the back alley, just outside the kitchen, two patches of light from the window and door illuminated the asphalt and glanced off the hood of Steve's truck.

Someone was in the kitchen.

Her pulse jumped and the hair all over her head prickled with dread.

Someone was here. The intruders had come back. And they were looking for whatever it was they sought, in the kitchen, again.

She had to call the cops, and quickly. Maybe they could catch them red-handed. She ran down the hall to her door, adrenaline pumping as she went for the phone, but with her hand on the doorknob she stopped.

Steve hadn't answered her knock.

Do you know where Steve was last night?

P.B.'s voice from after the last break-in echoed in her head.

There's good reason to believe something's hidden in this house. Why wouldn't *he try to find it?* P.B. had insisted.

Roxanne closed her eyes. It couldn't be. She knew what she was doing; she was fearing the worst because she'd just had the scary idea that she could fall in love with this man. Now she was trying to sabotage him in her head.

And yet . . . suppose it *was* Steve? No matter what she told herself, no matter what she felt for him, there *was* the chance that he was behind the break-ins. Would she be stupid not to admit that? And if he was behind them, if it was him in the kitchen right now . . . did she really want the cops to find him? *P.B.?* Did she really want Steve *arrested*?

She swallowed over a sudden lump in her throat and moved slowly back to the stairs. *Just call the police*, part of her said. *You've got to trust someone sometime, so trust now that it's not Steve.*

But she didn't. As much as she wanted to, she couldn't. It just made too much sense that the odd damage that had occurred at each break-in had been done by someone searching for something. Something that had been hidden pretty thoroughly, and a long time ago, if digging behind a brick foundation was any indication.

With quiet stealth, she slipped down the stairwell and opened the door to the back alley. Propping the door open with a rock she kept nearby for bracing it when she had groceries, she inched toward the back door to the restaurant and peered through the windowpanes.

The first thing that met her eye was the freezer, rolled toward the center of the room at an angle so that it didn't have to be unplugged.

Her stomach did a little jump. Then her hands rose and gripped each other at her mouth, as if holding in a scream. Wanting to cross the doorway, she ducked down below the door window and scrabbled left, then leaned against the wall on the opposite side. From this angle, she could see behind the freezer.

There, on the floor, with his hands tugging at a portion of the wall, was Steve.

She spun away from the door window, pressing her back against the outside brick wall, and squeezed her eyes shut. Disappointment and grief fell into her chest as hard as a piano from an upstairs window, followed quickly by a familiar sense of failure.

Stupid, she thought. How had she been so stupid? She *knew* she shouldn't have trusted him. She'd been duped again. Where was her judgment? Why couldn't she tell a good guy from a louse? How could she end up here again—used by another man who only wanted her for one thing? And it wasn't love.

Shit, she nearly said out loud, anger taking over. Had he slept with her so that she would overlook something like this? Or had that just been a perk?

P.B. had been right about Steve. She could hardly believe it.

She tipped her head back so it rested on the brick wall. She told herself she should be glad it was just Steve looking for his stupid document and not some hardened criminal with a weapon. But she wasn't glad. She couldn't be. This meant that Steve had lied to her more times than she could count. He'd pretended he knew nothing about the break-ins and he obviously had no intention of telling her if and when he found what he was looking for.

Whether or not she would be the rightful owner of that draft if he found it didn't matter. What mattered was that Steve decided it was better to lie and keep his actions a secret—allowing her to live in fear of being robbed—than to trust her and ask for her help.

She pressed the heels of her hands to her eyes and tried to stop tears from squeezing through her lids.

Great. She'd screwed up her restaurant and discovered she was involved with another liar, all in the same evening. Total personal and professional devastation.

She squatted down beside the door, then slid onto her butt, for some reason unable to move from the spot. She dropped her hands to the ground beside her, feeling the pebbly asphalt beneath her, the bits of broken glass and old tar and God knew what else.

If she sat here long enough, she thought, maybe it would turn out not to be true. Maybe when she opened her eyes and stood up she'd see nobody in the kitchen. Maybe she was so exhausted that she was sleepwalking and had hallucinated the whole thing.

But when she opened her eyes the patches of light were still on the ground, and the noise from inside the kitchen was soft but still there.

Unbidden, memories of the first break-in flooded back to her. That was the night she'd brought the bottle of wine to Steve's apartment. The night he'd been leaving for some engagement—with some kind of tool stuffed in his duffle bag.

She sat up straighter. *That's right*, she thought. She'd even commented on the handle, saying it looked like some kind of gardening equipment. Then he'd arrived home late, after she'd thought she'd heard glass breaking.

She covered her face with her hands. Why hadn't she remembered that before?

Because, she thought with sudden and cynical certainty, she hadn't wanted to know, hadn't wanted to see what Steve really was. Good old Roxanne, deluding herself again from the very beginning.

Chances were, if she sat here long enough, Steve would come out and find her.

What would he say? How would he explain? And more important, how would she react? Would she buy his excuses like she had with Martin all those years?

She had to think. She knew she would come to work tomorrow and find evidence of a new break-in, so she had to figure out how to respond.

Slowly she stood up and crept back to her apartment, suddenly more tired than she could bear. She'd figure this all out tomorrow. She'd deal with the new break-in tomorrow.

She'd decide what the hell to do about Steve *tomorrow*.

"I'm *going* to talk to her, Dana," Steve said into his cell phone, standing on the steps of the Library of Congress. It was a relatively mild day for winter and the sunshine felt good. "I'm just going to wait until after the weekend."

"Why?" she countered in her characteristically blunt way. "You're only going to agonize and work out speeches and water it all down until you say nothing at all."

She had part of it right, he had to admit. He had been agonizing and working out speeches.

"You don't understand," he said, watching three suited men in black overcoats get out of a black sedan and walk toward the Supreme Court building. "The restaurant's booked. We're just coming off of a hellish night. And Roxanne's still getting up before dawn to bake all the damn bread. I don't think springing the idea that I'd like to take apart a corner of her kitchen would go over very well right now. Especially considering there's probably nothing there anyway."

"Oh, for Pete's sake," Dana said. She was obviously in the van with her kids. Her language was way too clean to believe she was alone. "I'm not talking about your darn historical discovery or theory or whatever it is. I'm talking about your *feelings*, Steve. When are you going to talk to her about your feelings, you repressed clod?"

Steve sat down on the top step and leaned his backpack on the step below. "I was thinking I'd do it at the same time," he said, his head in one hand. "In my own cloddish way."

"What do you mean?" she demanded.

A car horn sounded in the background and Steve wondered if in her vehemence she was driving erratically.

"Should we get off the phone until you get where you're going?" he asked.

"They weren't honking at me. Tell me what you mean by doing it at the same time. You want to put your feelings in a historical context? Tell her your heart's been hidden all these years and you found it behind the freezer in her kitchen?"

"Hey, that's good. I should be taking notes."

"I'm serious, Steve," she said. "I don't want you opening up that bag of candy. That's for Daddy. You had yours in the store, remember?"

Steve lifted his head, squinting in the sunlight. "What?"

"Sorry, Steve, hang on a second."

Below him, he could hear water cascading over Neptune's statue in the fountain at the front of the building. A family of tourists stopped to look at it and the young boy raised a hand and said, "Ooh, look at the snake, Daddy!"

Steve thought about the box of rubber snakes and smiled. Dana had claimed that proved Roxanne had feelings for him. Nobody was that creative or went that far out of her way to prank someone unless they cared about him.

On the phone, Dana's voice achieved a tone Steve was glad she wasn't using on him, so reminiscent was it of their mother's. "Do you want me to stop this car, Justin? Because I will stop this car and take that away from you. Put it back in the grocery bag. *Now.*"

Steve pictured his nephew's mischievous face and smiled. The kid had spunk. He was the only one in the whole family who wasn't scared to death of Dana when she got mad.

"What I'm saying is," Dana said—and Steve waited to see who this was relevant to, him or Justin—"You've never talked this way about a woman before and I don't want you talking yourself out of what you're feeling for her. You're much better off just striking while the iron is hot."

"Are you talking to me or Justin?"

"Justin is much more emotionally mature. He knows to say 'I love you' when he feels it, don't you, sweetie?"

In the background Steve heard Justin singing, "I love you, Mommy! I love you, Mommy!"

"Great," Dana said, laughing, "now look what you've started."

"I didn't bring up the L word."

"See?" she exclaimed. "That's just what I'm talking about. Can you not even *say* it?"

"Dana, I'm going to talk to her. I've already said this a dozen times. My plan was to tell her about my discovery, then couch it in a kind of teamwork way."

"Teamwork?"

"Yeah, you know, if I find this valuable thing, of course it will be yours. I just want to use it in my book and then it will create success for both of us, or something like that. Stressing the 'both of us' part."

"Oh Steve," Dana said, her voice deadly serious and somewhat pitying. "That's just awful."

"Well it's not so easy, Dana. If I tell her about the hidden staircase, then tell her how I feel about her, she'll think I'm buttering her up so I can dig in her basement. Same problem if I tell her about my feelings, then tell her about the hidden staircase. The way I figure it, it has to be at the same time."

"That makes it seem like you think they're equally important."

"No, no, I had it better than that. It's written down in my notes someplace."

"Oh yes, be sure to bring your notes."

Steve put his head back in his hand as a chilly breeze kicked up. "Dana, if we talk about this any more I'm going to have your voice in my head when I talk to her and I won't be able to say anything."

"No, that's good. I'll *tell* you what to say."

He laughed.

"I'm serious. It's very simple. Just say ..." She paused. "Did I tell you you could open those Pop-Tarts?"

Steve shook his head. "Well, that's good, but that's not really the point I'm going for."

"Don't be stupid," she said.

In the background Justin sang, "Mommy said 'stupid'! Mommy said 'stupid'!"

"Quiet, honey." To Steve she said, "You just say, 'Roxanne, I'm in love with you.' Simple as that."

"Yeah, right." He scoffed. "I thought I'd say something more like 'I'd like to see more of you' and 'Maybe we could go out on an actual date sometime.'"

Dana sighed elaborately. "Jeez, Steve, don't go overboard or anything."

"Dana, if I go in there and say 'Roxanne, I'm in love with you,' she'll laugh at me."

"No she won't."

"Yes she will."

"Then why are you in love with a woman who would do such a thing?"

Steve thought about that. Because she *wouldn't* do such a thing. She wasn't mean. And she did care for him, he was fairly certain. So why was he so afraid of what she'd do?

He cleared his throat. "Look, she could have any guy she wants. She's gorgeous. And—"

"And she wants *you*. It's obvious. The woman has, what, two discretionary hours a week and she chooses to spend them with you? Come on."

"I'm convenient."

Dana clucked her tongue. "See, there again, I have to ask. If you believe that, why do you feel so strongly about her?"

"I don't know." He grabbed his backpack and stood up. "And I'm getting more confused by the minute. But right now I really have to go. If I don't get this research done today, I'll have to wait until Monday."

"No word from that editor you wrote to?"

"Nothing." He fought back the now-familiar despair. It had been weeks since he'd sent that letter.

"All right," she said. "I'll let you go. But here are my last thoughts to you. First, you need to figure out what's more important to you, the girl or the evidence for your book. If it's the girl, all you need to do is tell her you love her. That's what she wants to hear. Trust me."

"Whatever you say."

They hung up. Steve stood on the steps and looked up at the Library of Congress. He'd been working on this book for three years. It was the key to his future plans—he couldn't give that up for a girl he just met a couple months ago, could he? That would be idiotic.

But could he really put the book ahead of Roxanne? Ahead of the most amazing woman he'd ever met—who, inexplicably, seemed interested in him?

Was this really an either/or question?

No, he thought, but Dana was still right. This wasn't just a case of knowing what Roxanne wanted to hear. He needed to make a decision. What did he want to say?

Did he want to tell her he loved her?

He closed his eyes a brief moment, seeing Roxanne's sad, tired face from the night before, and answered the question with unexpected ease.

Yes, God help him, he did.

He arrived back home with just enough time to change and get down to the bar. Apprehension fueled his energy and he couldn't help worrying that his impression last night about a turning point, when she hadn't wanted comfort from him after the dinner fiasco, would prove correct. After all, what else could that mean, if not that she was pulling away from him? He was nothing to her but a convenience is what he thought it meant, but he hoped he was wrong.

He let himself in to the bar and saw Sir Nigel in the dining room fussing with tablecloths and moving silverware around. Rita came through the doors from the kitchen, tying her apron around her waist.

"Hey, Stevie," she said, impish smile breaking across her face upon seeing him.

"What's up, Rita?" He tried to sound lively as he

made his way around the bar to the service end, but he felt like a kid on the day his oral report was due. He was so sure something bad was going to happen, he couldn't act naturally.

"Nothin'." She approached the bar. "Don't you love this place now? It's so pretty here. And I love that there's no more smoke."

He smiled at her. "You love it here, huh? Well, who would have thought?"

She laughed. "I know, it's weird. But I do. By the way, I took a message for you earlier. Some chick called on the house phone. I wrote it down on a napkin."

Rita was about to sit on a bar stool when Sir Nigel spoke.

"Miss Rita, could I have a word?" He crooked a finger at her.

Rita turned to Steve and rolled her eyes. "The prime minister calls," she said in a lousy British accent.

Steve laughed and punched the cash button on the register to make sure there was money in the drawer. Yep. He pushed it closed and turned to shelve the rack of clean glasses sitting on the cold chest.

She was here, he was sure. She was always the first one here. He thought about going back to the kitchen for something, maybe he was in need of lemons or some other kind of garnish. But he was well stocked, another thing he'd accomplished last night in his insomnia.

Things were pretty calm as the crew set up, everyone moving quietly in the wake of last night's trauma. Just before five thirty, when the doors opened, Roxanne came out of the kitchen to the service bar.

He turned and smiled at her, taken aback again, as he

sometimes was, by how beautiful she was. But she did not return it.

"I need a pitcher of ice water," she said softly, looking toward the dining room.

"Sure," Steve replied in a voice too jovial to be real. If she knew him at all, she'd recognize that voice as rampant uncertainty.

"I remember!" Rita called from the dining room. "It was some woman who said she was an editor—Susan something. I put it on the liquor shelf next to the register."

Steve glanced at Rita, then back at the liquor shelf, where a cocktail napkin lay with Rita's big loopy writing on it. *An editor? As in, a book editor?*

"Thanks, Rita."

He grabbed a pitcher and looked at Roxanne, who was looking into the dining room.

"Anything else I can get you?" he asked. "Coffee? Tea?" The end of the joke—*Me?*—died on his lips as she settled her dark eyes on him.

"No," she said firmly.

Something was definitely up, he thought. Dread curled in his stomach and the cocktail napkin was forgotten.

He filled the pitcher with ice and used the soda gun to fire water into it. "Is everything all right?" he asked.

"Fine."

Oh God. He knew that 'fine.' There wasn't a woman alive who hadn't perfected the nuance of that.

"Roxanne," he said low, bringing her the pitcher, "what's wrong?"

She looked away again. "Nothing." She took the water, then added, "I'll talk to you later."

There was nothing reassuring in that statement, and Steve was tormented by it the entire evening. Though he tried to forget about it, write it off as part of her terrible mood from the night before, he knew it wasn't that. He knew, somehow, that whatever shit was about to hit the fan was coming straight for him.

The night was busy again, but he felt as if he dealt with it efficiently. He was getting used to this crowd and their brand of drinking. The white-haired gentleman was back, as he always was—the man Steve privately referred to as Red Top because he always had to call him a Red Top Cab—and Steve took particular pleasure in serving him this evening, knowing Sir Nigel was annoyed every time he poured the man another drink.

About halfway through the evening, Steve realized that in his distraction he'd forgotten to tell Roxanne how the cat had gotten into the kitchen. He'd secured the downstairs hole as much as possible last night, but she still needed to block the upstairs one. If she came out again he would tell her.

But she didn't come out. Despite the fact that he found himself stealing glances at the kitchen doors more and more often, he knew Roxanne would never emerge from them. No, she'd made it a point to try not to come into the front room when customers were present. He'd called her on it once, telling her she should come out *more* often, rather than less. That if people knew the place had such a young and beautiful owner it would get even more popular. But she'd slapped that idea down quickly enough. She seemed annoyed when anybody mentioned her looks, asserting that she would *never* use her appearance to try to increase business.

By the end of the night, he was exhausted and wired, as usual, but it was all tinged with apprehension. So when Roxanne emerged after the waitstaff had left and it was just the busboys mopping up the kitchen floor, he knew the other shoe was about to drop.

"Hey." He stopped wiping down the bar and came toward her, the towel still in his hands. "You look tired. Is everything okay?"

She stood stiffly at the end of the service bar, not meeting his eyes. "I am tired. I'm always tired."

"I know. It's been crazy. But I thought tonight went pretty well."

She nodded. "Comparatively."

"Listen, Roxanne, we don't have to talk here, or even at all tonight if you're too tired," he said, thinking for a moment that maybe, just maybe, this wasn't about him. "Or I can come up later, if you want, and you can unload your troubles on me. I'll even rub your back." He tried a smile.

Her eyes flashed up to his and he knew he'd made a mistake.

"Look, Steve," she said, and then paused for so long he had time to think he should leave, now, before she said whatever it was she was about to say.

Because it wasn't going to be good. He could see from the look on her face that it was not going to be good.

But he was too late to save himself.

"You and I both know," she began, taking a deep, seemingly fortifying breath, "that it's a bad idea to mix business with pleasure. I've been worried about this for a while now, and I've decided it's just not working."

For Steve, all the air left the room, as if he were in an airplane and a bomb had gone off.

"What do you mean?" he asked.

He knew what she meant. He knew exactly what she was getting at. She was done with him. Through. Finished. But what he wanted to know was why. What had happened that made her change her mind about him?

"I mean, we've had a nice fling." She swallowed. "And it's over now."

"A nice fling," he repeated. All he could do was stare at her, the bar towel now balled up in his hands.

"That's right." Her gaze turned steady, and her face was hard. Resolved, like a general demoting him to a private. "We got what we wanted from each other and now we're done."

"We're done," he repeated. Then, "We're done," in a more conversational tone, anger, disappointment and disbelief warring within him. "Well, that's good to know."

She didn't move. "I think you knew that it would happen sometime."

He shook his head, holding his hands up in exaggerated innocence. "I didn't. Really. So thanks for the update."

He should ask her why, he knew. He should sit her down, drag it out of her, see what this was all about. But he couldn't bear to hear her tell him that she just didn't feel anything for him. Couldn't bear to hear the words he'd said to so many others coming back at him.

Instead, he reacted with anger. Sheer, petulant, frightened-of-his-own-feelings anger. "Anything else, boss? Want me to clear out so you don't have to look at your mistake anymore or what?"

"You don't have to go," she said quietly. "Unless you want to."

He didn't hear the question in her voice. Just the suggestion.

"Oh I *want* to." He threw the towel onto the floor. Then he laughed. Throwing in the towel, as literally as possible. "I want to be as far away from here, and you, as possible."

He rounded the bar and let the service door slam down behind him.

She gave him a penetrating look. "Do you really?"

He stood as close as he dared and stared her down. "You bet I do."

Her eyes didn't waver, but she didn't say anything. She just continued giving him that stony look.

He didn't know what else he'd expected. It wasn't as if he'd ever talked about his feelings or treated their affair as anything other than a fling himself.

It was just . . . he'd just . . . he'd *felt* something, dammit. For her.

And she had felt nothing.

He had no right to be angry. He had no right to think ill of her. But he couldn't be around her, not for another minute.

Not without something in his chest breaking into a thousand pieces.

He took a last deep breath and said quietly, "Good-bye, Roxanne. And good luck."

He walked out the front door, wishing, as he did, that she had made it easier on them both and just killed him.

17

Dessert Special of the Day
Deep Freeze—cool and collected,
 until the room heats up
Champagne sherbet with lemon and orange syrup
 folded into Italian meringue

Roxanne wasn't sure why there had been no evidence of a break-in that morning, but it didn't matter. She knew what she'd seen and she knew what she'd had to do.

So why did she feel so awful about it?

Two days after she'd done it, she got a terse note from Steve saying that he was moving out at the end of the month. It wasn't exactly a surprise, but the feeling of despair it gave her was. How could she be sorry he was moving when he'd been, for all intents and purposes, vandalizing her property?

The following Friday night, Rita was the first to arrive at work—usually she was the last. Roxanne was in the kitchen pulling a *genoise* cake from the oven when the waitress came in.

Roxanne was startled to see her and her stomach flipped at the thought that Rita might have shown up early because she wanted to talk about Steve.

Roxanne knew they were good friends, and she knew everyone was unhappy he was no longer working there, but she had no desire to tell anyone about Steve's illicit search of her building. Not just because it was humiliating to her, but because she felt that if he was willing to move out and give up his search, she was willing to let the incidents go. He was just a man blinded by greed, who obviously felt he had to lie to get what he wanted. And what he wanted was that draft of the Declaration of Independence.

Not her.

With Steve gone, George had covered the bar the next evening—making it obvious how skilled Steve was. George could not come close to keeping up, and after that, Roxanne had hired a guy from the Italian restaurant down the street. She'd had to offer him a substantial raise in order to get him fast, which had not endeared her to his former employer, but it was that or let chaos reign.

"Hey, Roxanne," Rita said.

Roxanne turned the cake out onto a wire rack. It had to cool before she could fill it with butter cream, then layer it, glaze it all with apricot and ice it with *glacé royale*.

"Hi, Rita. You're early today." She wiped her hands on a towel, hoping against hope this had something to do with restaurant business.

"I know. I wanted to be sure to remember to give you this. I found it this morning." Rita reached into the large leather purse that was looped over her shoulder and pulled out a newspaper. "I couldn't believe it when I saw it."

She unrolled the tabloid, and Roxanne saw that it was *D.C. Scene*, a small entertainment paper that concentrated on the younger, more night-life-oriented type of subscriber.

"Read this," Rita said, pointing to a column that was headed WHO NEWS?

Roxanne took the paper from her and looked where she pointed. "In culinary news, Senator Robert Rush was seen canoodling with a very young, very blond, very pretty aide at the hot new restaurant in Alexandria, Chez Soi. In those intimate environs, cheating seems to be the rule, not the exception, as film director Francois LaBoroque was also seen there with a pretty starlet not too long ago."

Roxanne's face flushed and her palms went damp. "Is this true?" She looked up at Rita.

Rita shrugged, looking slightly surprised. "I know about that senator guy, I waited on him. And he was playing some serious footsie, if you know what I mean. I don't know about that French guy. But . . . don't you think this is good?"

"Good?" The word came out like a missile.

Rita looked taken aback. "Well, yeah. Uh, I mean, it's publicity, right? People like their restaurants to be cozy and romantic."

"But they don't like to be followed there by the paparazzi." Roxanne stepped closer and lowered her voice, since a couple of the busboys had just shown up. "Rita, you didn't talk to this paper, did you?"

"Me? No!" Rita held a fist to her chest and looked so spooked Roxanne wasn't sure if she was being honest or was just reacting to the look on Roxanne's face.

"No, of course you wouldn't," Roxanne said, collecting herself. Rita was not the type to go talking to a newspaper. "I'm sorry for even asking. I'm just . . ." She opened the paper again and looked at the column, digesting what this meant. It made the whole place sound like some sort of dirty, clandestine restaurant of ill repute. "I'm surprised, is all. And bothered, I guess."

"Bothered? I thought you'd be glad. It calls us the 'hot new restaurant in Alexandria,'" Rita protested, pointing to a spot in the column. "I think that's good. And you know how people love to see celebrities. I bet *more* people come here because of this."

Roxanne put a hand to her forehead. Maybe Rita was right. Maybe she was just primed for disaster because of that awful night when the reviewer was here.

And the awful moment when she realized Steve was the one behind the break-ins.

"Do you think so?" she asked doubtfully.

"Absolutely! I think we owe whoever wrote this a thank you. Especially if that reviewer decides to trash us."

Roxanne closed her eyes against the words and suppressed a shudder. *If that reviewer decides to trash us . . .* She didn't know what would have to happen for that reviewer *not* to trash them, but she still dreaded the occurrence.

"Are you okay?" Rita asked. "I shouldn't have shown this to you. I just, I really thought it was good."

"No, no. I'm fine." Roxanne turned back to her cake and touched it with a light finger. It sprang back perfectly. She looked at Rita. "And I'm glad you told me. Thank you. I just . . . well, I guess I have to think about it."

"Okay." Rita turned toward the linen closet and opened the door. She grabbed an apron, wound the strings behind her back and turned toward the swinging doors to the restaurant. Just before she pushed through she said, "Don't forget, Roxanne. There's no such thing as bad publicity."

Roxanne nodded and mustered a smile, one that died on her lips the moment Rita went through the doors. She looked at the door through which Rita had passed, the wheels in her head spinning wildly. Hadn't Rita said something the other night about an *editor* calling? Roxanne hadn't given it a thought at the time, but now she remembered the comment clearly.

In her mind's eye she pictured Steve's apartment. It was sparsely furnished and usually quite neat, except for one corner . . . that paper-strewn corner where his computer sat. What did he write? she wondered suddenly. She never even thought to question it before, just thought it was part of that hypothetical 'research' Steve was always talking about. But now she had to wonder. What on earth did Steve have on all those printed pages?

What would Steve be doing with an editor if he *wasn't* writing for a newspaper?

And if he *was* writing for a newspaper, if he were responsible for something like that gossip column, wouldn't he send his buddy Rita to see how Roxanne took it? Wouldn't he tell her to put a positive spin on it?

Was he doing it to get back in her good graces? Was he that desperate to stay and continue his search of her property?

But that was stupid. He'd made his search look like break-ins before; so why wouldn't he just break in again to search if he wanted to? He didn't need to work here for that. Didn't even need to live here. And he certainly didn't need to be sleeping with her.

Maybe he was doing it to get back at her. Make her restaurant look bad.

She put a hand to her head. She should have talked to Steve. Should have told him what she knew, that she'd seen him, and asked what he had to say about it.

She *would* do that, she decided, realizing she had to get down to work or the evening's desserts would not be ready. She would call him up, arrange a meeting, and clear the air.

Or maybe, just maybe, she would go have a look at what was on those pages . . .

Roxanne looked out her kitchen window the next morning and cursed under her breath. Steve's truck was still there. Fine time for him to start hanging around, she thought. The one day she'd like to get up there for a quick little look. Just a peek at those pages to see exactly what she was dealing with.

If he really was writing the column, would she take that as a good sign or a bad one? Would it mean he was trying to help her, or hurt her?

She couldn't stand the thought of him working

against her. Couldn't stand the idea that he might be so angry that he would deliberately try to sabotage her.

On the other hand, if he was trying to help her what would that mean? Would she forgive him for the break-ins? *Could* she?

She wasn't sure. All she knew was, she had to get in there and see for herself.

Two hours later, Steve was gone. She spent another twenty minutes watching the back alley to be sure he hadn't forgotten something and come right back, then she went up the stairs to his apartment.

She took the key out of her pocket and inserted it into the lock. But she didn't turn it.

She knew she hadn't a right to go in. She knew that what she was doing was illegal. Snooping. Spying. Breaking into his house to read his private documents.

She took the key out of the lock and stared at the door.

But how private were those documents if they contained gossip about her restaurant for the press?

She put her hand on the knob.

Don't be ridiculous, part of her scolded. *You have absolutely no evidence that he was behind that. None. Not one shred.*

She dropped her hand.

Except for that "editor" message.

She put her hand back on the knob.

And then, of course, there were the break-ins. Searching his apartment would just be tit for tat.

The break-ins. If he was capable of that, he was capable of any kind of duplicity. It was perfectly conceivable that he was behind the gossip column.

She took her hand from the knob and lay it on the

door, then put her head against it. She wasn't going to go in. She couldn't do it. It was an invasion of his privacy, no matter how she looked at it. Even though part of her hated herself for not being able to do what it took to investigate the matter, she could not let herself in.

After a second she pushed off the door and headed back down the steps, her footsteps heavy on the treads.

She needed to talk to him, that was all. She just hoped she didn't end up falling for any weak argument he offered because she missed him so much. After all she'd been through, surely she was stronger than that.

On Sunday, the review came out.

"It's not so bad," Skip said, sitting at her dining-room table with the magazine section in his hands the following Monday. "He says right here, 'I might give this restaurant another try after it's been around long enough to improve its service . . . '" He trailed off.

She turned a wry look to him as she emptied a pot full of water and put it back on the counter. "And the next sentence . . . ?"

"*If* it's around long enough," Skip read dourly.

Roxanne looked up at the dripping ceiling and adjusted the pot under it.

Skip continued reading.

"He said he loved the scallops of foie gras," he offered, "and the turbot gallettes with black butter sauce would have been 'divine' if they hadn't been cold. So really," Skip concluded, closing the magazine, "he didn't say anything bad about the food, except that it was cold and you didn't have a lot of what was on the menu."

Roxanne turned back to him, leaning on the counter.

"If you had read that review about any other restaurant, you would never plan to go there. You probably wouldn't even have noticed it said anything nice about the food. Just cold, late and not available. Not to mention the place was packed and everyone had to wait for their food."

Skip held out his hands, imploringly. "Hey, if the place was packed it says to me it's popular."

She smiled at her friend. "Thank you, Skip. But let's be realistic. The first line says it all."

She had memorized it. Or rather, it had emblazoned itself on her mind the first time she read it. *Going to a restaurant owned by a former* Sports Illustrated *swimsuit model should have been my first clue that the food would be scarce.*

"Yeah, he kind of blew your cover there, didn't he?" Skip acknowledged. "But you had to know it would come out sooner or later."

"I guess. I just didn't anticipate that when it did, it would be so public, or used so meanly." She sighed. "There goes my credibility."

"Roxanne, don't be ridiculous. If anything, that will help you. Look, you know the food is good, and if people want to come because of the celebrity factor, let them come. They'll find out what a great restaurant it is and come back for that. Whatever works."

"I know. That's not . . . well, okay." She hadn't meant her credibility with the public; she was thinking of Steve. Steve, to whom she had actually lied about being a model.

Well, she thought resignedly, maybe that made them even. He'd lied about vandalizing her building.

She felt a drop on the back of her hand and turned, looking up. Was the water coming from yet another crack? She leaned across the counter and flipped on the overhead light, but the bulb blew immediately.

"Dammit," she muttered, bending over to get another pot out from under the stove.

"What's going on over there?" Skip got up from the table and joined her in the kitchen.

She shook her head, positioning the new pot. "It's a leak. I don't know what to do about it. I guess I'm going to have to go up there and fix the stupid thing. It's probably the trap. The same problem I had with mine when I first moved in."

Though part of her was glad she now had a legitimate reason to let herself into Steve's apartment, another part, the moral part, didn't trust herself to do it without doing something she might later regret—like snooping around.

Skip looked at the water oozing through the overhead sheetrock. Then he looked at her. "When does he move out?"

Roxanne shrugged and didn't look at him. If she did, the sympathy on his face would make her cry, she was sure. "Two weeks or so."

"Have you seen him?"

She shook her head. "He's been pretty careful about going up and down the stairs, I think. I haven't even heard him except once. And that night . . ." She had to take a deep breath to keep the emotion from showing in her voice. "It was so late, he wasn't likely to run into me."

Where had he been? she wondered anew. Back with

that girl he'd been seeing before her? Out with someone new? Had he gotten another job? Maybe there was some other woman at some new bar with whom he hit it off. She had no doubt, in fact, that would be the case. Steve hit it off with everybody.

"Look at you," Skip said, with such kindness Roxanne felt the tears well in her eyes. "You're devastated by this. Have you even asked him about that night?"

Roxanne pushed off the counter and wiped a couple tears away impatiently. "I'm not 'devastated,' Skip. My God, he's just a man. One I've only known a few months. I feel hurt, sure, but I'll get over it. I've gotten over worse."

But had she? She'd asked herself this a lot over the past week, as she struggled to get out of bed and wrestled with herself to be productive. She even had to talk herself out of going upstairs and trying to start things up again—thefts be damned—because she just missed him so much.

But what kind of idiot would she have to be to go out with a guy she *knew* was dishonest?

In some ways this was different from the pain she'd felt after Martin, because this time she'd hoped she'd finally found a guy with some character. Not just someone to love, but someone who really *deserved* to be loved, someone who would never let her down. This was worse.

With Martin, she'd always thought he needed love for his character to blossom. He had so much weakness to be babied, so many mistakes to be excused.

Steve, however . . . she swallowed over the lump in her throat. Steve had been strong and sexy, and his confidence had been infectious. *How could he be a liar, too?* she wondered for the millionth time.

But she was kidding herself. Excusing his flaws just as she'd tried to excuse Martin's, time and again. Martin was a cheater, Steve was a liar . . . What was the difference?

"No, I haven't talked to him about that night," Roxanne added then, in a stronger voice. "I don't need to be talked into believing another con artist's excuses. You know that better than anyone."

Skip shrugged his shoulders, nodding. He couldn't argue with that, she could tell; he knew how she was. And besides, she'd shown him the area where Steve had been looking. He'd seen the damage to the plaster. So it hadn't been Roxanne's imagination.

"Thanks for coming by, Skip, but you don't have to worry about me. I'm upset, but I'll get through it. That's one thing the last couple of years has taught me."

"All right. You call me if you need anything." He patted her on the back and they walked toward the front door. "So what are you doing with the rest of your day off?"

She pulled a hairband from her pocket and finger-combed her hair into a ponytail. "Day off? What's that? I've already been up, baking bread, for your information. And now, since Steve's not home, I guess I've got to go upstairs and see what's leaking."

"You don't have to let him know you're coming? What if he's up there with—" Skip cut himself off.

But not before his words speared Roxanne's heart again. Not that she hadn't already thought of that. "In an emergency situation, which a leak qualifies as, I can go in without notice. But more important, I know he's not here because his truck's gone, as it has been every day since he quit."

"I'm sorry, Rox. I didn't mean to bring up—"

"It's nothing I didn't think of myself." She forced a smile. "You go on now and grade your papers. Thanks for offering to help, but I can handle it. I can handle it all."

Truer words were spoken every day, by everyone, Roxanne thought, as she let herself quietly into Steve's apartment. She didn't feel like she was handling anything, certainly not well. Mostly she felt as if she were bumping along in a rough current, just waiting to hit the next rock in the stream.

Though she'd knocked, long and loud, to be sure he wasn't there, she still felt strange opening the door to his private world. She knew she had a perfectly valid reason for being here today, but she felt like the snoop she'd almost been the day before anyway.

She went straight to the kitchen and set her toolbox down on the floor, willing herself not to look at the computer in the corner.

Glancing around the kitchen, she wondered if he had read the paper that morning and seen the review. Would he care that they'd been slammed? Would he say anything to her about the modeling thing? Maybe, now that they weren't seeing each other, it didn't matter to him what she may or may not have said about that in the past.

A few plates were in the sink, in which a few inches of water was still sitting. Apparently Steve had intended to let the dishes soak, but the water had instead run down the drain and leaked out of the trap. The top dish was covered with crumbs and despite her resolve not to poke around, she ran her finger through them, thinking of Steve up here alone, making himself some toast or a sandwich, and working at his computer.

Despite her resolve, she glanced toward the corner where all his papers lay. The question would plague her, she knew, until she found out for sure. Besides, what would it really hurt, just looking at a couple of pages? She wouldn't dig, she promised herself. And if it was anything personal she'd stop immediately.

Before she could change her mind, she strode over to the corner and picked up the top sheet of paper.

> *Portner's main concern at this juncture seemed to be in securing a home for his collections. Though no one was quite sure where he had acquired all that he sold, he was known in town as being a "purveyor of all things unique."*

She picked up a stack of papers and read a page in the middle.

> *In August of 1784, just after Jefferson arrived in Paris . . .*

She looked in a stack on the opposite end of the table.

> *Note: Portner's letter to Letitia, 1825.*

It was all history. Research. Notes about Portner Jefferson Curtis and those around him. She breathed a huge sigh of relief. There wasn't a gossip column in sight. In fact everything she laid eyes on was so academic in nature she found herself wondering if he was writing a book.

Could that be why it was so important that he find that draft?

Would that matter to her if it was?

She straightened the pages she had rifled through and stood back to look at the desk, making sure it looked the way she'd found it.

Then she turned back to the kitchen to get to work, wondering how on earth her heart could continue to ache over someone who had done her so wrong.

Steve stared at the first line of the restaurant review.

"You didn't tell me she was a model," his sister said, scooping another helping of scrambled eggs from a cast-iron frying pan. "No wonder she's a bitch."

The kids were upstairs and her husband had had to work today, so when Steve called that morning looking for someone to help him drop his truck off for service, he'd been invited for Sunday brunch.

"I didn't know," he said, wincing at the expletive his sister chose to describe Roxanne. "Turns out I didn't know anything about her."

He did, however, quite clearly remember Roxanne telling him countless times that she would never make a living off her looks, and that she didn't want to use her appearance to bolster business. He'd even mentioned once that she could be a model and she hadn't owned up to anything. In fact, as he recalled, she'd thrown it back at him as if he'd been a jerk for even bringing it up.

"Hmm, well," Dana said, refilling his orange-juice glass, "I guess that's understandable, in a way."

He looked at her. "It is?"

"Sure. Like the reviewer said, who would trust some rail-thin supermodel to have a decent restaurant?" She shoveled a forkful of eggs into her mouth.

"I guess you wouldn't publicize it, but that's no reason to keep it from people you're, you know, close to."

"Oh Steve," she said, in a tone so pitying he felt annoyed. "She didn't deserve you, you know that, don't you?"

"Thanks," he grunted.

He continued reading the review, feeling the pit of his stomach drop lower with every paragraph. "This is going to kill her," he muttered.

Dana looked up at him over her eggs, eyes alert. "So what?"

He dropped the magazine and met his sister's eyes. "I don't hate her, Dana. It'd be easier if I could, but I don't."

The two sat silently for a while before Dana said, "So tell me more about this editor who called. She's interested in the book?"

Steve nodded. "Yeah. She wants to see the whole thing when it's done. Which I told her would be in the next couple of weeks."

"So you're going to ask Roxanne about the basement before that? See if those steps are the ones?"

He rubbed a hand on the side of his face and shook his head. "I didn't tell the editor about that. I just told her about the mystery, the conflicting reports, that kind of thing, but that nothing had ever been found. The unsolved mystery aspect of it seemed to intrigue her."

"But if you found the thing," Dana insisted, "the book would be even better, wouldn't it? A shoo-in for publication, don't you think? I mean, jeez, something that's been hidden for two hundred years—something as famous as the Declaration of Independence. The whole country would be interested in that. That's the kind of thing you hear about on the news. I bet the *Post* would even excerpt the book. So why don't you just ask Miss Fancy-Pants, huh? What could it hurt?"

"I guess we'd find out, wouldn't we?"

"So you're going to do it?"

"I don't know." He shook his head. "I really don't know."

He didn't want to. He didn't want to ask Roxanne for anything. He had the answer to his question of whether she came first or the book did, he guessed. If he didn't want to ask her about excavating the basement now, apparently even *avoiding* her came first.

They sat in silence a few minutes more.

"Listen, why don't I get my neighbor to watch the kids, and I'll come over after we drop off the truck and help you pack some stuff up today."

Steve glanced at her, a half smile on his lips. "And why would you do that?"

"Because I'm a nice sister, that's why."

"Uh-huh. And?"

"And," Dana chewed a piece of toast, studying him. "We can get out that metal detector Mom gave you and see what's in that basement."

Steve shook his head, smiling ruefully. "I gave Roxanne back the keys to the restaurant. Besides, a metal detector wouldn't be much help looking for parchment."

Dana sighed. "Still. So there's no getting down there without her permission."

"That's right. But that would have been true anyway," he said with a firm look.

"All right, all right. I'll come help you pack anyway." At his expression she added, "Because I don't want to see you become one of those guys pining over the one that got away."

He was silent a long moment, wondering if that was what he was doing. Pining. If this hole in his gut and the vacuum in his brain was sorrow. If his inability to hold on to his anger was—he debated admitting this even to himself—love.

He took a deep breath. "Okay. Thanks. I could use an extra pair of hands."

They finished brunch and Dana unloaded the kids on her neighbor. Steve led the way to the mechanic and Dana followed in her car. After leaving the keys in the drop box, they got in her car and drove to his place.

"Jeez, no wonder you're in such good shape," Dana said as they tackled the last flight of stairs to his apartment. "I'll help you pack, but I'll be damned if I'll help you move. How'd you get everything up here, anyway?"

Steve laughed. "A little at a time."

They reached the top landing and Steve put his key

in the lock. Turning it left, however, he didn't feel the resistance of the deadbolt. Had he forgotten to lock it this morning?

He pushed the door open and was greeted by a *clink* of metal and a curse muttered in a female voice.

Dana behind him, he walked swiftly into the kitchen.

Shimmying out from under the sink, in a scene painfully reminiscent of the first time he met her, was Roxanne.

He narrowed his eyes as she pulled herself out from the cabinet, rubbing her forehead with one hand.

"Shouldn't you be wearing a swim suit for that?" he asked, trying to make his tone light but not quite succeeding. "No wait, that was your *last* job."

"Hello, Steve," she said, her eyes catching on Dana, behind him. She dropped her hand and there was a slight red mark where she'd obviously bumped her head. Her eyes moved back to his. "I guess you read the review."

He nodded, feeling a twinge of pity despite all efforts not to. "It wasn't so bad."

She looked up at him then with such appreciation in her eyes for that small comment that he could feel his resolution to stay angry begin to crack.

Her gaze dropped and her cheeks reddened. "I, uh, I know I misled you about—"

"Don't worry about it." There was no point discussing it. No point in hearing about how he didn't merit that bit of honesty in their relationship, if you could call what they'd had a relationship.

She glanced quickly back up at him. "Yes. I suppose

it doesn't matter now." She looked at the contents of Steve's cabinet strewn around her on the floor. "I'm sorry about this. Water was leaking into my apartment. Turns out it was the trap. I'm just finishing up."

It had been barely more than a week since he'd seen her, but his eyes drank her in like a nectar he hadn't tasted in years.

"The trap?" he said. "I've barely been home today to run the water. How would it be leaking?"

It sounded more like an accusation than he'd meant it to, and an injured look crossed Roxanne's face. He reminded himself to harden his heart. She had dumped him like an unwanted bag at Goodwill with barely a thought to his feelings. Why should he worry about hers?

"You left the sink filled with water." She gestured above her head to the counter, which was covered with the dirty dishes he now remembered leaving in the sink. "I guess the drain stop was leaking, too."

He didn't know what to say. They stared at each other a long moment before Roxanne's eyes shifted once again to Dana.

With a quick glance at Steve, Dana moved toward her. "Hi, I'm Dana."

She leaned down to shake Roxanne's hand, which Roxanne extended, but they both noticed the grease on it first.

"Oh, sorry." Roxanne laughed nervously and rubbed the hand on her jeans, then looked at it again and shrugged at Dana. "Nice to meet you."

Dana nodded, studying her. "You, too."

He could read the thoughts on Roxanne's face, the

question about who this woman was, the assumption that she was somebody she wasn't. It was funny, Steve never considered how his sister looked as a woman, exactly, but seeing her through Roxanne's eyes he realized how pretty she was, with her wavy shoulder-length hair and big blue eyes. He decided not to enlighten Roxanne about her.

"I can finish that," he said, for lack of anything else to break the silence. He gestured toward the pipes.

Roxanne shook her head. "That's okay. I think I'm done. Just, if you wouldn't mind, check it to make sure it's not still leaking in a little while."

He nodded. "Sure."

She started to put the bottles that had been under the sink back in the cabinet.

"I'll do that," Steve said. *You just go* was the subtext, and they all heard it.

Dana looked at him assessingly.

Roxanne stopped immediately and stood up. "Okay. Sorry to have interrupted." She put some tools back in her toolbox and turned back, her eyes seeking Steve's. With a quick glance at Dana she said again, "Sorry. Bye."

"Nice to have met you," Dana said as Roxanne passed on her way to the door.

"You, too," Roxanne said, not turning back.

"By the way, I'm Steve's sister," Dana called.

Steve gave her an exasperated look.

Roxanne stopped dead in her tracks, then turned swiftly. "You're his sister?"

The relief on her face was so obvious to Steve, he couldn't help wondering what the hell was going on.

Why should she care if Dana was his sister, when she was the one who had pronounced their 'fling' over?

"Oh, by the way, I didn't get a chance to tell you," Steve said, *because you dumped me quicker than lightning*, "but I figured out how Cheeto got into the kitchen that night. You might want to check the stove hole in the old chimney in your kitchen. He came through the one in the restaurant, behind the freezer. I found his fur on it."

Roxanne looked like she'd been struck. "Behind the freezer?"

He nodded. "Yeah. Sorry I didn't let you know earlier. Hope he hasn't disappeared again."

She shook her head, staring at him as if he'd just told her he'd discovered a ghost. "Behind the freezer," she repeated.

"Yeah, I did what I could to secure it down there, but you should block your end off."

"I will," she said vaguely.

They stood there another moment so awkwardly that Steve added, "That's all."

She blinked as if awakening. "Okay. Thanks." Her voice was dazed, then she shook herself out of it. "Oh, and Dana, it was nice to meet you. I didn't even know Steve had a sister." She gave them both a strained smile, then turned and let herself out the door.

Steve and Dana stood in silence.

"Wow," Dana said finally.

Steve sighed. "I know. She's a looker, that's for sure."

Dana turned amazed eyes to him. "No," she said. "Well, *yeah*. But that's not what I meant. Are you sure you understood her when she called things off?"

He crossed his arms over his chest to still the flash of

emotion he still felt, the desire he couldn't quell. She'd looked so vulnerable. How could that be when she'd so coldly rejected him a week ago?

He turned to his sister. "There was no *mis*understanding it, Dana. She could not have been clearer."

Dana looked at the closed door, shaking her head.

Steve frowned. "Why?"

"Because that girl is in love with you, Steve. I'd bet my life on it."

18

Bar Special
Scarlett O'Hara—<u>after all,</u>
  <u>tomorrow is another day</u>
Southern Comfort, cranberry juice, lime juice

Roxanne walked down the stairs in a trance.

What had just happened? Had he figured out what she must have seen and concocted a story for it?

She let herself into her apartment and dropped the toolbox, heading straight for the kitchen. She knew just where the old stove hole was. Behind a little useless cabinet that had been installed to camouflage it. For a while, the door to that cabinet had been falling open on a regular basis. It wasn't until this week, when she was desperate to keep herself busy during daylight hours so she wouldn't think about Steve, that she'd finally gotten a new latch for it.

Had that been Cheeto? Opening the cabinet and going for the hole? Could he possibly be that clever?

She went straight to that door now and unlatched it. She flipped on the overhead light, then realized she had yet to replace the bulb. Standing back so the window light would illuminate the space, she saw that the stove hole cover had indeed slipped off and lay on the floor. Soot dusted the old chimney face.

Something had been going in and out of the hole, that was for sure. She brushed her fingers against the brick, then rubbed their blackened tips together. Maybe the cat had been chasing a mouse.

She remembered how filthy Cheeto was the night he'd gotten into the restaurant kitchen. He'd been covered in food and dirt and dust, but some of it had been black. Some of it was soot.

She sat on the floor and put her head in one hand, looking at the sooty fingers of her other.

Steve hadn't been looking for that damn document that night, she thought. He'd been doing something *for her*. That's why there hadn't been any sign of a break-in.

She felt like crying. She wanted to run to him, tell him, apologize, to go right upstairs and plead with him to forgive her. But he was up there with Dana—his *sister*, thank God.

Besides, even though Roxanne might have been wrong about Steve, how could he forgive her for thinking the absolute worst of him? For accusing and convicting him, even if just to herself, of being a common criminal? What kind of person was she to have no faith in someone she cared about?

She'd blown it. She'd taken something that had been wonderful and had thrown it away.

She had ruined everything with her worries and her fears.

Or had she?

Several hours later, after the sun had gone down, Roxanne was standing on a chair in the front hall, reaching for the lightbulbs she kept on the top shelf of the closet to replace the one that went out in the kitchen, when she heard Steve and Dana talking as they came down the stairs.

It was nothing personal. Steve seemed to be thanking her for something and apologizing for getting her home so late.

Steve must be driving her home, Roxanne thought, and her nerves started to tremble at the knowledge that now was the time. She had to act. Quickly.

Her heart hammered as she grabbed the carton of bulbs, jumped down, and dragged the chair back to the dining-room table. Then she put the lightbulbs on the counter in the kitchen and glanced out the window to the alley below.

Steve's truck was already gone.

The coast was clear.

She wasn't sure how much time she had, so she rushed to the bedroom, carefully applied some makeup, took off her clothes, put on her black Chinese silk robe and headed for the door.

Roxanne hadn't been in Steve's apartment five minutes when she heard the front door open. She was sitting on Steve's bed, debating whether or not this was the most mortifying thing she'd ever done or the bravest, when the option of backing out of it was taken from her hands.

He was here.

Should she take the robe off? What did one do when one was hoping to seduce someone? Be subtle or blatant? Naked first? Clothed and apologizing later?

Then again, how subtle was it to be in his bedroom, robed or unrobed? She should have sat on the couch. Or maybe she should have waited until he came home and just knocked on his front door. She could have let the robe fall from her shoulders at the door, and she would have been closer to making a clean getaway if he didn't seem amenable.

Heart fluttering and hands trembling like autumn leaves in a stiff breeze, she leaned back on his pillows and tried to arrange her hair artfully around her. She had brought a candle so he would see it was her, but the room was still pretty dim. She wasn't sure he would notice it from the living room. She could be sitting here for hours while he worked on his computer or made dinner or something.

Come to think of it, she realized she didn't see any light coming *from* the living room either. Yet someone had definitely come through the front door. Why hadn't they turned on the light?

As quietly as she could, she pushed herself off the bed and tiptoed to the door.

Someone was rustling around in the living room, but from here it looked perfectly dark. She crept down the hallway, inching her head slightly forward around the corner until one eye could see the room.

In the corner stood a tall man with a flashlight, and he was going through Steve's papers.

Roxanne's heart leaped to her throat and she backed into the hallway. It wasn't Steve, standing there with a flashlight looking over his own papers. This man was bigger, bulkier . . . this man was shaped more like— Roxanne caught her breath.

It all made sense. He would know all the details, he'd been fascinated by the story, he was the one who had implicated Steve to her . . .

Roxanne's blood began to boil, and before she gave it a second thought, she flipped on the hall light and stepped out into the living room.

P.B. spun on his heels and issued a heartfelt "*Shit!*" the moment he set eyes on her.

Roxanne stood there with her arms across her chest and adrenaline pumping in overdrive. "Hello, P.B."

"Roxanne! I—hi—uh, where's . . ." He craned his head to look past her, as if expecting to see Steve emerge from the hallway behind her. When he didn't, P.B. frowned at her and said, "What are you doing here?"

"I was just about to ask you the same question."

P.B.'s face relaxed then, and he turned off the flashlight, putting it into his back pocket. "I was just picking up some stuff for Steve."

She looked at him in disbelief. A half laugh shot from her throat and she said, "*What?*"

His head swaggered a little as he cooked up his story—no doubt bolstered by her failure to deny that Steve wasn't here—and he put one hand arrogantly on his hip. "Yeah. Uh, Steve's at my place and he wanted some of his notes. So I, uh, volunteered to come pick them up. On my way back from the store."

It was then that Roxanne noticed the plastic grocery bag P.B. held, in which several pieces of paper had already been stuffed.

"So Steve's at your place, and you came here to get stuff for him."

"That's right." P.B.'s face was cocky. His eyes raked her from head to toe, no doubt taking in her obviously naked state beneath the robe.

Roxanne crossed her arms over her chest and pulled the neck of the robe closed with one hand. "Forgive me, P.B., if I tell you that I think you're full of crap. I think you're here ripping Steve off, just like you tried to rip me off."

P.B. chuckled, but a malicious gleam appeared in his eye. Roxanne suddenly wondered if she might be in some danger. P.B. was a cop. He had ways of making crimes disappear. His own crimes, that was.

"I don't know what you're talking about," he said lightly. "And you haven't answered *my* question. I thought you and Steve broke up. What are *you* doing here?"

At that moment, the front door opened and the lights in the living room came on. Steve halted in the foyer as he caught sight of the two of them.

"What's going on here?" His eyes swept from Roxanne, dressed as she was, to P.B., holding his grocery bag full of papers, and back again.

Roxanne and P.B. gaped at him.

Steve's expression went from shocked to confused to angry. "Someone want to answer me?" He let his gaze settle on Roxanne and his expression seemed to soften slightly. Then he turned to P.B. "P.B.? Why don't you go first?"

Roxanne breathed a sigh of relief. He couldn't have come back at a more opportune time.

"Yes, P.B.," she said, stepping farther out into the living room, arms around her middle to keep her stomach from leaping straight out of her body. "Why don't you tell Steve the reason you just told me for why you're here?"

P.B. looked from one to the other of them and tried to muster a chuckle. "It's funny, really." His eyes appealed to Steve. "You'll laugh, Steve-arino."

Steve pushed his hands into his pockets and walked slowly toward him. "I don't know why, but I doubt that, P.B. So let's dispense with the niceties until we get to the bottom of this, okay?"

He reached P.B. and took the bag from his hand, then looked inside. One by one he pulled the papers out, nodding as he read them as if it was all just what he expected to see.

"I, uh," P.B. began. "See, I was just, there was this, this thing, see. And after listening to you, um . . ."

Steve looked at him almost pityingly. "I'll tell you what, Peeb. I'll save you the trouble. I already know what you were doing here. And I have to congratulate you, you put your hands on a lot of the right stuff." He held up the pages.

"*She* was here first," P.B. blurted, gesturing toward Roxanne. "She was going through this stuff, I just took it from her. It's evidence, that's what it is."

"That's not true!" Roxanne gasped.

Steve turned and looked at her, his expression unreadable as his eyes searched her. Her cheeks reddened.

"She doesn't really look dressed for a robbery, do you think, Peeb?" He glanced back at his friend. Then he added, "But I'll deal with her," he turned back to her, pausing—and she wasn't sure, but she could swear she saw a slight smile—before adding "later."

Roxanne's entire body heated up at the prospect.

He faced P.B. again, then walked slowly around him to place the pilfered papers back on the desk.

"But you," Steve continued. "I finally figured out it was you behind the break-ins. After that last one. The one when you dug the holes under the steps."

"Me? Behind the—? What the—?" P.B. blustered, scoffing and rolling his eyes from Steve to Roxanne as if they were all in on the joke. "That's crazy. I didn't break in here. That was, that was . . ."

"Cut it out, P.B." Roxanne had never heard Steve's voice so cold. "I know I told you about the will, about how Portner had hidden something under a set of stairs in the house. I just didn't think you were that interested. So I kept thinking, who knew anything about history, about this obscure cousin and his possible theft, yet would bother to dig under stairs that any reputable historian knew were built after the Civil War? Then it struck me. I realized that I hadn't told you about that. Nor had I told you that the staircases had all already been investigated. You were the only person who might have known just one piece of that puzzle, and who would have been motivated enough and had access to go looking for this thing right now."

"Oh, come on. Lots of people would want to find a draft of the Declaration of Independence," P.B. protested.

"Sure, but nobody else believes it was really here. And why now? The issue has been dead for years in historical circles. *You* were the only person I told about those letters I found, the ones confirming the hidden document was one of Jefferson's. The *only* one, P.B. So it had to be either you or me. And I knew it wasn't me."

Roxanne swallowed. *She* hadn't. She had believed P.B. The obviously lying, sleazy, reprobate P.B. What was the matter with her?

"I was trying to help you, man," P.B. said, finally settling on a plan of defense. He slapped Steve's shoulder with a broad palm and gave a laugh of bravado. "Come on, I knew you were afraid to do it, 'cause of her. That's right." He nodded at Roxanne. "He wanted to look around, but he didn't want to piss you off, Miss High-and-Mighty. Thought you'd be an unreasonable bitch and not let him—"

"Shut *up*, P.B." Steve grabbed him by the shirt front, and even though P.B. was the bigger of the two men Roxanne saw uneasiness in P.B.'s eyes. "Who do you think you are? And who the *fuck* do you think you're talking to? You can't just make up anything you want and have us all believe it."

Roxanne cleared her throat. Both men looked over at her. "Is that why you told me you thought Steve was behind the break-ins, P.B.? Because you were trying to *help* him?"

Steve's eyes glittered as he turned back to his former

friend. "You said *I* was behind them? You told her *I* was the one digging up her basement? Is that . . . ?" He turned back to Roxanne, his face fierce. "Is that why . . . ?"

Roxanne looked down, too ashamed of believing P.B. over him to look him in the eye.

Steve looked back at P.B., then shoved him, hard, letting go of his shirt as P.B. stumbled back into the desk chair. He caught himself between the printer and the wall.

"Hey, you were the one doing all the investigating, looking for that copy of the Declaration of Independence," P.B. said belligerently, poking a finger through the air at him.

"For *the book*, P.B. Remember the book I'm writing? You knew why I was looking for that information, and it wasn't to start digging."

"Oh come on. You know you wanted to look. Besides, if you hadn't kept talking about it, telling everyone, making it into such a big damn story, I wouldn't have been interested in it at all. Nobody would have. Seems to me it could be *anybody* looking for that thing now. You made it sound so valuable and all."

"No, it couldn't have been anybody," Steve said, his voice low and barely controlled. "It could only have been somebody stupid enough to think they could break in and dig around and never have anyone be the wiser. It had to be a cop, *the* cop called to the scene so the report would never be filed. It had to be someone whose friend was inadvertently telling him where to look. Jesus!" Steve spun away from him, one hand raking through his hair as he tried to cool off. "How could I have been so stupid?" He turned back. "I *knew* that squirrel thing was bogus. What'd you do, scrape it off the road?"

P.B. looked away, not answering.

Steve glanced over at Roxanne, who straightened when his eyes fell upon her. "And you believed him?" he asked, his voice quieter but the emotion no less powerful. The disbelief in his eyes was painful. "You thought I was trying to rob you?"

She shook her head. "No." She cleared her throat. "No, Steve." She paused. "Not at first."

Steve exhaled heavily and gazed at her, the hurt clear in his eyes.

She spoke quickly, glancing at P.B. "At first I thought he was just jealous. Bitter, you know, about . . . about us. But then . . . then I saw you, the other night, after Cheeto got into the kitchen. I went downstairs and I saw you looking behind the freezer, pulling on some of the plaster wall, looking behind it. And I just . . ." She shook her head again. "It was just too easy to believe I'd made another mistake, that I'd trusted the wrong guy. Again. I'm *so sorry*, Steve. You can't imagine how sorry I am."

His expression did not change during this speech, but his eyes never left hers. She could see his breath moving his chest up and down, betraying his agitation, and wished she could go to him and hold him, tell him in every way she knew how, that she would be sorry for the rest of her days for not believing in him.

Several long moments of silence later, Steve turned back to P.B. with a sigh. "Listen, P.B., I don't know what to do about you. You've broken in to my apartment, you've betrayed me, you've lied, you would have stolen, if you hadn't been so inept. Tell me, would I be wrong to turn you in to your department? What would you do?"

P.B. sighed and looked at his feet. After a minute he looked up, his face contorted. "Hey, man, I answered your question for you. You don't have to look down there now. And I would've told you if I found something."

Steve shook his head. "I don't believe that for a second."

P.B. didn't look at him. "Okay, okay. I'm getting out of here. I can't deal with this right now."

He started toward the door, then turned as he reached it, realizing that nobody was going to stop him. "For what it's worth, Stevie, I'm sorry."

Steve just looked at him.

P.B. turned the knob and left.

Several minutes ticked by before Steve turned to Roxanne. She flushed from head to foot as he let his gaze take in her attire, then her position near the hall that led to the bedroom.

"I didn't know you were writing a book," she said softly. "I should have. I should have asked what all that research was for."

"You did. I just didn't tell you." He tilted his head. "And I didn't know you spent ten years as a model in major magazines. That makes me the more oblivious one, don't you think?"

She shook her head. "I made it sound like I'd never do that. I didn't want you to know."

He gave a short laugh. "I guess neither one of us knew much of anything about the other."

She looked at the floor. "I guess we just didn't know each other very well."

"Or trust each other very much."

She made a pained face. "I'm so sorry, Steve. I don't know what to say. I just didn't know who to trust. Not because of you, but because of me." She laughed once, shortly. "Talk about baggage."

She looked up at him. His face was impassive, contemplative. A long silence stretched between them.

"And what," he said finally, "did you hope to accomplish here tonight?"

Roxanne was relieved to hear a gentle tone in his voice. At least she thought she'd heard it.

"Well," she began, "I wanted to apologize. *Really* apologize. So I, uh, I thought if I came up here—"

She stopped as she heard his footsteps on the floor, looked up to see him walking slowly toward her.

"If you came up here . . . ?" he prompted.

Her hands knotted in front of her. "Yes, ah, you see, I thought I'd need to get your attention first, make sure you would listen and not just slam the door in my face." She let go of her hands and brought two fingers to play with the lapel of her robe. "Which is why I . . . wore this. Because we always seemed to, or rather we never had trouble with . . . you know. And I so wanted you to hear my apology—"

He reached her, then, and before she could finish the sentence he swept her up and off her feet, into his arms. Her hands went automatically around his neck.

"I don't want any damn apology, Roxanne," he said low, his face close to hers as he held her against his chest. "I want to know how you *feel*."

"How I feel?" she repeated, breathless. She couldn't take her eyes from his.

"About me," he added quietly.

Her eyes were swimming in his, their gazes locked as if they were each other's lifeline.

"Oh Steve," she said, her voice husky with emotion. "I'm in love with you. Totally. Completely. Head over heels."

A slow smile curved his lips and lit his eyes. "Head over heels, huh?"

She smiled back, tentatively at first, then more broadly. "That's right."

"That's all I need to know."

With that, he carried her down the hall and into the bedroom.

"And just so you know," he added, before he kicked the door shut behind them, "I'm in love with you, too."

"Head over heels?" she asked.

He laughed. "Over and over."

"Then that's all *I* need to know." She put her hands to his face and kissed him.

Epilogue

Six months later

Bar Special
Old-Fashioned—the way it should be
Bourbon, sugar syrup, angostura bitters, water

Dessert Special of the Day
Wedding Cake and Champagne—
   made for each other
White cake with raspberry cream filling,
   vanilla fondant, candied flowers,
   and the best bubbly $100 can buy

The knock on Roxanne's door came at 7 p.m. exactly. Roxanne glanced at the kitchen clock and smiled. He was right on time.

She checked her face in the hall mirror, brushed a finger beneath each mascara'd eye and pinched her cheeks. Then, smoothing the fabric of her sleek black cocktail dress one last time, she opened the door.

What she saw took her breath away.

Steve, in a tuxedo.

"When you said dress up, you meant dress up," she said, her eyes raking him hungrily from head to toe. He looked . . . classic. Like he belonged in a 1940s movie right next to Cary Grant. He'd even had his hair trimmed.

He stood casually, his hands in his pockets, and appreciated the sight of her with a low, "Mm, mm, mm." He tilted his head, and his eyes—she could swear they were actually twinkling—met hers. "You look incredible."

She smiled, unable to contain it. "Thank you."

He held out an arm. "Shall we?"

With a light laugh, she took his arm, closing the door behind her. "This is awfully fancy for a trip to our own restaurant."

"You're thinking about this the wrong way. We're not going to our own restaurant. We are going to have the Chez Soi *experience*. Just like any other patron. Though I suspect we'll be given something of the V.I.P. treatment."

She looked him up and down again. "I'll say. I can't wait for Rita to see you in that tux."

Sir Nigel opened the door for them with the broadest smile Roxanne had ever seen on his face. "Good evening, mademoiselle, monsieur. Your table is almost ready. Would you mind waiting at the bar a moment?"

It was a Wednesday night, but there was a fair number of people in the restaurant anyway. Two seats at the near end of the bar were open and they made their way to them, saying hello to some of the regulars as they passed.

Steve had just pulled out a bar stool for her when the white-haired gentleman who was always at the bar—the one Steve had said only ordered thirty-year-old single-malt Scotch—rose from his seat and came toward them.

"Hello," he said, his face creased and kindly. He was shorter than both Steve and Roxanne, so she sat to even them up a little.

"Mr. Shumaker," Steve said, taking his outstretched hand. "How are you tonight?"

"I'm fine, fine," he said, looking the two of them up and down. "You all look fit for a coronation. What's the occasion?"

"Just checking out the restaurant from the other side of the kitchen doors," Roxanne said with a smile. "Can we buy you a drink, Mr. Shumaker?"

"Well, that'd be lovely." His eyes crinkled when he smiled and he took the seat Steve offered him as Roxanne ordered their drinks. "Though I fear I have to take you to task, Miss Rayeaux, for depriving me of my favorite bartender."

Roxanne glanced up at Steve, who stood next to her, his arm circling her on the back of her chair. "Now don't go pinning that on me. Steve's the one who got his book published. Besides, he'll be back, part-time."

"No kidding. You got your book published?" Mr. Shumaker looked at him with delighted eyes. "The one about Jefferson's cousin?"

Roxanne laughed again. "Is there anyone you *didn't* tell that story to?"

Steve glanced around the bar. "Nobody here."

"And when is this book coming out, young man?" He looked expectantly at Steve.

"Next spring." Steve's smile was beyond gratified. The culmination of all his hard work had been better than his wildest dreams. The advance he had received had been much larger than he'd expected, and the publisher had decided to devote quite a bit to publicity, since there was already so much to be built on.

"They're even sending me on a book tour," Steve added. "Ten cities, can you believe it?"

"Wonderful, wonderful," Mr. Shumaker said. "I think I heard something about the discovery you made here. Do you mind if I ask a little bit about it?"

"Sure, fire away," Steve said.

To Roxanne's surprise, Mr. Shumaker pulled a pair of glasses and a small, spiral-bound pad of paper from his breast pocket.

"Tell me what led you to that spot in the cellar. In fact, tell me everything. Start at the beginning." He grinned and donned the glasses.

Happily, Steve launched into the story of how he'd followed the theories, studied the house's history, then found the letters and discovered the missing staircase.

Roxanne sipped her drink, watching Mr. Shumaker take notes while Steve talked. He continued to ask questions and Steve answered, warming to his topic like a mother going on about her newborn.

"So if it wasn't for the cat," Mr. Shumaker concluded at the end of the tale, "and that night that resulted in the first review of this place, the bad one, this 'fair copy' of the Declaration of Independence might never have been found."

"Maybe not," Steve said, "though I like to think I might have found it without Cheeto's help."

Roxanne corrected him. "Don't forget, we're calling him Sherlock now."

"That's right." Steve chuckled. "Mr. Holmes."

"So you dug at the base of where that hidden staircase would have been," Mr. Shumaker reviewed, "and found the . . . jar, was it?"

"Yes, an old pickling jar. One of the larger types, with the document folded once and rolled up inside." Steve leaned forward. "And it's interesting. Because Portner had sealed it with a combination of mutton tallow, beeswax and camphor, the parchment was protected from humidity. And being in a basement, which is a pretty constant fifty-five degrees, it was protected from heat. Finally, being buried, it was not exposed to sunlight. So despite being folded and neglected for nearly two hundred years, it held up incredibly well, better than the final copy we're all familiar with."

Mr. Shumaker shook his head as he finished writing. "That's just fascinating. So where is the document now?"

"It's on indefinite loan," Roxanne said, looking warmly at Steve, "to the Library of Congress."

Mr. Shumaker sat back in his chair. "Well, that's mighty generous."

"We haven't decided what we're going to do with it yet," Roxanne said, "but it didn't feel right to auction it off."

Mr. Shumaker tapped his pencil eraser on the table and looked at them both shrewdly. "I heard you also included a one-hundred-dollar donation. What was that about?"

Steve laughed. "Where'd you hear that?"

He smiled. "I have my sources."

Steve shook his head. "Restaurants. The last place you want to be if you have a secret."

Roxanne's hand found Steve's as she said, "I guess you could say that hundred dollars had been burning a hole in our pockets for quite some time, so we decided to give it away."

"At least for the moment," Steve murmured.

Roxanne glanced at him.

"Last question," Mr. Shumaker said, taking off his glasses and setting them carefully on the bar. "What ever happened to that big friend of yours, Steve? The policeman? I heard he was somehow involved in this. Unfavorably involved, I should say."

Steve and Roxanne both gaped at him.

"My God," Steve said. "How do you know all this?"

Mr. Shumaker smiled and looked down at his lap. "I'll be honest with you, Steve, because I like you. You too, Miss Rayeaux." He leaned toward them, his voice dropping conspiratorially. "I work for *D.C. Scene*. I have, you might say, a nose for news." He tapped the side of his nose with a gnarled finger.

Roxanne gasped as the penny dropped in her mind. "You're the gossip columnist."

Mr. Shumaker wiggled his eyebrows and grinned like an Irish leprechaun. "I hear things, I write them down." He patted his breast pocket. "But don't worry, I won't print anything you don't want me to. The only reason I printed that other stuff was because I was here that night the *Post*'s reviewer came . . . and well, I just wanted to be sure my favorite restaurant was going to be around for a while despite what he might write."

"You've got to be kidding," Steve said. "That was *you*? You *saved* us."

Mr. Shumaker chuckled. "Everybody loves a scandal. That's one constant about living in D.C. Not to mention everyone loves to dine with the rich and powerful."

"I don't know," Roxanne said slowly, unsure what to make of this turn of events. She still didn't like the idea of showing up in a gossip column. "I think it was Richards's second review that really saved us."

The old man's eyes twinkled as he looked at the two of them. "Richards owed me a favor. After I found out a little gossip about him."

Roxanne's eyes widened. "You *blackmailed* him to review us again?"

Mr. Shumaker laughed. "He was happy enough after he ate here again. Said he would have raved whether I had anything on him or not."

"Well . . . I just don't know what to make of that." Roxanne continued to look at the man curiously. He *had* saved them—that second review had brought the crowds rolling in—but had it been . . . ethical?

"Now don't give me that pretty look, missy," Mr. Shumaker said with a wag of one bony finger. "I'm not divulging what I had on him. That was part of the deal." He smiled impishly. "And you wouldn't feel sorry for the man, either, if you knew what I know about him."

Roxanne couldn't help it, she laughed.

"So what happened to the cop?" Mr. Shumaker asked again, looking at Steve.

Steve hesitated. "Oh, I don't know. I'd rather you didn't publicize P.B.'s part in this."

"No, no," Mr. Shumaker waved a hand. "Off the record. I'm just curious. Only thing I'm going to write about tonight is your book. With your permission of course."

It was all Steve needed to hear. He explained that after they'd discovered P.B. was behind the break-ins, they decided that they had to inform P.B.'s bosses. Even though they thought this was just a one-time thing, if he was so unscrupulous as to use his position to cover up something like that, they reasoned, they couldn't in good conscience let him continue to have the power of a police officer.

Lucky for P.B., his captain let him simply quit, telling him that a bad evaluation would be placed in his file so he could never work on a police force again, but that since Steve and Roxanne were not going to press charges, he could not be prosecuted.

"I never liked that guy," Mr. Shumaker said. "He was loud and disruptive. Not nearly as funny as he thought he was. A good way to ruin a nice Scotch on a winter's evening."

Steve laughed a little and looked down at his plate. "He's not so bad."

"Well, I'll leave you two to your drinks." Mr. Shumaker put his palms on the bar and stood up. "I hope you enjoy your dinner. I know I'll enjoy mine."

"Thank you," Roxanne said.

"Oh, one last question?" he asked, turning back to them with his impish smile.

"On the record or off?" Steve asked.

"Up to you."

Steve chuckled. "Depends on the question."

Mr. Shumaker raised a shrewd brow in his direction. "I'm just wondering about you two. What's next for Alexandria's hottest couple?"

"We're just enjoying the success of the restaurant," Steve said, leaning on the back of Roxanne's chair with a contented smile at her. "On the record."

"And the success of Steve's book," Roxanne added. "On the record."

Mr. Shumaker nodded. "Good to know. Best of luck to you both. And remember, if anything else develops I'll be right here to report on it if you want. Or rather." He looked toward his seat down the bar. "Right over there. Third stool from the right."

The three of them laughed and Mr. Shumaker moved back to his seat.

Sir Nigel appeared before them and with a short bow said, "If you'll follow me. Your table is ready."

Steve winked at Roxanne and they followed Sir Nigel across the room to the coziest table in the place.

Steve pulled out her chair and she sat.

"I could get used to this treatment," she said. "Not to mention the sight of you in a tuxedo."

Steve sat in the chair across from hers.

At that moment, Rita pushed through the kitchen doors with two glasses and an ice bucket containing a bottle of champagne. Without a word, she set the bucket next to Steve, placed the glasses on the table, then opened the champagne like the seasoned waitress she was.

Roxanne watched her in surprise. "What's this?" She moved her gaze to Steve, who shrugged innocently.

Rita smiled what could only be described as a shit-eating grin and said, "On the house."

Roxanne laughed. "How generous."

Steve was silent until the waitress left. Then he turned his eyes back to Roxanne, a smile playing on his lips.

Taking her hand, he spread the fingers out over his palm. "You know," he said with a smile, "I was tempted to give Mr. Shumaker a different answer when he asked what was next for us."

"Were you?"

Their eyes met, Steve's uncertain and Roxanne's curious.

"What did you want to say?" she asked. Something about the look on Steve's face made her heart rate accelerate. She curled her fingers around his.

"I wanted to tell him," he continued quietly, "that we might be getting married."

Roxanne's breath left her body. "*What?*" The word was a mere whisper.

Steve leaned back and pulled a small velvet ring box from his pocket. Placing it on the table between them, he added, "But I needed to get your answer first."

Roxanne gazed in shock from Steve's face to the box on the table. With trembling hands she reached out and opened it. Inside was a diamond ring, simple, elegant, and obviously expensive.

"Oh my God." She looked back up at him.

"So what do you say?" he asked, his expression growing nervous.

She laughed, so giddy her head was spinning. "I say yes. Of course!"

Steve exhaled as if he'd been holding his breath for an hour. "Oh thank God."

She laughed again and reached out to grab him. He kissed her then and they laughed together, until he pulled back and took the ring from its box.

"Here, let me," he said. He held her left hand and slid the ring on her finger.

"Steve, it's *gorgeous*." She gazed up at him, happier than she'd ever been in her life. "I love it."

"Good." He grinned. "Because I spent about a hundred bucks on it."

Author's Note

The missing draft of the Declaration of Independence I used in creating the subplot in this story was not entirely a figment of my imagination. Though it hasn't been proven, there is reason to believe a "fair copy" of the declaration did exist but was for some reason not preserved.

According to the U.S. National Archives & Records Administration (NARA), in 1823 Thomas Jefferson wrote that before submitting his Declaration of Independence to the Committee of Five (the group appointed by Congress to produce a document that would make the case for the colonies' independence to the world), he sent a draft to Benjamin Franklin and John Adams, "requesting their corrections ... I then wrote a fair copy, reported it to the committee, and from them, unaltered to the Congress."

According to NARA, however, that "fair copy" of the draft, incorporating the changes made by Franklin and Adams, if it existed, has not survived to this day.

Unless of course you believe in my fictional Jefferson cousin, Portner Jefferson Curtis, and his faithful biographer, Steve Serrano, both of whom *were* figments of my imagination.

*Fill your Spring with blossoming romance
brought to you by these new releases
coming in April from Avon Books . . .*

As an Earl Desires by Lorraine Heath

An Avon Romantic Treasure

Camilla, countess, sponsor, benefactress, has reached a stagger-ing level of social power and has used it to the full throughout her life. Only one man has managed to distract her attention from high society—and he has kept it with a passion he cannot hide. Now she who guards herself so carefully must learn to give the thing she protects most: her very heart.

She Woke Up Married by Suzanne Macpherson

An Avon Contemporary Romance

Paris went to Vegas to party away the sting of turning thirty all alone. But when she wakes up the next morning she's not alone anymore—she's married! To an Elvis impersonator! It seems like the end of the world as she knows it. But with a little hunk of Young Elvis's burnin' love, Paris is starting to think that get-ting married to a stranger is the best crazy thing she ever did . . .

A Woman's Innocence by Gayle Callen

An Avon Romance

Now that he finally has the infamous traitor, Julia Reed, in jail for treason, Sam Sherryngton hopes justice will be served. But suddenly facts aren't adding up. The more he learns, the more Sam doubts her guilt—and the less he doubts the attraction for Julia he's been fighting against for so many years . . .

Alas, My Love by Edith Layton

An Avon Romance

Granted no favor by his low birth, Amyas St. Ives managed through sheer will and courage to make his fortune. Now he thinks he's met a kindred spirit in the beautiful Amber, but when he discovers her true identity the constraints of social standing seem unconquerable. Yet with a passion like theirs, is there anything that love cannot overcome?